SHIRLEY CHISHOLM

Shirley

Chisholm

CHAMPION OF BLACK FEMINIST POWER POLITICS

Anastasia C. Curwood

THE UNIVERSITY OF NORTH CAROLINA PRESS

Chapel Hill

*This book was published with the
assistance of the Anniversary Fund of the
University of North Carolina Press.*

Manufactured in the United States of America
Designed by Richard Hendel
Set in Utopia and Real Text Pro by codeMantra

Jacket photograph: Representative Shirley Chisholm
campaigning for president in Framingham, MA,
March 25, 1972. © Michael Dobo / Dobophoto.com

Library of Congress Cataloging-in-Publication Data
Names: Curwood, Anastasia Carol, 1974– author.
Title: Shirley Chisholm : champion of Black feminist
power politics / Anastasia C. Curwood.
Description: Chapel Hill : The University of North Carolina Press,
[2022] | Includes bibliographical references and index.
Identifiers: LCCN 2022020614 | ISBN 9781469671178 (cloth) |
ISBN 9781469671185 (ebook)
Subjects: LCSH: Chisholm, Shirley, 1924–2005. | African American
women politicians—Biography. | Politicians—United States—Biography. |
African American women legislators—Biography. |
Legislators—United States—Biography. | African American
feminists—Biography. | Feminism—Political
aspects—United States. | LCGFT: Biographies.
Classification: LCC E840.8.C48 C87 2022 |
DDC 320.082/0973092 [B]—dc23/eng/20220527
LC record available at https://lccn.loc.gov/2022020614

Poems by Shirley Chisholm, "The Law of the Land" and
"The Albany Impasse of 1965," are reprinted with the permission
of the Shirley Chisholm estate.

For Carol
and
For Black girls who want
to be president

CONTENTS

ILLUSTRATIONS

TABLES

SHIRLEY CHISHOLM

INTRODUCTION
Beyond the Symbol

When Shirley Chisholm was a new member of the U.S. House of Representatives in 1969, an elderly white male southern member, she recalled, would grow agitated whenever she came on to the House floor. He would pull her aside and exclaim, "My! Imagine making forty-two five just like me!" referring to a recent vote to raise congressional pay to $42,500 per year. Chisholm was skilled at imitations, so when she told the tale, she echoed his southern accent in a staccato hiss, drawing out the five ("faaaaaaahv"), often to the delight of whoever was listening. The colleague, as she told the story, declared that she ought to kiss the floor, chairs, and whatever else was handy in gratitude for being paid the same salary as an older white man from the South. Chisholm grew exasperated, but she didn't explode. Having done her homework researching the background of all of her colleagues, she knew that he had cardiovascular problems and excess excitement might be bad for his health. So one day when he approached her on the floor, again repeating "forty-two five!" like a mantra, she was ready. "Look," she said. "I've come to the realization that what is bothering you more than anything else is the fact that I'm making forty-two thousand like you are." It seemed to be "eating up his innards." So, she told him, he should simply avoid her for his own well-being. "When you see me coming into this chamber each day, vanish. Vanish until I take my seat. So you won't have to confront me with this forty-two five." She then delivered an uncomfortable truth. "You must remember," she cautioned him, "I'm paving the road for a lot of other people looking like me to make forty-two five!"

Chisholm's aim to expand the possibilities in electoral politics for Black people, women, and other historically oppressed groups is how she paved that road. That she simply found her antagonist's vulnerability and used it as leverage to stop his bad behavior illustrates the savvy that got her through a decades-long career in the gritty world of American politics. By the time she got to Washington, she already had too much experience handling racism and sexism. For the first time, white segregationist congressmen had to work alongside not just Black men, but a Black woman—and she was not a subordinate but an equal. She had dealt with the New York version of Jim Crow all her life and was unimpressed with new colleagues' indignant racism and sexism. The descendant of outspoken Caribbean immigrants, she cared little for the idea of staying quiet and refusing to make any trouble. Instead, she wanted to shake up the status quo, both by creating a path for other Black women to Congress and in the functioning and priorities of the House itself. Her priority was change, not reelection, and she was completely unafraid of raising eyebrows. She once said that when she was gone, she wanted people to "say that Shirley Chisholm had guts."[1]

Shirley Chisholm: Champion of Black Feminist Power Politics is a historical and political biography of Chisholm's remarkable life and career: the daughter of a working-class Barbadian immigrant family who, through ambition and tenacity, became a national symbol of principled fearlessness—and Black feminism—in politics.[2] Chisholm's historic 1972 bid for the Democratic Party's presidential nomination has energized people across generations ever since. Her image is instantly recognizable; her quotes (actual and apocryphal) make the rounds of social media to inspire those fighting racism and sexism today. Less well-known is how she became such a symbol: her coming of age in the crucible of Brooklyn politics and her strategic deployment of whatever leverage she could get as a legislator over seven terms in the House of Representatives. Chisholm—like the rest of us—was a product of her own temperament and talents mixed with timing. In her case, it was a combination of self-confidence—in her own ability and in what was the right thing to do—and the zenith of liberal politics that cracked the door open enough for Chisholm's challenge to the status quo to slip through. When she did, Shirley Chisholm brought a radical vision of broad democracy into national political discourse.

BEYOND THE SYMBOL:
UNDERSTANDING THE CHISHOLM MYSTIQUE

Writing her biography has been challenging because Chisholm was complicated and it is difficult not to write hagiographically about the symbolic version of her. She is, with good reason, a heroine—but the true dimensions of her heroism are obscured behind our reflexive worship of her accomplishments. She left a readable and compelling set of two memoirs, but both of those capitalize on a mystique that she developed as a public figure: the superhuman who took on the entire political establishment for the sake of high principle. She, like so many Black women before her, separated her public life from her private life in order to maintain self-preservation while also taking on the political establishment.[3] Far from a straightforward accounting of events in her life, her memoirs contain gaps and inaccuracies.

2   INTRODUCTION

Where most members of Congress generate endless boxes of archives, much of Chisholm's official papers have gone missing.[4] These challenges have contributed to the persistence of a mythical version of Chisholm and the absence of her humanity. It also suggests why it has taken fifty years since her historic presidential run to publish this comprehensive biography.[5]

Behind the symbol is a brilliant strategist, inventive intellectual, and flawed human. In addition to the fearless, fighting Shirley Chisholm with her uncompromising persona, there are less-remembered aspects of Chisholm that make her even more significant. Her facility at connection and coalition contributed to her longevity in Congress and her lasting impact ever since. As a Black woman raised in a working-class Caribbean immigrant family, her very person was at the intersection of race, gender, ethnic, and class identities. She could no more ignore her Blackness than she could her woman-ness—so she didn't try. When it came to political issues, she felt bound to consider the simultaneous impact of racism, sexism, and economic justice on the enactment of democracy. She believed that, as Duchess Harris has written, "those who are most marginalized and disenfranchised in society should be centered, and through lifting up the most disenfranchised, everyone's standard of living would be in turn improved."[6] As a result, she was able to build a meaningful coalition with a multitude of people and organizations that represented varying American experiences. In fact, an imagined coalition of feminist, Black freedom, antiwar, Native, welfare rights, and lesbian, gay, bisexual, transgender, and queer (LGBTQ) activists was the inspiration for her presidential run. She was practicing intersectionality before Kimberlé Crenshaw coined the term and the theoretical framework to identify such work.[7]

The frank way in which she thought about self-determination for everyone is what I call *Black feminist power*: a vantage point across categories of identity that located points of intersection with common interests—and then used those points to bring pressure on the present configuration of power. In Chisholm's Black feminist political imagination, grounded in the era from the New Deal to the Great Society, the Democratic Party and electoral politics were the institutions that had the most potential to bring about change. Doing her homework, as she did with the colleague who harassed her about her salary, and mastering the workings of the legislative process were her favored methods for leveraging power. She had a good nose for locating where political capital lay and then pushed strategically on it. This was how she connected activists within the movements she supported to electoral politics. Chisholm was not only a practitioner of Black feminist power but also invented it as she worked—confounding existing categories of political ideology then and now. The ideas and solutions she championed came from her conversations with and voracious reading of thinkers in the Black freedom, feminist, antiwar, and other movements. Black feminist power meant that there was synergy between those movements and no gap between ideology and pragmatic politics: it was the idea that political power must operate democratically, in the service of self-determination for all. "It may very well take a Black woman to save our country," she told one audience during her 1972 presidential bid, implying that her vantage point at the intersection of race, gender, and power allowed her to see the true potential within American democracy.[8] Hers was a big-tent politics that recognized power as a malleable and moral force.

Notwithstanding the seriousness of Chisholm's democratic project, her skills at connection and coalition went beyond the issues. She was magnetic. In person, she was charming. A tiny woman, Chisholm radiated energy and warmth. She had a ready smile and a razor-sharp sense of humor with which she could disarm friends and foes alike. A clothes horse who looked good in just about anything, Chisholm was what one staffer called a "feminine cupcake with the heart of a lion."[9] She built warm relationships with colleagues of varied ideologies. She was a good and enthusiastic dancer and took the floor with anyone who would join her. She ran a congressional office full of young and largely Black and female staffers and built a workshop for democracy into the legislative workflow. And she was a formidable speaker, using equal parts pedagogy (she was trained in early childhood education) and soaring oration.

Chisholm also had some difficult interactions in her life, with both her family and political rivals. Her supreme self-confidence could seem arrogant at times, and she was ambitious enough to sacrifice personal connections for political gains. For all her belief in feminist coalitions and collaboration in politics, she was unable to practice the same when it came to her family of origin. Her relationship with her mother and sisters was mostly estranged after a 1960 dispute over an inheritance from her father that came just as she needed to fund her first campaign. From all outward appearances, Chisholm was happily married to a devoted man who supported her campaigns for nearly thirty years, then abruptly divorced to marry a dashing suitor, claiming that her first marriage had been unhappy for some time. Professional conflicts truly got under her skin. Almost from her beginning in Brooklyn politics she made enemies who thought her too ambitious to be a good steward of the neighborhood's representation in state and national government. One journalist saw her as an opportunist and nurtured a grudge for both their entire careers. Another nemesis sought to replace her as the top political force in Brooklyn and tried to win her congressional seat. A third dogged her in the press as insufficiently loyal to Black constituents in the late 1970s and eventually won Chisholm's seat after her retirement, despite the fact that she had already chosen a protégé to take it.

Similar tensions over her political ambition haunted her presidential campaign. Despite a cadre of supporters whose admiration and willingness to work for the campaign had no bounds, there were plenty of people who disapproved. Black political operatives, including most of her Congressional Black Caucus colleagues, thought that she was simply grandstanding and had not paid her dues via established Black political channels. Those white feminists who were allies when it came to legislative matters turned luke-warm when it came to endorsing Chisholm and supporting her at the 1972 Democratic National Convention. Most in the political mainstream seemed to write her off as irrelevant at best, disruptive at worst. They thought her delusional for actually running and claimed that she was crazy for thinking she could win.

As it turned out, Chisholm ran to win, but she did not actually think she would win. In fact, her plan would not work if she had won the nomina-tion. Her purpose in running was to build a coalition, a signature strategy of her Black feminist politics. That coalition was intended to respond to the turmoil of the late 1960s and early '70s: continued repression of Black activists, persistent sexism, entrenched poverty, and a seemingly endless and pointless Vietnam War. Alone, Black, brown, women, poor, antiwar, LGBTQ, and young voters made up small slices of the electorate and were running into walls of resistance. But together, Chisholm reasoned, they could be a "force to be reckoned with" in 1972. And she, at the intersection of those movements, was the one to do it. She wanted to sway the Democratic National Committee's party platform and pressure the nominee to appoint a Black vice presidential running mate, a woman secretary of Health, Edu-cation, and Welfare, and an American Indian secretary of the Interior by withholding votes until such an agreement was reached. In a broader sense, they would push the eventual nominee to expand democracy and bring the nation closer to the ideals of the Declaration of Independence. The fact that the coalition did not come together was not for Chisholm's lack of trying, but she did learn some of the limitations of Black feminist power politics within the Democratic Party.

What Chisholm's supporters and naysayers alike could not predict was that the early 1970s were a high point of liberalism in mainstream politics: liberalism that agreed in principle with full equality but was unwilling to risk political capital on making substantive change. American progress toward equality would not inexorably continue. Although Chisholm's attempt to change the platform did not work, the 1972 Democratic platform was none-theless the most responsive to left social movements of any platform for the next two generations. The party's nominee, George McGovern, lost in a landslide to Richard Nixon. When Jimmy Carter won the White House in 1976, he was the first Democratic president of Chisholm's congressional career, and she had high hopes for new sweeping social and economic legislation. But she was to find that, instead of returning to expanding the welfare state of the New Deal and the Great Society, the now-Democratic White House was tacking right on economic matters. When Carter was unseated by Reagan four years later, Chisholm fought like hell for existing domestic programs. Two years later, she was spent. In 1983 she left a Congress on the cusp of transformation by New Right politics and Democrats' attempted triangulation to keep as much power as possible. Chisholm was not done with politics just yet; she spent her last active decade at the helm of the National Political Congress of Black Women. Inside and outside the organization, she continued to mentor young people in politics, some of whom went on to careers in politics. Her fostering of the new generation of coalition-building feminist politicians resembles what Patricia Hill Collins has called "othermothering": Black women's practice of building kin networks based not on blood relationships but on the development of the comunity.[10] Chisholm never gave birth to any children, and her legacy lives through intellectual, not biological, descendants.

Chisholm came of age as the New Deal apparatus was built. She served as a legislator in the immediate wake of the Great Society and the foundational social movements of the twentieth century. She bowed out of politics gracefully and lived a long and full life afterward. She left the world as a new millennium opened alongside the rise of the New Right. She embodied the enduring tensions of her own time and of ours: the search for an expanded democracy alongside entrenched elites. She was an instrument, as she often said, for others to press their needs on the body politic. And no one else caught both the minds and imaginations of Americans quite like Chisholm did. Fifty years after her run, the United States has a historic number of women of color in Congress and has a Black and South Asian American woman as vice president.

   Chisholm's life—both its symbolism and its humanity—illuminate the way for new generations. It is hard to demystify our heroes. Still, we need to see them as human so that the humans of the future can see themselves as heroes.

DAUGHTER OF THE CARIBBEAN

───────── ★ ─────────

As a girl, the two female public figures Shirley Chisholm looked up to most were Eleanor Roosevelt and Mary McLeod Bethune, both of whom she met at least once—and both highly influential in the histories of U.S. Black feminisms. Late in life, Chisholm would credit Roosevelt, Bethune, and her grandmother Emmeline Seale as the three women who had the most influence on her: "influence in terms of the things they said to me."[1] Although the exact occasion remains unclear, Chisholm recalled that Roosevelt was present at an awards ceremony when the high school–aged Shirley accepted a prize. As Chisholm told the story, the First Lady complimented her intellect and exhorted the teenage Shirley to "never give up." Bethune, on an unspecified occasion, gave similar advice. These women also modeled womanhood that encompassed outspoken self-determination and, in the case of Roosevelt and Bethune, a deep engagement with public life. Roosevelt, a lifelong reformer and the wife of President Franklin Delano Roosevelt, asserted women's rights to participate in politics and media. Bethune was a builder of institutions and an advocate for Black women and men inside Democratic politics. Bethune and Roosevelt shared with Chisholm the belief that the government ought to work in the service of the people, including women. Bethune in particular, as a president of the National Association of Colored Women and the founder of the National Council of Negro Women, represented an intersectional and pragmatic advocacy for Black women that informed Chisholm's Black feminist power politics. Bethune's emphasis on reforming government and institutions to support those with little power and wealth would become bedrock within Chisholm's own thinking.[2] Years later, Chisholm would successfully sponsor a bill to erect the statue of Bethune that stands today in Washington, D.C.'s Lincoln Park.

But it was from Emmeline Seale, her Barbadian grandmother, that she learned the value of family, and of independence, both of which shaped her politics and her political vision. Shirley Chisholm's Black feminism grew organically from her family and place of origin. She was born in the United States to Barbadian parents and spent six years of her childhood on the island of Barbados. With a foot in two lands, Chisholm observed women's financial independence, how to maintain dignity in the midst of racism and poverty, how to succeed in school, and how to challenge authority. Her Barbadian grandmother taught her to be fearless about doing what she thought was right. Her Barbadian mother showed her single-minded tenacity. And her Barbadian father nurtured her intellect and her political education. Six years as a child in Barbados imparted a simultaneous identity as Black and immigrant, and Chisholm saw common threads between both throughout her life. Having been raised by self-determined women, she thought every option could and should be open to her regardless of sex.

But Shirley did not passively absorb the dictates of the adults in her life, no matter how much she respected them. Shirley's temperament, even as a young child, was opinionated, self-assured, and confident. Her feisty personality appalled her mother and some family members even as it delighted others, such as her father and maternal grandmother. This would be the case throughout her life, when some thought her too egotistical and self-aggrandizing while others admired her temerity and took inspiration from it. Young Shirley encountered her world with the conviction that she had the ability to make change, a belief that persisted well into her adult life. What she learned in girlhood built her sense of assertiveness over her own future.

ROOTS

Shirley Anita St. Hill was born in Brownsville, Brooklyn, New York, on November 20, 1924. But from the time Shirley was four years old to when she was ten, she lived with relatives in Barbados, her parents' home country—and a place rife with a history of European colonialism and slavery, like most Caribbean islands. Legal restrictions in the aftermath of slavery made it very difficult to own land, but Chisholm's family did own at least two small parcels. Both of Chisholm's parents came of age in Christ Church Parish, about eight miles from the capital and port city of Bridgetown. On a slight peninsula at the southernmost tip of the island, where the Atlantic Ocean and the Caribbean Sea meet, the neighborhoods of Bourne's Land, Below Rock, and Pegwell were home to grandparents, aunts, uncles, and cousins.

By the turn of the twentieth century in Barbados, Black Barbadians, known as Bajans, had experienced four centuries of creating wealth for Great Britain. Much of this wealth had taken the form of the sugar trade, but around the time Chisholm's parents were born in the late nineteenth century, the Barbados sugar industry took a steep decline. Planters held a monopoly on land ownership, and laborers were poorly paid, so establishing economic self-determination was increasingly difficult. Hurricanes in 1898 and 1922 worsened workers' conditions. As a result, Bajans began to leave:

first for what was then British Guiana, then for the Panama Canal Zone, Cuba, and eventually the United States. They joined other Black migrants from across the African diaspora arriving in the United States in increasing numbers during the first decades of the twentieth century, especially in the early 1920s. Between 1899 and 1932, nearly 108,000 Caribbean people entered through American ports.[3]

Chisholm wrote a much-abridged version of the island's and her family's history in her memoir *Unbought and Unbossed*. Regarding the push factors that drove Barbadians to the United States, she said only that "crop failures caused famines." She also stated that her father, Charles St. Hill, was "a native of" British Guiana. This, however, was not exactly true, a fact that Chisholm herself must have known. Although Charles had indeed been born in Guyana in 1898, it was to Barbadian parents, Thomas Jasper and Mary Malvina Weekes St. Hill. They were in Guyana for the short term, looking for a living wage. Shortly thereafter, they returned to their old neighborhood in the south point and eventually had their son Charles baptized in Christ Church Parish Church, allowing him to proudly call himself a Barbadian.[4]

Charles's great-grandfather Philip St. Hill and his grandfather George Sealy St. Hill were both coopers (barrel makers for rum) and had almost certainly been enslaved in the parish of St. George, to the north of Christ Church. Their occupations as artisans, and the passage of the skill from father to son, suggests that their status might have been higher than field laborers and provided them with more economic options. George was born around 1831, two years before the end of slavery in Barbados. His wife, Sarah Jane Crawford, a seamstress, was born around 1835. Her father was Mark Crawford, who was almost certainly enslaved also. The parish records that tracked births did so for both Black and white people starting in about 1800, but births of enslaved people did not note surnames, sometimes not until the 1840s in St. George. Therefore, it is impossible to know which George and which Sarah Jane of many people so named were the great-grandparents of Shirley Chisholm. In addition, their Thomas would be recorded as "mixed" on his birth certificate, suggesting that George, Sarah Jane, or both had some white ancestry, due to the rape of their enslaved foremothers by white men.

What is known is that George and Sarah Jane married in the Chapel of St. Jude in St. George's Parish in 1856. The couple lived at Golden Ridge Plantation, owned by the Yearwood family. Six years later, they had moved less than a mile to the northwest, to Sweet Bottom, a village founded by free Black people in the eighteenth century, and Sarah Jane gave birth to their son Thomas. By the time he was thirty years old he had become a carpenter and moved to Bridgetown. He met Mary Malvina Weekes, a domestic servant who lived near Pegwell in Christ Church, and married her in

December 1892 in the parish church. Mary Malvina was thirty-one years old when she married.[5] She already had one son, Moses Callender. In addition to Chisholm's father, Charles, the couple had Thomas Jr. ("Tommy"), who was the family rascal, Muriel, and James.

Many Barbadians moved to Guyana around the turn of the century because the sugar industry in that country was stronger than that in Barbados and the economy was more diversified. The Barbadian government had restricted out-migration in the nineteenth century, fearing that the sugar plantation workforce would disappear. But this changed by the twentieth century, when the St. Hills took the opportunity to go for a year.[6] They returned from Guyana to Christ Church. Not long after Charles was baptized at age ten, his mother died, followed shortly by his father. He remained in the home of his grandparents James ("Captain") and Hannah Weekes, who owned land in the Below Rock area nearby.[7] It was there that he would meet his future wife and Shirley Chisholm's mother, Ruby.

On her maternal side, Chisholm was born to a long line of women with strong familial connections and an equally strong sense of independence. Her great-grandmother Angelina Chase was a single mother who birthed Chisholm's grandmother Emmeline Chase (later Seale) in or around 1878. Emmeline had light skin and long hair, suggesting mixed Black–white ancestry. Angelina gave young Emmeline up to a white English woman who promised to send the girl to school. But years later, Angelina discovered that Emmeline had never been sent to school and had been doing household work instead. Emmeline never became proficient at reading, although she was gifted at doing mathematical figures in her head. Years later, Emmeline's children knew their grandmother Angelina as a kindly woman who sometimes gave them a ride to school in her pony cart on her way into town.[8]

In the later years of the nineteenth century, Emmeline and Fitzherbert Seale, a local plantation laborer, began a long courtship. Although Fitzherbert's birth record has not been located, his father, David Wiltshire King, was born on Industry Hall plantation in what is now Silver Sands, a few hundred yards from Bourne's Land. His mother's name has not survived, but it was most likely Seale, a name that belonged to a family of white Christ Church planters in the late eighteenth and early nineteenth centuries.[9] Emmeline and Fitzherbert married in Christ Church Parish Church in the summer of 1901, after they already had an older son Harold and daughter Violet, and only one month before Chisholm's mother, Ruby Leotta Seale, was born. Fitzherbert was twenty-three, and Emmeline was twenty-two.[10]

Fitzherbert left to work in the Panama Canal Zone in 1904 and returned a few years later, when he and Emmeline had two more children: Myrtle Seale (1908–1996) and Lincoln Seale (ca. 1908–ca. 1946). But their marriage did not last. Fitzherbert had brought back "Panama money," a nest egg of cash that friends and neighbors prevailed on him to give or lend to them. This money came with liabilities. For one thing, the sudden influx of cash into the Barbadian economy, and the sudden demand for land by men who possessed it, drove inflation in land and lumber prices.[11] The problem created by Fitzherbert's Panama money was personal, too. Having what people called a "soft heart," Fitzherbert freely gave of his assets. Emmeline, a "businesslike woman," was appalled that her husband had given away the family's money while they had five children to feed.

Muriel Forde, Shirley's sister, recalled the impact of Panama money on the neighborhood: "A lot of the village life then depended on what you call, Panama Money. Workers would send money home, as well as gold rings, which older Barbadian women still sport. Black workers often received silver instead. Grandmother [Emmeline] Seale bought land with the money, but by the 1960s it had been sold off in parcels to help her children and others leave for the US. The divorce occurred because Grandfather was too loose in lending money to people when he returned to Barbados from Panama, and also never got it repaid."[12]

Fitzherbert eventually left for Trinidad, where he had family, but he remained in contact with his children and sent money to Ruby so that she could go to the United States.

MIGRATION TO NEW YORK

Although structural factors, such as the push of poor wages in Barbados and the pull of better ones in the United States, doubtless influenced Charles St. Hill and Ruby Seale, they, like many Caribbean immigrants, most likely had more personal reasons for migrating. The St. Hill, Seale, and Weekes families all had histories of migration and independence—they moved to British Guiana and Panama, owned land, and engaged in artisanal occupations. Charles St. Hill had become a shoemaker by 1920, when he obtained a passport, and Ruby's immigration record shows that she was a needleworker in Barbados.[13] Both were products of the Barbadian education system and were proficient at reading and writing in English.

Still, the push factor of economic constriction came into play. The barter economy was changing and people needed cash. By the 1920s around 300,000 Anglophone Caribbean people, often fairly well-educated young adults, left for Canada or the United States. From 1900 to 1925, those who migrated to the United States typically settled in New York (Brooklyn and some in Harlem), New Haven, Hartford, and Boston after having worked to muster the money for the trip.[14] For many in Chisholm's parents' generation, the source of the fare and the "show money" was Panama money.[15]

Barbadian novelist Paule Marshall's mother put it thus: "If you was from the West Indies you had to have fifty big U.S. dollars to show to the authorities when you landed, to prove you wasn't a pauper or coming to the country to be a pauper. Back then, if you was black, you cun [couldn't] set foot in big America without fifty dollars cold cash in you' hand."[16] Fifty dollars in 1920 would be worth nearly $700 one hundred years later, no small sum.

Ruby, then Charles, managed to enter the United States before the Immigration Act of 1924 took effect, which would dramatically reduce Caribbean migration. In February 1922, at the age of twenty-one (she was not the "teenaged Barbadian girl" her daughter would write in *Unbought and Unbossed,* although she was only four foot ten and less than one hundred pounds), she left her mother's home in Hopewell and boarded the *Pocone,* a Brazilian-owned steamer on its way to New York from Santos, with twenty-five dollars in her pocket.[17] Although her own recollections of the eight-day trip do not survive, one might expect that her journey was similar to that of Paule Marshall's mother, Adriana Clement, in September 1923. The rough trip kept eighteen-year-old Adriana "puking and praying" up the Eastern Seaboard, but "all the same, I reach safe, yes. I saw New York rise shining from the sea," she would say, each time lifting her hands for emphasis.[18]

Although Ruby's daughter Muriel recalled that Fitzherbert had sent the money for the journey to New York, Ruby told the official who recorded her information that her older sister Violet had paid for her passage. She also declared that she merely planned a temporary stay of five years, after which she planned to return to Barbados. But she also stated her intention to gain U.S. citizenship. Once at the dock in New York, Ruby was detained overnight at Ellis Island, waiting to be collected by Violet and taken to her Baltic Street apartment in Brooklyn. The brief detention was probably because she only had twenty-five dollars of "show money." She quickly got to work, establishing a seamstress business.[19]

Charles joined a year later. He had left Barbados in 1920 and gone with his brother James to Cuba before taking the American ship *SS Munamar* from Antilla to New York in early April 1923. Both young men told the ship's officers that they were to be met by their "uncle" Joseph Agard at West 137th Street. Although they said that they did not plan to stay or seek citizenship, and would be departing within two years, they lived the rest of their lives in the United States.[20]

The community of Caribbean immigrants that young Charles and Ruby found was well established in Brooklyn and in Harlem. As Paule Marshall has documented, Barbadian girls carried everywhere the metallic sound of the two silver bangle bracelets that each one wore. The St. Hill kitchen hosted a cacophony of "real talk" among Barbadian women who called on

Ruby for a cup of tea or cocoa, as well as the smells of cooking.[21] Chisholm later observed that, though they worked hard, Charles and Ruby were not able to accumulate the wealth that other Americans did during the 1920s.[22] They were determined, however, to bequeath a more prosperous existence to their children. As Chisholm herself and sociologist Robin Cohen both noted, in the United States, Caribbean migrants tended to achieve economic independence.[23] Barbadian immigrants were particularly oriented toward building wealth, Paule Marshall has written:

> Bajans seldom socialized with the other islanders who had also immigrated to Brooklyn. Trinidadians were considered too frivolous, a people who lived only for their yearly carnival. Jamaicans in their view were a rough lot who disgraced the King's English by dropping their "h's" ('im dis and 'im dat). Those from the lesser-known islands such as St. Vincent and S. Lucia were dismissed as "low-islanders," meaning small, insignificant. As for American black people, they needed to stand up more to the white man. Bajans, meanwhile, had no objection to being called "the Jews of the West Indies" by other islanders—the term based on their ability to squeeze a penny till it cried "Murder! Murder!" and "to turn a dime into a dollar overnight." There was their known entrepreneurial chutzpah in general: "As soon as a Bajan gets ten cents above a beggar he opens a business."[24]

Homeland associations among Caribbean immigrants sprung up, including the Sons and Daughters of Barbados. The overriding goal of these associations was to foster prosperity for their members by offering sick or death benefits, as well as social occasions. A fictional version, the Association of Barbadian Homeowners and Businessmen, appears in Marshall's *Brown Girl, Brownstones*. That organization's motto was: "It is not the depths from which we come but the heights to which we ascend."[25]

Muriel Forde vividly remembered the culture of achievement in her parents' generation. "To be a Barbadian," she recalled, "it's about discipline, hard work, and . . . great ambition for your children. [Parents] had two things in mind when they went to the United States: to get a good education for their children because they always told the children, we have nothing of worth to pass on to you but one thing we can give you is a good education, once you have that, they like to say, then nobody can make a fool of you." This made Bajans acquire a reputation for being "too serious," in Forde's words. Prestige in the New York Bajan community came from having children who were doing well in school and buying a house, usually a brownstone. The St. Hills achieved both. They told their four daughters, "What's in your head can't take out," and instilled these and other ideals related to hard work and knowledge in Saturday afternoon "talks" at 1:30 each week.[26] But a good education, for Charles especially, included learning outside the classroom in the realm of politics.

Charles, who applied for citizenship in 1942, was politically engaged. Caribbean immigrants like him were overrepresented in leftist and Black nationalist organizations during the period in which Chisholm was born and raised. And Charles joined one of three Universal Negro Improvement Association (UNIA) chapters in Brooklyn. The UNIA, a mass movement with millions of members at its peak, was founded by the Jamaican Marcus Garvey. Garvey was a Black nationalist who advocated economic self-sufficiency for Black people worldwide. The UNIA offered fierce racial pride and a gospel of self-help through entrepreneurship. "If FDR was their hero, Marcus Garvey was their God," Paule Marshall has written about the popularity of Garvey among Barbadian and other Caribbean immigrants. Marshall characterized Garvey as the acknowledged leader of her parents' generation of Caribbean immigrants, a name that was "constantly invoked" around her mother's kitchen table.[27] There had been a thriving chapter of the UNIA in Bridgetown that had over 1,800 members by 1920, the year that Charles left Barbados for Cuba. And yet, even as the parents of Chisholm's generation flocked to political organizations, historian Winston James underscores that the second generation of Barbadian migrants tended to contain more radicals. Caribbean immigrants were particularly active in leftist and Black nationalist organizations during the period when Chisholm was born, and continued to be as she came of age politically. James has theorized that the characteristics of migrants, including their high literacy, experience with political organizing, and experience as a Black majority, interacted with the ideal of American democracy and the reality of American apartheid to push them toward radical activism. Chisholm's outspokenness and radical politics, and her simultaneous decision to work within the institution of the Democratic Party, is reflected in her heritage as a second-generation Barbadian American and in the lessons from her father.[28]

The distinctiveness of a Caribbean background would lead to intraracial ethnic tension during Chisholm's political career. "I have heard people grumbling for years," she wrote. She had heard the complaints "they're taking over everything," and "why don't those monkeys get back on the banana boat?" She thought that different experiences of slavery and emancipation, despite the common experience of the transatlantic slave trade and chattel slavery, lay at the root. For Anglophone migrants like Chisholm, emancipation had come without war and earlier than in the United States, as Chisholm pointed out as an adult. She noted fewer "race barriers" in the Caribbean and thought that "blacks from the islands tend to have less fear of white people, and therefore less hatred of them." Chisholm could not point to hostility directed toward her specifically but said "sometimes I can sense it."[29] She thought that animosity toward Black Caribbean migrants was an obstacle during her Brooklyn campaigns.

THE ST. HILLS OF BROOKLYN

Ruby had known Charles in Barbados because they had been neighbors near Bourne's Land. Just over a year after his arrival in New York, Charles met Ruby again and they "got better acquainted, fell in love, and married."[30] They set up their household on Jefferson Street in Brownsville. Charles began work at a bakery, and Ruby took in sewing. Shirley was born at home in 1924, the first of four: Odessa Leotta came along in 1926, Muriel in 1928, and Selma in 1931.[31]

Shirley's fiery temperament was evident from an early age. Her mother thought she was destined for great things, though she was not an easy child. "My mother couldn't deal with me. I was a very, very interfering child in everything. . . . I was talkative, I got into trouble."[32] Family lore held that she could read by the age of two and would sit other children down to lecture them. One day, after returning from a short errand to the store, Ruby found four-year-old Shirley with the infant Muriel in her arms. Shirley took it on herself to toilet train Muriel, because she loved to pull the chain on the old toilet. She placed the baby on the toilet and commanded her to "do it!" If she heard her sister "tinkle," she would be delighted for the chance to pull the toilet chain. If she did not, she would continue to badger her sister until Ruby came to the rescue of her youngest daughter. "I was into everything."[33]

Chisholm was proud of her defiance as a child. "I was not a bad child but I was mischievous. My mother, she was a young woman, she just couldn't handle me. My mother was soft, a very nice person. She just couldn't handle the little devil," she said in one interview.[34] In her memoir, she explains, "Mother was still only a girl herself and had trouble coping with three babies, especially her oldest." Of course, Ruby was twenty-three years old when her first child was born. Chisholm's description of herself as a young girl evokes Marshall's character Selina Boyce in *Brown Girl, Brownstones*. Selina's iron-willed mother Silla echoes what Ruby might have said about Shirley. Selina asserts her own identity as herself, not the dead brother who haunts the Boyce family, and as a product of both American and Bajan influences. In one scene within the novel Selina stalks away from her mother. While regarding her rebellious daughter's "small back as unassailable as her own" retreating away from her, Silla marvels, "But look at my crosses. . . . Look how I has gone and brought something into this world to whip me."[35] Ruby might have felt a similar wonder at her oldest daughter's rebellions.

Perhaps Shirley's challenging temperament was a factor in the St. Hills' decision to send their daughters to Barbados to stay with family. But there were other considerations, too. Chisholm thought that the education in Barbados was part of the decision, because reading was taught at age three and writing was taught at age four. Also, remitting wages to the island to support the girls was far more cost-effective than keeping Ruby home to care for them. Having two full-time working parents and fewer mouths to feed would also enable the St. Hills to accumulate savings for the eventual goal of buying a house. According to Muriel, "[Ruby] was interested in two things: she was interested in all of her children, four children, getting a college education, and this was back in the 1930s. And buying a home. Those were her goals."[36]

The St. Hills booked passage on the SS *Vestris*, a British ship on the Lamport and Holt line, for mid-November of 1928. Ruby, her daughters, and her older sister Violet's four children were all ticketed on the 550-foot ocean liner. But those plans would prove to be a false start and the basis for a family legend about Ruby's tenacity. About five days before the ship sailed, Ruby awoke from a nightmare. In her dream, the *Vestris* had sunk. When she awoke, she informed her husband that she refused to set foot on the *Vestris* and that they would have to rebook on another ship. "And my father was furious, you know," Muriel recalled. "Everything had been arranged, he had gone to the trouble of getting the trunks they had packed for the trip carried down, but she said, we're not going." Exasperated, Charles informed his wife that if she wanted to change the booking, she herself would have to make the arrangements and reship the trunks. Chisholm's aunt Violet had a similar reaction. Appalled by Ruby's fixation on her intuition, Violet was nevertheless unable to overcome her younger sister's legendary determination. Ruby had made up her mind and informed Violet that she could send her four children ahead on the ship with somebody else, but that Shirley, Odessa, and Muriel would not be on the *Vestris*. Seeing that this was an unacceptable option, Violet grudgingly agreed to the switch. Ruby and Violet, with baby Muriel, set off for the shipping agent's office, arguing all the way. Disaster nearly struck: Violet, who held Muriel, tripped and fell on the subway stairs and the eight-month old baby rolled onto the subway platform, miraculously unhurt. The tickets were changed to the SS *Voltaire*, which sailed two weeks after the *Vestris*, and the issue was put to rest.[37]

Ruby's dream and her insistence on acting on it saved the family. Three days after the *Vestris* departed, newspapers reported the tragic news that the ship had sunk off the coast of Virginia. One hundred and eleven of the crew and passengers, including all of the children and most of the women aboard, perished. Those who survived told of growing panic and a too-late SOS from the captain. Following the custom of women and children first, two lifeboats of women and children were loaded on the side that faced the heavy weather. The boats, one of which was reported to have a hole patched with tin, banged down to the water and "went to pieces," sinking into the violent ocean. Surviving passengers, some of whom were clinging to debris, watched in horror as the bodies of drowned women were "flung about in the waves."[38] Results of the British and American investigations into the disaster, one of the worst since the *Lusitania*, were that the captain had radioed for help hours after he should have, vital hatches and scuppers were not closed when they should have been, and the crew completely lacked effective emergency procedures. Had Ruby and the children been on the ship, they almost certainly would have been among the dead. One of the few bodies that was recovered belonged to Mildred Headly, the five-year-old daughter of a Barbadian immigrant and his wife who were headed back to Barbados. Both parents and Mildred's two siblings had gone down with the ship. "After that my father never imposed when [Ruby's] mind was made up," Muriel recalled. "Even if she couldn't give a reason, just a feeling or intuition. [He] never imposed after that."[39]

Ruby and the seven children sailed on the *Voltaire on* November 24 with thirteen of the survivors from the *Vestris* who had decided to travel again. The sister ship of its unfortunate fleet mate, the *Voltaire* and its lifeboats were shining with fresh paint. It would have been reassuring for Ruby to see that the lifeboats' lowering apparatus was positioned ready for action. Along the way, the ship's passengers and crew conducted a brief memorial ceremony, according to Muriel. At the spot off the coast of Virginia where the *Vestris* had gone down, all aboard the ship went to the rail and tossed wreaths overboard.[40]

Emmeline, doubtless having heard about the shipwreck, was very anxious as she waited for her daughters and grandchildren to arrive and must have been relieved when the *Voltaire* sailed into the capital city of Bridgetown. Ruby and the children would have been met by a cacophony of sights and sounds. The port was filled with vendors selling everything from ackees (mamoncillos, sweet pulpy fruits surrounding a large stone) to mauby (a drink made from the bark of the soldierwood tree). Barbadian women carried loads of coal on their heads to waiting ships. In preindependence days, the city was inhabited by a mix of British colonial officials, merchants, and laborers. Shirley recalled a long customs and health inspection delay at the port, and then the bus ride to Vauxhall along unpaved roads, sometimes encountering animals blocking the way. When Shirley got off the bus, she came face to face with her grandmother Emmeline Seale for the first time.

Emmeline Seale modeled Black feminist qualities of self-determination and dignity for her granddaughter. As an adult, Chisholm credited Emmeline for "where I got my nerve." Emmeline appeared as a "stern, unafraid woman" to her granddaughters. She was tall and beautiful, usually dressed in white, with "an hourglass figure," and long hair pulled back into a bun. She taught her grandchildren to carry themselves upright and was a strict disciplinarian, but managed to embolden rather than intimidate Shirley. "She was so commanding and she always told me, don't be afraid of anything, child. You must grow up and you must do what you believe you have to do." Chisholm recalled that Ruby thought her daughter and her mother were very much alike "in terms of my spirit, my attitude, and everything. I got those qualities, if you will, from my grandmother. And that's how it came back. She was a great influence in my life."[41] Though she would only spend six years with Emmeline and never see her again after returning to the United States, Chisholm often credited her grandmother for her willingness to speak plainly, take risks, and make provocative decisions.

The daily routine of living in Vauxhall could not have been more different than Brooklyn. Vauxhall was a few miles closer to Bridgetown than Bourne's Land, but still in the country. Shirley quickly had to learn to do chores that city kids did not. Drawing water from the well and carrying it on her head with her back very straight, and gardening for the kitchen, which included sweet potatoes, yams, tomatoes, and other vegetables, were all part of her duties. The family lived on the produce in the garden, plus an abundant supply of flying fish. They also had turkeys, chickens, goats, and one or two cows for milk, and children's chores included cleaning their pens and chaperoning grazing on unfenced pastures. Shirley recalled that one memorable turkey was "vicious" but beloved, and he disappeared at Christmas. The children figured out that he was their Christmas dinner and refused to eat him—but otherwise, such refusal to enjoy the food they raised and caught was uncommon. She also had to become accustomed to the noises of the verdant and crowded island at night: chickens, cows, sheep, crickets.[42]

There were also more relatives. Shirley's maternal grandfather, Fitzherbert, by then was living permanently in Trinidad, but there were others. Like her grandmother, most relatives had modest four-room houses and extensive vegetable gardens. Ruby stayed for six months, and when she left it was the children's twenty-year-old aunt Myrtle who most often had to care for Shirley and her sisters and cousins. Their uncle Lincoln also lived in the household and worked for a newspaper in Bridgetown, one of the few journalists among Black Barbadians in the interwar years. The extended family and surrounding community were important to the children because

Emmeline Chase Seale.
Courtesy of the Muriel Forde family.

Emmeline worked full time as a cook of some renown. She left at five or six in the morning, and, because her white English employers had the habit of lingering at the table late into the evening and would not offer to carry their cook home, it was sometimes not until ten at night that she was able to return. Both Muriel and Shirley vividly remembered the stress of those late evenings. Mornings were often stressful, too, as Aunt Myrtle wrangled seven children's preparations to leave for school. The family lived across the road from the school, but the children were often late because Myrtle insisted that all seven leave the house simultaneously and someone was always lagging.[43]

Later in life, Chisholm almost romanticized the strong discipline that her elders used when dealing with them as children, though she was also proud of her own defiance. Childrearing in the Seale household was very strict: speak only when spoken to. Her grandmother's sternness worked to keep the young Shirley in line: "one look—she didn't even have to hit you." Communal mores about children's behavior upheld expectations of proper decorum at all times: neighborhood adults would complain about poor manners if any child passed by on the road without a greeting. As Muriel recalled, "Sometimes a slap, or a personal apology on our part would be in order if we happened to be around when the complaint was made. Our aunt would be chagrined to think that someone believed she was raising rude and ignorant children," even though she happened to dislike the neighbor in question.[44]

Children were also expected to stay completely out of any conflicts between adults. But Shirley did not, at times shocking adults with her outspoken opinions on whatever was at issue. She habitually sat down in the same room when adults paid calls, and on one infamous occasion was unable to keep her nose out of the grownups' business. The visitor that day told Aunt Myrtle that her husband was to preach a sermon the next Sunday. Shirley piped up and said, "He's going to preach? He's so boring!" The visitor was outraged and left "in a huff," as Muriel remembered, with Myrtle frantically trying to repair the damage as the guest packed up. After her angry departure, Myrtle angrily turned to Shirley. "Your mouth have no cover," Myrtle complained, promising punishment if the girl continued to insist on sharing unsolicited opinions.[45]

Although Chisholm would become known for her democratic pedagogy during her political career, she still admired the more authoritarian style of teaching used by her school. Bajan children were caught between two unyielding authority figures: their parents and their teachers. Chisholm had the same admiration of tough discipline at school that she had of her grandmother's iron will at home, and considered an adversarial relationship between children and adults to be beneficial to learning. Chisholm later recalled, "The teachers and parents were in league against you. . . . But you learned."[46] Teachers had authority to punish students physically, and then parents, after finding out about their children's transgressions, might well spank them again on their return from school. Inside the small Methodist church that served as the Vauxhall Primary School during the week, seven tiny classrooms, with children from ages four to eleven, were sectioned off by screens. Despite the inevitable carrying of sound from one section to

Vauxhall Primary School.
Author's photo.

another, "we learned very well." Shirley could read and write by age five, practicing on reusable slates that the children cleaned with their spit. Muriel protested not going to school with the other cousins, so at age four she was allowed to sit quietly in the classroom. She quickly learned to read shortly after she began attending lessons.[47]

Although the Barbadian schools seemed, to the St. Hills and to Chisholm later, to be more effective than those in Brooklyn, they, too, were problematic. Barbadian authorities recognized only a responsibility to teach children to read and write. Education as a source of social mobility was most certainly not the colonial government's objective.[48] Chisholm herself recalled that most Barbadians did not expect to go to college, working instead as artisans or laborers.[49] Learning and living in a majority-Black country, however, taught the young American children that Black people were fully capable of self-determination and leadership.

RETURN TO NEW YORK

The St. Hill girls and their cousins remained in Barbados until their mother sent for them in 1934. Ruby missed her daughters and feared that they would grow up without knowing her, but Shirley was bereft when she had to leave Barbados. She would never see many of her relatives again, including her grandmother. After an eight-day boat ride, the family was reunited at 110 Liberty Avenue in Brownsville, where most of their neighbors were not Black Americans but Jewish—some first-generation immigrants from eastern Europe.

The girls returned to a changing Brooklyn. In the most recent census of 1930, Black people numbered about 69,000 and made up 2.7 percent of the Brooklyn population. Black households had grown beyond the few pockets they had established in the first decade of the twentieth century: downtown, on Bridge Street (where most residents were servants living close to white employers), Weeksville (in what is now Bed-Stuy), and Fort Greene. After World War I, they began to establish households near the Navy Yard and the waterfront, and were also a growing presence along Fulton Street and Atlantic Avenue. The percentage of Black residents grew to 4 percent in 1940 and would grow even bigger during Shirley's later years of high school and her college career, as World War II brought in more emigrants from the U.S. South.[50]

At the cold-water railroad flat, Shirley and her sisters endured frigid winter days while their mother was away procuring sewing materials by huddling together in bed. Striking one of the few negative notes in her description of her childhood, Chisholm alluded to the trauma of this time, disclosing in her memoir that "to this day, I'm still afraid of the cold." The experience led her to empathize with poor Americans later in her career. She also learned more about Jewish life in Brooklyn, knowledge that would be helpful when she ran for office later. She recalled that she loved to sit on the fire escape and watch worshipers coming and going from the synagogue next door, fascinated by this glimpse of religious life. Her memoir contains a slightly different version: she and her sisters "giggled" at the synagogue's members; when caught, Ruby punished them. Chisholm's descriptions of her mother's relationship with their neighbors suggest that Jewish women apparently came to rely on Ruby for making sense of bills and other bureaucracies. Ruby sat with Jewish neighbors on fair days in the park, sometimes laughing over shared jokes. Beyond this camaraderie, however, was Ruby's deep respect for religion, even when it was not her own. She belonged to a small English Brethren church and took her daughters to services three times each Sunday.[51] Ruby showed Shirley and her sisters how to make alliances across racial and religious lines. In addition to learning about new neighbors, the girls had to reacquaint themselves with parents they had not seen for six years. Shirley chafed against the rules set by her mother even as she delighted in her father's pursuits. Like other women from Barbados, Chisholm later recalled, Ruby was "thoroughly British in her ideas, her manners[,] and her plans for her daughters." Ruby was a reserved person, especially in contrast to her mother, and, like her daughters Shirley and Muriel, very small. She and Emmeline agreed that one must always dress well, with shined shoes, ironed dress, and combed hair, when one went out. Despite tight finances, her seamstress skills and some hand-me-downs from wealthy white employers made certain they were all well presented. Chisholm would enjoy dressing well throughout her life. But she did not like the restrictions on behavior that Ruby imposed. Where Emmeline had encouraged Shirley's outspokenness and independence, Ruby's "old world ways" discouraged this and felt stifling and embarrassing to her oldest daughter. Charles was more inclined to allow a freer rein, and Shirley recalled that "sometimes he would lecture Mother, trying to persuade her that she was an immigrant and should adapt more to the ways of her new country." But he deferred to Ruby's rules. The girls were expected to be rigorously punctual to parties, but to leave after exactly one hour, just when the party would be getting going. Permissible Saturday amusements included the public library, the movies (although not coming home in time for supper prompted Ruby to go retrieve the girls holding a strap), and outings with Aunt Violet and the cousins at Jones Beach or Coney Island. She was also expected to learn piano. Ruby's rules were especially strict when it came to her daughters' sexuality. As a high school student and even as a college student, Shirley was discouraged from dating and expected to study hard instead. She rebelled by playing popular songs and jazz on the piano and allowing boys to walk her home and kiss her on the front step.[52]

For Shirley, who had spent formative years in Barbados, loyalty and closeness might well have been stronger with Emmeline and Aunt Myrtle.[53] She remembered her mother as "an austere individual" whose piety and religious orientation were more pronounced than her engagement with "things of the world" such as civic activism. At least two of her sisters, she said, were closely aligned with Ruby's outlook, but Shirley felt like an iconoclast. Still, parts of Ruby's personality did rub off on Shirley. She would have observed her analysis of the world in those kitchen rap sessions with other Bajan mothers.[54] Ruby explicitly taught her daughters what she hoped would be protective lessons on social protocols. In counseling them to trust very few people, she repeated to them, "In this life you have one or two friends. Everyone else is an acquaintance." Forde thought that her mother did not want them to trust others too easily, and to exercise extreme care when confiding in people. She also told them to keep trying when they met any sort of barrier. "You might not be able to go straight through," Muriel paraphrased. "You look for ways to go under it, around it, or over it . . . never sit back and complain." As a grown woman, Chisholm would possess a similar reserve and resourcefulness, remaining very private and excelling at solving seemingly unsolvable problems.[55]

While Ruby often represented restraint to Shirley, Charles helped her see possibilities for her future in politics. He was fairly egalitarian when it came to gender, seeing the importance of a college education for all of his daughters. Her father, a "very handsome," "remarkable," union man who was about five foot six, would have been a great scholar had he been able to attend college himself, Shirley believed. His appetite for reading led him to buy multiple newspapers each day, to the chagrin of his budget-conscious wife. When Shirley returned to the United States in 1934, Charles was working for a commercial cake bakery and a proud member of the Confectionary and Bakers International Union. He would later take a job at a burlap bag factory where, before the advent of plastic bags forced him to retire, he was president of his union and vice president of his Brooklyn local. He invited his friends for whiskey-fueled, long political conversations at the flat (whiskey, too, was an unnecessary expense in Ruby's eyes). "I could sit in a couch or chair and listen to him for hours" as he told stories about Garvey and railed against the British colonial system in the Caribbean, Chisholm recalled. He even took his oldest daughter to hear Garveyite speakers discuss Black nationalism.[56] In almost every interview she gave, once her political career had started, Chisholm credited her father with developing her political awareness and claimed that she had been his favorite daughter. She maintained that her interest in politics came from the political stories that he told about Marcus Garvey and the Roosevelts. She asserted that he didn't "brag about" the other three girls as much as he did about her, though Muriel insisted that Charles was equally proud of all of his daughters. At any rate, he did not see politics as a male-only domain and freely shared his ideas with his daughter, nurturing her political thinking and encouraging her to pursue politics as she got older.

Shirley had more adjustments to make once back in New York. The three girls returned not only to their parents but also to their youngest sister, Selma, who had been born in September 1931. Shirley and her siblings and cousins were also shocked at the lack of discipline in American classrooms, with their spitball throwing and disrespect of teachers. Having been schooled out of the country, Shirley did not know U.S. geography or history and was put back to the third grade at PS 144, two grades behind where her age and skills placed her. Bored, she became an expert spitball thrower. Ruby and Charles recognized the discipline problem as boredom, hired a tutor for the missing subjects, and arranged for Shirley to be promoted several grades. The discipline problems stopped, and Shirley became an academic star.[57] The cold-water flat that the family lived in was affordable enough that Ruby could stay home and take in sewing while Charles worked at the bakery. He attempted to earn more money by switching jobs to a burlap bag factory, but the work was inconsistent. Eventually the desire for better housing required Ruby to take a job doing domestic labor for a wealthy Jewish family. This meant longer hours, and, as the oldest, Shirley was in charge of taking care of her sisters. She wore a house key on a string around her neck and was required to bring her sisters home for lunch during the day. Each Tuesday, her mother gave her a quarter for day-old goods from a local bakery. Those would serve as lunch for the next few days. She also retrieved her sisters from school each afternoon. In the summer, she was home with them. Ruby instructed her to keep them on a rigid schedule, which she did: outside early in the morning to play, back in by noon, back out at 3 for another hour of play, back in by 4:30 in time to meet Ruby when she arrived home at 5 or 6. On weekends, the family would go to church and then Sunday School. By Muriel's recollection, Shirley loved having authority over her younger siblings. She was "domineering" and beat her sister when she disobeyed, and Ruby approved. "We all obeyed her without question," Muriel said. Shirley was also "very outgoing. She was very good at organizing and managing things. She had the ability to make friends easily, and a lot of school friends looked up to her." Shirley also made sure she looked her best every day. She loved clothes and would sometimes get up first in the morning so that she could have her pick of the outfits, many of them sewn by Ruby, and be the best dressed.[58]

According to her memory, all of the children were well aware that the St. Hills needed to earn every available penny so that they could buy a brownstone and understood why childcare fell to the eldest. The savings from Shirley's babysitting and additional income from Ruby's labor allowed a series of moves that would eventually lead to purchasing a house. First they moved to Bedford-Stuyvesant around 1936, into 420 Ralph Avenue, which had central heating.[59] However, the city had plans to tear the neighborhood down and erect the Kingsborough housing project, so around 1940 the family made a temporary move to 316 Patchen Avenue, across the street from where the Breevort Projects would be built in 1955. Charles took a second job as the building's janitor, which meant free housing, and Ruby was able to stay at home once again with the girls. Once the Kingsborough Projects were completed in 1941, the family moved into the modern apartment complex of sixteen six-story buildings, with a total of 1,100 units. Though spartan and plain, it had thirty-six employees who gardened, painted, repaired, and secured the premises. Although many displaced poor and nonwhite families in slum-clearance projects were left to "self-relocate," the city sought "model tenants" who were employed members of the working classes, and the St. Hills managed to fit the bill.[60] This was where the St. Hills would live through most of Shirley's high school and college years. Later, living in the Kingsborough Projects would anchor her belief that affordable public housing was essential to building financial independence. But in the short term, the changing neighborhoods represented a challenge and a culture shock for Shirley, who was constantly getting lost and whose Barbadian accent was mocked by other children. She used storefronts as landmarks, but when these changed, she often lost her way. She also had to break her habit of walking and playing in the street, as she had done in Barbados, and learn to use the sidewalk.[61] More and more, Barbadians were moving southward from Bedford-Stuyvesant into Crown Heights. The St. Hills themselves would buy a brownstone there on Prospect Place in 1945, and Chisholm would live in Crown Heights throughout her congressional career.

The girls also had to learn more about Blackness in America after their return from the majority-Black island and their move to Bedford-Stuyvesant. While they had been one of a tiny number of Black families in Brownsville, living in Bed-Stuy brought them into sustained contact with Black American culture for the first time. It also forced more reckoning with overt racism in Jim Crow America and "being made to feel inferior." This seems to have been the moment when Shirley became aware that white Americans saw her race as primary and her ethnicity as secondary—or irrelevant. Shirley became more conscious of "dislikes of my people," and she heard racial slurs such as "nigger, kike, Jew bastard, black son of a bitch." As one of a very few Black children in Brownsville, she had been less aware of overt racism, but as she listened to her father's conversations with other adults about how Black people were in dead-end jobs and other experiences of various adult workers, she became angry.[62] Later she would claim that she was more resilient when it came to racism than her sisters had been: "My sisters could not fight discrimination. My sisters are not fighters. They gave up along the way."[63] Ruby and Charles attempted to insulate their daughters from white supremacy by instilling a sense of confidence in their own intellectual abilities. Muriel recalled that time with more nuance about her own attitudes than Shirley perceived. "We were brought up in a very hard world for black people," she told an interviewer. "And yet we were brought up without any feeling of antagonism toward whites. We lived among whites for most of our lives. We went to school with them. And a good many of them helped us along our way. . . . We were always taught [to] take people as they are. You wait and see how they treat you or what their attitudes are." "My parents had a saying," Muriel recalled. "'Brains have no color.' You know. Everybody has been endowed by God with some degree of intelligence. Except it's up to you to evolve it to the highest point that you can."[64] Therefore, racist treatment was never an excuse for poor grades.

However, a belief in uplift and achievement was no match for the pervasive and institutionalized racism in the midcentury United States, even for the St. Hill girls. Despite getting the highest grade in her class, for example, Muriel was not awarded the history medal. Although she recalled that such snubs only made her work harder, and that upon graduation from high school (which she finished at age sixteen), she earned more prizes than anyone else, such discrimination served as reminders of racism's power. Furthermore, Muriel's winning those medals had an impact not only on the pride of the St. Hill family, but as a vindication for Black people in the city. "I wanted it also for the colored people of Brooklyn," she said. "Because we were real tired of going to these ceremonies and our kids not being up there when it came time for awards and medals and what not."[65]

Shirley took her parents' exhortations to heart and worked hard to succeed in school, too—not just because she wanted to vindicate Black intellect but also because she was ambitious and liked to be on top. By the time she returned from Barbados and was enrolled at the appropriate grade level, she was old enough for middle school. She attended PS 28, Junior High School 178 at Saratoga and Dean Streets, and then graduated from Girls' High School in 1942. At Girls' High, which was integrated, she was very involved with extracurricular activities: the Arista Honors Society, the "Pan-American Club," the "Literary Strollers," the Knitting and French clubs, the yearbook, and tutoring, and served as a teacher's aide. Her nickname was "Shorty," and her popularity was evidenced by scores of autographs across the pages of her yearbook.[66] These diverse interests suggest young Shirley's interest in international relationships, literature, and teaching. She was also winning accolades. She won the French medal and the Junior Arista Society (honors) prize. It was at a prize-giving ceremony that Eleanor Roosevelt witnessed Shirley's acceptance speech and Mary McLeod Bethune gave her instructions to work hard and persevere.

Shirley St. Hill's upbringing blended American and Caribbean life, lessons about race and gender, her ambition and drive to achieve, and the coming of age of her own outspoken character. The encouragement of her heroes, in both Barbados and the United States, resonated with her growing sense of her own capacities and her conviction that she ought to do good in the world. She wanted to emulate the three women heroes of her early life: her grandmother Emmeline Seale, Roosevelt, and Bethune. She wanted to exercise power over the world around her. And so, as a Barbadian American Black girl with big ambitions, she took their mandate with her and embarked on her college education.

2

IN PURSUIT OF THE HIGHEST IN ALL
The Making of a Young Intellectual

Although Shirley Chisholm would eventually be a formidable Black feminist political force, young Shirley St. Hill was ambivalent about pursuing politics during college and her early career. She was inspired by Mary McLeod Bethune's leadership and wanted to emulate it, but she was focused on earning a degree that would lead directly to professional employment. She did not think that she had a future in electoral politics and thought she could make change by following in Bethune's footsteps and becoming an educator. Teaching was one of the few professional opportunities for bright Black women, she knew, and she made plans to start teaching after college. She chose a sociology major even though she excelled at and was energized by political science.

She made these choices in part because she carried the hopes of her family on her small shoulders. She became the first person in her family to attend a college or university. Eventually, two of his four daughters fulfilled Charles St. Hill's hopes by winning scholarships for college; not having to use their savings to pay tuition allowed Charles and Ruby to purchase a brownstone on Prospect Place for $10,000. Shirley was offered scholarships to four institutions, including Vassar and Oberlin. She wanted to go out of the city to a residential campus, but boarding away from home was not included in the scholarships and was expensive. She reluctantly enrolled instead at the city's public Brooklyn College (BC), which had no tuition and no residence halls, and lived with her family. The campus, built of red brick, lush with trees, was relatively young, having been opened at its present site just five years before. BC was free and thus accessible to students from all class backgrounds, but women had to possess a higher grade point average than men to gain admission.[1] Shirley was excited by the possibility of "making it" as her parents wanted for her. Her grandmother had always told her that "determination, not distinction," would prevail—and Shirley thought that her perseverance and determination gave her a "strong character" and were the reasons for her success at college and, later, in politics.[2]

Shirley St. Hill, high school graduation photo.
Courtesy of the Muriel Forde family.

In addition to providing a credential for a professional career, going to Brooklyn College transformed Shirley. It was the "opening of my entire personality," and the moment of realization that her ideas were worthy of attention. While she characterized herself as having been somewhat introverted in school since her return to the United States, college life encouraged her to speak out more. Having read ten or eleven books per month between ages ten and eighteen, she had a lot to talk about. She was active in many student organizations and became known as a crack debater. As a "bookworm," Shirley did not often attend parties, although when she did she surprised the boys with her impressive dancing abilities. Because of her school performance, she gained a reputation as being "too intellectual" to date. But her studious habits did not mean that she was uninterested in socializing or in finding a beau. She was sometimes ashamed of her clothes because they were not as new or fashionable as those of other students, so dating and socializing likely led to some embarrassment. And she was unwilling to sacrifice her academics for the pursuit of romance. She spent many hours in the library instead of at parties, she explained later, because she did not want to squander her opportunity to get a good education. Still, she eventually experienced her first serious love affair during her senior year.

Even though Shirley declined to major in political science or plan for a political career, she continued to develop her Black feminist power political outlook. Through her extracurricular activities with other Black men and women students and her voracious reading, she built personal and intellectual commitments to the antiracist and feminist thinkers of the past. She practiced her speaking skills through debating and developed political savvy through coursework and conversation. And she even chose teaching as a vocation in part because, as she admitted, she liked to be in charge. Shirley's college and early career years did not represent an inevitable march toward her future accomplishments; rather, she determined which of her skills were the strongest and assessed how she could use them for the common good.

EDUCATION INSIDE AND OUTSIDE OF THE CLASSROOM

Chisholm recalled that BC had only sixty Black students because, despite free tuition, the 89 percent grade point average required was not achieved by most of the city's Black high school students. Within her graduating class, only nine other students in the yearbook appear to be Black. There were many white women, however—more than before the United States entered World War II. President Harry Gideonse remarked on this in his yearbook comments to the graduating class: "The girls came to take the places which the boys had left vacant."[3]

One of the first lessons Shirly learned at BC was that leftist politics could be dangerous in the midst of the Cold War. She saw that the institution walked a fine line between being "radical" and "red." Chisholm remembered BC as a "radical" institution for its day, with multiple student organizations that were "ultra-progressive." She hastened to add, however, that the place was hardly "riddled with Reds." In this she was alluding to the scrutiny that BC and its fellow institutions (City College, Hunter College, and Queens College) underwent in the early 1940s. The Rapp-Coudert Committee, a New York state version of the House Un-American Activities Committee, investigated faculty and staff for communist and subversive activity. Although it claimed an interest in fiscal and administrative responsibility, the Rapp-Coudert Committee's ultimate aim seemed to be curbing teacher unions and decreasing public spending on higher education. It was successful at removing faculty it deemed as communist-affiliated, without due process, even if (and perhaps because) the faculty member was a strong teacher and scholar. Gideonse, who was appointed in 1938, cooperated with and even anticipated the concerns of the Rapp-Coudert Committee so that suspected communist infiltrations were not made public. The result was that, by the time Shirley enrolled at Brooklyn, there were indeed no overt communist sympathizers on the faculties of city colleges.[4]

Shirley was quite active in extracurricular activities. She joined multiple organizations in quick succession, ultimately dropping many of them—something that she did for the next twenty years. Her dissatisfaction, she maintained, came from her frustration with organizations that made promises but failed to get things done.[5] But there were several that drew her in, especially the Harriet Tubman Society, Ipothia, the Debating Society, the Political Science Society, the Pan American Club, and the Social Service Club.[6] Her senior yearbook explained that the Harriet Tubman Society of seventy members "holds discussions and forums in an attempt to arrive at some definite conclusions concerning the racial problem." Chisholm remembered the new organization (it was founded during her first year) as the first place she heard people other than her father discuss race and racism. She also recalled that she was able to participate in these discussions, but "more out of my reading than my experience," meaning that she did not relate to the lifelong experiences with American racism that other students had because of her Bajan upbringing. Thus, the Tubman Society was an essential education and an opportunity to learn from her African American peers whose families had lived in the country for generations. Through the new club she read about Tubman, Frederick Douglass, W. E. B. Du Bois, George Washington Carver, and African history. She also joined the

Brooklyn chapter of the National Association for the Advancement of Colored People (NAACP), but in her own words "was not too active." She also dabbled in community service through the Urban League and the Brooklyn Home for the Aged.[7]

The social club Ipothia was her particular pride. The name came from an acronym of "In pursuit of the highest in all"—a phrase that Chisholm identified with and characterized her approach to social justice and politics. She cofounded the club, intended to function as a sorority for Black women, with other members Edna Blanding, Carmen Skeete, and Ena Williams, who were also in the Harriet Tubman Society. In Chisholm's words, "We were tired of trying to get into white groups, and decided, 'who needs them?'" But the group also recognized the need for Black women to identify their own interests independently of Black men. She recalled that Ipothia reached a high point of twenty-six members—no small feat considering that there were fewer than one hundred Black students at BC.[8]

Shirley discovered her oratorical skills in the Debating Society. Debates were often over current events, and the society argued about the integration of the armed forces, capital punishment, and poll taxes. Shirley needed only a page of notes to guide her through a "fiery" closing speech, as she was the designated final speaker during many debates. Her team "won more often than it lost."[9] Shirley found herself unbothered by holding views that others did not always agree with, and she noticed that other students tended to respect her opinion. She discovered she had the courage to state and hold her position, an ability to influence others, and an "ability to hold an audience" when speaking.

Membership in the Political Science Society showed her how difficult working with white-run groups could be. The group conceived of itself as "progressive," but Shirley noticed that Black people were treated with the expectation that they could not hold real power alongside white members. Even Black students with more talent and intelligence than the white members who held power in the organization did not hold leadership positions. Chisholm, in hindsight, credited this experience with showing her the reality of national political power. "I perceived that this was the way it was meant to be: things were organized to keep those who were on top up there," she wrote. "The country was racist all the way through."[10] The society invited a white politician to speak on campus, probably Assemblyman Irwin Steingut, father of future Brooklyn Democratic Party leader Stanley Steingut. He proclaimed that Black people could move ahead, but only under white leadership. "That stuck in my throat," she wrote, and she credited the moment with sparking her eventual devotion to electoral politics. As scoldings in Barbados had emboldened her to be more outspoken, so did Steingut's dismissal of Black political agency. She grew skeptical that attempts to solve problems through talking with "the leading people," as she termed prominent white citizens, would lead to real change for Black citizens.[11]

She found an encouraging mentor in Louis Warsoff, whom she called "Proffy," the one white political science faculty mentor who encouraged Shirley without reserve. In *Unbought and Unbossed*, she identified him as the first white man she trusted, and she recalled that he showed her "that white people were not really different from me." A blind man, Warsoff was willing to have "long talks" with his young protégé. And, after she acquitted herself particularly well in a debate match, "Proffy" identified Shirley as a likely prospect for a career in politics. She demurred because politics connoted corruption and opportunism to her. And, even though it rankled, she realized that it was nearly unheard of for Black women to participate as candidates. She also claimed to have little interest in politics and campaigns, but at the same time she despised comments like Steingut's that wrote off Black political participation.[12]

She did not major in political science. She instead chose a degree she thought was more practical: a major in sociology and a minor in Spanish. She planned to become a teacher, one of the few professional options available to her as a Black woman. In *Unbought and Unbossed*, she recalled the cautionary tale of her sister Muriel, who graduated magna cum laude from BC in 1950 with a major in physics and was unable to find a job in any laboratory. She thought that sociology would lead to more job prospects for a Black woman than political science; fluency in Spanish helped her reach and teach students and, later, constituents. She found herself still planning to become a teacher but intrigued by the exhortations from others that she become a change agent. Teaching, she thought, would utilize her talents and serve society through educating children about what she herself was learning. But in college she began to think more seriously about racism, what she called doing "something about the way whites treated my people."[13]

FIRST LOVE, FIRST JOB, AND FIRST MARRIAGE

Shirley's personal life took a dramatic turn during the spring of her senior year when she fell in love. As she matured, she had become, in her words, "an attractive enough quiet little girl with long hair." During Easter break in 1946, Shirley took a job as a jewel setter in a Manhattan costume jewelry factory. She would recall it as the worst job she ever had, requiring her to clamp tiny stones into their seats on necklaces and bracelets. "At the end of a day," she recalled decades later, "my eyes would be aching and tearing; my fingers would smell of metal, and the back of my neck would be pained due to the constant bending over."[14] However, those discomforts had an upside that came in the form of a new romance. Her mother, perennially protective of her daughter's sexual innocence, had ordered Shirley to avoid socializing with the mixed company there. At first Shirley obeyed, but, as usual, she found it challenging to conform to her mother's rules. She was eating lunch by herself in her first week of work when a dashing Caribbean man in his late twenties approached her. R—, as Chisholm called him, "was an excellent conversationalist, and communicated a feeling of warmth and nearness to those about him," and he served as an informal leader in the eyes of other workers. Surely it was all right to speak with a fellow West Indian, and such a polished one at that, the young woman might well have reasoned.

The admirer swept Shirley off her feet and into a love affair. The characteristically private Chisholm gives a hint of the whirlwind character of this romance, tinged with amusement at her younger self, in *Unbought and Unbossed*. However, she wrote an even more detailed version in an unpublished draft of the book.[15] In the published version she recounted that she threw away her packed lunch every day for her remaining time at the factory so that she could eat lunch with her suitor. Once Easter break was over and she returned to classes, the lover invited himself to the St. Hill home on a Saturday, over Shirley's misgivings ("he wouldn't take no for an answer"). Ruby was appalled. For one thing, she was "primed to hate him on sight," and she disapproved of the man's choice of sport coat and slacks rather than a suit.[16] The man also walked into Ruby's bedroom, ostensibly to fix his tie, without permission, a grave invasion of privacy and propriety. Charles St. Hill, alternatively, was charmed and enjoyed talking to R— about current events.[17] He lacked Ruby's instincts, which warned her that this older man was untrustworthy, and chided his wife to be "less of an islander and more American in her views," as Chisholm later put it. Chisholm wrote that "the battle began" after the man's departure on that first visit, and that she threatened to leave if Ruby's disapproval drove her to do so, which ended the argument. "She's only growing up," Charles reassured his wife, and an uneasy truce prevailed.[18]

After she graduated in 1946, her relationship with the handsome suitor seemed to be progressing toward marriage. Still, Shirley set about looking for a means to attain economic independence and advance her teaching prospects. No matter how in love she was with R—, she was apparently unwilling to sacrifice her professional pursuits. Like other Black women in the twentieth century, Shirley was prepared to combine marriage and career ambition.[19] She had graduated cum laude and hoped to find a teaching job quickly with this sterling credential. Admittedly, not all of her motivation for wanting to teach consisted of high ideals. As she had since her childhood years, she liked to hold power, and she wanted to teach in part "because it made me feel big."[20] However, as she grew older she began to admire her chosen profession more.

She had a difficult time getting started as a teacher. Racism restricted where she would be hired, and she also was extremely young looking—she was just over ninety pounds, with a pageboy haircut and the appearance of a high school student. Interviewers told her that she did not look old enough to teach or be responsible for children, one way to encode racism into rejecting her. She found herself being passed over for jobs in favor of other BC classmates, even though she was better prepared. "I wore out shoe leather day after day," she recalled.[21]

She heard of a possible opening for a preschool teacher at the Mt. Calvary Child Care Center, housed at the Mt. Calvary Methodist Church in Sugar Hill, Harlem. At the time it was one of Harlem's tonier neighborhoods, to the north of the commercial strip and hustle and bustle of 125th Street. Having scored an interview, Shirley was not at all sure she had made a favorable impression on the somewhat stern-seeming director, Eula M. Hodges. Hodges asked at the interview whether Shirley could handle a group of children even though she looked like a child herself, and the younger woman "blew up," stating her case forcefully. Hodges, unfazed and able to see past first impressions, asked Shirley to come back several times to answer more questions. Hodges was so impressed by Shirley's tenacity that she did hire her, saying, "Well, if you're game enough to try, I'm game enough to try you."[22]

Shirley St. Hill took her first classroom of four-year-olds and proved herself as a teacher. Her pedagogical creativity led to her playing the piano and singing to students, teaching them dances (the horse trot, the duck walk, and the elephant run), and writing plays for the children to perform. When she eventually received older school-age students in an afterschool program, she taught them embroidery. She and Hodges came to respect each other deeply. Hodges was impressed when Shirley delivered her monthly reports in front of the entire staff from memory. Chisholm eventually rose to the position of assistant director and left in 1953. "I turned out to be one of the best teachers," she bragged. She also developed a social network at Mt. Calvary. In addition to Hodges, she befriended fellow teacher Margaret Ormsby, and she participated in the teachers' bridge club. Shirley was the one to name the club Les Femmes Gaies (The Lively Ladies) and, despite not knowing any card games before starting, became an "expert" player.[23]

Not long after being hired at Mt. Calvary, Chisholm entered the master's degree program in early childhood education at Columbia University. She attended night classes, commuting to Mt. Calvary each morning, then eating a quick dinner and taking the subway over to Columbia once the school day was over. She studied while commuting on the subway and earned her degree in 1951 while also teaching.[24]

She was still planning to marry R—, the man from the jewelry factory, but she had caught the eye of another suitor. Conrad Chisholm, while walking from class to a meeting one evening, introduced himself and "persuaded [her] to stand still long enough to get acquainted."[25] Conrad, "a stocky, quiet, handsome Jamaican," was a forty-one-year-old recently arrived immigrant when Shirley first encountered him. Conrad grew up in Summer Hill, about twelve miles from Montego Bay, in St. James Parish, as one of nine boys and three girls. His father, John, never finished "elementary high school" and was listed as a "planter" on Conrad's birth certificate. Still, he was well read and served as chair of the Parish Council School Board. His mother, Zillah Knott, was a skilled cook and taught her son to cook, which was very useful because "when I married [Shirley], she couldn't cook. Her mother kept her out of the kitchen. And she couldn't boil water. She couldn't burn it, so to speak." Conrad himself attained middle-class status in Kingston through a high school degree from Calabar High School, one of the most prestigious in the country. Conrad's education propelled him to a good civil service job after graduation, and he worked as a statistician in the Labor Department in Kingston. He said that he was "recruited" to come to the United States to work during World War II, though it is unknown by whom. Conrad was attracted to Shirley because of "her strength of character," he said. "She was one of those people that was a fighter. She was tenacious."[26]

When Shirley met Conrad, she was still head over heels for her fiancé, R—, but the engagement failed. As late as the summer of 1948, things had seemed to be on track. R— had ambitions to become a criminal lawyer and was accepted to law school in the fall.[27] But Ruby turned out to be correct about R—'s trustworthiness. Shirley first noticed something was wrong when she returned from a three-week vacation upstate and R—was at Grand Central Station to meet her, but looked exhausted. "I was to learn much later," she wrote, "of the terrific mental strain he was then undergoing trying to control the events he had set in motion, always afraid that one slip might prove fatal and uncover his carefully spun web of deceit and fraud." Then R— sponsored a woman from Jamaica to migrate to New York. Shirley, under the impression that she was an old friend to whom R— owed a favor, eagerly helped by finding accommodations and winter clothes for her. When the woman arrived, Shirley found her oddly standoffish but continued to provide help and friendship. One day, the woman angrily confronted Shirley about her engagement to R—. At this moment, Shirley finally grasped that her fiancé's relationship with the woman was romantic. Shirley fled R—'s house, whereupon she ran into R— himself at the subway station.

He followed her home, "pleading and cajoling," but she was unmoved. She refused to speak to him.[28]

The final blow to the relationship was when Shirley discovered about a month later that R— was awaiting deportation on Ellis Island. She visited him once, whereupon he told her that he had overstayed his visa and had been discovered through the supplier of his fraudulent birth certificate.[29] He was most likely in deeper trouble still as a coconspirator in a major immigration fraud scheme. Real estate salesman Edward Stewart, investigators found in 1948, had collaborated with court clerks in South Carolina who helped him obtain false U.S. birth certificates. He then sold them to Jamaicans who wished to immigrate to the United States, for $50 to $350, and brought them in through the Port of Miami. There were thirty other coconspirators arrested in connection with the fraud, and Shirley's fiancé was most likely one of these.[30] His female friend had also been arrested. Still angry but willing to help, Shirley agreed to pack up the woman's things to ship them for her. As she did so, she inadvertently discovered letters to the woman signed "Your loving husband, R—." Armed with certain knowledge of her lover's lies and betrayal, Shirley left the room and visited Ellis Island one last time to inform R— that she would not continue to help him in any way. The man "glared at me for a few silent moments, then turned on his heel and walked away." He and his wife were shortly deported to England.[31]

In *Unbought and Unbossed,* Chisholm described a mental breakdown that occurred afterward. "I couldn't sleep; I couldn't eat," she recalled, and her family sent her to "a farm in New Jersey, owned by old family friends," to recover. There, "in the quiet, surrounded by fresh air and affection, tempted by country cooking, I groped my way back to reality." Chisholm's discussion of such a personal matter—a failed love affair and then a subsequent mental breakdown—was quite rare. This passage in *Unbought and Unbossed* is exceptional for her candor regarding her romantic fortunes and her mental health. It is difficult to tell whether she exaggerated her mental state after the betrayal or if she really did become so despondent that she "considered suicide" and sank into what sounds like a deep depression. She explained it by saying that she had to "grope" her way back to reality and become "in control of [her]self," implying that it was youthful notions of love that pushed her into mental illness.[32] Even so, her experience suggests a vulnerability that she took pains to conceal during her career but which emerged at later times. It is not clear how or when she took a leave of absence from her position to go to the farm in New Jersey in what was probably late 1948. She remained employed at Mt. Cavalry until 1953, however, so her job survived the personal turmoil. Indeed, she claimed in *Unbought and Unbossed* that she returned from her ordeal having "decided that my future would be one of complete devotion to my profession of child welfare and early childhood education. And one of spinsterhood."[33]

As she tells the story, however, Conrad Chisholm "learned I was back in circulation" and set about wooing her "with infinite gentleness and patience." He was aided by Ruby, who approved of Conrad's manners and welcomed him into the family's brownstone. Conrad reciprocated Ruby's affection. Shirley did her best to discourage him with "glacial aloofness, standing him up, angry sarcasm, avoiding him." According to Conrad though, the issue was Chisholm's ambition and preoccupation with books and education that caused her hesitation. When he first proposed, he recalled, he told her that she ought to settle down and get married, that there was more to life than books. Shirley did not entirely believe him, he recalled. She, however, wrote that Conrad succeeded because his "inexhaustible sympathy got through" to her and she "realized that this was a different kind of man"—someone she admired for "being a good storyteller and spiffy dresser." They developed a rapport in which she was pampered and protected, and they enjoyed ballroom dancing together. To Shirley, who had recently experienced profound betrayal, Conrad must have seemed to be a safe haven. Her parents were almost certainly relieved to have an older, financially stable husband for their daughter. After a bridal shower at Margaret Ormsby's house and a June engagement party at the St. Hill brownstone, they married on October 8, 1949—Conrad's forty-third birthday. Shirley was twenty-five. Her trousseau contained a host of embroidered linens, hand-painted china, ceramic ashtrays and knickknacks, and fine glassware. Her sister and cousin made all of the dresses for the women in the wedding party. Her trousseau included a travel outfit of a blue suit with matching beret, a bag (with red lining), wine lizard shoes, and red and blue luggage pieces. The teachers from Mt. Cavalry—led by Eula Hodges—worked from nine in the evening until three in the morning decorating the church on the "sunny and mild" wedding day. Shirley dressed with the help of her sisters. Odessa, as maid of honor, set the veil on her sister's head, and Shirley pinned a corsage on her mother's dress. The party lined up on the steps of 1094 for a photograph: Shirley, Charles, eight bridesmaids, a ring bearer, and a flower girl. After the ceremony at St. Phillip's Episcopal Church, the 150 guests proceeded to the Stuyvesant Community Center on Decatur Street for a reception. Later, the new Mrs. Chisholm dressed for her honeymoon, and the couple departed for Grand Central Station and a train to Montreal. After a weeklong honeymoon, they moved into the second floor of the St. Hill brownstone for a time before moving a few blocks away to a small apartment on Park Place.[34]

In her marriage, Chisholm insisted on continuing her career—and Conrad had no choice but to assent. The marriage worked because "we had

Conrad and Shirley Chisholm at their wedding, 1949.
Courtesy of the Muriel Forde family.

compromises," Conrad would later recall. Chisholm's assertive public persona did not mean that she was always so assertive at home:

It was a give and take proposition. There were certain times when she didn't get out of hand but she was overbearing. And at other times I went out and I stayed out and things like that but we did compromise with that. But the thing about it is, the marriage worked because I knew what I had. And she recognized what she had. We were both

Shirley Chisholm and Ruby and Charles St. Hill at her wedding, 1949.
Courtesy of the Shirley Chisholm estate.

individuals. Mature individuals who were working for a good cause, that is [this] whole marriage. So that's the whole thing about it. . . . She was the fighting Shirley Chisholm in public but at home she was not.[35]

The St. Hills liked Conrad. "He was a very good-natured person. And very humorous. I am partial to people with a sense of humor," Muriel recalled.

Although Charles was "a more serious type" than Conrad, they got along quite well.[36] For fun, the couple went to movies and dances at the Audubon Ballroom (she was a better dancer than Conrad, he admitted), and they enjoyed trips to the mountains. Both had a good sense of humor. "Whenever she danced, everyone would just stop dancing and look at her. She's tiny, oh yes, she's tiny. And she dances and knows all the right moves. And she'd dance with anybody. She was a very kind-hearted, loving individual." They walked, worked, and talked together. Later, during her political career, if she was speaking at a church on Sunday he would help her prepare a sermon, drawing on his education at the Baptist-founded Calabar High School. They both loved to eat, and go to picnics and parties on Bear Mountain. And they traveled up the Hudson to Saratoga Springs during horse racing season.[37]

But Chisholm was not a stay-at-home wife. She also would not bear children, although, as became even more apparent later, Collins's "othermothering" is what Chisholm embraced as a teacher and as a politician.[38] She finished the coursework for her master's in 1951 from Columbia and was promoted up the ranks at Mt. Calvary. She was serving as assistant director at Mt. Calvary in 1953 when she was offered the position of director of the Friend In Need Nursery School, a private primary school in Brownsville that served forty mostly middle-class Jewish and German children. The school's rather old-fashioned name had originated in the nineteenth century, from its founding as an institution for poor children. It had since begun a long decline, with financial problems plaguing the board of directors. Chisholm was hired to try to turn the school's fortunes around. The board was hesitant to hire a Black woman as their director, but Chisholm came highly recommended and they were desperate to resuscitate their school. She was the second of two Black teachers working in the four-teacher school.

Chisholm, with her characteristic take-charge approach, soon discovered the weaknesses that had driven the school toward obsolescence. While the parents and students appreciated Chisholm's fresh perspective, the white and mostly female and elderly board insisted on an antiquated, Victorian model of behavior from its teachers. Summoned to the monthly board meetings by a little bell and placed on a chair in the center of the room, Chisholm was expected to answer questions about both the school and her own personal life. In her telling, she was amused rather than intimidated by such treatment, and she set about correcting it immediately. She rebuked the board for "poking into" her personal life and informed them that they were paying her to run the school. When one of them pushed back, informing her that she was simply to do as she was told by the board, she rejoined with "there are certain things, such as pride and dignity, that an individual never gives up." She then moved her chair from the center of the room to the edge of the circle with the board members. Under threat of her resignation, and with the support of three of the board members, she successfully changed the format and culture of the meetings. Still, she was all too aware of the racial suspicion with which she was treated by some on the board, even as she experienced admiration and respect from parents and students. She doubted whether any questions about her personal life would have emerged had she been white.[39]

She was already eyeing new opportunities but found that racism was still an impediment. Now that she had demonstrated her leadership abilities at Friend in Need, she submitted her dossier to the New York State Employment Agency as a candidate for administrative positions. But even though she was an attractive candidate on paper, when employers realized that she was Black, the job would suddenly be unavailable. On one memorable occasion the agency's coordinator told a private school principal in the northwest Bronx (possibly the prestigious Riverdale Country School) that Shirley was the ideal person for the job. When she called on the phone, in her most professional voice, she was told to come to the school for an interview. After getting off the train and walking to the school along tree-lined streets, however, she began to doubt whether she would be hired in the predominantly white neighborhood. "It was beautiful, and I knew it was too good for black people. They would never let me have it." Matters became worse when she encountered a very cool receptionist who all but ignored her. This cool demeanor turned to fluster when Shirley told the receptionist that she was there to be interviewed for the teaching job, and the receptionist retreated into the principal's office. When she was finally shown in to see him, he had invented a spurious reason for why he could not hire her. Shirley was "floored to no end" and challenged him to admit that he had not known she was Black on the phone. Years later, Chisholm recalled her resolve: "If I had an opportunity, White America would not forget me. . . . They will pay for this." She named this incident as a key moment: "I began to get certain feelings churning inside me . . . I began to get involved in community life and organize people" just as she'd done at Brooklyn College.[40]

After the Riverdale debacle, the placement officer recommended her for the directorship of the Hamilton-Madison Child Care Center in the Alfred Smith Projects near city hall. The Smith Projects were part of the massive redevelopment of the Lower East Side under Robert Moses; urban renewal had torn down old tenements, leaving a ribbon of housing projects from 23rd Street to the Brooklyn Bridge. The Hamilton-Madison Center was a settlement house that oversaw the Child Care Center and served a large Black and Puerto Rican population. Director Geoffrey Weiner recalled later that Chisholm's principled stance on what she believed was right made her job challenging. But "she never moved an inch," he said, "especially if it was in the interest of the children and their families."[41] Because of Chisholm's fluency in Spanish, she was able to communicate well with all 150 of the students, to whom she wanted to teach reading and writing beginning at age four.

It was at Hamilton-Madison that Chisholm began to revisit her earlier attraction to politics. Not content to leave her involvement with students to the hours they were in school, she started to invest herself in their lives outside of school, attending meetings of neighborhood groups and becoming involved with the surrounding community.[42] From there she helped organize public housing tenants to take their problems with the housing authority about substandard buildings and facilities before the city council. The Bureau of the Budget was making allocations, and Chisholm joined the effort to steer more city dollars to poor residents. She was a natural spokesperson, she recalled later, because she "had the tenacity and the determination to withstand all of the insults, humiliations and abuses that the big boys would thrust in the direction of poor people." Accustomed to such treatment, members of the community often felt powerless and disengaged from government. But Chisholm drew energy from these kinds of struggles. Those same people who felt disenfranchised ultimately pushed her toward public office.[43]

From her relentless focus on academics in college to her appointment as an administrator at a major educational facility, Chisholm stayed focused on winning credentials and climbing the career ladder. She had even found a supportive husband who seemed unthreatened by her ambitions and her developing Black feminism as a personal and political philosophy. But politics, remaining at bay as a vocation, gradually returned to her life as an avocation. By the mid-1950s, Chisholm would be immersed in the Brooklyn political scene.

3
BROOKLYN POLITICS

———— ★ ————

When she entered politics, Chisholm joined a tradition that was at least as old as the Black presence in New York City. She would say later in life that she went into politics because of the problems she saw in her neighborhoods and wanted to solve: Black people suffering and being ignored by the local politicians. But she also joined a tradition of Black Caribbean immigrant political involvement, in place since at least the 1910s. "People often ask me how I managed to burst on to the national political scene so quickly," she said in 1970. "What most people fail to realize is that in Brooklyn there have been black people working toward political freedom for over twenty years."[1] Of course, it was longer, but that is what she saw in her lifetime. And she herself would become Brooklyn's most skilled activist at "convert[ing] grassroots organizing into formal political power."[2] Chisholm would add Black feminism—her analysis of intersecting racist and sexist forces—to electoral savvy in the struggles for power that her political forebears had begun.

In order to gather her own political power, Chisholm had to navigate the existing system in Brooklyn: one in which local officials deferred to local assembly district leaders in a complex system of favors and patronage. Existing Black elected and appointed officials tended to work within that system. She entered political activism, however, at a time when alliances and the balance of power were shifting. She cast her lot with the insurgents—those who sought to take power from the established players and old patronage networks and create an interracial leadership coalition in Bedford-Stuyvesant. The coalition held more opportunities for the development of women leaders, too. Among Chisholm's new colleagues was her political mentor and future campaign strategist Wesley MacDonald Holder, who recognized her political talent. Starting as an activist knocking on doors and attending meetings, she proved a quick study at detecting which way the winds of power were blowing and finding herself on the winning side. Black feminist power meant being able to locate and then challenge power to act on behalf of Black men and women. Chisholm's skills bore fruit: after a decade of involvement in local politics, she would wind up poised to win her first elected office.

BROOKLYN POLITICS: BOSSES AND BLACK VOTERS

Trading patronage jobs for votes was the Democrats' chief strategy for gathering power across the city, and it had worked well for decades. New York City Democratic politics had developed a system of political clubs at the assembly district level, where district leaders parceled out the patronage and favors. These district leaders reported to the party boss at the county level, who in turn reported to the state's Democratic Party leadership. Shirley Chisholm was to have a complicated relationship with this system as both an insurgent and a collaborator. She would emerge as the figurehead of a multiracial Democratic club that dethroned the existing white-controlled one in her own New York State Assembly district, the Seventeenth. But she would also participate in—and sometimes cooperate with—the Brooklyn Democratic Party organization, especially after 1968. As with other institutions, Chisholm came to shape this political dynamic to her favor as she rose in the ranks, even as she developed a Black feminist power politics.

Prior to the Great Migration and Chisholm's parents' generation, most Black New Yorkers voted Republican because, like their peers across the United States, Black voters maintained an allegiance to the party of Lincoln. However, this changed beginning in the 1920s. Across the river in Manhattan, the county-level Democratic political organization Tammany Hall responded to the influx of Black residents to Harlem by beginning to run Black candidates in the early 1920s. It simultaneously developed patronage relationships with Black voters by helping them get city jobs. Charles Murphy, Tammany leader from 1902 to 1924, developed a close relationship with the city's leading Black Democrat, Ferdinand Morton. Morton's United Colored Democracy became the clearinghouse for patronage toward Black residents. Marcus Garvey allied himself with Tammany, too. Caribbean migrants did not have the same relationship with the party of Lincoln as United States–born Black New Yorkers did. Many Black Brooklynites descended from people who had been enslaved within British and sometimes French or Spanish colonies across the Caribbean and had no personal family memories of the Civil War and Reconstruction. The American political party alignment did not resonate with them in the same way. Therefore, at least in Manhattan, Black New Yorkers were quicker than the rest of Black Americans to switch their allegiance to the Democratic Party.[3]

The willingness of Black Caribbean New Yorkers to vote for and run for Democratic Party candidates eventually meant that they found themselves getting elected. By the time the Democratic Party consolidated power during the Roosevelt administration, Black politicians across ethnic lines had begun to get elected to office from Harlem. Shirley St. Hill as a girl would have been familiar with Black political leadership in the city. Adam Clayton Powell Jr. was elected to city council in 1941 and then to the House of Representatives for Harlem in 1944. After Powell left his city council seat, Benjamin J. Davis, a communist with strong ties to organized labor, was elected. Hulan Jack, an immigrant from Guyana, won a New York State Assembly seat in 1940. Black Democratic political clubs also rose to prominence with leadership by Caribbean immigrants in Chisholm's parents' generation: Barbadian Herbert Bruce's the Beavers was formed as early as 1933, and J. Raymond Jones, an immigrant from St. Thomas, led the Carver Democratic Club in Harlem in the 1940s.[4] Within a generation, Shirley Chisholm would be leading alongside these Black men to represent her own constituents.

Brooklyn, and Bed-Stuy in particular, was somewhat slower in allowing Black elected representation. It was also slower to develop a Black majority population. But in the late 1940s, southern Black veterans were buying houses in Bedford-Stuyvesant, while Caribbean families, the St. Hills included, gained citizenship and bought in Crown Heights. Where Black people made up only about 4 percent of the Brooklyn population in 1940, they numbered over 210,000 and made up 7.6 percent of the population in 1950. The center of Brooklyn's Black population moved also, toward Bedford-Stuyvesant, where 60 percent of all Black Brooklynites lived in the 1940s.[5] The Democratic Party had started to revise its Brooklyn strategy as early as 1930, when it had lost a New York State Assembly seat to the GOP. Party leadership began to court Caribbean Black voters specifically in an effort to build loyalty. Roosevelt's New Deal in the 1930s provided a helpful platform. But the most influential factor, which would provide Black Democratic votes for the next generation, was the United Action Democratic Association (UADA), formed in 1933 in the aftermath of the GOP upset and FDR's election. Founded and led by Bertram Baker, a Caribbean migrant from Nevis of Chisholm's parents' generation, UADA was something of a Black auxiliary to the regular Democratic county organization.[6]

Baker quickly became the elder statesman of Black Brooklyn politics. He was born a minister's son in 1898 in Nevis and moved to the United States in 1915 to live with his grandmother. Having been well educated in the Caribbean, he attained the job of accountant for a chandelier company after completing a correspondence course in accounting, and then built his own private accounting business out of his Bedford-Stuyvesant home. He successfully applied for U.S. citizenship in 1924, the year Chisholm was born, and then worked his way up to a district captainship in the regular Seventeenth Assembly District (AD) Club by 1925. Eight years later, he gathered his Caribbean friends and allies, along with a handful of African Americans, in the UADA's founding meeting at St. Phillip's Episcopal Church. County leaders found in the UADA a mechanism for winning Caribbean migrants to the party.[7] The UADA was successful in dramatically increasing the number of Black citizens on the Kings County (Brooklyn) Democratic Committee: from six in 1932 to thirty-nine in 1936. In 1935, the UADA's reach grew due to the insurgent Brooklyn district attorney campaign of Samuel Liebowitz, the defense attorney for the Scottsboro Boys, who was running against the establishment Democratic candidate William F. X. Geoghan.[8] Liebowitz did not win, but his campaign manager, a Guyanese immigrant named Wesley McDonald Holder, turned over the list of local activists who had supported the campaign to Baker. Owing to his rising profile and growing organization, Baker was appointed deputy collector of internal revenue for the city and then to a job in the borough president's office.[9] Caribbean immigrants were clearly influential in politics, something not lost on Chisholm.

Baker was an organization man, unfailingly loyal to the Democratic Party leadership and heavily invested in traditional lines of authority. As the most prominent Black person in politics, he received support from the NAACP, the American Labor Party, the Urban League, and the Black Elks. His gradualism and temperament earned him criticism from Brooklyn civil rights activists, including Chisholm herself (she dismissed him in *Unbought and Unbossed* as part of "the old Brooklyn machine"). He made little effort to support other Black political figures, tending to stand behind the party organization's candidate even when there was a Black office seeker in the race. By some accounts, he was authoritarian, stubborn, autocratic, and cold. He appointed only women as his coleaders, apparently because he believed that other men would "try to outshine him."[10]

Even Baker could not breach the color wall within the Kings County Democratic Party without the help of interparty competition from Black political activists. It took him over a decade to win the support of party bosses for a run for elected office. In 1946, Ada Jackson (American Labor Party) and Maude Richardson (Republican Party), both Black women, ran for the New York State Assembly seat from the Seventeenth AD. Jackson won about 4,000 votes, but Richardson won 9,614, only 77 fewer than the winning white incumbent Democrat, John Walsh, with 9,691. Baker used the occasion as a wake-up call for the Democratic Party leadership, arguing that the election results amounted to "a racial vote in protest.": an indication of real dissatisfaction from Black Brooklynites. His argument was strengthened the following year when Jackson made a credible bid for a Brooklyn City Council seat. She lost the race but won most of the Black votes in the Seventeenth AD.[11] The Democrats realized that they would almost certainly lose the seat if they continued to run only white candidates. In 1948, district leader Stephen Carney convinced the incumbent Walsh to withdraw from the race, and Baker finally had his chance, winning the Seventeenth AD seat over Maude Richardson, whose success two years before had helped Baker convince the Democrats to run a Black candidate at all.[12]

The year 1948 was significant in Black Brooklyn politics for another reason. That year, in the climate of Cold War anticommunism, a Black lawyer named Lewis A. Flagg successfully defended the president of the Brooklyn chapter of the NAACP, Fred H. M. Turner, against charges of communism. Turner had belonged to the National Negro Congress, which later had communist leadership. With such obvious legal skills, Flagg made his first entry into formal politics in 1949, allying with the American Labor Party to run for a municipal court judgeship on the Republican ticket.[13] He lost, but he did not give up. When a judge of the Second Municipal Court District died in office in 1953, New York mayor Vincent Impellitieri appointed white Democrat Benjamin Schor to fill the seat even though Flagg was a logical choice. At the time, all forty-nine of the municipal court judges in Brooklyn were white, although a majority of the citizens who appeared before them were Black and brown. To add insult to injury, Schor spoke before the Brooklyn and Long Island Lawyers Association, comprised of Black lawyers, and taunted them: "I have [the judgeship]. If you want it, come and get it."[14] Black political activists decided to do just that.

BLACK INSURGENTS IN BEDFORD-STUYVESANT POLITICS

The snub to Flagg, in the context of both a growing Black presence and the beginnings of deindustrialization in Brooklyn, was a watershed event for Black Brooklyn politics. Black people were growing tired of being passed over for jobs, whether as janitors or judges. They had moved to Brooklyn because of opportunities in housing and in jobs. Now, during demobilization and the disappearance of war jobs, and the ongoing discrimination in housing, Black Brooklynites found themselves steered into downwardly mobile neighborhoods and living on downwardly mobile wages. White residents departed for suburbs farther away from Brooklyn's city center. The Brooklyn Navy Yard, a reliable source for job opportunities in the 1940s, began to lay off workers after the end of World War II and eventually closed in 1966. By 1960, the nearly 370,000 Black residents (about 14 percent) had far worse economic prospects than their white counterparts.[15] In 1953, Flagg being passed over for a judgeship illustrated the refusal of white officials to share power, as those same officials remained indifferent to economic inequality.

These frustrations catalyzed Chisholm's political career. She had met Wesley McDonald ("Mac") Holder, the campaign organizer for Samuel Liebowitz's district attorney campaign, before. Now Holder emerged as the head of a movement, and Chisholm joined. After Schor's taunts, Holder challenged Black lawyers in the community to run for the judgeship, this time on the Democratic ticket. Flagg was the one who accepted the challenge, on the condition that Holder run the campaign. Holder agreed and, with other community activists, formed the Committee to Elect Lewis S. Flagg. Chisholm joined the campaign and began to learn politics from Holder. Holder enlisted support from prominent Brooklynites, Black and white, sent mass mailings, and won the necessary support of the United Electrical Workers Union, the United Auto Workers, and the American Labor Party.

His campaign workers, including Chisholm, also canvassed the neighborhoods. The challenge was that many voters in the district were in the habit of voting for the straight party line on Election Day. Therefore, they had to alert voters to Flagg's viability as an independent candidate. They went door to door, convincing voters one by one to vote for Flagg, no matter how else they voted. On election night, Holder went so far as to hire private detectives to guard the entrances to the room where the ballots were stored. Flagg narrowly won the Democratic primary, a result that was challenged in the state supreme court. Then the court-mandated recount found that he had won by a slightly larger margin. Flagg went on to win the general election by a wide margin. In 1953, Black insurgents had won their first victory over the Democratic establishment in Brooklyn.[16] Chisholm had had her first taste of what it meant to challenge entrenched power—and win.

MAC HOLDER AND THE
BEDFORD-STUYVESANT POLITICAL LEAGUE

Chisholm had met her future mentor and collaborator Mac Holder through her hairdresser while she was in her senior year at Brooklyn College. Beauty shops have historically been sites of political discourse for Black women, so it is no surprise that her hairdresser, Cleo Skeete, was the one to introduce Chisholm to Holder. Whatever conversations Shirley had with Skeete are undocumented, but it seems likely that the two of them discussed politics during their appointments. The result was that two of the most influential figures in Brooklyn politics—one present, one future—met for the first time. Chisholm would later join Holder's organization. Holder made a big impression on her. A "tall, quiet-looking man, partly bald, with light-rimmed glasses," she admired how Holder seemed unafraid to confront the existing power structure head-on.[17] He also seemed unthreatened by women participating as equals in public life. Her partnership with Mac Holder would last throughout her political life. Holder was, Chisholm would say later, "the shrewdest, toughest, and hardest-working Black political animal in Brooklyn, probably in New York City, and maybe elsewhere."[18] Her political learning curve accelerated under his mentorship, and meeting him was the beginning of her climb toward national office.

Mac Holder would turn out to be instrumental in Chisholm's entire political career. He was in Chisholm's parents' generation, born and raised in 1897 in Guyana (then British Guiana), where he started a career in teaching. In 1920 Holder decided to become the first of his family to leave Guyana for the United States and joined Garvey's Universal Negro Improvement Association (UNIA) in New York. He enrolled at what was then City College, where he would eventually earn a degree in mathematics. He served the UNIA for five years and became a liaison to the South and Midwest for the organization. He began working as a journalist after that, as a reporter and then as Brooklyn editor for the *New York Amsterdam News*. In 1935, he was asked by Liebowitz to run the campaign for district attorney. Liebowitz, the "pilot of a countywide insurgent machine," lost in the primary. But Holder had built an organizational structure behind him that remained, and the future Assemblyman Bertram Baker approached him about taking it over. Holder, then working up the career ladder at the *New York Amsterdam News*, gladly gave it, and Baker folded Holder's organization into the UADA.

Holder took a brief respite from politics during World War II, but could not stay away. He moved to Washington, D.C., to become a statistician for the War Productions Board in 1942. With his City College degree and a sharp mind, Holder rose meteorically through the government pay ranks. When his white supervisor expressed surprise that Holder had originally been hired at such a low level, Holder put the man on the spot: "Mr. Barr, when I came in here, if I'd asked you for a grade 5, would you have given it to me?" Barr did not respond, but Holder had made his point about employment discrimination. In 1946, the year Chisholm graduated from Brooklyn College, he returned to Brooklyn to work as an analyst of crime statistics in the district attorney's office. There, he noticed that Black people's arrests were far more common than white people's, despite similar offending rates across racial lines. He was drawn back into local civil rights struggles. In 1948, the year Baker was elected to the state assembly and Flagg made his first, unsuccessful bid for a judgeship, Holder led a campaign to desegregate downtown Brooklyn's Towers Hotel with the help of his allies in the district attorney's office. Because of Holder's more radical stance and willingness to challenge leadership structures, his and Bertram Baker's relationship had become more conflicted and rivalrous. Holder had grown dismissive of Baker's rise to state office. He thought the Democratic Party's "White Fathers" had recognized the need to run a Black face in the race and simply chose him as their proxy.[19]

Chisholm would cast her lot with Holder's more radical stance, rather than the party line of Baker's strategy. In the 1953 Flagg campaign, Chisholm discovered she still loved politics even though her education career had grown successful. She was named Brooklyn College Alumnus of the Year in 1957 for her work in early childhood education. In 1959, she began consulting for the City Division of Day Care. As the supervisor for ten day care centers, she oversaw over one hundred city employees and the budget of about $400,000. She spent her days evaluating centers, city and private; attending conferences and meetings; and lobbying local leaders for more and better day care facilities.[20] But at the same time she had been involved in tenant activism at the Governor Smith houses, and, finding herself with spare time while Conrad was on the road for work, she began looking for opportunities to get more involved in Brooklyn politics. She joined Holder's Lewis Flagg campaign through someone she knew from Brooklyn College.[21]

She soon discovered that her local Democratic Club was teetering on the edge of a political succession by Black Brooklynites. Against the backdrop of the Flagg campaign and a growing Black population in the district, Baker had been given the district leadership and assembly seat of the newly apportioned Sixth AD, which included most of Bed-Stuy, in 1954. The Seventeenth AD once again had a white assemblyman, but tenuously. Crown Heights made up a large part of the oddly-shaped gerrymander. But Crown Heights, which had been mostly white, had a growing Black population. There were two new housing projects with mostly Black tenants: the Albany Houses, where Chisholm had been involved in tenant activism, and the Breevort Houses. Black residents became a majority by 1957 and put increasing pressure on white Democratic politicians to be represented by one of their own.[22]

Baker had won a measure of power in the aftermath of the Flagg campaign despite, or rather because of, his lack of involvement with the insurgents. He maneuvered his way to nominating the next three judges—all Black—in Brooklyn. He bridged relations between the UADA and insurgents, naming Lewis Flagg's wife, Marie, as his coleader. He also received moderate support from Holder and Flagg themselves, who attended a few UADA meetings. It was an excellent training ground for a young, ambitious educator and politician like Chisholm.

But Chisholm and her fellow reformists were still unimpressed with Baker. Except for him, Brooklyn's representation was all white and mostly male. And he had been put in power by white party bosses. She recalled that "there were still no black elected officials from Kings County, on the state, city, or national levels," but she glossed over the fact that Baker was already in the state assembly.[23] Like her mentor Mac Holder, Chisholm perhaps didn't consider him a true ally of Black Brooklynites.[24]

She was frustrated at how the white Seventeenth AD club leadership held power over Black and brown constituents. Needy residents of the district were permitted to visit the club on Mondays and Thursdays in order to plead their cases in front of Vincent Carney, who elevated to district leader when his brother Stephen died and extracted votes in exchange for help with problems. Such problems were most likely to be about housing, employment, or government agencies. In order to reinforce the supplicant relationship of constituents, Carney and "his flunkies," as Chisholm called them, sat on a dais at one end of the room, while petitioners sat in two de facto segregated lines and were expected to wait patiently.[25] Chisholm challenged the hierarchical waiting system because "I just wanted to see what they would do," so she walked directly up to Carney at the dais and claimed she had an urgent topic to discuss. He heard her out, but her one-person protest did nothing to alter the dehumanizing ritual.[26] He and the party had very little understanding of the issues that poor and nonwhite people faced in the district, such as discrimination in housing, jobs, and services. Still, Carney's power was eroding, and he was doing little to include Black participation. Had he done so, he might have headed off the political succession that would come in 1960.[27]

Meanwhile, the grassroots alliance from the Flagg campaign raised political consciousness among Black Brooklynites and continued its insurgency against the Democratic machine throughout the 1950s. After the successful 1953 Flagg campaign, Holder transformed the organization into the Bedford-Stuyvesant Political League (BSPL), which was "in effect, an insurgent political club." Its goal was to "increase the political representation of the Negro people and peoples of other minority groups" within government, and to "educate the citizenry as to the political, economic, and social needs and aspirations of the Negro people and of the minority groups within our community."[28] In 1954 the BSPL sought to bring the first hospital to the Bedford-Stuyvesant district. It also ran a full slate of candidates: Congress, state senate, assembly, and, of course, Holder as district leader. Campaign literature contained fiery Black nationalist language: "The Bedford Stuyvesant Political League demands fuller and fairer political representation for Negroes. It supports vigorous, militant Negro leadership!" The effort failed, however, and no one from the slate was elected. Black voters were not yet persuaded to vote for nonmachine candidates.[29]

The BSPL was never able to duplicate its success from 1953. It held voter registration drives, and Holder ran several times for assembly and for state senate, never victorious. In 1956, the BSPL "forced" the Seventeenth Assembly District Club to elect its first Black officer: Shirley Chisholm. Holder recalled that it was on his recommendation that the club elected her as vice president. That same year, the BSPL proposed a civil rights plank for the Democratic National Convention. Chisholm was present when Holder submitted the proposal to Brooklyn City Council chief Joseph P. Sharkey. But another BSPL activist, Tom Jones, remembered that Holder had done little with the organization. Holder had taken a new job, and left Jones and Chisholm to shoulder much of the duties within the organization.[30]

In 1957, the already strained relationship between the BSPL and the party regulars broke down when Baker quietly promised a city council seat to Mac Holder but failed to follow through. Chisholm went with Holder and two attorneys to a meeting with Baker and Carney. Once there, Holder reminded Baker that Baker himself had taken over the leadership of what became the UADA from Holder over twenty years before. Doing so reminded those present that Holder himself was no political novice and that Baker owed his success in part to Holder's aid. Then he disclosed Baker's promise of the council seat, hoping it would force Baker's endorsement of him. The gambit didn't work and instead showed Holder's weak hand.[31] Chisholm noticed and began to make her own plans for leadership. Chisholm was a vice president and, in her trademark ambitious style, had her eye on the presidency of the group. As she told it in her memoir, it was the grassroots members who, impressed by her speeches at rallies and leadership of delegations to Brooklyn City Hall, urged her to run. Still, a reluctant candidate or not, she openly sought the post. "I felt stubbornly that I had a right to run," she said.

Holder was "furious," and a rift opened up between the two. While he believed that others in the club were using her for their own gain, she declared that there was nothing in the BSPL's constitution that granted Holder presidency for life. He marshaled all the forces he had against her candidacy, raising campaign money through his connections at the Mount Lowery Zion Baptist Church and packing the election meeting with church members who signed up for BSPL membership as they came in the door. That night, at Paragon Hall on Fulton Street, he circulated three-page, single-spaced pink flyers denouncing Chisholm, accusing her of trying to "snuff out the life of independent political action," of being a "stooge," and of trying to "destroy the organization by taking over and so nullifying its effectiveness as to make it nothing more than a social club." Contrasting his own catalogue of successes as president of the BSPL, he implied that Chisholm would not work as hard, devote as much time, or have the expertise to handle the league's business, as he did. He also painted her as an ingrate: "For three years I've pushed Shirley Chisholm forward. Tonight, as a reward, she is trying to push me—out." He included an open letter to Chisholm, signing it "Your friend, or should I say former friend, Wesley." The soon-to-be infamous flyer worked, and Chisholm lost. Holder stayed, though the organization was weakened as a result. When Holder was seriously ill in 1963, it became weaker in his absence; in 1966 the treasury was divided among the active members and the BSPL was dissolved.[32]

THE SEVENTEENTH ASSEMBLY DISTRICT
AND THE UNITY DEMOCRATIC CLUB

Still, Chisholm was not without a political home. She had joined the Seventeenth AD Club sometime in 1954 or 1955. She and her hairdresser Cleo Skeete also attended meetings of Baker's UADA. She was still working for the party machine in the early 1960s, after Samuel Berman took over the leadership, which would have made her tenure in the Seventeenth AD Club at least five or six years. The fact that she wrote in *Unbought and Unbossed* that her membership in the regular club was much earlier suggests some ambivalence on Chisholm's part regarding her membership in the party organization while she was simultaneously working with the BSPL. Clearly, she wanted to convey the impression that she joined the club early in her career, was always an outsider, and could not be controlled by the bosses. She explained that she belonged to the club because she thought she might be able to effect change in the political machine by working on the inside. It is possible, if not probable, that Chisholm was more invested in the work of the Seventeenth AD Club than her maverick image suggests.[33]

Nonetheless, Chisholm sought to change the sexist and racist practices of the club. She made some limited progress by energizing women in the Seventeenth AD. She spoke proudly of her skills in organizing women: "The women have always loved me. I don't know, it's a fantastic thing I have with women." In this case, perhaps it was her creative talents: she was tasked with the work of making boxes to hold raffle tickets and money at the yearly card party. After hunting down boxes from local candy stores, she painted them, cut out pictures to glue on, and presented the impressive fruits of her labors to her fellow women club members. But, as she said, she went beyond her assigned role after that. At the next party committee meeting, she pointed out the elephant in the middle of the room: women were expected to organize fundraisers but excluded from sharing power. She noticed how often the men at the club used the word "power," which equaled control, but assumed that women would only play a supporting role. And she persuaded the others to raise the issue at the next club meeting.[34]

Chisholm's ideas won the battle, but she recalled that it earned her a reputation for being a troublemaker. At one meeting, a woman she identified as Molly stood up and successfully made the case for the party commit-tee to get a budget. The women got the money that they needed to put on the events—$700 that they turned into $8,000 through the fundraiser—but Chisholm felt that she had been marked as a "problem." Rather than being "their 'good black woman' in the club, a sort of show dog," she had disrupted lines of power and a backlash began.[35] Carney and his deputies' first tactic to neutralize her was to put her on the board of the club with ten white men. Their hope was that once given the trappings of power by sitting on the board, she would not make any more fuss. Chisholm was instead "appalled at what they discussed in the backroom" and the expectation that she would keep quiet about misallocating funds and other unfair practices. Chisholm left the meeting and told women members about what was being discussed. She was removed within three weeks. She did, however, remain in the club's rank and file, continuing to be an "irritant," asking about police protection and enforcement of housing codes in the neighborhood.[36]

At the turn of the decade, Chisholm found the group that was to be her base of power for the next two decades. Fellow Black Brooklyn activist Tom Jones gathered together an interracial group of allies starting in 1958. Chisholm and Jones were both protégés of Holder, both of Caribbean back-ground, and both politically ambitious. The Democratic political organiza-tion that formed out of Jones's group, the Unity Democratic Club (UDC), would seek to become a true coalition—as well as a rival with the Seven-teenth AD Democratic Club for control over the district.[37]

Tom Jones was also a child of Barbadian parents, born in 1913. His father, Thomas S. Jones, was a podiatrist and a Garveyite, and had moved to New York in 1908. Thomas Senior and his wife, Mabel Ward Jones (daughter of the family that produced Mount Gay Rum), were the first Black family on their block, and they formed the first block association in their neighborhood. The younger Thomas recalled attending UNIA rallies and had vivid memo-ries of Garvey's voice exhorting "up, you mighty people!" He went through the New York public schools and then earned his undergraduate and law degrees from St. John's University. He also moved toward socialist politics and the antifascism movement, which he encountered through Brooklyn's Carleton YMCA. The issues of the day were Mussolini's encroachment on Ethiopia and the Spanish Civil War, and Jones flirted with the idea of skip-ping the bar exam and going to fight in the Abraham Lincoln Brigade. But he stayed in New York and was admitted to the bar in 1938; he then enlisted in the army in 1941, eventually rising to the rank of first lieutenant. He was part of the Normandy invasion and eventually became a court-martial judge in 1944. Jones would later recall that his activist education was solidified in the army. He witnessed firsthand the irony of fighting for democracy abroad while he, like so many Black soldiers, was treated as a second-class citizen in the military. He also noticed an "upsurge of awareness" in New York and other northern cities when he returned to the States. Like Holder, he returned to Brooklyn after the war and jumped right back into local activism. He joined the local NAACP and campaigned against police brutality. When he attempted to join the Seventeenth AD Club, only to be turned away and steered toward Baker's UADA, his disdain for the Democratic establishment was sown.[38]

Jones participated in political campaigns after that, in Harlem for Adam Clayton Powell's congressional campaign and in Brooklyn outside of Democratic circles. He was recruited by some YWCA members to work on Ada Jackson's American Labor Party campaigns in 1946 and 1948. He left the American Labor Party in 1950, however, because he felt that the party was insufficiently committed to Black representation. He also felt professionally slighted by the other lawyers on the left: though he was a member of the bar, sympathetic to trade unions' cases, and in need of work, he was never hired by them. When he did represent prominent leftists in court, he found himself being red-baited alongside them. The cases he worked for Paul Robeson and others earned him skepticism, not support, from Black activists who assumed that he could not be Black and red at the same time.[39] In Holder's Lewis Flagg campaign, Jones came home to Black Brooklyn politics, but this time it was through an insurgent Democratic Party movement. Holder, Jones, and Chisholm had much in common: they were proudly Caribbean, outside the established Democratic Party, and charismatic leaders. They also valued achievement, prestige, and formal political recognition. Even as they advocated on behalf of the collective, they prized individual success. It was not surprising, therefore, that Jones and Chisholm would eventually make a move to assume power within Brooklyn insurgent politics. When Holder's BSPL imploded, Jones struck out on his own.[40]

Chisholm recalled the founders of the UDC as "about six persons, of which I was one," aiming to take over the political organization of the district and "boot out the failing but still potent white machine." It was an interracial vision with Black leadership. Jones was propelled by two things: the southern Black freedom struggle that had resulted in the Montgomery Bus Boycott and the beginnings of nonviolent direct action, and the local Democrats' "divide and conquer" strategy toward Black Brooklynites. Also, even though he stopped short of saying so directly, he believed that Holder had sold out to the white leadership. Perhaps this was because, in 1962, Holder ran against Jones for the assembly on the regulars' ticket. He was aware of the necessity for a unified Black vote, so he did not challenge Bertram Baker in the Sixth AD for either the district leadership or the assembly seat.

Instead, Jones turned his ammunition on the Seventeenth AD, an island of white leadership in a majority-Black district. In 1960, the Seventeenth was a boomerang-shaped parcel surrounding Baker's significantly more coherent Sixth. Both existed within the heart of Bedford-Stuyvesant, roughly bounded by Myrtle to the north, Howard to the east, Park Place to the south, and Washington Avenue to the west.[41]

Jones's group became the "Thomas R. Jones Committee (for full registration and adequate representation in Bedford-Stuyvesant)" for the 1960 Democratic primary. At an April meeting, Chisholm, in an early example of her push for coalition, led the discussion about allying with other campaigns. The committee decided in favor of partnering with another insurgent club and ran Jones as the candidate for assembly on the same ticket. They achieved the considerable coup of having Chisholm's hero, former First Lady Eleanor Roosevelt, address a rally that attracted 400 spectators. Actor Harry Belafonte lent his name as a sponsor for the UDC's letterhead. Jones ran on integration, schools, jobs, higher wages, health care, housing, transportation, youth services, city services, and Black and Puerto Rican representation. The joint initiative, the Committee for Full Registration and Adequate Representation, recruited and trained volunteer canvassers and poll watchers. Berman won the assembly seat over Jones, 3,082–2,033. But the Thomas R. Jones Committee saw that margin as a victory. If, after only one year of activity, it could come within 1,000 votes of defeating the machine, an electoral victory was a real possibility.[42]

The UDC was formed on June 1, 1960, in response to Jones's failed, but energizing, campaign. It moved into quarters in the old UNIA building at Bergen and Nostrand, and then quickly moved to Knickerbocker Avenue and began to attract a multiracial, heterogeneous group of loyal supporters.[43] The organization took off in part because of Jones's left-inflected, powerful mobilization style and the perception that the regular organization was not doing enough for poor and nonwhite residents. About thirty to fifty people usually showed up for the regular meetings. The neighborhood had a node of interracial marriages, including that of Jones himself, who was married to the radical Jewish activist Bertha K. Jones, Ruth and George Brooks, Jocelyn and Andrew Cooper, and Marshall and Ethelyn Dubin. Other Black married couples participated: Jones's sister Grace was married to radical Black novelist John Oliver Killens. Ruth Goring, a Black nurse, was a central figure and eventual president of the club. Others included white activist Mary Woods, white artist Joan Maynard, and Black painter Ernest Crichlow. All of them were sympathetic toward socialist politics (James Shaw would later recall socialist teas). Chisholm was there, too, although no UDC member besides Chisholm herself recalled that she was present at the founding meetings.

The minutes of at least one strategy meeting indicate her presence, but she was also involved with the regular Seventeenth AD Club simultaneously, a fact that several club members recalled clearly.[44]

All of the UDC members believed that the Seventeenth AD Club was not addressing the real problems of the community. While it is possible that they exaggerated the power of the outgoing club, they saw little Black and working-class representation, and few services for residents of the district.[45] Their strategy was to register people to vote and then make sure they did so. Those who entered the headquarters in need of assistance or information sometimes stayed for the business meetings and got involved that way. The UDC also created alliances with traditional community organizations: block associations, school parent-teacher associations (PTAs), and tenants' rights groups, all of whom would later find political benefit from Chisholm's political othermothering. In the "Operation Employment" project, Andrew Cooper led an effort to get unions to accept Black members and promote them to leadership positions within the locals. Operation Employment also successfully pressured employers—Sheffield Farms, a division of Sealtest Dairies, and the Ebinger and Bond bakeries—to hire Black people at all levels.[46]

The UDC also began a citizenship education program, headed by Ruth Brooks, a social worker. Within about a year, they became very popular and well attended. As Brooks put it, the program taught local citizens that "politics was deliberately made mystical." Participants learned the basics of politics: the significance of the Democratic primary and its greater importance than the general election, the process of choosing delegates, legislative processes, and the inner workings of local politics such as patronage. They also heard guest speakers: Sam Meyers of the United Auto Workers; Joseph Collier of the Transport Workers Union; New York City Council member Paul O'Dwyer; J. Raymond Jones; Harlem City Council member Herbert Evans; James Booker of the *Amsterdam News*; Hortense Gabel, assistant to the mayor for housing; labor lawyer Milton Friedman; and others.[47]

In 1962, the UDC finally broke through. Jones ran for both Seventeenth assembly and district leader, with Ruth Goring as coleader. His opponent was Sam Berman, with Carrie Lark, a Black woman, as his coleader. The New York Committee for Democratic Voters, which was a citywide organization supporting insurgent campaigns, lent the UDC their backing. In what looked like, and probably was, a desperate effort to hold on to power and appeal to Black voters, Berman nominated Holder for assembly. But Holder, a member of neither the Seventeenth AD Club nor the UDC at that point, stood no chance of winning over the increasingly popular Jones. Holder also blamed a bad case of chickenpox, which interfered with his ability to campaign. The

Democratic leadership then tried another tack: they asked J. Raymond Jones to speak with Tom Jones about conceding the district leadership to Berman and settling for the assembly seat only. Tom Jones brought the proposal back to the UDC membership, which strongly objected. In the end, a fracture in the Democratic leadership created an advantage for the UDC in the backing of the up-and-coming Brooklyn assemblyman and Eighteenth District leader Stanley Steingut, who was making a bid for county Democratic leader. And the UDC had become a force in the local election: its voter registration and education campaigns lent an estimated 500 additional voters to the 1962 primary. In the end, those votes were decisive: the UDC's ticket beat Berman, Lark, and Holder by about that same number. Jones was now district leader and assemblyman for the Seventeenth AD.[48]

Chisholm was involved on both sides, a fact that she never discussed in interviews or writings. She had made donations, purchasing a typewriter and giving cash to the UDC. Conrad advertised his private investigations agency, Halcon, in the club's newsletter, and the couple donated funds toward the 1961 annual dance. She had paid her dues literally and figuratively, serving at meetings, on the executive committee, and on the staff of the UDC newsletter, representing the UDC at Central Brooklyn Coordinating Council meetings, as well as organizing dinners and teas. Chisholm's relationship to the UDC would prove complicated. Nearly twenty years later, Jones disclosed that he hadn't known that Chisholm "was carrying water on both shoulders"—that is to say that she had been working with both him and with Brooklyn party leader Sam Berman at the same time, at least in 1960. Certainly this was not a point that Chisholm wanted to belabor, as she had implied in *Unbought and Unbossed* that she was finished with the regulars after her brief stint on the executive board. But Jones recalled that she had still been participating in the Seventeenth AD Club during the birth of the UDC. That she did so suggests that the ambitious Chisholm was assessing the best path for her own political advancement and was loyal to neither faction.[49]

In the aftermath of the 1962 victory, the UDC encountered impediments to its momentum. For one thing, the patronage opportunities that came with control of the district were not made clear to Jones. Second, the caseload of residents who needed assistance securing government services was huge. And third, many members noticed that Tom Jones stepped away from his commitment to interracial participation. This was for two reasons. First, many of the white members were aligned with socialist and left politics, and he was concerned about accusations of communism within the UDC. This might well have been because of his new alliance with Stanley Steingut, who was now the leader of the Brooklyn Democratic Party. Jones was in line for a judgeship. He wanted economic stability after a lifetime of hardscrabble law practice, and he feared that redbaiting could derail his candidacy. Some UDC members also felt that the leftist members' objections to Jones's deal with Steingut led Jones to cut those leftists out. Second, in a move that presaged what would happen within some civil rights groups later in the decade, Jones pushed out white members. Echoing the Seventeenth AD Club's gender politics, Jones also retreated on women's leadership opportunities in UDC. He introduced rhetoric about the importance of male leadership in the UDC, arguing that local youths needed to see a Black male role model in charge, and then brought in Black captains who had worked under Berman to be the senior leadership of the UDC. This alienated the Black women who had been organizers within the club since its inception.[50] Chisholm was persistent and continued to work in the UDC. She had made some enemies, however. Her critics characterized her role as opportunistic and coercive. The two most vocal ones were Andrew Cooper, a labor activist, and the UDC's president and eventual district coleader Ruth Goring. Cooper, in particular, would become Chisholm's most outspoken antagonist. In oral histories, he claimed that she was at best a lukewarm UDC supporter before the 1962 victory. She became more interested in the club, he said, once it actually held electoral power. She did little of the day-to-day work like canvassing, he recalled. He believed that she had ingratiated herself with Tom Jones in order to advance in the club.[51] Goring, who emphatically denied that Chisholm had been present at the founding of the UDC, asserted that Chisholm used the club for her own political aspirations. Goring also observed that Chisholm started red-baiting in the UDC and targeted Walter Linder and his wife, Esther. Goring suspected Chisholm of having taken a logbook of office activities in order to gather information on members and also resented Chisholm's admonitions in club meetings to avoid associating with communists. For her part, Chisholm had shown "resentment" toward Goring, though she tried to heal the rift by planning a tea in Goring's honor during the 1962 campaign.[52]

Jones found Chisholm useful, however. His strategy, many observed, was to use Chisholm and another member, Pat Robinson, to carry out the purges. "Tom made some deal with Shirley," Mary Woods recalled. "I got the feeling that Shirley Chisholm had her eye on what I wrote in the newsletter; I had the feeling she was there to watch me," explained Walter Linder, a communist and UDC member, who went on to say, "It got worse as she advanced. She wasn't the most honest person." Ruth Brooks had some choice words to describe Chisholm: "She's nasty, but she's not strong." Brooks characterized Chisholm as an opportunist without true convictions.[53] Jones did not earn the same contempt for his actions, even as it was widely perceived that he had tasked Chisholm with carrying out his wishes.

Jones eventually was offered the judgeship and took it, leaving his assembly and leader positions. He left a leadership vacuum in the UDC and many members who grieved the loss of their hopes for the future of the UDC. Chisholm stood poised to step into the breach, but she was not welcomed with open arms. She had made some lasting enemies, especially Andy Cooper. Still, Chisholm had learned the lay of the political land over the past decade and had developed enough influence and supporters in the club to continue her career in politics. When a seat opened up in the state assembly, Chisholm would use what she had learned to run and win. She would have to push past the sexism of rivals within the UDC to do so. They underestimated her at their peril. "All through my political life, men misread me," she would say at the end of her life. "They always . . . they didn't realize that I don't have fear of people. I'm not afraid of people."[54] This outward appearance of fearlessness in the face of weaponized and politicized sexism and racism came to define her earliest forays into politics and paved the way for future generations But first, she had to win.

4
THE FIRST VICTORY

─────────── ★ ───────────

In 1964, Chisholm's Black feminist power politics grew into formal elected political power. Chisholm turned her ambition and talent toward gaining office within local and state Democratic Party organizations. While she won the Seventeenth Assembly District (AD) through a combination of commitment, hard work, engagement, and local knowledge, she also had qualities that are expected from men candidates but criticized in women: the ability to spot and exploit an opportunity and a single-minded determination to win power. Her recorded memories of her early political career overwhelmingly concern principle over politics, although she certainly employed politicking to accumulate power. Others, including those in her own family, recalled her entry into politics as less principled and begrudged her success. As was the case for other politicians then and now, the enemies that Chisholm made on her way up would hound her for the rest of her political career. The intersecting problems of racism and sexism led to additional strain, as would the opening of a permanent rift in her family of origin. Still, she finally found herself elected to office. And she finally got to wield her political muscle, making strategic alliances with those she thought could be valuable allies.

LOSS AND CONFLICT IN THE ST. HILL FAMILY

The 1960s began with personal hardship for Chisholm when her father died after a stroke in 1960. He died while she and Conrad were still living on one floor of the family house on Prospect Place. Chisholm had remained close to her father and continued to think of herself as his favorite daughter. He would sit in the front row in local committee meetings and listen to her speak. "You have something in you—use it well," he told her, and he also told her not to let her sex restrict her. After his retirement, she recounted, he would go to a nearby park to play checkers and brag about his Shirley. He said he "was so crazy about me" because of her successes in school and her career.

Chisholm had begun to worry that her father was ailing, though he was keeping himself very busy. On one day she stayed home from her job at the Bureau of Child Welfare and looked out into the small backyard to see her increasingly frail father gardening. Concerned that he was subjecting himself to hot weather without a hat, she called down to him and cautioned him to be careful. Not long after that, the two went for a walk in the park together. Chisholm recalled that he was particularly anxious to share stories of his childhood and youth in the Caribbean. But he also complained of not feeling well and told her, "Shirls, I know you're going to be a great woman. . . . I'm not going to live to see it." Chisholm was frightened to hear him discuss his mortality. The next afternoon, Charles had a cerebral hemorrhage after working for several hours in the garden. He died before Chisholm was able to get to his side. Incapacitated by grief, she left work for five weeks, only returning when she thought to herself that "Papa" would want her to continue and that she couldn't let him down.[1]

Charles's death was especially difficult because Chisholm had a far more distant relationship with her sisters and mother. She felt that she "became alienated" from her sisters because she thought of herself as her father's favorite. Her mother was far less encouraging when it came to politics. Ruby was committed to her Brethren church, which Chisholm thought made Ruby hostile to political pursuits. Chisholm also thought that, in contrast to Ruby's own mother, Emmeline, Ruby held more rigid beliefs about the place of women. "[They] never supported me in the political arena," she complained late in life about her mother and sisters. "I couldn't even get them to go out and get a page of signatures for me. They said, no. No woman had any right to be in politics. . . . This is the most fascinating thing about my life. I had absolutely no support from my family for politics. None."[2] While this categorical declaration excluded her father's support, and her sister Muriel's approval, it was true that her remaining family of origin had little involvement with her career. Conrad, in his recollection, was Shirley's source of family support. He did not feel threatened, but instead "I felt as a helpful . . . mate, that I would help her achieve what she wanted to do. And that would make me feel big."[3]

Her conflicted family relationship was due to the disposition of Charles's estate. Fully half of the total inheritance, $8,000 to $10,000 from a life insurance policy, went exclusively to her in what she called a "trust fund." The remainder of the estate was divided evenly between his survivors, because Charles had left no will. Chisholm, until her very last interview, insisted that she had not made any financial request from her father. But, she conceded, "to this day this is what [has] kept me separated from my family. They cannot accept the fact that I did not tell my father to do it. This was his way of rewarding me for moving ahead so nicely. Because he realized that my mother and my sisters were acting against me. And he said he had to look out for me. But he did not tell me that he was going to set up a will or what have you. That was what caused the breakup of the entire family. It was a very sad thing. Very sad."[4]

Chisholm did of course have the option to heal the rift by sharing her inheritance with her mother and sisters, but she did not. She needed the funds because her political career was beginning in earnest, and by the time the will was probated, it would likely have been the end of 1961 when Chisholm received all funds. Her inheritance would equate to over $85,000 in 2020 dollars, a nice nest egg for beginning a bid for public office. Chisholm's strong ambitions coupled with the distance between Chisholm and her mother and sisters might well have been an acceptable cost to her for a financial jumpstart in politics—and if her family of origin did not support her, she would win over Brooklyn's voters and find her family among her new constituents.

CONFLICT AND COALITION IN CENTRAL BROOKLYN POLITICS

Chisholm did not have a ready-made electoral base, even as she stepped into Tom Jones's shoes—and she even seemed to relish making her own. She declined to renew alliances with some of Jones's supporters and collaborators. Jones had had a strong relationship with the nonviolent direct action campaign of Brooklyn CORE (Congress of Racial Equality).[5] Founded in 1960 by allies of Tom Jones and the Unity Democratic Club (UDC), Brooklyn CORE staged a series of daring campaigns focused on housing, employment, municipal services, and public education. The chapter cooperated with the UDC's Operation Unemployment in 1962 in efforts to integrate the workforce in Ebinger's Bakery retail stores. Jones, while running for assembly in 1962, supported Brooklyn CORE's innovative tactics when it protested inadequate sanitation by delivering a load of rubbish to the steps of Brooklyn Borough Hall. When the chapter protested discriminatory hiring for construction jobs at the building site of the future Downstate Medical Center in 1963, it had attracted the attention and support of Malcolm X. Brooklyn CORE was progressively growing more outspoken and confrontational, and was successfully mobilizing on the basis of nonviolent direct action during the very years when Chisholm was building a base of support within the UDC.[6]

But Chisholm was drawn to less confrontational activism and kept Brooklyn CORE at arm's length. In the early 1960s she seemed to prefer avenues for social change that worked through civic advocacy. Notable among these for its support of her campaigns was the Brooklyn branch of Key Women,

Inc. A Black women's organization founded in New York City in 1954, Key Women undertook local social welfare projects such as sponsoring college scholarships, counseling women in prison, and finding foster homes for needy children. By 1962, it had chapters in Westchester, Queens, and Brooklyn. Chisholm belonged to this last branch, and after being elected as recording secretary, she helped organize a garden party at the Brooklyn Home for Aged Colored People and a luncheon honoring Mallie Robinson, mother of baseball player Jackie, for her service to humanity. In 1963, Chisholm herself was a recipient of an award at the Key Women Luncheon, held to benefit King's Southern Christian Leadership Conference that year. When Key Women President Belle Thompson left on an extended overseas trip, Chisholm assumed her position. The Key Women would be crucial supporters for Chisholm's political ambitions.[7]

Chisholm also rose to leadership within another civic organization: the Central Brooklyn Coordinating Council (CBCC). The CBCC was a reform organization created to combat juvenile delinquency in the late 1950s. It had been headed in its early years by Maude Richardson, the Republican Party candidate who helped push Brooklyn's Democratic organization to put forward Bertram Baker as a New York State Assembly candidate in 1948. Later, public school secretary Elsie Richardson (no relation to Maude) would become the group's most prominent activist. Originally the Central Brooklyn Coordinating Council for Youth, its first major initiative was to place two dozen teenagers in summer jobs with local businesses. In 1962, the organization's agenda expanded into liaising between citizens and Brooklyn's leadership in matters of housing, schools, social services, urban planning, and rehabilitating the neighborhood's image in the local press, all issues on Chisholm's agenda. In the fall of 1962, CBCC reorganized itself to deploy political pressure on city government in a one-hundred-person strong meeting at the Bedford YMCA. It is likely that Chisholm was pulled into the CBCC because of her activities with Key Women, and after the CBCC's reorganization in 1962, Chisholm was elected third vice president and chair of the Program Committee, with the well-known physician Cecil Gloster as president. Chisholm's role was to represent the UDC.[8]

The CBCC was quite active during Chisholm's tenure. She created a list of 1963 priorities that the council approved, with housing at the top, followed by education reform and youth programs. Under her leadership the CBCC supported James Meredith's desegregation efforts at the University of Mississippi in late 1962, and in early 1963 recommended which neighborhood the city's slum clearance efforts should target. The CBCC also attempted to guide the opening of a Department of Labor office in Bed-Stuy, including helping choose its director, but was dismayed to find itself left out of the process. Chisholm, who had been identified as a possible director, was one of those who criticized the decision to hire a man from Westchester. "We have had grave fears about this very thing," she lamented, arguing that a person more familiar with local needs would have been a better choice. But it was the CBCC's efforts to establish a funded youth program that got the most meaningful commitment from the city government. That November, Chisholm was among the group of CBCC leaders who lobbied Mayor Robert Wagner to negotiate more job training investment, and the city came through with $26,000 to hire staff. Then, when President Lyndon Johnson announced the War on Poverty in January 1964, Chisholm and Richardson's groundwork in connecting activism to government programs helped make the CBCC a key partner for the federal government. But in the meantime, on the heels of Johnson's announcement, Wagner offered an additional $40,000 and created Youth In Action, the organization that would figure prominently in the federal War on Poverty. In addition, its board was a local repository of political clout in Brooklyn.[9]

Despite work in the Key Women and the CBCC, most of Chisholm's energies went to maintaining leadership in the UDC. Power struggles were causing turmoil inside the UDC, and she was at the center of them. Her eventual rise to coleader in the UDC was, to some members, a "diabolical plan" enabled by Jones's abdication. As UDC member and state senator James Shaw saw it, Chisholm and fellow member William Thompson developed a plan to take over the election district structure. They managed to convince Tom Fortune to help them, which he did by pushing existing members, including Andy Cooper and Ruth Goring, out. Although he had intended for Chisholm and Fortune to take over, Jones later complained that they changed the focus of the UDC from the issues that he had championed, that they would not take his advice, and that they did not acknowledge their careers' debt to his mentoring. "They cut relationships off from me," he said. "I don't blame them, I am not quarreling with them, but they never consulted me, they would never seek out my counsel, and they would never treat me with any deference." Other UDC members felt that Jones had completely abandoned the club. He "disappeared into the woodwork," founding member Pat Carter would recall later.[10]

Nevertheless, Chisholm had money, ambition, and now connections and name recognition. She lobbied hard for the nomination and in 1964 Chisholm emerged as UDC's candidate for New York State Assembly. Some UDC members recalled the process of selecting Chisholm as the UDC candidate as anticlimactic, suggesting that she was simply in the right place at the right time. According to Pat Carter, Chisholm had only recently migrated from the Seventeenth AD Democratic Club. But she had an existing political

66   THE FIRST VICTORY

constituency from her previous activism, and she was the only person that the UDC membership could agree on. And at that point, Carter recalled, Chisholm "was a courting person." She was working hard in the organization, raising money, sending out mailings, and engaging with the community. She used her own money to buy a mimeograph machine for the club. As Cooper put it, she had the advantage of "no children, few financial worries, and could afford to finance her own campaign." Her eagerness and hard work, in addition to her magnetic personality, made her an attractive candidate. At the same time, Goring, who might have seemed to be a logical successor to Jones, did not want to serve in an elected office. Goring was also acerbic, difficult, and "not the kind of person who made a lot of friends."[11]

Despite being one of two women poised for election from the UDC to the assembly, Chisholm still encountered some sexism. She recalled telling the Unity Club: "Don't tell me that because I wear a skirt that I don't have the ability to be in politics." Rather than the group's foregone decision that Carter recounted, Chisholm had to ask for the designation to take Jones's assembly seat, and she prepared to fight hard if she didn't get it. As she recalled, the UDC leadership assured her that they had always intended to designate her. She was not convinced, however. She thought that any hesitation to put her forward as its candidate was due to her sex. "One can use a woman for whatever they have, but to put her in a position of power is another thing," she said later. Although she had proven skills and ability, she believed that men were afraid to campaign against her because they knew she was a superior candidate. She also recognized that she might have been politically "expendable," and that the establishment feared she might "take over Kings County." But she had no intention of doing so: "If you give me a piece of the pie, no trouble from me." Notwithstanding her suspicions of sexism, she did get the UDC's endorsement and set to fighting the Seventeenth AD candidate in the primary.[12]

THE QUEST TO REPRESENT THE SEVENTEENTH ASSEMBLY DISTRICT IN THE POLITICAL LANDSCAPE OF 1964

Chisholm wanted, above all, to be elected to representative office. She cast this in altruistic terms: "As a politician, I wanted to represent the people in a very wholesome way. . . . for the benefit of the people." In discussing her motivations, she renounced the "game" of politics because she preferred to be truthful to the people at all times, even if it was unpopular. Her record after gaining office bears out her commitment to better government on behalf of the people. Yet she clearly relished politics, and in 1964 she embarked on a nearly twenty-year career in elected office. "Many of my friends actually wondered how I stayed so long in politics. They always thought I'd get thrown out along the way. But for some reason, I survived. And I survived because I think precisely because of confidence that was built up in me, because of how I pursued the political trail when I did."[13] Of her frequent campaigning, she said, "I don't know how I haven't collapsed . . . but I swamped 'em each time."

Chisholm was a clever campaigner. There were numerous primary candidates for state legislative jobs in Brooklyn, but Chisholm theorized that the only argument opponents could mount against her was her sex. Therefore, she strategized her campaign based partly on gender, by targeting women's groups for support. In the Seventeenth AD, Black women outnumbered Black men in the voter rolls three to one, meaning women were necessary for a victory. "I hate to do this," she claimed, preempting any accusations that she might be pandering to women's groups. What she did not say was that she already had a base of support in Brooklyn Black women's networks such as Key Women. She spoke to women in Bushwick and Green Point housing projects, and to the Women's Day luncheon at Brown Memorial Baptist Church. The strategy paid off. Aided by the power of Brooklyn's Democrats and the now-hegemonic UDC, Chisholm handily defeated her opponent in the primary, with 4,290 votes to his 1,729.[14]

Chisholm's election year, 1964, was a pivotal moment for liberalism nationwide. In his January State of the Union address, President Johnson announced a War on Poverty. In inspirational language, he declared a bold new initiative that would "galvanize poor people across the United States" and "raise the hopes of poor black city- and country-dwellers, inspired and ignited by visions of community control and economic self-sufficiency." Poor people developed vibrant grassroots community organizations in response.[15] Conceptualized by the Kennedy administration in 1962, the War on Poverty was intended to solve what Kennedy called a "bedrock problem" of America. Kennedy was not motivated by worries over appeasing the civil rights movement or rising welfare expenditures as much as he was by economic policy concerns: his economic advisors believed that poverty was a drain on economic growth and that its existence was immoral in the context of American affluence. Johnson enthusiastically endorsed the ongoing effort after assuming the presidency in November 1963. The refined plan focused on funding community organizations, christened "community action programs," and would be administered by its own agency under the leadership of Kennedy's brother-in-law Sargent Shriver. Johnson announced the expansive initiative in January 1964, promising to end poverty but to do so without cash "handouts." The initiative's flagship legislation, the Equal Opportunity Act, moved quickly through both houses of Congress despite being somewhat vague on the details. It created the Community Action Programs, as well as legal assistance to the poor, the Job Corps, VISTA, and Head Start. Forgoing cash assistance, despite the efforts of Shriver himself and Wilbur Cohen of Housing, Education, and Welfare, the programs provided an infusion of jobs in poor communities. A political backlash against welfare was also on the rise in the early 1960s, and passage of the bill depended on distancing it from cash assistance and venturing "off into the wild blue yonder" away from the Aid to Families with Dependent Children system.[16]

Second, the Civil Rights Act, stuck in Congress since the previous summer, was finally pushed through, assisted by the forceful personality of Lyndon Johnson. Although it did not address the disenfranchisement and violence that Black southerners lived through daily, it did outlaw discrimination in public accommodations and in employment. Importantly for the women's movement, a last-minute addition of the word "sex" to Title VII of the act made employment discrimination against women illegal, alongside discrimination on the grounds of race, color, national origin, or religion. Chisholm was delighted at the bill's passage. Her response to the act was rather unusual for a politician. She liked to write poetry in her spare time, and she wrote a poem about the new law for the *New York Amsterdam News*:

LAW OF THE LAND
The day was July 2nd in the year of '64
The temperature was high and tempers were hot
The sit-ins, the wade-ins, the actions of Core [*sic*]
Were all part of the struggle in the "melting" pot . . .

Chisholm went on to praise Lyndon Johnson's "stroke of a pen" that "ended discrimination and segregation as a way of life." But she also hinted that the matter was far from settled:

The struggle has begun in spite of the past
For bigots and dixiecrats [*sic*] will not easily comply
True Americans somehow will rise to the task
And show with their actions and words, even a cry
That the day of reckoning has finally come.

That stroke of a pen meant that "our preachments of democracy will now ring true," she wrote with a flourish at the end of her poem.[17]

Even at the time the poem was published, however, Chisholm knew that the rhetoric of democracy was far from reality. Liberalism had, so far, passed sweeping legislation but was woefully inadequate at protecting those who directly confronted the nation's white supremacy. The year 1964 was also

Mississippi Freedom Summer, when the Council of Federated Organizations (COFO) brought Black and white student volunteers through the Student Nonviolent Coordinating Committee (SNCC), CORE, and the NAACP to the state. Freedom Summer exposed the facts that, despite the new Civil Rights Act, white supremacy still inflicted terrorism on Black Americans and the Johnson administration would only go so far to protect civil rights. COFO's task was a voter registration drive, and the outcome was an insurgent state Democratic organization called the Mississippi Freedom Democratic Party (MFDP). COFO's volunteers were under constant threat, and three of them, James Chaney, Andrew Goodman, and Mickey Schwerner, were murdered by the Klan just a few weeks after Chisholm's primary victory. In the shadow of their disappearance, the MFDP held its own primary and sent its own delegation to the Democratic National Convention in Atlantic City. The MFDP argued its case before the convention's credentials committee: their delegates had been democratically elected, while the regular Mississippi delegation had excluded Black Mississippians from the polls. The MFDP was in compliance with all national rules for Democratic primaries. The MFDP also promised unity with the national ticket; the regular party had made no such pledge and ultimately supported the Republican Barry Goldwater for the presidency. The MFDP's bid to be recognized and seated on the convention floor faced concerted opposition, however, led by President Johnson. Johnson feared losing the support of other southern delegations if he allowed the MFDP to vote in the convention, so he deployed his soon-to-be vice presidential nominee Hubert Humphrey and the FBI to block it. Humphrey negotiated with civil rights leaders for a compromise, while the FBI surveilled those same leaders in order to get advance information on their strategies. In the end, Johnson's pressure persuaded the members of the credentials committee not to consider the challenge, and the administration offered a compromise of two at-large seats to the MFDP. The MFDP (and most of the regulars) turned down the offer, choosing instead to conduct a sit-in on the convention floor using sympathetic delegates' credentials.[18]

Chisholm would have followed the developments closely. The UDC's delegates to the convention were supportive of the MFDP's position. Pat Carter, whose name had come up earlier as a possible candidate for the assembly seat that Chisholm sought, and Andy Cooper served as delegates for the state of New York at the Atlantic City–based Democratic National Convention. Their position, however, had not been approved by Jones and his new allies in the Brooklyn party organization. After their return they found themselves ostracized from local Democratic Party politics because of their support of the MFDP. The UDC, with Steingut calling the shots, fired Cooper and Carter from the voter registration project and installed

Chisholm as its head instead. Cooper and Carter left, disillusioned, and turned their attentions to forming a new organization, the Mid-Brooklyn Independent League.[19] Cooper would be hostile to Chisholm herself for the rest of their respective careers.

Finally, the local fight against racism served as a backdrop to Chisholm's campaign. Brooklyn CORE conducted protests against police brutality and threatened a "stall-in" during the opening day of the World's Fair in New York City in April. That same month, City Councilman Thomas Weiss introduced a bill that mandated a civilian review board for instances of police use of force. Weiss had no support and the bill failed, while police brutality continued. In July a fifteen-year-old Black youth, James Powell, was killed by a white off-duty police officer, Thomas Gilligan, on the Upper East Side of Manhattan. Powell was shot three times and was unarmed. On the day following Powell's death, a peaceful protest by CORE at the site where the incident occurred was met by police wielding nightsticks. The next day, the day of Powell's funeral, 250 people who had been attending a Harlem CORE rally marched in protest to a nearby police precinct. When police began an attempt to disperse the crowd, violence erupted, a rain of bricks and bottles fell down on the streets from the rooftops, and the crowd grew. The police, lacking organization, became increasingly aggressive. After someone threw a Molotov cocktail toward a police car, officers began firing their guns into the air, and shooting continued until dawn. There was a break in the conflict until night fell again, and then again the following night, when it spread to Bed-Stuy following a Brooklyn CORE rally at the corner of Nostrand and Fulton. Civil rights leaders from both Manhattan and Brooklyn tried to calm the streets without success. The uprising ended after two more nights of protest.[20] For some, it confirmed the idea that Brooklyn, and New York City as a whole, "was in a state of steady decline." *Look* magazine published an illustrated article detailing the damaged neighborhoods of Harlem and Bed-Stuy for a wide readership. This narrative also led to increased attention from Democratic politicians who were invested in the War on Poverty. Three days after the city calmed, Mayor Wagner designated funds to create an organization, Youth In Action (YIA). YIA's mandate was to assess the state of Bed-Stuy: juvenile delinquency, housing, health, employment, recreation, and social welfare. He also invited Martin Luther King Jr. and Bayard Rustin to tour the city and offer solutions. As Joshua Guild has noted, however, "substantively, the new program offered little to black Brooklynites . . . what it promised instead was further study to confirm a reality black Brooklynites already knew too well." Still, YIA's leadership would move the organization beyond Wagner's limited vision and create a community center that provided legal aid, youth programs, and job training. It was able to do so in large part because YIA would be, in 1965, designated a Community Action Program under the War on Poverty's Economic Opportunities Act.[21]

In the midst of these local and national headlines, Chisholm campaigned in the general election. None of her public comments on the riots survive. It seems that Chisholm continued to lobby for votes through appearances at various gatherings, such as the local Masons' dinner dance and an eight-dollar-a-plate fundraising luncheon at the sleek new Hotel Americana (now the Sheraton New York) in Manhattan, sponsored by the Women's Committee for the Election of Shirley Chisholm. With the Democratic nomination secure, the full might of the Democratic organization was behind her. Chisholm was put forward on a slate that included Tom Jones for municipal judge, Tom Fortune for district leader, and William Thompson for state senate. Despite predictable, less progressive opposition, she won in a landslide with 18,151 votes. Her Republican challenger, Charles E. Lewis, got 1,893 votes, while Independent Simeon Golar only received 922. In winning the race, she was one of a handful of Black women to win new posts in state legislatures; Indiana and Missouri both added Black women, and she was joined in Albany by Constance Baker Motley, who had been reelected a state senator. Nine Black legislators were headed to Albany in January, three more than had served in the prior session. Among these was Arthur Hardwick, the first Black assemblyman from outside New York City, a Buffalo liquor store owner.[22] On top of these historic gains, the Democratic Party was now in control of the assembly for the first time in twenty-five years.[23]

ENMITIES AND ALLIANCES

Celebrations soon gave way to internal conflict that bubbled up into public view. The day after the elections, *Amsterdam News* columnist Daphne Sheppard enthused over Chisholm's victory: "Brooklyn's effervescent Democrat, Shirley Chisholm, her feathered Robin Hood cap perched at a jaunty angle and trailing a beige-lined scarlet cape from her irrepressible shoulders," had won a decisive victory. That victory was all the more notable because Chisholm, fluent in Spanish, had won over much of the Latinx constituency in the district. However, the Black middle class had been less supportive. She quoted Chisholm's barb about the "nose-in-the-air black bourgeoisie" who had cut into her victory. Chisholm had held much more appeal to "the man in the street," the assemblywoman-elect opined. This statement was likely the subject of much discussion among Bed-Stuy activists, including the disgruntled Andy Cooper, recently departed from the UDC. In early December the *Amsterdam News* published Cooper's criticism. An elected official ought to be sensitive to the "particular sore spots that might be present on the community Body Politic," he asserted. By bringing up a possible division between the Black and Puerto Rican/Latinx voters in the district, she had "hit one of the sore spots right in the area where it hurts most." Implying that Black voters had not supported her wholeheartedly, after her convincing victories in both the primary and the general election, was at the least irresponsible and at worst suggested that Chisholm was intentionally dividing the community. Cooper demanded an apology from Chisholm, which it appears she never gave.[24]

Assemblywoman Chisholm seemed to welcome controversy and was eager to wade into politicking. After a postelection vacation to Montego Bay in Jamaica in December, Chisholm returned to New York and her waiting assembly seat. She took a trip to Albany during the week before Christmas for a meeting about the possibility of redistricting Bedford-Stuyvesant in the U.S. Congress. The Bedford-Stuyvesant Committee for a Representative Congressman was lobbying to have the districts redrawn and pointed out that gerrymandering had divided the Seventeenth AD up to be represented by no fewer than five members of Congress. The group spoke to the presumptive majority leader of the state assembly, Stanley Steingut, as well as the outgoing minority leader in the assembly, Anthony Travia. Travia pledged support to an effort in 1965 for redrawing the lines. Steingut's position on the matter was not on record.[25]

Steingut's silence and Travia's support proved decisive once the 1965 assembly session officially opened. In a continuation of Travia's fight with Steingut that had originally begun over the party leadership in Kings County (Brooklyn), the two were engaged in a struggle over the Speaker's chair. Because Democrats had won a majority in the assembly chamber, they were now entitled to choose a Speaker. Travia had been Democratic minority leader and was poised to take over as Speaker, supported yet again by Mayor Robert Wagner. But the matter was far from settled. Steingut began to plan a bid for the position as soon as the general election was over, and he had the support of another big player in New York state politics, Senator-elect Robert F. Kennedy. As the clock ticked down to the first day of the new session on January 6, he gathered enough support to split the state Democratic Party, and two days before Christmas he won a preliminary poll of existing and newly elected assembly members.[26]

Steingut still faced a fight. Although the official vote for the Speaker was ordinarily a pro forma matter on the first day of the new session, Travia's supporters decided to block Steingut. Because they had the required number of votes to block Steingut but not enough to elect Travia, neither Steingut nor Travia won the seat. Unofficial negotiations back at the DeWitt Clinton Hotel, the accommodations for most assembly Democrats, failed because of constantly shifting lines of allegiance. Each Democrat was expected to stop by either Steingut's or Travia's suite each night after dinner and reassure the respective candidate of his continuing support, and if he failed to show, he was tracked down by each side's team. The mood at the Ten Eyck, the hotel where the Republicans stayed, was one of "great glee" as the Democrats were busy "snatching defeat from the jaws of victory," as Chisholm quipped. The impasse went on for thirty days (Chisholm wrote hyperbolically that it was double that at two months). On the twenty-eighth ballot, on February 4, Travia prevailed and was elected Speaker.[27]

Chisholm supported Anthony Travia, a bold move given that party boss Steingut had been a past friend to the UDC. Steingut had paved the way for Tom Jones to win his assembly seat in 1962 and had elevated Jones to the bench. Still, Steingut was unpopular with other Black legislators and with the Black press: the *New York Amsterdam News* castigated him for "hand picking" a candidate for majority leader in the state senate whose "record reads like a Goldwater Republican" on matters of civil rights, and argued that Steingut could not be trusted on racial justice. Most of the Black Albany legislators, with the exception of Arthur Hardwick of Buffalo and Mark Southall of Harlem, stood behind Travia, who had publicly supported the push to redraw Bedford-Stuyvesant's congressional district in a way more favorable to Black voters. Bertram Baker made a nomination speech on Travia's behalf and was joined in his support by Chisholm, Percy Sutton of Harlem, and Kenneth Browne of Queens, all Black.[28]

In choosing Travia, Chisholm made a strategic move to engage a wider civil rights agenda rather than protect her local political bank of favors. Chisholm recognized the potential in the liberal national mood while also seeing the need for continued pressure for antiracist and antipoverty policies and would proceed accordingly as a legislator. But supporting Travia was also politically savvy: she might well have seen indications that Steingut's power was waning and Travia's on the rise. She did not, however, discuss her choice in either those terms. Instead, she claimed that, because Travia had put long hours and much energy into the job of minority leader, she believed he ought to be given the chance to serve as Speaker. "No one had given me any specific reason to vote against him," she wrote in *Unbought and Unbossed,* and "it would have been wrong, just wrong," to deny Travia the top seat after his previous hard work. Too, she admitted to some mutual dislike between herself and Steingut. "Stanley and I had been feuding for years," she recalled, explaining that "he could never accept my outspoken style." It didn't help that she had been in the audience at Brooklyn College when his father, Irwin, said Black people needed white leaders two decades earlier.

In her memoir she glossed over the fact that her allegiance to Travia was public knowledge before the session even started. She described with some

Shirley Chisholm and Anthony Travia dancing at Governor
Rockefeller's mansion, February 1968.
Bettman via Getty Images.

sense of amusement how astonished the other Democrats were over her choice. As she told it, Albany Democrats assumed that, as Jones's replacement, she was a Steingut supporter. As such, she had been exempted from the required evening check-ins at Steingut's DeWitt Clinton Hotel suite. She relished the telling of an encounter with one colleague who casually commented one day that he was glad he and Chisholm were on Steingut's side, which he believed would win. Chisholm asked him how he knew she would vote for Steingut, to which he replied, "Everybody knows that." Chisholm shocked him by declaring that she planned to vote for Travia. At that point, word got back to Travia who, similarly surprised, summoned Chisholm to his suite so he could hear for himself. She explained that she respected his previous work and so would vote for him although, she warned, "there will be times I will disagree with you."[29]

Meanwhile, back in Brooklyn, the UDC leadership was appalled that Chisholm refused to support Steingut, their most powerful supporter. Tom Fortune and coleader Ruth Goring, aghast, called Chisholm in Albany.

Goring in particular was a strong Steingut ally and was galled by Chisholm's response. According to Goring in a later interview, Chisholm stated that she had been sent to Albany by Bed-Stuy, but now that she was there she was obligated to vote her conscience. Enraged at this unilateral political decision, Goring left the UDC shortly afterward, leaving Chisholm to become coleader with Fortune.

Chisholm's legislative aide Allan Fagan had a less dramatic version of the story. The UDC was indeed concerned, he recalled, because Steingut had been instrumental in the voter registration drives that got Jones and then Chisholm elected. But not voting for Travia would have been a mistake, he thought, because it would have disrupted the rules for ascendency in the assembly and would have hamstrung Chisholm from making a legislative impact.[30]

Chisholm, who seemed to enjoy the excitement of the Speaker fight, composed another poem marking the occasion. "'Twas the days before Christmas when all through the House," she penned,

> Every legislator was stirring—yes, even a mouse
> The patronage was hung by the chimney with care
> In hopes that the majority would soon be there . . .
> Again we marched forth on the following week
> In hopes that we wouldn't have the same old repeat
> They swarmed into the Capitol—200 odd strong
> Nay, never did one see such an animated throng.
> Straight to the DeWitt Clinton to store away each bag
> Then scampering all over as if playing tag
> First up one floor then down three or four
> To get the latest news . . . nothing less, nothing more. . . .
> Well, bless my soul, the battle is o'er
> A coalition has finally opened the door
> We must be about the business of the state
> We can now move forward . . . 'tis never too late.[31]

Chisholm's exuberance at being in the halls of political power and her delight at having defied "politics as usual" emerge between the lines of her homemade poem. She had risen to the top of the UDC and the assembly race and had made it to Albany. She was already building alliances and demonstrating to her colleagues and constituents that she would not conduct old-fashioned patronage politics as usual. And, as an elected official, she finally had access to the legislative process and the ability to enact Black feminist power.

5

BRINGING WOMEN'S RIGHTS
AND CIVIL RIGHTS TOGETHER

───────── ★ ─────────

Once in the assembly, part-time poet and full-time assemblywoman Chisholm developed the approach to Black feminist power politics that she would use for the rest of her career. She joined a coalition of other recently elected Black legislators who worked together on antipoverty and antiracism bills. Ongoing assembly redistricting meant she had to run for her own seat twice more, so she was continually bolstering her influence in War on Poverty–era Bed-Stuy. She also identified her own priority issues: economic justice for poor women workers, women's political equality, and, eventually, abortion rights. Chisholm's years in the assembly were also the beginning years of the so-called second wave women's movement, which Chisholm joined in its early stages.[1] It was through the women's movement that Chisholm would raise her national political profile. Her early adoption of feminism contrasted with her relative lack of engagement with the "big four" national civil rights organizations: the Southern Christian Leadership Conference (SCLC), the Congress of Racial Equality (CORE), the Student Nonviolent Coordinating Committee (SNCC), and the NAACP. Perhaps her preference for electoral politicking and coalition making made it more practical to remain neutral with regard to an organizational home—or perhaps she perceived fewer opportunities for women in those groups. Nevertheless, Chisholm's understanding of and sometime involvement in local civil rights activism, coupled with her political tenacity, influenced her legislative priorities as an assemblywoman. Her performance would eventually lead to her election to national elected office from Bedford-Stuyvesant. Hers was a brand of Black leadership that crossed color and gender lines, one that became a model for future politicians. She had determination, a keen understanding of local politics, and the alliances that allowed her to work toward the next step in her political career.

WORKING IN THE ASSEMBLY

After the Speaker matter was settled, Chisholm threw herself into her duties as an assemblywoman. Having bet on the winning horse in the Speaker fight, she was rewarded with a plum committee assignment: Education.

She and Percy Sutton of Manhattan, who had been named to Social Welfare and Relief, became allies in Albany and back in the city. Early on, she became involved in social programs, participating in an endless series of events focused on left-leaning causes between her arrival home on Thursday evenings and her return to Albany on Monday mornings via train or bus. She listened to testimony at a meeting convened by the reform Democrats (the New York Committee for Democratic Voters) on addiction treatment, abortion, birth control, and housing; attended a working lunch about the problems facing teenagers convened by the Bedford-Stuyvesant Boys' Club; spoke at the awards luncheon of the Zeta Phi Beta sorority; discussed child discipline with teachers at PS 138; and addressed a community cleanup day in her old Patchen Avenue neighborhood. She collected a community service award from the women's committee at the Concord Baptist Church and an honorary plaque at a Brooklyn testimonial dinner. During the week, when she was not on the assembly floor, she was holed up in her DeWitt Clinton Hotel room doing her homework of reading bills and reports.[2]

Other legislators did not work quite as hard. David Dinkins, elected to the assembly in 1965, recalled "almost nightly receptions and parties thrown by lobbyists. We would frequently read the papers the next day to find out what we had done the day before in session. Sometimes the process was so complex and convoluted that we didn't know what the hell we were doing."[3] The social life among the legislators in Albany excluded Chisholm, for the most part. Most attended lobbying dinners and cocktail parties, which Chisholm declined in favor of room service in the hotel. Whether she was hurt or relieved by her exclusion from fellow legislators' socializing is difficult to discern. On the one hand, Barbara Winslow and James Haskins theorized that it rankled Chisholm more than she admitted. She did, after all, love to dine and dance. Haskins quoted her as saying that "Men don't like independent women. Not many knew I was a regular gal."[4] But on the other hand, Chisholm implied that she disapproved of the "convention"-like atmosphere of the legislative session and especially the conduct of some of her colleagues who were far from home and family. First, she did not want to participate in the lobbying, which she saw as purchasing legislators' allegiance with lavish meals or more. But, perhaps more importantly, she encountered the sexual harassment that is familiar to Black women in the United States. "There is an active, shall we say, night life," she sniffed. "I took no part in it, in spite of the fact that a few of the male legislators made persistent and sometimes ingenious efforts to get me to." This not-so-veiled allusion to sexual propositions suggests that Black women, no matter their status as elected legislators, might well have been seen by her white male colleagues as a Jezebel figure, an image that has harmed Black women for centuries.[5] She was not bereft of friendship in the assembly, however. In addition to her ally Percy Sutton, she befriended Arthur Hardwick of Buffalo, another first-year legislator. Her relationship with Hardwick would eventually deepen into romance.

BLACK FEMINIST POWER IN ALBANY

Chisholm began to develop her brand of pragmatic radical politics. In the office, she had hired Unity Democratic Club (UDC) member Allan Fagan as her aide. Fagan joined the UDC in 1964 and helped with the voter registration drive that lent key momentum to Chisholm. He was hired because he had experience with writing political newsletters and other documents, and this is what he did for her: drafting bills and writing *Shirley Chisholm's Report from Albany*, the constituent newsletter, on a periodic basis. Fagan recalled that each bill he drafted on her behalf, and that she then dropped into the hopper, represented "what she thought was right." Although "she was not afraid to commit political suicide," as Fagan put it, pragmatism was also necessary in order to move those bills along. She started the session with no fewer than ten initiatives that she "tossed into the legislative mill." She (or Fagan) drafted bills to expand social education; include domestic and hospital employees in unemployment insurance; mandate police training in civil rights and liberties; replace substitute teachers in cities with permanent faculty at the junior high level; outlaw residential redlining; establish state-funded day care; establish all-day kindergartens and after-school programs; identify scholastic abilities in historically oppressed groups; and reestablish minimum distances for the sale of alcohol, building on the issues in Brooklyn that compelled her to enter politics.[6]

Chisholm's legislative efforts met with some successes. While some of her bills were sent to the Ways and Means Committee, never to emerge, her bill to expand unemployment insurance of $500 or more per year to include domestic workers was passed by the assembly in April. She also pushed through her bill to identify scholarly ability in students who belonged to "culturally deprived" groups, and one that would ensure that teachers who took maternity leave would be able to count years of service prior to their leaves toward tenure.[7]

Chisholm's antipoverty work came from her critique of the War on Poverty as not going far enough. She was an ally to those engaged in enacting War on Poverty policies; the Central Brooklyn Coordinating Council (CBCC) had spun off Youth In Action (YIA), the eventual designee as Brooklyn's Community Action Program, and she continued to liaise with the CBCC even though she no longer served in its leadership. In December 1964, as an assemblywoman-elect, she had participated in the CBCC's conference on the War on Poverty. In 1965, the organization provided a forum for politicians to speak about their efforts on behalf of Bed-Stuy in the federal War on Poverty. Chisholm was one of those speakers, as were Senator Jacob Javits, Senator Robert F. Kennedy, and the city's candidates for mayor.[8] But once she reached Albany as a legislator, she went beyond the War on Poverty's attempt to remedy economic distress without cash assistance. She focused on the cracks that poor people often fell into that the War on Poverty did not cover: widening the unemployment safety net, increasing educational opportunity, and mitigating sex discrimination against women teachers.

She was particularly critical of the sexist and racist assumptions built into the War on Poverty. These included the casting of Black men as irresponsible and Black women as domineering, two facets of the same idea that Black people's own dysfunction was the reason so many Black people were poor. In 1965, Assistant Secretary of Labor and Director of the Office of Policy Planning and Research Daniel Patrick Moynihan wrote *The Negro Family: The Case for National Action* (widely known as the Moynihan Report). Although the Moynihan Report liberally cited Black social scientists such as E. Franklin Frazier, Horace Cayton, Kenneth Clark, and Thomas Pettigrew, and echoed some of their concerns with racism and economic injustice, its author ignored the intent of those scholars' works and placed the bulk of the responsibility for inequality at the feet of a pathological Black family.[9] Moynihan knew that Lyndon B. Johnson's administration was, in the wake of the 1964 Civil Rights Act, desperately trying to take control of the civil rights agenda. When Moynihan arrived at the conclusion that the major problem facing African Americans was the disintegration of family life, members of the Johnson administration were relieved. Here was a problem they could take credit for solving proactively. It conveniently took blame away from economic discrimination. It also fit neatly with what historian Robert Self has called "breadwinner liberalism," that is, public policy that sought to economically support a male-headed nuclear family, which the War on Poverty policies often assumed.[10] The report took as its starting premise that African Americans were behind in the "competitions of American life," one of which was the right of an American man to be the financial and executive head of a household. As the government looked for ways to increase the likelihood of equality of results, he wanted to point out that halting the disorganization of "the Negro family," which was the source of the destruction of Black people's very "fabric of society," would take a significant step toward this goal.[11] The picture Moynihan presented of Black families was likely intended to be shocking and accessible to laypeople, for his audience would be politicians and not sociologists.

Moynihan's denigration of Black women who had the responsibilities of supporting their families but none of the prerogatives of manhood particularly rankled Chisholm. Moynihan concluded that matriarchy was holding "the Negro community" back. Black youth were "caught" in what he called "the Tangle of Pathology." He correlated lower intelligence scores and the likelihood of juvenile delinquency with the absence of a father, and suggested that enlistment in the armed forces could counteract the effects of such a disorganized and matrifocal family life. The military would also enable Black (male) youth to "feel like a man."[12] While Moynihan mentioned poverty and unemployment, he asserted that Black women's power—central to Chisholm's vision of a more equitable society—had become the worst hindrance for the advancement of Black people.[13] Chisholm did not question his assumption that Black men had been emasculated and that Black women had to be responsible for holding families together. She even said that, along with perseverance, Black women developed "dominance." But she disagreed with the use of the term Black "matriarch" for its negative connotation, one Moynihan perpetuated in his report.[14] Although she was incorrect that white sociologists had coined the term (it had been sociologist E. Franklin Frazier), she was correct that it served a divisive and negative function. She would find out just how divisive it would be within the next few years of her political career.

Chisholm learned that she had become a lightning rod for persistent Bed-Stuy problems. Grumblings about the job she was doing soon spread outside the UDC. She bristled when an anonymous reader wrote to the *New York Amsterdam News* that she was "blind" to the problems facing her constituents. Specifically, the reader criticized Chisholm for allowing the yard and a portion of the fence surrounding the Brooklyn Home for Aged Colored People to remain in a state of disrepair. Chisholm shot back the following week that such things were the responsibility of the home's board of directors, and that she could not possibly "correct the many ills and wrongs that beset our community." Responding to the reader's accusations that the lack of attention to the home's garden suggested that Chisholm had forgotten from whence her support came, she replied, "I also know that when the time comes I have only my [legislative] record to present to the people."[15] Although this was likely not the first time that Chisholm heard complaints about her performance as an elected official, it was the first time they were publicized, and it foreshadowed future criticism as well as the frustration that Chisholm would feel as a result.

The assembly redistricted the Seventeenth Assembly District (AD) into the Forty-Fifth AD during the 1965 legislative session, and so Chisholm had to run for her seat again. According to James Haskins, she was "furious" and complained that "they" (most likely Stanley Steingut and his allies) were attempting to harass her. However, this restricting mandate came not from the Democratic leadership but from the U.S. Supreme Court, which had ruled that state legislatures must be redistricted to equalize populations and approach "one man–one vote" as much as possible. A Republican-led lame duck session in December 1964 came up with a plan to do so, affirmed by a federal court, which mandated redrawing districts and requiring some legislators to run in both 1965 and 1966. Reflecting her evolving political sensibilities, Chisholm experimented with a more militant tone during this campaign. She and her father had discussed Malcolm X and the Nation of Islam up until Charles's death in 1960, and Chisholm maintained an interest in the now-independent activist. In the wake of Malcolm's assassination in February 1965, she quoted him in campaign speeches.[16] Despite her unhappiness with having to run again, she was unopposed in the primary and won easily in the general election. At the same time, once reelected, she acquired a colleague who would later become a nemesis: Sam Wright. In the new Thirty-Ninth AD, Wright defeated Ray Williams by a margin of 2–1, thus gaining the Democratic nomination for the seat, and easily took the election in November. Wright, a lawyer from Brownsville who had worked for the Corporation Counsel Office, would be the third Black assemblyperson from Brooklyn in addition to Chisholm and Bertram Baker.[17]

Chisholm's sophomore year in office corresponded with a new interest in Bed-Stuy from the federal level—but Chisholm was stung when she was not sought out for consultation. The new senator Robert F. Kennedy took the initiative for his own antipoverty project in the state of New York. On a tour of Brooklyn with Central Brooklyn Coordinating Council members and now-Judge Tom Jones, Kennedy received lukewarm support—even a young boy who answered the door at one apartment abruptly shut it in Kennedy's face. Ten months later Kennedy announced a major new program at CBCC's community development conference. Flanked by a cadre of powerful white men behind the podium—Senator Javitz, Mayor John Lindsay, and Robert Wood of the Department of Housing and Urban Development—he announced the new Bedford-Stuyvesant Renewal and Rehabilitation Corporation, which would combine housing, employment, health care, home loans, a community center, and urban beautification. Chisholm sat in the front row of the auditorium. But she was not on the stage and felt slighted by Kennedy. After her election to Congress, Chisholm would recall that she had received the most votes of any official in the area "but Kennedy never sought me out. . . . I think there were some people who kept him from me."[18]

Chisholm continued to cut her own path in the legislature, poised for reelection yet again in what would become the Forty-Fifth AD in January

1967. As one of the "most militant advocates of Negro rights" in the assembly (Percy Sutton was the other), she continued to introduce bills and argue for her district's interests. She and Sutton formed the Council of Black Elected Democrats the year before, which rotated meetings between their two hotel rooms while the legislators were in Albany. She opposed an increase in real estate taxes that would burden the tenants and homeowners in Bed-Stuy and collaborated with Bertram Baker to pass a bill that regulated alcohol sales near schools. She defended unlicensed car services, citing their usefulness for Black and brown people who were passed by regular taxis when they attempted to hail a ride in a poor neighborhood. She hosted her beloved Key Women twice in the state capital, for a luncheon and a tour. And, illustrating her growing participation in political power brokering, she led the decision of several of her Black Democratic colleagues to demand a lieutenant governorship for a Black candidate in 1966. This, they reasoned, would put a Black person in the position of actually setting state policy and being responsible in the absence of the governor.[19] Chisholm's chosen candidate for governor was Frank D. O'Connor, but Nelson Rockefeller won the seat in November.[20]

Chisholm was most outspoken over education, reflecting her first career and her move from the schoolhouse to the state house. When the state assembly voted overwhelmingly to pass a bill allowing the loan of public school textbooks to private and parochial schools, Chisholm told the *New York Times* that it violated the separation of church and state. She thought the policy would siphon resources away from public schools. The bill's supporters, she said, were having an emotional reaction and were deluding themselves that they were helping underserved children.[21] *The New York Times* editorial board supported Chisholm's position the following day, citing her concern that once the state lent free books to private and religious schools, the ground would be laid for loans of teachers or even buildings.[22]

Even closer to Chisholm's heart, however, was expanding access to higher education for nonwhite and poor students. In 1966, twelve years after *Brown*, fewer than 3 percent of students in the City University of New York (CUNY) system were Black. When Anthony Travia, in consultation with Governor Rockefeller, introduced a bill for the massive expansion of CUNY, Chisholm and the other Black members of the state legislature saw their opportunity. They offered their colleagues two choices: they would kill the present bill or amend it to provide access for more Black students to the campuses in the CUNY system. In a "shirt sleeve session" (Chisholm remained in her jacket, surrounded by jacketless male colleagues) at the *New York Amsterdam News* offices, the legislators hammered out an amendment.[23] The clout of the nine Black legislators had risen when in 1966 they determined that their votes were needed to reelect Anthony Travia as Speaker. Capitalizing on this, Chisholm and Percy Sutton led a visit to Travia's DeWitt Clinton Hotel room one night early in the 1966 session. In this "midnight march," the Black legislators seated themselves on the radiator and the edge of the bed and presented their demands frankly. In exchange for their support for the CUNY expansion, including a $400 million construction fund and a greater matching contribution from the state, the Black state legislators wanted a provision that would increase access for poor students. The plan they came up with during their "shirt sleeve" session was to create a $2 million fund that would provide support services such as testing and tutoring to poor students in order to prepare them for college. In the first year, 1,666 students would be admitted under the initiative. Later, such students would be allocated 5 percent of seats at CUNY. In order to fund this effort, the group proposed charging wealthier students—about 55 percent whose families earned over $10,000—a tuition fee. Up until this point, tuition had been free to all. The tuition provision was designed to appeal to upstate Republicans, who had long complained about the fiscal irresponsibility of charging no tuition at all. The Black lawmakers hoped that the fee would also create more spaces for less wealthy students.[24]

Their efforts worked. When Travia's bill was introduced two days later, it contained a provision for $1 million to be allocated to a testing and tutoring program of 1,000 poor students who had placed in the bottom third of their high school cohorts. While Sutton, Chisholm, and their colleagues did not receive all they had requested, and Harlem senator Basil Patterson called the funding "a drop in the bucket," the provision was there nonetheless. With Rockefeller's support, the assembly passed it easily the next day, and the senate did the same a week later. Rockefeller signed it into law immediately. In August, the city Board of Higher Education, having christened the program for poor students SEEK (Search for Education, Elevation, and Knowledge), allocated an additional $400,000 so that the program could be expanded to 2,000 students. By August the program was full, and nearly 700 of the students had been nominated by YIA. Within one year, Brooklyn College found that SEEK students dropped out at a lower rate than other students.[25]

Chisholm was very pleased with SEEK, often speaking of it as her proudest achievement from her days in the New York state legislature. Two thousand students were served in 1966, with another 2,000 in the 1967–68 academic year. Her penchant for exaggeration led her to imply that she was the only state legislator to draft and push the bill. Indeed, she wrote in *Unbossed and Unbought* that it was the result of a bill that she had introduced (one of eight that passed out of fifty total).[26] She tended to deemphasize that she had worked with other Black legislators to get the amendment added to an existing CUNY expansion bill. The SEEK program itself was likely conceptualized by CUNY professor Julius C. C. Edelstein, who had lobbied Chisholm on the Education Committee. She responded to his request, delivering a moving speech on the floor of the assembly and fiercely advocating for the program.[27]

Chisholm also took a keen interest in the fate of Long Island University's (LIU) Brooklyn campus. LIU, a private liberal arts institution, had begun in Brooklyn and expanded to two other campuses. The cost of doing so, however, had raised tuition. After a high-profile controversy in which the provost resigned in 1966, the City University of New York made an offer the next year to buy LIU's Brooklyn campus, planning to move its business school to the site. Student and faculty reaction was swift and outraged. Citing the need for a small, private liberal arts college in the heart of Brooklyn, several state legislators, including Chisholm, formed a commission to look into the sale. Two weeks of hearings were held, and although nothing came of the hearings per se, CUNY cancelled the planned purchase and the LIU Brooklyn campus remained.[28]

CONGRESSIONAL REDISTRICTING IN BEDFORD-STUYVESANT

Chisholm was keeping an eye on a possible opportunity to advance to the U.S. Congress. Back in Bed-Stuy, a nascent movement to elect a Black U.S. legislator from Bed-Stuy was taking root. Eddie Pinckney and Etheline Dubin, grassroots activists, led the new Committee for a Negro Congressman from Brooklyn (CNC). The object was to elect a new Black representative from the Eleventh District. It was on the eastern edge of the borough, covering Cypress Hills, Bushwick, eastern Brownsville, and the southeastern corner of Bed-Stuy. They enlisted a star-studded cast of honorary chairs: Chisholm, Rev. Milton Galamison, Ruth Goring, and Joseph Tepedino. Over seventy community members had endorsed it. The committee's statement, released in April 1967, pointed out that Brooklyn's "liberal reputation" was belied by its all-white representation in Congress, and urged that a Black candidate be put forward for the election that fall.[29]

The committee encountered a sticky problem, however. Although Brooklyn's Black population had been growing since Chisholm's birth, the congressional districts were divided up in such a way as to dilute Black voting power. The most recent congressional lines had been drawn by the Republican-led state legislature in 1961. The Eleventh District had some of Bedford-Stuyvesant, but there were three other districts that included slices of it. The Tenth, a vertical slice of Brooklyn from Myrtle Avenue in the north all the way down to Bergen Beach, was represented by Emmanuel

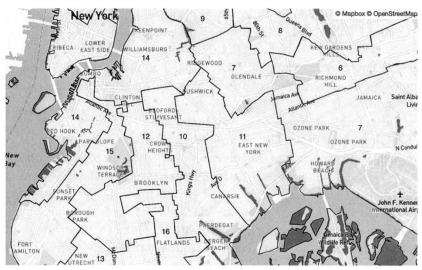

Brooklyn's Ninetieth U.S. Congress districts prior to redistricting,
1968. From Lewis, DeVine, Pitcher, and Martis, *Digital Boundary
Definitions of United States Congressional Districts, 1789–2012.*
© Jeffrey B. Lewis. © Mapbox. © OpenStreetMap.org.

Celler. The Twelfth, represented by Edna Kelly, ran along Nostrand and
Bedford Avenues from Lafayette down to Tilden Avenue, then ended in a
wide crescent encompassing Kensington and Borough Park. John Rooney's
Fourteenth District, an oddly bifurcated parcel on the western edge of the
borough, was cobbled together from Greenpoint and the Brooklyn Navy
Yard, plus the northwest corner of Bed-Stuy, at the north end and a long
southern end running from Red Hook almost all the way to the Verrazano
Bridge.[30] The result of these geographical patterns meant that Bed-Stuy, a
relatively straightforward block in the heart of Brooklyn, was represented
by no fewer than four white congresspeople in Washington, none of whom
owed their seats to the Black and brown voters in the neighborhood.[31]

The committee was not successful, and a white fellow Brooklyn College
alumnus, Frank Brasco, was elected to the Eleventh District seat. But the
work had garnered broad support, and the committee gained steam from
this effort. Resistance to the all-white Brooklyn delegation would take the
form of changing the district boundaries themselves.

The assault against racial gerrymandering would be led by none other
than Andrew Cooper, Chisholm's former fellow UDC member and now
detractor. He decided to file his own lawsuit, *Cooper v. Power*, naming the
state commissioner of elections as his lead defendant. Joining with fellow

former UDC member Joan Bacchus [Maynard] and Paul Kerrigan, a white liberal Republican, Cooper filed on June 23, 1966, against the commissioners of election, Governor Rockefeller, the attorney general, all of the congressional officeholders from Kings County, and a slew of state legislators and party leaders. The suit alleged that the congressional district lines were "so torturous, artificial, and labyrinthine" that no "proper purpose" for their existence was evident. The districts, it argued, effectively eliminated the necessity for representatives to concern themselves with Black constituents. Citing the Fourteenth and Fifteenth amendments of the U.S. Constitution, the suit requested that the court mandate redistricting that would consolidate the political power of the then 370,000 Black voters in Bed-Stuy. It further stipulated a stay of elections for the House of Representatives until such redistricting could take place.[32]

A federal judge of the Eastern District of New York affirmed the lawsuit as a "substantial federal question" in August 1966 and called for the formation of a three-judge panel to hear the case the following March. Cooper, in preparation, sought support from Brooklyn's Black leadership, including Chisholm and the UDC. Roy Wilkins of the NAACP and Floyd McKissick of CORE filed affidavits, and the NAACP filed an *amicus curiae*.[33] But Chisholm did not play any part in Cooper's suit, an inaction that Cooper would never forgive. He said he wrote to her at the time he filed the suit, asking for her support, but she never responded.[34]

Chisholm's reason for not responding to Cooper's missive was likely because she was aware of another challenge to Bed-Stuy's gerrymandering, one that she probably thought was more likely to win. A few weeks before Cooper filed his suit, the New York Liberal Party filed *Wells v. Rockefeller* in the New York Eastern District federal court, asserting that the current congressional districts in the state were gerrymandered. Pointing to the vast differences in population of several districts, party leader Donald Harrington and David Wells of the International Ladies Garment Workers Union alleged that the districting completed in 1961 by the Republican-led state legislature gave the advantage to Republican voters. The present scheme crammed voters who were more likely to vote Democratic into larger districts, thus reducing the effect of each voter's vote. The Twelfth District was the largest in the state. Next door, the Fifteenth was one of the smallest. It started in downtown Brooklyn and encompassed the largely white neighborhoods of Prospect Park, Park Slope, and the neighborhoods at the foot of the Verrazano Bridge. This districting outcome was directly in opposition to the U.S. Supreme Court's 1964 "one man–one vote" ruling in *Reynolds v. Sims* that mandated districts to have relatively equal populations.[35]

The court would affirm Harrington's suit, ruling in May 1967 that the New York state legislature must redraw the congressional districts. Citing a "seemingly bizarre structure of the present Congressional districts," it pointed out the vast population differences between districts in Brooklyn and that two of the districts were not contiguous. Stating that the current districting indeed violated the Supreme Court's recent "one man–one vote" ruling, the court mandated new districting in time for the 1968 elections. "The 1968 and 1970 (even possibly the 1972) Congressional elections ought to be held in districts far more equalized than they are at present," the court wrote in its decision. "There are enough changes [using 1960 census date] which can be superimposed on the present districts to cure the most flagrant inequalities." Immediately, the Liberal Party appealed, albeit unsuccessfully, to Governor Rockefeller to call a special legislative session for redistricting. Instead, Rockefeller appealed the Southern District's ruling to the Supreme Court.[36]

Cooper's suit, meanwhile, had been heard by a panel of three federal judges in late March, but they reserved the decision. Eventually, they would dismiss *Cooper* nearly a year later, in March 1968, because *Wells v. Rockefeller* had been affirmed by the Supreme Court. Two of the three judges declared that, in light of the Supreme Court's decision, the state law in dispute had been repealed and new districts had already been established in time for the 1968 elections.[37] Cooper would appropriate the *Wells* victory as his own, writing that "in 1967 the Supreme Court ruled in our favor and ordered that the districts must be 'compact, contiguous, and of equal size.'" He took credit for the creation of the new Twelfth Congressional District and portrayed Chisholm as the naysayer who came around due to the effort's success: "Shirley Chisholm was suddenly very interested," he recalled. He would remain one of her most vocal critics and successfully convinced contemporaries that his suit had brought about Chisholm's seat.[38]

In the hope that Bed-Stuy's redistricting would indeed be upheld *in Wells v. Rockefeller*, Chisholm spent much of 1967 raising her national profile. She traveled to Washington, D.C., for the Council of Elected Democratic Officials, along with other Black women who were involved in electoral politics: Yvonne Brathwaite Burke of Los Angeles, Alice Johns of Chicago, Barbara Jordan of Texas, and Victorine Adams of Baltimore. Together, the group minced no words when criticizing state Democratic parties for being indifferent to the issues of Black citizens. A few months later, Chisholm served on the steering committee for a conference of Black elected officials at the University of Chicago, a group that was cochaired by her assembly colleague Percy Sutton.[39]

JOINING FORCES WITH FEMINIST MOVEMENTS

However, it was the nascent feminist movement that drew Chisholm into the swirl of national politics in an unprecedented way. Although she had thus far built her career on representing Black and brown constituents from Brooklyn and the state of New York, she had not forged strong ties to the nominal leaders of the nationwide Black freedom struggle. Perhaps this was because those organizations were weighted toward the South and Midwest: SCLC in Atlanta, CORE in Chicago, and SNCC diffused across the South. Only the National Urban League and the NAACP had roots in New York City, although Chisholm did not have close relationships with those organizations. She also did not ally herself with Brooklyn's chapter of CORE, even though it had collaborated with the UDC on Operation Unemployment.[40]

The center of the women's movement, however, was in Chisholm's backyard—New York City—and perhaps this was why she quickly allied with it. The National Organization for Women (NOW) had its largest branch there and was home to its founding national president, Betty Friedan. New York was also a center of welfare activism. The Citywide Coordinating Council and Brooklyn's own Welfare Recipients League were founding organizations within the National Welfare Rights Organization. Founded in 1967, the Brooklyn Welfare Action Council would become the largest chapter for the National Welfare Rights Organization by 1968. New organizations emerged from the New Left: New York Radical Women in 1967, and Redstockings (founded in the aftermath of New York Radical Women's dissolution) in 1969.

While none of these organizations shared identical concerns or strategies, all of them reconceptualized the personal into the political. Issues that had seemed to be merely the idiosyncratic problems of women now emerged as national issues: childcare, reproductive justice, access to work and money. As historian Robert Self argues, it was women's growing presence in the waged workforce, alongside the prevailing male breadwinner ideal, that energized the movement. Between 1945 and 1960, wives and mothers almost doubled their percentage in the workforce, while the percentages of men and childless, unmarried women there remained the same. Married women and mothers worked out of financial necessity or to satisfy their own ambitions, but they were also expected to do "the second shift" of work at home, taking care of family and household, once their waged work was done. This was exacerbated for poor and nonwhite women, whose work was often essential for household survival. The growing number of women who engaged in both family and waged work were unfairly handicapped in the latter in terms of raises, job retention, and advancement.[41]

As a New York state legislator, she saw the women who led such organizations as her constituents. Until 1967, Chisholm had not explicitly identified with women's issues in politics even though she came out of a woman-dominated profession and often commented that her sex was always a part of her political journey. She had, however, promoted legislation that recognized and remedied injustices facing women: the lack of unemployment benefits for the overwhelmingly female and nonwhite domestic and hospital workforce, equitable tenure rules for women teachers on maternity leave, and the lack of affordable childcare. Signaling her identification with labor feminists, who advocated for protective legislation that acknowledged women's differences from men, she introduced a bill in 1967 that proposed a maximum forty-eight-hour, six-day work week for women in New York state.[42] She would back away from this approach shortly thereafter, recognizing that protective legislation in practice protected men's access to certain jobs, overtime wages, and promotions. Instead, for most of her career, she would follow Pauli Murray's legal framework of asserting women's equality to men while acknowledging that women's childbearing and childcare responsibilities were not the same as men's. Therefore, women needed freedom to seek employment while they needed protection to do so on an equal basis with men.[43] Furthermore, Chisholm allied herself with welfare rights activists who asserted women's rights to remain out of the paid workforce in order to parent full time.

In 1967, Chisholm began her efforts for explicit equal rights for women. She teamed up with the other three women in the New York State Assembly to sponsor a bill making it illegal for employment agencies to discriminate on the basis of sex. The bill, also sponsored by Constance E. Cook, Gail Hellenbrand, and Dorothy H. Rose, was passed and signed by the governor in April and took effect on September 1, 1967. She also joined a coalition of twenty-nine assembly colleagues to cosponsor a bill liberalizing the state's abortion law. This would decriminalize abortions and allow the state health commissioner to authorize hospitals to provide so-called therapeutic abortions under certain conditions. It was not successful, however, and neither was a reintroduction of the bill in 1968.[44]

Still, Chisholm's efforts had begun to establish her bona fides with feminist activists. In 1967, she began to seek formal connections to the leadership of the growing women's movement. She decided to reach out to the National Organization for Women—specifically its founder, Betty Friedan. NOW was founded at the 1966 Conference for State Commissions on the Status of Women. Founded in response to John F. Kennedy's Presidential Commission on the Status of Women, and its 1963 report, the state commissions had been holding national conferences since 1964. At the 1966 meeting, there was a critical mass of delegates who had grown frustrated with the Equal Employment Opportunity Commission's refusal to enforce Title VII of the 1964 Civil Rights Act, which prohibited discrimination based on sex as well as race. Fifteen of these delegates adjourned to Friedan's hotel room one evening to discuss forming a new group, though they made no decision. The next day, however, in response to the refusal of conference leaders to allow a vote on a resolution calling for EEOC's enforcement of Title VII, a group of women decided to form a nongovernmental organization to advocate for women's equality. They formally created NOW at a founding meeting that October, with Friedan as national president and Kay Clarenbach as the chairman [*sic*] of the board.⁴⁵

Chisholm became involved in the new organization, becoming vice president of the New York chapter, founded the previous fall, by April 1967. That month, fresh from her nondiscrimination bill victory and perhaps aiming to raise her national profile, Chisholm wrote to Friedan introducing herself and pledged that she would "work to the best of my ability in fulfilling the aims and goals" of NOW.⁴⁶ She enclosed a short biographical article and summary of her 1966 legislative achievements from the assembly. The article explained that, as the first "Negro" woman in the state assembly, she was establishing a distinguished record of advocacy for education and domestic service employees.⁴⁷ Friedan's response does not survive, but their relationship continued after that point. Chisholm would remain aligned with NOW for the next several years, and perhaps to show that the political street went both ways, Friedan would serve as a delegate on her behalf in the 1972 presidential election.

Chisholm also worked on behalf of NOW during the New York state constitutional convention in 1967 to add abortion rights to the state constitution. Running from April to September, it involved 186 delegates elected from across the state the previous November and was led by Anthony Travia. Nine of the delegates were women, eleven were Black, including Thomas Jones, and four were Puerto Rican, including Herman Badillo. The convention had been called in large part because of the redistricting implications of the Supreme Court's "one man–one vote" rulings, but many more issues besides congressional lines were up for debate. The developing women's movement used the convention as an opportunity, aided by Chisholm. Two weeks after the convention began, a NOW demonstration at Albany marked "the first public march for women's rights since women won the right to vote in 1920." Calling the developing women's movement "the second great civil rights movement of the 1960s," the marchers drew attention to NOW's two proposals regarding the new constitution. Proposal I sought to add the word "sex" to the section that prohibited discrimination on the basis of race and other factors. It mandated that sex, marital status, pregnancy, or parenthood could no longer be grounds for denying education, employment, or housing, and withdrew state public funds from any entity that thus discriminated. However, the only nondiscrimination clause to survive concerned race, religion, and national origin in any school supported by state monies.[48] Chisholm was designated head of the campaign for Proposal II, which simply stipulated that "the right to terminate a pregnancy shall be deemed a civil right." She also, in her capacity as NOW New York's vice president, cosigned a "Dear Delegate" letter that went out to all elected delegates. It outlined the two proposals, enclosed a copy of NOW's letter to Travia requesting an appearance to testify at the convention, and the press release.[49] Their efforts resulted in some token gestures from the convention. Chisholm accompanied Friedan and several other NOW representatives to observe the convention floor at a June session, and Robinson requested that Travia officially welcome them, which he did.[50] The abortion clause was defeated, however.

After defeat on the abortion clause, Chisholm stayed peripherally involved in the proceedings. When members of a Black sorority, Lambda Kappa Mu, visited Albany to observe the convention, Chisholm welcomed them.[51] When the convention was over on September 26, however, Chisholm came out against the new state charter, which the convention had voted to present as an entire package rather than piece by piece. She joined her other New York City Black assembly colleagues, the NAACP, and the Urban League. She explained that "the faults outweigh the gains," and being forced to vote on the entire constitution deprived voters of a democratic process to approve or dismiss specific aspects of the document.[52]

Throughout 1967, Chisholm continued to build her national profile. She won her final assembly race, this time for the Fifty-Fifth District. She attended the Conference of Elected Democratic Officials in Washington, D.C., where she advocated for the national party to be more responsive to Black and Latinx voters.[53] She was on the steering committee for another conference on Black politics in Chicago.[54] By the end of 1967, she had developed strategic alliances in New York and nationally. There was a movement afoot to elect a Black congressperson, and there were two legal challenges to the current districting; she was building city and statewide support from the women's movement, and she had raised her profile within the Democratic Party. When the door opened, she would be ready to step through.

6

UNBOUGHT AND UNBOSSED

★

Chisholm's signature slogan, "Unbought and Unbossed," implies an independent, principled, fearless warrior. And in Chisholm's case that descriptor is indeed true. But the slogan had more mundane origins in the fact that in 1968 Democratic Party bosses declined to choose her as the arm of their organization in New York's Twelfth U.S. House District race. Therefore, Chisholm did not have access to the cash that the party's candidate did, but neither was she beholden to any party leadership. She was literally a free agent and set about turning the party's snub into an asset that would define her career. Black and women voters gave Chisholm the 1968 congressional election. In the process, her profile would develop from a mainly local figure into a national one.

But winning local support was not simple, as her district was fracturing before her eyes. Her political ascension was also a signal of a cultural sea change in New York. The city had been a working-class stronghold through World War II. Between the time Chisholm graduated from Brooklyn College and when she ran for the House of Representatives, the city became politically and culturally dominated by white-collar workers.[1] As Black politicians and voters became more visible, ironically, working-class people, which included most Black New Yorkers, became less visible. "Two New Yorks" developed during 1967 and 1968: one white and largely Jewish and Catholic, the other Black with a few white allies, a racialized political split between white liberals and Black radicals that colors New York politics to this day.[2] Therefore, Chisholm not only had to gain the votes of her district's Black majority; she also had to acknowledge and get support from the significant number of white voters who remained. She did so by appealing to women.

Chisholm's congressional race occurred at a time when other Black candidates were seeking congressional seats nationwide with a good chance of winning. Cleveland and Chicago were other cities in which either redrawn districts or changing demographics had led to Black majorities among the voters. If Black candidates won in all three races, the number of Black congresspeople would increase from five to eight.[3] Nationwide, the *Chicago*

Defender estimated that about 200 Black candidates were running for various elected offices in the fall of 1968, including seats on state legislatures, school boards, and city councils.[4] But these electoral successes occurred alongside multiple challenges. White Americans were losing patience with the human rights demands of the Black freedom struggle and were alarmed by the news that showed urban rebellions flaring in cities from coast to coast. Their suspicions of urban Black Americans were further nurtured by the "law and order" mantra of Richard Nixon and the rising Right.[5] Considerable conflict within the Black freedom struggle created complications. Black Power activists, ascendant after 1967, developed an explicit critique of white supremacy and advocated for self-defense, even when it turned violent.

The Black freedom struggle had always contained elements of the argument for Black self-determination that would come to be called Black Power, including armed self-defense, but popular media made much of the change in tactics. Black Power's Black nationalist strains clashed with the integrationist model of the civil rights establishment, but this discrepancy in tactics had already existed on a grassroots level within the larger movement and became crucial in implementing and broadening the Black freedom struggle after 1968. Recent Black Power scholars have demonstrated it was Black Power itself that led to the political gains by Black politicians in the late 1960s. Three core ideas guided the Black Power ideology: self-determination, pride in "blackness" (the term "Negro" was seen as having been imposed by white Americans), and international racial solidarity. And, to quote Peniel E. Joseph, "Black Power loomed over the year 1968."[6] If Chisholm did not openly court Black Power activists or mirror Black nationalism, she adopted the self-determination element of Black Power's core tenets: she insisted that political power for Black Brooklynites was at stake during the congressional election. She later observed that the labels Women's Liberation and Black Power created reactivity and a lack of critical thinking about how the movements could connect, especially through and among Black women. But in 1968 she represented the candidate who was most open to the aims and rhetoric of Black Power.[7]

Chisholm combined Black Power with Black feminism, insisting on self-determination, pride, and solidarity for Black women. The political quest for simultaneous antiracism and antisexism that emanated from this intersectional approach was Black feminist power. Ultimately, her Black feminist power approach won by navigating the fissures between the local and the national, between Black and white New Yorkers, and within the city's Black activist circles by creating rapport and building alliances with white voters in the district. And she targeted the sometimes overlooked but numerous voters to whom she had special appeal: women.

THE FIELD

By 1968, Chisholm had acquired stature as an experienced, charismatic legislator. "In the Assembly Chamber when she debated . . . she would sit there and you would just be in awe to watch this woman. And whenever she debated, it was amazing how you could drop a pin and hear the pin drop. Everybody paid attention," journalist and biographer Susan Brownmiller recalled. Her colleagues recognized that she always knew her facts, and those who debated her were usually aware that they needed to have done their homework also in order to keep up. But Brownmiller, then a writer for the *New York Times Magazine*, met Chisholm in 1968 and also saw her as a square. She was "a typical West Indian," Brownmiller said, who used to wear "those starchy white blouses with the collar that was up high."[8]

In December 1967, Chisholm and other Black political activists got the news they had been waiting for. The redistricting lawsuit, *Rockefeller v. Wells*, was upheld. Rendering its decision on December 17, 1967, the U.S. Supreme Court simply affirmed the opinion of the lower court.[9] Although the ruling was not the declaration of racial inequality in districting that Andy Cooper's suit had hoped to elicit, everyone expected that the new district lines would not dilute the Black vote this time. The legislature would indeed create the new Twelfth District, which encompassed most of Bedford-Stuyvesant and consolidated Black voting power. Cooper's suit would be dismissed the following spring, with two of the three judges declaring the case moot in the light of recent redistricting.[10]

It was far from a foregone conclusion that Chisholm would run for the congressional seat. The Supreme Court's decision signaled the beginning of a major contest between would-be Black congresspeople. Chisholm was one of six who were identified early on as possible candidates. The others were state senator William C. Thompson; Brownsville assemblyman Samuel D. Wright; Rev. Milton Galamison; and James Farmer, the former national director of the Congress of Racial Equality (CORE). Even Tom Jones briefly considered running for the seat, and a "Jones for Congress" storefront appeared. But by the time he approached Tom Fortune to ask for his support, Fortune and the Unity Democratic Club (UDC) had already committed to helping Chisholm. "He came around to the club but there wasn't much support for him," Fortune told Brownmiller. He thought that Jones's recent absence and the feeling that a judge should be "above politics" dampened enthusiasm for his candidacy. Jones had also spoken to

Robert F. Kennedy about his congressional ambitions but reported that Kennedy convinced him not to run so that he could continue his work with the Bedford-Stuyvesant Restoration Corporation. Also, Thompson dropped out and allied himself with Kennedy.[11]

Members of the UDC, Central Brooklyn Coordinating Council (CBCC), Youth In Action, and other Black Brooklynites anticipated the glut of candidates and developed a rigorous interview process to screen possibilities. In a deliberate effort to prevent Steingut's Democratic organization from deciding on its own puppet candidate, Etheline Dubin led an effort by the Brooklyn groups to create the Committee for a Negro Congressman (CNC) and a candidate interview process. The CNC had been strategizing since the spring of 1966 to get "a black man" elected. It had collaborated with Brooklyn CORE in a protest against gerrymandering in front of Emanuel Cellar's home. In June, it held a dinner dance fundraiser with Chisholm as one of the featured speakers. Now that the Supreme Court had ruled, the CNC proceeded with interviewing potential candidates—twelve in all, with Chisholm as the only woman. At 11:45 on December 23, 1967, Chisholm got the phone call: she had been unanimously chosen to be the congressional candidate. She was "excited, somewhat overwhelmed, and very excited."[12]

Chisholm was sure that the committee had selected her because she was the only candidate who had the "nerve" to disagree with them on some things, her confidence, and her proven record of being what she began to call "unbought and unbossed" at the polls. "I had, I knew, been the only one of the potential candidates who talked back and disagreed with them, about things they would have to expect from a nominee," she said. "I did not go to them with my hat in my hand, and this is what they liked. "I was the kind of voice that [the CNC] wanted in Washington." As she heard it, the only objection that came in the form of "underground rumblings" was that she was a woman. But, she felt, her real problem was that she had little money after using much of her inheritance to get to Albany.[13]

Officially, the CNC announced that it had made its "enthusiastic endorsement" because "Mrs. Shirley Chisholm has already established a reputation for political independence." The CNC affirmed its commitment (and, by extension, that of its candidate) to jobs, housing, and education for Bedford-Stuyvesant. Chisholm herself announced, "I now suddenly realize that the greatest fight in my life is about to take place, and once again the people in this community will determine my political destiny on the basis of my record, my independence, and my courage."[14]

Others recalled the CNC's decision with less enthusiasm. Etheline Dubin, then executive secretary of the CNC, recalled that Chisholm wound up getting the nod because another logical choice, Ruth Goring, had lost her coleadership of the UDC. Chisholm had a long history with CBCC, had an existing political constituency, and was not completely tied to the Democratic machine. Dubin was undoubtedly aware that Chisholm did have political alliances, but Steingut still ran the Brooklyn Democrats and he had not forgotten Chisholm's refusal to vote for him as Speaker in the state assembly in 1965. Chisholm was clearly independent from him.[15]

Steingut, for his part, would not accept the committee's choice and supported former state senator and current city councilman William Thompson instead. He and the county Democrats did not officially endorse anyone, however. Rather, at a meeting held after the Citizens' Committee announced its choice, all eight white Kings County district leaders and members of the assembly voted against endorsing Chisholm. Chisholm and Tom Fortune, both present at the meeting, were the only two votes in her favor. Steingut's county organization decided to "let the people decide" in word but support Thompson in deed. Chisholm was sure that the voters could see through this, and said so in *Unbought and Unbossed*: "White people think black people are stupid, but it came through to the community that the organization could not bring itself to endorse me because I would not submit to being bossed by any of them." And of Thompson, she told Brownmiller, "Willie felt the white boys were going to get out the vote for him." Thompson was supported by most of the white party leadership. The outcome of Chisholm's rejection by Steingut's organization was not all bad, however. He had little connection with voters in the district. One of Lyndon Johnson's aides was reported to have said that "if you gave [Steingut's] crowd a pocketful of free subway tokens, they couldn't find their way to Bedford-Stuyvesant, or what was going on with the Negroes when they got there." And Chisholm drew righteous energy from her independent status. It was in response to the non-endorsement from Steingut and the county organization that she adopted the slogan "Unbought and Unbossed."[16]

The third primary opponent would be Dollie Lowther Robinson, a labor activist. She had worked in the Women's Bureau under Assistant Secretary of Labor Esther Peterson and had participated in a 1963 meeting on "The Problems of Negro Women," part of the President's Commission on the Status of Women's activities. She had also been the New York Constitutional Convention delegate in 1967. Her unfortunate campaign slogan was: "Hello Dollie, We Like Dollie—For Congress." She was supported by her former Sixth Assembly District coleader Bertram Baker, A. Philip Randolph, Rev. Gardner Taylor, and many trade unions. Chisholm thought that Robinson was in part put forward by the county organization to spoil Chisholm's chances. They even "threw in a woman too," she said, to split the female vote.

But Chisholm suspected that Robinson's prime rival would be Thompson, because they were from the same neighborhood.[17]

James Farmer, passed over by the CNC, would not run in the Democratic primary. He would later claim that Steingut had supported him, perhaps having missed the open secret that Steingut stood behind William Thompson. Farmer allied instead with the Liberal Party, architects of the redistricting lawsuit. Farmer had left the directorship of CORE in order to join the Johnson administration and help with a literacy program effort. When that had not materialized, he took a teaching position at Lincoln University in Pennsylvania. But he was looking for his next step. He found it in the Twelfth District's congressional race. As he recalled it, the Liberal Party had been the one to approach him and that he had agreed on the condition that his candidacy was not just a token one.[18]

He rented an apartment on Herkimer Street at Nostrand. Announcing his Liberal Party candidacy at the Bedford-Stuyvesant Liberal Club on Nostrand, he proclaimed his status as a "militant black independent." Although he denied advocating violence—militancy for him translated into slum elimination, employment, and education—his embrace of the term "militant" indicated that he might not be aware of the delicate dance needed to win white voters. Still, his candidacy would be formidable. In May, the Republican Party adopted him as its candidate, so he became a joint Liberal-Republican candidate in the general election. But even this endorsement had an Achilles' heel. It had not been local GOP leadership who had backed this move—Chisholm had heard that the national party pressured local Black Republican leader Arthur Bramwell to withdraw the Black attorney Robert Murray and add to their ticket. "I had nothing to do with it. I certainly did not choose," Bramwell complained. "He appears to be the candidate of Lindsey, Rockefeller, and Javits." "Everybody, Republican, Democrat, black and white, male and female, resented the intrusion," Chisholm said. Still, the newspapers seemed to think that he was the favorite to win in November.[19]

THE NEW DISTRICT AND THE 1968 ELECTIONS

When the race began in January, the 1968 state assembly session had yet to meet and redraw the district lines. Chisholm still had her term to serve, and it started just a few days after the CNC's announcement of their endorsement. She was joined by nine other Black legislators, the largest number yet. The nine sought to form a bloc with which to influence their colleagues in an extensive legislative agenda. They were in for "a grinding session." In addition to creating the new districts that the Supreme Court had mandated in *Rockefeller v. Wells,* the lawmakers would decide how to fill the vacant seat left by Rep. Adam Clayton Powell, who had been removed from Congress

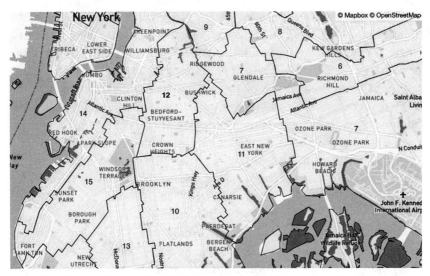

Brooklyn's Ninety-First U.S. Congress districts after redistricting, 1968. From Lewis, DeVine, Pitcher, and Martis, *Digital Boundary Definitions of United States Congressional Districts, 1789–2012.* © Jeffrey B Lewis. © Mapbox. © OpenStreetMap.org.

after an ethics violation. They would also vote on a bill to liberalize the state's abortion law, grant permission for police to use additional force, and expand Rockefeller's budget to rehabilitate poor neighborhoods and increase public school funds.[20]

Travia and the rest of the leadership hammered out a redistricting plan in February. Twenty-nine of New York's forty-one districts, most of them in New York City or nearby, acquired new lines. One sitting member, Edna Kelly of the Twelfth, would likely be unseated, to her great resentment.[21] As expected, her district was parceled out into other ones in order to equalize the population in each. The greatest portion was attached to Emmanuel Celler's, and, though she would go on to challenge him in the primary, his status as "the dean of the state's Congressional delegation" kept his district safe. In order to replace Kelly's district, a new Twelfth was drawn, with half of the voters living in Bedford-Stuyvesant. The other half were in adjoining neighborhoods including the mostly white Bushwick. The bill passed easily, was signed into law the same day by Governor Rockefeller, and approved by a federal court within the month. The new Twelfth District seat had become a reality.[22]

The redistricting might have been uncontroversial in the legislature, and as Chisholm and Travia danced together at Governor Rockefeller's annual ball outside Albany much attention focused on the fact that the new district would likely elect a Black representative. Indeed, one of the drafters of the apportionment bill conceded that the legislature "had to give Brooklyn a Negro because of pressure from the courts." The result was a district that had 60 percent Black and 10 percent Puerto Rican residents. The courts had merely required contiguous and evenly populated districts, and the redistricting was hardly a blueprint for reform. Indeed, in the bill that its bipartisan architects rushed through the assembly, the machine Democrats' overall position had been strengthened. Eight hundred and fifty thousand Puerto Rican residents, despite their number, were divided in the redistricting so as to break up their voting power. The lack of controversy and debate surrounding its passage suggested that the leadership had already decided on how to reshape the districts with a minimum of disruption to the present balance of power. But journalists and Brooklyn residents alike were well aware of the racial succession that would now take place.[23]

In national politics, the top of the ticket in 1968 was far from settled by the primary in June, a result of disarray in the Democratic Party. Johnson had been running for a second elected term, but the party bosses nationwide who had helped deliver his votes in 1964 were no longer in charge. When the New Hampshire primary results made clear that the Johnson campaign was on the ropes, Robert F. Kennedy decided to enter the race. There was also Senator Eugene McCarthy of Minnesota, who had been in the race since late 1967, drafted by Citizens for a Democratic Alternative. Both McCarthy and Kennedy were antiwar candidates, supported by Chisholm and Thompson, respectively. The charismatic Kennedy and the somewhat plodding and poetry-quoting McCarthy prepared for a long fight against Johnson. But Johnson threw a curveball in late March, simultaneously announcing that he would attempt to negotiate peace in Vietnam and withdraw from the election. The field would be further attenuated when Kennedy was shot on June 5, just after winning the California primary. The series of shocks to the Democratic Party left a breach that might have favored McCarthy. However, Vice President Hubert Humphrey had been polling higher than McCarthy even before he actually contested any primaries. Humphrey, as Johnson's successor, would eventually win the Democratic nomination for president.[24]

THE CAMPAIGN TEAM

Although the assembly had yet to draw the district, the fight was on and Chisholm put her campaign team together. Her old friend and erstwhile foe, Wesley McDonald "Mac" Holder, immediately stepped up to manage the campaign, joining the team officially in late March. Who approached whom is unclear, although Chisholm wrote in *Unbought and Unbossed* that she was surprised to receive a call from Holder offering his help. "Twenty years back, he said he wanted to live to elect a black judge and a black congressman," she explained. "Now he thought he saw a chance of reaching the second, greater goal with me but, he told me, I couldn't win without him and the people in the streets. Looking back on it, I think he was right." This version also appeared in James Haskins's biography. However, other accounts suggest that Chisholm recruited Holder. "As the first order of business," Nancy Hicks wrote, Chisholm went to Holder and "told him that she could not run without him." Regardless of who made the first overture, Holder was initially ambivalent about taking the post. He told the *Amsterdam News* that it took him "several weeks of soul searching" to decide to reenter politics.[25] Holder oversaw the strategy, finances, and organization, so that Chisholm could "stomp the streets."

Chisholm had acquired a few young and energetic aides. She had attracted the allegiance of young Puerto Rican activist Victor Robles. Robles met Chisholm when he was working for Gilbert "King" Ramirez in the New York State Assembly. Chisholm was impressed by his loyalty to Ramirez. Robles then went into the military for two years, and when he returned he saw the posters for Chisholm's congressional campaign. "I was thrilled, and I reached out to her," he recalled. Robles sought many opportunities to tell the district's voters that, like their parents or themselves, Chisholm's parents came from the Caribbean seeking opportunities for their children.[26] His case was helped by Chisholm's facility with Spanish, which continued to prove a useful curricular choice from her days at Brooklyn College. He would remain close to Chisholm for years, as she developed into an othermother figure for him. Allan Fagan, her aide in Albany, was also a team member. Fagan's job in the campaign was to work under Holder to convey Chisholm's message to people: "not just personalities, but ideas."[27] Fagan was himself running for the assembly seat in the Forty-Third District, where Democrat George Cincotta was the incumbent.[28]

Conrad Chisholm was a stalwart of the campaign. In 1968, he was a Medicaid applications investigator in the New York City Department of Social Services. "Roddie," as Shirley called him, was a cheerleader and morale booster for his wife, especially when the Democratic organization withheld its support early on. "She cried every night," he recalled. "She came home to me and she said, I want to run. I have the ability and I can run. And I can win but the men won't let me. So I said, go out there and run. You have a shoulder to cry on here. Come home, I'll give you all the support you need. I'll get my friends, get petitions signed, and get all the work done, canvassing and things like that. And so she did. She went out there and did a beautiful job."[29]

Chisholm had three formidable organizational allies behind her: the UDC, a grassroots campaign organization, and local labor. Tom Fortune at the UDC was quick to endorse his coleader, announcing that her New York State Assembly experience and her participation in local politics made her his choice.[30] Citing his admiration for her outspoken advocacy for people in the community, he saw no reason to discontinue his alliance with her for the congressional race.

A grassroots organization had also dedicated itself to her campaign. What had originally been organized as Women for Chisholm quickly expanded to include men and became the Shirley Chisholm for Congress Committee (SCCC). It formally endorsed her on February 24. Annie Bowen and Norman Adams served as cochairs, with Alice Lee and Conrad Chisholm as honorary cochairs. In the words of Bowen, the committee believed Chisholm "would wage a showdown fight" on behalf of Bedford-Stuyvesant in the House. Where the Key Women had supported Chisholm's assembly run, this new interracial, mixed-gender organization would be a major booster for her congressional campaign.[31] It was no coincidence that the organization had been founded by women and retained women in multiple leadership positions. Conrad bragged that Shirley could "pick up the phone and call 200 women and they'll be here in an hour." And Chisholm was proud of her effect on women. She told a story that became her creation myth for the campaign: on a winter night in early 1968 (she told Brownmiller it was February and the Schomburg interviewer it was a Sunday morning), she was surprised by a knock at the door. One or more Black women, who might have been elderly or might have been welfare mothers (the story varied slightly in different published versions), explained that they had been talking about politics at a meeting and had decided to take up a collection for Chisholm's congressional campaign. They had gathered $9.62 in coins in a paper bag, which they presented to her. This was the moment, Chisholm said, when she decided to run, although, of course, she had already been designated by the committee. More important than the details of the story was Chisholm's repetition of it. She wanted it known that she was the people's candidate. Black women of small means wanted her to represent them in the national government.[32]

Cochair Annie Bowen was the mastermind of the SCCC. She was an activist in her church, Brown Memorial, and a strong believer in women's leadership capabilities. Well aware that women did the bulk of organizing in churches and civic organizations, she was outraged to find out that some local ministers would not support Chisholm because of her sex. "Men are weaklings," she scoffed, fuming that women worked hard on behalf of their communities but men were the ones to get support as leaders. "If women are doing the work at home, they should be able to represent us in a higher office," she reasoned.[33] From her home on St. Marks Avenue, she ran the "forever-in-motion body of women" to raise funds for Chisholm, whom she adored.[34] The two had met before Chisholm was elected to the assembly. Bowen, thinking it was a long shot, found Chisholm's phone number somehow and called the candidate with an invitation to speak at Brown Memorial Church's women's day gathering. To Bowen's delighted surprise, Chisholm answered the phone—and accepted. Then Bowen blurted out a burning question: how did the ambitious and active Chisholm stay married? Chisholm replied that Conrad had known that Shirley's "time belongs to the people" before their marriage, and that the marriage would have been impossible had he not understood this. Bowen "fell in love" with Chisholm at that moment. She would later say that she wanted to emulate her idol— and that she was delighted when sometimes people actually mistook her for Chisholm.

Four years after their first meeting, Bowen still admired her assemblywoman and wanted her "fiery female blood" down in Washington. Besides the personality traits that Bowen treasured in her candidate ("she's honest and she's not afraid"), Bowen thought Chisholm had the best understanding of Bedford-Stuyvesant's problems and the most democratic approach to solving them. Crime, lack of childcare options, low wages, lack of education opportunity and disrupted, chaotic classrooms, and insurance redlining had turned the vibrant local streets that Bowen recalled from childhood into a place she feared, especially at night. The presumptive opponent in the general election, James Farmer, would not understand this change because he was unfamiliar with the neighborhood over time. Furthermore, Chisholm's experience working with children demonstrated her "motherly instinct," a positive trait to have as an elected official.[35]

Notwithstanding Bowen's complaints about men's lack of support, the SCCC did expand to include men and to have a male cochair. "Petty jealousy" prevented some male clergy from supporting Chisholm, but there were several, including the minister at Brown Memorial, who lent conspicuous support. A broad base of "housewives, doctors, men, and women" contributed to the campaign, eventually raising over $8,000. Chisholm herself attended all of the meetings (over the objections of Bowen, who thought that the candidate needed to get more rest). The SCCC held several fundraisers, starting with the "Shirley Sip" at Old Paragon Hall in March and then a dinner and dancing fundraiser for her at the Grenada Hotel in May. Bowen was working on getting an endorsement from James Brown by the time of the general election (though no record of such an endorsement exists).[36]

Third, Chisholm had local labor organizers' support. Over the course of her campaign, she would be endorsed by the statewide New York AFL-CIO, as well as Local 3 of the Bakers and Confectionary International, Local 1199 of the Drug and Hospital Workers Union, Local 140 of the Bedding Curtain and Drapery Workers, District 15 of the International Association of Machinists, the Aero-Space Workers, and the Central Labor Council.[37] Etheline Dubin, head of the CNC, and her husband, Marshall, were also active in multiple union activities in Bedford-Stuyvesant. Etheline was from a Black Caribbean family, and Marshall was white and Jewish. In addition to her CNC role, Etheline was active in the PTA and tenants' rights organizations. Marshall was an organizer and area director for the Hospital Workers' Union, with a domain of New York, New Jersey, and Connecticut. Both had been UDC members from early on. Although the Dubins had some ambivalence about Chisholm's political ambitions, they both publicly supported her. The Hospital Workers' Union had formally endorsed Chisholm for Congress.

Marshall Dubin liked Chisholm's candidacy in part because she was a woman. As the organizer of a hospital workers' union, with many women members, he thought that women should have a role in "determining their own conditions." He was appalled by the objections he had heard based on Chisholm's sex, and by the fact that no Black woman had yet served in Congress. He also admired Chisholm—her educated and intelligent leadership, and the Caribbean roots she shared with his wife. Plus she was dark, and "one of our own," and she most certainly was "not one of the boys." Speaking for the community that he identified with, Marshall declared that Chisholm had "captured the imagination of our people."[38]

Dubin also liked her stance on the issues. He had not forgotten Chisholm's work in the assembly on unemployment insurance for hospital workers. Outside of issues directly related to organized labor, he supported Chisholm's emphasis on education. Indeed, he shared Chisholm's call for community control of public schools, even though he felt torn by the simmering conflict in Ocean Hill and Brownsville that was between Black parents and a largely Jewish teacher's union leadership. The school situation was "dynamite," he reflected. He had been disillusioned by "conservative talk" he had heard from Jews involved with the teachers' union, and chastised them for trying to reform Black neighborhoods without the input of Black residents. Black parents' "whole lives had been managed by white people," he noted. It was time for them to have a say in their children's education. Dubin did concede, however, that Chisholm was not as radical or as far left as some wanted her to be. Some might even consider her to be "on the more conservative side of some issues." At the same time, she sought to discern and address the needs of the community. And in this wholehearted belief in the people she was unique. Marshall Dubin appreciated her pragmatism. For example, she was not opposed to the Vietnam War on ideological grounds: that the war was in itself immoral and that the United States must leave now. Rather, she saw its consequences for Bedford-Stuyvesant: the war diverted funds from domestic programs that affected the community. The community's perspective as a whole mirrored Chisholm's. Bedford-Stuyvesant voters did not like the war, but they were not simply motivated by an abstract desire for peace.[39]

Judith Berek, the organizer for Local 1199 of the Hospital Workers' Union, ran the union's support for Chisholm. Berek, raised in a white, middle-class family, had been a research lab tech in a hospital before labor politics pulled her in. The Dubins had introduced her both to the union and to the Chisholm campaign. Both Chisholm and the union shared similar goals—in particular, helping people help themselves. Local 1199 provided volunteers and funding as well as a voter registration drive. When Berek visited hospitals to recruit and collect grievances from union members, she also gave out voter registration forms. Chisholm's lack of patronage from Steingut's local Democratic organization meant that it was even difficult to print up buttons and literature. But the presence of white union activists on the ground in the community, visibly aiding the campaign, helped show that Chisholm really could bridge Black and white community members.[40]

UNBOUGHT AND UNBOSSED: THE PRIMARY STRATEGY

Chisholm had the endorsements of several key players but would have to win over as many voters as possible. Campaigning began soon after the calendar turned to 1968. She made her formal campaign announcement on January 19, at a kickoff cocktail party at the Clinton Hill house of the leftist interracial couple Pete and Hortense "Tee" Beveridge.[41] After making her announcement to the 200 guests there, she listed her campaign platform:

Decent low cost housing
Equality [sic] education for our children
Extension of day care facilities and federal support for these centers
Adequate hospital and nursing home facilities
Enforcement of anti-discrimination laws
Increase of tax exemption from $600 to $1,000 per person

The platform, she conceded, was composed of familiar issues, but she asserted that "we have never had anyone looking like us to consistently and persistently hammer away at these matters."[42]

The campaign set up its headquarters at 1103 Bergen Street near Nostrand Avenue. Holder had insisted on a dedicated campaign office and staff after the staff at the Unity clubhouse had missed thousands of names when creating mailing labels for campaign literature. The party at the Beveridges' was followed by a swirl of events: Lambda Kappa Mu sorority honored Chisholm at its Founders' Day celebration in early February.[43] Chisholm "held court" at a meeting at the Astorian Manor banquet hall in Queens later that month.[44] The Queens Committee for a Negro Congressman, led by Grace Robinson, held a cocktail party fundraiser for Chisholm at the Red Carpet Lounge. She flew to Atlanta for Martin Luther King Jr.'s funeral that April to pay respects as well as show her visibility. In June, just prior to the primary, the SCCC produced a "Festival of the Arts" in her honor at Lefferts Junior High School.[45]

The campaign strategy used knowledge of demographics to target messages to voters. Ironically, even though the nonwhite population had increased in Brooklyn by 35 percent since 1960, white voters were still the majority. Only about 15 percent of Black voters turned out for presidential primaries. Therefore, it was white voters whose votes in the primaries would be decisive, even though their population in the Twelfth District of Bed-Stuy and Crown Heights was only about 40 percent. And, because Brooklyn was a Democratic stronghold, it was essential for Chisholm to win the primary on June 18. Winning over white voters was imperative.

The mythology of the new Twelfth District was that Andy Cooper's lawsuit had created a Black district, which was far from the truth. *Wells,* not *Cooper,* was the relevant case and had merely dictated districts that were "compact, contiguous, and of equal size." The result was that the new plan placed a number of majority-white neighborhoods, along with most of Bedford-Stuyvesant, into the Twelfth. This brought criticism from both the right and the left when observers incorrectly read the new district as entirely Black. Congressman Emmanuel Celler complained that he didn't "believe in carving out a new district for the Negro. It's segregation in reverse." White Democratic leaders in Greenpoint fretted that their districts had been, in the words of Jason Sokol, "ripped from their natural home and moved forcibly into an African-American district." Paul Kerrigan, one of the original *Wells* plaintiffs, complained that the Twelfth District's voters were only 50 percent Black and that white incumbents had consolidated their power in other districts. Kerrigan's numbers were incorrect: the district was approximately 60 percent Black, 30 percent white, and 10 percent Puerto Rican.[46] Chisholm herself kept her feelings about the matter private, setting about instead to become the first Black congresswoman by attempting to win over all constituencies: Black Americans, Caribbean or not; Jews; Puerto Ricans; and Irish, Polish, and Italian Americans.

The campaign strategy consisted of reaching individuals one on one. "I don't think there's any politician who works as hard as I do on a personal level," she told one interviewer. Chisholm was proud of her organizing ability. She told another that she based her campaign on appealing directly to voters' hearts, in person. "You have to let them *feel* you," she said [emphasis

Shirley Chisholm campaigning from a sound car in Brooklyn, October 1968.
Leonard Bazerman / AP Photo.

in original]. Her sound truck, plus cars of supporters, would drive through housing projects. "Ladies and gentlemen of the Breevort Houses," Chisholm would announce through the loudspeaker, "This is Fighting Shirley Chisholm coming through." People would open their windows and lean out. Chisholm would keep up a stream of talk. "My mother tells me I was born fighting," she joked. "She says I was kicking so hard in the womb she knew I was aching to get out and fight." Her campaign workers would then hand out about 2,000 campaign flyers per stop.[47] She did door-to-door canvasses raising money, holding coffee-klatches in the housing projects. Reciting the story of the group of women who had brought her $9.62, she courted small donors. A "Soul for Shirley" fried chicken dinner with dancing to soul music attracted about sixty supporters to a campaign worker's home and raised $400. Allan Fagan recalled that there was even an option on donation slips to choose a twenty-five cent contribution to the campaign, which would have been substantial money for many voters in 1968.[48]

Appealing to voters across racial lines became the campaign's decisive edge. Chisholm for Congress targeted young people, Puerto Ricans, and people in the neighborhoods outside of Bedford-Stuyvesant. She courted the 16,000 largely white registered voters in Bushwick by staying there for several days, broadcasting that she would "liberate us from the machine" from her sound truck. She focused on Bushwick's women in particular. Thompson won the Steingut-controlled Bushwick—but by only fifty votes. Chisholm considered that a victory.[49]

Chisholm also did her best to assure Black voters that she was on their side. She took a stand against the Nixonian "law and order" politics emerging within the Republican Party and the rising New Right. In March 1968, Chisholm was one of seven Black New York state legislators who criticized Republican Governor Nelson Rockefeller's policy choices on the grounds that they were leading to racial unrest. Specifically, the legislators cautioned that his cuts in state medical benefits and the pending law that would give more discretion to police to use their guns were alienating Black people. They went so far as to suggest that services and programs that benefited Black people were being cut in order to protect the interests of the wealthy. She also exhorted middle-class Black New Yorkers to involve themselves in politics, particularly regarding community-controlled education: "We must step forward forcefully and not too late because this is when radical groups fill the empty vacuum," she warned.[50]

Her commitment to Black Brooklynites and her cross-racial appeals notwithstanding, her secret weapon was an appeal to women voters. Chisholm insisted that she only did so under duress and made much of being "forced" to strategize her campaign along gender lines. But she and Holder had calculated their chances and come up with a central campaign strategy. In the new Twelfth Congressional District, women outnumbered men in the voter rolls by three to one. There were 10,000–13,000 more women than men. In her memoir and in interviews, she often repeated the statistics and boasted how she and Mac Holder were smart enough to figure that out and use it to their advantage. "I hate to do this," she claimed, making it sound as if she had simply appealed to women as a pragmatic but slightly distasteful strategy. In reality, her investment in the political implications of women's empowerment dovetailed neatly with her ambition to get elected. She still sat as the honorary president of the New York chapter of NOW, and shortly after her formal candidacy announcement, future national NOW president Dolores Alexander wrote a *Newsday* piece praising Chisholm as an exemplar. "One of NOW's resolutions urges women to run for office at local, state, and national levels," Alexander wrote, and she predicted "radical changes in the power structure of the country" if more women like Chisholm heeded the call. Perhaps her heavy involvement with feminists was a calculated political choice, but it was one that went well beyond simply making an effort to appear at PTA meetings and coffee-klatches.[51]

Chisholm found herself on the cutting edge of the women's movement through her stand on abortion rights. In April 1968, Chisholm cosponsored a bill that would liberalize New York's abortion laws. The current law was that abortions were permitted if the mother's life was in danger. The proposed law expanded permitted abortions to circumstances in which a woman's mental or physical health was in danger, the child would have a mental or physical disability, or the pregnancy resulted from incest or rape. Chisholm was joined by two of the other three women in the assembly and Albert Blumenthal of Manhattan. Under strong opposition from Roman Catholic assembly members, however, the bill failed. Chisholm was appalled, saying that the current law had "driven thousands of women in this state to unskilled practitioners" in order to obtain abortions. Blumenthal would introduce a bill again in December for the 1969 session.[52]

Chisholm's campaign strategy worked, but just barely. On a day when the polls were open for seven hours between 3:00 p.m. and 10:00 p.m., turnout was not large in Bedford-Stuyvesant. There were also allegations of non-operational voting machines and incorrect party assignment to registered Democrats. At the end of the evening, Mac Holder sat in campaign headquarters, waiting for the poll watchers to bring the results of each precinct's voting machines to him. At 1:30 the next morning, having posted all of the incoming precincts on a blackboard, Holder declared victory by about 600 votes. Chisholm's assembly district came out for her by a margin of three to one. But the other districts were closer. The official results: Chisholm had received 5,431, Thompson had 4,634, and Robinson had 1,751. She won by 788 votes, surprising the pro-Thompson pundits as well as Thompson himself, who had been so confident that he took a vacation on Cape Cod during the last days of the campaign. His consolation prize was the state senator seat over Bertram Baker. It was also a day of victory for Unity's other candidate, Waldaba Stewart, who beat ex-Unity member and Chisholm's detractor Andy Cooper for the Eighteenth District state senator nomination.[53]

Chisholm credited her "integrity and sincerity" for her victory. In the *New York Times*, she said the issue that had carried the day was peace. She thought that the winner of the Democratic primary for Senate, Paul O'Dwyer, had won as a peace candidate. She opined that her constituents preferred domestic spending on programs rather than defense spending on Vietnam, and because they were disproportionately represented among the casualties of the war. Harlem titan Hulan Jack, however, thought that Black people voted for O'Dwyer because he was strong on civil rights. And even though Edna Kelly, who had been unseated from her Twelfth District congressional seat, had run in the Tenth against Emanuel Celler on reducing crime and negotiating peace in Vietnam, she still lost by a wide margin. But Chisholm more likely had won the race as the "unbought and unbossed" candidate of women across the color line.[54]

Chisholm suddenly found herself to be a new Democratic Party darling. Having turned back the establishment candidate, she had established herself as the "titular head of the Democratic Party in Brooklyn." With the national leadership in flux, she took advantage of an opening to raise her national profile. Like the statewide Council of Elected Negro Democrats, which in February announced its disappointment with the national Democratic Party's unequal distribution of power and patronage, she felt that Johnson was insufficiently responsive to Black politicians. Robert Kennedy had been a likely ally, especially given his previous relationship to Bed-Stuy, but to Chisholm's disappointment he seemed to be in Thompson's corner during the primary and declined to support her publicly. The campaign had more successfully cultivated national alliances with Eugene McCarthy, who personally had called Chisholm for a half-hour chat in the primary campaign.[55]

The general election campaign geared up and Chisholm was out in the district, riding the sound truck and visiting churches. But her politicking was interrupted by a health scare. Conrad, concerned by the number of times that she had to get up during the night, lobbied hard to get Chisholm to visit her doctor. When she finally did go, after reluctantly canceling three campaign meetings, the doctor diagnosed her as either pregnant or carrying a large abdominal tumor. His exam led to an immediate referral to a gynecologist for a biopsy, over Chisholm's protests that she had multiple meetings scheduled for that evening. She experienced no pain and had not been aware that the tumor had been growing for up to two years prior because, she said, the tumor was "concealed in the pelvic basin." She was admitted to the hospital, and the biopsy result arrived the next day: the tumor was benign, and both Conrad and Shirley breathed a sigh of relief. But her relief soon turned to impatience, because she still needed surgery. On July 18, she underwent a hysterectomy surgery at Maimonides Hospital, which included the removal of a hefty uterine fibroid. The recovery from the surgery necessitated a ten-day hospital stay and strict bed rest afterward. She lost seventeen pounds, considerable for someone who ordinarily weighed in at under one hundred. "I looked at myself in the mirror and wept," she said. "I was so emaciated from the waist down that I looked like Twiggy." And, as she rested at home in Sterling Place in August, she could hear Farmer's sound trucks making their circuits of the neighborhood. Rumors that she was dying of cancer began to circulate, and she noticed that "my people became demoralized."[56]

Against doctor's orders, she attended the Chicago Democratic National Convention at the end of August 1968. New York Democrats had put her name forward as one of two representatives to the national committee. Edna Kelly had previously served as national committeewoman for the state; now, as she had replaced Kelly as the Democratic nominee for the Twelfth District, Chisholm was likely going to replace Kelly on the Democratic National Committee (DNC), too. The Democrats had specifically decided to name a Black woman to the seat and sought to increase the numbers of Black and Puerto Rican delegates to the convention. There was a list of five other names, but Chisholm felt confident that she would get the nod, especially after Harlem Democratic Party stalwart Hilda Stokeley withdrew her name. Chisholm flew to Chicago but remained in her hotel room, too weak to participate on the floor. Her previous engagement with McCarthy paid off when his pledged New York delegates nominated her on the first day of the convention. The next day, Tom Fortune called to say that the New York delegation voted unanimously to install her, a marked contrast to the divided vote over the state committeeman and the violence between protesters and police that would erupt outside the next day. Chisholm was now the first Black woman to be a member of the DNC.[57]

She finally returned to the streets of Bed-Stuy and Crown Heights in September. She won Conrad over to her cause, pointing out to him that "the stitches are not in my mouth." Reluctant to argue with her, he complied when "she asked me to bundle her up and take her down two flights of stairs to the car, and I had pillows to prop her up and she went campaigning." She immediately felt better after she went out on the sound trucks and saw the enthusiasm of her supporters. Even the postoperative pain seemed to lessen. "Ladies and Gentlemen," she proclaimed, "This is Fighting Shirley Chisholm and I'm up and around in spite of what people are saying."[58]

In Chicago, against the backdrop of Mayor Daley's police fighting antiwar protesters in the streets outside, Hubert Humphrey emerged as the Democratic nominee. Chisholm quickly fell into step behind him. On Labor Day in 1968, Democratic presidential nominee Hubert Humphrey met with members of the state Democratic leadership who pledged their support, Chisholm among them.[59] Chisholm told Humphrey that he would "come across strong" in New York.[60] She was hopeful that she herself would, too, so that she would become the first Black woman sent to national elected office.

7
FIGHTING SHIRLEY CHISHOLM

———————— ★ ————————

The general election for the Twelfth District seat was, in many ways, like starting over for Chisholm. For one, she had to reenergize her campaign after recovering from surgery, no easy feat for a woman politician in particular. And she had to win over the white voters yet again in the district. This was not a foregone conclusion, even though the district was overwhelmingly filled with Democrats. The state and local parties were in a disarray that mirrored the national situation. With Robert Kennedy gone, there was also a statewide power vacuum in the Democratic Party that Brooklyn organization leaders said would be filled by county leaders. But the Brooklyn county leader, Steingut, was licking his own wounds, having had Thompson defeated by Chisholm in the primary. All of this confusion inspired considerable optimism within the Republican ranks for capturing the seat with James Farmer as a Republican. Richard Nixon had trounced Nelson Rockefeller at the GOP's Miami convention that summer; thereafter, Governor Rockefeller endorsed James Farmer in the race for the Twelfth District congressional seat.[1]

While Chisholm lay recuperating in Maimonides Hospital, Farmer opened his general election campaign with a rally in late July, positioning himself as the underdog and the candidate in favor of people's power. His one hundred interracial volunteers would stand at subway stations, handing out leaflets twice a day. They also passed out mock ballots that advocated ticket splitting by voting for Humphrey for president. He had taken pains to distance himself from Nixon and Agnew at the top of the ticket, previously declaring on the radio that "Nixon has been on the wrong side of so many issues involving civil rights that his comments in the last few weeks do not convince me that he is sincere." Instead, he pledged support to Governor Rockefeller, who had been shown in a Farmer-commissioned poll to be ahead of Hubert Humphrey among Black voters. Despite his new affiliation with the GOP, Farmer maintained that he still considered himself to be "an independent black American" and that the Democratic Party should not take the Black vote for granted: "And above all don't be wedded to any political party in this upcoming campaign. Keep them guessing."[2]

Farmer was hopeful for victory because of his name recognition from the Black freedom movement. His campaign manager was Simeon Golar, who had unsuccessfully run against Chisholm for state assembly four years earlier. Telephone polling showed him ahead by a five-to-one edge when callers identified themselves as calling from his office and three to one when they said they were from Chisholm's office. However, his central dilemma was that people tended to vote the Democratic Party line, and the district was over 90 percent Democratic. In the general election, people tended to vote for Democrats all the way down the ballot. Furthermore, troubled by the possibility of his party affiliation giving votes to Nixon, Farmer endorsed Humphrey. This angered Republicans, and the party reduced their financial and political support.[3]

The general election demanded Chisholm's finesse in building both momentum and coalition. As conflict between parents and teachers in the Ocean Hill-Brownsville school district intensified and polarized voters across the color line, she sought a solid majority. She employed two related strategies that could appeal to voters. One was to continue her slogan of "Unbought and Unbossed," an image of maverick politics that short-circuited the tyranny of political party organizations. And, as Jason Sokol has argued, this slogan enabled her to appeal to the entire electorate across lines of race, class, and political affiliation, focusing on people over party.[4]

Her other talking point was local leadership. She was, she argued, the only homegrown candidate who truly understood the problems of the district. She repeatedly asked her rally and debate audiences why Farmer did not run in his home borough of Manhattan. The political opportunities of the question allowed her to inform voters that Farmer had simply been chosen in a top-down, cynical political decision by the Republican Party in a bid to gain the congressional seat.[5] Her point that a born-in-Brooklyn candidate should represent the district in Washington worked as a potent signifier for voters across racial lines. It would appeal to white voters because they saw Farmer's decision to run as a "Black militant" with some skepticism regarding whether he might represent them in Congress. It would appeal to Black voters, especially those who advocated for self-determination. The Chisholm campaign paid a camera crew to film him leaving his Manhattan apartment and commuting to Brooklyn to campaign.[6] Chisholm would later claim that she was confident in her ability to beat Farmer because of that local connection. "It makes no difference to me if he's running or not because I live in the community and he doesn't. He comes across the

Brooklyn Bridge every day to run in the community. He's not known in this community," she said.[7]

Chisholm did not have to dig very deep to project righteous indignation about Farmer. It probably galled that former Unity Democratic Club (UDC) devotee John Oliver Killens was cochair of the Citizens Committee for James Farmer for Congress. Most of her camp was appalled that he had the temerity to carpetbag in the district. Her pet name for him was "the national candidate," a label that managed to capture the sense of intrusion he inspired. Allan Fagan called him "Travelin' Jim" and pointed out that he represented the party of Nixon and segregationist Strom Thurmond. "It is not fair for an outsider to come into a neighborhood and claim to represent them," he complained. It was even worse to represent the Republican Party, which sought to cut welfare and other domestic programs and roll back civil rights legislation, and accept money from them. Farmer's bumper stickers urged a vote for "Row A," which contained Nixon and Agnew at the top of the ticket, despite Farmer's claim to support Humphrey. "Honorable men don't do things like this," Fagan said. "If he wants to sell his soul, let him do it someplace else."[8] UDC stalwart Marshall Dubin was quite bothered, labeling Farmer a "glamour candidate" who was "nothing to Brooklyn," having no roots in the community. Another Brooklynite was similarly scornful. Farmer should give his sponsors "their money back because they're placing their bets on the wrong horse," he said, "and because it's an insult to the community." Farmer was clueless about appealing to the Caribbean migrant population, not to mention existing intraracial politics in the district. Locals felt that other Black politicians had paid their dues by working their way up through local organizations. They had relationships with local residents and realized that the problems facing the community would take longer than two years to fix, as Farmer advertised. To some, it was naïve and insulting for Farmer to say Bedford-Stuyvesant did not have sufficient homegrown leadership for the House of Representatives. To imply that the community was leaderless was to ignore the facts on the ground and to play into mythologies of Black neighborhoods' dysfunction. Local politicians, including Thompson, Jones, and Goring, were of Caribbean descent and understood the importance of immigrants in the community despite occasional "grumblings," as Chisholm put it, that people from the islands were taking over.[9]

In truth, Farmer's and Chisholm's politics shared more similarities than differences. They simply worked hard to distinguish themselves from the other. They appeared with Ralph Carrano on WNBC's *Direct Line* program in early September. Farmer unveiled a plan to sell government bonds to raise money to develop poor neighborhoods. Called "Martin Luther King,

Jr." local development bonds, they would pay the same interest rate and mature in the same period as defense bonds. He was to meet with some U.S. senators and Congress of Racial Equality (CORE) leadership to ask them to add the bonds to a bill that they had introduced, which would create local development corporations. He also said that he would improve police-community relations by instituting town hall meetings. Carrano stressed the need for law and order. Chisholm agreed with him up to a point, but argued that both Black and white citizens were entitled to law and order, and that the "root causes" of lawlessness had to be addressed as well. Chisholm also advocated for more subsidized housing—over 1 million units. Farmer agreed and said that "small unit housing" should be built and subsidized loans should be offered to buyers to purchase them. They both had a history of wanting to end redlining by home insurance companies: Farmer by asking the New York state superintendent of insurance to set up an emergency pool after many Black residents saw their policies cancelled, and Chisholm by advocating for legislation in the 1965 session of the assembly.[10]

Both candidates had complicated relationships with Black Power. Black Power, the nascent nationalist political ideology that advocated for Black self-defense and self-determination, had begun to make national head-lines. Stokely Carmichael, the director of SNCC who had visited the UDC, published *Black Power* with Charles V. Hamilton in 1967.[11] It was in 1968 that Black Power became ascendant in Brooklyn, centered on the explo-sive Ocean Hill–Brownsville schools conflict, which "help[ed] crystallize an emergent black cultural nationalism in Brooklyn."[12] Both Farmer and Chisholm had to figure out how to respond in ways that would cement Black support but not alienate white voters. Local activists had established a Black-controlled school board, headed by Rhody McCoy, in the summer of 1967. The United Federation of Teachers (UFT), which functioned in tan-dem with the Board of Education bureaucracy, opposed the Black school board. The UFT was largely composed of left-leaning white teachers and was led by Albert Shanker. The conflict over so-called community control split racially and ethnically: supporters tended to be Black or elite Protestants, and Manhattanites, while those opposed tended to be middle class, white, Jewish and Catholic, and from the outer boroughs.[13]

The split solidified as the conflict over Ocean Hill–Brownsville's schools worsened. The community-controlled board fired nineteen white teachers deemed hostile to community control in May 1968. In response, the UFT organized a citywide strike when school started the next September. Here-tofore estranged Jewish and Catholic teachers and voters united behind the strike, as did most middle-class white people across the city. Black New Yorkers and their elite allies, including Mayor John Lindsay, stood behind the community-controlled Black board. The split deepened when some Black teachers and activists made anti-Semitic statements. In the end, Lindsay was forced to compromise and the teachers were reinstated. But the damage was done: Lindsay and other liberals who had aligned behind community control were now seen as "tainted" by white middle-class voters. And Chisholm would have to navigate multiple political alignments in order to win.[14]

Chisholm was in favor of community control of schools, but she made it clear that she thought it was the business of parents, not Black Power activists, who should be negotiating with the state. Just prior to the primary in June, she had given two back-to-back speeches to groups of Black women on the necessity of Black middle-class parents' involvement in the school controversy. In Albany that spring, she complained, she had watched as "extremist groups" had made the journey to lobby legislators, rather than the "parent groups" she thought should have done so. If "we" (presumably middle-class Black women) did not act visibly and decisively, "it may be [too] late," she warned. Appealing to moderation and to women was an ongoing component of Chisholm's political strategy.[15]

Still, in late September she and Farmer both came out publicly in support of community-control leader Rhody McCoy and the local governing board. She accused Shanker of "using the people to advance the power of the UFT" at the expense of students. Farmer said much the same thing, proclaiming that the governing board's "struggle is the struggle of all men who demand for themselves the rights that others enjoy in a democratic society." He went somewhat further than Chisholm in expressing his skepticism of the fairness of due process in the situation. "The African American is an expert on injustice and due process has often been his enemy. The faithful observance of 'law and order' frequently has been to keep the Black American in his place and stifle his aspiration," Farmer said. In October, Chisholm joined the interracial committee founded by Ocean Hill and Brownsville residents in Brooklyn to stop the closing of an experimental, community-controlled school.[16]

Chisholm's role here illustrated her uneasy relationship with Black Power in Brooklyn. Though she shared advocacy of grassroots activism and institutional transformation with those activists, she criticized the militant political tactics activists used. The most prominent Black Power activist in Brooklyn, Sonny Carson, had been pushed toward Brooklyn CORE by Malcolm X after Malcolm had observed the chapter's increasingly militant actions earlier in the decade. By 1968, the Brooklyn chapter had seceded from national CORE.[17] Carson was heavily involved in the school's conflict but had declined to support Chisholm. Marshall Dubin thought Carson had snubbed Chisholm because of sexism: "Some militants feel it is the black man who has to come to the fore. Their view of the black woman . . . is that because of conditions in this country . . . the black woman has had the power and the authority in the black community." He noted that, even though Chisholm had no interest in keeping Black men down, the idea that men should be dominant and protective hurt Chisholm among militants. Ollie Leeds, the former head of Brooklyn CORE, also disliked Chisholm, Dubin said. But Leeds was an equal opportunity critic, having labeled both Chisholm and Farmer as "within party machines."[18]

Farmer tried to appeal to Black militant men by encouraging young Black people to become involved in politics. He seemed to believe that his ace in the hole was his maleness and his repudiation of the 1965 Moynihan Report. He deployed a "black male mystique" to try to win the race with Black militants, projecting "an image redolent of Africa and manhood," in Brownmiller's words. He hired young Black men in dashikis to drive around to subway stations to campaign on his behalf. They would say, "We need a man in the Congress of the United States," and beat bongo drums. His literature stressed the need for "a strong male image" in Congress. Sometimes Chisholm would be catcalled by them: "Here comes the black matriarch!" She believed that he thought he could beat her because she was a woman, and he would say in speeches that she was a frail "little old schoolteacher."[19] She made his talk about "machismo" a center of her campaign, emphasizing that Black men's concerns were equal to but not more important than those of Black women. "The black man must step forward, but that does not mean we have to step back," she said in at least one speech.

Several years after the race, Chisholm recalled that Holder decided to target women voters in the district because of Farmer's masculinism. While this belies her accounts elsewhere that she herself had noticed the large ratio of women in her prospective constituency prior to the primary, it certainly speaks to her sense of justification in focusing on women in the campaign. She had never intended to use her sex "as an asset." But Black men were "sensitive about female domination," she noticed, and "were running me down as a bossy female, a would-be matriarch." If Farmer had understood the district better, however, he would have realized that there were a great many female-headed households in Bedford-Stuyvesant, led by women who were longtime residents and registered voters. So she decided to turn what Farmer thought was his competitive edge into his point of vulnerability. "[W]hen someone tries to use my sex against me, I delight in being able to turn the tables on him, as I did during the congressional campaign," she admitted.[20]

The *New York Times* bore out the Chisholm campaign's observation that national media and public stars alike focused on Farmer. It started its coverage relatively evenhanded, but rather patronizingly referred to Chisholm as "Woman" in a late October headline: "Farmer and Woman in Lively Bedford-Stuyvesant Race." Farmer, it said, had a "national power base" while Chisholm had "local interests and power." The article presented the choice between them as "personal," because both advocated more housing and jobs, and both were strong advocates of school decentralization, which was a major issue at the time in the area. Farmer was looking to become a representative of Black people in the government, while Chisholm had stronger community ties.[21] The article characterized Bed-Stuy as a neighborhood of juxtapositions: drab public housing and the very poor mixed with upwardly mobile residents of brownstones. The author did pick up on the necessity of winning over white voters because Bed-Stuy was surrounded by Crown Heights, Williamsburg, and Bushwick, and Chisholm and Farmer might split the Black vote. He also acknowledged that Chisholm had an advantage because most voters in the district were Democratic. The reporter had talked to Chisholm "in the neat living room of her house at 1165 Sterling Place, decorated with plastic-covered sofas, African and Chinese art and photographs of herself with Senator Kennedy and her husband, Conrad Chisholm, a private investigator." "My power comes from the people," she told him. As if to punctuate her claim, the *New York Amsterdam News* endorsed her on the same day the *Times* story was printed. The editorial said that their choice was based on Chisholm's "long service to the Brooklyn Community and her proven legislative ability."[22]

Lawyer and Black feminist Pauli Murray read the "Farmer and Woman" article and was outraged by Farmer's claim that Congress needed his masculine presence. She wrote memos to twenty-five people, enclosed the clipping, and urged them to support Chisholm in the race. Her subject line was "Fair Play in the Shirley Chisholm Congressional Campaign" and explained that Murray had already sent a contribution to Chisholm but that Farmer's claims had prompted her to write the letter. "I am convinced that stooping to *sexism* is as unfair and reprehensible as stooping to *racism* in a political campaign" [emphasis hers], she wrote. She reminded her letters' recipients that Farmer would have been appalled had literature recommending that a white man be elected to Congress been distributed. Even if Farmer himself had not written the literature, she held him responsible for it.[23] Murray also wrote to the *New York Times* to complain about their coverage. She then wrote to Chisholm herself, enclosing the fifty additional copies of the letter that she had run out of stamps to send.[24]

Chisholm was likely pleased to have the alliance of Murray and the network of feminists she had alerted to Farmer's and the *New York Times*'s masculinism. She took full advantage of an invitation from the Emma Lazarus Federation of Jewish Women's Clubs Brooklyn chapter. The Emma Lazarus Federation was an organization of leftist and progressive women, founded during World War II, that had historically allied with civil rights causes. Farmer sent his campaign manager for a short speech raising the specter of George Wallace in the Democratic Party and Farmer's leadership "among freedom-loving people." But Chisholm, albeit late, attended herself and employed her full oratorical powers honed at Brooklyn College and in the state assembly. She was well aware that a nexus between antiracism, feminism, and local politics was located within the "Emmas."[25]

After Chisholm was introduced, she began: "Four and a half years ago I was the first black woman state legislator from Brooklyn . . ." but was promptly interrupted by applause. She went on to recount her repertoire of political bona fides: her local roots, that she moved into politics from community organizations, and that she had been urged to run by others rather than seeking power on her own. She juxtaposed her status as an "unbought and unbossed" political outsider to Farmer's as a political insider with the national Republican Party. "He has the right to run, but if he's so interested in people of the community, why did he not go to Harlem to work in politics there? Why did he decide to trek across the Brooklyn Bridge?" she inquired. Before turning to her platform, she emphasized her gender. "Ladies, you have to understand one thing," she said in a confidential tone. "It is very important . . . and I'm going to be very prejudiced and biased. . . . It is very important that we get more women emerging in the political arena." She lamented that she even had to deal with "this whole question of sex," and she claimed that she had only begun expressing the issue three weeks ago, despite the fact that her lifelong campaign strategy rested on gathering women's votes. But "because the undercurrent in the movement that we don't want a woman in Congress really took hold" among Jewish women, she focused on her sex as the pivotal point.

Turning to the issues, she addressed the war in Vietnam ("immoral and unjust") and education (busing won't solve problems; universal quality education will). On education, she conceded, "We are not interested in separatism." Instead, she advocated for affordable housing in cities. She concluded her statement in a stirring tone that was an early version of a statement she would make throughout the rest of her life. "I do not want to be remembered as the first black woman to go to the US Congress," she said. "I want to be remembered as "a symbol and a hope for the young men and young women . . . who have become disillusioned" as someone who fights for what she believes and owns herself. "I come to you with nothing but myself to give." She concluded to sustained and enthusiastic applause, and most attendees expressed respect for the candidate.[26] She had won over this audience of women, it seemed.

The last several weeks of the campaign were a series of decisive rallies and appearances.[27] She spoke at fundraisers inside and outside of the borough, including one held by her former Mount Cavalry supervisor Eula Hodges in Harlem and a series of teas with white women in Bushwick.[28] The highest stakes of these appearances was a debate with Farmer at Community Church. After a brief lecture on the history of racism that alluded to Wallace's and Strom Thurmond's rise to power as analogous to the Tilden-Hayes compromise of 1877, Farmer spent most of his time outlining his plan for a new Community Development Corporation. He had already been in conversation with his prospective future colleagues in the U.S. House of Representatives about getting seed money for the project. He named other problems he planned to solve: insurance protection for Black homeowners, comprehensive education, and a school decentralization bill that would respect teachers' rights as employees.

Chisholm's opening remarks, by contrast, began and ended with her deep roots in the community and her desire to be elected on the basis of her record of service to Bedford-Stuyvesant. Her agenda included redirecting spending from the war in Vietnam to domestic antipoverty work and high-quality education everywhere. To eradicate poverty she proposed not only a guaranteed annual income (which she acknowledged was just a Band-Aid), but guaranteed annual work, which would "heighten aspirations," provide jobs, and help families. To allow women to go to work, she proposed a new system of day care centers. On schools, busing, she knew, was not the answer—she was aware of young children who had been traumatized at unwelcoming schools far from home—good schools everywhere was the answer. She had fought unsuccessfully in Albany for decentralization but still felt that communities should be able to control their own schools. Farmer rebutted as a breadwinner liberal, however: women should not be "forced" to go out to work. He also did not feel that a guaranteed annual income reduced initiative, and reiterated his independence from the Nixon-Agnew ticket. Finally, in response to a question about whether "Black racists" should be denounced, Farmer agreed with Chisholm's statement that neither Black nor white people should be racist. But he went further by cautioning that not all "Black pride" activists were racist. His impassioned defense received strong applause, suggesting that his alliance with Black Power had been strengthened.[29]

At a rally protesting the presidential candidacy of Alabama governor George Wallace, the UDC had come together for Chisholm. Tom Jones gave a barn burner of an introduction, endorsing Chisholm by pointing to what was at stake in her election and in the presidential race. Chisholm started with much the same thread. Wallace wasn't "just a nut"; he posed a real threat to progress in equality and justice thus far. But Chisholm only got that far before she was interrupted by a heckler who expressed the volatility of the Ocean Hill-Brownsville standoff. "We don't have to wait for George Wallace," the heckler shouted. "Albert Shanker is already [taking community control]! Why isn't this an Anti-Shanker rally? Shanker's doing Wallace's dirty work!" With practiced and characteristic calm, Chisholm waited until the man left (his departure was cheered by many present) and then explained that the outburst hadn't bothered her and that she and her "brothers" had been arguing over the issues. "We are in constant conversation," she said. "But youth is impatient. It doesn't bother me." She cautioned the audience, however, that "we must not as a people take it out on the Jewish people." Instead, she wrapped up, we must see Wallace as part of a racist "sickness" in society that must be healed. The crowd enthusiastically applauded.[30]

The anti-Wallace rally was not the only occasion where Black Power–aligned hecklers interrupted the proceedings. At an October 31 rally for vice presidential candidate Edmund Muskie, Chisholm introduced him to both applause and boos. Almost immediately, audience members began to shout. While one man complained that Muskie was not practicing what he preached, others yelled to let the candidate speak. A shouting match began: "We can't trust these people. Black Power for black people! [Muskie] is just a confidence man. Power to the people! Eldridge Cleaver for the next President of the United States!" Muskie tried to stay on message. "All I can do is to begin the conversation with you," he managed, as someone shouted "oink oink!" "I will do what I can to build a country in which each of you, as well as anyone else. . . . can have decent jobs, decent homes, decent education, and a chance to build a better future for your children," Muskie said, but his last line was punctuated by a protester stating, "Eldridge Cleaver for President!"[31]

As the Muskie rally made clear, Chisholm's tenuous coalitions were fragile, as coalitions often are. She spoke to Black voters at Newman Memorial Church just days before the election, acknowledging that she had not been in Bedford-Stuyvesant as much recently. She explained that she had been speaking to white voters in the district because they were crucial to her victory plan. "I need to be sure I have the backing of white constituents in Bushwick, Green Point, Williamsburg. This is why you have not seen me as much, because I assume that you know about me. You know what kind of individual I am. I have not had it easy in politics, and I won't equivocate now," she declared. She had been across the district about 150 times, she estimated, and at six or seven meetings each night. "I have visited in homes where there have never been Black people before." She also reported that she had been told by white voters that they planned to vote for her for Congress but Nixon for president. When the audience laughed, she told them not to. Voters saw both her and Nixon as "outspoken," and planned to vote for them on that basis. However, if Black people did not vote on Election Day, Chisholm might win but so might Nixon.[32]

In addition to the debates, fundraisers, meetings, and rallies, Chisholm and Farmer both took to the streets in the last days of the campaign, seeking to win over voters one at a time. On one corner, passersby were urged to "Come and say hello to the honorable James Farmer. The man of dignity, the man of know-how, the man of knowledge, the man of ability!" The announcer emphasized the word "man." Then Farmer would come on the loudspeaker. "Vote for me on column A or D. Please don't look for me on column B because the Democrats wouldn't let me in their primary. . . . For far too long, the Democratic Party has [had this district] in the bag." Then bongo drummers and singers would play to the tune of *Funga Alafia*, a West African welcoming song: "Farmer for Congress, Ashay, Ashay! We want Farmer, Ashay, Ashay!"[33]

At another corner, at Fulton and Nostrand, Shirley Chisholm's emcee stood exhorting residents to vote column B, which was Chisholm for Congress and Paul O'Dwyer for Senate. He reminded them that the ticket stood for jobs, education, housing, federal day care, and unemployment insurance for domestic workers. Then Chisholm pulled up on a sound truck, speaking with conviction. "Vote for a congressman [sic] who belongs to this community. Vote for someone who has fought valiantly for you in the state legislature," she boomed. "You know my record in the state legislature. You know what I have stood for. You know that I'm unbought and unbossed." She disembarked and stood next to the sound truck, meeting voters, and then made an address. She reminded those present that she had been born and educated in the neighborhood, that her sex did not matter but her record in the state assembly did, that she would refuse to keep quiet as a first-term congressperson, and that Farmer was there to "reap the spoils" of the new seat in the district. Then she spoke in Spanish, repeating her instruction to get to the polls on November 5. Returning to English, she laughed, "I don't think I did too badly!"[34]

The rally was recorded by an oral history interviewer who then canvassed the crowd, disclosing that those standing nearby had opinions that ranged from indifference to conviction. A Chisholm supporter praised her and other Democrats, in part because "she pronounces her syllables more distinctly." One person had been unaware of the candidates in the race, but supposed he would vote for Farmer because of name recognition. When told about Chisholm being from the neighborhood, he changed his mind. A woman refused to share her choice, but spoke highly of Farmer as "honest, trustworthy." A Caribbean man was confident that she would win. Another pair of men with Caribbean accents did not want to see a woman doing what they saw as a man's job, for Congress was "a little too rough for a woman." One man was undecided and would decide on Election Day.[35]

The race was close leading up to November 2. At the last minute, civil rights giant A. Philip Randolph endorsed Farmer, a rare political commentary for Randolph.[36] Chisholm's forces organized a sixty-car caravan of supporters that wound its way through the district on October 19, led by a sound truck and then Chisholm in the first car. In "a dramatic black-and-white cape and the spiked high heels that she never tired of," Chisholm addressed whoever was nearby at the multiple stops along the way. When the Farmer campaign found out, it dispatched a flatbed truck with a loud band to play music wherever the caravan was. Chisholm supporters remained behind, pointing out that Chisholm did not need flashy music to show that she cared about the issues.[37]

Farmer's efforts were not enough and he lost. He had miscalculated. While he was courting famous Black people, Chisholm had recognized that women—Black, white, and Puerto Rican—were decisive in the election. She had capitalized on both the Democratic Party loyalty in the district and on Farmer's carpetbagger status. She won by an over 2.5-1 margin, a spread that was evident within about an hour of the polls closing. The official tally would be Chisholm, 34,885; Farmer, 13,777; Carrano (Conservative Party), 3,771.[38] The polls had long lines and had to stay open late to accommodate all voters who had showed up. Farmer had been waiting with about 150 of his supporters at his headquarters, listening to his campaign band of bongo and flute players and watching the returns on two televisions. About two hours after the polls closed, he conceded. He sent a gracious telegram to his opponent: "May I congratulate you on your victory. It has been a hard fought race and I want to assure you that I will work to help you fight for better housing, equal employment, and the other things so necessary to make this district a better place for all its residents, both black and white." Even in his concession, he ignored Puerto Rican residents.[39]

Chisholm gave her victory speech with Conrad standing on one side and Holder on the other. She exclaimed that she was "deeply grateful and deliriously happy." "I am most happy this night for myself and for the many poor soldiers who have encouraged and supported me in every political effort," she said, and went on to thank Holder and Fortune explicitly.[40] Furthermore, she could not have succeeded without Conrad, "this wonderful man."

She credited "the people" who "know what I stand for" for her victory and pledged to represent them in Washington, Black and white. She would not forget from whence she had come. While she refused to make any promises, she named her early priorities as better antipoverty programs and accessible college educations. Finally, she said, "Although I'm making history, this evening, I'd love to believe that my victory tonight is a symbol of hope."[41] She was thinking that the moment was the beginning of a more democratic society.

The election won, Chisholm had much to do. First, she had to restore her health. She weighed ninety-six pounds at the time of her victory and had lost seventeen pounds during the campaign. She and Conrad took a long trip to Jamaica to refresh themselves, though Chisholm was recognized and followed by reporters and fans there. They also bought a new row house on St. John's Place in Crown Heights, a few blocks from their Sterling Place apartment, that came with a baby grand piano. She also had to make the rounds of gatherings that were planned in her honor. Chisholm was immediately in demand as an honored guest at the Antioch Baptist Church, Youth In Action's postelection reception, and a 1,000-guest victory gala dinner in December at the Saint George Hotel. At the latter, the event's program juxtaposed Chisholm's achievement with Phillis Wheatley, Harriet Tubman, Sojourner Truth, and Chisholm's own personal hero, Mary McLeod Bethune. The list of dais guests read like a Who's Who of local Democratic leaders, and ascendant state Democratic star Howard Samuels gave the keynote on race relations.[42] Chisholm's victory did not renew close relations with her mother and sisters, however. Her sister Muriel Forde was, as she recalls, "rather startled" when Chisholm won the congressional race. She was living in Manhattan by then and was not in touch with Brooklyn politics. "But we were very proud and happy when she did it," Forde hastened to add.[43]

Forde might well have found out about Chisholm's victory from the *New York Times*, which, with other national media, suddenly discovered Chisholm. Indeed, Chisholm was overwhelmed with nonstop calls from ABC, CBS, NBC, the *New York Times*, the Associated Press, and reporters across the country. She also received well wishes from Assistant Secretary of Labor Esther Peterson. "Your election has given a tremendous boost to those of us who believe so deeply in what you stand for. Please call on me if I can be helpful in *any* way."[44]

Chisholm also had to plan for her first term. She immediately announced after winning that she would not be "a quiet freshman Congressman." Although she was aware that the custom was for first-termers to "be seen and not heard," she did not plan to follow that custom.[45] "My greatest political asset—which professional politicians fear—is my mouth, out of which comes all kinds of things one shouldn't always discuss, for reasons of political expedience," Chisholm told the *Washington Post*. She suspected that her new male colleagues, seeing her slight frame, might assume that she would be a pushover.[46] "I just want to do a good job in Congress. I'm not only going to represent my people but also fight for white people," she declared. She was proud of being "beholden to no one" and of taking no machine money, thus making her no one's pushover congressperson.[47]

She also made a visit to Washington, where she outlined a Black feminist power agenda to reporters. She told them that her first policy priorities would be to end the war in Vietnam and to put money instead into antipoverty programs and jobs training. She thought that women legislators had an advantage over men who, she said, "get bogged down with such things as transportation, banking, shipping, etc. that the social aspects of legislation don't get enough attention. . . . Women don't get hung up making deals the way that men do," she theorized. She also observed that Black people, and especially youth, had lost patience with studies and data. "They are ready to join those movements that are ready to suit the action to the word. And if the group happens to be militant then we will have to be militant."[48] Having pledged leadership that responded to the least powerful among the electorate, she was ready to take the oath of office for her first term.

BUILDING THE CHISHOLM MYSTIQUE

──────── ★ ────────

As a new member of Congress, Chisholm said that she was well aware her "freshman" status carried limited influence. That, along with the fact that she was Black and a left-liberal ("the smallest faction in the House"), meant that she did not expect to get much legislation passed. "I do not see myself as a lawmaker, an innovator in the field of legislation," she remarked. Still, she deployed Black feminist power politics in pragmatic ways. She felt keenly her responsibility to represent the 15 percent of the U.S. population that was Black, and the overwhelming problems of her own district with securing adequate housing, employment, and education. "I work to be a major force for change outside the House even if I cannot be one within it," she said to a pair of interviewers.[1] She decided to concentrate on two fronts. First, her office conducted a large amount of "case work," the assistance to individual constituents and sometimes nonconstituents who requested her help. Second, she sought to push the federal government to enforce antidiscrimination laws, preserve or create programs, and make grants to her district.[2] But Chisholm's power and influence would rise in response to her less tangible qualities: a fearless and uncompromising image that coexisted with warmth, charm, and genuine idealism.

Much of her approach to office and to people is reflected in *Unbought and Unbossed,* which she wrote in her first term. I use it here to develop what I call the *Chisholm Mystique* of the congresswoman's professional and legislative style. Chisholm deployed two kinds of leadership while she was on Capitol Hill: publicized and symbolic leadership, and pragmatic pedagogical leadership. Her simultaneous use of both made her more effective than she otherwise might have been.

(UN)WELCOME IN THE CAPITOL

On the morning of January 3, 1969, Conrad pinned an orchid on Chisholm's jacket just as she left her offices in the Longworth building for the opening session of Congress.[3] Her suit was red wool, with black velvet trimmings. She arrived on the floor of the House late, after the roll was called, and in her haste forgot to remove her coat and hat. Informed by several colleagues that she was violating a House rule, she hastily retreated to a cloakroom, then took a seat directly across from the Speaker's podium. Many admirers from both sides of the aisle greeted her, including Melvin Laird, the incoming secretary of defense, congressional colleague Adam Clayton Powell, and George McMahon of Texas. She was immediately struck by the relative lack of formality in the House compared to the New York State Assembly. "Members walked around shaking hands and slapping each other on the back, talking without paying attention to the proceedings," she recalled. Their conversation drowned out the parade of speakers to the podium who each read a minute of their speeches, then handed it to a clerk for publication in the *Congressional Record* "as if it had been really given and the other members had listened to it."

The swirl of being welcomed to the Capitol made Chisholm chronically overcommitted. She was "flooded" with interview requests and party invitations. She satisfied as many interview requests as possible but, as she did in Albany, she avoided parties ("the cocktail and dinner party circuit is mostly made up of hangers-on, dealers, and self-promoters," she declared). She was late to many of the functions she did agree to attend, such as a reception at the Capitol Hill Hotel, with political supporters and poor residents of Bed-Stuy, as well as family and friends. When two busloads of people had ridden down to see her, because of the day's schedule, she was only able to spend ten minutes at the party and arrived two hours late. The mayor and D.C. city councilman Walter Fauntroy had been there to congratulate her, but she missed them as they could not stay long enough. Plans for a reenactment of her swearing-in ceremony had to be scrapped. She missed entirely an appearance at a National Women's Party/National Organization for Women ceremony. She was also honored at a reception by the Metropolitan Democratic Women's Club in the Gold Room of the Rayburn office building, for which she was nearly two hours late. Nearly 300 invited guests waited patiently for her, including Mayor Walter Washington, House Majority Leader Carl Albert, and Charlie Diggs. When she arrived, however, her charisma made everyone forgive her. In her speech she proclaimed that she represented not only her Twelfth District, but Black Americans, doubtlessly leading to more requests for interviews and help.[4]

But the reception from many of her colleagues was not so warm. Indeed, initially, Chisholm was "very, very unhappy" in the Capitol, lonely because her colleagues were standoffish, even hostile. Some of them made her feel like she was "somebody coming out of the moon," she recalled years later. She had arrived in Washington with the reputation of being "a hellcat," and despite her diminutive size, she suspected that she was frightening to most of her congressional colleagues. As time went on she "realized that everyone had been expecting someone else, a noisy, hostile, antiwhite type." Sometimes the lengths others would go to in order to avoid her were almost comical. One day early in her term, she inadvertently took a seat at the table that was unofficially designated for the legislators from Georgia. While sitting there alone, reading the *New York Times*, a Georgian approached. After informing her that she was at "his" table, he seemed to expect her to move immediately. But she refused. She suggested that he sit at another table and, assuming that he would be embarrassed to admit that he did not want to sit with her, to tell whoever asked why he was not at the Georgia table. He was, however, not at all embarrassed to do just that. As she watched, her Georgia colleague jumped up and intercepted all of the arriving Georgia legislators to tell them that she would not move and that they all had to move tables. Eventually they settled uncomfortably at a smaller table, while the tiny Chisholm sat alone at their usual large one.[5]

Trouble predictably and most often came from white southern congressmen. She dealt with such insults with a sense of humor and attempted to embarrass the offender. The slights lasted for about the first five months of her term. The colleague who exclaimed that he could not believe her salary was $42,500, just like his, was clearly undone by having a Black woman as his equal. Another representative from Arkansas always seemed to have a coughing fit when she came near him. Politely, she would always say "God Bless You" to this individual. Brock Adams, a colleague from Washington, eventually pointed out to her that he was spitting, not coughing or sneezing. He seemed to be coughing so that he could spit into a handkerchief and then in her face. She bought a handkerchief herself, which she put into the pocket of her "beautiful sweater suit." As she approached the spitter, she pulled her handkerchief out when he pulled his out, and spat into hers directly in front of him. He, too, was cured of his behavior. Another colleague from Georgia gleefully and maliciously remarked, "We will have fun with you!" "The fun works both ways," Chisholm replied.[6]

She also, much to her chagrin, had to assert her right to respect from citizens who came to see her. After her arrival in Washington, she was shocked when "Black men, militants, extremists, or whatever you want to call them, come into my office and put their behinds right up on my desk." They would then proceed to list what they wanted her to do. "But eventually," she explained, "I look at them and I say, 'I'm ready to talk with you, but I can't talk with your behind in my face. Now you get off that desk, because you wouldn't do this to any other congressman and you know it." Furthermore, she would call them out on not being registered to vote. The offenders, she recalled, would be stunned that Chisholm was so direct and unintimidated.[7]

THE CHISETTES

In direct contrast to the disrespect that some congressional colleagues showed Chisholm, her office staff was loyal and energetic. She had begun the hiring process late, because she had taken three weeks to travel to Jamaica after the general election, so in December she scrambled to find her staff. And she had already decided not to simply award positions to her previous supporters, because "what I needed was experience, to make up for my own inexperience in Washington, and after that, of course, I needed competence and loyalty." The women she initially hired, four Black and two white, would do their best to support their new boss. The fact that the staff was all-female was not a coincidence—Chisholm wanted to provide opportunities for advancement to women on the Hill. Furthermore, when she arrived, she found that women, students, and American Indians wanted to work for her. Initially fewer Black people did, causing her to wonder whether they thought that she shouldn't have run for the office. One notable exception was Pauli Murray, who, citing "how proud I am that you represent Negro/Black women particularly," sent her résumé and contact information in case Chisholm ever needed Murray's expertise.

The diverse staff, which was what she wanted, were there "so that people can see each other and learn to appreciate each other—[they] were supportive and enthusiastic." They would notice that she hadn't eaten all day and go get supper for her. The bond that they had was "created out of respect." According to Chisholm, "They saw that even though they were my help and everything, they knew that I was interested in them. . . . If they got into any personal problems . . . I'd get right in there and help them." Brownmiller noticed "an unusual feminine ambience: the girls are more attuned to each other's incipient moods and sniffles than a male or mixed staff would be." The office staff acted somewhat like a family, and some staff even brought their children to work at times. They dubbed themselves the Chisettes. Eventually they would be joined by male staffers, but the Chisholm Mystique was emboldened by the novelty of an all-female Washington office.[8]

Administrative assistant Carolyn Jones Smith would be the foundation of the office. A Black woman in her twenties from the Tidewater region of Virginia, Smith had an earthy sense of humor and a fierce protectiveness of her boss. Smith was working for Congressman Charles Waylan of Ohio at the time Chisholm won her office, and a staffer in the House of Representatives personnel office thought that Smith might be a good fit for Chisholm's workforce. Smith resisted at first, thinking that Chisholm looked "tired and old" (she was still recovering from surgery at that point) and would probably not last long in the Capitol, but the personnel staffer convinced her

"The Chisettes," 1969. *From left*: Alice Pannell, Karen McRory,
Travis Cain, Shirley Chisholm, Shirley Downs,
Carolyn Jones (later Smith), and Pauline Baker.
Courtesy of the Shirley Chisholm estate.

to go interview for the job of personal secretary nonetheless. Unlike some representatives, Chisholm interviewed people herself, with Mac Holder, in the borrowed offices of outgoing member Joe Resnick (D-NY). "We hit it off right away," Smith remembered. The two of them got into a bantering conversation about a bandage on Smith's foot. Chisholm reportedly said, "Well, you certainly are not a put-on!" to which Smith replied, "No, what you see is what you get!" Smith was hired. The two would become quite close, working side by side every day when Chisholm was in Washington, sometimes traveling to speaking engagements together, and maintaining a genuine mutual affection. Chisholm became godmother to one of Smith's daughters. Chisholm could "read" Smith's face and know at a glance whether something was wrong. Chisholm appreciated Smith's ability to keep her "cool, calm, and collected," in Smith's words. Smith knew what to touch and what not to touch on her boss's always neat desk. Although Smith was fairly quickly promoted from personal to executive assistant, the personal part of her job never disappeared. "She had all of the faith in me and I loved her dearly," Smith recalled.[9]

At first, Smith privately referred to Chisholm as "the old lady from Brooklyn." She realized eventually that Chisholm's hairstyle, a page-boy style with tight bangs, was one reason she looked old. Smith got her to go to Smith's own hairdresser, but Chisholm would revert back to her old style as soon as she herself did her hair. Finally, in the spring of 1969, Smith had an inspiration. When she suggested a wig to Chisholm, the congresswoman enthusiastically embraced the idea. "I had a friend, another friend who owned a wig shop . . . [fix] up a few of them and I brought them in and put 'em on her, combed them and she said 'Oh! Oh, this is going to be great!' And I said, 'see how much time it can save! And you can throw those little curlers that you roll that little doo-doo roll bangs up on and the page boy—just throw it away!' And she said 'Fine!' And that's how Shirley Chisholm got to start wearing her little wigs!"[10]

Smith soon expanded her role as Chisholm's stylist. Smith helped Chisholm update her wardrobe, after Chisholm complimented Smith's style and asked for help. Smith wanted to change her "little old schoolteacher" look, even though Chisholm reminded her that she had actually been a "little old school teacher." Smith visited a shop called the French Poodle on Connecticut Avenue and arranged to send clothes that Smith had chosen up to the office for Chisholm to try. Although she tried in vain to get her boss to shorten her skirts, or wear pantsuits, Smith successfully outfitted her in colorful, stylish suits and three-piece knits. The congresswoman insisted on picking out her own shoes and handbags, however. "And the shoes," Smith recalled. "She continued to wear the Shirley Chisholm high heels. She has that New York walk, you know that pip-pup-dup-pip-pip-pip, you could hear her coming down the halls. . . . So I would tell the staff, 'here comes Mrs. Chisholm!' And I'd peep out the door, and here she coming, just struttin', just struttin.'"[11]

Chisholm's concern with her appearance, and Smith's insistence on helping create it, emerged from their experiences as Black women. As political scientists Nadia Brown and Danielle Lemi have written, Black women political officials have an even more fraught set of decisions regarding personal aesthetics than other politicians. Black women are all too aware of stereotypes regarding both Blackness and womanhood and thus "face unique pulls and pushes in presenting an acceptable image in the eyes of voters."[12] Chisholm also faced the gazes of her new colleagues in the House and Senate, many of whom were hostile. Smith understood this pressure and ensured that her boss's clothes and hair were on point each day.

Smith and Chisholm enjoyed an informal and respectful rapport. Chisholm recalled conversations she had with other women members of Congress who complained about their staffs. "Everybody must have a Carolyn in their office," she would tell them. Carolyn herself recalled the astonishment of colleagues when Chisholm told them how candid Carolyn was:

> So they said, "a Carolyn?" So she said, "yes, my Carolyn makes me laugh. She keeps me grounded. She tells me when I am wrong and what have you" and she says—And they said, "you haven't fired her?," [and] she says, "Oh, no way. No, that's my Carolyn and I'm going to keep her. . . . You know, the woman had the nerve to call me from the House phone one time and said, "Carolyn, tell me something funny." I said, "you don't pay me enough."

When Chisholm was in the District, Smith made sure all of her boss's needs were taken care of. This included making sure that Chisholm had appropriate housing, that she was properly fed, and even that her clothes and wigs were cleaned and maintained. She or another staffer ventured to the cafeteria each day to pick up Chisholm's lunch, because she preferred not to eat in the members' dining room. The Black staff in the cafeteria eventually learned to recognize Chisholm's staffers and often moved them to the front of the line. The staffer would bring the lunch back up to Chisholm, who would eat at her desk wearing paper cuffs that she had purchased from a catalog (she loved catalog shopping) to protect her sleeves. Smith's husband, Richard (she had married him during her first year on the job), escorted Chisholm to functions at the White House when necessary.[13] Chisholm stayed in Washington Mondays through Thursdays, and Smith usually drove her to the airport at the end of each week.[14]

Chisholm had encountered housing discrimination prior to moving to D.C. After arranging to view an apartment close to the Capitol, she arrived at the appointment to discover that it was suddenly not available. She let the agent know that she was a congresswoman, and suddenly there was an available apartment again.[15] But she bypassed that rental and took a place in southwest Washington, in the Capitol Park complex, not far from the Capitol. Unfortunately, word spread that she lived there, and within three weeks her apartment was burgled and about $540 worth of clothing was taken. Chisholm herself had been away in New York for the weekend, but it "frightened the devil out of all of us," Smith said. She wondered whether Chisholm had not locked all of the locks, or whether the intruder had indeed broken in. Smith and Chisholm both wondered whether Chisholm had been a specific target. While the robbery might have been part of a larger pattern of crime in D.C. that the city's political leaders were struggling with, and the mayor was embroiled in a controversy about police use of guns in the District, she thought that she might have been singled out. The *Chicago*

Defender's pseudonymous political columnist, "Diggs Datrooth," warned readers, "Don't believe those stories that New York's Congresswoman Shirley Chisholm is frightened because burglars ransacked her apartment. The spunky little Representative declares that she's from New York and nothing shocks her." But Chisholm also said that she thought the theft was an "inside job."[16] She moved out the next day.

Mac Holder had found a private home in northeast Washington owned by a Freedman's Hospital nurse named Annie B. Pharr. The house was on a quiet street and had an alley that provided discreet access to the back door. Pharr agreed to prepare meals and host the congresswoman. "Annie Pharr waited on her hand and foot," an aide recalled, and she even supplied food to the Secret Service when Chisholm ran for president. Chisholm did not have to think about cooking or cleaning. Chisholm was, given the break-in, very private about the location of her home. She refused to give her address to the *Washington Post* for its feature on congressional home addresses. Her home numbers in both the District and at home in Brooklyn would be unlisted and very difficult to obtain (she got a new home number in Brooklyn and transferred all calls from the old number to her district office). All she would say was that her commute to her new home inside the District was about twenty minutes.[17]

Shirley Downs, Chisholm's legislative assistant (later legislative director), would be another longtime Capitol Hill staffer in Chisholm's office. She was often assisted by three college student volunteers who ran down materials in the library for her. The "brilliant" but somewhat eccentrically dressed (Smith called her a "flower child") young white woman called her boss "Chizzy," and was not afraid to argue with her over how to vote in committee. In these instances Downs would get very agitated and indignant, and Smith suspected that Chisholm rather enjoyed the verbal sparring. Nonetheless, Downs admired her boss's appetite for information. "She's like a vacuum cleaner," Downs said. "I mark stuff for her to read and the next day she comes in and says, 'Let's get together at 2 o'clock and discuss it.' She reads anything and everything."[18]

In 1969, Downs was a self-described "child of the 60s." She had grown up in a small town in Ulster County, New York, in a family that valued education above all else. Her interest in politics had been sparked by a great aunt, a professor of history, who quizzed Downs on current events each time she visited. She started her education at American University's School of International Service but found her peers to be less interested in scholarship than she was. She was much happier after she transferred to Skidmore College and concentrated her coursework on developing nations. Although a career in the State Department might have aligned with her interests, she learned that women were more likely to advance through careers on Capitol Hill. In 1964 she took a job with fellow Ulster County native Joe Resnick, who was running for Congress. When he won, she followed him to Washington. She was known across the Hill for her rather outlandish style of dress. One of her favorite outfits was a "purple and lime green striped dress . . . [that] was very short, and I wore knee-high purple boots, and one lime green stocking and one purple stocking." But she hastened to point out that, while Chisholm was lenient on wardrobe matters (she would simply ask men to have a tie at the ready just in case), it was another member's staff person who scandalously showed up in hot pants to work one day.[19]

Chisholm hired Downs after Resnick had lost his Senate bid in 1968. His staff, including Downs, Travis Cain, and Karen McCrory, were packing up his office. Cain was a Black woman from Texas who, along with Downs, had been working on grants, constituent issues, and economic development. She had written to Chisholm asking for a job. When Chisholm traveled to Washington to interview Cain, the three offered Chisholm the use of Resnick's office for that interview and others. "We knew who she was . . . the pepper pot from Brooklyn," Downs recalled. They were also charmed when they met her because "she just telegraphs and projects this warmth." "It was fun to be with her and it's almost as if you had always known her." For her part, Chisholm was charmed, too. Having observed Resnick's staff working together, she ended up offering jobs to all three women in her own office.[20]

By hiring Downs, Chisholm was one of the first members of Congress to employ a female legislative assistant. Downs was responsible for coordinating all of the legislative work in the office. Chisholm introduced only one bill during her first term, to create a memorial to her hero Mary McLeod Bethune in Washington. She tended to sign on as cosponsor instead, though committee work and collaborations with other members kept Downs busy.[21] Once Chisholm took a seat on the Committee on Education and Labor in 1971, Downs would write legislation having to do with day care, early childhood education, vocational education, women's rights, and pensions. Downs also recruited candidates to work within the office, although Chisholm always interviewed the finalists. But most of Downs's work was within the committee meetings and hearings, where much of the real work happened in Congress. She did not work for Chisholm only, but for the larger functioning of the committee: she organized meetings, invited constituents and interest group members to testify, wrote amendments, and wrote back-up statements. In some ways, she recalled, her job was more like lobbying in the sense that she exposed committee members to the ideas of advocacy groups like the Children's Defense Fund or the League of Women Voters. When Herman Badillo, elected to the House from the Bronx in 1970, arrived at Education and Labor meetings, he would ask Downs, "Which way are we voting?" knowing that he would agree with Chisholm's interpretation of a given issue. At an Education and Labor subcommittee meeting, she crouched behind the seats of Chisholm and Louise Day Hicks, the Boston antibusing advocate, handing materials to both women. Hicks had expressed interest in advocating for a minimum wage for day care workers, and so the two women, who were seen as natural enemies, were collaborating on pushing forward a childcare agenda. Such cooperation was exhilarating to Downs because Chisholm supported the cause without needing all of the credit.[22]

THE WORK

Downs and others enjoyed working for Chisholm because of the congresswoman's collaborative ethos. Downs interpreted Chisholm's Black feminist power politics as "the true, the right, and the beautiful." The objective was to redistribute political power to become more inclusive to those who had been excluded. This extended beyond the Twelfth District to American Indians, citizens of U.S. territories, Latinx people, LGBTQ people, and poor people. It also spread beyond Chisholm herself; her project was not to get reelected as much as it was to solve problems. "She wanted her energies to be spread out with helping the downtrodden as she called them," is how Carolyn Smith put it. She liked how Chisholm refused to place people on War on Poverty program local boards because of patronage, instead accepting the community's nominations. In hindsight, Downs likened her boss to Nelson Mandela in the sense that he was "non-tribal even though he came from an important tribe" and had an expansive view, a "different mindset." Chisholm seemed to be able to see the connections between widely differing groups.[23]

Downs noted that a pedagogical approach characterized Chisholm's relationship with disempowered voters (those who had "been dealt out of politics," as Downs put it). She modeled a belief that all could be represented and that all could participate. "Come on in, the water's fine! You can do this too," was how Downs quoted her boss on participation in politics. Furthermore, she loved people who were new to the process, so that she had the opportunity to teach them—a predilection that caused her to say yes to countless college campus speaking engagements. Chisholm's warmth and personable affect enabled her to work with the diverse constituency in her district and beyond. "When she went out into the country, she would . . . talk to any group," Downs recalled, including conservatives. She understood that "government was a compromise . . . because if people thought things were just shoved down their throat, then . . . they wouldn't buy in." Along the same lines, she did not hesitate to work with conservative colleagues. By helping them feel comfortable, she was able to get them to "buy in," which in turn would create support for new legislation. She was also cordial, generous, and genuinely interested in what other people thought, even when she did not agree. The result was that she projected an unusual degree of "inclusiveness."[24]

Charm seemed to become part of Chisholm's repertoire. Aided by Carolyn Smith's fashion consultations, she developed a put-together look with matching shoes and bags. She conversed easily with all of her colleagues. She was even, according to one of her later aides Laura Murphy, "kind of a flirt" and, as mentioned before, "a feminine cupcake with the heart of a lion." She surprised many of her colleagues with cards on their birthdays. When Speaker John McCormack was struggling with his wife's terminal illness, Chisholm escorted him to the chapel for a prayer. "She sees into people, and connects with them at their level emotionally," Downs explained. "On the Hill, it wasn't that she didn't think that there were lots of prejudiced son of a bitches. She knew that there were, but she never gave up hope that they would change."[25]

Colleagues also realized that Chisholm and her staffers could explain confusing pending legislation. Ever the teacher, Chisholm could break down concepts into manageable units and help her colleagues put them together. She freely admitted that it was her staff who enabled her to do so, because Downs and others discussed the nuts and bolts of policy with her. Other staffers would "give [members] this piece of legislation and they would read it not knowing what the hell they were doing when they get over there to vote," Smith recalled. She got lots of invitations to lunch from those who needed a tutorial on House bills, and not just from Democrats.[26]

Correspondingly, the office worked in an egalitarian fashion. That meant an unusual level of autonomy for staff, and, in the Chisholm offices, interns were held in the same regard as permanent staff. "Everybody got face time" with the congresswoman, especially if they were working on an issue. And she was unusual in that she allowed all staff and interns to work on issues that interested them. "Even if she was dissatisfied with the way you had done something . . . she had a way of giving you advice without stripping you of anything," recalled Andrea Holmes. The office felt "like a family," said Downs. Chisholm had not left her educator strategies in Brooklyn; she thought that her staff were all undergoing a learning process and that their best education would come from learning by doing. She wanted them to "always aim high." As Downs saw it, Chisholm's Washington office was a "training ground" for young developing political operatives. Carolyn Smith said that staffers would "learn not to want for everything, to give back," and to educate oneself, one's children, and one's community. She also trusted her staff to do their homework and prepare documents thoroughly. Sometimes there was no time for her to review all of what a staff member had prepared herself, but she would enter meetings with the script her staff had prepared, trusting that the staff member in question had taken Chisholm's position and the relevant facts into account. If a cause aligned with Chisholm's desire to help disempowered people, she would support a staffer's pursuit of it. For example, Downs recalled an intern from California who adopted the issue of abolishing the navy test range on the Caribbean island of Culebra. The young man investigated the issue thoroughly and prepared an insert for the *Congressional Record* under Chisholm's name. He later became a lawyer in a legal services program back in California. Having staff who moved through the office and then struck out on their own was part of Chisholm's plan: she was attempting to build a political network.[27]

Because of heavy constituent needs, Chisholm hired Andrea Tracy Holmes as a caseworker in 1971. She was attracted by the reputation Chisholm had developed as a fair and encouraging employer. A Washington native and a Black woman with three children, Holmes was "not only excited to be working for the first African American woman of Congress but she was also helping me to put food on the table." Holmes's casework helped contribute to the Chisholm Mystique by fulfilling the congresswoman's plan to assist her individual constituents directly. Holmes acted as an ombudsperson, inquiring at government agencies on behalf of those who had been denied services or ignored ("I basically wrote letters all day long and was on the telephone all day long"). In Bedford-Stuyvesant the needs of constituents were vast and covered a range of issues: social services, military, and immigration. Pleas for help ranged from problems with employment to those with army authorities, immigration, and the criminal justice system. She might contact the Social Security Administration because someone had been denied benefits, or write private immigration bills to send to the Judiciary Committee. She saw her mission as helping people organize to advocate for their concerns. She might even accompany constituents to hearings on the Hill, if they were granted. The work was "depressing at times" because the need so outweighed the resources Holmes could muster, but any victories were exhilarating. Thank-you letters disclosed how casework intervention had improved constituent lives: "Words cannot express my sincere gratitude"; "I want to thank God for women like you"; "Only through your co-operation and influence was this possible and I will be ever grateful to you"; "I can truthfully say you are the most outstanding woman I have ever met. Bless you."[28]

Chisholm's aides drove her everywhere, since the congresswoman still did not have a driver's license and had nearly weekly speaking engagements. Years later, Smith still vividly recalled an occasion on which she accompanied Chisholm to a speech that was not well received. In 1970 or 1971 the two traveled by car to Harpers Ferry, West Virginia, to a panel discussion. Chisholm was dressed in a faux leopard coat that Smith had picked out for her. After the prespeech luncheon, Smith began to get concerned that the audience would not welcome Chisholm's outspokenness. She cautioned Chisholm, "When you get up there just be calm, just talk." But the congresswoman defied the suggestion. She gave a "fire and brimstone speech" and refused to stop even when Smith stood in a prearranged spot and made desperate gestures signaling that the speech should end. When Chisholm finally did end, Smith hustled the two of them out the door to the parking lot, where they were intercepted by a man who said, "'You should be ashamed of yourself.' And of course she stops in her tracks. 'What do you mean?' And he says, 'There you are with a leopard skin coat on! You should know better than to kill! Don't you know how many animals it took to, to, to, make that coat?' I said, 'For your information, it's fake! The only thing it hurt was her pocketbook! Come on Mrs C, let's go!'" Rattled by the confrontation, and with their hosts nowhere in sight to assist their departure, Smith drove them out of town at breakneck speed into the rapidly darkening night. The road was winding and hilly, and Smith feared that they would not make it to the highway. Even Chisholm uncharacteristically admitted that she was getting nervous. The two finally made it to the highway, and Smith took a deep breath. "And I looked over at that girlfriend and she was snoring," Smith recalled with amazement. Chisholm slept peacefully as they finished the trip back to Washington. Once safely home, the two joked about it. "Has anybody sent my check?" Chisholm inquired. "No, let's go back up there and get it," Smith dared her boss. She did eventually get paid for her appearance.[29]

Chisholm's staff also enjoyed lighter moments together. "She loved to at the end of the day kind of kick back and relax," Holmes said. The congressional offices on each corridor pooled their cash and held hall parties just before breaks at Easter, Memorial Day, and other holidays. Everyone would bring a dish to share. Carolyn and Richard Smith also held New Year's Eve parties at their home. Chisholm usually joined her staff and danced at the parties. "She loved to dance, she loved to have a good time," Andrea Tracy Holmes remembered. She also shopped out of catalogues and bought presents for her office staff and their children at Christmas.[30]

THE WEEKLY SCHEDULE

Chisholm spent "four long days in the capital and three longer ones back home" each week. She left her office by 7:30 p.m. each night, occasionally going to speak in the area but usually heading home. Once there, she ate dinner and would "get in bed with the memorandums, reports, and letters" she needed to catch up on. Each Thursday, Smith or another staffer dropped

Chisholm off at the airport for her return to Brooklyn, and took Chisholm's wigs to get serviced at the shop. Conrad Chisholm collected his wife from the airport and from there the couple went home (eventually he and Smith insisted that Chisholm not do any speaking at all on nights she flew back from Washington). On Fridays, she spent the day in her district office at 587 Eastern Parkway. On Saturdays she usually worked the streets in her district, and on Sundays she made the rounds of churches, often having a speaking engagement. "It's a good thing I'm *not* a party type," she declared, "because I just don't have the time for it."[31]

Conrad continued his role as her helpmate husband. In Brooklyn, Conrad was the one to take her clothing to the cleaners and other things to make sure she had her basic needs met. He was a source of comfort: "When I'm disturbed, distressed, and distracted, I simply go home and cry on his shoulder. . . . He is a wonderful lover because, first, he is my friend." While she was in Washington, he worked out of her district office, running errands for Mac Holder and the other staff: case worker Victor Robles, secretary Arlene Doren, and William Howard, the accountant. The couple didn't go out often after she was elected to Congress, because she was recognizable and would often attract unwanted attention. Sometimes they did go out to dinner to places where they knew that they wouldn't be disturbed. But Conrad seldom traveled to Washington or attended official functions. Indeed, Carolyn Smith's husband, Richard, often served as her escort. Conrad trusted the Smiths, and the couples were friendly. Both wives worked long hours, and both husbands did much of the cooking. After the Chisholms bought a house in St. Thomas, the Smiths vacationed there with them (on that occasion, Conrad did the cooking, because he was expert at preparing Caribbean fish dishes).[32]

Besides Mac Holder, the other fixture in the district office was Victor Robles, the young Puerto Rican activist who had worked on the campaign. Fiercely loyal and protective of Chisholm, he and most others thought of him as Chisholm's adopted son (years later, he still sent Chisholm Mother's Day cards). She was an othermother to him, and he acted as a son at times. He spent most of his time at the office or at the Chisholm home, acting as case worker, bodyguard, and general assistant to Mac Holder. In Brooklyn, while Chisholm was in D.C. all week, Robles would make appearances on her behalf, at demonstrations or PTA meetings. He worked all week, then met her at the airport with Conrad, and accompanied her all weekend as well. He did not mind because "I really saw her not as my boss, I really saw her as my mother." He was a bachelor, and young, and was happy to play that role. He often communicated with Spanish-speaking constituents, and acted as a general case worker within the district office. When he traveled with Chisholm, he escorted her to her hotel room and made sure "no one dared go near that room." He prepared her tea (she was not a coffee drinker) and took care of her when she was sick.[33]

On the rare occasions the Brooklyn staff would come to D.C. or vice versa, there was a bit of tension between Carolyn Smith and Mac Holder. Smith's theory was that Holder felt that he, and not Smith, should be the one telling Chisholm what to do and looking out for her. Smith suspected that he felt a sense of rivalry with her and perhaps was frustrated that he could not control her. Downs had a different memory: to her, "he was really incredible. He was fun, he was funny, he was politically wired."[34]

Back in the Capitol office on Mondays, Chisholm caught up on paperwork because there were no sessions, and Smith would often take calls from people to whom Chisholm had promised something or other while she had been in New York. The week might also include a trip to make a speech or lecture. Chisholm was "deluged with mail from people wanting her to be here, there, and everywhere," according to Carolyn Smith. In her first one hundred days in office she received over 3,000 speaking requests. She had to turn most of them down, but she still traveled the country making appearances.[35] She spoke to women's groups, Black groups, educational institutions, churches, and political groups. She was asked to lend her support to newly founded organizations: the Southern Elections Fund, the National Association for the Repeal of Abortion Laws (NARAL), and the New Democratic Coalition.[36] Her roll-call vote attendance was 55 percent in her first term, well below the average Democratic member attendance rate of 85 percent. One explanation was that she only voted on matters that she thought of real concern, but it was also true that she was frequently on the road.[37]

Chisholm used such speaking engagements to articulate her larger political beliefs and to comment on the state of the nation. In February, Chisholm told local members of the Emma Lazarus Federation of Jewish Women's Clubs that the country needed a "revolution of women" to solve problems:

> The women of this country now must rise again as we did some 100 years ago and take over the world leadership of the nation! . . . There is a communication gap between younger and older generations and all about us we see confusion. . . . It is the woman, I believe, who is ultimately going to bring our country back. . . . The one great fear in the capital is that some day the women of this country will band together and fight for justice and freedom on every level. We have got to make this happen.[38]

To students at Georgetown University in April, she predicted that "a coalition of college students and black people will save American society." While she did not approve of student riots, she understood the motives behind them. She also observed the irony that Black people have long been told to improve themselves, but now that they were doing so, white people were anxious.[39] In June, she electrified an audience in Chicago with a no-holds-barred speech on racism and politics. Speaking at a benefit dinner for the interracial First Presbyterian Church in Woodlawn, she expressed hope that youth would cause change in the status quo.[40] A commentator gushed that she "literally wrapped her audience in a box and could easily have carried them back to Brooklyn with her. The dynamic and petite congresswoman from Bedford-Stuyvesant is all power and guts and femininity."[41]

THE BEGINNINGS OF COALITION

Such accolades were in stark contrast to the hard slogging that Chisholm was doing in Washington. From her first day in office, Chisholm found herself swimming upstream, and especially on the key issues of Vietnam, civil rights, women's rights, and poor people's rights.

She did not stand alone on any one of these issues. But her political standpoint had coalesced into Black feminism. She believed that none of these issues excluded any of the others, and she pursued them all simultaneously, from the first day of her first term. She picked and chose coalitions with various allies who shared her view on specific issues. For example, on the issue of bilingual education, she not only worked with Spanish-speaking groups but also American Indians (who at that time did not have representation in Congress), Samoans, Italian Americans, and Russian Jews.[42]

The most famous coalition that Chisholm joined was the Democratic Select Committee, which would later become the Congressional Black Caucus. In her first term it was an informal grouping of the nine Black members of Congress, led by Charlie Diggs of Detroit, plus Senator Ed Brooke from Massachusetts. Diggs, already a seven-term veteran of the House, had assembled the nine representatives on the morning after the Democratic National Committee met in January 1969 for a breakfast with outgoing Vice President Humphrey. All Democrats, the nine were Diggs, Chisholm, Adam Clayton Powell of Harlem, Robert Nix of Philadelphia; Augustus (Gus) Hawkins of Los Angeles, John Conyers of Detroit, Bill Clay of St. Louis, Louis Stokes of Cleveland, and William Dawson of Chicago.[43] Clay had just won in 1968 after a hotly contested Democratic primary in which he ran against an opponent who openly appealed to white supremacy. Stokes had just been elected after federal courts mandated that Cleveland's districts be redrawn.[44] Powell's seat for the Ninety-First Congress was hard won. He had legal troubles dating back to 1960, and although he won the election in 1968, he was at first not permitted to take his oath of office. The House did allow him to take the oath once he was stripped of seniority and fined $25,000. Powell believed that his unseating was racially motivated, an interpretation that Chisholm would publicly agree with. Chisholm and the seven other seated Black members voted to reinstate him, first without any censure and then for the compromise amendment that included the fine and loss of seniority. This was their first time voting together, though it would not be their last by any means. But they certainly would not always agree. The nine were "nine different human beings, of different ages and backgrounds, different interests and dispositions, and from different kinds of communities," Chisholm remarked. The highly heterogenous group experienced "jealousies and rivalries," something that Chisholm said should have been expected. She found it "naïve" that white politicians and pundits had assumed that the bloc would automatically band together as a unit, with a designated leader.[45]

They saw themselves representing all Black Americans and not just their own constituencies. Brooke did not participate at all, and neither did Dawson, elected a quarter of a century previously. A loyal Daley machine Democrat, Dawson seemed afraid of appearing as though he was voting for Black interests only. He would break with the informal Black caucus most of the time during the coming year. Adam Clayton Powell and Robert Nix were on the periphery. Most active and vocal were Chisholm and six men: Stokes, Conyers, Mitchell, Diggs, Clay, and Hawkins. Diggs was the leader.[46] For her first two terms, Chisholm was the only woman in the group. "Because of the accident of being the only black woman member," she said, she received a disproportionate share of media attention. She disavowed any desire to become the de facto leader of the small group. Some of her colleagues, Downs thought, were unaccustomed to women being as "forthcoming and assertive" as Chisholm was. She found that she could smooth the way and lessen resentment by sharing credit with the others. Chisholm believed that if others could share the credit and think that things were their ideas, work could get done.[47]

But she had no illusions about how much work could indeed get done. "At present, the ten black members of Congress must be considered mainly for their symbolic value," she lamented. Because of their small numbers, even if they voted together and cooperated with each other more often, their effect was "negligible." She was heartened, however, by the numbers of Black elected officials in localities across the country, and by the increasing success of candidates who were willing to make principled stands on issues.[48]

THE COMMITTEE ASSIGNMENT

Chisholm refused to blindly join and follow any group, even the Democratic Party leadership itself. This would become evident in an event that grew

The Democratic Select Committee, 1969. *From left, seated*:
Shirley Chisholm, John Conyers, and Charles Diggs. *From left,
standing*: Augustus Hawkins, Parren Mitchell, and William Clay.
Courtesy of the Shirley Chisholm estate.

the new congresswoman's notoriety. As a new member, Chisholm would
be assigned by her party to one of the twenty standing House committees.
She knew that the House's seniority system (which she referred to as the
"senility system") made it unlikely that she would get her first choice. She
had hoped for an assignment to the Education and Labor Committee, and
sent a cover letter with a résumé to each Democratic member of the Ways
and Means Committee requesting Education and Labor, then Banking and
Currency, then Post Office and Civil Service, and finally Government Operations. All of those committees, she argued, would either use her skills or
allow her to address issues relevant to her constituents. When she found out
she was placed on Agriculture and on a Forestry subcommittee, she thought
it a "ridiculous assignment," even though in hindsight she acknowledged
that Agriculture's jurisdiction over food stamps and migrant labor interested her. "Apparently all they know here in Washington about Brooklyn
is that a tree grew there," she quipped. Allard Lowenstein, another antiwar
new congressperson from New York, was assigned to Agriculture, too. Jacob
Gilbert of the Ways and Means Committee defended the assignments by
saying that there were so many members from New York that not all of their
requests could be honored. Also, the committee would be discussing food
programs and consumers' legislation. *Washington Post* staff writer William

Greider was not convinced and mused that this was an example of how the power structure kept outspoken people in their proper place. Bronx congressman Jacob Gilbert had been responsible for the assignment, and protested that he faced a dilemma of how to allocate New York's twenty-six members among twenty committees.[49] Chisholm recognized the "pressures of geography and seniority," but she made a moral argument based on fair representation of Black people. "It is time for the House of Representatives to pay attention to other considerations than its petrified, sanctified system of seniority, which is apparently the only basis for making most seats," she said. She went on to argue that if 10 percent of Americans were Black, then forty-three U.S. representatives should be Black. Surely the nine in Congress now could be allocated to appropriate committees with real import for Black people, she thought. She thought that would encourage them to "work effectively to help this nation meet its critical problems of racism, deprivation, and urban decay."[50]

Chisholm, in a nearly unheard of move, approached Speaker John McCormack in protest. Unfailingly polite, McCormack listened and then gently told her, "Mrs. Chisholm, this is the way it is. You have to be a good soldier." Chisholm's reply startled him. "If you do not assist me, I will have to do my own thing," she warned. Perhaps afraid of Chisholm causing an open conflict, McCormack reluctantly approached Wilbur Mills, chair of Ways and Means, who then approached the chair of Agriculture, William R. Poage of Texas. Both Mills and Poage were unhappy with the freshman congresswoman ("Poage, I heard later, really blew his stack and made some very unpleasant remarks," Chisholm recalled). The answer was no.[51]

Chisholm had one more strategy to try: the Democratic caucus where all members approved the assignments. She had been warned by Brock Adams of Washington that she might not even be recognized at the meeting, and it was indeed a struggle. Every time she rose, other more senior colleagues did. Because seniority dictated who was recognized, she kept getting passed over. Such action was deliberate; colleagues were "smiling and nudging each other" as they watched her efforts. She finally rose and made her way down to the well in front of the Speaker, where she stood and waited to be recognized. Mills, McCormack, and Majority Leader Carl Albert conferred for a moment, and then Mills asked Chisholm her business. Chisholm gave a short prepared speech about reasons she protested her committee assignment, not the least of which was that there were only nine Black members of the House and they ought to be placed strategically to have the most opportunity to right inequality. She proposed that she be removed from Agriculture and that the Committee on Committees make a new assignment for her, to be voted on at the next month's caucus. She returned to her seat, and Wilbur Mills recognized her to offer it formally. The amendment passed. Chisholm was pleased that she had prevailed. She said, "I don't know where I'll end up . . . [but my constituents] will know they have a Representative who won't sit back and take the system."[52]

Chisholm won both admirers and detractors. As the Democratic members filed out of the chamber that day, male colleagues informed her dolefully that she had committed political suicide, even though they agreed with her in principle. The story was widely covered in the press, with all three major television networks carrying interviews with her. "Some of the Washington press corps clucked over my actions and waited for the thunderbolts to vaporize me," she wrote in her memoir. Others lectured her in print about how Congress really worked.[53] The *Washington Post* was admonitory in its reporting of the story: apparently, Chisholm "offended many colleagues with her brashness" and "privately, they accused her of grandstanding a bit." A "northern liberal" commented that "this was good politics for her district, but it was bad politics in the House." The *Post* didn't dare quote any southern Democrats, whose numbers were dwindling as its ranks began to strike off for the Republican Party. Chisholm had commented that she knew that she could not always get her way as a freshman congresswoman, but "only nine black people have been elected to Congress and those nine should be used as effectively as possible."[54] The *Chicago Defender* published an editorial favorably remarking on her stance. It reported that she "stood up in the Democratic Caucus" to make the remarks that were widely printed. In response, the *Defender* wrote that "At long last we have a representative in Congress who will not be whiplashed into silence."[55]

Chisholm was not vaporized, as it turned out. Three weeks after her refusal to sit on the Agriculture Committee, Chisholm was assigned to the Veterans Affairs Committee and welcomed by its chair, Olin Teague of Texas.[56] Apparently she was unable to be appointed to Education and Labor at that point because there were already three New York Democratic members on the committee.[57] But she was reasonably pleased with her new assignment, and she had made her point. She would not avoid making waves in her efforts to advocate for her constituents. And, whether she had angered senior Democratic officials or not, she now had more speaking engagements and press attention than she ever could have imagined. Black newspapers nationwide picked up the story and reported approvingly on her successful challenge.[58]

THE CHISHOLM MYSTIQUE IN THE NATIONAL PRESS

The national attention paid to Chisholm continued. In April 1969, Susan Brownmiller's feature article, "This Is Fighting Shirley Chisholm," was published in the *New York Times Magazine*. Brownmiller was a young journalist in 1968, on the staff at ABC News as a writer and freelancing for the *Village Voice* and other publications. When Brownmiller had first asked the *New York Times* about writing about Chisholm in early 1968, the response was, "Who wants to hear about a little old black lady in Brooklyn?" However, after Chisholm won the primary, even though there were many people who wanted to write the story, the editor did remember that Brownmiller had been the first to ask. The result was a long feature story in the magazine. Brownmiller vividly described Chisholm as having "the bearing of a queen" and being a gifted public speaker.

In the New Journalism style, Brownmiller wanted to trail Chisholm everywhere, including at meals, but Chisholm insisted on taking her meals privately. Brownmiller thought her subject was "kind of square." Dressed in knitted suits, straightened hair in pageboy, with "weird wing glasses," Brownmiller recalled that Chisholm "exuded a school marmish look." She never felt a "sisterhood" with the congresswoman but did find Conrad "much easier to get along with." "Her defenses were . . . really high, but it was the way she could survive. . . . But that's the political game and that part of it she didn't play well," concluded Brownmiller.[59]

What was clear from the article was that Chisholm would not follow the script for anyone who expected her to fall into step. She criticized Democratic reformers, Black Power activists ("woolly heads" [*sic*] and "spear carriers"), and white liberals ("Don't you know that white liberals are our favorite parlor conversation?") alike. She took aim at the media for playing up Black anti-Semitism, arguing instead that Black Brooklynites were protesting the establishment, which just happened to be Jewish (she seemed to ignore the anti-Semitic rhetoric that had accompanied such protest, however). And she was suspicious of the new buzz phrase "Black capitalism," suspecting that it merely amounted to "a tax-incentive plan for white businessmen."[60] The article eventually became the genesis for Brownmiller's biography of Chisholm targeted to young adults, published the following year. Whether Chisholm, in Brownmiller's opinion, was good at playing politics, she certainly was a good story and Brownmiller sought to tell it.

Chisholm ended her first year as something of a celebrity. The Hallmark Gallery (run by the greeting card company) chose her as one of its celebrity designers for its Christmas tree display. Together with Joe Namath, the Lindsays, Cab Calloway, and Johnny Cash, Chisholm submitted her instructions for her tree's decorations. It was to be a "brotherhood tree," covered with dolls from the world's nations.[61] She was sought out for interviews and book projects: her former state assembly colleague George Metcalfe was writing a book of profiles of Black leaders, Susan Brownmiller's biography was forthcoming, and other biographers had expressed interest.[62]

The Chisholm Mystique would turn the new congresswoman into an enduring symbol. From a curiosity to a coalition builder, Chisholm had assembled a formidable team of staffers and had begun to take on the micro and macroscale problems that stood in the way of power shared among all American people. And she had gathered no small amount of notoriety. On Capitol Hill, she started to develop publicly what had been driving her personally: her Black feminist politics.

9
BLACK FEMINIST POWER POLITICS
ON CAPITOL HILL

As a new lawmaker in her first term, Chisholm sought to translate her beliefs into political change. Such an undertaking was challenging. The year Chisholm took the oath of office in Congress, 1969, represented a cultural and political maelstrom. Richard M. Nixon was inaugurated as president of the United States. American troop numbers peaked, at over 500,000, in Vietnam. Neil Armstrong took "one small step for man, one giant leap for mankind" on the moon. The Boeing 747 and the Concorde took their first test flights, Elvis opened in Vegas, John Lennon and Yoko Ono staged a bed-in, and thousands flocked to Woodstock, New York, for its famous rock festival. Young people protested politically and socially: Harvard students took over the administration building, radical feminists organized an abortion "speakout" in New York City, and LGBTQ New Yorkers stood up to police in the Stonewall riots. Two massive anti-Vietnam war demonstrations came to the nation's capital. Amid the chaos and conflict, Shirley Chisholm served the first year of her first term in Congress, oftentimes championing the challenges brought by U.S. social movements on the left.

At the time she took office, Chisholm was not only the first Black woman in the House of Representatives, but she was also the first Black feminist. What this meant was that she supported social justice broadly from her standpoint of being both Black and female. She furthered the agendas of multiple movements—those of antiwar, civil rights, women's, and poor peoples' activists—in an integrated strategy that helped move those movements "from protest to politics," as civil rights organizer Bayard Rustin wrote in 1965, suggesting that activists bring transformations in social justice from the streets to the halls of national government.[1] Claiming political power was central to Chisholm's vision. And her Black feminism was expansive. She built common cause with white-led feminist groups such as the National Organization for Women (NOW), Women's Equity Action League, and National Association for the Repeal of Abortion Laws (NARAL), but she also recognized that they did not always represent everyone. She knew that poor, Black, and brown women were concerned with their children's education and other practical concerns.[2] As historians Robert Self and Dorothy Sue Cobble have explained, equal rights feminists protested "forced domesticity and denial of access to the market" while working-class women activists protested "forced market labor and the denial of full-time domesticity."[3] Chisholm was more identified with the latter, though she certainly allied herself with the former. As a Black woman who was the daughter and granddaughter of Black women who had worked in service occupations for low wages, and as a feminist and Black freedom advocate, she saw Black women at the nexus of political and economic justice issues. For many Black women, this manifested as the problems of being a female head of a household in a political system centered around what Self calls "breadwinner liberalism," the idea that a nuclear family needed to be supported by men's market wages and women's domestic labor, and that the state should support that end economically.[4] But for the women Chisholm had in mind, women often provided for the financial and domestic well-being of their families. "We were acutely aware" of the problems of female heads of household, Downs said, "because it occurred with the Black population first. But then it just was spreading, and spreading, and spreading, and spreading."[5] The issues that the office tackled addressed the challenges that single women heads of household faced.

At the moment Chisholm was elected to Congress, she joined a national effort by Black feminists to unify the intersecting concerns within the Black freedom struggle and second wave feminism. Chisholm joined other Black feminist thinkers from her time and throughout the history of Black feminist thought. Chisholm advanced her agenda in Congress and published *Unbought and Unbossed*, with its series of essays on feminist issues, alongside the work of Flo Kennedy, Frances Beal, Mary Ann Weathers, Linda LaRue, Pauli Murray, Michele Wallace, Toni Cade Bambara, the National Black Feminist Organization, the Combahee River Collective, bell hooks, Maya Angelou, and Audre Lorde.[6] Like them, she grasped and sought to explain the inextricable linkages between Black women's issues and other social justice concerns, but unlike contemporary Black feminists, she pursued those issues from within the halls of the national legislature.

Black feminism, emerging from multiple sources within the Black freedom movement, coalesced as white women activists from the New Left and Chicana feminists from Chicano activism built their movements in the late 1960s and 1970s. Nearly simultaneously, welfare recipients organized into a national movement in 1967. These activists were in part energized by the infamous Moynihan Report of 1965. All had distinct roots, but all shared common goals for women's self-determination.[7] Chisholm's feminism was based on an intersectional analysis: the idea that forms of oppression were interrelated and inseparable from each other. She understood that Black women found themselves in a unique position because Blackness and femaleness were not merely additive, but intertwined within the American polity. Chisholm acknowledged the particulars of her experience as a Black woman, but, as a politician, she emphasized possibilities for coalition across movements. She adopted a critique of politics that advocated for an expansive recognition of common needs and interests, while still recognizing the specific issues facing members of various groups. Her activism parallels what Ula Taylor has called "community feminism": the idea that Black women not only must seek self-determination but also justice and empowerment for their larger community. She also applied her career to what Kimberly Springer has named "interstitial politics"—that is, a politics "between race and gender but cognizant of both."[8] Chisholm's words and actions embody a Black feminist praxis of coalition building in the service of shifting power relationships that echoed the work of Frances Beal in "Double Jeopardy: To Be Black and Female." Beal maintained that Black women were part of an overarching system of oppressions in which all humanity was caught, and that all "revolutionaries" in the struggles against oppressions must be regarded as equals, regardless of sex. Chisholm addressed both Black men, who feared that Black women would aggrandize power to themselves or even undermine Black men, and white women, who did not understand that they must fight racism and economic exploitation in order to eradicate the roots of sexism. In sum, she argued, all forms of oppression must be destroyed, not just one or another.[9]

THEORIZING THE INTERSECTIONS

Chisholm's analysis, especially earlier in her congressional career, vacillated between seeing the Black freedom struggle and feminism as parallel and seeing them as intersecting. At times, she insisted on naming sexism as the oppression that most affected her personally. She made this argument in high-profile venues: on the floor of the House and in committee hearings. In May 1969, Chisholm reintroduced the Equal Rights Amendment (ERA), a bill that had been introduced by multiple legislators as far back as 1923. In accompanying remarks, she made her first of many public statements that she had experienced more discrimination based on gender than race within politics, and she informed her colleagues that sexism was just as unacceptable as racism, a rhetorical strategy that likely pleased her feminist allies as much as it might have angered or perplexed her Black male colleagues.[10] When testifying about sexism before her congressional colleagues in 1970, she asserted unequivocally that she had experienced more obstacles related to sexism than to racism in her career. Chisholm's remarks marshaled relative yearly income to prove that women were disadvantaged relative to both Black and white men in the labor market. She used her own experiences in politics to show discrimination there, where her "chief obstacle," she said, was "to break through the role men assign women." This role was that of invisible labor to organize political organizations ("handle the details") without being rewarded with power in those organizations. However, although she made the claim that sexism was worse than racism, she made a detailed analysis of how the two forms of oppression connected. Both sexism and racism were so pervasive that they seemed normal. Some people were both Black and female, like herself, and when she added analysis of class she noted the many Black women who were heads of households and poor. Her policy prescriptions were based on that knowledge: Chisholm continued to emphasize that she had been discriminated against more on the grounds of sex than race. It was here that she quoted Pauli Murray on the framework of Jane Crow, that racism and sexism were equally unjust and dehumanizing. On the other hand, she did begin to advance an intersectional argument when she discussed poor female heads of household, pointing out that 25 percent of Black families in 1970 were headed by women, and 62 percent of those were poor. She also called for childcare for working women and the enforcement of existing anti-discrimination statutes[11]:

> If we are sincerely interested in solving our welfare problems and helping our poor and working class families we must recognize the correlation between their problems and the battle to provide equal opportunities for women. For these women, their income is not a supplement; it is essential for the survival and well-being of the family unit. They must have more and better job training opportunities and equal pay and a fair opportunity for advancement. Finally they must also have adequate day care facilities. Right now we have 5 million preschool children whose mothers have to work, but day care facilities are available to only 2 percent of our women. Without adequate day care, we have seriously handicapped women and in some cases doomed them to failure on the job market.[12]

She made the argument about the relative effects of racism and sexism in an even more visible venue later in 1970. In a guest column in *McCall's* in August, she declared, "Of the two handicaps [of her race and sex], being Black is much less of a drawback than being female." Not only that, but it would be harder to eradicate sexism because "women in America are much more brainwashed and content with their roles as second-class citizens than Blacks ever were." She continued, asserting that women had a unique and invaluable contribution to make in politics. In such a public forum, her statement about the relative impact of racism versus sexism caught the notice of the Black and mainstream press.[13] Some of her contemporaries publicly disagreed with her. Frankie Freeman, an attorney from St. Louis, Missouri, on the U.S. Commission on Civil Rights, explained that "I do not know that we can say that women are equally discriminated against [compared to Black people]," even though she supported the legislation under discussion. She thought that Chisholm had spoken from her own background as a northerner, and Freeman did so from hers as a southern Black woman. The Nineteenth Amendment had done little to help Black women in the South because Jim Crow disenfranchised most Black people, and Freeman personally had been excluded from public accommodations because of racism. Feminist lawyer Flo Kennedy made a more blunt statement on television. She said that when feminists got shot by police, as Chicago Black Panthers Fred Hampton and Mark Clark were, she might see sexism as worse than racism.[14] It is possible Chisholm used rhetoric ranking oppressions to convince men of the impact of sexism. As Kimberly Springer reminds us, Black feminism did not transform from an either/or framework of understanding racism and sexism to a both/and framework in one isolated moment.[15] Neither did Chisholm. Her conception of overlapping oppressions in 1970 was based more on parallel concerns than intersecting, interconnected ones. But despite her rhetoric and increasingly over time, she took on a set of issues that targeted multiple forms of oppression simultaneously: law enforcement's targeting of Black Power groups; women's equal opportunity in education; equal pay for women; universal childcare; and legal representation for poor citizens. She introduced her first bill: a memorial for her hero Mary McLeod Bethune (its successful outcome resulted in a statue within Washington's Lincoln Park). And later in 1970 she modified her statement: "This country, as far as I'm concerned, has been just as much antiblack and antifemale," she told the New York City Commission on Human Rights.[16]

BLACK FEMINIST POWER POLITICS IN COALITION

Chisholm's developing intersectional framework was embodied by her continuing rapport with Black women. A national figure now, she took her ideas on the road. She addressed meetings of Black women in the National Council of Negro Women and the Black Independent Women's Political League.[17] In January 1970, Chisholm made her first public trip west, to Southern California. The guest of honor at a local education foundation's banquet, she met Los Angeles's Black women leaders, including Yvonne Brathwaite (soon to be Burke), currently in the California state legislature; Ruth Washington, manager of the *Los Angeles Sentinel*; and Johnnie Tillmon, a national leader in the welfare rights movement. The local press was enamored. The *Sentinel* printed a summary of Chisholm's outspoken stances on various issues, which "astonished many of the press used to generalized partisan cliches from politicians." In an interview with the paper's reporter, Chisholm declared herself a militant, hinted that there was a "national conspiracy" against the Black Panthers, and called for attacking racism at "the roots."[18]

Black women advocated on Chisholm's behalf, too. When the New York Democratic leadership criticized Chisholm for endorsing Republican mayor John Lindsay, Black women from all five boroughs of the city rallied to her defense. They founded the United Black Women's Political League in August 1969. Etheline Dubin was Brooklyn's borough chair. Careful to distinguish their support of Chisholm from any implied support of Lindsay, the organization's spokeswomen nevertheless identified racism within conservatism as its driving issue and identified Lindsay as the mayoral candidate who best served racial justice. The group's first meeting, on September 13 in Town Hall, drew 700–1,000 people and an illustrious roster of speakers. Chisholm herself received a standing ovation with an electrifying speech. "We will be a force to reckon with and nobody will take us for granted any longer," she exclaimed to the rapt crowd. Black freedom movement veteran Fannie Lou Hamer told the audience that the fates of Black women in the North and the South were inextricably intertwined. Also on the program was a young ACLU lawyer and soon-to-be Lindsay appointee to the city's Commission on Human Rights, Eleanor Holmes Norton. The group's mission was to organize "as an independent force, within existing political organizations, and in concert with Black men, so that our considerable voting power elects officials who serve the interests of Black homes and families." Chisholm hoped that her crossing of party lines portended the demise of the two parties' monopoly on the political system.[19]

Reviving the ERA was a key goal of Chisholm's feminist supporters. The ERA represented a feminist challenge that Chisholm was eager to take up. Members of Congress had unsuccessfully and repeatedly introduced it over the past five decades. Months after being sworn in for her first term, Chisholm picked up the baton and introduced a bill reviving the ERA.[20] In accompanying remarks, she again cited the fact that she had experienced more discrimination based on gender than that based on race within politics, and she informed her colleagues that sexism was just as unacceptable as racism. Unfortunately, she had noticed that understandings of the wrongness of sexist discrimination, especially in employment, were missing. She made similar points about employment discrimination when she addressed Black women. The ERA, Chisholm said, directly affected all women, regardless of race. The ERA was not solely a law to benefit middle-class white women, as many assumed, but would also affect Black women, who worked for wages in great numbers. Those women had deep experience in their jobs but almost never held better-paid supervisory positions. The ERA, she argued, would provide a legal basis for challenging those inequities and others that any woman faced in her workplace, in any industry.[21]

Though her strongest supporters were and would continue to be Black women, Chisholm also maintained formal alliances with feminist organizations that were largely middle class and white. The ERA had been a priority of historically white feminist organizations for decades, and her championing of the bill strengthened her relationships with them. She accepted the Women's Equity Action League's invitation to join its national advisory board.[22] She also cosponsored a bill to increase family planning services. She was named a vice president of the New York City chapter of NOW, although her position was largely symbolic, and she also accepted the honorary presidency of NARAL. Chisholm would explain in *Unbought and Unbossed* why she formed an alliance with the mostly white-led organization. She had supported abortion reform in the New York State Assembly that would have expanded the medical grounds for abortion and simplified the process for obtaining approval, she pointed out. By 1969, however, when NARAL approached her to become president of that organization, she had decided that laws should leave the decision to end a pregnancy entirely up to a woman and her doctor. Her reasoning was thus: first, she personally knew women who had been harmed by illegal abortions; second, Black and brown children would benefit from being raised by prepared and willing parents; and third, poor people have little access to education about birth control. All three of these reasons to support NARAL directly affected her constituents, even though she was aware that some Black nationalist leaders had labeled birth control and abortion for Black women "genocide." A precursor to the reproductive justice movement, she took pains to point out that Black, brown, and poor women were generally in favor of access to birth control and abortion, and were disproportionately affected by lack of access to legal abortions. Her first public stance on behalf of the legalization of abortion came in September, when she appeared at a NARAL press conference in support of a lawsuit brought by four physicians against the state of New York. She also praised a recent California Supreme Court decision that the state's abortion law was unconstitutional.

Inside Congress, on the urging of NARAL, Chisholm considered and drafted a bill that would legalize abortions, but because she was unable to build sponsorship across political and party lines, she did not introduce it. She felt that such a coalition would be crucial to a bill's progress through the House, and that her political capital would be better spent in changing public opinion. She did continue to advocate for legalization, however. She testified in early December 1969 in front of both the House's and Senate's population growth task force panels. In both testimonies, she argued that abortion laws might more properly be thought of as compulsory pregnancy laws. Because the most dependable method of contraception, the pill, was not a failsafe, and complete abstinence was not practical, women who found themselves with an unwanted pregnancy were, in the United States, subject to compulsory pregnancy. Wealthier white women had access to medically indicated "therapeutic" abortions, which were financially out of reach for most women. In addition, not all unwanted children were illegitimate. Although many illegitimate children, who were financially costly in terms of Aid to Families with Dependent Children benefits, were the result of unplanned pregnancies, Chisholm marshaled statistical evidence to suggest that nearly a quarter of married pregnancies were unwanted. For poor families, additional children deepened poverty. Chisholm's impassioned testimony to both committees asked her congressional colleagues to consider which was more immoral: ending a pregnancy or consigning a child to a life of poverty with an unprepared mother. Furthermore, to those Black nationalists who maintained that abortion was a path to genocide, Chisholm remarked that Black women should never be required to have abortions, but should nonetheless have the option of obtaining them. Chair of the House committee George H. W. Bush of Texas thought that her well-researched presentation was so helpful that it should be inserted into the *Congressional Record*.[23]

In addition to NARAL, Chisholm worked closely with NOW on a variety of issues. She corresponded with NOW national president Delores Alexander in early 1970 about the still-current practice of segregating men and women (or "ladies" and "gentlemen") in the House gallery and counseled Alexander to hold a protest about it. NOW also tried to get her appointed to the House Committee on the Judiciary in 1970. A petition with over one hundred signatures was hand-delivered to Wilbur Mills during the Senate hearings on the ERA, urging him to place her on that committee, though he never did.[24] Chisholm cosponsored the Women's Strike for Equality, organized by NOW, in August 1970. The event, with its emblematic slogan "Don't Iron While the Strike Is Hot," commemorated the fiftieth anniversary of the Twentieth Amendment's passage and urged passage of the ERA. Chisholm marched in the parade down Fifth Avenue with Betty Friedan, Flo Kennedy,

Eleanor Holmes Norton, Beulah Sanders of the National Welfare Rights Organization, her soon-to-be colleague in the House Bella Abzug, and former congresswoman Jeanette Rankin.[25]

Chisholm's developing ideas on the interlocking realities of race, sex, and class and her collaborations with others built a foundation for her legislative priorities. Her presence as a Black feminist on Capitol Hill would shape the fights that she took on, both over policy and in elections. While she found common cause and partnerships, implementing her ideas in practice was challenging. The president and a good number of congressional colleagues stood in opposition. Chisholm would have to devise ways to move around the obstacles and enact Black feminist policy through legislation.

10
GUNS, BUTTER, AND JUSTICE

It comes as no surprise that Chisholm's work as a government official who was defining Black feminist power politics cut right across America's dividing lines. In 1969, race, sex, and Vietnam divided Americans, and Richard Nixon exacerbated these issues. Although he presented himself as the Great Conciliator, he immediately set about exorcising Great Society ghosts by consolidating his anti-Black support among the Silent Majority and in the South. He delayed civil rights policy implementation and cracked down on protesters to impose "law and order." Far from planning peace in Vietnam, as he had promised on the campaign trail, he escalated the war and began illegally bombing Cambodia. He had a disdain for congresspeople and senators, claiming that "they had the luxury of criticism without responsibility."[1]

Chisholm stood perpendicular to most of Nixon's ideology. On both "guns and butter" and civil liberties issues, Chisholm and her other Black colleagues in the House clashed with President Nixon often. Although the nine made up only 2 percent of the House, this number was half again the number of Black members in the previous House. Besides criticizing the Vietnam War, the informal group's concerns centered on domestic policy and priorities. And despite having been elected from left-leaning Brooklyn, she faced an uphill battle as national politics turned right. Through the first half of her congressional career, she would become increasingly frustrated with Nixon as an obstacle to what she believed to be necessary political reforms. She began to think that meaningful reform would have to wait until the end of the Nixon administration, even as she grew alarmed at the political repression of his tenure.[2]

Still, she contributed to change as effectively as she could. Her energies were expended on intertwined concerns: opposing the war in Vietnam on Black feminist grounds, collaborating to protect the gains of the Black freedom struggle and transform the movement into policy change, making the federal government responsive to the economic needs of the American people, and attending to her New York Democratic organization and constituents.

Chisholm's first floor speech in the House of Representatives was about Vietnam. Although she had not identified strongly with the New Politics of 1968, her intersectional perspective led her to see the war as a major obstacle to American equality. Allard Lowenstein, erstwhile of the campaign to draft Eugene McCarthy and now a representative from Long Island, organized a four-hour "talk-in" on the war with the help of Chisholm and William Fitts Ryan for March 26. The atmosphere in the House was more charged than usual that day because black-garbed protesters from Women Strike for Peace were crowding one corner of the gallery. About 1,000 mostly white, middle class women protesters had converged on Washington, D.C., for a "Vietnam Protest Lobby" against the Vietnam War, the first such protest since Richard Nixon's presidential inauguration two months before. Chisholm herself had encouraged members of Women Strike for Peace to attend. There had been some shuffling and grumbling in the gallery because Capitol officials had only allowed fifty women in at a time for fifteen-minute shifts until antiwar representatives interceded and opened one entire side of the gallery for the protesters.[3]

What compelled Chisholm to speak was not her opposition to the war per se. Rather, she was moved by the juxtaposition of increased spending on defense with cutbacks on programs for poorer Americans: on the very same day Nixon had announced a new missile defense system, he also announced budget cuts to the Head Start program in Washington, D.C. "For whatever it was worth, even if it would only get it off my chest," she wanted to express her disgust with the hypocrisy of government spending priorities, she recalled. "As a teacher, and as a woman, I do not think I can ever understand what kind of values can be involved in spending $9 billion—and more, I am sure—on elaborate, unnecessary, and impractical weapons when several thousand disadvantaged children in the Nation's Capital get nothing," she lamented. She vehemently disagreed with those who said that domestic spending on city schools would have to wait until the Vietnam War ended, which Nixon's Secretary of Defense Melvin Laird had said would take at least two more years. "Two more years," Chisholm fulminated, "of high taxes to feed the cancerous growth of a Defense Department budget. . . . Two more years of too little being done to fight our greatest enemies, poverty, prejudice, and neglect here in our own country." Chisholm ended her speech with a declaration that she would vote "no" on any defense funding bill brought before the House until that day "when our values and priorities have been turned right-side up again" and spending was once again on "people and peace."[4] As she later recalled, "I could not vote for money for war while funds were being denied to feed, house, and school Americans." She also pointed to what she saw as wasteful spending on audits of local nonprofits and the Job Corps while only a handful of auditors monitored the far greater sums exchanging hands through defense contracts. Her speech did not lead to any action by Congress or even the support of colleagues who did not already agree with her, though she had gotten it off her chest and NBC did cover it on the evening news.[5]

The response was enthusiastic in the activist community, however. Chisholm's stance on the war as "neither just nor unavoidable," and her public articulation of it, won her support among peace activists and particularly among youth. She attracted increased attention from students and "began to be drowned in requests to speak on campuses." The *Chicago Defender* also reported favorably on her speech, likening her to a "female David with a slingshot going up against the mighty Goliath" and reporting that "the galleries resounded with applause." Later, Women Strike for Peace would use Chisholm's words to urge New York mayoral candidates to participate in a taxpayer's revolt in protest of military spending.[6]

The Speech against the War, as she called it, was the beginning of several high-profile criticisms she would make. In May, she cosponsored New York colleague Ed Koch's bill calling for an immediate 100,000 reduction in troops and an immediate cease-fire.[7] She also refused to malign the protesters who sought an end to the war, saying instead that U.S. universities must address the root causes of student unrest or pay the price in the form of destruction of property.[8] Later on in May she brought that perspective to the House when she addressed a subcommittee of Education and Labor on the same issue. Unlike conservatives who wanted to remove federal aid from institutions where demonstrations took place, Chisholm argued that Congress ought to take the complaints of the students seriously.[9] June continued Chisholm's crusade as a high-profile antiwar figure. Chisholm was one of forty-five national legislators who signed a report that called for a drastic reduction in troops in Vietnam, the formation of a coalition government there, a moratorium on nuclear testing and missile defense systems, a new office for reviewing defense expenditures, and more congressional supervision of defense priorities.[10] Then she publicly supported a group of largely Quaker protesters who were staging weekly meetings for worship with readings of the names of the Vietnam War dead on the Capitol steps. Chisholm, alongside colleagues Ed Koch, Don Edwards, and George Brown, signed a letter to her colleagues that asserted that the First Amendment rights of the group were being violated by their repeated arrests.[11] Chisholm and her fellow signatories decided to join the protesters but avoided arrest even as the Capitol Police took many of the Quakers into custody. She and the other members of Congress continued to read the names for a short time after the arrests.[12] She also cosponsored a resolution that sought to limit the arms race with the Soviet Union and spoke out in support of a constituent in her district, Johnny Woodfin.[13] Woodfin, a private in the army, had circulated a petition against the war and led a public antiwar event. He was now at risk of a dishonorable discharge. "Soldiers are citizens too," she remarked, "and they should be afforded all the rights and privileges of civilians." Although she could not stop the processes in place against Private Woodfin, she asked her colleagues to act to prevent such cases in the future, and she called for military justice reform.[14]

As the summer of 1969 gave way to fall, opposition to the war spread and Chisholm remained visibly supportive of the protesters and critical of Nixon. The public opinion scales were shifting in her favor. Approval of Nixon's handling of the war slipped from 47 percent in June to 35 percent in September, while the percentage that disapproved went from 45 to 57 percent in the same period. The draft was coming to seem increasingly capricious and unfair, and Nixon had promised to reform the process into a truly randomized one in May, but a new policy had failed to materialize. Congress struggled to push meaningful draft reform through legislation. Over the summer, multiple congresspeople submitted draft reform bills, though no hearings had been scheduled, and nearly 3,000 draft resistance cases were on federal criminal court dockets nationwide.[15] Chisholm joined Frank Thompson of New Jersey's coalition of thirty-eight congressional colleagues to support a randomized draft lottery bill, which Thompson submitted on October 3. Thompson's bill extended student eligibility for draft deferments and established a method to process deferments uniformly and fairly. It never got out of committee. Then Whitney Young of the National Urban League, who had long refused to speak out on the war, publicly condemned it and thus became the first Black leader of a major organization to publicly oppose the war since Martin Luther King Jr. had done so in 1967.[16]

Days after Young's statement, the Vietnam Moratorium Committee organized a massive nationwide demonstration: a day of speeches, rallies, and demonstrations in communities across the country on October 15. Chisholm herself made two appearances. In the Capitol late the night before the big day, she addressed the floor. Wondering aloud why American mothers were refusing to display gold stars, or accept the American flags from their sons' coffins, she answered herself by explaining how American citizens had realized that Vietnam was an unjust war. To counter claims of anti-Americanism on the part of protesters, she argued that it was the hawks in government who subverted the Constitution, refused to listen to the "voice of the people," and thus were un-American. Then she flew back to New York, where she spoke at a large gathering in Bryant Park.[17]

The day of demonstrations did not go unnoticed by the House Armed Services Committee, which subsequently voted to send Nixon's draft reform bill to the floor of the House, where it passed 382–13.[18] But Chisholm and four of her Black congressional colleagues (Clay, Conyers, Diggs, and Hawkins) were among the thirteen House members who voted against the bill on the grounds that it was too little, too late. On the floor of the House, Chisholm objected on the grounds that substantive reform and genuine debate over the bill had not occurred. The new draft still privileged white, affluent Americans, and remained unequal at its core. In her comments to the press, she pointed out that those most affected, nonwhite and poor young Americans, had had no opportunity to present their views in testimony on the bill.[19] Shortly afterward, when the New Mobilization Committee to End the War in Vietnam (the New Mobe) organized a second massive protest for November 13 and 14, Chisholm formally endorsed their efforts. Three hundred thousand people were present at the Washington rally, the largest in Washington's history, and a few thousand took part in activities in other cities.[20] The war continued on, however, while the new draft lottery was held for the first time on December 1, 1969.

Chisholm's opposition to the war, on moral and economic grounds, had not been the top priority of her campaign. But it was the urgent issue of 1969 and pitted outsize military spending over funding for domestic programs— the classic guns versus butter conundrum. Chisholm came down squarely on the side of butter, because that was what her constituents needed. But her actions did not escape notice by young activists, and her credibility as a rare politician who was willing to challenge unchecked military might dramatically rose among them.

THE DEMOCRATIC SELECT COMMITTEE

The war in Vietnam was inextricably linked to the Black freedom struggle as Black men were disproportionately drafted and killed in the war. But furthering the Black freedom struggle for Chisholm required both defense and offense. Defense meant repelling Nixon's encroachments on gains from the War on Poverty and the civil rights era to date. Through his first term, Chisholm and her Black colleagues on the Democratic Select Committee continued to be at odds with Nixon over domestic issues, and registered objections wherever possible. His administration was an unfortunate change of fortune for liberals on the Hill, who had become accustomed to getting their legislation passed during the Johnson era. Nixon himself was somewhat indifferent to domestic policy except, significantly, school integration, the blocking of which was the cornerstone of his Southern Strategy.[21] What was more, people distrusted him. "There was a nervousness about him even before Watergate," Shirley Downs remembered. He had a history of participating heavily in the House Un-American Activities Committee during his early days in Congress.[22]

At first, the Black legislators mostly played defense against Nixon's Southern Strategy. Nixon had figured out that disgruntled southern Democrats were ripe for the Republican Party to pick. Enduring disapproval from not just Black congresspeople but also from the public at large, he increasingly turned to his allies in the South for support. Chisholm and her Black colleagues publicly decried his obstruction of civil rights initiatives. In April, they wrote to Nixon that they believed his administration was attacking the Equal Employment Opportunity Commission in order to reverse the gains of the 1960s, including awarding contracts to companies that had racist policies. All of the Black representatives signed except for William Dawson.[23]

Black members of Congress soon found themselves engaged in another fight against the president's determination to win support in the South. In a stroke of opportunity for Nixon that May, both U.S. Supreme Court chief justice Earl Warren retired and liberal associate justice Abe Fortas resigned. Nixon nominated and easily won confirmation for the relatively uncontroversial Warren. E. Burger for the chief justice position. But, in a political calculation designed to build support in the South, he nominated South Carolinian Clement Haynsworth, of the U.S. Court of Appeals for the Fourth Circuit, for the associate justice seat. A firestorm commenced. Haynsworth's record showed that he had delayed school desegregation and had favored the employer in five labor-versus-management cases. Civil rights activists and politicians were appalled.

The unofficial Black bloc in the House mobilized against Haynsworth. Chisholm and the other Black representatives (minus Dawson) signed a statement that John Conyers read in front of the Senate Judiciary Committee. Chisholm followed Conyers with testimony against the nomination. She predicted that Haynsworth would impede the progress of equality as an associate justice. "The Supreme Court," she said, "is the one institution that has given us hope when everything else has been lost on the city and state level." Furthermore, she warned that rioting would become a more attractive option to pursuing rights through the courts in the future. She was backed up by her colleagues Charlie Diggs, Bill Clay, and Louis Stokes, plus Clarence Mitchell and Joe Rauh of the Leadership Conference on Civil Rights. It seemed to Chisholm "that the effect was visible" on the senators present, although she admitted to not knowing whether the action had actually changed any votes. The committee room was conspicuously missing southern senators James Eastland and Sam Ervin during her testimony. Regardless, the experience left an indelible impression. "It was during the Haynsworth affair that I most clearly saw racism at work in the Congress," she recalled, noting that "the contempt that radiated from some of the Judiciary Committee was astonishing," with most members except for Birch Bayh projecting indifference to witnesses who criticized the nominee on the basis of his racism. Once the pro–civil rights witnesses were finished, Senators Eastland and Ervin reappeared, and the panel continued its proceedings. Eventually corruption allegations sank Haynsworth's nomination, although Nixon still refused to withdraw the nomination. It was eventually defeated on the Senate floor, 55–45, in November.[24]

Nixon's next nominee was even worse, however. In January 1970 he chose Harrold Carswell, a "good ol' boy from South Georgia" who sat on the U.S. Court of Appeals in New Orleans. No doubt hoping to signal his friendliness to southerners, Nixon quickly found that his dog-whistle move was all too audible. An ad that Carswell had used during his 1948 bid for a seat in the Georgia state legislature that stated his undying commitment to segregation surfaced. His efforts to keep a golf course all-white did, too.[25] Confirmation hearing testimony alleged Carswell's racist actions up until 1966.[26] Chisholm, with Bill Clay, Louis Stokes, and five other House members, began a campaign to convince their colleagues in the Senate to oppose Carswell. Their strategy was to organize voters in their home states to urge senators from those states to vote against the nomination.[27] Senators, even Republican ones, refused to back Carswell. Eventually the nominee was rejected by the Senate and Nixon successfully nominated Harry Blackmun, who would eventually write the majority decision in *Roe v. Wade*.[28]

But Chisholm and the Democratic Select Committee kept an eye on Nixon's nominations. When Nixon, at the suggestion of Senator Strom Thurmond, nominated segregationist attorney Joseph Rogers to be the U.S. attorney for South Carolina, Chisholm was among those who requested a Senate hearing on the appointment.[29] Late that June, after rumors that the administration was planning to slow down school integration, Chisholm and her Black colleagues sent a sharp statement to Nixon. Swerving from the current plan in any way would be "a betrayal" of Black Americans, and the president's refusal to uphold the Constitution by following the guidelines showed that he would sell "the birthright of black children for political considerations" and that his campaign promises were "worthless," they wrote.[30]

The colleagues who signed that letter—Chisholm, Clay, Conyers, Hawkins, Powell, Nix, Diggs, and Stokes—were not too far off when they suggested that Nixon was sacrificing civil rights to political expediency. Because much of Nixon's remaining support was in the South, and because he had been advised by his aide and former Strom Thurmond staffer Harry Dent that it was possible to win a majority of southern voters over to the Republican Party, he sought to please southern political allies. This meant turning back civil rights and nominating southerners for federal posts. Chisholm was incensed when news leaked that Nixon, at the behest of Senator John Stennis of Mississippi, sent a memorandum urging a slowdown of school desegregation to several high officials in his administration. The memo resulted in Secretary of Health, Education, and Welfare Robert Finch successfully convincing a federal judge to move the desegregation deadline in Mississippi.[31] Chisholm issued a statement in which she accurately described the Southern Strategy: "Nixon's statement [about the memo] this week was veiled in a dense fog of vague, fine-sounding phrases," she remarked. "But it was also loaded with code words like 'neighborhood schools' and references to school busing that made it easy for southern segregationists to understand what it means. Nixon is paying off another installment of his 1968 debt to Dixie, and trying to store up credit for 1972." She was less accurate, however, in her prediction that Nixon's appeal to segregationists would "be his Vietnam" and that the country would "refuse to take" the direction toward undoing the gains of the civil rights era.[32] As her time in Congress continued, the preservation of those gains would begin to eclipse the efforts to score new ones.

Still, supporting the Black freedom struggle involved playing offense, too. Chisholm and the other Black Democratic Select Committee members brought the anti-apartheid movement to the fore when they jointly signed a statement asking for a sanction on South African Airways. Released by Diggs in his capacity as chair of the Subcommittee on Africa of the Foreign Affairs Committee and his affiliation with the American Committee on Africa, the statement's 162 Black signatories argued that to allow South African Airways to fly to the United States was to support apartheid. They also pointed out that some Americans—Black Americans—would not be welcome on the flights and at the posh tourist spots that the airline promoted in its advertisements. The statement was the idea of longtime activist (and erstwhile Farmer supporter) A. Philip Randolph. Chisholm would continue to criticize South Africa in the years ahead.[33]

BLACK FEMINIST POWER POLITICS ON ECONOMIC AND POLITICAL FREEDOM

Chisholm saw economic justice as a logical next step in the Black freedom struggle. She would promote redistributive policies during her entire time in Congress. In April of her first year, she spoke to a group of Black women antipoverty activists visiting the Capitol, the first of many such groups she would welcome.[34] The agendas of poor people drove her policy ideas. She advocated for cash payments and training in financial literacy rather than food stamps or food banks, because she said lining up for food or handing over stamps insulted people's dignity. "Who wants to be told what to eat?" she asked rhetorically. It was better to issue funds with fewer strings attached.[35] In July, she spoke on the House floor about improving the fairness of tax laws. "People who earn an income below poverty level pay Government taxes while millionaires play on Florida islands. Workers sacrifice essential goods so that Lockheed can continue to receive a 7 percent investment credit," she said. Slightly over a week later, she cosponsored Patsy Mink's bill that called for a higher personal income tax exemption. The bill sought to ease the burden on poor and middle-income taxpayers. She endorsed the National Conference of Anti-Poverty Agency's meeting at Columbia University, called in response to Nixon's policies, and led an interracial coalition of thirteen representatives calling for General Motors to increase its accountability to Black Americans.[36]

At the end of 1969, Chisholm began to align visibly with Black Power activists. In September, Chisholm and Adam Clayton Powell, together in a convertible, gave the Black Power clenched fist sign as they waved to crowds at a Harlem parade.[37] The Democratic Select Committee, together with some liberal white colleagues, jointly condemned the police killing of Black Panthers Fred Hampton and Mark Clark in Chicago that December. Hampton, the twenty-one-year-old charismatic leader of the Chicago branch, had already experienced police harassment and the party's phones had been tapped through the FBI's COINTELPRO program. Although Chicago police insisted that they had been let into Panther headquarters, and then had been fired upon first in the early hours of December 4, forensic evidence suggested that police had actually broken into the apartment and begun shooting while the residents were asleep. Now she joined with several Black and white colleagues (William Dawson was conspicuously absent, despite representing Chicago) to call for an extension of the soon-to-expire National Commission on the Causes and Prevention of Violence so that it could look into the incident. Eventually, the Justice Department conducted its own grand jury investigation, which failed to indict any police officers, although the Illinois state attorney who had issued the order for the raid was resoundingly defeated in the next election.[38]

In the aftermath of what had transpired in Chicago, Chisholm attacked the McCarthy era McCarran Act as the House Committee on Internal Security debated its renewal. The McCarran Act had been passed during the Korean War in 1950, at the height of anticommunist and anti-espionage fervor. Now, twenty years later, Chisholm was one of a group of legislators who feared that the act could be used to jail people "merely on suspicion," as Patsy Mink put it. Chisholm called out the racist double standard in the application of the act's provisions and, indeed, in the attitude of the Justice Department. While conservative groups such as the Ku Klux Klan and the Minutemen had stockpiled arms and prepared for violence against other Americans, especially Black ones, they encountered relatively little interference from law enforcement. Unsurprisingly, groups on the left, such as the Black Panthers and Students for a Democratic Society, that also prepared themselves for violence in the name of self-defense were targeted by the police. Over the past two years, the McCarran Act had been used to repress Black activists to the extent that $1 million had been allocated for internment camps, and local police nationwide had raided Black Panther headquarters. The killings in Chicago and the persecution of the Chicago Seven were simply the most visible incident. "It has become apparent in America that dissent can no longer be tolerated particularly if said dissent exposes the grievances, insults, mistreatment, and injustice towards black people who have been the most loyal citizens of this country despite the tremendous abuse of us as a people," Chisholm argued. She expressed fear for democracy itself and that Black Americans were similarly afraid. The McCarran Act must be repealed, then, in the interest in preserving American democracy. Chisholm was careful to say that she did not agree with all of the Black Panthers' ideas and actions, but there was no double standard for justice, she argued. All "civil and personal liberties of all people in this country must be protected until proven guilty," she told her colleagues at the committee hearing. One of them was appalled that she would defend the rights of Black Panthers. William Scherle (R-IA) declared, aghast, "With all due respect, I sure feel sorry for you." Chisholm quipped back, "I can understand why you would feel sorry for me, so it is quite mutual, sir."[39] Ultimately, Chisholm's view would prevail. The McCarran Act was repealed in 1971, and a new Non-Detention Act specified, "No citizen shall be imprisoned or otherwise detained by the United States except pursuant to an act of Congress."[40]

Chisholm was also speaking out on behalf of Black Power at the podium. Her spring 1970 speech at Wellesley College was billed as an Earth Day address, but she explained to her audience how racism was a "cancer eating away at the heart of America" and called for fair treatment of the Black Panthers.[41] She also released a statement in defense of Joan Bird, a twenty-one-year-old Bronx Community College student who was a member of the New York Black Panthers. "Joan Bird," Chisholm explained, "is one of millions of women who as a result of suffering the deepest oppression on every level of social, economic, and political life are then jailed for trying to change the conditions which they didn't create but of which they remain the victims."[42]

In addition to protecting democracy, welfare reform was central to Chisholm's Black feminist power vision in her first term. As Robert Self has pointed out, in the late 1960s welfare was unpopular across the political spectrum. It had also come under heavy criticism from recipients themselves, not because of their objection to its existence but because of the invasive surveillance by the state that accepting it brought upon them and the paltry amounts disbursed. Welfare rights activists reconceptualized the receipt of welfare as their right as citizens.[43] They argued that a country as wealthy as the United States ought to ensure citizens had a basic income, with access to the necessities of life.[44] Chisholm began her advocacy for federal welfare reform a few months into her first term. Like others in Washington, and even Nixon himself, Chisholm critiqued the current welfare system. But Chisholm did so from the standpoint of welfare rights activists, who stood at the heart of Black feminist power's intersectional concerns. Chisholm and her fellow New York representative Allard Lowenstein cowrote a bill, cosponsored by eighteen others, to increase the federal share of welfare and Medicaid payments from 50 to 90 percent. The bill would also provide minimum standards of aid and remove the cap on the number of covered children. In Chisholm's view, "The thrust of this bill is to begin the process of removing the worst injustices of the present law and establish a more equitable base of support for social service programs." But it did not get out of the Committee on Ways and Means.[45]

The issue came up again, however, in Nixon's proposed Family Assistance Plan (FAP).[46] The 1970 bill guaranteed an annual income of $1,600 for a family of four and provided job training. Chisholm, like most welfare rights activists, including George Wiley of the National Welfare Rights Organization, saw the bill as providing much too little. She pointed out that the U.S. Department of Labor set $6,207 as the minimum figure for an "acceptable" standard of living in a city. She also criticized Nixon's scheme as amounting to forced labor because of its compulsory work provision. "If Congress can take the liberty to grant themselves a raise to $42,500 a year and at the same time expect that a family of four can live on $1,600 a year, then it is time for deep evaluation of what we are trying to accomplish with our programs," she suggested on the floor.[47] She was in the minority, however; the bill passed the House, although it stalled in the Senate.[48]

NEW YORK: CONSTITUENTS AND LOCAL PARTY POLITICS

Notwithstanding the powerful national currents that Chisholm navigated, she still remained the representative for Bedford-Stuyvesant and the committeewoman for New York's Democratic Party, and she had to get reelected in 1970. She worked on local issues: the redevelopment of the closed Brooklyn Naval Yard and funding for local social services, including the McDonough Street Community Center, the Opportunities Industrialization Center, the Charles Drew Neighborhood Health Center, the Brooklyn Local Economic Development Corporation, and the Consumer Action Program of Bedford-Stuyvesant. She helped a local technology company get a Department of Defense contract and a local bus company get its charter to operate, and attempted to mediate an acrimonious conflict between the board and director of a neighborhood health clinic.[49] She cooperated with the Bedford-Stuyvesant branch of Jesse Jackson's Operation Breadbasket to expose discrimination in the city's Manpower programs.[50] A group of schoolchildren who documented abandoned buildings and cars, trash-strewn vacant lots, and filthy streets and sidewalks in the district briefed her staff.[51] Chisholm lent her public support to a group of largely Black and Puerto Rican women hospital workers who were striking in order to demand the right to unionize in Fort Greene, Brooklyn. She and Percy Sutton, now Manhattan borough president, also supported a similar Charleston, South Carolina, strike, which they compared to the 1968 Memphis strike that Martin Luther King Jr. had been aiding when he was shot. At issue, they said, were human dignity, fair pay, and the right to unionize. She also supported a community group in Manhattan that protested Pratt Institute's purchase of a housing development, and turned down an honorary degree from Pratt when a tenants' group telegraphed her asking her to do so.[52]

Chisholm also kept a hand in contentious local Democratic Party politics. Nationally, she called for the Democratic National Committee to employ more Black staff. She advocated for reform of the New York state Democratic Party's elections guidelines.[53] But party politics in New York City were more important to her own political fortunes. She had miffed a few in the Unity Democratic Club by moving outside the club's district when she bought the row house in Crown Heights. Tom Fortune was finding it "easier to deal with Congresswoman Chisholm through Conrad Chisholm," and he did not approve of the congresswoman's protest against her original committee assignment.[54] She also found herself in a struggle for power citywide. Early in the year Chisholm herself had been rumored to be considering a run for mayor of New York City. Democratic New York City mayoral candidate James Scheuer had sought Chisholm's counsel in choosing a Black person to run on his slate with him, and she supported his eventual choice, Manhattan Assemblyman Charlie Rangel, for city council.[55] But Brooklyn Democrats (led by Steingut and new leader Meade Esposito) were seen as the Democratic organization that was most able to draw votes in the city.

They favored Hugh Carey as the Democratic nominee.[56] Chisholm, having abandoned running for mayor herself, came out for Scheuer, bucking the Brooklyn leader. Mincing no words, she leveled strong criticism at the local Democratic leaders who were, she said, "only interested in feathering their own nests, and not in the people's welfare." She and Percy Sutton strongly endorsed Charlie Rangel for city council in their capacity as cochairs for the Citizens Committee for Rangel.[57]

When her chosen candidate did not win the Democratic primary, Chisholm would make her endorsement of Liberal Party candidate John Lindsay instead, much to the consternation of Democratic leadership. Lindsay was the incumbent, who had been elected as a Republican previously. Lindsay had won his first term as mayor as a liberal Republican. He was something of a paradox. On the one hand, he was, as Charlayne Hunter-Gault has described him, "a square-jawed Yale-educated, tennis- and squash-playing W.A.S.P. from a well-connected family, a Republican, who entered politics representing 'The Silk Stocking District' of New York to boot." On the other hand, he had utilized War on Poverty money to create empowerment programs for poor and nonwhite empowerment programs, sought to curb police brutality, raised taxes to provide social services, appointed nonwhite officials to high-profile city positions, and personally ventured into Harlem and Bedford-Stuyvesant to meet with his Black constituents. As vice president of the Kerner Commission, charged to assess the reasons for the urban violence that had combusted in 1967, Lindsay and two of his staffers had written the signature phrase, "Our Nation is moving toward two societies, one black, one white—separate and unequal."[58] He had also supported the Black advocates of community control during the Ocean Hill-Brownsville strike. Hoping for support from nonwhite and liberal white voters, Lindsay decided to stay in the race as an independent candidate and chose to run on the Liberal Party ticket.

His base was in the city's Black residents, on the one hand, and middle-class white liberals, on the other. A conspicuous absence among his supporters were working-class Italian, Irish, and Jewish voters. Indeed, Lindsay may have exploited the class and ethnic differences between himself and the supporters of his Democratic opponent, Mario Procaccino, who skewed far more working-class and white ethnic. He and his camp sometimes caricatured Procaccino as an emotional Italian and his supporters as anti-Black racists. Unfortunately for Procaccino, the stereotype stuck. It was not helped by his ill-advised remark to a group of Black voters that "my heart is as black as yours." He was referring to the discrimination that he had faced as an Italian American, but the comment fell flat on the audience of people who lacked the ability to assimilate into whiteness at all.[59] In other words, local

New York politics bore some resemblance to national politics: the ascendant politics of law and order, and the struggles of liberal politicians to hold onto some power. This was New York City, however, and the national rules didn't quite apply.

In the summer of 1969, Lindsay found himself casting about for supporters as he tried to get his independent campaign off the ground. Lindsay saw an opportunity to attract more liberal Democratic voters and managed to garner the endorsement of the New Democratic Coalition in mid-July. Getting Shirley Chisholm to sign on would be a coup because of her status as state committeewoman in the Democratic Party and as a powerful symbol of Black political power in the city. She decided to side with Black New Yorkers over the Democratic Party, and publicly announced her decision at a church in Baltimore. Saying that "all the liberal and reform people have to support Lindsay," she declared that she would officially endorse Lindsay at a press conference, with the mayor, at Gracie Mansion on the following Tuesday.[60] This was news to her home district; Brooklyn political figures Tom Fortune, Sam Wright, and William Thompson all heard of her decision via the radio. For their part, they had refused to support the Democrat, law-and-order candidate Mario Procaccino, but had decided to abstain from a vote on whether to endorse him instead of voting "no."[61] At the press conference, Chisholm explained that she was supporting Lindsay because "he has appealed to our hopes rather than our fears," referring to the racial pluralism that Lindsay had shown during the Ocean Hill-Brownsville conflict and its contrast to Procaccino's law-and-order dog-whistling.

The Democratic Party establishment was displeased. According to the state's election laws, the party did have the authority to remove any member for "disloyalty to the party, corruption in office, or enrollment in another party," although the rule was seldom observed. Leader Esposito chided Chisholm: "As Democratic National Committeewoman, Mrs. Chisholm owes responsibility to the Democratic Party. You can't take the honors and shirk the responsibilities." Some from Procaccino's camp advocated expelling Democratic Lindsay supporters from the party. Others, including her congressional colleague Emanuel Celler, called for removing Chisholm's Democratic committeewoman seat from her as discipline for breaking party lines. Chisholm herself had to reassure her local supporters in a hastily called meeting at her district office after the rain of criticism—which she did by pointing out that no other local leaders had the political courage to stand up to the Democratic machine. "Let the chips fall where they may," she declared. "I am still and will continue to be unbought and unbossed."[62] She used her favorite line again to reinforce her political agenda as distinct from those who followed political money more than political principles.

Chisholm had calculated her position correctly. Democrats were hesitant to make a martyr out of Chisholm and further drive away Black and Latinx voters. Procaccino and the state chair declined to censure Chisholm, sensing that it would drive liberal voters further away from him. As the *New York Times* put it, "Mrs. Chisholm has become something of a national liberal symbol and some Democrats argue that even criticizing her will drive liberals away from Mr. Procaccino."[63] Indeed, the New Democratic Coalition would publicly praise Chisholm for her choice. Having escaped unscathed, Chisholm and Lindsay collaborated on a few appearances, including meeting with the Secretary of the Navy in an effort to preserve jobs in the Brooklyn Navy Yard and traveling to the 1969 Southern Christian Leadership Conference meeting. When rumors flew about a breach in the two politicians' relationship, Chisholm reaffirmed her support of Lindsay in powerful terms. "He wants to fulfill the American dream so that people like us can be a part of it," she told a crowd of supporters at the official dedication of her new district office.[64] Despite the fact that fewer Democrats lent their support than he would have liked, Lindsay managed to log a victory and continue on to a second term as mayor. He would eventually join the Democratic Party. As a result, Chisholm seemed prescient.

Chisholm also deployed her growing power in the next year's governor's race. In early 1970, Chisholm formally endorsed Howard Samuels for governor and took on the role as cochair for his support committee.[65] At the New York State Democratic Convention, drama over the election intensified. The state leadership chose Arthur Goldberg as its candidate. Samuels had not won the party's backing, but Chisholm exerted what influence she could over the next name on the ticket. She pushed her colleagues to tap Basil Paterson, a son of Caribbean immigrants and in the same generation as Chisholm, as lieutenant governor. In one version of the story, her colleagues were reluctant to endorse a Black man, arguing that Goldberg's Jewishness was already enough of an electoral liability. One delegate charged that Chisholm was part of a "sinister cabal" within the state party that advanced the agenda of "minority special-interest groups." Whether a "cabal" or not, Chisholm led two walk-outs from the convention floor by Black delegates. In one version of how the second walk-out started, Chisholm accused fellow delegates of being "nothing but robots and automatons." When someone shouted at her to get off the stage, she retorted, "You come and get me off." In another version, Paterson's endorsement was already a done deal and Chisholm was simply grandstanding. At any rate, Paterson did gain the lieutenant governor nomination. She would not give up on Samuels, however. That June, she solicited support for Samuels in the upcoming primary and campaigned against Goldberg. Again, she came under fire— and this time her erstwhile allies Percy Sutton and Tom Fortune distanced themselves from her. Samuels lost in the primary (though he did well in Bedford-Stuyvesant, thanks to Chisholm), and Goldberg won the nomination.[66] The Democratic ticket of Goldberg and Paterson would lose the general election, however.

Chisholm herself won her own reelection handily, by an over 5-to-1 margin.[67] This time, she was endorsed by the Liberal Party for the Twelfth District, which had been redistricted again and lost part of Crown Heights while it gained part of Ocean Hill-Brownsville. It was now 66 percent Black. Her challengers were "two political unknowns." The Republicans had even considered endorsing Chisholm. Unsurprisingly, Chisholm declared that she was not "actively campaigning," because she did not take her opponents seriously and she had much work to do in Washington. She conducted a "low-key" campaign, walking the streets to chat with constituents and publishing one newsletter.[68]

She had emerged as the most prominent Black voice in the city, illustrated by the fact that leaders of a Queens prison uprising demanded to be allowed to meet with her. In the last days of her 1970 campaign, prisoners in the Long Island City branch of the Queens House of Detention grabbed the keys from their guards and started unlocking cells. The uprising came after a small uprising at the upstate Attica correctional facility's metal shop and presaged the larger one at Attica the following September. They took over several cellblocks with twenty-three guards and civilians as hostages. Inmates from three other prisons quickly followed suit, creating "perhaps the worst crisis in the history of the city's prisons." The takeover was a protest against racism, brutality on the part of the guards, bad food, overcrowding, and the selection of a true jury of their peers for the thirteen New York Black Panthers presently awaiting trial. Hostages declared that they were well treated, and some were even sympathetic to the cause. Protest leaders at Long Island City demanded to see Chisholm and her colleague Herman Badillo, Nation of Islam leader Louis Farrakhan, and Mayor Lindsay, in order to negotiate a resolution. After a long overnight session with Chisholm, Badillo, and Farrakhan, judges were dispatched to the jail to hold immediate bail hearings.[69] Chisholm had become a symbol of Black political power to everyday people.

At the end of her first term, Chisholm had signaled her priorities from her Black feminist power standpoint. With the help of strategic allies she had questioned the Vietnam War, pushed to protect the gains and activists of the Black freedom struggle, and developed a critique of economic and welfare policy in coalition with other Black feminists. She had sought to respond to her New York constituents while deepening her influence in the state's Democratic Party. She had also developed a following of devotees. But the work was still uphill in the climate of the Nixon administration. She needed more momentum. Having established her bailiwick and a core of support in Congress, she sought to create a manifesto of sorts: a book that would explain her origins and priorities to a national audience. The result would be *Unbought and Unbossed*.

11

THE BOOK
A Black Feminist Power Manifesto

Amid her growing fame in 1971, Chisholm published an autobiographical book that would considerably enhance the mythology of charisma, idealism, and ambition that surrounded her. The resulting volume, called *Unbought and Unbossed,* would not only help launch Chisholm's presidential run but also become the definitive source on Chisholm's life for the next several decades. Almost everything that scholars know about her life story comes from this book, a second one published three years later about Chisholm's presidential campaign, and a handful of interviews. It seems that, when it comes to Chisholm, historians have abandoned their usual skepticism toward autobiography.[1] And, as much as it seems that the book is a straightforward accounting of Chisholm's life up until 1970, it is of course a constructed presentation that imparts a particular perspective on the politician. Indeed, the book is where electoral politics meet the politics of memory.

In *Unbought and Unbossed,* Chisholm described the making of her Black feminist power persona and beliefs. She retrospectively wrote about her fearlessness and political education by her doting father. She portrayed herself as beholden to no one, principled, a maverick, and a self-made woman by dint of qualities that existed in her from girlhood. Her style was defiant and blunt. Given such an auspicious beginning and a penchant for speaking out, her readers see that it was foreordained that she would always speak her mind and bring pragmatic radicalism to party politics.[2] Of course, such an image is that which Chisholm, her staff, and her publisher wished to convey. The reality was far more complicated. While Chisholm was indeed unusually forthright and devoted to a Black feminist power political vision, her political life contains contradictions. Comparing the *Unbought and Unbossed* version of Chisholm with her life events shows which stories mattered to her. We can see that she sacrificed her relationship with her family, courted establishment politics slightly longer than she would have liked to admit, and did have something of a politician's ego.

The story of how *Unbought and Unbossed* came to be written and published, as well as its inconsistencies with other accounts, suggests that Chisholm's political legacy is simultaneously less idealistic and more achievable than it appears at first glance. On behalf of herself and other executives at the press, Joyce Hartman, New York editor at Houghton Mifflin, approached Chisholm in April 1969 to ask about a possible book. Eldridge Cleaver's *Soul on Ice* and Ann Moody's *Coming of Age in Mississippi* had been published in 1968, and Maya Angelou's *I Know Why the Caged Bird Sings* was just about to be published, signaling a willingness on behalf of mainstream publishers to put Black radical voices in mass circulation. Chisholm was arguably the most prominent Black politician in the nation; a book from her made publishing sense—and history.

Hartman visited Chisholm and Mac Holder, still her chief elections strategist, in the district office. Hartman found Chisholm "gracious and direct," "acutely aware of her unique position and its historic importance." Holder, who was tasked with handling all arrangements, was "laconic, circumspect," and "may know a lot about precinct politics but little about publishing." Hartman outlined to him plans for a book much like the one that would eventually be published: part autobiography and part essays about her political ideas and hopes for the future. After a few months of consideration, Chisholm signed a contract that included a $25,000 advance and 15 percent of list price in royalties. Both the publisher and the author had a significant interest in producing a book that sold well.[3]

While the publisher was delighted to land the contract, Chisholm's proposed title of *Unbought and Unbossed* engendered initial ambivalence. Hartman, "despite its belligerence," liked it. But it "didn't stir much enthusiasm," the editor-in-chief Richard McAdoo reported of the meeting in which the title came under consideration. "It is somewhat clumsy to get the mouth around, and it struck some as having a somewhat negative pitch. Obviously you don't want to relay this reaction verbatim to Mrs. Chisholm since she has made the phrase her campaign slogan."[4] The remaining discussion is lost, but Chisholm prevailed in the dispute. It is difficult to imagine the book with any other title now, because it did so much to cement Chisholm's reputation as an independent and incorruptible figure.

With publication plans in place, Chisholm had to get the book written. Through Downs, Chisholm had met the young journalist Lee Hickling, who had covered politics for a local New York state newspaper. She dictated her life story and her thoughts to Hickling, who then wrote down what he heard and organized the material into chapters.[5] He was also the one to correspond with Joyce Hartman on editorial matters. When he sent the autobiographical chapters plus the first two topic chapters, McAdoo personally read them. He sent unvarnished criticism to Hartman. The chapters on Chisholm's family and early years were good, he thought, but after Brooklyn College he thought it seemed rushed. Then, too, was the problem of Chisholm's tone. The task was to "file down the sharp edge of the author's ego which shows through often enough to alienate the reader." He thought more modesty and humor would make Chisholm more appealing to readers. Where the manuscript read "I refuse to bow to political expediency," McAdoo's response was "come down off this sort of lofty perch." Hartman softened these remarks and sent a diplomatic request for more details and less ego to Hickling. When the editors got the second part of the manuscript, the essay chapters, they were less than thrilled. The language was boring and they lacked a personal feel. The abortion law repeal chapter was way too long and should maybe even be eliminated, and McAdoo in particular thought the chapter on Women's Liberation "tedious, but maybe this is because I'm not a woman." Duly, Hartman sent Hickling a letter asking him to add more anecdotes and personal reflections. Whether he did is unclear, but Hickling did create chapter titles while the editors created the four section titles. Hickling also arranged for book jacket photographs to be sent by Gordon Parks Jr. The collage of four photographs that would appear on the cover were all of the same event, some of Chisholm in midsentence, gesturing, and one of her with a hand on her hip, smiling. Galley proofs were done in July, and the book was in print (with a first run of 15,000 copies) by September.[6]

Unbought and Unbossed fits the genre of political autobiography in that it presents Chisholm's life as an inexorable march toward principled public service. It is a hybrid structure of autobiography and essays: the first one hundred pages document Chisholm's life and career up to her first congressional floor speech (against the Vietnam War), and the following seventy-five pages are a collection of writings on the workings of Congress, abortion, coalition politics, Black politicians, women's rights, antipoverty, antiracism, and youth.

Like other autobiographies, the book contains inaccuracies about places and dates. Chisholm wrote a much-abridged version of her family's history in it. She wrote with nostalgia and fondness about the six years she spent in her parents' home country, Barbados, from age four to ten. As much as Chisholm deplored poverty in American cities, she painted life on the British colonial island in a rosy glow. Regarding the push factors that drove Barbadians to the United States, she said only that "crop failures caused famines," but did not discuss the racism and inequalities that kept Black Barbadians poor. She also gave herself broader roots than just Barbados in stating that her father, Charles, was from Guyana.[7] She romanticized the harsh discipline in Barbados's households and colonial schools. Teachers had authority to punish students physically, and then parents, after finding out about their children's transgressions, might well spank them again on their return from school, she remembered in positive terms. Her view of life back in Brooklyn once she had returned is less rosy, except for her accounts of her father, whom she adored. She declared that she was his favorite and that he was her first political mentor, but she admitted that his decision to name her as the beneficiary of his life insurance policy caused a rift between her and her three sisters. It was not her fault, she claimed, though she did not elect to share the proceeds. All in all, she seemed to want readers to know that her background had set her up for political success: the strictness of her upbringing on the island and her father's mentoring led her to a culture of political achievement on behalf of disempowered citizens.

Chisholm's story also departs from a strict chronology when it comes to her commitment to reform and insurgency, a strategy that makes her seem even more principled and independent. In *Unbought and Unbossed*, she says that her "interest in politics grew gradually" in the late 1940s, and as a result she joined the local Democratic club, the Seventeenth Assembly District, around the time of her college graduation in 1947. But interviews and archival evidence suggest that she actually did not join the Seventeenth until 1954 or 1955, and she stayed at least four years. The conflicting dates suggest some ambivalence on Chisholm's part regarding her membership in the regular club. Clearly, she wanted to convey the impression that she joined the club early in her career, was always an outsider, and did not stay long. She explained that she belonged to the club because she thought she might be able to change the political machine by working on the inside. But it seems possible that Chisholm was more invested in the work of the Seventeenth Assembly District Club than her maverick image suggests.[8] And when the insurgent Unity Democratic Club formed in 1959, the organization that would support her political rise, Chisholm joined it. She was still involved with the Seventeenth, a fact that she never discussed in interviews or writings, preferring to convey the impression that her loyalties had shifted to Unity immediately and entirely.[9]

Her telling of the successful campaign for Congress in 1968 emphasizes that she had to battle the party establishment at every turn. Chisholm was sure that the committee had selected her because she was the only candidate who had the "nerve" to disagree with them on some things, her confidence, and her proven record of being "unbought and unbossed" at the polls. "I had, I knew, been the only one of the potential candidates who talked back and disagreed with them, about things they would have to expect from a nominee," she said. "I did not go to them with my hat in my hand, and this is what they liked." As she heard it, the only objection that came in the form of "underground rumblings" was that she was a woman.[10]

The essays as a group serve as a manifesto for the Chisholm Mystique by making her guiding principles explicit and bringing Black feminist power politics to a wide, new audience. Chisholm started the set of essays with "How I View Congress," an argument against seeing Congress as an august body to be revered. Instead, she asserted, it was merely a fiefdom of old men. A tiny group of them controlled the body's activities and were not responsible to their constituents or the U.S. public. Many of her colleagues were alcoholics, she disclosed, and instead of carefully considering their votes, they would ask their friends what to do. She found the hearings on Capitol Hill to be time consuming, expensive, and ineffective at getting justice for everyday citizens. The trips that committee members took were less about fact finding and diplomacy than expenses-paid junkets. And "the people," unlike every other group in the country, lacked a lobby. Even the Democratic Study Group, a coalition of about one hundred left-liberal members, faltered when things became controversial. The result was that most citizens did not get their needs met. A second result was that Chisholm, who previously considered herself a moderate, had become "a militant."[11]

Chisholm then turned her attention to reproductive freedom in an essay called "Facing the Abortion Question." In it, she described her evolution from a reformer who thought that it should be easier for women to get so-called therapeutic abortions (that is, mediated by laws and medicine) to an abolitionist when it came to all abortion laws. The precipitating event for her reflection was being approached by NARAL (then the National Association for the Repeal of Abortion Laws) as a candidate for its founding national president in 1969. Though she was unable to accept their invitation, accepting instead an "honorary presidency," in her deliberations over the matter she more fully developed her thinking. In recent years, she had become more aware, through personal acquaintances, of the impossible bind that women with unwanted pregnancies found themselves in. Faced with such a bind, women would seek out abortions—whether safe and legal or dangerous and illegal. Given this fact, Chisholm declared unequivocally that she wanted women to have access to safe and legal procedures. She publicly proclaimed herself an advocate of women's rights to abortions and promptly received an onslaught of "one of the heaviest flows of mail to my Washington office that I have experienced." Although there were some "temperate and reasoned" letters that disagreed with her stance, she was surprised to find most of the letters were in favor. Some even pleaded with her for information on where one could obtain an abortion. To be sure, most of her male colleagues were puzzled—not because they disagreed per se, but because they thought she would lose votes and reelection. Chisholm chided them in her essay for worrying more about the political repercussions of any decision rather than the rightness or wrongness of it. On the urging of NARAL, Chisholm considered and drafted a bill that would legalize abortions, but despite her efforts she was unable to build sponsorship across political and party lines, and she did not introduce it. She felt that a strong coalition would have been crucial to a bill's progress through the House, and that her political capital would be better spent in changing public opinion. Bringing public pressure to bear on the legislative process, she thought, was the best path to ending "compulsory pregnancy."[12]

Chisholm's third essay was the story of her decision to back Liberal Party candidate John Lindsay for the New York mayoral race. She explained her political dilemma. Mario Procaccino emphasized "law and order," as Nixon did, and appealed to white Americans who felt forgotten and silenced, as Nixon did, but with a New York twist. With his strong Italian ethnic and working-class identity, Procaccino had the support of ethnic white New Yorkers from the outer boroughs, who saw themselves as having fought ethnic discrimination and now needing law and order to protect what they had. These were the same voters who had supported the white teachers in the Ocean Hill-Brownsville strike. Both the major party nominees were "conservative," as Chisholm put it.

Chisholm recalled that Lindsay had a staffer phone and asked her whether she planned to support Procaccino. As she recalled in *Unbought and Unbossed*, she replied, "In good conscience, I cannot." To her, Procaccino and the Republican candidate both seemed reactionary and hostile to Black people. But at the time of the call, she didn't give the aide the answer he or she wanted. She still did not know what to do with regard to the race. "The situation was a king-sized headache for me," she wrote, "because I was not only a leader of the black community in one of the five boroughs, I was also a Democratic national committeeman." Other Black politicians were "straddling" as a way to avoid the issue. Conrad, Holder, and others discouraged Chisholm from breaking party lines and endorsing Lindsay, sure that her doing so would spell disaster. After much rumination, she decided that "too much was at stake" for Black voters, and she felt that Lindsay was the best chance for improving life in the city for them. She called Lindsay and told him she would support him.[13]

Chisholm pointed to Lindsay's win as one for coalition politics, which, she said, revolve around issues and not around parties. Coalition "is not a comfortable kind of political action for its leaders," she observed in the essay, "because it involves creativity, innovation, change, and commitment to the people instead of to personal advancement." In order to achieve such a coalition, leaders would have to offer power and real representation to "in-groups" and "out-groups," and genuinely "broaden the base" for political decision making.[14] Chisholm would later pay an uncomfortable price for her defection from the Democrats.

Her next essay directly addressed racism and politics. Titled "Black Politicians and the Black Majority," it focused more on her own analysis of the workings of racism than on Black politicians themselves. She began with her frustration at the cynicism of the now-defunct Brotherhood Week (founded by the National Conference of Christians and Jews in 1934 and continuing until the 1980s) in which "hypocrites pretend to cleanse themselves of the racism they practice the rest of the year." She acknowledged that most Americans seemed unaware of their hypocrisy and lamented that she was repeatedly asked by white people some version of the question, "What do you Negroes want now?" Her response was to invoke the fact that eradicating racism was very much unfinished business, and she would cite specific examples throughout the essay. "Racism is so universal in this country, so widespread and deep-seated, that it is invisible because it is so normal," she pointed out.[15]

"Black Politicians and the Black Majority" then wandered somewhat as it reached Chisholm's conclusion that, first of all, racism served as a distraction from the fact that most people—Black and white—lacked political power. Instead, a small group of white people controlled wealth and power. Quoting Frederick Douglass, she made a call to arms: "Power concedes nothing without demand." In her opinion, the civil rights movement had been about integration and it had failed. Now, she sympathetically turned to Black Power. "We must move forward together," she declared, "and we must do it ourselves," as other ethnic groups had done in the past on the way to political power. The pressing issues now were jobs and housing, and equality in education was the longer-term goal. Eschewing industrial education, she quoted Malcolm X on the figure of Uncle Tom and the necessity of "repudiating" worship of Great Man figures like George Washington Carver. But she did echo liberal caricatures about the supposed violence of Black Power. "Basically I agree with what many of the extremist groups are saying—*except* that their tactics are wrong and too often they have no program," she wrote (emphasis hers). In this divergence, she told Black Power audiences, "I'm not a fool . . . I'm a pragmatist." She saw fighting within electoral politics ("the system") as the only practical choice, even for a "militant," a label she had proudly claimed in "How I View Congress."[16] Her critique of Black Power was not unique, but her militancy and her radicalism as labels are also grounded in a classic understanding of *radical* to mean getting to the *root* of a problem.[17] She knew that electing Black feminists like her to office would make a difference for constituents who were Black, brown, young, female, and/or poor because her priorities were different.

In the last pages of the essay, she turned to the role of Black politicians. Repeating her conviction that the ten Black legislators in Washington were largely "symbolic," she also cautioned that Black politicians were uniquely vulnerable. It had been easy for Sam Yorty, a white candidate for mayor of Los Angeles in 1969, to paint his opponent, the Black retired police officer Thomas Bradley, as antipolice, for example. Yorty simply invoked "law and order" politics. Adam Clayton Powell had been persecuted for behavior that a white congressman would have gotten away with. It was possible for Black politicians to win races where the electorate was not majority Black, but only if they followed Julian Bond's six points, published in Mervyn Dymally's 1971 anthology *The Black Politician: His Struggle for Power*. After quoting him at length, she summarized Bond's points thusly: "For our freedom struggle to advance in the political arena, black politicians have to accept their blackness. They have to form an ideological base from which to operate, and that base has to be founded on their color." Pointedly, she said the electorate also should be open to women as well as men candidates and be willing to vote across party lines in the interest of making the best choice. Finally, she reminded her readers that attractive ideology was only part of the strategy: the basics of voter registration, financing, and campaigning were absolutely necessary. After all, she herself had paid her dues in this regard, and that is how she eventually won national office.[18]

"A government that cannot hear its people" was Chisholm's critique of the War on Poverty as well as of Richard Nixon. First, the War on Poverty: while well intentioned, it had been designed by middle- and upper-class people who had no idea of the real challenges facing poor people. Not only that, but the architects failed to account for racism as an obstacle to eradicating poverty. Still, the Community Action Programs had politicized Black and brown people somewhat, and the best illustration of its success in this area was the anxiety of politicians over community self-help and other organizations. The result was an attempt to gut the Office of Equal Opportunity programs that did the most good, such as Head Start and the Job Corps. When it came to Nixon, Chisholm saw him as a paradigmatic politician who refused to hear the people: his administration sought to dismantle the main protections of the Voting Rights Act, discontinue school desegregation, and nominate racist judges to the Supreme Court. On this last point, Chisholm offered one of her characteristic zingers. When Nixon put forward the name of Harrold Carswell after the defeat of Clement Haynsworth (see chapter 10), she instructed her office staff not to put any reporters through who might want Chisholm's comment. She told them to tell the press, "She says she can't be bothered to make a statement every time Nixon appoints a racist to the Supreme Court." Nixon's worst failing, she said, was his "cynical, callous attitude" toward nonwhite people. She predicted that his Southern Strategy to attract white southern Democrats to the Republican Party would be "his Vietnam," that is, his undoing. In this, she would prove quite wrong.[19]

Chisholm next turned to the developing feminist movement in "Women and Their Liberation." While the term intersectionality did not yet exist, Chisholm used an intersectional lens in this essay. She analyzed the links between discrimination against women and nonwhite people, especially in economic and occupational realms. She adapted passages nearly verbatim from her January 1970 *McCall's* article, "Racism and Anti-Feminism," that explicitly connected race and gender. "This society is as antiwoman as it is antiblack," she explained, and sexism, like racism, was largely invisible. One of these passages would become something of a manifesto: "In the end, antiblack, antifemale, and all forms of discrimination are equivalent to the same thing—antihumanism," she stated.[20] But Black people were radicalized and women were not. Even as Chisholm sought passage of the Equal Rights Amendment, the law could not in itself eradicate sexism. Women themselves "must become revolutionaries." They needed to embrace their "femaleness" and claim political power. On the former point, just as Black people had done, women should embrace womanhood as a positive attribute for leading within society. Second, women should enter politics as candidates and officials, especially because they were already doing the political work ("laboring anonymously in the background"). However, they should also be prepared for sexism from men as they did so. In both of these arguments Chisholm articulated a social feminist vision: women had unique female attributes that were more principled and moral, and thus beneficial to the citizenry.[21]

Chisholm's final essay concerned "Youth and America's Future." Lamenting that there were no major youth leaders coming to the fore, she emphasized that she did not wish to become such a leader. She did, however, make time to speak to student groups in order to help them "force change." "My role, I think," she speculated," is more that of a catalyst. By verbalizing what is wrong, by trying to strip off the masks that make people comfortable in the midst of chaos, perhaps I can help get things moving." She disclosed how much she identified with "the kids," saying that she as well as they were "tired of being lied to" and that they shared a mission to push the United States to live up to the promise of true democracy. She both admired them and feared for them because they were willing to die for causes that aligned with their beliefs. Older people unfairly scapegoated youth, but she wished to see more youth involved in politics and hoped that lowering the voting age (the Twenty-Sixth Amendment would pass in 1971) would help with this.

Chisholm ended this essay, and the entire volume, with a statement of her raison d'être. She saw her main accomplishment in winning office not as being a "first," but because she won "unbought and unbossed." This meant that she had rejected money and a secure footing in party hierarchy in favor of her own convictions and political autonomy. The sometimes meandering and nonlinear essays of her political philosophy were meant to illustrate how the biographical details in the previous sections translated into her own pragmatic radicalism.

Historians are right to be wary of such political and politicized autobiography as a stand-alone source, but such self-framing matters for feminist historians as well as political historians who are seeking a stronger sense of the era in which someone is writing while in politics. Hearing her on her own terms is important, and giving her the context for which she wrote is significant for understanding *Unbought and Unbossed.*

Reviewers for the most part responded positively to her "nettling candor," as Charlayne Hunter (later Hunter-Gault) put it in the *New York Times Book Review.* Hunter conceded that the book was "no great work of literature" and criticized Chisholm's unabashed self-promotion, but praised Chisholm's "honesty and vigilance." The book, Hunter said, was possibly the most important thing that Chisholm had accomplished since taking office, and she did "expose" the problems that white male members of Congress ignored. The *Boston Globe's* reviewer, Glendora Putnam, said that "the reader almost feels [Chisholm's] rebellious spirit" and that the book was "perfectly titled." Putnam thought that the biographical sections were better than the essays, although the essays had useful material for both women's liberation and Black militants. UN ambassador Marietta Peabody Tree, writing in the *Washington Post,* called it a "tremendously impressive book," written in "clear direct prose devoid of the fuzzy generalities of the New Left." The Washington *Evening Star's* reviewer found the book compelling, describing it as a genuine "political philosophy" that was not a craven appeal to voters in an election year. John Kenneth Galbraith provided a puff that he had "recently concluded on the basis of careful research that Shirley Chisholm is the best member of Congress. This book confirms it." The exception to much praise was the *Boston Herald's* review, which called it "too obviously a message book."[22]

Unbought and Unbossed announced its author's intentions to disrupt politics as usual. It also contributed much to the Chisholm Mystique: a principled, no-punches-spared, fearless new face on the political landscape. She placed herself squarely within an African American literary tradition of autobiography as a way of setting the story straight. But the book was not legislation. As a member of Congress, Chisholm would have to use what toehold she could get to solve the problems facing her larger constituency. The toeholds she had were coalitions and institution building.

12

INSTITUTION BUILDING
The Congressional Black Caucus and the National Women's Political Caucus

Chisholm's second term in office was devoted to much the same substance as her first term. But in 1971, Chisholm's work turned increasingly toward institution building within the alliances to which she already belonged, especially among other Black and female congresspeople. Chisholm's coalition approach bridged the politics of race and gender as she worked with both Black male colleagues and feminist colleagues inside the House of Representatives.

Her second term brought Chisholm the committee assignment she had been waiting for: Education and Labor. Conventional wisdom on the Hill was that she got it because of her loyalty to Hale Boggs in his successful quest to move up from House majority whip to majority leader. Winning had required that Boggs, an establishment candidate, court the nonestablishment members like Chisholm. But Chisholm maintained that she had endorsed no candidate for leader and that she had simply requested the assignment in a meeting of the New York delegation, which had unanimously supported her choice. She was one of four other Black members and two other women members on the larger committee. Her subcommittee assignment was the Select Subcommittee on Education, but she would find herself and her staff lending expertise across subcommittees.[1]

Her Black feminist power pragmatic approach—democratic and collaborative—makes her work difficult to find in the archival record. Her effectiveness as a legislator would come not so much in the form of sponsoring bills and passing her own legislation. Rather, her strategic handling of committee work and legislative procedure laid groundwork for later successes, and solved problems without fanfare. Victory was usually slow in coming, and some battles would need to be fought more than once. Indeed, the fronts for those battles were not only on the floor of the House or even in committee meetings, but in the informal networking across the Hill. The unwritten nature of Chisholm's contributions makes it difficult to track her impact on national policy, but she and her staffers were convinced that they were able to get further by working off the record. Having experienced the limelight of the Chisholm Mystique, the congresswoman knew that such notoriety could backfire. She thus leveraged her influence to share or give credit to her colleagues and erase her own work in the historical record. Passing legislation that would benefit her national constituency of poor, nonwhite, young, and/or female Americans was Chisholm's priority, and she didn't care whether her name was on it or not.

Chisholm also considered the future implications of new laws in terms of governance—it was one thing to get legislation passed but another to have it implemented effectively. "There is so much legislation on the books," she told a UPI reporter in January 1970, "but the difficulty is in the implementation of these laws."[2] Getting support from a broad base was essential for implementation, and the best way to build support was to solicit ideas and input from everyone, even those who differed ideologically. Thus, she or her staff approached colleagues from across party or ideological lines when an issue might call for collaboration. They might write the legislation or amendments that other members then introduced. Her staff was empowered to act autonomously to communicate with staffers across the Hill, a responsibility they took seriously. But collaboration did not mean abandoning the office's guiding principle of doing "the true, the right, and the beautiful." Chisholm constantly reminded staff that change would be limited without an intersectional approach.[3]

THE CONGRESSIONAL BLACK CAUCUS

Chisholm had been part of the congressional Black coalition, the Democratic Select Committee, from January 1969 to early 1971.[4] In 1971, in response to the growth and rising expectations of its members, as well as Nixon's civil rights conservatism, the group formalized into the Congressional Black Caucus (CBC) with a slate of officers, an executive committee, and subcommittees on February 2, 1971. Charlie Diggs was elected chair. After some discussion about a name, during which "Congressional Committee on Minority Rights" was floated, the group decided to use the term Black because all of them prioritized what they saw as Black interests.[5] The founders intended to represent Black Americans as a whole and advance their interests. Indeed, the CBC boldly declared its members "representatives of the black population," and some speculated that it sought to step into the leadership vacuum left by the death of Martin Luther King Jr. and the decline of the major organizations of the 1960s Black freedom struggle.[6] Its members said they were careful not to cover the same territory as the NAACP and Urban League, but rather came together to "concentrate our energies" in Washington. Its founders wished for strength in both unity and diversity. In its early years, the CBC's best and most lasting success came through gaining better committee assignments for its members, an effort that Chisholm's action to change her own assignment from Forestry and Agriculture in 1969 had started.[7] They decided that they ought to serve on diverse committees so as to promote the needs of Black Americans in multiple places. The focus on Black people did not preclude consideration of other Americans besides Black ones; in fact, the CBC pointed out wherever it could that some issues that affected Black Americans were not exclusive to Black people.[8]

The elections of 1970 had brought five new members in January 1971. Charles Rangel replaced Adam Powell as the representative for Harlem after a rancorous race during which Powell called Chisholm "Aunt Jemima" for supporting Rangel. Chisholm had been a supporter of Powell's during her first term and applauded him at an honorary dinner in February, but by June she had settled into Rangel's camp. Other new faces were Ron Dellums, representing Oakland, California; Ralph Metcalfe of Chicago (replacing the party establishment loyalist William Dawson, who had died in office); and Parren Mitchell of Baltimore. Walter Fauntroy had been a director of the Washington chapter of the Southern Christian Leadership Conference and national coordinator of the Poor People's Campaign in 1969, and would be added in early 1971 as the nonvoting delegate for the District of Columbia. Charlie Diggs of Detroit was chosen as the leader over his colleague John Conyers, who was seen as too vocal and militant to be the public face of the group. Chisholm was named chair of the Military Affairs Committee within the CBC. They also acquired a small treasury of $250,000 as a result of a $100-a-plate fundraiser at the Sheraton Park Hotel. Celebrities and high-ranking Democrats attended: Hubert Humphrey, George McGovern, Edward Kennedy, Edmund Muskie, Coretta Scott King, Jesse Jackson, Ralph Abernathy, and Joe Rauh. Ossie Davis was the keynoter, and Dick Gregory and Bill Cosby performed at no charge. The fundraiser allowed the group to hire a full-time staff member.[9]

Chisholm was still the only woman. Almost immediately, there was friction between Chisholm and her male CBC colleagues. When she asked many questions, as was her style, she noticed resistance. "They used to grumble, 'she wants to know everything,'" Chisholm observed. She also recalled that colleagues viewed her as a woman who stepped out of her "place." She recalled complaints that she had too much "women's lib" support and was not sufficiently focused on Black issues. Bill Clay claimed that she was not supportive of the idea of the CBC in the first place and was "uncooperative." The conflicts would come to a head over her presidential campaign later in the year. Still, she had her allies. The three most supportive men on the CBC were Parren Mitchell, Ron Dellums, and at times John Conyers. Dellums tried to educate the others, but "it made no difference. It's something I'll never forget as long as I live: how this question of being a woman got in the way of everything." "They used so many strategies to stop me but nothing stopped me," she explained later.[10]

One source of disagreement was that Chisholm thought that the caucus needed to move beyond racial lines to build coalitions with white lawmakers. While going "off into isolated enclaves of blackness" would "satisfy the emotional needs of some of our people," it would not "bring about help in some kind of concrete way," she argued. While she was "ever mindful that my first priority is the liberation of Blacks from second-class status in America," she also held "the belief that on many issues, the concern of groups other than Black ones is just as great as our own." By collaborating with others whose interests aligned, legislative accomplishments could be greater. This would be one way the CBC could move beyond rhetoric and into the mechanics of legislation. But not all of her colleagues agreed. In an interview with a Howard University oral historian, Chisholm regretfully and reluctantly acknowledged that there were "several black personalities, who have psychological needs, political needs and social needs" that drew their focus away from helping Black people. Her implication was that power and fame motivated some CBC members more than the actual welfare of Black constituents, especially after the caucus had a meeting with President Nixon.[11] However uneasy a coalition, the newly named group was lumped together as many colleagues in Congress saw them as uppity grandstanders and made accusations of Black separatism. Even labor unions and the established civil rights organizations were skeptical.

Early on, the group took Nixon to task. The CBC's first coordinated action of 1971 was to boycott Nixon's State of the Union address on the grounds that he had still not responded to Diggs's 1970 request that he meet with the Democratic Select Committee. They were just looking for publicity, Nixon aide John Ehrlichman said. Next they turned to the major television networks to request air time for a response. When a first request was denied, they sent a second and "buttressed their case with a long discussion of the legal and constitutional issues they say are at stake."[12] Nixon claimed that he had previously not thought it necessary to meet with the group because he had already "met with a number of blacks" and had invited the CBC members to his receptions and briefings. Unofficially, the White House had a general disdain for legislators, and Nixon still believed the CBC only wanted publicity. He thought of their concerns as "special interests," not substantial issues. Vice President Spiro Agnew, famous for his unwillingness to temper racist remarks, said the group "arrogated unto themselves the positions of black leaders, those who spend their time in querulous complaint and constant recrimination against the rest of society." He contrasted the "constant complaining" of "these people" with the Kenyan, Ethiopian, and Congolese leaders who were "grateful" for United States aid.[13]

The continued public pressure of the legislators and their boycott of the State of the Union, plus some brokering through Senator Ed Brooke, yielded an invitation in late February. The meeting itself finally took place on March 25 in the White House's Cabinet Room. Nixon, the picture of solicitousness, greeted each congressperson in turn. Chisholm was still fuming that an army bus had at first been sent to pick up her and her colleagues, although the mistake was quickly rectified and limos were sent instead.[14] The CBC had convened a task force that evaluated 400 position papers in preparation for the meeting. They drafted a sixty-item document about Black and poor people's issues in preparation for the meeting, including "poverty, voting rights, equal employment, revenue sharing, welfare, housing, racism, health, and foreign policy."[15] The CBC wanted withdrawal from Vietnam by the end of the year, the end of "no-knock" policing laws, sanctions against South Africa for apartheid, and a $6,500 guaranteed annual income—not, as had occurred in the past, "equality as a rhetorical promise." Chisholm's remarks concerned the treatment of Black veterans and the need for a civil rights division within the Department of Defense. "Following the conference, the representatives expressed satisfaction with the President's response," a front-page *New York Times* story said, which was to appoint a five-member committee to handle the concerns the CBC had brought. Nixon had also admitted that if he were the CBC, he "would be over here fighting for the rights of black people," and that "black Americans had been treated unfairly and are still being treated unfairly." The next day, the CBC gave Nixon two months in which to craft a response to their recommendations, choosing the seventeenth anniversary of *Brown v. Board of Education*, May 17, as the deadline.[16]

Any optimism that Chisholm felt in the aftermath of the meeting with Nixon was dampened in May. First, Nixon's formal response to the March 25 meeting, although detailed and thorough, indicated that he believed he was already making progress on the demands the CBC had presented and did not feel the need to do much more. The White House also convened its own "black caucus," of about thirty, mostly Republican Black officials, who could spread pro-administration talking points.[17] The CBC's response was that Nixon's response was "deeply disappointing," especially on the issue of welfare. Chisholm was among a small group within the CBC that outlined a plan for building political power going forward. The CBC would campaign in strategic districts and use what power it had to reward its white allies and freeze out "enemies," she said at a May 24 press conference.[18] Then, in a move that was clearly a nod to southern conservatives, Nixon put forward segregationist Albert Watson, a former member of Congress and failed gubernatorial candidate from South Carolina, as a possible appointee to the U.S. Military Court of Appeals. Chisholm announced that Watson was in the running at a CBC press conference, where she vowed to do everything she could to block Watson's nomination. It would, she warned, "undo all of the progress and goodwill that the White House has claimed in its response to the Black Caucus' [sic] recommendations." In her capacity as chair of the Military Affairs Committee, she argued Watson's white supremacist politics made him unfit for the post. She wasn't the only congressperson who objected; the hue and cry Watson's candidacy engendered led Nixon to withdraw it.[19] Still, she was even more disgusted by June, when she criticized the lack of progress on employment discrimination in the construction industry. Nixon was failing to back up his words with deeds and "has never had a commitment to black citizens," she complained.[20]

As Nixon dragged his feet, the CBC forged ahead with a legislative agenda that mirrored their original demands. In conversation with the National Welfare Rights Organization (NWRO), the entire CBC cosponsored the Adequate Income Act of 1971, a response to Nixon's Family Assistance Plan (FAP) bill that had cleared the Ways and Means Committee.[21] Nixon's bill established an income floor of $2,400 for a family of four with a work requirement, while the NWRO/CBC plan was for $6,500, with aid available for families making up to $11,000 per year.[22] Chisholm argued against Nixon's bill on the House floor. She was an advocate of welfare reform, she said, but only reform that actually made an improvement to the existing system. Nixon's plan fell short in the dollar amount allowed for a minimum income, yes, but it also perpetuated discrimination against women, and women of color in particular, by requiring work while ignoring childcare and the need for well-paying job opportunities. Minimum wage was $1.60 per hour, which meant an annual income of $2,400 for a full-time job. Given that the average income for women, whether they worked full- or part-time, was just over $3,000, and the same figure for Black women was just under $2,000, the FAP needed to provide access to jobs paying above minimum wage and with childcare in order to be an improvement over the current situation. But it made no provision for training for highly skilled jobs or creating good jobs, leading her to agree with the NWRO contention that the FAP was intended to "subsidize low-wage paying employers rather than enable poor people to become self-supporting."[23] H.R. 1, as the FAP bill was known in 1971, would "only replace an inadequate system with one that is equally ineffective," she argued. Furthermore, she said, the bill's stinginess was "part of the overall pattern of discrimination against women, especially minority women, in this country." She saw the bill as useless in helping poor women find employment that would provide an adequate income.[24] Chisholm perceived a central contradiction within the FAP's demands that single mothers work.

As the legislation came to a vote, Chisholm and the CBC found themselves joining conservative colleagues in voting against Nixon's measure, which won in the House anyway. In the Senate it fared worse. It got bogged down in the Finance Committee by critics from both the left and the right and never went to a vote. No welfare reform passed at all, a situation that had been predicted by the *New York Times* in an editorial just before the bill reached the floor. "It would be ironic," the editorial board wrote, "if black and liberal Congressmen who believe that this reform is not generous and compassionate enough were to defeat the bill by joining with reactionaries opposed to any improvement." Senator George McGovern attempted to reintroduce the CBC's $6,500 figure in a new bill, but it got nowhere.[25] A guaranteed annual income for Americans would not come into existence.

Though some of her relationships were contentious, there was one CBC colleague with whom Chisholm immediately clicked. Ronald Dellums, representing Oakland, California, was the first Black person elected to Congress from a majority-white district. Oakland was, of course, not just any district—its new congressman saw it as an "incubator" for multiple movements, not just one or the other. He won by building a coalition on the idea of "justice for all." He was already one of Chisholm's admirers, having read *Unbought and Unbossed*. Once he arrived in Washington, he painted his office a "vibrant, forbidding orange" and appalled his neighbor Barry Goldwater Jr. (R-CA and the son of the 1964 GOP presidential candidate) with an exhibit of photographs of Vietnam War atrocities. He outraged Edward Hébert of Louisiana, chair of the House Armed Services Committee, by taking reports of atrocities by Vietnam Veterans Against the War seriously. His antiwar and other progressive stances would eventually land him at number sixteen on Nixon's infamous enemies list. Dressed in Italian suits, with an Afro just starting to go gray, the tall (six foot four) congressman was a striking contrast to the petite Chisholm. But the two shared much in common. "For some reason she took a liking to me," he would recall. He thought that America at the time needed a straightforward speaker like her to be very clear about the issues. They became good friends. In part this was because, as Chisholm did, Dellums considered himself a coalition politician. He insisted that "people do indeed operate on more than one dimension," necessitating collaboration across identities and movements. He understood that Chisholm's race and gender intersected with both the Black freedom struggle and women's liberation and applauded her investment in both. Both of them wanted the CBC to develop coalitions where Black people had common interests with others. For example, they both appeared, with Parren Mitchell and Charlie Rangel, on the Capitol steps in solidarity with antiwar protesters.[26]

Chisholm and Dellums were perhaps the most invested in getting out of Vietnam of all of the CBC members, and it was for this purpose that they collaborated on cochairing unofficial hearings into racism in the military. They had, they said, classified documents that showed the Department of Defense had made agreements with other countries to limit numbers of Black soldiers. As chair of the CBC's Military Affairs Committee, Chisholm sent her aide Thaddeus Garrett to Turkey, Greece, Italy, and Germany to investigate allegations of racism against Black service members. The report he made said that he did find racism, and that the "explosiveness which prevails is made more serious by the amazing fact that many of those in command positions on all levels refuse to realize that . . . racism can and does exist."[27] Then two GIs approached her for help after going AWOL from the U.S. base in Germany because of what they said was a trumped-up rape charge. The information Garrett gathered, plus the plight of the accused GIs, prompted ten CBC members' visits to military bases (Chisholm visited Fort Dix in New Jersey) and three days of hearings. The night before the hearings began in November, over one hundred Black soldiers were arrested at a demonstration against racism at Alabama's Fort McClellan. They had experienced several days of racist violence, including an incident in which a white military police officer hit Black personnel with a car, sending several to the hospital. The majority of those who got arrested were members of the Woman's Army Corps (Fort McClellan was the group's headquarters), who were joined by Black men as they marched toward what they thought would be a peaceful meeting with commanding officers at the base's football field. Violence broke out along the way, and what resulted was a "Gestapo-like round-up" of the Black servicemen and women. The hearings themselves attracted considerable press attention and the filling of the vacant assistant secretary of defense for equal opportunity position. More quietly, in 1971 Chisholm also testified before the House Armed Services Committee about eliminating the draft and voted for several bills and amendments limiting the draft and war spending.[28]

Chisholm's involvement in an internal split within the Democratic Party was one of the occasions on which Chisholm found herself at odds with a CBC colleague or two. She was on the side of the insurgent candidate for chair of the Democratic National Convention Credentials Committee, a white man, Senator Harold Hughes (D-IA). Hughes had been the one to nominate Eugene McCarthy at the Chicago 1968 convention and was part of the party reforms in the aftermath. The establishment candidate, chosen by party chair Lawrence O'Brien with the customary lack of consultation with presidential hopefuls, was a Black woman, Patricia Roberts Harris. She was the first Black woman to serve as a U.S. ambassador (to Luxembourg, named by Lyndon Johnson). In the interim she had been dean of Howard Law School and was now a partner in a D.C. law firm with Hubert Humphrey's close associate. On the face of things, she would have been a logical figure for Chisholm to support. But Harris was anointed by the party leadership, and Chisholm revolted. When Democratic Party reformer Senator George McGovern put Hughes forward and sought support from other Democrats, Chisholm signed on, even agreeing to place Hughes's name into nomination at the upcoming Democratic National Committee meeting. She explained that "the time has come for the rhetoric of party reform to be transformed into action. The test now awaits all those, including [DNC] Chairman O'Brien, who have preached reform for the Democratic Party for so many years to display their conviction by supporting the man whose dedication to fair play stands unquestioned."[29] Apparently those who supported Hughes saw Harris as a mammy figure, coopted by her white bosses. In a seeming departure from the usual, it was the southern Democrats who favored Patricia Roberts Harris. Their rejection of a Black woman was politically perilous, so perhaps McGovern was strategic when he asked Chisholm to be the face of the opposition. Despite these efforts, the southerners won and Harris was voted in. Southern committee members voted almost unanimously for her (except for three).[30] Chisholm did not escape criticism. Cleveland's Mayor Carl Stokes, a Hubert Humphrey (establishment) ally and brother of CBC colleague Louis Stokes, criticized Chisholm for aligning against Harris. Chisholm, John Conyers, and Georgia state legislator Julian Bond responded in *Jet* magazine that they thought Stokes was simply positioning himself to be tapped by the Democratic establishment should they look for a Black running mate.[31] The breach with Stokes and others would persist into the following year's presidential race. And Harris would chair the very committee that decided whether Chisholm's 1972 presidential delegates would be seated at the next convention.

By the end of 1971, Chisholm had forged a sometimes-fragile, sometimes-effective alliance with the other Black legislators in the House. But her CBC colleagues were by no means uniformly supportive of her legislative agenda, particularly when it came to blending feminism with the Black freedom struggle. Chisholm was forced to pave her own road toward realizing an intersectional Black feminist power legislative agenda, and to pick and choose allies who would help her do so.

Chisholm enacted her Black feminist power vision in feminist legislation and in forging alliances with feminists, too. She cofounded the Women's Political Caucus and played instrumental roles in the passage of two landmark feminist bills, one that became law and another that did not. The Education Amendments of 1972, which added Title IX to the Higher Education Act of 1965, prohibited sex discrimination in all aspects of college and university life and would be signed by President Nixon in the summer of 1972. The Comprehensive Child Development Act would have provided for universal childcare, but was vetoed by Nixon.

She did so with an additional outspoken ally. Starting in January 1971, Chisholm was joined by another avowedly feminist colleague in the House: Bella Abzug. Like Chisholm, she spoke in plain language, forceful, impassioned rhetoric, and with an emphasis on coalition. The two were friends and collaborators. Chisholm had supported Abzug's congressional campaign from the beginning, and Abzug had even been called "a white Shirley Chisholm."[32] They both participated in a special social justice swearing-in ceremony on the Hill. Chisholm herself expressed delight that Abzug was now a colleague. "Now I can say I'm going to get my sister Bella to take you on," she bragged.[33] They would also experience rivalry. Abzug would argue that Chisholm sold her vote for Speaker to get her change in committee assignment, and also said that Chisholm did not like to work with groups as much as Abzug herself did. Abzug, for her part, could be mercurial. She was at times "volatile . . . profane . . . and abusive" to her staff, six young women under thirty and one man, a Vietnam veteran. One of her legislative aides, Judy Wolf, said that Abzug used both "conventional" methods and the press and public opinion to get things done. Eight months into her term, she had already lost her top aide, who said working for Abzug was "the most demanding" job she had ever had.[34] Chisholm even hired a refugee from Abzug's office, Andrea Tracy Holmes. Holmes worked only a short time before growing weary of the Manhattan congresswoman's abrasive relationship with her staff. "A very brilliant woman but a difficult person to work for and with and things just kind of came to a head," Holmes explained. (Smith was more blunt: "You could hear her screaming and yelling at her staff all the way down the hall.") Chisholm needed a caseworker, and Holmes successfully applied for the job. "Going to work for Shirley Chisholm was like stepping from the fire into Nirvana, Utopia," she recalled.[35]

Rivalries and personal friction aside, Abzug and Chisholm moved in tandem on feminist issues in 1971. They corroborated each other's testimony before hearings on the Hill, testifying on the same day in favor of a bill that would become the Equal Employment Opportunity Act of 1972.

The bill added litigation authority to the Equal Employment Opportunity Commission (EEOC) and expanded its reach to smaller companies and all government employers. Chisholm made a bold assertion of the importance of sex-based EEOC cases, correcting what she perceived as an assumption that race-based cases were more important. "For those who think that the women's liberation movement is a joke vaguely connected with burning bras and getting in the 'men only' bars," she said, "may I disabuse you of that notion; it is about equal pay and equal opportunity in the job market." Half of nonwhite people were women, for whom employment discrimination had devastating consequences. With Patsy Mink, they wrote a "Dear Friends" letter instructing nationwide allies to go visit their representatives over the August recess to lobby for the bill. But on the day the bill was debated on the floor and voted on, Chisholm and Abzug split. A Nixon-backed amendment added by John Erlenborn (R-IL) removed the EEOC's cease-and-desist powers as called for in the original bill, and Chisholm refused to vote for it on those grounds, while Abzug still did. The bill would go on to pass the Senate and be signed into law by Nixon without the cease-and-desist provision.[36]

Chisholm and Abzug collaborated on two other projects in 1971. The first was the National Women's Political Caucus (NWPC). In response to the fact that only twelve representatives and one senator were women in a country with a 53 percent female electorate, the NWPC sought to coordinate women's political power to increase representation. In July, Chisholm joined Abzug, Gloria Steinem, and Betty Friedan to found the organization. The women, aided by the organizational powers of Liz Carpenter, who had been Lady Bird Johnson's assistant, convened about 300 others from widely divergent political backgrounds at a meeting July 10 and 11 at Washington's Statler Hilton. After an initial plenary session, they broke out into workshop groups. The gathering was a highly heterogeneous one, with women from across the political spectrum. Steinem had begun to serve as a "bridge" between generations of feminists, and in her remarks reminded those present that they shared having been shut out of political power. Chisholm had made sure that Black women were included, and, on behalf of the Black women present, she introduced a resolution that the caucus would withhold support from any racist political candidate. She warned that some white participants had seemed to be willing to endorse a racist candidate, so long as she was a woman, which had alarmed Black participants. While they were sympathetic with the women's movement, "we are also part of another movement—the liberation of our own people," she said. Other Black women present were Dorothy Height, Myrlie Evers, Beulah Sanders, Jane Galvin Lewis, Eleanor Holmes Norton, Marian Wright Edelman, and Fannie

Lou Hamer. Aileen Hernandez, formerly of the EEOC and now president of the National Organization for Women (NOW), chaired a plenary session to hammer out the new organization's policy stances. In sum, as the political arm of the women's liberation movement, the NWPC would seek to promote feminist reforms and candidates in electoral politics. The caucus hoped "to get more women involved in politics, to consider running, to form a network of people that they could call upon, to talk to."[37] The resolutions called for caucuses to form in each state, and for a national registry of women political candidates, which would then allow more support and fundraising. The gathering adopted a twenty-point program centered on eradicating sexism, racism, violence, and poverty.[38] And it took on the task of enforcing party rules for gender equity at both parties' conventions, with 50 percent female representation in state delegations and committees. Its efforts would take immediate effect: participation of women delegates at the Democratic National Convention increased from 13 percent in 1968 to 40 percent in 1972.[39]

Chisholm herself had high hopes for the NWPC as a coalition-building moment between women and Black activists. "I believe we have taken a step in that direction," she said.[40] Two days later, and "bubbling with enthusiasm," she looked back on the weekend's events: "For the first time in a movement such as this we had many Black[s] participating. Two hundred seventy five in all came. And, they came from all classes, all colors, and all political persuasions. And they are committed to the one thing bringing us together, the need to organize to bring political clout to bear on the direction in which this country is moving."[41] Chisholm was likely delighted when Audrey Colom, a twenty-four-year-old teacher from Washington, D.C., saw news of the meeting and called Chisholm's office. The two spoke "at length," and Chisholm urged Colom, as a young Black woman, to get involved at the grassroots level. Chisholm's words carried much weight for Colom, who credited Chisholm for having "gotten rid of a lot of hang-ups I have about not offending white men." Colom responded by attending the first D.C. chapter meeting and agreeing to serve as its president.[42]

The need for such an organization was illustrated by the fact that Nixon, Henry Kissinger, and Secretary of State William Rogers openly mocked the photos of Chisholm and other cofounders at the NWPC, laughing that the scene looked like "a burlesque." Rogers teased Kissinger that Steinem was "Henry's old girl friend." Nixon's record on appointing women to positions in the executive branch was poor, a fact that he and others attributed to not being able to find qualified women. In one media blunder, Nixon thought inviting the wives of cabinet members to a meeting would make him look woman-friendly. His policy interests were also tone-deaf to women's issues.

From left: Gloria Steinem, Bella Abzug, Shirley Chisholm, and Betty Friedan
at the founding of the National Women's Political Caucus, 1971.
Charles Gorry / AP Photo.

But Chisholm remained unruffled. "We will indicate to them in 1972 what
can happen when women . . . get together."[43]

The organization set up national offices with the help of Liz Carpenter and her mentee Virginia Kerr. However, once she had helped found
the NWPC, Chisholm did not become a regular attendee of the meetings,
electing to send Downs in her stead. In part this was because she traveled
often and was out of the district. Also, the meetings were long—discussions
would continue until there was a consensus. According to some, Friedan
and Abzug's strong personalities and struggles for power (which Chisholm
reportedly mediated at times) could be exhausting. Chisholm also thought
that the organization should be run by the next generation of women political activists, whom she thought were the most important decision makers.
Finally, Chisholm had some frustration with NOW and the NWPC because
she wanted them to focus more attention on the needs of poor women and
economic justice. Whatever her reasons, some in the NWPC were miffed.
Downs thought that their irritation might have had an effect on Chisholm's
run for president later.[44]

Chisholm and Abzug's other major effort, for which they were joined by
Democratic representative Patsy Mink from Hawaii, was to pass the 1971
Comprehensive Child Development Act (CCDA) with a provision for uni-
versal day care. The CCDA had been developed in coalition with the NWRO,
NOW, and the National Council of Negro Women and introduced in the

Senate by Walter Mondale and in the House by John Brademas, a Democrat from Indiana who was chair of Chisholm's Select Subcommittee on Education. The bill aimed for a key victory for feminism in the late twentieth century by introducing universal childcare and thus affirming the rights of all women—not just poor ones—to participate fully in the labor marketplace. Were women able to work for wages without being constrained by lack of childcare, then a long-standing constraint on their career advancement and economic independence would be lifted.[45] The bill called for the establishment of universal day care facilities, to be phased in over the course of three years. Chisholm, Abzug, and Mink envisioned that children across all classes would be eligible to enroll in the facilities, thus avoiding the appearance that the program was an antipoverty or welfare program alone. They also called for a highly trained and professional staff that would provide high-quality educational services so that families would wish to enroll their children in public day care facilities.

Chisholm worked hard on the bill because of her on-the-ground experience in Bed-Stuy. She had encountered constituents who were on welfare because they lacked access to safe and meaningful childcare. She also knew that Black and brown women were the canaries in the coal mines for white women, and that the economic problems that nonwhite women experienced would reach white women, too.[46] For her, what was at stake was not only all women's self-determination to climb the career ladder freely, but the survival of poor women and their children. She and Abzug held public hearings on the need for universal childcare at the Veterans Administration Building in Manhattan in February, inviting a host of experts and community activists.[47]

The Committee on Education and Labor held hearings for the CCDA in the spring of 1971. Both Abzug and Chisholm testified, and they both stated that Brademas had introduced "a good bill." But they both argued that it did not go far enough. As a result of the New York hearings and a consultation with Marian Wright Edelman of the Children's Defense Fund, they had written their own version with significantly increased funding and introduced it on the day they testified. Under their bill, the first year's funding would be $5 billion, increasing to $10 billion over three years, because that was the amount the congresswomen had determined would be needed for the number of high-quality childcare facilities required. To those who might see such a number as astronomical, Abzug pointed out the $70 billion budget of the Department of Defense. Chisholm agreed: $10 billion was doable were Congress to invest in domestic programs as a top priority. If the Nixon administration were serious about getting people off of welfare, adequate childcare was a necessity.[48] Predictably, the Abzug-Chisholm version was not adopted by the subcommittee. But Chisholm tried another tactic. She went over subcommittee chair Brademas's head to appeal to Carl Perkins (D-KY), the chair of Education and Labor. She had a good working relationship with both Perkins and Albert Quie (R-MN), the ranking minority member on the committee. In response, Perkins chose Chisholm to be on the bicameral Conference Committee to reconcile the Senate and House versions of the bill, even though it was usually the chair of the subcommittee who served in that capacity. The result was a less fiscally ambitious version that preserved some of Chisholm and Abzug's changes, including provisions for small communities. But it compromised on the income limit and local control because of a competing coalition of southerners, conservative evangelicals, and antifeminists who worried about racial and gender changes as a threat to social order. Brademas added it to the 1971 reauthorization of the Economic Opportunity Act.[49]

The entire bill passed both houses with an appropriation of $2.2 billion for the first year, and some, including Health, Education, and Welfare secretary Elliott Richardson, thought Nixon would approve and that it was politically expedient to do so. But a political storm was gathering. Antifeminists feared that the childcare legislation, in allowing women unrestricted access to the labor marketplace, would cause women to abdicate their motherhood duties and place child-raising into the state's hands. According to historian Robert Self, "To abandon motherhood was a sacrilege. It was to undermine the nation itself." At the same time, southerners feared the local, rather than state, control of childcare centers and the potential racial integration that would bring.[50] Nixon was under lobbying from conservatives and his aide John Ehrlichman, and faced a reelection challenge from the right in the New Hampshire primary, Representative John Ashbrook (R-OH). The opposition correctly identified a major underlying objective of the bill: women's economic citizenship.[51] Despite messages of support from Republican legislators and a coalition of left-leaning groups, Nixon got far more vehement opposition from a developing coalition of antifeminists and Vietnam hawks who sought to reduce the government's domestic role, not expand it. He rejected the Economic Opportunity Act extension with a scathing veto message. On the child development provisions—which he called the "most deeply flawed" aspect of the bill—Nixon criticized it for its "fiscal irresponsibility, administrative unworkability, and family-weakening implications." He claimed it would diminish parental authority and involvement, tear families apart, and create communal, rather than parental, child rearing. It was, in short, a "radical piece of social legislation." This rhetoric, it was rumored, had been written by none other than Daniel Patrick Moynihan, author of *The Negro Family* report six years earlier.[52] The universal childcare bill was dead.

Chisholm, meanwhile, had forged ahead with her Black feminist power agenda to expand government on behalf of poor and nonwhite women. She addressed the first convention of the National Committee on Household Employment, during which the National Association of Household Workers was founded.[53] She contributed a foreword to *Abortion Rap*, a book by feminist lawyers Florynce Kennedy and Diane Schulder. Kennedy and Schulder had gathered depositions from women as part of a lawsuit, *Abramovicz v. Lefkowitz*, that they hoped to get to the Supreme Court as a test case. Reiterating her argument that outlawing abortions amounted to "compulsory pregnancy," she blamed illegal botched abortions for maternal injuries and deaths. In countries that had liberalized abortion laws, the death rates from illegal abortions had dropped.[54] She worked to get the Fair Labor Standards Act extended to preschools, which was interpreted by the Department of Labor to encompass day care workers. For this effort, she worked with the top lobbyist for the AFL-CIO, Kenneth Young. Young made sure that the chair of the subcommittee, Edith Green, knew he was involved behind the scenes.[55]

Chisholm collaborated with Edith Green, chair of the Higher Education Subcommittee, and her Education and Labor colleague Patsy Mink on what would eventually become the landmark legislation against sex discrimination in colleges and universities, Title IX of the Higher Education Amendments of 1971. Green, a Democrat from Oregon who had been in the House since 1954, held hearings in 1970 about sex discrimination in colleges and universities that most of the male members did not attend. Mink was a Democrat from Hawaii, elected in 1964 and a strong feminist leader who also challenged racism throughout her life. In 1971, however, with new allies on the Education and Labor Committee, including Chisholm, and with a large education bill in the works, Green seized the moment. She introduced the bill in April and quietly inserted a provision on sex equity among the more hotly contested items regarding financial aid and busing. Still, it attracted some negative attention. In the subcommittee, Republican Alfonzo Bell moved to strike it from the bill, much to the dismay of its proponents. After hearing this, Shirley Downs, Chisholm's legislative aide, stormed straight to the Republican counsel. "What did you do?" she exploded at him. "Why did you offer this? How did this happen?" The aide backed away. "No, no, Al offered it but it was given to him by John Brademas and we offered it for John Brademas." Stunned, Downs went to find out why the Democrat Brademas, who had worked for comprehensive childcare, was standing in the way of this particular sex equity legislation. It turned out that Brademas's legislative aide had attended an all-male college that he did not want to see integrated by sex. Downs mustered all of the women congressional staffers, members

of the press, and party fundraisers she could. She approached other Brademas aides and even women who dated the unmarried congressman, and
she talked to the wives and daughters of other congressmen. All lobbied
Brademas to reconsider his legislative aide's recommendation. Brademas
relented, and the Title IX amendment was sent to the full committee.

Green, hoping to keep the provision under the radar, did not even broach
the topic of Title IX until a meeting of the full Education and Labor Committee, where she could count on her allies Chisholm and Mink. Downs did not
take any chances this time and summoned a network of women to push its
passage. She befriended Carol Burris, who led the Women's Lobby. A coalition of women, including older suffragists, congressional caseworkers, and
secretaries, sat in on the committee vote. The efforts worked; the provision
survived the full committee intact and was reported to the House in October.
It came up for debate in November. Again Erlenborn offered an amendment
to reduce the impact of the law, as he had done with the Equal Employment
Opportunity Act. He wished to exempt undergraduate admissions at private institutions from the requirement for sex equity and was supported by
presidents at multiple elite schools. Although Green and Mink vehemently
protested and marshaled statements from other presidents of top schools,
the amendment passed by a narrow margin . Chisholm was, notably, absent
from the chamber for the vote. She did arrive in time to argue unsuccessfully
against John Ashbrook's amendment releasing school districts from the
responsibility to bus students in order to integrate. But the months of effort
did yield some reward. The entire bill passed, including Title IX, and was
sent to the Senate.[56]

Also successfully passed by the House in the fall of 1971 was the Equal
Rights Amendment. Although it had been introduced every year since 1923,
it had never successfully gotten out of committee. Chisholm had joined the
effort as a cosponsor since 1969. Martha Griffiths, the Democratic representative from Michigan who had successfully inserted the prohibition against
sex discrimination into Title VII of the Civil Rights Act of 1964, was the one
who finally got it out of the Judiciary Committee. In 1970, Griffiths cajoled
218 of her colleagues to sign a discharge petition, and the House ultimately
voted in favor of the ERA. The Senate, however, did not. But in 1971 Griffiths
again got the bill passed in the House, and the Senate would approve it in
1972.[57] It still needed ratification by the states, however, and Chisholm would
continue to advocate for it throughout the rest of her career.

Chisholm's first two terms were a high-water mark of attempting to realize the promises of liberalism to the Black freedom struggle and the feminist movement through Congress. Chisholm's radicalism—in the sense of

getting to the roots of vulnerable Americans' problems and solving them—was expressed in direct attempts at legislation and in institution building. Black feminist power depended on working intersectionally, advocating for both woman and Black Americans simultaneously. Chisholm sought to bolster Black feminist power through developing collaborations and coalitions that met at the intersections of humans' identities. She theorized that anti-humanism resided in antifeminism and anti-Blackness. The converse was that humanity was at the intersection of feminism and the Black freedom struggle. As she worked, she came to two realizations: her humanistic vision would not be realized with a hostile president in office with veto power, and she herself was eligible to run for president.

13
CHISHOLM '72

★

Shirley Chisholm's presidential campaign was an attempt to win that acknowledged the impossibility of winning. "Presidential Politics is a big-time, high-stakes game, and it is played by tough, sophisticated politicians with plenty of money and plenty of skill," she wrote in her second book, *The Good Fight*. "My own participation in 1971 and 1972 was a unique, one-shot phenomenon, an effort by an amateur supported by a crowd of idealists."[1] But she knew someone had to go first, and she felt compelled to do it. She simply felt that she was positioned to run a serious campaign that would "open up the doors" for Black candidates and women to seek the office in the future. "That was it. I wasn't even thinking what would happen if I got it . . . I really didn't think about these things at all. All that was on my mind was that I had to do it. I had to open the door ajar." She campaigned in Florida, California, Massachusetts, New York, New Jersey, Michigan, Minnesota, Colorado, and North Carolina, and appeared on the ballot in a dozen other states.

The idea was to bring a substantial bloc of delegates to the Democratic National Convention in Miami so as to be in a negotiating position. She had no illusion that she would actually win the nomination. She was, in fact, ruthlessly pragmatic. No Democratic candidate would be able to beat Nixon, she maintained during and after the campaign, except for Senator Edward Kennedy with Arkansas representative Wilbur Mills as running mate. Her analysis rested not on her particular affinity for Kennedy and Mills but on her calculus of what voters would do on Election Day: vote for a recognized name at the top of the ticket with a southern vice presidential candidate just below.[2] She was determined to see the campaign through the convention; to help turn the convention toward drafting Kennedy if possible; to influence the platform and get promises from the eventual nominee; and to "prove a point" that someone besides a white man could run.[3] She only succeeded at the latter. But in so doing, she violated political protocols that included paying one's dues and working through established channels. She insisted on following her own script when it came to running her campaign. The result was irritation mixed with grudging admiration from Black and women colleagues and activists as well as concern that she might be able to block the nomination of another candidate that might win loyalty from Black and women delegates otherwise.[4]

Far from seeing her catholic relationships with the Black freedom struggle and women's movement as liabilities, Chisholm's Black feminist vision of political power made her think she was uniquely suited to build a strong coalition. She envisioned a campaign organization and voter base of people who were Black, female, young, poor, or all four. By introducing racial and gender equality simultaneously, through the symbol of her own person, she thought that she could build a voluminous tent that would encompass Americans of all identities. In her dream, those within the tent would recognize each other as allies and come together as a committed electoral coalition that would bring enough clout to the Democratic Party to move the platform and the eventual nominee leftward. She repeatedly called herself the "instrument" through which all constituents had a voice.[5] As it would turn out, the coalition would never come to be, although she would become the first woman and Black American to carry delegates at the Democratic National Convention.

It was irrelevant to Chisholm that her unilateral decision to run annoyed other Black politicians and feminists. She was asserting her right to run, despite her extremely slim chances. And she had an unshakeable amount of confidence in herself and her convictions. "I ran because someone had to do it first," she wrote. "In this country everybody is supposed to be able to run for president but that's never really been true. I ran *because* most people think the country is not ready for a black candidate, not ready for a woman candidate."[6] Her Congressional Black Caucus (CBC) colleague and strongest supporter Ron Dellums admired the campaign for the sheer "audaciousness of it." She "was not demanding to get in; [she was] asserting her right to be in," he observed.[7] Shirley Downs agreed that it was Chisholm's self-confidence that allowed her to run. "She certainly thought she was smart enough to be president," Downs said, and there were people who called her an "egomaniac" for running. "But virtually everybody that runs has to have that little self-confidence," Downs admitted. Still, Chisholm saw the campaign as an empowerment exercise and not an attempt to gain personal power. Not only could anyone "fight city hall," Downs explained, but "you can become city hall." The result was a political education for both the National Organization for Women and the Black Panthers as both organizations became empowered within the political process.[8] Armed with the courage of her convictions, "I had a mind of my own, you can't tell me what to do," Chisholm would say later. In her view, her great strengths were "self-confidence, aggressive, no-nonsense, articulate, [and] decisive." She added, "I really can't think of my weaknesses," though acknowledged that others might criticize her stubbornness and iconoclasm.[9] She conceded that "I had too much confidence at times . . . maybe at times. I don't know. I was such a confident person. I was not afraid of anything or anybody."[10] Later in life, and perhaps even in 1972, Chisholm admitted that she did not think that someone so forthright and outspoken could actually be elected president, because of the money and lobbyists needed to win.[11] Yet one of her campaign workers recalled that on the toughest days on the campaign trail, Chisholm would wonder at the condemnation aimed at her, suggesting that she was unaware of how her persona rubbed influential people the wrong way.[12]

Nevertheless Chisholm found herself reaching across racial and gender lines out on the campaign trail and attracting a wide coalition of supporters. Indeed, she was able to raise $250,000, most of it from small donations (though total expenses were close to $300,000, and it took three years to pay off the remaining debt once the campaign was over).[13] She had been stunned when supporters in Florida and Minnesota, many of them women, raised $10,000 between them within a month. She had challenged their insistence that she run by pointing out that she would need money to do so, and they proceeded to do just that. "When they sent me the money, I was very much . . . I was very much afraid. It shook me a little bit. Because then if I didn't run, they'll have called my bluff and I'd say, oh gosh, what have I gotten myself into? And that's how it began to grow." Eventually she would have sixteen or seventeen satellite offices. Throughout the campaign, supporters were creative in their fundraising. They held chicken fries, fashion shows, and dances. The most that any one group raised was between $4,000 and $5,000, which alarmed Chisholm because she knew much more would be needed. But she said that the enthusiasm and her following kept her going.[14]

"A WOMAN PRESIDENT? IT'S NO JOKE, BUB": THE DECISION TO RUN

With a heightened national profile, a loyal cadre of students and women urging her to run, and an awareness that the Democratic Party took much of its base for granted, it now seems like a logical decision for Chisholm to think about a presidential bid. At the time, however, it was anything but. The supporters were vocal but few in number. The "New Politics" Democrats and Chisholm's own CBC colleagues seemed to never have thought about women as candidates. The coalition who understood overlapping constituencies—feminists, Black politicos, and young antiwar activists—was only composed of a few within each of those groups, and they argued among themselves.

Still, Chisholm was intrigued. For one, the student audiences wherever she lectured kept pleading with her to run. She had built a strong image among college students for her opposition to the Vietnam War and because of her many speeches on university campuses. In these speeches, she attempted to do what she outlined in the "Youth and America's Future" chapter of *Unbought and Unbossed*. She pushed students to see themselves as the catalysts for transformation. She was especially in demand during commencement season, giving speeches at Rutgers's Douglass College, Hampton University, and Howard University, plus many others. She encouraged Howard graduates to fight, but to "fight intelligently." She was interrupted nineteen times by applause from the crowd of 11,000, who cheered the loudest when she mentioned her refusal to vote for any military appropriations until there was a ceasefire in Vietnam.[15] The students pushed her to consider a run. "When are we going to change things?" asked a young man at one southern university. Chisholm did seem to gather strength from the overwhelming receptions she received, which was in marked contrast to the doubts and rebukes from her critics. And she thought that the response she got from young people was important politically. She believed that the failure of the Democratic Party in 1968 had come about in large part because of a split between younger radicals and the liberal establishment, and she thought that she could bridge the liberal-radical gap. And she loved the idea of being a trailblazer.[16]

Chisholm had begun her explorations of running for president in the late spring of 1971, looking for opportunities for coalition between her multiple constituencies in order to demand a response from the government. Groups in twenty-five states "organized . . . in their own way" for her as a presidential candidate. Their support pushed her to run, even though she knew that "hell was going to break loose."[17] By summer, Chisholm was warming to the idea. She was a featured speaker at the National Welfare Rights Organization's (NWRO's) fifth national convention on the campus of Brown University in Providence, Rhode Island, and used it to float the idea of running. The convention was focused on electoral politics; George Wiley, head of the NWRO, had envisioned a convention in which members would be encouraged to participate in electoral office, either as candidates for office or delegates to the national convention.[18] On July 31, she spoke to about 1,200 members of the NWRO in a stirring address, telling of her hopes of a coalition between young voters, women, Chicanos, Indians, Black people, and poor people. Dressed in a yellow suit with a "Welfare Not Warfare" button, she urged the cheering audience to seize political power. She shared her analysis that welfare was essential as "the recognition on the part of the government that the American system has failed to provide adequate educational opportunity and job training for all Americans. It is further recognition that it is the absolute right of every human being in this country to have an adequate diet, sufficient clothing, decent housing, and proper medical care."[19] At that moment, she explained, her CBC colleagues were holding meetings across the nation requesting that their colleagues make no firm commitments to political parties so that no party would take Black votes for granted. In conclusion, she raised her right fist in a Black Power salute to thunderous applause. At the news conference after the speech, Chisholm disclosed the exciting tidbit that she might run for president in 1972 and she was open to the possibility of running as a third-party candidate in case there was no acceptable Democratic nominee. The *New York Times* covered the announcement and concluded that Chisholm was running "not as a black candidate, but as a feminist," seemingly under the impression that the two were mutually exclusive.[20]

Chisholm was not the only one thinking of getting a Black candidate into the race. Other Black leaders had started to consider a strategy for 1971. The CBC had at one point tossed around John Conyers as a possible candidate. Jesse Jackson, head of Operation Breadbasket, of the Southern Christian Leadership Conference (SCLC), was reported to be pushing for a Black presidential candidate. He envisioned a third party for this purpose that would draw together Black and antiwar voters. Conyers was his chosen candidate, and, despite disagreement between Jackson and the CBC over the third party issue, he claimed he would be consulting them as he made electoral and legislative plans going forward. At the same time, there were rumors that he would be working with Carl Stokes, the Black mayor of Cleveland, on pressuring the Democratic Party to run a Black vice presidential candidate.[21] In September, *Jet* magazine released the results of a readers' poll it took on whether a Black person should run for president. Ninety-eight percent of the respondents said yes, with 30 percent choosing Georgia activist and state representative Julian Bond. Stokes got 27 percent, Conyers got 13, Massachusetts senator Edward Brooks got 7, and Chisholm got 5. Of the group, only Conyers and Chisholm had expressed interest in running.[22] Meanwhile, Black male leaders were strategizing. Chisholm agreed with her male colleagues on two counts: that the Democrats were taking Black voters for granted, and that they could take a Black bloc of delegates to the national convention and thereby influence the nominee and the platform. But she was not part of the conversations.[23] In August 1971, the National Democratic Party of Alabama, a multiracial rival to the state party, sponsored the Southern Black Political Caucus in Mobile, Alabama. Bond, Alabama gubernatorial candidate John Cashin, and Fayette, Mississippi, mayor Charles Evers led the gathering. Among invitees were all Black elected politicians in the South, the New Democratic Coalition, and the New Party. About 400 participants came. Chisholm, along with several of her colleagues in Congress, had originally planned to be there but did not attend. Among the workshops was one on delegate selection, which armed participants with the specifics on how each southern state would choose its Democratic delegates to the national convention. *The Nation*'s analysis of the meeting suggested that a Black "man" should run for president because, first of all, it would shock and surprise "the average white." Also, a Black presidential candidate would motivate many Black voters to register and vote, and perhaps run for delegate seats themselves. By doing so, and by fully taking advantage of the DNC reforms, these voters could bring pressure to bear on the national Democratic Party. However, Bond urged those present not to endorse any candidates yet. "No permanent friends, no permanent enemies, just permanent interests," he cautioned.[24]

Bond, with now Manhattan Borough president Percy Sutton, Congressman Gus Hawkins, poet and activist Imimu (Amiri) Baraka, and Coretta Scott King, brought Black political figures together again in Northlake, Illinois, near Chicago in late September, to what was supposed to have been a secret meeting. Bond was developing a "favorite son" plan: run popular local candidates in states and districts that had significant Black populations in order to win primaries, build blocs of Black delegates for the convention, and get Black voters to turn out. His idea was that local communities would choose their candidates, but already names were being floated. All of the CBC was invited to Northlake, along with the leaders of the major civil rights organizations, but Chisholm did not go, feeling at that point she might become a "center of dissension," and neither did Conyers, Stokes, and Ralph Abernathy of the Southern Christian Leadership Conference. Chisholm sent her aide and future campaign director Thad Garrett, who reported back that Baraka and Roy Innis of the Congress of Racial Equality (CORE) had stationed bodyguards at the base of the staircase leading to the meeting room. "I might remark that no elected black officials I know have bodyguards," she stated crisply, "only the self-anointed and media-anointed ones, and they must know better than I why they need them."[25] Chisholm's colleague, Washington, D.C., delegate Walter Fauntroy, was present and would eventually decide to run as a favorite son. Richard G. Hatcher, mayor of Gary, Indiana, and a California assemblyman, Willie Brown, also were dominant voices at the gathering. They planned a convention for the next year. Some of them were optimistic about Chisholm's candidacy.[26] However, Bond and Brown,

208   CHISHOLM '72

in particular, agreed that they thought Black politicians from New York had too much say in planning the direction of Black politics. Whether because of Chisholm's New York origins, her sex, her absence from the meeting, or a combination of those factors, those present followed Bond's and Brown's leads and declined to support her.[27]

Undeterred, Chisholm grew even more convinced that she needed to go forward. "The fact is," she observed, "that there was a vacuum into which I was propelled." The Northlake meeting had failed to produce a consensus Black candidate. She felt more strongly that somebody would have to press the white candidates on platform and policy. She thought she could bring a coalition together that could pressure the DNC. By November 1971, she had some grassroots "scouts" in over twenty-four states and plans to run in at least five primaries. Her momentum was building: one journalist wrote that she was "probably the most powerful black woman in the United States."[28] Chisholm seemed to be behaving as if she was. She certainly thought that she was the best candidate "because, paradoxically, I was not only a black candidate [but also a woman candidate]." She thought herself to be the most able to get votes, to have the largest dedicated pool of volunteers, and to have genuine grassroots support, because she envisioned her candidacy as bridging racial, ethnic, and gender lines. She was the candidate of anyone who wanted to change the status quo of who held power in America, which was a large group.[29]

And there was the rub. Black men politicians and activists expressed concern that Chisholm would represent women more than she would represent Black people. At the Northlake conference, an unnamed person had argued affirmatively that the first Black presidential candidate should be a man. She ran into sexism again soon after that. In October, she was invited to Jesse Jackson's Operation Breadbasket Expo. As she took that stage, she walked by a group of men standing together. One pointed her out to the other: "There she is—that little black matriarch." Chisholm was incensed, and she felt the sting of angry tears. When she reached the podium, she abandoned her planned speech about Black unity. Instead, she addressed sexism: "Women were intruders in politics in the eyes of men like these, and most black men were like these." She repeated her claim that she had encountered more barriers as a woman than as a Black person, and then announced that she would not ask permission of Black men to run. "Black men, get off my back!" she exclaimed. She then questioned Black men's dedication to all Black people. While she was seeking support from her male colleagues for the Free Angela Davis campaign, they had been mute, she pointed out. Thus, Black men leaders had no business questioning her commitment to helping Black Americans, she angrily declared.[30]

If anything, the resistance from male colleagues made Chisholm more determined to make a bid. Their disapproval grew at the CBC's conference of Black elected officials at Washington's Omni Shoreham Hotel in late November. Chisholm had been named as chair of a panel on early childhood education but had no leadership role in the heart of the conference's business, a session on national political strategizing. Louis Stokes had named an all-star panel for this task: his brother Carl Stokes, mayor of Cleveland; the up-and-coming state senator Barbara Jordan from Texas; Percy Sutton; and Howard Lee, mayor of Chapel Hill, North Carolina. The panel was fielding questions from the audience of elected officials when a fellow National Women's Political Caucus member and Black state representative from Florida, Gwendolyn Cherry, asked the room why "our Presidential candidate is not here" for a discussion on increasing political power. Cherry had publicly endorsed Chisholm in late September, acknowledging that her chances for a victory "seem very slim" but arguing that Chisholm would "make some of the candidates address themselves to the human necessities of life." Dramatically, Chisholm rose from the audience and took the microphone. It was "incomprehensible," she announced, that as a presidential candidate, the highest Black woman elected official, and the DNC's state committeewoman from New York, she was not invited to take part in the discussion. "You had better wake up," she snapped, in a criticism aimed at her male colleagues. Louis Stokes and the panel made no overt response to Chisholm, though Sutton did take a dig at her idea of coalition politics, claiming that Black activists needed to "coalesce within ourselves" first. Representative Bill Clay was incensed at Chisholm. Chisholm knew about the session on national strategy, he would write later, and was simply sowing seeds of discord in the CBC. Chisholm's "broadside of immeasurable venom" left him "flabbergasted by the unexpected and justified intrusion." In private, congressmen, who refused to be named in the press but who likely included Stokes, explained that they thought an all-Black meeting should decide which candidate to run, despite the fact that two prior meetings had failed to settle on one. In other words, Chisholm had jumped the gun in defiance of those who saw themselves as national Black leaders, and that leadership's snub broadcast their anger loud and clear.[31]

Chisholm forged ahead. She was adding more primaries to her incipient campaign and seemed committed. As the fall went on, she got more attention. The *Boston Globe*'s Mary McGrory called Chisholm a "whiplash of a woman" who was not afraid to act alone: "While the men were meeting in the backroom of a Chicago motel last September, trying to figure out which of them would go first, Chisholm slipped out and threw her hat into the ring." She told McGrory that she would announce in January or once she had raised $250,000, whichever came first.[32] In a November testimonial dinner in her honor at the Americana Hotel, she said that she would make an announcement in January. Mayor Lindsay was in attendance and wore a "Chisholm for President" button, though he did not make a formal endorsement.[33] Appearing with Bella Abzug at an Albany conference on women in electoral politics, Chisholm again asserted that she would run—in North Carolina, Florida, California, and Wisconsin at least.[34] When Ed Koch asked if she could be his running mate, she replied with a wink, "I don't think the country is ready for a Jewish Vice President."[35] At a campaign stop in East St. Louis, Illinois, in December, McGovern conceded that Shirley Chisholm had a "good record, but it's no better than George McGovern's record. I was fighting for the same thing she supports long before she entered Congress."[36]

Her staff was incredulous at first that their boss was serious about running. "I thought she was out of her ever-loving mind," Carolyn Smith recalled. "I was not the only one. Shirley Downs thought she had lost it," and so did her colleagues. But Downs understood: "Shirley Chisholm basically makes up her mind herself. She doesn't go running around consulting with people . . . she consults herself and then tells you." Chisholm's press aide Pat Lattimore was concerned about her safety, as was Conrad. "She gets the hate mail and the threats," Lattimore said, "but she'll plunge into a crowd full of all kinds of militants. I get very worried." Her family was surprised, too. When her sister Muriel Forde heard that Chisholm was running for president, she was living in Barbados, where she had moved in 1971. "Well, I thought, maybe she wants to try it, why not?" Forde said.[37] Thad Garrett, concerned, warned Chisholm of the work that was involved in running a presidential campaign, in addition to a congressional campaign every two years. Some CBC colleagues were hostile, such as Bill Clay. In contrast to Clay, Dellums was supportive and understood that she was trying to pave the way for others. Charlie Rangel was also supportive. Despite the fears about her sanity, safety, and/or corruption, Chisholm felt driven to try. "It's almost somebody from above, from the brother of God telling me, you can do it. Go do it," she recalled. "The thing about it, for better or for worse, I have tremendous confidence in myself. Tremendous confidence. Maybe too much. Always have."[38]

PRIMARY CHALLENGERS AND CHALLENGES

Chisholm's opponents in the Democratic primary were much better funded white men and included early favorite Edmund Muskie, then the U.S. senator from Maine; George McGovern, U.S. senator from North Dakota, the eventual nominee and the chair of the committee that reformed national conventions after the debacle of 1968; Henry "Scoop" Jackson, U.S. senator from Washington; her old ally New York mayor John Lindsay; former vice president Hubert Humphrey, who had won the nomination in the previous cycle; and Alabama governor and demagogue George Wallace. Her respect for these men was tepid: she would later say that Muskie and Lindsay felt a sense of entitlement, though Humphrey turned out to be "kinda nice."[39] She also faced an uphill struggle with the press, who concentrated on the race's favorites and thus gave her little exposure, creating a self-fulfilling prophecy. She was limited by the increasing reliance of presidential candidates on television appearances and what would later come to be called sound bites. With her slight lisp (she had this all her life) and formal demeanor, short video and audio did not do her justice. She had the capacity to energize audiences, but this worked best in longer-format appearances. Coupled with sexism and racism toward her candidacy, these challenges represented a major obstacle. As one reporter who covered the 1972 campaign for the Washington bureau of the *Los Angeles Times* put it, "There's always the con-cept in political journalism of a tier system," in which the judgment of the reporters would decide which candidate was the top priority to cover. "And you have a first tier and a second tier and a third tier. I would say in 1972, Shirley Chisholm was in the fifth tier," the reporter recalled.[40]

Chisholm spent the first half of 1972 holding down two jobs: as congress-woman and presidential candidate. Her weekday schedule on the campaign trail was to get up and have office hours in Congress, then sit in the House chamber at noon when it convened, and then at around two or three in the afternoon leave to fly to a campaign stop, even though the House session would go until six or seven. If possible, she would return to the District at nine or ten. She usually had an aide with her, and in the final two months four or five Secret Service officers with her, but did not travel with many people.[41] She recalled that she made her rivals, Scoop Jackson in particular, nervous when she showed up without an entourage. The other candidates would be getting last-minute briefings or makeup, and she would walk in by herself.[42]

Before Chisholm was polling above 5 percent nationally, she had no Secret Service protection. Humphrey, Muskie, McGovern, Jackson, and Wallace got Secret Service guards, but Chisholm did not. The criteria were that an announced candidate had to get 5 percent or more in a Harris or Gallup poll.[43] Even though Chisholm had gotten more than 5 percent in another public opinion survey, she was not guarded by the Secret Service until mid-May, when George Wallace was shot at a campaign stop in Mary-land. Conrad Chisholm and Victor Robles stepped in as bodyguards in the meantime. Conrad gave up his insurance fraud investigations, and he trav-eled everywhere with his wife, often listening to comments around him as he sat incognito in the audience. Robles got a permit to carry a gun to protect her. Because of her threat to the status quo, Robles was often afraid for her safety. "I would have given my life to make sure that Shirley Chisholm would continue to be what she is," he swore.[44]

Once a Secret Service detail was dispatched to the campaign in May, the Chisholms set up a base of operations for the agents in their home in Brooklyn. There were three shifts, and although the agents were overwhelmingly male, each shift had a woman on duty so she could accompany Chisholm to the restroom. The agents were delighted that the Chisholms provided a room with a card table and television set in their home, a gesture that no other candidate made. Apparently, guarding Chisholm became a plum assignment. The agents would show their affection by gifting the congresswoman with a binder at the end of the campaign that contained photos of the Special Agent in Charge John Paul Jones and agents on each shift, as well as Chisholm's campaign and office staff, and complete itineraries from the two-month period in which they guarded her.[45]

Although Chisholm would prefer to avoid discussing the campaign's physical dangers for the rest of her life, her run carried real risk. She was aware of three attempted attacks on her life. On one occasion, she had finished speaking in a large ballroom and then began to greet people in the room. The Secret Service noticed that there was a man shadowing her as she moved, and when they saw his hand go into his pocket they apprehended him. He had a large knife and had planned to stab Chisholm in the back. Robles also recalled that someone tried to enter Chisholm's room during a campaign trip in the South. A chandelier in Boston mysteriously crashed to the ground where she was standing moments before. She also received hate mail—some simply questioning her right to run, and some of it threatening. It did rattle her. When stopping in Memphis, she resisted staying in the Lorraine Motel, where King had been assassinated four years before. There was no other choice of accommodations, however, and Chisholm wound up keeping her aide Helen Butler up all night fretting about being attacked. Her staff was jittery also, and insisted on having one of them travel with her and help reassure her "and calm her down." They could be threatened, too. On one staffer's trip to North Carolina, he waited at the airport baggage claim for his boxes of brochures and bumper stickers, each of which had a sample of its contents stuck to the outside. The boxes rolled out on the carousel with "Nigger go home" handwritten across them.[46]

Far more numerous and visible than those who wished her bodily harm were Chisholm's devoted supporters. Observers of the crowds at her speeches were impressed by their enthusiasm. Although some thought that she was physically unattractive and noticed her lisp when she began, the audience invariably became adoring as she spoke.[47] One Massachusetts voter wrote: "If [the press] could have heard the supporters of Shirley Chisholm and felt the granite-like solidarity of their movement, they would not ignore her impact upon American thought."[48] A faculty member wrote from a community college in Baltimore that he was a McGovern voter but that he and other Black Americans could not love McGovern "as we can love a Shirley Chisholm."[49] Humphrey once remarked to her that if his campaign workers worked as hard for him as hers did for her, he would have been elected.[50] A former Democratic committeewoman from Minnesota wrote, "Smart, though-minded, and shrewd, [Chisholm] could put together a small surprise package at Miami Beach."[51]

Chisholm was the public face of the campaign and a woman, but there was a group of men behind the scenes: Conrad, Mac Holder, Thaddeus Garrett, and Victor Robles. Conrad continued to take care of Chisholm and their home. He cooked her meals and cleaned the house ("Conrad Chisholm was liberated!" said Robles). Holder was her campaign manager. "Genius. He was a genius," Chisholm would recall later. Mac Holder and Conrad were both sources of encouragement. Late in 1971, they had listened to Chisholm's complaints that her candidacy was not taken seriously and encouraged her to go ahead and announce in January. Thaddeus Garrett served as a manager of sorts in Washington. Both Holder and Garrett were good tacticians but "found it quite difficult to really manage" racist invective toward the candidate. Garrett had been elevated after the first campaign manager, Gerald Robinson, resigned during the Florida campaign. Garrett, a serious young Black Republican, did most of the press work. Robles remembered Garrett's formality. "We used to kid him, because . . . what black man went around calling himself Thaddeus Garrett III?" he remembered. "I mean, he made sure [he] emphasized the III." Robert Gottlieb, a summer intern in 1971 who went on to work on Chisholm's campaign in Florida, described Garrett as a "counterbalance" who was "more establishment." Garrett's presence was valuable as someone who was comfortable working with House leadership himself and who put white male politicians at ease.[52]

Bob Gottlieb was a white Cornell University senior from New York City. He had gone to work for Chisholm in Washington as a congressional intern in the summer of 1971, because of her principled stances and willingness to fight "the white establishment." But he quickly learned that his boss was also "savvy politically." Chisholm appointed him national youth coordinator for her campaign. Though he had almost no experience ("I really didn't know what I was doing"), he found himself in charge of a major aspect of the campaign, traveling to North Carolina, Florida, Wisconsin, and California, as well as upstate in his native New York. He was not paid enough to cover rental cars, gas, or hotels, so he slept in dorm rooms or people's homes. Campaigning on college campuses was very inexpensive, and he found himself to be operating as an advance person for such appearances: he would approach student leaders, ask them if they wanted to help organize a rally, and then contact local media about the event. Eventually he was promoted to "field coordinator." He had some successes, though he also felt like an "outsider" as a white man working with Black supporters.[53]

Chisholm had made the decision to run and put her team in place. Now she had to build the voter coalition and make her case to the voters that her Black feminist power approach to electoral politics was precisely what the country needed to address sexism, racism, and Vietnam as the cultural fissures dividing the United States.

14
THE CHALLENGES OF COALITIONS
ON THE CHISHOLM TRAIL

Chisholm's strategy to bring delegates to the Democratic National Convention depended on the creation of a broad electoral coalition. The coalition would represent those who were usually unrepresented. In numbers, she hoped, people from those populations—Black, brown, poor, young, and/or female—could bring some power to bear on the Democratic Party candidate and platform of 1972.[1] She theorized "that if we all bind together, we don't necessarily have to agree with every little point in the agenda. But if we bind together, numbers are important. We will become a force to be reckoned with at the convention."[2] She would require the nominee to promise a Black vice presidential nominee, a woman secretary of Health, Education, and Welfare, and an American Indian to be secretary of the Interior. She enjoyed strong support from people in each element of the coalition, with many enthusiastic volunteers. Ron Dellums, himself a coalition politician, explained why he thought her approach was the best option:

> At the end of the day I believe coalition politics are the most difficult but simultaneously the most sophisticated form of politics in this country. This is a country that is racially diverse, ethnically diverse, etc. . . . Coalitions force you to think about common interest. What we have to always remember is that people move for their reasons [and] not ours. And so it's finding people's self-interest that's important and bringing people together so that their common interest brings together a force capable of achieving the objective you want to achieve. For people who are in the minority . . . in terms of numbers . . . or ideas, in order to expand the numbers or to expand the power of the idea forces you to reach out beyond your own environment, beyond your own smaller group in order to bring in a broader range of people. So coalition politics are important politics . . . and ultimately the only real politics that makes sense.[3]

Chisholm's Black feminist power vision necessitated an intersectional coalition that explicitly included people who were Black, brown, female, or poor—and who oftentimes held more than one of those positions.

As Chisholm's experience shows, the difficulty of coalition was in maintaining it long enough to accomplish change. Too, creating and sustaining a national coalition rather than a locally focused one was much more difficult. Chisholm's vision was expansive, not exclusive, but some in constituent movements had separatist leanings, whether acknowledged or not. Tension existed between women's liberation and Black political activists, even though both groups had common roots in the Black freedom struggle in the late 1960s. But they had different theories on roots of oppression. Black activists were a mix of Black Power proponents, focused on poverty and police violence in cities, and establishment politicians. Meanwhile, the women's movement had emerged from a multigenerational activist network, some of whom were focused on equal access to middle-class opportunities while others took cues from Black Power and demanded human rights and the necessities for survival. Chisholm observed that "the women's movement has been a white middle-class phenomenon," while Black men and women were concerned with "survival," meaning access to basic resources. As a Black feminist, Chisholm wanted to bridge the perceived gap between Black men and white women's political priorities via electoral politics.[4] "And heavens, [my supporters] fought," she would recall later. "They fought like cats and dogs. Because I ran into the opposition and furor [between] the black people and the white women." In particular, Black men and white women "just could not come together. And in doing that, they destroyed themselves in the process." Bob Gottleib put it more bluntly: "Everybody hated everybody in that campaign." He spent much of his time smoothing over conflict in the New York office. "They all spoke the lingo, they all talked the talk," he recalled, but "everyone was in it for themselves."[5]

COALITION CHALLENGERS: BLACK COLLEAGUES

While Chisholm gravitated toward thinking intersectionally, not all of her supporters did. Both feminist and Black would-be coalition members created obstacles to coming together. "Black folks were seeing her as part of the women's movement campaign, and the women groups [sic] were seeing her more as a black candidate," one campaign aide explained.[6] Chisholm herself recalled, "If it was a black man that was running, I think it would be different. If it was a white woman that was running, I think that would be different. But here, a woman and a black person running, it just couldn't come together." She worried so much about the failure of this coalition that she lost weight during the campaign, and it took her several months afterward to recover.[7] "It was a helluva position to be in, really," she admitted.[8]

In addition to the internal rifts within Chisholm's supporters, she experienced pushback from both Black politicians and women's movement leaders. Because of her ideological and personal location at the intersection of race and gender, and her resistance to representing any one group in favor of an intersectional approach, she had multiple sources of power. This disturbed Black leaders, who questioned her loyalty to them, going so far as to say that she had "contempt" for Black male colleagues.[9] Black politicians complained "she had not taken any of us into her confidence and never discussed her plans for seeking the highest office." She had "jumped the gun [and] didn't give us a chance to put our strategy together." Julian Bond remarked that hers was "a unilateral candidacy. A great many Black politicians resented it. She went off entirely by herself."[10] They argued that Chisholm had become "captive" of the women's liberation movement. Carlos Russell, dean of contemporary studies at Brooklyn College and a member of the *New York Amsterdam News* editorial board, complained that for Chisholm "almost every issue is reduced to male vs. female . . . vaginal politics, so to speak." She was all talk and no action, he said, and took the Black vote for granted.[11] An anonymous Black leader complained that "she's a militant feminist and she rubs us the wrong way."[12] Chisholm believed such remarks were sexist, plain and simple. "Deep down inside their hearts," she theorized, "many of the blacks had a fear about women being in politics."[13] Such allegations carried additional weight because of the recent humiliation of the Moynihan Report and the increased criticism of male behavior by women's activists.

Not all Black male politicians withheld their support. In addition to Ron Dellums, Parren Mitchell supported Chisholm's challenge to George Wallace in the Maryland primary. At a joint press conference in Washington, Mitchell declared that Chisholm "might be the miracle we need to demonstrate that Wallace is antithetical to everything that is good and constructive."[14] Her former state assembly colleague Percy Sutton convened an advisory board on her behalf in February, after "weeks of secret and complex negotiations." Jesse Jackson and Richard Hatcher, mayor of Gary, Indiana, signed on. Sutton explained: "Shirley was out there and we had to make a decision. She put a number of us on the spot. I found I could not run around the country committed to a black Presidential candidate concept and not supporting Shirley. Then I decided, if I join her, she is accountable to me." Sutton, Jackson, and Hatcher visited Congressional Black Caucus (CBC) members in Washington to try to convince them to support Chisholm. There had been some deal making: Chisholm would agree not to run in Washington, D.C., where

Walter Fauntroy was a favorite son candidate, and Ohio, where current CBC chair Louis Stokes's brother Carl Stokes was mayor of Cleveland. The Stokes brothers wanted the option to keep Black Ohio delegates uncommitted until the national convention. As of early February 1972, Charlie Rangel approved of the effort. John Conyers was working out some final negotiations before making an official statement of support (he would eventually decide to support Chisholm in states where she had entered the primaries, and McGovern elsewhere). Sutton thought that Clay was leaning toward supporting Chisholm (he would eventually oppose her). However, the alliance was fragile because of "lingering bad feelings" over Chisholm's perceived unilateral decision and concerns that she was too loyal to the women's movement.[15] And it would not hold together in March at the National Black Political Convention in Hatcher's hometown of Gary. Black voters at large overwhelmingly supported Humphrey in the primaries, another reflection of the fact that many younger Black voters sat out primary elections. The older ones who did vote likely remembered Humphrey's early civil rights stance and might have regarded Chisholm's candidacy as symbolic.[16]

Constantly refuting accusations took a toll. Both Conrad and Mac Holder were concerned over the amount of energy she expended in educating people on her stance on women's liberation. While she made an effort to conceal the emotional impact of Black leaders' rejections, she did show her anger sometimes. One of her campaign workers in California recalled an occasion when Jesse Jackson preceded Chisholm on the stage. When Chisholm walked off, there was Jackson, kneeling, mock-worshipping and declaring his affection for her. Rather than feeling honored, however, Chisholm seemed to bristle. She felt that Jackson and others didn't truly take her seriously, and commented at times that they were "jiving" her. Bob Gottlieb heard her comment more than once that "they were going to kill me," meaning the negative forces coming from Black politicians threatened to exhaust and demoralize her.[17]

Chisholm's announcement disrupted calls for Black solidarity by other politicians. Many leaders saw that keeping Black voters unified in a bloc would be a powerful force within the Democratic Party—but they were far from unified on how to make that happen. Georgia state legislator Julian Bond floated the idea of forming a Black Party. The Black arts movement poet Amiri Baraka wanted to create an African People's Party. A group of activists and Black business people were already negotiating with the DNC and had among their demands 20 percent Black staffers and committee members. Julian Bond said he was inclined to support Chisholm but did not want to be "tied down" to one particular candidate. He would, in a "curious development since Julian was one of the earliest and most vocal supporters of the concept of a Black candidate and a Black strategy," support McGovern.[18]

The most visible break between Chisholm and other Black politicians was when she did not go to the National Black Political Convention in Gary, Indiana, the second weekend of March. The convention seated 4,000 delegates from fifty states. Its leaders, which included her CBC colleagues in the House, Charlie Diggs and Walter Fauntroy, plus Jackson and Baraka, were somewhat divided between nationalist and integrationist goals, and between endorsing a presidential candidate or not.[19] Just a few days before the Gary convention opened, Chisholm publicly announced that she would be campaigning in Florida instead. She implied that it was because she had already planned her campaign schedule before the Gary schedule was ready.[20]

But there were more complicated reasons. Chisholm was still not garnering concerted support from Black political leaders. She felt that she had little to gain and much to lose from attending. Chisholm saw little possibility of coalition between those who advocated separatism and integrationists (like herself) who hoped to demand racial and economic justice from within the political system. Worse, however, were the rumors she had heard of questionable alliances between Black convention participants with white politicians, promising votes for favors. She thought the convention's organizers were disingenuous: while thousands of Black delegates willingly spent their savings to travel to Gary for the meeting to decide on a Black strategy, she believed that some of the conveners were already privately pledged to a candidate. This drastically reduced the leverage for bargaining with candidates.[21] And then there was the sexism. Women were noticeably absent or few among the organizers and speakers. She recalled later that she heard some organizers of the convention had wanted a Black male candidate to run and intended to discredit her. "To me, the [Gary convention] was called primarily to oust Shirley Chisholm," she concluded.[22] She took a calculated risk to travel to Florida instead of Indiana because she thought she would lose publicly if she went to Gary.

Observers wondered whether it was sexism that kept the convention from endorsing Chisholm, or whether it was Chisholm who was "foolish [as] the only announced black [presidential] candidate to stay away from the gathering in the face of implied repudiation."[23] New York Amsterdam News political reporter Chuck Andrews seemed to think that, given the lack of consensus among those headed to Gary about endorsing her, she was well advised not to go. The Amsterdam News's executive editor, Bryant Rollins, corroborated that there was risk to Chisholm by reporting that the New York delegation had decided not to endorse their native daughter.[24]

Chisholm's candidacy was a major fault line at the convention. Jesse Jackson was still backing her, as was her old ally Percy Sutton. But there was plenty of criticism: she was a woman, she had decided unilaterally to run, and she envisioned an integrated coalition instead of advocating for Black Americans only. The convention did decline to endorse her (or create a new political party, for that matter). Carl Stokes, mayor of Cleveland and brother to Chisholm's CBC colleague Louis Stokes, was a Humphrey supporter and one of the forces behind the decision not to endorse Chisholm. "Admittedly," he said in 1973, the decision not to endorse "was to stop them from joining Congresswoman Shirley Chisholm on her ego trip in the presidential primaries." Given its seemingly unbridgeable divides, the convention's main outcome was a National Black Assembly that agreed to meet next in Philadelphia in 1976.[25]

Most of Chisholm's Black colleagues and the Gary convention were focused on forming a Black bloc of delegates at the convention and voters in the ballot box. Coalitions across racial lines were not a major consideration. Therefore, Chisholm's cooperation with feminists and antiwar activists ran counter to what the loudest voices within Black politics were saying.[26]

CHALLENGES IN THE WOMEN'S MOVEMENT

Chisholm's relationship with women's movement leaders was similarly fraught. 1972 was the first presidential election year in which a broad-based women's movement received attention from most of the candidates. Chisholm was explicitly profeminist, but in a marked change from 1968, every other candidate made an effort to signal his friendliness to women's concerns, too. The Democratic candidates took pains to add "and women" to every mention of the word "men," and McGovern had pledged to appoint women to his cabinet. Even Nixon had appointed a woman to his Committee for the Re-Election of the President, and the Republican Party had produced a brochure full of tips on how to properly behave toward women.[27] The National Women's Political Caucus named as its top priority the equal representation of men and women and political party conventions in 1972. This recommendation had been issued by the McGovern Commission reforms, and the National Women's Political Caucus (NWPC) needled Democratic and Republican Party leadership to follow through.[28] They were excited because this was the first major-party run by a woman that campaigned in many states, a fact that Chisholm herself was proud of.[29]

But they were also ambivalent, especially feminist leaders. Bella Abzug and Betty Friedan publicly praised Chisholm but stopped short of fully adopting her as the NWPC's candidate because they also did not think she would win. Chisholm was deeply disappointed in her former collaborator

Abzug, who "turned out to be kinda a traitor of the cause," after indicating that she would endorse Chisholm but never doing so.[30] When Friedan introduced Chisholm at the National Organization for Women regional meeting in New York City, as "the first woman President of the United States," she hastily added that vice president was also acceptable. Chisholm immediately reminded the audience that she was indeed running for the top office.[31]

Chisholm laughed about NWPC infighting with reporters, but she really thought that the failure of the women's movement to stand wholeheartedly behind her was racism. She suspected movement leaders assumed a white woman candidate would be more competitive. Carolyn Smith thought that Chisholm's iconoclasm and resistance to being directed by the movement's leaders was part of the problem ("she and Betty Friedan, oh they used to fuss back and forth on the phone, you know"). Friedan and Steinem wanted Chisholm to be a spokesperson for them, Smith thought, and their vision of the movement.[32] Her one-time biographer Brownmiller seemed unaware of Chisholm's coalition and delegate pressure strategy, saying, "I am sure that many women in the Chisholm campaign shared Chisholm's delusion that she had a chance." Calling Chisholm supporters "rank and file women," she implied that they were not savvy enough to understand how politics really worked.[33]

White feminists offended Black activists at times. Sometimes, white women would point out that their financial contributions should let them have a greater voice in the campaign.[34] Worse, some white feminists' interactions with Black activists and voters were unappealing or downright offensive. Betty Friedan was excited about Chisholm's campaign and determined to be involved, but some of her interventions were tone-deaf and did not make a good impression on Chisholm supporters. One observer said that "she ranted in a breathless manner and the folks in Brooklyn wanted to know who that woman was and why Shirley let her speak." Friedan had hired a public relations firm and threw a fundraising party for herself as a Chisholm delegate without sharing the money with the Chisholm campaign, which created more tension. Then disaster struck. Friedan decided to campaign for Chisholm on the Saturday before the New York primary with a "Traveling Watermelon Feast," a plan to distribute watermelon to Harlemites from a flatbed truck carrying a band. Chisholm delegate candidates were horrified. The *New York Amsterdam News* put it bluntly: "Yes, Betty Friedan was coming to Harlem, band and all, and to distribute watermelon to the natives." The campaign hurriedly canceled the event, though not before Friedan's plan had managed to offend political allies.[35]

Within the National Organization for Women's leadership, Wilma Scott Heide and Muriel Fox publicly encouraged donations to Chisholm's campaign. Steinem was Chisholm's staunchest supporter among white movement leaders, meeting with Chisholm and holding on the longest.[36] Steinem had recently tapped Chisholm to serve on the board of her Women's Action Alliance advocacy organization, although she qualified her support for Chisholm by naming her alongside Bella Abzug as the best woman candidate. But Steinem already had a close working relationship with McGovern dating back to 1968.[37] When it came to the convention, many feminist leaders would support McGovern, including Steinem. Author Kate Millett explained in an interview: Chisholm was "far and away the best candidate," but Steinem was pragmatic in "trying to see that a white, male candidate represents women's interests."[38] This pragmatic approach that white women could take for white men was not possible for Black women and was the source of a significant fissure in the U.S. women's movement of the 1970s.

BLACK WOMEN, YOUTH, AND LGBTQ SUPPORTERS

In contrast, Black women were some of Chisholm's most reliable advocates, and Chisholm, for her part, had a strong desire to impart confidence to future Black women in politics. Lawyer and Black feminist radical Flo Kennedy became an unfailing supporter. Kennedy and Chisholm had both joined the New York chapter of the National Organization for Women in 1967: Kennedy as a leader and organizer and Chisholm as an advocate in the state legislature and ceremonial vice president. They had worked together on changing New York's state abortion laws, and Chisholm had written the foreword to Kennedy's *Abortion Rap*, a book that included selected testimonies from the *Abramowicz v. Lefkowitz* class-action abortion rights suit Kennedy had prosecuted in 1970. The two had also cooperated on the public campaign to free Angela Davis. Chisholm and Kennedy's ideas on the necessity of coalition mirrored each other. Like Chisholm, Kennedy believed that coalitions of other groups with the Black freedom struggle were necessary to create real change. It "never occurred to [Kennedy]" "that a women's movement would not also fight against racism and imperialism."[39]

When Chisholm announced her campaign, therefore, Kennedy was a ready ally. Kennedy immediately saw the coalition-building opportunities the campaign presented. She institutionalized her support for Chisholm after a group of Queens College students asked her how they could campaign. Eschewing complicated organizational charters and bylaws-writing, Kennedy simply set up a group, the Feminist Party, for the purpose of recruiting a cross-racial cadre of college students to support Chisholm's bid. Her strategy was to set up Feminist Party chapters on college campuses, which eventually numbered over twenty nationally, and recruit Chisholm-pledged delegates to run in New York's Democratic primary. She also sought greater

Supporters listening to Rep. Shirley Chisholm,
St. Paul AME Church, Roxbury, Massachusetts, 1972.
Michael Dobo / Dobophoto.com.

media attention to the Chisholm campaign. As Chisholm herself argued, Kennedy campaigned not because of an expectation that Chisholm would win, but in an effort to steer press coverage and political negotiations toward recognizing Black feminist priorities.[40]

On March 2, led by Kennedy, the Boston chapter of the Feminist Party announced its formation and support of Chisholm's candidacy, urging Massachusetts voters to vote for her in the April 25 primary. They believed that Chisholm would bring "feminist values . . . into the major areas of American life." Those values would transform the country from one at war to one at peace. They reminded voters that gender hierarchy in society easily became racial, ethnic, and religious hierarchies. And they wanted to bring the strategy of consciousness-raising into politics. They typed up information sheets telling people what the ballot would look like and how to vote for Chisholm.[41] The Boston chapter made awards to local journalists, a local artist, and Chisholm's campaign organizer Saundra Graham. And the national Feminist Party held demonstrations in support of Chisholm at the Miami convention. Kennedy and filmmaker Sandra Hochman led a group of Feminist Party members at the Democratic National Convention into a demonstration to protest the lack of Chisholm coverage.[42]

Not all Black women embraced Chisholm, however. She perceived that some were deterred by the pushback they got from Black men's arguments that Black women should stay in the kitchen or support men's political ambitions, not run for office themselves. After Chisholm's angry speech in 1971 at Operation Breadbasket in Chicago, other Black women privately said that they sympathized with her but were "afraid" to defend her for fear of being attacked as man-hating. Chisholm believed that such fear of being labeled a race traitor was the reason the National Council of Negro Women and Black sororities did not publicly endorse her.[43]

Young voters were the core of Chisholm's coalition. The Twenty-Sixth Amendment, allowing eighteen-year-olds to vote, meant that a new crop of young supporters could add their sweat equity as well as their vote to her campaign. In all, she recalled later, one-fifth of her votes came from college-age youth. They were attracted to her, she thought, because she seemed authentic: "They felt a certain kind of sincerity in me, they said I sounded real."[44] She estimated that she went to about seventy-five college campuses and spoke to packed auditoriums during the campaign. She thought that they liked the fact that she would sit on the floor with them to talk and joke, and she was touched by their concern for her safety: many of them were afraid that she would be assassinated. The faith of the students bolstered Chisholm. "There's nothing like knowing people believe in you," she said.[45] However, a groundswell of newly enfranchised young voters would not materialize at the polls.

Chisholm also had a constituency of LGBTQ voters. Chisholm thought that one of the reasons that they supported her was that they, too, saw her as sincere, and that she explicitly condemned discrimination against gay people as part of her platform (no other candidates did).[46] Ron Dellums argued that Chisholm's "putting a face" on racism, sexism, homophobia, and environmental destruction made it impossible for other candidates to ignore those issues. "Shirley's contribution . . . was to be an articulate person on these issues," he recalled. "Sometimes standing out there on some issues, perhaps even more clearly and more focused because when you have nothing to lose then you can risk it all. . . . I believe that once, as a politician, you free yourself of any consideration of winning and losing, then the focus becomes something much larger, something much more significant, and that is the integrity of the debate."[47]

But other would-be allies accused Chisholm of divisiveness. Her potential as a divisive figure in the 1972 presidential race was criticized by Democrats and, in at least one instance, was seen as an asset by Nixon's Committee for the Re-Election of the President (CREEP). G. Gordon Liddy's original plan to defeat the Democratic Party in 1972 ("Operation GEMSTONE") included

"Operation COAL," a plan to send financial support to Chisholm. He thought that supporting her could "force Democratic candidates to fight off a black woman, bound to produce ill-feeling among the black community and, we hoped, cause them difficulty with women." Attorney General John Mitchell immediately dismissed the plan, implying that Nelson Rockefeller was already carrying it out. Liddy dropped Operation COAL from the plan, though other "dirty tricks" were in the works.[48] Such machinations were a further threat to the already fragile coalition behind Chisholm's candidacy.

THE CAMPAIGN TAKES A STAND

Chisholm set up a Washington, D.C., campaign office at 20 E Street N.W., the old Dodge House, in January. She hired Kentuckian Lori Collier and Princeton junior Lizabeth Cohen to run the office and started producing position papers (likely penned by Thaddeus Garrett).[49] There would be eight papers in all, under the banner "Shirley Chisholm Speaks Out," on international aid, the Middle East crisis, African foreign relations, the economy, the American justice system, the environment, consumers' rights, and housing equality. As a group, they sounded central themes: the Nixon administration's indifference or hostility to everyday citizens; the same administration's friendliness to corporations and industry to the detriment of most Americans; Chisholm's priority of butter over guns—domestic programs over military spending; and the outlining of policies that would benefit poor, Black, and brown people.

The first three position papers were on foreign relations and advocated for the United States to prioritize its support of democracy and peace overseas, rather than tolerating repression and militarization. On international aid, Chisholm denounced previous programs as maintainers of the status quo, and declared the United States the "chief arms supplier of mankind." She posited a program of building infrastructure and education instead, in order to aid poor and dispossessed people. Striking a similar tone on the Middle East, she pledged to "remember the human element" in both sides of the Israel-Palestine conflict and to recognize all countries diplomatically. On Africa, Chisholm pledged an "attitude of sympathetic solidarity" with African countries in order to bolster America's standing in the world. She promised to expand economic aid and trade with Africa, while condemning any governments or European colonial powers that stifled democracy.[50]

The next four position papers concerned domestic policy. On economic issues, her central assertion was that Nixon was influenced more by "big business" than the needs of everyday Americans. He followed the "time-honored Republican tradition of 'what is good for General Motors is good for the country'" by allowing prices to rise and subsidizing corporations.

Chisholm disagreed with such a strategy. She pointed out that, under such a doctrine, unemployment and the cost of living were rising simultaneously, while the economy's rate of growth was decreasing. Economic inequality, she said, should be laid at the feet of the government's overly friendly policies toward industry. To remedy the situation, she outlined an eight-point plan to end poverty: get out of Vietnam; add a guaranteed annual income of $6,400; increase taxes for wealthy corporations and individuals; reduce spending on space, defense, highways, and farming subsidies; create half a million public service jobs; ensure equal opportunities for women; add a national day care system; and support nonwhite businesses.[51]

Chisholm had similarly critical words for Nixon's "law and order" doctrine. With such rhetoric, Chisholm baldly stated, he had "declared war on blacks, non-whites, and the young." Adding insult to injury, law-and-order policies were unconstitutional and failed to stem a rising crime rate. Nixon committed "sins of omission" by not restricting gun sales, not providing drug or other rehabilitation, not reforming courts, allowing continued police misconduct, and ignoring common sense calls to decriminalize some behaviors. Meanwhile, his "sins of commission" included politicizing the Department of Justice and encouraging counterviolence, as well as appointing Supreme Court justices who sought to roll back civil rights gains and looking the other way when civil rights were violated. If elected, Chisholm said, she would prohibit handguns; add Black, brown, and female judges and law enforcement officers; replace J. Edgar Hoover at the FBI; reform prisons to add a prisoner's bill of rights; add treatment for substance abuse and separate treatment from punishment; create civilian review boards and increase funding for police; create better information sharing between agencies; support the federal Civil Rights Commission; uniformly apply criminal laws; abolish indeterminate sentencing; and enforce federal antitrust laws.[52]

Chisholm's next two position papers turned to tempering the influence of corporations in order to protect the environment and consumers. Despite Nixon's address to Congress on the environment and his signing of the Clean Air Act in 1970, Chisholm thought that Nixon's captivity to big business hindered his response to environmental crises. The result was continuing air pollution, water pollution, power brownouts, and sprawl. Her emphasis was on what is now called environmental racism. In direct opposition to GOP orthodoxy that environmental regulations cost jobs, she argued that environmental cleanup could generate jobs and growth. She applauded the revival of the consumer movement, which had been founded at the turn of the century and called on the federal government to institute food and drug standards. Its resurgence in the 1960s demanded consumer protection from corporate avarice. Chisholm saw the movement as a necessary "attack [on] the injustice, irrationality, and unfairness in our society." Holding business accountable regarding the quality and safety of the products it offered would reduce business's outsize influence and restore power to the people. She promised her administration would immediately create a federal consumer protection agency, create standards and requirements for product safety, and allow consumers greater opportunities in the courts.[53]

Chisholm reserved the issue of residential segregation, which she placed under the heading of "Housing," for her last and longest position paper. She acknowledged that Americans of all races were among those in inadequate housing, and attributed the problem to a lack of support for urban Americans in general. The heart of the problem, though, was the existence of two housing markets: one Black and one white. Black citizens were paying more for comparable housing and were still restricted to ghetto neighborhoods. There, they encountered poor public facilities and services, including schools, sanitation, transportation, and food shopping options. Such inadequate resources led to a lack of economic mobility, to "wasted lives and manpower," and, occasionally, to rage and riots. The solution was fourfold: a change in zoning laws that would allow affordable housing units in more places, including wealthy suburban neighborhoods, enforcement of non-discrimination laws, reduced property taxes, and subsidies where needed. An eleven-point list encompassed these and related promises to improve life in cities.

Chisholm did not create specific position papers that addressed women's rights and the Black freedom struggle, choosing instead to weave the concerns of those movements within each topic. She did discuss abortion and gay rights on the campaign trail, topics her competitors avoided.[54] Usually, she named issues that already concerned liberal Democrats and incorporated solutions designed to increase racial and gender equality. For example, instead of writing a solely antiwar position paper in response to the antiwar movement, she wrote three position papers outlining a progressive foreign policy. Such an approach stepped away from the politics of politicized identities and toward an intersectional analysis. Her headline issues were familiar ones to other Democrats and did not necessarily depart from their positions in substantial ways. In early 1972 the liberal Americans for Democratic Action (chaired by Allard Lowenstein) rated Chisholm at 97 percent, its highest score except for that of Edward Kennedy at 100 percent (conversely, the conservative group Americans for Constitutional Action rated her the lowest of all presidential candidates, at 18 percent).[55]

As her platform took shape, she was also shaping a claim to Black feminist political power—both through her own person as a potential holder of presidential power and in empowering those who had been denied political power in the past. She understood that many Black, brown, female, young, and poor voters lived at the intersections of more than one of those categories. And the more humane world that she outlined in the position papers would help all of the people, regardless of identity. She kept her agenda focused on her constituents, seeking to build a coalition of voters who could mobilize together for political reform. Her kind of reform, if successful, would ultimately transform politics in the United States. But it was also a radical approach in that she wanted to use politics to create solutions for the problems electoral politics itself had created. Her platform in place, Chisholm set off on the campaign trail.[56]

15
WINNING DELEGATES
ON THE CHISHOLM TRAIL

Chisholm's road through the primaries in the first half of 1972 brought her Black feminist power politics to all corners of the continental United States. The campaign was like her usual lecture circuit, but with many more appearances and this time with a concrete goal of shifting political power. New audiences encountered the Chisholm Mystique and were swept into action by her charisma. She exposed each audience to her Black feminist power political vision. Every location where Chisholm campaigned was its own political ecosystem, in dialogue with others through the conduit of Chisholm for President. The effort drew in new voters and activists, some of whom would remain in politics for the rest of their lives. Chisholm herself became a truly national figure in the process, with a national reputation and a new platform for her ideas.

The point of campaigning in the states was to get delegates for the 1972 Democratic National Convention in Miami. Delegates would be the currency for negotiations there. Empowering a Black feminist political agenda required obtaining loyal delegates, state by state. A contested convention was expected, and candidates in a narrow contest might be willing to make promises in exchange for delegate votes. Each state's Democratic Party made the rules for how delegates were apportioned from the results of that state's primary. Chisholm hoped that, by focusing strategically on states that might have a bloc of voters behind her, she would win delegate representation at the convention. Chisholm hit the trail in January and began the rounds of a handful of states that, she hoped, would yield a substantial delegate count. She was already registering in the national polls, though in small amounts. Gallup showed that Ed Kennedy was in the lead, but he had not declared his candidacy. If Kennedy was not included in the tally, she had 2 percent nationwide, suggesting that she and Kennedy were attracting some of the same voters.[1]

The official launch of the campaign before setting out was in the school auditorium at Bedford-Stuyvesant's Concord Baptist Church on January 25. The audience of about 500 was filled with Black women and students from the church's elementary school.[2] Chisholm began with a statement that was a manifesto for Black feminist power politics; her stance at the intersection of race and sex allowed her to define herself as a universal people's candidate:

> I stand before you today as a candidate for the Democratic nomination for the Presidency of the United States.
>
> I am not the candidate of Black America, although I am Black and proud.
>
> I am not the candidate of the Women's Movement of this country, although I am a woman, and I am equally proud of that.
>
> I am not the candidate of any political bosses or special interests.
>
> I stand here now—without endorsements from any big name politicians or celebrities or any other kind of prop. I do not intend to offer you the tired and glib clichés which have for too long been an accepted part of our political life.
>
> I am the candidate of the *people* and my presence before you now symbolizes a new era in American political history.

The speech showed off her electric speaking style and expressed her faith in the promise of American democracy for all. She pointed out that the federal government had made fundamental mistakes such as Vietnam and an economic policy that left behind millions of citizens in unemployment or poverty. She blamed the Nixon administration for these problems and lifted up "the American people" as those who would save the nation—specifically naming "Women, Blacks, Browns, Indians, Orientals, and Youth" as members of this vanguard. She believed that people would move beyond racism and sexism to vote for a nonwhite, nonmale candidate; indeed, a "new sensibility" would lead them to demand substantive change. In her vision of "a new America," citizens would be free from war and violence, poverty and discrimination—and have access to the fundamental necessities of life such as housing, health care, jobs, clean water, and clean air. She ended with a specific plea for those who had previously felt left out of politics to join her.[3]

The campaign had an undeniable energy and optimism. Responses to the announcement were ecstatic in some quarters. The *New York Times*'s editorial board was approving. Chisholm did not harbor false hopes of winning the nomination, the editorial acknowledged. Rather, Chisholm "projects herself as a symbol and a spokesman for what ought to be rather than what is." Chisholm might well have been pleased with the essay's closing remark: "Hers is a venture in the politics of hope."[4] But other press opinions were lukewarm at best. The *New York Times* also warned that perhaps it would be best for Black Americans to "concentrate their efforts behind a man they regard as best on the whole range of issues," implying that Chisholm's womanhood somehow limited her relevance on the issues.[5] The *Amsterdam News* declined to endorse her. "While we welcome her candidacy," the editors wrote, "we are not, at this point, prepared to offer an editorial endorsement of Cong. Chisholm."[6] *Boston Globe* columnist Martin Nolan was fairly dismissive. He predicted that McGovern's and Lindsay's campaigns would be "crippled" by her declaration and saw her and McCarthy as "equally frivolous." And he said she was "defeatist" for acknowledging that Nixon had the silent majority vote. An anonymous *Globe* editorial wisecracked that Chisholm weighed only ninety-eight pounds, but "many presidents have been lightweights."[7] Columnist Mary McGrory noted that some "members of the Black Caucus are mourning in private that a symbol of their centuries-long matriarchal dominations should be their standard bearer."[8]

Bolstered by the enthusiastic reception she got at the campaign launch speech, Chisholm mounted her campaign. She would campaign heavily in Florida, Massachusetts, California, and New York, with smaller efforts in North Carolina, Michigan, Wisconsin, Minnesota, and New Jersey. She knew that she had to generate delegates—the purpose of any presidential political campaign. Therefore, she tended to choose states that had a lot of delegates available and awarded them proportionally. But she also wanted to get new voters involved and empower women and Black, brown, young, and poor people to use electoral politics as a way to improve their own lives. Therefore, she campaigned in states where it was difficult to win delegates if there was a local campaign organization that gathered enough funds. The candidate carried her own dreams as well as those of many newly energized organizers and voters.

FLORIDA

Chisholm was pleasantly surprised by the large amount of support that she received in the South. In Alabama, Mississippi, and Georgia, white supporters established campaign offices, belying the warnings of those who said that she would not receive any southern support and that she should write the region off. In contrast to waffling liberal politicians in the North, she recalled, southern politicians would give their unstinting support once they had pledged it to a candidate. Four years later, there would still be Chisholm for President groups in some southern states. Later in life she reflected that her travels to the South had pushed her to think about people as humans and not labels.[9] While it was true that most formal political power was held by white men who were indifferent or hostile to her agenda, there was a diverse coalition of southerners who worked hard on expanding democracy in their states.

Chisholm was convinced to run in Florida due to a coalition that included Black women political activists, students, and feminists. Their enthusiasm led Chisholm to think that there was potential for her to get some of Florida's eighty-one delegates in the March 12 primary. She had strong support in the northern panhandle, as well as enthusiasm from women in the international city of Miami down south. Gwen Cherry, the state representative who had passionately advocated for her at the Congressional Black Caucus conference the previous November, was the campaign's engine in Florida. Cherry called Chisholm's Washington office and explained to the congresswoman "that Chisholm for President organizations were ready to swing into action in several parts of the state if I would say the word." Chisholm agreed to try a concentrated campaign in the state.[10]

She set out for a tour of north Florida during the first week of 1972. She discovered there that local Black politicians, especially men, were lukewarm, but students and women were enthusiastic.[11] Her devoted core constituency of Black and white students, white feminists, and Black women activists was helpful in the uphill battle, and they welcomed her enthusiastically. Her strategy was to visit with Black and women's organizations (including National Organization for Women [NOW] local chapters) and speak on college campuses. There would even be some dancing at a Miami nightclub. The January tour brought her to a largely white audience at Florida State University that turned out 2,000 strong and another excited audience at Florida A&M, a historically Black university.[12] A Florida liberal caucus in late January would award McGovern 83 percent of the vote and Chisholm 8, providing some cause for hope.[13]

However, Chisholm's effectiveness on the stump was undermined by the disorganization and discord within the campaign organization. Campaign offices had opened in several cities, but the volunteers were very difficult to coordinate.[14] The initial state coordinator "quit in frustration" because volunteers on the ground could not stop fighting, and also because he "thought this was a real amateur campaign." Nobody was fully in charge. Some tasks were done multiple times while others went neglected. Press were directed to show up at the wrong locations. Volunteers forgot to invite members of the community to campaign stops.[15] In an infamous incident, a white driver and a Black driver both arrived at the Cocoa Beach airport to pick Chisholm up. "When I came off the plane, came down the ramp, I saw these two groups apart and I sensed that something was wrong." What the two groups were fighting about was whose motorcade—the Black men's or the white men's—Chisholm would ride in. "And they forgot me for a moment. And they were tearing up . . . it was embarrassing. So I saw a little white man . . . standing on the side and he was there for me. He had . . . spelled my name wrong.

'Chisholm for President.' C-H-I-Z-U-M. But nevertheless, he was for me for President, and he was so excited by everything that was going on. So I went over to him. . . . And when they saw me get into the man's car, all of them ran for their cars [laughter] trying to run after me. It was so funny. Because I couldn't stand there any longer and deal with this kind of fight that was going on."[16]

As in other states, the volunteers were a heterogeneous—and sometimes unconventional—group. One of her two remaining staff members "didn't know how to dress. He wore a lot of hippy clothes, but he was so sincere" and very committed and hardworking. He understood that his habit of going barefoot in shorts and a ratty T-shirt might harm Chisholm's image, so he tended to stay in the background. Although there were a number of hippies who worked for her, Chisholm recalled that "all kinds of people" worked tirelessly for the campaign. She was amused by visiting satellite offices and seeing the variety of people who would walk in. Robert Gottlieb, her other staffer, was very young but made up for it with "intelligence and energy."[17]

There were also internal divisions over priorities. In south Florida, Chisholm had a devoted group of white women working for her. On the one hand, they successfully coordinated media attention and other aspects of her visit. On the other hand, they prioritized abortion, childcare, and equal rights for women at the expense of other Black feminist priorities. They also appointed themselves as the gatekeepers to the candidate, which left other parts of the Chisholm coalition fuming. Chisholm thought that this was due to women's past exclusion from electoral politics, but the women, unlike Black activists, "find it hard to believe that they have a great deal to learn" about political organizing. As for Spanish-speaking supporters, whom Chisholm had thought would be numerous in Miami, they were relatively few among sometimes-conservative Cuban refugees.[18]

Florida was George Wallace country, and he would eventually win the state's primary almost thirty points ahead of his next challenger. The reason for such a wide margin of victory was school integration. In Florida, white antibusing proponents had responded to a recent federal decision that mandated busing with a ballot initiative to amend the state constitution. Unsurprisingly, Wallace's strength in the state was directly related to his "stand in the schoolhouse door": his public opposition to integrating the University of Alabama in 1963 and now to busing in 1972. He also appealed to southern Democrats who remained loyal to the party even as they deplored recent civil rights legislation, promising that he would move the Democratic Party rightward again.[19] The focus on busing carried over to the presidential primary. On every one of her visits to the state, Chisholm took questions related to her own stance on busing to integrate public schools. She was, as it turned out, not a proponent of busing, though not for the same reasons Wallace opposed it. She criticized busing on the grounds that it was not an effective way to provide an equal education to children across racial lines. As she wrote in *The Good Fight*, simply moving children from one school to another would not correct the "root cause" of segregation, which was racism that trapped Black families in poor housing with underfunded schools. However, she was all too aware that any criticism of busing would be seized upon by segregationists as support for their cause. Therefore, she addressed the underlying premise of busing in her responses: if schools were more equal to begin with, busing would not be necessary. However, "an artificial solution was better than none." Furthermore, Black and brown children had been bused to schools far from their homes for years, with no public outcry. Her candor drew praise from an unexpected source: George Wallace himself remarked that at least Chisholm "says the same things in Chicago that she says in Florida." He was not the only one to notice what Chisholm and Wallace had in common: James Bevel, formerly of the Southern Christian Leadership Conference (SCLC), thought that a Wallace-Chisholm ticket would be one that could honestly represent the people.[20] Although his idea was immediately dismissed by Chisholm, suspicions that she was collaborating with Wallace would persist.[21] Photomontage artist Alfred Gescheidt added Chisholm's and Wallace's heads to the figures in Grant Wood's *American Gothic*, entitling his creation *Politics Makes Strange Bedfellows*.

Florida's existing Black male political establishment was not impressed with Chisholm. This seemed to stem from hostility to the idea of a woman running for president, or worries about seeming to be led by a Moynihanesque Black matriarch. Older Black men would "tend to watch silently" as she made campaign stops. The *New York Times Magazine's* writer described these skeptical voters' behavior: "She is tasted like a new food. Voters ask what her husband thinks, what kind of education she has, whether she would favor Blacks over whites."[22] Some Black voters were outwardly supportive and showed up at rallies but would not make an effort to vote or raise money for Chisholm.[23] The state NAACP field secretary, Marvin Davies, predicted that Chisholm would not win much of the Black vote. "They admire her for taking the mystique off the Presidency, but I don't think Blacks in Florida right now feel they are ready for a lady President," he commented. A local Miami official said that Chisholm might gain a "sympathy vote" but that "the intelligent people that I have heard talk are going to cast their ballots for Humphrey and some for Muskie." Other unnamed leaders complained that Chisholm was "putting many Blacks on the spot and in some cases neutralizing Blacks who otherwise would have supported white candidates." They felt pressured because they did not want to be "accused of being Uncle Toms" for not supporting her, but wanted to back a candidate they thought could win.[24]

At least one local Black politician was overtly hostile. Alcee Hastings was a fiery civil rights lawyer and a candidate for U.S. Senate. He worked on school desegregation cases from his office in Fort Lauderdale. He had been horrified by Wallace's strong showing in the 1968 Florida primary, and worked to no avail on Governor Rubin Askew to convince him to run for president. Chisholm, however, was undeserving of Hastings's support, he said, because "she hasn't done her homework and she's simply not known in Florida among Blacks."[25] After "flirting with" the idea of supporting Lindsay, and a brief stint supporting Muskie, Hastings decided to mount a "favorite son" candidacy himself in 1972. When Chisholm announced her intent to run in Florida, he was dismayed. He angrily withdrew, stating that he would rather vote for Wallace than for Chisholm. He sent 500 letters urging Black activists and leaders across the state to vote for Muskie.[26] Just after the primary, he would opine that Black Floridians did not want to vote for her because she represented the "Black matriarchy." Later in life he explained his lack of support was simply because he did not believe she could win and did not want to support her "just because she's Black."[27] This was not because of personal dislike, he said, and later in life he remembered Chisholm's campaign as an engine of change.

There were also strong allies. Two Black lawyers facilitated two days of events in North Florida: rallies, speeches at businesses and colleges, and media interviews. They thought attracting Black voters in the Florida panhandle—which had more in common with the Deep South than Miami—would substantially improve her showing in the state. They invited a host of Chisholm's Brooklyn supporters from Brooklyn, including William Thompson, now a city council member. They chartered a bus, the "Chisholm Express," for Chisholm and her entourage. Aboard the bus, the mood was "jovial," and regularly "a blond-haired girl with a thick southern drawl would strum her guitar and sing the campaign song she had written." At Florida Junior College in Jacksonville, she spoke to about 375 applauding students.[28] The bus stopped in other towns with large Black populations—Quincy, Gretna, and Marianna—and the campaign held rallies at their courthouse squares. Chisholm was struck by the heavily rural character of the area, and the obvious poverty that mere statistics did not convey. She preached her vision of a coalition between Black, Indian, Chicano, poor, and women voters, and campaign workers passed buckets for coins and dollar bills. In Quincy, a mostly Black crowd of about 1,200, many of whom were elderly, cheered with Black Power salutes. The SCLC's Ralph Abernathy took to the podium to make a statement of endorsement. In Marianna about 300 supporters, overwhelmingly Black, cheered for her on the spot where Wallace would hold a rally later the same day for about 500 white people. Chisholm was nearly overwhelmed by the symbolism of her speaking from the steps of a building that represented oppression to Black Americans, with its nearby statue of a Confederate soldier holding a rifle that "seemed almost to be pointing at me. A feeling came over me about the courthouse," she wrote, "a place of fear for Blacks for a hundred years, where white justice had been dealt out to them." The symbolism was not lost on her audience, one of whom told her that he never thought he would see a Black speaker on the courthouse steps.[29]

Wallace was the runaway winner in Florida with 41 percent, and Humphrey was a distant second. Lindsay won about 6.5 percent. Chisholm won 3.5 percent with 43,989 votes, beating McCarthy, Mills, and Yorty.[30] She had spent about $13,000 in the state, far less than the estimated $500,000 each that Lindsay, Humphrey, Muskie, and Jackson had. Although Chisholm forged ahead undaunted, the fact that Black voters had not come out decisively for her was likely a disappointment. Chisholm was already finding the campaign trail to be draining. Her days in Florida were fourteen hours long and included endless campus speeches and media appearances. In one interview in Miami, she seemed to break. "I am tired. I am tired of fighting, fighting, fighting all the time," she lamented. "I just bought a fabulous home in the Virgin Islands. I just want to sit in a rocking chair and look at the sky." When this attracted negative press attention, Bob Gottleib had to explain that she felt pulled in two directions by women and Black voters, and that while she had strong support from college voters, "the big boys . . . are hitting her on the head." He went on: she was very resilient and managed her energy well on the campaign trail. The interview occurred after other appearances and she was tired and let slip some candid comments, he explained.[31] But Chisholm's remarks showed just how exhausting the battle for delegates was. And there were still other states to go.

MASSACHUSETTS

Chisholm was drafted into the April 25 Massachusetts primary. One hundred and two delegates were at stake. A group of Chisholm supporters in the state initiated the campaign. They drafted her through a liberal state caucus in January. The Chisholm campaign had not committed to the caucus, and Chisholm herself was already scheduled elsewhere on the date. But a group of Chisholm backers, led by Black Cambridge city council member Saundra Graham, planned to use the caucus to persuade Chisholm to run in the state. They also hoped that Black people would participate in the primary and help win a seat in the Massachusetts legislature for Boston activist Byron

Rushing.[32] McGovern won the caucus with 60 percent, but Chisholm was a strong second with 23 percent.[33] Chisholm's success was a surprise that bolstered the Chisholm supporters. Chisholm herself telegrammed her praise for the Massachusetts team from California. Impressed by the strong showing, McGovern's team decided to negotiate with their Chisholm counterparts about possibly joining forces. McGovern was worried the Democratic race in Massachusetts was going to be an uphill climb and his campaign was willing to negotiate coalition slates. A new state law would allow delegates to vote for whoever won in their district, and allow candidates to concentrate their campaign in districts where they thought they could win.[34]

Eventually, Democrats in four congressional districts formed coalition slates of Chisholm and McGovern supporters.[35] Graham was named the statewide chair of the campaign. Graham, a working-class Black activist who had a strong commitment to Chisholm's Black feminist power agenda, built the campaign from scratch. There was also Wendy Curwood, treasurer, who weekly unlocked the campaign headquarters, a small storefront located next to a motorcycle shop at 229 River Street in Cambridge. The headquarters had no furniture, so when Wendy collected the modest donations from the mailbox she seated herself on the floor to sort it. She was a white Boston University student, married to Steve Curwood, a Black journalist who had graduated from Harvard in 1969. Both of them were twenty-four years old, excited to be caught up in a grassroots movement to elect a candidate who, more than any of the others, could stand for them.

Convinced by the enthusiasm of supporters, Chisholm decided to run in Massachusetts and made her way to the state in February.[36] Chisholm announced her official Massachusetts primary candidacy to 300–400 people in the gym of the Cambridge Community Center. A small portion of the audience were white liberals and women's liberation activists, but the majority were Black. Many were women, and their children attended, too. The speech hit Chisholm's talking points about coalition. "It's time for the have-nots in this country to get together," she exclaimed. "I decided it was time when the powerless and the helpless did not have to select the lesser of two evils and choose between Tweedledum and Tweedledee." She drew parallels between Latinx people in the Southwest, Indian reservations, Black people stuck in segregated neighborhoods, and Appalachians in coal mining towns: "What difference does it make if you are white or Black?" she asked. "You are both suffering." She reiterated her plan for influencing the agenda at the DNC, and demanded a Black vice president, a woman as secretary of Health, Education, and Welfare, and an Indigenous secretary of the Interior. Her comments were met with a chorus of "right on, sister." She then took a walking tour of Harvard Square. As she campaigned in the

Rep. Shirley Chisholm embracing activist Elma Lewis,
St. Paul AME Church, Roxbury, Massachusetts, 1972.
Michael Dobo / Dobophoto.com.

streets, a campaign worker preceded her, shouting, "Step right up; Here's Shirley Chisholm; Harvard Square will never be the same again!"[37]

On her next trip to the state in March, she visited the heart of Black Boston, Roxbury, for a rally at the Charles Street AME Church. Community organizer Elma Lewis introduced her and her delegates, and then she launched into one of her speeches.[38] Precisely what happened next has been told in multiple versions. But all of the stories agree that a group of gay men in drag, wearing their Sunday best, entered the church to hear the candidate. They shouted encouragement: "Hiya Shirley!"[39] "Tell them Shirley, tell 'em!"[40] Her initial response was embarrassment, not because the men were gay but because she feared the congregation would not take her campaign seriously if her supporters violated church decorum by shouting. "It was very, very embarrassing to me," she admitted. "And at the same time, it struck my funny bone. I had to prevent myself from laughing."[41] "The Black people are really very conservatively oriented anyhow . . . and these gays had taken up their church for Sunday morning!" Chisholm used the opportunity to engage in some coalition organizing: "I told the people in the church that don't forget that gays are human beings too." She variously remembered that there were twenty-one or sixty visitors in drag. "We went through the sermon, the minister went through the sermon really quickly and honey, I got out of there fast. And I got on the sidewalk, there were a whole group that had made a big semi-circle, they had me in a semi-circle and they were hugging me and I will never forget that."[42] The men were aware that Chisholm was the only candidate who had nondiscrimination against LGBTQ people as part of her platform. One of them said that he was aware of the conservative attitudes about gay people in Black churches and that he wanted her to tell the congregation to support gay people.[43]

Chisholm had built up a following among students and in the cities of Cambridge, Boston, and Springfield. Over several visits to the state she spoke to students at Simmons College, Boston University, Harvard, Springfield State College, and Boston State College (now University of Massachusetts–Boston). She also courted local feminists and Black activists: the Feminist Party, Eastern Massachusetts NOW, and the Boston NAACP.[44] She held a press conference, dropped into radio stations, and took advantage of the free TV time for all primary candidates in the state by visiting the major network affiliates. She said in one interview that she hoped half of her pledged delegates in Massachusetts would win despite lack of funding for the campaign. She was not "beholden" to large donors, however, and not dismayed by a lack of endorsements from those in power, because she was "the kind of person that threatens holders of power . . . my power is from the people."[45]

Rep. Shirley Chisholm campaigning for president,
Roxbury, Massachusetts, 1972.
Michael Dobo / Dobophoto.com.

In a column published on the day of the Massachusetts primary, Chisholm wrote that "Blackness is an attitude"—not one of style, words, and appearance, but a genuine desire to see all people out of poverty and empowered equally. She made a dig at Black nationalists: "Many of our would-be leaders are running about and trying to start and maintain an elitist revolution in the name of social revolution. No one man has ever been right about everything nor has one group or civilization." Black people can't just be focused on rights for Black people. Her definition of a social revolution reflected a Black feminist power ethos: "I am talking about the basic right of everybody to share in the building of a better society and the right to receive fair and equitable payment for that contribution. I believe that at bottom the ideals of democracy are sound, but I do not believe that those ideals have ever been practiced, except in terms of an elitist few."[46] With that last plea for coalition, voters went to the polls.

McGovern won a decisive victory in Massachusetts among both "antiwar liberals and disgruntled working people." He appeared to be on his way to the nomination, to the surprise of many experienced politicians in the state and nationwide. He won nearly 53 percent, followed by Muskie at 21, Wallace at 8, Humphrey at just over 7, and Chisholm at 3.6, or 22,400 votes.[47]

Lindsay, who had hoped for a victory in Massachusetts, dropped out of the race. Chisholm did best in Black precincts (where McGovern ran second, his only statewide defeat) and among students. McGovern had 89 of the 102 delegates. Chisholm had a total of five. All would have to vote for McGovern on the first ballot, but then they could vote for their favorite candidates.[48] Still, they had some influence: Black delegates Jim Pitts and Ellen Jackson were elected to the party platform committee and Saundra Graham won a spot on the convention's credentials committee.[49] The Massachusetts campaign had earned a ticket to the convention, and a handful of delegates for Chisholm.

CALIFORNIA

Chisholm had initially decided to bypass California because of its winner-take-all primary. The Democratic Party's McGovern Commission in the aftermath of 1968 had recommended that state primaries award delegates proportionally to the popular vote, but California had been granted an exception for 1972. Hubert Humphrey and Scoop Jackson were challenging the exception with a lawsuit, and Chisholm accepted Humphrey's invitation to join it on the chance that she could get some delegates out of the process.[50] Still, she insisted that she did not expect to win the suit or any delegates from California. And she worried that her run might have a downside: it could jeopardize Ron Dellums's reelection support from the party.[51] She nevertheless went ahead because the campaign had drawn new people in to politics and she did not want "to disappoint some of the strongest supporters I had anywhere." She delegated all California campaigning to local volunteers and did not send any national campaign funds or personnel, an approach that miffed some supporters. But plenty of enthusiastic campaign workers remained, and they set up regional organizations in the Los Angeles and Bay Areas.[52] The Los Angeles campaign was an organization of feminists associated with NOW and the National Women's Political Caucus. In the Bay Area, the campaign had strong ties to Black Power organizations and was mostly staffed by Black activists. As usual, students loved her. The coalition accomplished more than either of the main constituent groups could have alone. Although Chisholm's campaign was run on a shoestring, it gathered strength from both Black Power and radical feminists. Chisholm's fiery extemporaneous speeches, tempered by her sharp sense of humor, offered hope in the aftermath of assassinations and years of Vietnam.[53]

In terms of energizing Black voters, there was a lot to gain in the state. One estimate was that Black people made up 10–12 percent of potential voters in California, and that it would be these voters and Chicano voters who would decide the Democratic primary. Experts thought that those who were over thirty-five were committed to Humphrey. But young Black voters were at present uncommitted, and were largely deciding between two choices: McGovern and Chisholm. Chisholm's appeal came in large part out of Black activism in the state. Black Power and Black nationalism were popular among younger Black voters, and Chisholm was the candidate most identified with Black Power. To her supporters, she seemed to genuinely care about the issues, not self-interested power brokering. Those supporters wanted their support for Chisholm to broadcast their views to the political establishment.[54]

Black Californians were invested in politics, after six years of high-profile activism by the Black Panther Party and others. They wanted equality "beyond civil rights to broader participation in the financial and political structures." Some thought that their support of Chisholm was "a symbol of their political awareness."[55] Others were emphatic that the campaign was not merely symbolic. They recognized the campaign as "an exercise in political reality called 'get a toe in the door!'"[56] of party politics. Indeed, the party used Chisholm's candidacy to energize a voter registration campaign. They convened a Black Community Survival Conference in March at which 10,000 free bags of groceries were distributed and Black political candidates spoke.[57] The hope was that first-time voters would turn out in droves.

As in Florida, there was much skepticism by established Black politicians, who worried her campaign would split the vote.[58] In general, established Black political leaders, mainly men whose power base lay in mainline civil rights organizations and the clergy, eschewed Chisholm's campaign in favor of the more mainstream candidates in the hope of brokering goodwill that would come in handy later.[59] There was a rumor that one or more of them had been paid $35,000 to campaign against her.[60] Some, such as state senator Mervyn Dymally, supported Humphrey even as he acknowledged that "Mrs. Chisholm is the most attractive one of the lot."[61] Other Black activists jumped on the McGovern bandwagon and campaigned on his behalf in the state. Coretta Scott King, Jesse Jackson, and Julian Bond all made appearances on behalf of McGovern.[62] Some Black Californians supported McGovern from the outset. Most prominent among these was Willie Brown, at that time a San Francisco assemblyman and the leader of McGovern's campaign in the state.[63] At the Gary convention, Willie Brown and UCLA student body president Lamar Lyons cochaired the California delegation, the second largest.

Another source of hostility toward Chisholm was the California McGovern campaign itself. Because of the winner-take-all nature of the primary, even a small percentage of votes could help shift who would win a plurality, and McGovern campaigners worried Chisholm would take votes from their candidate. When Chisholm supporters suggested that the liberal

California Democratic Coalition issue a joint endorsement of McGovern and Chisholm, for example, McGovern supporters demurred, even though it meant McGovern would fall short of the votes needed for any endorsement at all.[64] Chisholm also became aware of a whispering campaign that alleged she was there in order to undermine McGovern's bid on behalf of Humphrey. McGovern supporters had become convinced that anything other than support for their candidates was a corrupt conspiracy.[65] They were wrong about a Humphrey-Chisholm plot, but they were correct that there was deception afoot. A Nixon aide had hired lawyer Donald Segretti to implement a "dirty tricks" plan intended to seed Democratic intraparty conflict in California. Segretti's operatives stole or printed stationery mimicking that of several campaigns. On a sheet of bogus Humphrey stationery, they typed a press release alleging that Chisholm was mentally ill and had been committed to a Virginia psychiatric hospital in 1951 after being found dressed in men's clothing and behaving aggressively on the streets of Richmond. She was still under psychological care, it alleged. The operatives mailed it to reporters at the Associated Press, local papers and TV stations, and the Los Angeles office of Johnson Publications (home of *Jet* and *Ebony* magazines) three days before the primary. Another letter was sent out to Democratic delegates on Humphrey stationery that suggested McGovern should be stopped at all costs and the Chisholm campaign agreed a vote for Humphrey was the best way to do this. The FBI did eventually investigate and discover that the fake releases were part of the Watergate scandal but not until the following year. In the meantime, suspicion between campaigns ran high; at least one Humphrey staffer thought that the McGovern campaign had created the mental hospital press release.[66]

As elsewhere, Chisholm's own supporters were devoted. In Northern California, college students Barbara Lee and Sandra Gaines ran the campaign. On the first campaign trip, Chisholm stopped at Oakland's all-women Mills College, where Frances Mullins was teaching a course entitled "Candidates, Campaigns, and Constituents," a hands-on practicum in political organizing. Lee and Gaines, both single mothers and juniors, were two of the students in the course. Gaines was raising three sons and had won a Ford Fellowship to attend college. Lee was president of the Black Students Union and was also a "community worker" for the Black Panther Party: fundraising, handing out flyers, and working in the party's school. Chisholm had been invited by the Black Students Union to give a speech, and Lee and Gaines attended. Lee had previously feared she would fail Mullins's course because she was not interested in any of the candidates she knew of: Muskie, McGovern, or Humphrey. The issues that Lee cared about were aligned with Black feminist power: access to day care, good housing, health care, and education. When Chisholm spoke, Lee discovered that not only was Chisholm fighting for the things Lee cared about but also that the congresswoman was running for president. At the conclusion of the speech, the "awestruck" Lee approached the candidate.[67] Chisholm recalled being approached by "this little Black girl," who appeared younger than her nineteen or twenty years, wanting to start a campaign organization for Chisholm. Not having paid staff, Chisholm could not be choosy. She agreed to allow Lee to proceed.[68] Lee herself recalled that she asked Chisholm where she could start and who she could call. "My dear," the congresswoman said, "the first thing you must do is register to vote." Then she explained the constraints: "If you really believe in me and believe in what I stand for, you'll go out and make it happen. We don't have a lot of money. We don't have a national campaign, and so, for those who care about me, we go out and do it." Undeterred, Lee created a campaign with the guidance of Professor Mullins. She and Gaines would become campaign leaders in the region. Their connections to both the women's movement and the Black freedom struggle in Oakland would make them effective bridges between white women and Black men and led, Chisholm believed, to her eventual strong showing in Alameda County. They opened an office and began a series of fundraising events—teas, fashion shows, and dinners. Lee lobbied her contacts in the Black Panthers to become involved in a voter registration drive and primary campaign on behalf of Chisholm.[69]

Lee and Gaines ultimately put together a coalition of Black power, faith community, and women's activists. They were careful to emphasize common concerns and issues—and also to educate groups within the coalition about the specific challenges facing others within it. The Black Panther Party was beginning its foray into electoral politics, organizing on the precinct level to get out the vote: registering voters and handing out literature.[70] The campaign office opened in the Fillmore district of San Francisco, a Black neighborhood, with some shabby office furniture and a handful of phone lines. They were eventually joined by a professional campaign organizer: Wilson Riles, a young Black Peace Corps alumnus who had helped his father win a statewide office and had worked for a professional campaign management firm. He had been hired by NOW. While Lee and Gaines had not chosen Riles, the three managed to get along.[71] There was a small amount of friction between Riles, a man who had professional credentials and was paid, and the unpaid Black women who had the contacts within the community. When Riles arrived and suggested that their new office needed curtains, implying that the women should take care of that detail, Lee and Gaines told him bluntly to buy them himself. But Riles quickly realized they deserved his respect as strategists. "They had their own ideas and concepts of what needed to be done in order to change things," he said. "More often than not, they were right."[72]

The Bay Area campaign was aided tremendously by Lee's contacts in the Black Panther Party. Chisholm's campaign came at a time when the party was looking for increasingly direct involvement in politics. The party's two founders, Huey Newton and Bobby Seale, were working on increasing Black political power. They remembered that their intellectual progenitor Malcolm X had begun to emphasize voting as a civil and human right before his death in 1965. Seale had already encouraged Ron Dellums to run for Berkeley City Council and saw the Chisholm campaign as a continuation of party efforts to organize the grassroots.[73] The party "used the Chisholm campaign to test their political machinery," Seale recalled. Chisholm's priorities aligned with those of the party's leadership and of the rank-and-file members, many of whom were college students with sophisticated knowledge of history and the political economy. A large force within the party had already dedicated itself to a precinct-by-precinct voter registration campaign in Alameda County, which included Berkeley and Oakland. Workers were delegated to small sections of precincts and charged with getting to know the voters in each, with a hierarchy of leaders coordinating the overall effort. Voter registration was also mandatory for recipients of free bags of groceries at party events. By the time of Chisholm's bid, the apparatus was ready to go and the party had registered 11,000 voters. Seale and others cared less about the fact that Chisholm was female than they did about her platform for using the political economy to effect social change. The party slogan of "All Power to the People" included women, said Seale, who recalled, "I'm just proud that we were there to stand behind Shirley and work to get votes for her."[74]

In April, Newton formally endorsed Chisholm's campaign in a statement read by party chairman Bobby Seale at St. Augustine's Church in Oakland. Newton proclaimed that the party sought to usher along the trend of transferring power to the masses by supporting Chisholm's campaign. She was the best "social critic of America's injustices" of any presidential candidate. He directed "every Black, poor and progressive human being" to vote and work for Chisholm, and offered to make the party offices a resource for individuals looking for ways to get involved.[75] The candidate publicly accepted the endorsement, with some explanation that she had not solicited it but instead the Panthers "came to the conclusion that in terms of their own hopes and aspirations I could be the best candidate. . . . What has happened to them as an oppressed group in America, being used to the meaningless platforms and empty promises, has led them to come to the conclusion that perhaps with me there is hope."[76] Chisholm was pleased, but she experienced some pressure to disavow the party. Most Americans thought of the group as violent extremists, despite the social welfare work that took up much of the party's agenda by 1972. As Chisholm recalled, however, there was never any question of whether she would accept their endorsement. The party thought that she was the candidate most likely to act in their interests, and she would not turn them away.[77] Furthermore, she wanted to encourage organizing for political change. She liked the fact that they were not hung up on her gender, which led her to credit them with more "political maturity" than more established Black political leaders. She thought that refusing their support would be "arrogant and inconsistent with my strongest principles."[78]

The peak moment of the party's support was a fundraiser at Huey Newton's Oakland penthouse, the "Night of 1,200 Lights," on May 18. Newton and Seale had generated the idea, and Barbara Lee provided most of the organization work. It was interesting for Lee to see the "Black bourgeoisie," party members, and white liberals all there.[79] Just over sixty nonpaying dignitaries attended, including Ron Dellums, while about seventy supporters paid their way, including a large group from the Mills College Black Students Union. The night was magical, with the lights of the city spread out below. The presence of the Secret Service presented a dilemma, because the party and the Secret Service mutually distrusted each other. The campaign successfully brokered a compromise. Newton himself and party members would not attend, and the Secret Service officers would remain very inconspicuous in the back of the room. The event was a great success. The candidate appeared and gave a brief speech. "Panthers, I know it's been hard, it's been rough. You might make the difference here in California, and I'm glad you are giving the electoral process a chance—with me." A party proxy presented Chisholm with a $1,000 check and a copy of Newton's book, *To Die for the People*. The next week, the *Black Panther* newspaper ran a full-page ad in support of Chisholm and Ron Dellums.[80]

Shortly thereafter, Newton released a statement, "Why We, the Black Panther Party, Support Sister Shirley Chisholm." Her platform echoed, he said, the party's own survival (social services) programs. Both Chisholm and the party shared "the same history and the same victory over death" that included slavery, racism, and violence. Compared to Humphrey, whom Newton labeled a sellout and war criminal, Chisholm was "a beautiful Black Woman who is giving her life for poor Black People." Supporting her would send a signal that Black voters would demand more for their votes in the future. "We love her, we support her," he wrote.[81]

Chisholm also spoke to establishment venues. Riles convinced a reluctant church to have Chisholm come speak during the campaign and was vindicated by an overflow audience and a huge collection for the day.[82] She spoke at San Francisco's Commonwealth Club, a distinguished civic organization that had been hosting prominent speakers since the 1920s. "There was a debate among us whether or not Shirley ought to go there, because you know, this was a kind of mainstream, you know, right-ist kind of forum," Wilson Riles remembered. After consultation with the national campaign, they decided to accept. He was delighted with the results.

> I was blown away by the speech that she gave at the Commonwealth Club. I mean, I had known a little bit about her positions and so forth but hadn't really seen her directly speak very much about these issues before. She had spoken to audiences that were mainly Black about issues that were concerned to Black folks. And she got up in front of the Commonwealth Club and gave the most in-depth, knowledgeable . . . speech about the economy and all of that economics and what was going on in the economy that was helping or hurting poor people and people of color and how changing a few things, we could move in a more positive and just direction to lift people out of poverty.[83]

Chisholm would eventually make her best California showing in Alameda County, where Oakland was the county seat, with 9.6 percent of the vote. Dellums believed that many of those voters might not have voted or participated in the election had it not been for the Chisholm campaign.[84] The consequences for Barbara Lee's life were substantial: she got an "A" in her Mills College course, joined Ron Dellums's staff, later became a state representative, and eventually inherited Dellums's seat in Congress.[85] As for the Black Panther Party, Bobby Seale ran for mayor (he finished second) and then Chair Elaine Brown ran for the Oakland city council the following year. Using this electoral experience, the party put together a coalition to help elect Oakland's first Black mayor, Lionel Wilson, in 1977.

The Southern California campaign was led by Los Angeles NOW organizer Arlie Scott and a Santa Barbara grandmother, Jean Sunderland. The campaign organization was dubbed the Chisholm NOW Committee, a partnership between Los Angeles NOW and the Southern California section of the NWPC, which had endorsed her for president.[86] Scott was a graduate student in history at the University of Southern California and joined the campaign because she had seen Brownmiller's *New York Times Magazine* feature on Chisholm in 1969. Suddenly, she found herself officially involved: at one early rally Chisholm told supporters to be sure to give their contributions to Scott herself.[87] Jean Sunderland and her husband were longtime political activists on the left, and she had been a founding member of Women Strike for Peace and of the Southern California section of the NWPC. She saw the Chisholm campaign as a chance to draw together a coalition across race, gender, and age that would involve new people in politics.[88]

There was a lot of enthusiasm for Chisholm in Southern California. The campaign booked her for popular college campus events; Chisholm spoke to standing ovations at Whittier College, Claremont Graduate School, and the University of Southern California ("one of the largest and most enthusiastic gatherings in recent history").[89] A large Los Angeles rally—1,750 people were present with about 300 turned away—cost $1 to attend. Former NOW president Aileen Hernandez introduced the candidate, and Yvonne Brathwaite presented her with a contribution check. The speech itself "just blew everybody away." Chisholm spoke for thirty-five minutes, pausing often for applause from audience members who leapt to their feet. Booker Griffin, a radio personality on soul station KGFJ and a state assembly candidate, was beyond impressed by the rally. It was "the biggest and most successful political rally in this town since Bobby Kennedy's closing rally in 1968," he proclaimed. He said that Chisholm "offers a positive type of militancy, a productive way with concrete goals to say "hell no" to the establishment. . . . This woman possesses a definite and undeniable electricity that cannot be denied." Griffin also had withering words for Black political leaders who were conspicuously absent from campaign events. They were, in his words, captives of a "plantation system" that was "so secure in its control of Black political apparatus that it has Blacks, several in elected office, doing the hatchet job on Shirley for their plantation bosses." The *Los Angeles Times* reporter was less enthusiastic calling her "articulate, tough, bright and probably brilliant, tireless, vain, gutsy, honest, but demagogic, combative, loquacious, and charismatic." The reporter argued that Chisholm was energizing her campaign "with an emotional appeal rather than with a specific platform."[90]

Scott worked on raising enough money to make the campaign as credible as possible, to the candidate as well as to voters. This was not easy. She had, when Chisholm designated her as the recipient of campaign donations, immediately opened an account at the student bank on USC's campus. The staff were very skeptical when they learned what the account was for. "When I got up to the teller," Scott recalled, she said, "I want to open an account please. And [the teller] took a piece of paper and said, what is the name? I said it's an account for an organization. And she said, what is the name of your organization? And I said, Shirley Chisholm for President. And she said, all right. What was she running for President of? And I said, of the United States. And she drew back a little bit. I felt that her foot was going back towards the alarm system and then she finally realized that . . . I was no threat, I was harmless."[91]

After the account was set up, Scott had to look for a headquarters and recruit other local supporters to work the campaign. The need to get 15,000 signatures on a qualification petition to get Chisholm's name on the ballot by March 24 was a useful organizing tool. Sunderland canvassed eight counties, supervising the twenty-five Chisholm for President offices that had sprouted. She drove a camper van, dubbed the "Chisholm Trail Wagon," on her rounds. "Just because of the fact that she's running, we can't lose," Sunderland explained to a reporter. Responding to the sense of urgency, volunteers fanned out in search of supportive signatories and met the deadline with about a week to spare. McGovern, Muskie, and Lindsay had gotten there first, but Chisholm's name would appear fourth on the ballot, above Humphrey's.[92]

Early on, Scott encountered the tendency of her NOW colleagues not to take the campaign and the coalition it represented seriously. Many did not seem to grasp the idea of bringing delegates to the convention and thus pressuring the eventual nominee on reproductive rights and more diverse representation within the Democratic Party. Instead, she observed, they chose the established but riskier strategy of allying with the candidate they thought could win (McGovern) in the hope that he would support their issues in return. When Scott asked them about their support for Chisholm, they would often express that they liked Chisholm, but that McGovern was "the best of the male candidates." They thought that a vote for Chisholm would be meaningless, because she was unlikely to win the nomination. Some Black leaders felt the same way, or their sexism meant that they did not want to support a woman. Despite Scott's frustration with both lines of thinking, she remained diplomatic and a unifying figure. This was no small feat as Black Chisholm supporters accused white women supporters of "dominating the whole scene." This was compounded by the fact that the California campaign had very little direction from the national campaign, which might have buffered disagreements. "Arlie really understood the dynamics between the feminist movement and, and African-American women and Shirley Chisholm," Barbara Lee explained. "I mean, she was very helpful in . . . reducing a lot of the tensions and a lot of the . . . divisiveness that could have occurred . . . she was, really, a phenomenal woman." Scott, for her part, wished that she had had more time to pull a coalition together before the campaign.[93]

Scott proved to be a capable fundraiser. She made a promise to Chisholm that the California campaign would not generate any debt, and she fulfilled it. The state campaign alone raised between $40,000 and $50,000 throughout California's forty-three congressional districts, compared to the national campaign's figure of $250,000. Most money came from small donors and fundraisers, quite a feat considering Chisholm only visited three times. There were a few large donors: a wealthy woman, divorced from her McGovern-supporting husband, donated between $5,000 and $15,000 herself. Diahann Carroll, who had hosted fundraisers for the Student Nonviolent Coordinating Committee in the past, held a fundraising party for Chisholm at her Beverly Hills home in late April. Carroll wanted to meet Huey Newton and was delighted when he attended the party. Her cohost, the comedian Flip Wilson, donated $5,000.[94]

The last hurdle was media coverage, which was overwhelmingly concentrated on the two front-runners. A case in point was the scheduled June 4 appearance of McGovern and Humphrey on the ABC television show *Issues and Answers*. Having learned of the broadcast, Chisholm (and Sam Yorty) realized that the program was actually set up as a debate and should thus be open to all candidates per Federal Communications Commission rules. She filed suit with an appeals court in San Francisco and lost. The justices decided that the appearance was a "bona fide news interview" and not subject to equal time regulations. Undaunted, and despite the fact that she only had a few days, she decided to file suit. She approached young Maryland attorney Tom Asher, who had recently founded a public interest firm called the Media Access Project, asking him whether, on short notice, he could fight to have her included in the debate. Chisholm and Asher appealed to the U.S. Circuit Court in Washington, D.C., and this time they won.[95] The court also dictated that NBC and CBS, which had both excluded Chisholm from joint interviews with McGovern and Humphrey, must give her time in the few days remaining before the primary. She did so from New York: too exhausted from constant campaigning, Chisholm participated in the programs remotely.[96]

Despite her television appearances, and a late endorsement by the SCLC's Western Region, Chisholm fell short of the 200,000–300,000 votes she had hoped for in California. McGovern won with 1,550,652, Humphrey came in second with 1,375,064, and Chisholm came in fourth, earning 157,435 or 4.4 percent of the vote.[97] Under a proportional system, however, that number would be enough to bring twelve delegates to the convention the next month.

NEW YORK

The case Chisholm sought to make in her home state was simple: the Democratic Party nomination was not sewn up, and she needed delegates to keep the party accountable. But the late June home state primary was surprisingly challenging. First, Chisholm's own name would not appear on the ballot. Voters would select delegates only, and the names of the candidates to whom those delegates were pledged appeared nowhere on the printed ballots. The election of Democratic National Convention delegates in the state of New York was itself a confusing and complicated process.[98] Second, local political alliances, feuds, and shifting allegiances created an anti-Chisholm contingent in her own Brooklyn district. Chisholm was still hopeful. As a New York committeewoman, she herself had a delegate vote at the convention. She thought she would have at least six, and possibly as many as nineteen, delegates from New York. She was the only candidate besides McGovern who was actively campaigning in the state, and multiple constituencies were behind her.

In her home district there was some grassroots support, including people from her church, those who knew her from her teaching career, and constituents whom her office had helped. William Thompson remained steadfast and helped field a Chisholm-committed slate in the district. She also had committed slates in Westchester County, Buffalo, and Syracuse.[99] Small fundraising functions were "springing up all over the place in the city and even statewide."[100] There was a group called Black Women for Shirley Chisholm for President, which included luminaries Dorothy Height and Dorothy Pitman Hughes.[101] Flatbush Women for Shirley Chisholm held a dinner fundraiser; Harry and Julie Belafonte held a star-studded cocktail party at their home.[102] Julie Belafonte also teamed up with Diahann Carroll for a "Stars for Shirley" evening fundraiser with Lena Horne, Ruby Dee and Ossie Davis, and Roberta Flack.[103] The Coalition of 100 Black Women invited her to their meeting, and there was a benefit performance of Van Peebles's *Ain't Supposed to Die a Natural Death*.[104] The *New York Amsterdam News,* after extensive interviews and discussion, endorsed her.[105] The state organization People for Chisholm held a cocktail party—this one at Harlem's Doll House restaurant.[106] In Manhattan, her support was strong among feminists because Betty Friedan herself was running in Harlem as a Chisholm delegate.

But she had opponents in Brooklyn who engaged in "throat-cutting, back-biting, and petty jealousies."[107] This was a major obstacle to the campaign, and Chisholm had hesitated about running slates in New York because of her uncertainty that she could work out support with local Black politicians. After local megachurch pastor Rev. William Jones criticized her record in Congress and mused aloud about running against her for the Twelfth District, Chisholm hit back. "Please don't send a boy to do a man's job," she warned, "since this 100-pound featherweight would enjoy nothing better than slaying a behemoth of a man."[108] But the conflict with the pastor was not the only one. A rift opened up between Chisholm and former rival William Thompson on one side, and her former supporters Assemblyman

Tom Fortune and state senator Waldaba Stewart on the other. Fortune and Stewart collaborated with Chisholm's rival Assemblyman Samuel Wright to devise a new uncommitted delegate slate in the Twelfth District. They regarded Chisholm as an "ingrate who has ignored them during the two terms that she has served" because she was not supporting their reelection campaigns. They were appalled that she neither consulted nor informed them of her plans to run for president prior to announcing in January. They refused to support her at the Gary convention in March, and Fortune was quoted in the *New York Times* as now regretting his assistance to her campaign in 1968. "She was spending so much time with women's lib and gay lib that she was forgetting all about Black lib here in Bedford-Stuyvesant," he said.[109] Although the *Amsterdam News* had formally endorsed her, one editorial board member, Carlos Russell, proclaimed his support for McGovern, and made his infamous "vaginal politics" assertion about Chisholm. He went on: "As much as I searched, all I hear is James Brown's 'Talking Loud and Saying Nothing.'"[110]

The three men were right that Chisholm had support among women's movement leaders, even as they assumed that such support compromised Chisholm's commitment to Black voters. Chisholm, alternatively, saw no such conflict and continued to bring Black and women supporters into a coalition in the state. At the New York Women's Political Caucus in Syracuse, ninety-one-year-old congresswoman Jeanette Rankin proudly wore a Chisholm for President button. For the primary Chisholm's delegates represented a cross-section of social movement leaders with a large presence of feminists: Betty Friedan, Gloria Steinem, Jacqueline Ceballos, and Flo Kennedy, plus Manhattan Borough President Percy Sutton and Reform Democrat Paul O'Dwyer. New York NOW would throw her a campaign party, although there was some dispute over who would pay for it.[111] Black women were, as elsewhere, the most devoted supporters. One reporter discovered that "most women" in Harlem planned to vote for Chisholm even though they feared they were backing a losing candidate, because "Shirley is the only one up there who is saying anything" about poverty and racism.[112]

Chisholm's campaign planned a packed month of June in advance of the primary. At the National Youth Movement luncheon she received the endorsement of its young leader, the Reverend Al Sharpton.[113] People for Chisholm organized a rally for her on June 12, at the Edison Theatre in Manhattan, with a message to "send the feminists to the Democratic convention."[114] The next evening, she appeared on local television for an interview by the *Amsterdam News* editorial board. Asked if she was a "serious" candidate at a fundraiser the next night, she emphatically told her audience, "What do you think I've been doing for the past seven months, crisscrossing the country? Why do you think I have stayed in when others with big-name endorsements and big money have dropped out? Of course, I'm serious."[115] The Saturday before the primary, she was back home in Brooklyn, reviving her 1968 campaign style with a sound truck and motorcade, this time made longer by the addition of Secret Service vehicles. At stops along the way, she exhorted onlookers to vote for the "Chisholm Team," "The Team That Cares": her delegates and also the candidates for local seats that she had put up against her rivals.[116]

But the whirlwind campaigning fell short. In the primary, McGovern's delegates did even better than expected, winning 240 of the 248 delegates up for grabs. Chisholm had been nearly shut out. Even in her home district, her delegate slate had been beaten by Stewart and Fortune's uncommitted one, which would probably go to McGovern.[117]

OTHER STATES

Chisholm campaigned lightly in other states. She won one primary, the uncontested one in New Jersey.[118] In the midwestern states she targeted, her best showing was seven delegates in Minnesota. She fared slightly better in southern states. In Georgia, she had five committed delegates, most from the Fifth Congressional District on the west side of Atlanta, where there was an energetic student-led campaign for her. Only one of the Fifth's delegates was not pledged to her: Julian Bond.[119] She won four delegates in Tennessee.[120] Chisholm did not enter the early May Washington, D.C., primary, despite her popularity in the District and the lack of travel expenses required. Walter Fauntroy, delegate to the District of Columbia, had personally asked Chisholm to stay out because he would run as a "favorite son." He promised his delegates to her on the second or third ballot, and reminded her that he was a minister and so his promise was genuine. In Chisholm's telling, she "took him at his word" and did not run there. She nearly reconsidered when a faction of District Democrats and the editorial board of the *Washington Post* accused Fauntroy of employing antidemocratic "dictator tactics."[121] Despite the fact that she felt she had disappointed some by not running there, Chisholm wished to avoid infighting with Fauntroy over the issue and stayed out.[122] Fauntroy won the primary in D.C. with almost 72 percent. She would regret her decision when Fauntroy handed all of his delegates over to McGovern.[123]

Chisholm ran in the less competitive North Carolina primary and won 7.5 percent of the vote, a distant third to George Wallace and former governor Terry Sandford. That share did not yield any delegates, however. It also contributed to talk that Chisholm was a stalking horse for Wallace. Rumors continued when George Wallace was shot in an assassination attempt during the Maryland primaries two weeks later. Chisholm was deeply shaken by the shooting, which occurred when Wallace got up close to voters and shook hands, as she often did. She was relieved to get Secret Service protection after that point, but still felt that she could easily have been in Wallace's situation. She decided to make the hour-long trek from the Capitol up to Silver Spring, Maryland, to visit Wallace in the hospital, accompanied by Thaddeus Garrett. Catching her as she emerged from the hospital, the press asked what she was doing for the nearly fifteen minutes she had spent at Wallace's bedside. She explained: she had decided to express her sympathy to Wallace. The visit was "pleasant," and the two had a brief discussion in which they agreed on "government unresponsiveness to the people," symbolized by outsize corporate interests and taxation.[124] Speculation swirled. Were she and Wallace brokering some sort of Faustian bargain? Or was Chisholm using Wallace's injury as an opportunity to display collegiality? But Chisholm still disagreed with Wallace on fundamental issues. When a *Washington Post* writer asked her about her rumored support of Wallace as a vice presidential nominee, she "exploded with 'Jesus Christ!'" and described how their views on most issues were diametrically opposed.[125] She would keep having to explain her visit to Wallace for years afterward.[126]

The primaries were over after June 20, and Chisholm had learned hard lessons about maintaining a diverse coalition and the extreme difficulty of fundraising. She had won about 2.7 percent of the popular vote. In Chisholm's view, she had thirty-one delegates (the *New York Times* counted twenty-eight). The night after the New York primary, she was still upbeat, proclaiming her exhaustion but vowing to "remind the big boys of the people when they start wheeling and dealing." She spent the first week of July resting in the Virgin Islands.[127] Then she headed for Miami.

16

THE CHISHOLM COALITION
ON THE NATIONAL STAGE
Miami '72

The 1972 Democratic National Convention in Miami had a completely different complexion from the one in 1968. Major reforms, adopted after 1968's chaos and violence, yielded a delegate body that was younger, more Black and brown, and more female. Out of 3,085 delegates at the DNC, 15 percent were Black and 40 percent of the credentialed delegates were women, both tripled from 1968. Far fewer delegates held elected office in 1972 than they had in 1968.[1] A symbol of the new inclusiveness, Yvonne Brathwaite, a Black woman and front-runner for a California congressional seat, was named DNC vice chair. This did not come without resentment from party officials and labor leaders, many of whom lost out to the newcomers.[2] The result was a convention that was part aspirational and part conservative. Energy from those experiencing new levels of participation gave the convention an air of possibility. The front-runners were concerned with winning, and their policy positions and promises were secondary to this enterprise. But party stalwarts were also concerned with preserving earlier power arrangements, and the DNC's power as an institution. The Miami convention was thus an explosive mix of competing interests. It would also be a defeat for Chisholm's campaign. However, Chisholm would emerge from the convention with increased power as a legislator and as a political force in Brooklyn.

Chisholm was there to exercise Black feminist power politics. In other words, she was using what leverage she had to push the party and the nominee toward her vision of political equity within the intersections of race, sex, and class. She wanted pledges to support government programs for equity and would demand a Black vice president, a woman secretary of Health, Education, and Welfare, and an Indigenous secretary of the Interior. But she also hesitated to dictate a program. She, above all, wanted to be "a rallying point, a catalyst," to stimulate the seizing of political power by her coalition, not dictate an agenda.[3] To do so, she still needed more delegates. With the delegate count so close between Humphrey and McGovern, her hope was to have a consequential number of votes with which to bargain. There were still delegates, mostly Black, who could be persuaded to vote for Chisholm on the first ballot—that is, to remain uncommitted to either front-runner. Still, McGovern seemed to be tying up more and more votes from Black and women delegates. Chisholm was aware of, and disappointed in, the political games underway in the delegate race. "There was a lot of dishonesty that was going on with these big, fat white gentlemen with these big stomachs running around, it was not right," she remembered. In particular, she suspected that campaigns were buying delegates for money. She was also disappointed by a lack of support from those she considered allies. Even Humphrey, with whom she found common cause in challenging California's winner-take-all system, and whom she saw as essentially decent, tried to appear to be more of a supporter than he really was. Bella Abzug similarly declared herself a supporter but did nothing to help Chisholm's campaign. Steinem, too, was a self-declared Chisholm supporter but led the NWPC into backing McGovern. Chisholm thought it would have been embarrassing for them not to support her, as a woman, but she discovered any embarrassment was outweighed by their desire to back a winner on the first ballot. She was similarly frustrated by the lack of support from most Black political colleagues. Despite these frustrations, and the fact that Chisholm was glad when the campaign was over, she was glad she had done it. "I never lost faith in the Democratic process," she stated later.[4]

Chisholm was the object of some curiosity from convention delegates, the press, the public, and the front-runners. For some she inspired admiration; for others, anxiety or hostility. Joe Harris, a member of the Connecticut delegation, for example, noticed that hers was the only national campaign that had Black campaign workers in a "large number."[5] Columnist George Frazier of the *Boston Globe*, on the other side, characterized her as an unqualified spoiler who would take Black votes away from McGovern and help Nixon win. But one of his readers answered in Chisholm's defense: "Mrs. Chisholm paid her dues just by being a woman in a country where men like George Frazier can have their ideas published. Right on Sister Shirley."[6] McGovern claimed to take the Chisholm campaign "very seriously." Equality for both Black people and women were "two very important matters" for him, though "of course I hope she won't take votes away from me," he said.[7] Some Black delegates did hesitate to move into the McGovern camp as long as Chisholm's name would be in nomination at the convention.[8] Humphrey, too, was anxious that he would lose supporters to Chisholm. Democratic Party leadership even offered Chisholm a seat on the Steering Committee as a consolation prize in exchange for her delegates, which she declined.[9]

The political game of negotiating for uncommitted or wavering delegates began weeks before the convention itself. The 400-plus Black delegates were very much divided over whom to support. Some, such as California delegation leader Willie Brown, were backing George McGovern, placing their bets on the favorite in the hope that McGovern would repay the favor later. Others remained uncommitted, waiting to see whether they could bargain with their votes at the convention to help put one candidate over the top, since McGovern was just 150–200 votes short. And Chisholm still had her stalwart supporters, spread out across the states.[10]

Despite these differences, newspapers seemed to see Black delegates as part of a "bloc" that would vote in unison. Competition among Black politicians to be the top power broker of this bloc was fierce. The *New York Times* credited Yancey Martin, a Black McGovern campaign staffer, and Julian Bond with being in charge of Black delegates. The *Washington Post*, however, identified Walter Fauntroy as the main mover and shaker.[11] Others were bargaining with McGovern: the three chairs of the Gary convention, Richard Hatcher, Amiri Baraka, and Charlie Diggs, announced their support after reaching an agreement with the candidate. Chisholm's Congressional Black Caucus colleagues Louis Stokes, Walter Fauntroy, and Bill Clay also extracted some promises from McGovern, claiming they could deliver enough delegate votes to clinch the nomination.[12]

The 1972 Democratic Party platform was the most liberal party platform yet in the history of the nation. The 150 members of the Platform Committee met in Washington in late June. Chisholm had one delegate who was a member: Jim Pitts of Massachusetts.[13] Although McGovern himself, citing "exhaustion," did not appear at the meeting, Chisholm did. She suggested that "the Democratic Party . . . shake off the old custodial type of liberalism with its litany of welfare projects, its stress on numerical quantitative aspects of problems and politics, and its self-styled pragmatists, contemptuous of those who challenge the familiar routine of power politics and Main Street wisdom." She advocated for the repeal of all laws that targeted LGBTQ people for repression. She also rejected the labels of "radical left" or "moderate center." She said, "It's too bad everything has to be labeled. We need to write a humanistic platform . . . and if we're concerned about human beings in America we won't get hung up on labels." The platform committee responded with a standing ovation, the most positive response given to any of the candidates.[14] But Chisholm would be disappointed with the platform regarding its vagueness on abortion rights, the Vietnam War, and economic revitalization.[15] She would try to improve on these shortcomings at the convention.

Shirley and Conrad Chisholm, and most likely Mac Holder and Thad Garrett, plus eight Secret Service agents boarded a plane late on the night of July 8, bound for Miami. There was an "air of excitement" aboard, and several starstruck passengers shook Chisholm's hand and wished her good luck. There was a small cluster of press and supporters at the airport, but the Secret Service hustled the candidate past them and into the motorcade. "I remember thinking this must be what it is like all the time when you're the president, or a queen," Chisholm recalled later. More well-wishers greeted her outside the Deauville Hotel with hand-lettered signs, because the management would not allow banners, and so crowded her car that it took some time for the agents to clear her path. An impromptu rally ensued. Kenneth Gibson, mayor of Newark and chair of the Platform Drafting Committee, was there to greet her and gave a short welcoming speech on the stairs to the mezzanine, after which Chisholm spoke.[16]

It was very exciting for Chisholm to finally have arrived, but she knew she was in for an uphill battle. Challenges came from multiple fronts: the media, the other candidates, and party leaders. "Oh, boy, the media was just waiting for Shirley Chisholm to come in," she recalled.[17] The McGovern camp itself was on the seventeenth floor of the Doral Hotel, and the fifteenth floor of the same hotel was where "the most powerful leaders in black America assembled."[18] The young Rev. Jesse Jackson was there and gave an interview to the *New York Times* that made clear his allegiances had switched to McGovern. Jackson was now saying Chisholm had irritated Black leaders by declaring her candidacy without waiting for their approval. He rehashed the original grievance: "several meetings of men politicians" had floated candidates to unite behind, including Carl Stokes and John Conyers, Jackson told the *Times*, but Chisholm had "blocked those possibilities" when she declared her decision to run. He seemed to blame her for the Black leadership's major error of not uniting behind a Black candidate early in the process, even though he had been a supporter earlier.[19]

Other erstwhile supporters were wavering. Ron Dellums was under considerable pressure from California Democrats to throw in with McGovern. Chisholm remembered later, referring to Dellums, that this made the convention "hell because the persons who were supposed to nominate me backed out at the last moment because some of the other . . . candidates got to them." She said that "Percy Sutton came to my rescue" to make the nominating speech.[20] Thad Garrett was expressing pessimism privately. First he was worried that Chisholm's nomination at the convention would not occur. Then he thought that Chisholm would "make somebody mad" at the convention. Then he feared that Dellums would switch sides once he arrived. Chisholm called Carolyn Smith, due to give birth to her first daughter imminently, and therefore still in Washington, every day. So did Garrett. Smith counseled Garrett, who complained that he "couldn't control her," to just tell Chisholm his opinion and then she would make up her own mind based on his information.[21]

The morning after her arrival in Miami, Chisholm appeared on *Meet the Press* with McGovern and Humphrey. Moderator Laurence Spivak opened the interview asking about the California delegation. Why, if Chisholm and many of her supporters were ideologically allied with McGovern, did she support changing the rules of the California delegation? "I have always believed," she replied, "that if you are going to talk about representative government, that the vote of every man and every woman must count. It doesn't make sense to me to have someone just securing approximately 44 or 45 percent of the vote in a particular state and then come home with all of the delegates. What happens to the other 59 or 60 percent? That's not democracy." The interviewers pressed harder, arguing that she favored the "anti-McGovern position." Chisholm responded with her typical directness. "I do not put it in that light at all," she said crisply. The matter rested on principle, she declared, the very same principle on which the McGovern commission had rested its reforms. Her stand had not changed since the start of the campaign and would not change no matter the candidate in question. McGovern's stance, alternatively, had changed as soon as it was his own nomination in question. Although his commission had favored proportional representation in state primaries, he was, in Chisholm's words, "like all the rest of them. It's politics as usual, maybe just under the name of reform."[22]

The interviewers also wanted Chisholm's predictions on the general election. What did she think "the drag down effect" would be if McGovern, polling badly against Nixon, won the nomination: would other Democratic seats be lost in races further down the ballot? And what would "the black vote" do in the general election? About the general election, she would only say that some of her House colleagues were indeed concerned about their chances in November. On the "black vote," she corrected her interrogators. "I have no idea as to how that black vote will go," she said, "because the black vote is not a monolithic vote. I think we are finding that out more and more. There is no one black leader in this country, today, that can control the black vote. There is no group of black politicians that can control that black vote."[23] In other words, assuming that all Black people and politicians would feel the same way and behave as an electoral bloc was missing the entire landscape of Black political thought, with its tremendous diversity on ideology and tactics. As to the nomination itself, Chisholm was clear that she would support any Democratic Party nominee—except George Wallace. She repeated that the best hope of the party was a Teddy Kennedy–Wilbur Mills ticket that could unite the various factions of the party: Kennedy was still very popular and Mills, as a moderate southerner, might be able to circumvent Nixon's southern strategy.[24] But acknowledging that it was very likely McGovern would win the nomination eventually, and did not need Black support to do so, she reminded McGovern that he would need Black votes in November.

The stakes were high for the ongoing disputes over convention delegates that were still pending. Chisholm argued that Black delegates could play a consequential role only if the proportional California delegation was seated. "What would be the use," she asked rhetorically, "of going through the motions and agreeing on a program and trying to get unified support for it, when something close to half the black delegates were already delivered to McGovern?" Her first mission was to do everything she could to sway Black delegates into remaining uncommitted, or at least uncommitted to McGovern. If there was no clear winner, Chisholm could bargain with her delegates to ask for some promises from McGovern. "Six or seven of us," she said on the day of the nomination ballot, "would go to see him to discuss with him what we feel and know the things are that must be done to salvage whatever we can of the [platform] planks that were not supported, and to bring in a solid black vote in November."[25]

THE BLACK CAUCUS AND BLACK LEADERSHIP

Outside Chisholm's campaign, other Black leaders assumed that she just wanted to be at the head of the power brokers out of self-interest and did not trust her to negotiate on their behalf. Whether because of sexism, their frustration that she had not consulted them, or irritation that their own plans were not working out, they seemed incapable of imagining that Chisholm had a principled strategy. Julian Bond was peevish. "The central issues is who will broker [for Black voters]," he said. He and others had negotiated promises from McGovern, and "now that it's clear he'll win, a lot of people want to get in on it. . . . Why should I let you come in late and take over?" Amiri Baraka also lumped her in among the broker wannabees, even though his strategy of remaining uncommitted and then negotiating with the candidates was not far off from Chisholm's. Walter Fauntroy accused Chisholm of being the center of the stop McGovern movement.[26]

Chisholm's main opportunity to make her case was at the Black caucus meeting later on Sunday, where all the candidates would speak. The Black caucus was made up of Black delegates and alternates, a total of about 645, and presided over by Charlie Diggs.[27] Chisholm saw the Black caucus speech as her last chance to "change the script" about supporting McGovern. Aware that a year of political planning and meetings had not yet unified Black voters and political activists, she decided to try once more to make her best argument for Black political agency. She reasoned that conventions had a "superheated emotional atmosphere" and that she might be able to impress on delegates the historic opportunity they had to make demands of the DNC leadership. She slept little the night before, restless with anticipation. Walking into the caucus meeting, she was buoyed by a wave of applause: "The way the room erupted into shouts and cheers gave me a thrill of hope," she recalled. She began to speak, in "a voice made husky by air-conditioning."[28]

The following speech "rocked the house." In an openly emotional plea, she accused Black political leaders of having sacrificed their integrity for false promises from other candidates. In particular, they had accepted promises of $50,000 to $75,000 for voter registration funds in exchange for supporting McGovern. "Don't sell your vote . . . our people are watching us," she urged the delegates present, and reminded them that they had paid their own way to the convention and owed nothing to anyone. The audience repeatedly interrupted her with "stomping and cheering," especially the "younger and more militant delegates." In contrast, the Congressional Black Caucus members present sat stone-faced, refusing to applaud. Chair Diggs even got up and left the platform while she was speaking.[29] After less well-received speeches from McGovern and Humphrey, Charles Evers, mayor of Fayette, Mississippi, and an uncommitted delegate, spoke. All candidates should release their Black delegates to vote for Chisholm, he argued. Then Chisholm could negotiate with the front-runner, whether McGovern or Humphrey. His words and Chisholm's pleas had some effect: the Black caucus held a vote to ask all presidential candidates besides McGovern to release their delegates to Chisholm for the first vote.[30]

However, as Chisholm won that limited support from some in the Black caucus, she lost a key supporter. Ron Dellums, who had originally planned to make Chisholm's nomination speech several nights later, was "on my back and just strategizing from my hotel room" in the Doral, seriously ill with bronchitis. He would watch the nomination on television from his bed. On the night of the Black caucus meeting, he reluctantly decided to back McGovern. He explained his decision as a pragmatic one. "If there's any kind of way that . . . we had thought that it could have been Shirley, then that would have been . . . fantastic. We wouldn't even be here discussing it. It would be the greatest moment in the history of the world. But, that wasn't about to be. Nobody was that naïve." In his recollection, because the platform was very progressive and McGovern was clearly progressive, endorsement made sense.[31] Despite his illness and public support of Chisholm up to that night, his lack of appearances at strategy meetings and absence at the podium on her behalf seemed a betrayal to Chisholm's candidacy. To make matters worse, the *Los Angeles Times* reported on Monday morning that Dellums had dropped his support for Chisholm because, he was quoted saying, she was allied with an anti-McGovern "coalition of expediency and power . . . deathly afraid of the new forces moving to assume leadership and expose hypocrisy in this country." While Dellums might well have been referring to the front-runner Humphrey and not Chisholm in his "expediency and power" comment," the way his comment was reported made it seem that he was repudiating her, too.[32] Chisholm, stung, also seemed unaware that he was indisposed and blamed his withdrawal on pressure from others. Chisholm's and Dellums's relationship survived the convention intact, although some of Chisholm's supporters, perhaps unaware of Dellums's illness, were angry that he had not made the nomination speech.[33] Wilson Riles of the California campaign was especially disappointed: "I don't think that there was at that time anyone else in the country but Ron Dellums who could've put it as well as succinctly and as memorably about what the importance of Shirley's campaign was and what the importance of those issues were."[34]

THE WOMEN'S CAUCUS

The next opportunity for Chisholm to solicit delegates was at the women's caucus meeting in the Carillon Hotel the day after the Black caucus meeting. It was the first anniversary of the founding of the National Women's Political Caucus (NWPC).[35] Perhaps no occasion better indicates the difficulty of maintaining a unified feminist front. The NWPC had expended much effort in the run-up to the convention, including nationwide educational meetings on delegate selection.[36] Compared to the 1968 convention, where women were 13 percent of delegates, 40 percent were women in 1972. Out of the over 1,100 women delegates at the convention, perhaps 300 were active NWPC supporters. Among them, there was some disunity. Gloria Steinem and Bella Abzug, who served as the convention floor leader, were at odds with cofounder Betty Friedan over whether to push for Chisholm as the vice presidential nominee. "I'm so disgusted with Gloria," Friedan reportedly said, with a litany of accusations that Steinem was racist and opportunistic. Chisholm herself was not interested in the vice presidential position. Friedan, however, would not give up. Encountering the National Council of Negro Women representative Jane Galvin Lewis in the lobby of the Deauville, Freidan angrily accused Lewis of "playing both ends." Lewis was a Chisholm ally, but she had suggested Steinem as a vice presidential nominee at the NWPC meeting because the group was generating a list of names. "What kind of black are you anyway?" Friedan shouted at Lewis, implying racial disloyalty.[37]

About 300 women delegates at the convention attended the July 10 meeting. Each candidate was invited to speak. The most anticipated speeches were from Chisholm and McGovern. As she had been at the Black caucus, Chisholm was greeted with the warmest applause of the day. People stood on chairs and shouted for her for about ten minutes. Moderator Liz Carpenter said, "This shows where you stand in our hearts," implying that even though the delegates might not vote for Chisholm she was their favorite. Chisholm pushed back, saying that "you know that deep in your hearts, you put me beside any candidate and I have a deeper commitment to those issues that are important to us than any of them. You have to make the decision whether your commitment to women is going to go down the line for a woman candidate or whether women go for the male candidate like they always do." The loud cheering was despite the fact that fewer than twenty-four were actually voting for her. One Michigan woman explained: "That's why I'm clapping so hard . . . I'm clapping out the guilt. But this is politics and she's not going to win."[38] McGovern's performance was not nearly so well received.[39]

White feminists bemoaned their conundrum at the convention and after the fact. One writer explained that she could not "adore" Chisholm as she did Bella Abzug because of Chisholm's lisp, wigs, and exhortative speaking style. She even alluded to a "very real possibility that she might be unhinged." But this writer, Vivien Leone of *off our backs*, grudgingly acknowledged Chisholm's relative legislative effectiveness when compared with Abzug, and the fact that merely running as a serious candidate was a huge step. Leone acknowledged that it was easier for women at the Democratic National Convention to see McGovern as a "realistic candidate" because of his maleness. After reading this assessment, Gloria Steinem wrote in, relieved, saying that Leone had put into words exactly what Steinem was thinking.[40] "I didn't think she was crazy [to run;] I thought she was crotchety," said Susan Brownmiller years later. "I think her strengths as a politician were more symbolic than real," she mused, and recalled that Chisholm was not "real pally" or a good dinner companion with the other NWPC members. She was also unaware of Chisholm's performance record in Congress.[41] Such calculations would mean that women delegates, including NWPC members, would decline to vote for Chisholm on the floor.

THE CONVENTION FLOOR

The first order of business at the convention itself was settling which delegates were entitled to be seated. And the challenge to California's winner-take-all method of delegate selection had the most effect on the candidates' fortunes, even more so than the nomination balloting would. McGovern, as the top candidate from that primary, was in the ironic position of arguing against his own reform so that he could win back all 271 delegates from the state and sew up the nomination. Humphrey, for his part, wanted proportional representation so that he could keep his significant number of California delegates and stay in the race for the nomination. Chisholm's twelve California delegates knew that they could help tip the count toward either Humphrey or McGovern, provided that they were recognized. But they were running into trouble. Suspicions were running high in the McGovern camp that Chisholm was a spoiler on behalf of Humphrey.[42] The Chisholm delegates needed microphone time to make their case, but Willie Brown, cochair of the California delegation, would not yield any.[43] The first night, the proportional California delegation had been seated with some difficulty, because Brown had engineered that credential badges be withheld. Eventually, Riles had to "basically threaten someone" to get the badges and got the California Chisholm delegates on the floor with minutes to spare.[44] But they would only be able to stay a short time. Brown, a former activist-turned-assemblyman, took the podium to deliver damaging comments about the proportional delegation. He claimed that his winner-take-all delegation was the most diverse in the country, and that the convention therefore ought to vote unanimously in order to preserve all of their voices. He singled out the twelve Chisholm delegates for breaking with the majority of the delegation to support a previous challenge from South Carolina. Alluding to his background in the Black freedom struggle, he argued that allowing the delegation to vote their individual consciences would violate their civil rights more than requiring them to cast a unanimous ballot would. In a spirited crescendo, he cried, "Give me back my delegation," dramatically waving his fist. The opponents of the challenge had a tough act to follow, but they tried to counter this spirited defense, arguing that the winner-take-all system violated the McGovern reforms. But the tide had turned. On a roll call vote that was completed just after two in the morning, the winner-take-all system won, 1618.28 to 1238.22.[45] The California Chisholm delegates lost their credentials and were escorted from the hall.[46] Barbara Lee was suspicious and angry: "I was very mad, I mean very angry at the people who did that, especially my dear friend, Mayor Willie Brown. I was so furious." Chisholm's California delegates did stay and participate in Black caucus and platform meetings, and consoled themselves that they had forced McGovern to take their issues into account.[47]

With the nomination for McGovern all but sealed, Chisholm's coalition and the NWPC had less leverage. So did the other candidates; Humphrey and Muskie folded on Tuesday morning.[48] Chisholm's campaign fought on for a sliver of influence. Aware that his effort was in vain without his California delegates, Humphrey announced that he would release ninety-seven Black delegates to vote for Chisholm on the first ballot, the result of extensive lobbying efforts by Thaddeus Garrett and others.[49] Charles Evers made a pitch to the Black caucus that, now that Humphrey had released his Black delegates, those delegates should show their "racial solidarity and pride" by voting for Chisholm. But he was working uphill. Pro-McGovern Black delegates—chair Richard Hatcher, Louis Stokes, Jesse Jackson, Bill Clay, Walter Fauntroy, Julian Bond, and Alderwoman Anna Langford of Chicago— all accused Humphrey of using Chisholm "in a final desperate effort to block McGovern." His release of Black delegates was a stunt, they thought, to pressure McGovern delegates into voting for Chisholm, too. The possibility that Chisholm—though aligned with Humphrey on the California challenge— had her own aims and strategy separate from any other candidate was never entertained. Chisholm, for her part, could not afford to turn away a "badly needed windfall" of almost one hundred delegates.[50] Discussion at the Black caucus meeting was "sharp, shouting, swearing debates." Julian Bond said Chisholm had "sold out" to Humphrey. Fauntroy, confronted by the threat of revolt by his own Washington, D.C., delegates who had been moved by Chisholm's speech, told them that the Humphrey move was an effort to defeat McGovern on the first ballot. Humphrey should have given all of his votes to Chisholm, Fauntroy argued. McGovern made no move to release his Black delegates, and they remained steadfast.[51] When Garrett tried to convince McGovern delegates in the room to support Chisholm as their vehicle for making demands, he was met by "jeers." At the same time, Fauntroy had a tough time of it when he spoke on McGovern's behalf. And at the end of the meeting those who hadn't left in frustration agreed to support Chisholm on the first ballot.[52]

Though Chisholm delegates were now no longer in play as bargaining chips for a nominee, they still had votes to cast on the party platform. The July 11 session set a record for the longest a Democratic National Convention session had ever gone, at nearly twelve hours. It began with a few preliminaries, including the uncontested election of Yvonne Brathwaite-Burke as vice chair. Then the platform debates started. Chisholm's delegates got a memorandum about her stances on each platform challenge.[53] She was opposed to the minority reports that advocated for adopting George Wallace's conservative new platform on capital punishment (allowing states to execute convicted felons).[54] A group of opponents, including Massachusetts Chisholm delegate Jim Pitts, refuted each of the proposed planks. The Wallace minority report lost on a voice vote.

Chisholm was in support of Minority Report No. 5, the National Welfare Rights Organization's (NWRO's) $6,500 minimum income plank. All week, the NWRO demonstrated and lobbied for a $6,500 per year minimum income to be written into the Democratic platform. After a roll call vote, the plank lost by about a two-to-one margin, however.[55] Minority Report No. 7 concerned a reproductive freedom addition to the plank on women's rights. A sentence would be added that read, "In matters relating to human reproduction, each person's right to privacy, freedom of choice, and individual conscience should be fully respected, consistent with relevant Supreme Court decisions." The plank failed on a roll call vote, 1101.37 to 1571.8.[56] Finally, Minority Report No. 8 concerned sexual orientation. It called for a plan that "would affirm the right of all persons to express their own sensibility, emotionality, and lifestyle," freedom from police harassment and employment discrimination, and the repeals of all laws governing sexual acts between consenting persons. Chisholm supported this plank, too, but the majority of those present did not, and it lost on a voice vote.[57] Despite the losses for the NWRO, gay and lesbian rights, and reproductive freedom proponents, the platform was the most liberal for a major party to date.[58]

The nomination process itself was next. July 12 was an ordinary hot and humid summer day in Miami, but it would become an extraordinary date. That night Chisholm would become the first Black person to have her name entered into nomination at a major party convention, and the first woman to be nominated at the Democratic National Convention.[59] She was still angling to bring some pressure on McGovern on behalf of Black, brown, poor, and women voters. An "unending stream" of delegates had been coming by the Deauville hotel suite, recruited by Garrett and Sherry Friedman, a Chisholm campaign worker, for Chisholm to lobby for a vote on the first ballot. After two days of this, Chisholm was feeling optimistic, even telling a reporter she thought that she had 300 delegates. She picked up some from Garrett's home state of Ohio, Mississippi, Louisiana, Pennsylvania, and even Florida, even though delegates from the Sunshine State were pledged to Wallace and risked arrest because they were under Florida jurisdiction. Friedman also convened a secret meeting with Florida delegates to outline a plan that, if there was a second nomination ballot, up to seventy of them might vote for Chisholm.[60] Another cluster of Black caucus members present revolted against pressure by Fauntroy to switch to McGovern and chose instead to endorse Chisholm.

That night, the convention heard nomination speeches. Each candidate would be nominated by one delegate and then seconded by two additional delegates. The Chisholm campaign was still reeling from Dellums's backing out of the nomination speech. But Percy Sutton stepped up. He addressed the convention: "Madam Chairlady, Mr. Chairman, if my mouth dries up on me, if my tongue becomes large in my mouth, if my voice becomes quavery," he said, it was because the moment was such a historic one. He recalled "years of shame for America" during Jim Crow, with the humiliations of segregation and the terror of racist violence. Now, he announced, Chisholm's "presence, action, and conduct" signified change. She had coalesced "the forces of dissatisfied women, struggling minorities, the poor and the young," and had assaulted unfairness and injustice. His nomination was greeted with applause and cheering.[61] Barbara Amram, the Minnesota Democratic leader, seconded Sutton. "Shirley Chisholm speaks for the rehumanization of this nation," she announced. She was "a catalyst for change so that the lights will turn on again for those written off by others: blacks, Latins, Asians, Chicanos, Indians, youth."[62] Charles Evers, brother of Medgar Evers and then the mayor of Fayette, Mississippi, also seconded the nomination. Chisholm would stay true to her word and to the people she represented, he said. "We would like to ask all of you here who have claimed so long you want to see black folks and white folks and poor folks represented," he exhorted, "I would like to beg you to let's go out [sic] and vote on the first ballot for Shirley Chisholm and let the country know that all of us poor folks, all of us black folks, and all of us folks who were left out so long are not going to let nobody put us in their hip pocket on the first ballot."[63]

Then came the long process of balloting. This was a fraught experience for many delegations, some of whom wanted to signal support for a particular candidate while eventually casting votes for the now-presumptive nominee McGovern.[64] As the first roll call wrapped up, McGovern had won 1,728.35 votes, Jackson had won 525, Wallace had won 381.7, Chisholm had won 151.95, and former North Carolina governor Terry Sanford had won 77.5. There would be no second ballot. Chisholm's greatest number came from Ohio, the twenty-three votes for which Garrett had lobbied. She also had support in southern states; Louisiana had 18.5, Mississippi and Georgia had 12, Tennessee had 10, and Virginia had 5.5. In addition to Ohio there were other Rust Belt delegates, too: 9.5 from Pennsylvania, 6 from Minnesota, 5 from Wisconsin, and 4.5 from Illinois. Colorado had seven, and her home state of New York had six. But then states were permitted to change their votes, and fourteen of them reduced their votes for Chisholm.[65] Delegations began requesting changes to their tallies, enough to strip Chisholm of 50 votes and give McGovern another 136. Jackson, Wallace, and Sanford lost votes, too, but none would lose as many to McGovern as Chisholm did.[66]

As news came in that she had peaked at just under 152 delegates, Chisholm decided to release them. From her Deauville suite, she telephoned Thad Garrett on the convention floor and informed him to tell Chisholm delegates

Shirley Chisholm at the Democratic National
Convention podium, July 12, 1972.
Thomas J. O'Halloran / Library of Congress.

to vote their conscience.[67] Victor Robles, serving as a delegate from New York, refused. It was his first and only national convention. He was disgusted by the political wheeling and dealing that he saw there. In protest, he and the other three New York Chisholm delegates, including Annie Bowen and Mary Pinkett, held up the roll call. Bronx congressman Herman Badillo and Garrett tried to persuade them not to. Finally Robles was called to the front to take a phone call, and it was Chisholm herself, releasing him and the others as her delegates. They finally relented.[68]

As officials were counting the changed votes, Chisholm made her way down to the floor to concede in a short speech:

> For seven long months and maybe more than seven months, a large number of us have been going up and down the paths of this country trying to take a certain kind of message to the American people. And you know, in the Democratic Party we always have our fights and our struggles and our battles, but we now know that the most important thing that lies ahead for us is to be able to unseat the incumbent in November. (Applause.) And therefore, in unity there is strength. I also want to make it quite clear that it was the delegates here that made history tonight, the delegates that made history tonight. (Applause.) So in closing, God be with all of you and I pledge myself to criss-crossing this country once again in terms of voter registration campaigns to swell those rolls to unseat the incumbent, Richard Milhous Nixon in November.[69]

She was met with a wave of applause that belied the fact that she had not won the nomination. Chisholm recalled the delegates "went crazy" cheering for her. Even the George Wallace delegation applauded her.[70] By the end of the changes in balloting, close to 1:00 a.m., McGovern had 1,864.95 votes, Jackson 485.65, Wallace 377.5, Chisholm 101.45, and Sanford 69.5. She was the first woman to be nominated and carry delegate votes in the Democratic Party. And she was the first Black American to do the same in any national political party.

THE CONVENTION AFTERMATH

In the final analysis, Chisholm thought that the mere fact that she ran, not expecting to win but making a good faith effort to do so, was a powerful message. She thought that "the next time a woman of whatever color, or a dark-skinned person of whatever sex aspires to be President, the way should be a little smoother because I helped pave it." Chisholm tried to boost her supporters' spirits at the end of the campaign. "Let's just say this has been a wonderful trip we have taken together," she told them, acknowledging she had learned much along the way. Indeed, she wrote in her memoir of the campaign, she marveled at "how much we accomplished with next to no money, with a haphazard, volunteer organization, and with no planning worthy of the name." "How far could we have gone," she mused, "if we had done it right?" Many of her delegates went home energized to participate in local and state, or even national, politics, and far less complacent about the assurances of self-appointed Black leaders.[71] Nonetheless, they were also disappointed by the fighting and rancor they had witnessed. Hopes for unity within the Chisholm coalition were dashed. Many in the women's movement felt betrayed by the convention's focus on nominating McGovern himself rather than a commitment to egalitarian ideas. Chisholm, alternatively, saw victory in the fact that the unprecedented number of women delegates had been able to force the convention to debate Vietnam, abortion rights, and poverty. She was not surprised that the abortion plank was voted down, for instance, but was glad that women had fully participated in the process.[72] For Chisholm, the greatest disappointment was that a critical mass of Black delegates did not cohere or agree on a strategy, and thus become a political force. As for McGovern's nomination and then loss in the general election, she thought both were inevitable. A more unified Black bloc probably would have nominated McGovern anyway, and his campaign was no match for Nixon's. She still thought, a year after the race, that the only winning Democratic ticket would have been Ted Kennedy with Wilbur Mills. There were bright spots in the 1972 election, however: a more robust voter registration effort and more Democratic campaign funding.[73]

Shortly after the campaign, few in the media bothered to analyze it. A notable exception was Gloria Steinem. Steinem theorized that Chisholm might well have pushed the front-runners to the left. "The Chisholm candidacy didn't forge a solid coalition of those people working for social change," she admitted. "That will take a long time. But it began one. If you listen to personal testimony from very diverse sources, it seems that the Chisholm candidacy was not in vain." Chisholm's greatest impact, Steinem thought, was on individuals. She published a set of comments from sixteen observers and participants in the 1972 race in *Ms.* One interviewee, a household worker, described her friends' transitions from thinking of the Chisholm campaign as a "joke," to being angry that she hadn't let a Black man run, to proud admiration. Flo Kennedy pointed out that the campaign had "freaked out" those who "thought they were revolutionaries but discovered that they couldn't dig her wig." The editor of *Newsweek* decreed that the peak moment of the convention had been her speech to the Black caucus meeting. Fannie Lou Hamer described her pride in casting a vote for Chisholm on the first ballot because, she said, Chisholm talked about "the real issues in this country" that the male candidates had not talked about, and refused to "bow to political pressure." Arlie Scott recalled the political education nonwhite and women Californians got, and the remarkable moment of coalition when she found herself in a lunch meeting with both Bobby Seale of the Black Panther Party and Aileen Hernandez of the National Organization for Women. Tom Wicker of the *New York Times* expressed amazement that men had not wanted her to run, but she had done it anyway. And the ten-year-old daughter of Harry and Julie Belafonte declared her intention to run for the presidency.[74]

Others analyzed the lack of formation of the "Black bloc," as Chisholm had warned at the beginning of the week and, indeed, throughout the campaign. By week's end, Andy Muse, director of the DNC Minority Division, was saying the same thing: "The watchword for this delegation [of Black people] is independence, in the sense that they don't owe anybody anything."[75] Billy Rowe of the *Amsterdam News* was disappointed. "I think it was wrong that Black leaders throughout the country failed to throw their support behind the Presidential candidacy of Congresslady Shirley Chisholm," he wrote. "It seemed to me that their backing right up through the last ballot of the Democratic convention would have really given Black Americans bargaining points."[76] But the events of the convention showed that Black unity was unrealistic, given the heterogeneity in Black politics.

Ron Dellums continued to admire his colleague. He had thought some of the criticisms of Chisholm at the convention were untrue and calculated. "And that just made . . . Shirley more endearing to me," he said. "It just made me want to hug her even more." He had not meant his endorsement of McGovern to say anything negative about Chisholm, and he believed that she did not interpret it as such—which might well have been the case—but her campaign workers never did forgive him for it. As for the result of the general election, Dellums thought that the party was not ready for a more progressive agenda. "Maybe that's why Shirley and I are simpatico," he mused, because "we had the audacity to be on the edge and to take risks," even inside the party structure.[77]

Barbara Lee, a California Chisholm delegate, was transformed by participating in the campaign. "It was such a good feeling to be able to [become involved in politics] and to know that we were making a difference," she said. It was her first time to a convention, and it was especially meaningful to be able to be a delegate.[78] She was convinced that, had the campaign been better funded, it would have gone much farther. By any account Lee thought that the campaign "really opened up a whole 'nother world to us, and it is a world that we can't turn our back on. . . . Shirley showed us that, even with attacks and even with hassles and even though she had many, many difficult days, she stayed the course, and I believe—especially for African-Americans and for women and for people of color—if you stay the course, you stand on principle, if you stick with what you believe in, if you do the right thing, you're a winner, and other people will see that. And, you know, you will influence the course of the world."[79]

THE GENERAL ELECTION

The final order of business for the convention was to nominate a vice president and present McGovern's acceptance speech. Chisholm's substantive role was over, but Black leaders and feminists still angled for leverage. Both would be disappointed. Chisholm told the NWPC that she would not accept a nomination for vice president, thus putting an end to any talk about picking her. Five Black leaders, not including Chisholm, were summoned to McGovern's headquarters where the candidate informed them of his top five picks. Under the impression that McGovern wanted their opinions, the five returned downstairs to discuss the merits of each. As they were deliberating, the television showed an impromptu press conference in the hotel's lobby. The campaign announced that Missouri senator Thomas Eagleton, who had not been on the list McGovern shared with them thirty minutes before, was the candidate. Bill Clay realized, he wrote later, that "McGovern . . . had no intention of involving blacks in the nuts and bolts decisions for a victorious campaign."[80] This was a lesson that Chisholm and her supporters had already learned.[81]

The McGovern presidential bid did not work out so well, as many party stalwarts had predicted. Shortly after the convention, vice presidential nominee Eagleton disclosed that he had previously been hospitalized for mental illness and withdrew from the race. Sargent Shriver, Johnson's War on Poverty captain and now ambassador to France, was named in his place during an extra session of the DNC.[82] But the troubles extended into the ideological. As journalist Jules Witcover recalled, "The Republicans effectively stamped McGovern as an irresponsible, wild liberal." The "demonization of McGovern and liberals were major contributors to his lopsided defeat.[83] The freewheeling delegate fight on the floor of the convention, which took so much time that McGovern's acceptance speech was in the wee hours of the morning, contributed to this impression. Prime-time television viewers saw the seemingly chaotic delegate fight and slept through the nominee's acceptance speech.[84] Activists on the left felt abandoned by McGovern as he moved to the center in order to contest the general election. NWPC activists were still furious about their treatment.[85] Chisholm's ally the young Reverend Al Sharpton complained that McGovern included very few Black youths on his campaign team.[86]

The candidate did not seem to appreciate or wish to use Chisholm's willingness to campaign on his behalf. After weeks of ignoring her, McGovern did call in early September to alert her that his wife would be visiting her district, which Chisholm already knew. She grew irritated that McGovern had squandered her experience campaigning on a grassroots level, and also that a group of Black leaders who had formed after the convention had decided not to include her either. She announced later that month that she would decline to do any active campaigning on his behalf. Still, she said, "I guess we'll have to vote for McGovern."[87] Eventually McGovern asked her for substantive help in turning out Black voters. He personally called to ask Chisholm to participate in a Bedford-Stuyvesant rally and to speak with him at Chaney State College, a historically Black institution outside of Philadelphia.[88] Chisholm politely agreed to do so and also supported McGovern in printed material. She called McGovern "a fine and decent man, with real sympathy for the issues women are concerned with" in *Glamour* magazine's October issue.[89] She sent out a twelve-page preelection newsletter supporting the McGovern-Shriver ticket and her own reelection.[90]

Chisholm's campaign to retain her congressional seat was more of a coronation than a battle. Earlier in 1972, the Republican-controlled New York state legislature had redistricted the city. They had taken pains to maintain safe seats for Chisholm, Rangel, and Badillo, so as to avoid gerrymandering lawsuits in defense of these high-profile representatives. However, Republicans had divided Black and brown neighborhoods around those safe districts, diluting the voting power. Assemblyman Sam Wright accused her of complicity in the arrangement.[91] Despite labeling Chisholm "something of a disappointment in her second term" due to her absences while conducting an "abrasive" presidential campaign, the *New York Times* endorsed her. Chisholm won her district in a landslide with nearly 88 percent of the vote (57,821) to her Republican opponent's 10 percent. Her mentee Vander Beatty also won a state senate rematch primary against a Chisholm detractor, then went on to win in the general election. The Beatty victory signaled that Chisholm was still the prime political power in Black Brooklyn.[92]

Chisholm had won a third term, though she was not unscathed in the 1972 election. The lack of support nationally for her attempt at coalition was a great disappointment. She returned to Congress for ten more years of service. Ron Dellums "didn't get the feeling that Shirley lost fire and lost heart because she continued to be the same woman getting up in the well of the House and fighting back."[93] She would fight for Black feminist power priorities for the rest of her congressional career.

17

COALITION POLITICS IN
CONGRESS, 1972–1976

★

Chisholm still had an undaunted sense of her own political voice after the 1972 campaign. She marveled, "In this hour in America the white power structure stands in awe because they are a little bit afraid of Shirley Chisholm."[1] She kept working within that white power structure to make legislation because she saw it as the best option. But she further developed her Black feminist power ethic of self-determination and political agency for the most vulnerable Americans. She remained in Congress for ten years after her run, serving six more years on Education and Labor, where she advanced Black feminist legislation, and four on the powerful Rules Committee, where she used her accumulated power to make pragmatic prodemocracy decisions. Her reputation as a fiery idealist belied the real power that she began to wield within the Capitol. Those who might have thought that she was too busy making paid speeches and running for president in her first two terms would not be able to make that criticism beyond late 1972. "Philosophically I remain involved," she told a religious education organization in 1973, "because it is the only way I can express my love toward a different America, an America that does not yet exist in time and space."[2]

Reflecting on the state of American politics in the Watergate era, Chisholm began to fear that the United States bore some unsettling similarities to Rome before its fall. She felt war-weary, as she told an interviewer in the spring of 1973, but she also knew that Black, brown, female, young, and poor people engaged in politics with and through her campaign and that was a win to her. The disaffection of Americans from the political process concerned her, as did the fragmentation of coalitions into unconnected identity groups. The "bizarre dress" that she observed in young protesters was a sign of how little they trusted previous generations, she thought. Chisholm hoped that something good for Black people would come out of the present sense of upheaval, though she also realized the chaos might only increase because those in power would fight hard for the status quo. The children of the middle class who rejected middle-class conventions gave her cause for optimism.[3] As for the Democratic Party and its shortcomings, she felt that she had no choice but to continue to participate—she was, in her words, "not hung up on labels any longer. I am hung-up on humanity." The party was the best hope, she thought, of bringing justice to poor Black people who represented humanity to her. If there were ever a viable alternative for structure and organization, she would change parties. At the same time, leadership for Black political advancement would have to come from the grassroots, from "Black indigenous leadership." Politicians were necessary for carrying out the work inside the government, but Black politicians were not equipped to bring together an actual coalition because of their self-interest.[4] The same was the case for women's leadership. "Democrats gave her the blues," one of her staffers recalled, because the party still functioned like "an old guy's social club" and still did not take issues of gender seriously.[5]

Chisholm was still reeling from the venom Black men politicians had aimed at her during the presidential campaign. After the presidential campaign, she went through "a long process" of assessing what had happened. She took a vacation to St. Thomas, during which she "did a lot of reflection" and made peace with her decisions on the campaign trail. She stood behind her decision to run a coalition campaign. In the sense that her efforts resulted in participation by a host of Black, brown, female, young, and poor people in politics for the first time, she felt she had been effective. A year later she was still saying, "What hurts me more than anything else is this, that if the brothers—and I'm talking about the brothers in politics, I'm not talking about the masses. . . . If the brothers would only leave me alone, and stop attacking me so much and stop giving out the wrong statements about me, I'd continue." But she was feeling fatigued from fighting Black men's political animus toward her. "I want to be left alone," she told another interviewer, who said that despite Chisholm's claim that she felt merely "hurt" and "deep sadness" about Black men's hostility, "her voice betrays a deep residue of bitterness and barely contained rage." In June 1975, she definitively ruled out running for president again, She would have needed at least $750,000 to start and a dedicated fundraising team, which she lacked. "I am sure," she declared, that "the American people will not raise this kind of money for a Black woman."[6]

Some of her self-reflection appeared in a new memoir. In May 1973 Chisholm published a book-length memoir of the campaign trail, *The Good Fight*.[7] The book documented the 1972 campaign from July 1971 to Nixon's reelection in November 1972. Chisholm made an evaluation of Democratic politics since 1968 (still, even after the party reforms, "white men's politics"), youth energy, and the state of Black politics.[8] She then documented the progress of the campaign through the convention and ended with several essays. The first, "Black Alternatives," espoused her belief that Black

Americans could not get ahead by assimilating into white institutions but must instead claim political and economic power. The purpose was not revolution, she cautioned, but to transform separation imposed from without into organizing to change political fortunes. And leaders would not accomplish this merely by wearing Afros and dashikis but by also developing a "practical politics" of organizing for democracy.[9] In "Coalition Politics," Chisholm once more articulated her vision for working across difference for real political change. She read Nixon's landslide reelection as a signal that the nation was moving rightward, largely driven by racism and sexism. To overcome this, coalitions that involved real power and decision sharing, not just top-down leadership, were necessary. For example, trade unionists and Black people need not squabble over the few good jobs available; they should mutually recognize a common need for well-paying jobs for all.[10] The volume concluded with a selection of Chisholm's position papers and speeches.[11]

Chisholm was returned to Congress with a consolidated hold on political power in Brooklyn, but the hard fight had costs at home. One was her energy, which she restored somewhat by enjoying herself at Brooklyn's Annual West Indian-American Day festivities. "It's the one day a year that I can get away from politics and see some joyful, happy faces," she explained.[12] After a burglar was caught in the St. Johns Place house in the early hours of Friday, October 13, she and Conrad moved to an "elegant new home" on President Street to the east of Prospect Park.[13] But no vacation, festival, or move could erase the rancor that had emerged from Black men political colleagues and would remain for years.[14] She began to openly mull retiring from Congress, telling one reporter that she would perhaps run in 1974 but definitely not in 1976. She got involved in citywide politics: her name was floated as a possible New York City schools chancellor, and she seemed to be intrigued.[15] In the 1973 New York mayoral race, Chisholm supported her colleague in Congress Herman Badillo in the Democratic primary, but switched to endorsing the primary's winner, Abe Beame, for the general election.[16]

She was growing weary of her home district politics and political rivals there. Former assemblyman Sam Wright, principal architect of the anti-Chisholm effort in Brooklyn in the previous year's presidential primary, would repeatedly run candidates against Chisholm's allies and oppose Chisholm in the Democratic primary for Congress in 1976. The trio who had opposed her presidential run, Tom Fortune, Waldaba Stewart, and Wright, disagreed fundamentally with Chisholm on a political approach. While Chisholm favored a coalition model, the three men followed a more traditional path of rewarding loyalty through patronage and cooperating with party organizations. "Hell," Tom Fortune said, "it's been going on since time immemorial, you understand . . . but we just found out where all that patronage was coming from. Now, just when we're getting the door open just a little bit, she tells us we shouldn't take it." Chisholm thought such thinking was unethical and led to scandals, such as those over well-paid jobs in federal agencies and local school boards going to party leaders' contributors and relatives. At the same time, one anonymous source said, control over those local programs did not translate into influence with white political leaders, which Chisholm did have. She was "rubbing their noses" in that fact. "Her personality makes it difficult for them to admit to her that they've made a mistake. They feel castrated," the source said, disclosing gendered resentment.[17] Indeed, her feminism and popular following did seem to anger male colleagues. Sam Wright would prove especially troubling in the coming years. He was raised in Ocean Hill, where he had been a prominent community-controlled schools movement leader. He had a formidable appearance; he once was a professional boxer and had a ridge of scar tissue across his eyebrows. After four years of backing local candidates in opposition to Chisholm, he himself would eventually run against her for Congress in 1976.[18]

In Washington, Chisholm still had a foe in the form of Richard Nixon, who was returned to office for four more years. Resigning herself to this fact, Chisholm remarked that "the next few years of the Nixon Administration are a detour from the path of progress that we experienced under Kennedy and Johnson. I just have to look on it as a detour for the moment and hopefully in 1976 there will be in power a person who is more committed to alleviating social ills."[19] As the Watergate corruption came to light, her criticism of Nixon grew even more pointed. By mid-1973 she was on the record calling for his impeachment. When the Congressional Black Caucus (CBC) learned that all members had been included on Nixon's enemies list, she called his administration "fascistic."[20]

Chisholm's transition from political lightning rod in 1972 to a lower-profile role as effective legislative negotiator and collaborator took place in the context of her willingness to build unlikely coalitions for specific political purposes. She leveraged her higher profile and what she had learned on the national campaign trail into building more coalitions on Capitol Hill. Chisholm acquired even more of a "reputation . . . for a willingness to work with Republicans as well as Democrats, conservatives as well as liberals, in pursuit of her goals."[21] Chisholm's ability to explain things clearly led other members of Congress to respect her expertise. Carolyn Smith recalled that Chisholm's training as an early childhood education teacher easily transferred to communicating with the wide range of intellects among her colleagues. Smith recalled that "she would really explain pieces of legislation to the guys who really didn't understand anything."[22] Her focus remained on remedying the intersecting problems of racism, sexism, and poverty that she had addressed during her presidential run. She fought legislation that would roll back civil rights laws, such as antibusing bills, and supported legislation that promoted equal educational and economic opportunities. The result was a raft of legislation that did not carry Chisholm's name but represented untold hours of her behind-the-scenes work and made material differences in Americans' lives. She also took seriously her responsibility to "bring home the bacon" in the district, in the form of federal grants.[23] And her casework load on behalf of constituents did not let up.

PEOPLE AND POLICIES ON CAPITOL HILL

Chisholm continued to work in her signature legislative style. For all of her genuine Black feminist convictions, she was also politically savvy enough to realize that coalitions between legislators from sometimes divergent ideological camps were also the best hope for getting things done. She credited herself with bringing more federal dollars into Bedford-Stuyvesant, but lamented the fact that newer members of Congress like herself still did not have the seniority required to move bills out of committees. Comparing herself to Adam Clayton Powell Jr., she noted that Powell had held the chair of Education and Labor, and had been able to determine what legislation would reach the floor. In 1973, most bills that nonwhite and women members introduced were languishing in committee. Therefore, alliances with more senior, often white and male members were necessary.[24] This was especially true as the nation's politics swung rightward.

Nationally, Black Americans saw her as their advocate within the federal government. As soon as she returned to full-time legislating in late 1972, ten Black servicemen at Laredo Air Force Base took over a mess hall in a protest against racism on the base, and one of the demands was to communicate with Chisholm. In Washington, about fifty inmates at the District of Columbia city jail took eleven hostages in a protest against poor conditions, the housing of juveniles with adults, and unfair bail and trial policies. Chisholm joined then Board of Education chair Marion Barry in negotiation with the inmates. She spoke to them through a megaphone outside the first-floor window of Cellblock 1. While they had begun the standoff refusing to settle for nothing less than unconditional release, she was able to convince them to bring their concerns to an emergency court hearing, where the judge prescribed reforms and prohibited reprisals against them. All hostages were freed. Chisholm was credited as a "magician" who turned the inmates away from their determination to die or go free to a willingness to speak with the judge.[25]

The 1972 campaign trail had taken her away from the House, but she returned with new energy. Her attendance at roll calls had been very spotty during the first half of 1972, with the exception of the Economic Opportunity Act amendments bill hammered out by Education and Labor.[26] After the convention and her trip to St. Thomas to recover, she was back on Capitol Hill full-time. The challenges were many. For one, the CBC had not itself coalesced around a common strategy or set of priorities. The bitter 1972 conflicts over presidential politics and Chisholm's candidacy had made it evident that the CBC could not effectively serve as the unified leadership committee of Black America. After the bitterness in the presidential race, its members were not unified. Chisholm continued to insist that "we cannot function on our Blackness alone," that is, it would be necessary to develop cooperative relationships with white congresspeople in order to get votes.[27] It had hired new, more experienced staff and was narrowing its focus to brokering relationships within Congress. Rather than being "grandiose case-workers" for all Black Americans, the members would focus their efforts on legislation and leave casework and problem solving to the CBC staff.[28] The members appeared to be getting along better, although Chisholm was occasionally sparring with Louis Stokes and Bill Clay.[29] The new CBC started out 1973 with a bill that would make Martin Luther King Jr.'s birthday a national holiday, something members could all get behind.[30] The CBC also made a unified response to President Nixon's State of the Union address with their own "True State of the Union Message" delivered on the House floor, with each member taking on a section.

Chisholm returned to committee and Democratic caucus work as well. Her expertise as an educator and administrator had earned her the respect of her colleagues on Education and Labor. Even though she lacked official seniority, she had forged alliances with more senior members, including Chair Carl Perkins, who respected her knowledge and appreciated her ability to educate them on thornier policy points.[31] Chisholm was appointed a member of a new subcommittee on gender discrimination within the Labor Subcommittee.[32] Colleagues also named her assistant secretary of the House Democratic Caucus.[33] Her work was issue-driven, and she did not mind who got the credit: "She was not concerned about herself, she was concerned about the issue," recalled Shirley Downs. "She would give the credit to other people. She didn't care. She didn't have to have a press release with her name on it. She only cared that the truth was written and the beautiful got done."[34]

The office in Washington, now in 123 Cannon, added more staff. Thaddeus Garrett would leave the office in 1975 to become a special assistant to Vice President Rockefeller, and then was appointed to the Consumer

Product Safety Commission with Chisholm's endorsement in 1976.[35] Carolyn Smith, Shirley Downs, and Andrea Tracy Holmes remained as more staff joined. Mia Cole started as Downs's secretary and then moved into legislative work herself. Brenda Pillors and Helen Butler joined the team. Senior Legislative Assistant Patsy Fleming came on to work on antipoverty legislation, especially food stamps, and then was replaced by Muriel Morisey in 1975.[36] Although she was not a Chisholm staffer, Northern California campaign coordinator Barbara Lee came to work on the Hill for Ron Dellums and became close to Carolyn Smith, calling her when she had questions and staying in contact with her mentor.[37]

In January 1973, the CBC delegation grew by three. Chisholm, now nearly fifty years old, was joined by two other Black women in the House and one Black man, Andrew Young. Barbara Jordan was thirty-six years old and represented a district in downtown Houston that had recently been redrawn. Yvonne Brathwaite-Burke was thirty-nine and represented a new district in Los Angeles that included Watts. Both were lawyers. Inevitably, the three Black women were compared to each other in the press. One Black columnist opined that "Barbara is smarter and Yvonne is prettier" than Chisholm.[38] Jordan was characterized as "cold and calculating" by one white man interviewer, who called Chisholm "screeching" and "emotional" by contrast.[39] Jordan had served as president pro tempore of the Texas State Senate and, in that role, had technically been governor of the state for one day while the governor and lieutenant governor had both taken a day off.[40] Barbara Jordan told Chisholm that she was "a Texan first and a Black second," a philosophy that Chisholm did not agree with. In Smith's recollection the conversation went thus: "Well I'm sorry, Barbara, I can't be that way," she said. Jordan shot back, "You're going to run yourself into the ground, woman."[41] Jordan's fame would come in part from her participation on the Judiciary Committee Watergate hearings and her displays of legal knowledge.[42] Yvonne Brathwaite-Burke was a civil rights lawyer and NAACP activist-turned-state legislator. The *Washington Post* alerted readers to the arrival of Brathwaite-Burke, reassuring them that she was "as tough and stubborn as Shirley Chisholm, but she almost never displays those qualities openly." By example, it reported that when Brathwaite-Burke experienced housing discrimination as a legislator in Sacramento, she simply filed a complaint with the Fair Employment Practices Commission and got the apartment. She was "not another Shirley Chisholm, who might have picketed the restaurant and apartment house and held press conferences on the sidewalk," apparently unaware of the fact that Chisholm had encountered racism in looking for D.C. housing and had neither picketed the building nor filed a complaint. The article heavily emphasized Brathwaite-Burke's quiet

An interracial feminist coalition at the Capitol, January 1973. *From left*:
Martha Griffiths, Shirley Chisholm, Elizabeth Holtzman,
Barbara Jordan, Yvonne Brathwaite-Burke, and Bella Abzug.
Bettman via Getty Images.

manner, fashionable good looks, and recent marriage to political consultant William Burke.[43] Chisholm warned Brathwaite-Burke about the pitfalls of media attention: some might "want to see you in a specific image that may not be what you are," she said.[44] Cardiss Collins became an unexpected fourth Black congresswoman after her husband George Collins, who had been reelected from Chicago the previous November, was killed in a plane crash near Midway Airport. The four did not move in lockstep, but they appeared on a National Urban League panel together in August in Baltimore, where they candidly strategized how Black people, and Black women, could increase their political power.[45] They also joined forces to write an open letter to Health, Education, and Welfare secretary Casper Weinberger protesting the forced sterilizations of a family in Alabama.[46]

Chisholm was still collaborating with nationally organized feminists. She flew to Houston in February 1973 to open the first annual meeting of the National Women's Political Caucus (NWPC) with Gloria Steinem and Bella Abzug. Having weathered its first party convention cycle, the NWPC was ready to decide on organizational priorities. One priority would be the Equal Rights Amendment, which had passed both houses the year before but was shedding momentum in its quest to be ratified by thirty-eight states.[47] A

Goldwater supporter and mother of six named Phyllis Schlafly had started an organization called STOP ERA. Schlafly's organization had managed to slow the rate of ratification in the states by getting several to reject the amendment and a few to begin procedures to rescind ratification. Now the convention had to generate a strategy for how to turn back the growing conservative backlash. Chisholm was the keynote for the opening session of about a thousand cheering delegates, presenting a speech entitled "Can a Woman Be Elected President?" She did encourage those women present to run for office on broad platforms that recognized the wide variation in women's concerns and took up more issues than the usual feminist ones of abortion and the ERA. She criticized women for not supporting her presidential campaign because they thought she had no chance of winning. And she forcefully suggested that new grassroots leadership begin to step in ("I am sure that Betty, Gloria and Bella are as sick of seeing their faces as I am of seeing mine," she said). She also continued to lay out her argument for antipoverty policies. She framed it as a fight against Nixon's attempt to direct Congress's agenda, particularly regarding fiscal priorities. His recent budget cut plans, which would defund the Office of Economic Opportunity and other domestic programs, were a direct rebuke to congressional appropriations decisions. She thought the NWPC, and the movement in general, ought to prioritize such issues in order to expand its focus beyond white middle-class women.[48]

BLACK FEMINISM IN LEGISLATIVE ACTION

As the 1973 session got underway, Chisholm began a focused campaign for antipoverty policies, guided by a Black feminist power framework. She would start with a defense of the Office of Equal Opportunity (OEO), which Nixon threatened to dismantle. She would then fight for a minimum wage bill that would increase the minimum wage and expand the workers covered. She would also cosponsor the Older Americans Act. She brought antipoverty grant money to the district for the Bed-Stuy Restoration Corporation and other programs.[49]

Chisholm mounted a full-on defense of the OEO when Nixon unilaterally announced the discontinuation of the War on Poverty–era agency, claiming the cut would save $8 billion. Chisholm did not yet have the votes among her colleagues to save the program, so she set about convincing them. In February, Education and Labor's new Subcommittee on Equal Opportunities began a series of hearings in multiple cities that would make the case for preserving the OEO, and Chisholm was one of the seven members. At the first hearing, she skewered Nixon's administration for emphasizing the need for a work ethic among Americans while planning to "completely disembowel or eliminate programs that would help people to get in the direction of the work ethic that everybody talks about." She still wanted a realignment of priorities toward services and away from the Vietnam War. When it came to public programs, she was insistent that most poor Americans were acting in good faith, wanting to participate in the labor marketplace, but stymied by discrimination and lack of opportunity.[50] At one of the sessions Chisholm questioned Nixon's Acting OEO Director Howard Phillips, zeroing in on Phillips's ideology to suggest that his personal political beliefs interfered with his carrying out the responsibilities of the office. He was a cofounder of the conservative Young Americans for Freedom, and she attempted to ascertain whether he was ideologically opposed to the fundamental mission of the OEO. She pressed him hard about whether Nixon had instructed him to eliminate the OEO programs.[51] She found his answers were "evasive and misleading."[52] When the OEO hearings convened for two days on Chisholm's home turf of New York City, she pressed even harder. She closely questioned witnesses, her remarks often meeting with applause from the packed audience. She elicited testimony from the chair of the city's main antipoverty agency that transferring OEO functions to Health, Education, and Welfare would not maintain the same level of services. She encouraged witnesses who ran Community Action Programs in upstate New York to discuss how the programs benefited many white people as well as Black and brown people. Other topics were the value of the Legal Services Corporation and the practical impact of Nixon's proposed cuts.[53]

Chisholm judged the hearings a success. Congressional colleagues local to the cities where they were held professed a new understanding of the problems faced by poor, Black, and brown people. Chisholm marveled at the white congressmen who listened to the stories of witnesses with tears in their eyes. Given that, before the hearings, the predominant sentiment was that the Community Action Programs authorized by the OEO gave too much political power to local people through the idea of maximum feasible participation, the fact that so many colleagues eventually voted to save the OEO was remarkable.[54]

Continuing to take aim at poverty, Chisholm took the opportunity to address welfare reform on the House floor. Just after the end of her presidential run in 1972 she criticized the need for cash assistance at all, citing widespread structural inequality in education and employment in the United States. She told her colleagues she was preparing a minimum wage bill that would extend minimum wage protections to service workers, and argued that covering more workers would reduce poverty and welfare rolls. If families must receive welfare, she argued further, their needs ought to be met fully. To this end she entered the debate over funding welfare programs in the District of Columbia. The Washington City Council was considering

284   COALITION POLITICS IN CONGRESS

a flat-grant system whereby families would all receive the same amount of cash assistance regardless of individual circumstances. This was wrong, Chisholm said, because the specific needs of the children must be taken into account.[55]

Nixon had not made good on any of his promises to the CBC for establishing adequate welfare payments, ending the maltreatment of recipients, or providing paid work opportunities, she told the House in early 1973. His $2,400 guaranteed income figure was much too low to support a household, the public sector employment program started in 1971 was thoroughly inadequate, and job development and training programs had been frozen. To add to Nixon's failures, he had vetoed the childcare bill that would have allowed millions of women to join the workforce while imposing an oppressive workfare scheme that would require people to take jobs at subminimum wage. He had proposed a 1972 budget that gutted social services.[56] Together with Orwellian methods of surveillance of families and the demonization of people on public assistance, Nixon's tactics, Chisholm stated, were a cynical appeal to Nixon's "silent majority" white voters who projected shiftlessness on to welfare recipients. In order to address the true needs of poor Americans and help them overcome the need for welfare, Chisholm argued, the opposite of Nixon's policies needed to happen. The minimum wage law needed to be extended to poorly paid service workers, many of whom were women of color, and no welfare reform bill should permit subminimum wages for program participants. More job development initiatives and government jobs were needed, in addition to childcare services. In short, the policies needed to allow Americans to "earn a living with dignity and self-respect."[57] In April she released a press statement and again took the House floor in opposition to cuts to welfare services and benefits that would require work by recipients but not provide day care for children. These cuts came not through a budget or appropriations bill that the Nixon administration sent, but rather through policy guidelines inside the Department of Health, Education, and Welfare. Chisholm's remarks signaled that the executive branch's end run around Congress had not gone unnoticed.[58]

Notwithstanding her persistent efforts to reform welfare, Chisholm's signature legislative achievement in the early 1970s, and perhaps ever, would be raising and expanding minimum wage protections. Chisholm had started a push for a new minimum wage bill while still running for president. The bill would extend federal minimum wage laws to domestic workers, day care employees, and certain government employees. She had keynoted a 1,000-strong convention of the National Committee on Household Employment in the fall of 1972, where she was "cheered wildly."[59] "These are the working poor," she reminded her House colleagues. "They are not on welfare or asking for handouts. They are working hard, skimping and scrapping [*sic*], to keep their families together. I think it is high time we rewarded them for their efforts and provided at least the basic minimum wage."[60]

Starting in January 1973, Chisholm coordinated forces to expand minimum wage coverage to household workers. She was working closely with the National Household Workers Union. Her staff had put in considerable time talking to labor and women's rights organizations and researching wages and cost-of-living data. Her office had become an unofficial headquarters for the almost forty groups with input into the legislation. Chisholm herself had lobbied fellow members of Congress, enlisting the help of Edith Green and Martha Griffiths. Worried colleagues confronted Chisholm in the cloakroom, fearing what it would mean if they were forced to start paying their household workers better. "You know, Shirley," one colleague told her, "last week my wife gave our maid a beautiful bundle of clothes. And my maid never complains. We asked her how she felt and she said she was happy." Chisholm, noting that much opposition came from southern colleagues who saw themselves as entitled to the low-wage domestic work of Black women, realized that she was in a fight over the economic power of Black women. Her legislation was "upsetting a tradition many of the Southern Congressmen have been enjoying for years." She doubled down on her efforts to convince her colleagues of the folly of their thinking. She therefore individually lobbied these men, inviting them to come to her office for a cordial visit. When they came, she said, "Some of them didn't want me to let other Congressmen know that they were in my office. But the interesting thing was the beginning of a change of attitude; that they would come to a Black woman's office who had sent for them, and who wanted to talk to them, and they would sit and listen." Thanks to her hospital visit in 1972, she even enlisted George Wallace in lobbying some of her colleagues. She estimated her conversion rate at nine out of ten, although she conceded that it took a huge amount of energy to do so.[61]

She intensified her public crusade for wider minimum wage coverage on May 1, when she gave a floor speech, with nine pages of accompanying data in the *Congressional Record*, in favor of extending minimum wage protections to 16 million service workers not covered by the Fair Labor Standards Act. Again she called out the Nixon administration for its hypocrisy: it claimed its proposals would foster a work ethic, but its proposal not to extend the minimum wage ran counter to the idea of fair pay for work done. The wage bill that had recently emerged from Education and Labor did not extend coverage to all 16 million, but it did at least cover about 6 million domestic and day care workers, as well as some government employees not currently covered.[62] She explained her concern for domestic service workers, because pay was so low and yet so many women, especially Black women, were forced to take such jobs. The median wage for domestic work was $1,800 per year, well under the poverty line and not nearly enough to support a family, as many women had to do. The idea of receiving fair wages for hard work cut across political factions, she pointed out. Then, to bolster her case for expanding minimum wage protections, Chisholm inserted into the *Congressional Record* a list of civic groups who were in support of her proposal, including women's rights, labor, religious, and civil rights organizations. She added an investigative article published in the *Washington Post* about the number of domestic workers in the nation's capital alone who worked but still remained in poverty, and a report from a Senate subcommittee that about 20 percent of American workers were making wages under $80 a week. She provided state-by-state census data about the yearly incomes of domestic laborers, and letters signed by the CBC and women of the House in favor of extending coverage.[63]

Chisholm refused to dilute her proposal. She took to the floor of the House to argue against her fellow Education and Labor Committee member John Erlenborn's substitute bill. Erlenborn wanted to remove her provision to cover the 6 million additional workers. He conceded that the minimum wage needed to be raised, so Chisholm was mystified as to why he would not seek to extend it to all workers. Again, she made an argument to cover domestic workers and pointed out that many Black women, including her own mother, did such work. Many women who did domestic work were also heads of household, and the minimum wage provision would merely provide more means to make a living for their families, not paid vacations or health and retirement benefits. She ended her remarks with a moral barb about her colleagues' hypocrisy: "All that rhetoric about welfare cheaters and loafers is nothing but a lot of hot air because you never meant for people to be able to work and earn a wage adequate to support themselves."[64] Chisholm's hard work was effective. A version of the bill, H.R. 7935, passed the House that would raise the minimum wage to two dollars per hour in late 1973 and to $2.20 in July 1974, and domestic workers would be included. It passed the House, then the Senate, too, after Hubert Humphrey presented Chisholm's data.[65]

Nixon vetoed H.R. 7935 in September on the grounds that it would cause inflation. But the fight was far from over. Carl Perkins, chair of Education and Labor, led an effort to override Nixon's veto. Chisholm almost immediately stepped to the lectern when debate opened. The most important reason to override the veto, she argued, was humanitarianism, regardless of the issue of inflation. She again pointed to the nearly 1 million household workers who would be covered under the bill's provisions as of July 1974 so that they could make the very modest wage of eighty-eight dollars per week. Inflation had already been very unkind to the working poor, who had to cover expenses with inadequate wages and wanted nothing more than to work for a living. The House came twenty-eight votes shy of overriding Nixon's veto.[66] Still, the chapter on the bill was yet to be closed; Chisholm reintroduced it in the next session and kept up her lobby, and Nixon would sign an almost identical one in 1974.

"TWIN JEOPARDY" AND BLACK FEMINIST POWER POLITICS

As she worked on legislation that would benefit Black, brown, and poor women, Chisholm had begun to articulate an explicitly intersectional vision of Black feminist power in politics.[67] In public, Chisholm opined on what would need to happen in order to create a powerful coalition of Black political interests. One necessary condition was for Black men to take women's equality seriously. In an essay she published in the *Black Scholar,* she argued that racism was neither more nor less important than other forms of discrimination, including gender and sexual orientation. "Mediocre men," she said, reduced the pool of possible competitors for the highest status positions by limiting women's and Black people's access. To change this, Black and brown people, women, and anyone else facing some sort of discrimination in economics and politics needed to unite. Black people—and in particular Black men, for Black women already understood oppression on two fronts—needed to realize that it was in their own interest to identify and join with other oppressed groups. To those who thought Black people needed to be liberated first, "I say that there is no need to fight two different battles, but we should fight both at the same time." Black women were supporting families and had ambitions beyond housewife or service worker status, and ought to have a shot at more options. And to those who argued "it is time for Black women to step back and let Black men take the lead," she offered instead that Black men needed to step forward.[68] She similarly told an oral history interviewer that achieving racial equality required the work of both Black men and women, strongly repudiating the idea that Black women should step back to allow men to lead.[69]

Chisholm drafted a statement in July 1973 that evolved into a speech she would deliver multiple times over the next several years, a Black feminist power call to arms. The crux was that Black women were in a unique position to assess social justice for many groups because of their vantage point at the intersection of multiple oppressions. Chisholm saw Black women's problems as overlapping with other social justice concerns but simultaneously distinct. She referred to this intersection as "twin jeopardy."[70] Explaining that neither the Black movement nor the women's movement addressed Black women's concerns adequately, Chisholm also noted that Black women often faced class discrimination. Although she credited the National Council of Negro Women and Black sororities with political strategies, she argued that Black women were overwhelmingly uninvolved in politics. "Both races of women have traditionally been limited to performing many brainless tasks," she explained. "The minimal involvement of Black women exists because they have been systematically excluded from the political process, and they are members of the politically dysfunctional Black lower class. Thus, unlike white women, who escaped the psychological and sociological handicaps of racism, Black women's political involvement has been a most marginal role." She then pointed to the current politically active role that Black women were playing in order to reverse their historical disempowerment.[71] Chisholm's language of "twin jeopardy" was undoubtedly influenced by Frances Beal's groundbreaking essay "Double Jeopardy: To Be Black and Female" (1970), which Chisholm had read in her personal copy of Cade's *The Black Woman* anthology in April 1973, according to her carefully written notation inside the front cover.[72] Chisholm changed Beal's language somewhat, from "double" to "twin," perhaps wishing to emphasize the similarities between sexism and racism. Staff recalled that Chisholm often invented her own language for points she desired to make.[73]

Chisholm supported the growing Black feminist movement by delivering a version of her speech at the inaugural conference for the National Black Feminist Organization (NBFO) in New York City in November 1973. Hastily called after thirty Black women founded the organization and announced its formation in August, the meeting was labeled as the Eastern Regional Conference but attracted women from all over. Michele Wallace, who would author *Black Macho and the Myth of the Superwoman*, was a crucial organizer. Chisholm's fellow speakers were Flo Kennedy and founder Margaret Sloan, and she was introduced by Eleanor Holmes Norton. In front of the 250 women gathered there, her keynote critiqued the matriarchy thesis advanced by the Moynihan Report, published eight years before but still holding much rhetorical power. Because of white sociologists and policy writers (meaning infamous report writer Daniel Patrick Moynihan), she told the NBFO founders and several other audiences, Black women had been labeled "matriarchs," who desired to usurp power from Black men. She pushed back against Moynihan and called out suspicion from Black men of Black women's desires to speak for themselves. On the issue of reproductive freedom, she continued to disagree with some Black nationalist leaders who had labeled birth control and abortion for Black women "genocide." Black women's concerns and desires centered on simple "survival" for themselves and their families, echoing language used by the Black Panther Party in its own survival programs. Black women were interested in pragmatic changes like day care and a livable minimum wage for all. "Why are we in favor of these goals? Because they are part of survival," she said. "Black women have been unable to accept many of the focuses of the white women's movement because they are not geared to survival. That is the reason for the National Black Feminist Organization coming together," she declared. Furthermore, Black women's activism was directed toward helping all Black people survive, and their talents should be utilized as fully as possible.[74] Black women ought to contribute to Black liberation struggles alongside, not behind, Black men, she argued, and both Black men's and women's strengths and intellects were needed in ongoing movements. Black women ought to shed the "albatross" of racial and sexual stereotypes and participate fully in contemporary movements for change. "We can't be divided by the 'enemy' who tells us Black women are keeping Black men back," she insisted. The mood was electric as Chisholm's words resonated throughout the room, the audience alternately quiet and cheering.[75]

The acclaim that she got from the NBFO contrasted with the criticism from some white feminists, who were quick to conclude that Chisholm's rhetoric signified a lack of commitment to or understanding of feminism. For example, Rita LaPorte, president of the lesbian organization Daughters of Bilitis, professed sympathy with the idea of solidarity when she said that "the white lesbian and the Black heterosexual woman have something in common, namely, a vicious oppression that in a sense competes in the soul with the oppression of racism." But she ignored the intersectional position of Black lesbians, and then dismissed Black feminists by asserting that their concerns for Black men were "amusing" and that they had "suspicion of or hatred for the white feminist movement." And she claimed that Chisholm "courted Black votes rather than women's votes" and thus deserved to be written off.[76]

White feminists directly questioned her on what they saw as poor teamwork from Black feminists. In an interview shortly after the founding NBFO conference, Chisholm explained to a reporter that nonwhite women had a different set of priorities than the largely white feminist leadership. In reply the reporter asked whether there had been "much of an attempt on the part of minority women to understand the position of white women?" Chisholm, summoning patience, stated that she thought Black women had indeed made such an attempt and that Black women saw much that was positive within the women's movement. But she reemphasized that Black women were far less invested in combating the feminine mystique and an adversarial relationship with men than they were in full political inclusion. Black women's problem with white feminists was that, for all of white feminists' language about "sisterhood," the relationship did not seem to be mutual. Black women were not included in all activities, and their concerns were not reflected in white leaders' priorities and rhetoric, yet Black women were often called on to support those same leaders. It was these conditions that had led to the founding of the NBFO, she explained.[77]

Black feminist priorities guided Chisholm's approach to policy issues. As a member of the Committee on Education and Labor and several sub-committees within it, Chisholm addressed them head-on. Key among these was the Subcommittee on Equal Opportunities, newly formed in 1973. In the first July of its existence, the subcommittee held hearings on H.R. 208, a bill that would authorize Health, Education, and Welfare grants to further sex equity in education and establish a council on women's educational programs.[78] This was right up Chisholm's alley. She made a brief opening statement about the necessity of exploring gender stereotypes. This was not just a fringe issue pushed by "women libbers," she explained, but a real problem in that women's full capacities were being wasted. She then participated extensively in the questioning, starting with the head of the Women's Equity Action League Arvonne Fraser and continuing through the sessions. Chisholm asked Fraser whether school administrators and guid-ance counselors did not need training in recognizing stereotypes, and to a representative from the American Council on Education she posed a ques-tion about whether standardized tests fostered inequality. She pushed Black Philadelphia physician and city council member Ethel Allen to address the necessity of racial inclusion on the commission that the bill would establish, for the purpose of making sure women of all races would benefit from the legislation. As the hearings continued, she continued to press the issues of changing the mindsets of those in power about gender roles and ensuring that the bill would benefit a racially diverse population.[79]

As 1973 ended, Chisholm was meeting with some legislative success but was plagued by what she felt was harassment by the Office of Federal Elections in the General Accounting Office (GAO). The elections office announced that it had found several presidential campaign finance rules violations, the central one being the possible misappropriation of a $23,000 campaign surplus. All of the problems stemmed from incomplete or non-existent bookkeeping. While the report submitted to the attorney general showed a $6,000 deficit, the books, kept by Conrad, in fact showed the sur-plus in question. Auditors discovered it in July, and Conrad pledged to file an amended report. By November he had not, and the agency recommended that the Justice Department take up the matter. The penalties for such viola-tions were up to one year in jail and a $1,000 fine for each, though the GAO seemed not to recommend making any formal charges. Chisholm saw the investigation as politically motivated harassment by the Nixon administration because of her strong criticisms. It was a "fishing expedition" to attempt to catch her out, not a bona fide endeavor. She tried staying lighthearted when speaking about it, but angry tears betrayed the stress of the situation. She explained that her campaign had not been professionally managed due to lack of funds, asserting that the lack of recordkeeping was by no means intentional. Furthermore, when the audit was done, there appeared to be a surplus because not all bills had yet been paid. As of now, the surplus was gone. Defiant, she stated that she would be fully cleared.[80] She had spent tens of thousands of dollars of her own money to finance the campaign. Now the fallout of insufficient resources was costing her dearly. Backed by a nine-page report her committee had prepared for the GAO, she disclosed that total income for the national campaign had been $118,620.62. Chisholm herself had paid $32,599.50 and had been reimbursed for $14,974.34 of that. Paid staff had numbered only six, and Chisholm vehemently denied the insinuation in early reports that she had misused any funds. When all bills had been paid, the reported surplus had not just vanished but a deficit was evident, and a fundraising dinner plus a personal check from Chisholm had covered the remaining debts. In April 1974, the Justice Department cleared Chisholm's campaign of any alleged misconduct. Chisholm was relieved and exhausted. She told veteran D.C. reporter Ethel Payne, "I'm sick and tired of the whole situation. . . . If I said what I really think, it would be unprintable and unspeakable."[81]

DEPLOYING BLACK FEMINIST POLITICAL POWER FOR ECONOMIC JUSTICE IN 1974

Despite her exhaustion, Chisholm had weathered the challenge and was still fighting in 1974. Her Black feminist power approach had evolved and begun to bear legislative fruit. As the biennial election cycle started up, Chisholm conducted her usual rounds of speeches, including one at Al Sharpton's National Youth Movement's first Minority Youth Day celebration along with rivals Sam Wright and Tom Fortune.[82] She also got a boost from a documentary film about her; *Chisholm: Pursuing the Dream* was released in May. It was produced by two young filmmakers, Bob Denby and Tom Werner of the new company New Line Cinema, who had followed Chisholm on the campaign trail in 1972.[83] Her hold on the Twelfth Congressional District was solidified when she won re-election in the fall.

In Washington, Nixon—wounded but not yet ousted from office over the Watergate affair—remained an obstruction. Chisholm nonetheless finally got the minimum wage bill passed. Despite Nixon's veto the previous year, Chisholm was determined to pass another bill that raised the minimum wage for 36 million workers and drew domestic and farm workers under its provisions. It passed in late March, with a larger majority than its predecessor. It landed on Nixon's desk March 30, where he reluctantly signed it, claiming worry that the bill would lessen employment prospects for domestic workers. But the chances of Congress overriding his veto this time were high, and he likely felt pressure from the worsening Watergate situation, so he did sign.[84] Chisholm's dogged efforts had paid off. The bill raised the minimum wage from $1.60 to $2.30 an hour. There were nearly 20 million domestic and farm workers who would be newly covered by the protections. She would name this legislation as one of the proudest moments in her congressional career.[85]

Even as she won the fight over wages, the battle to save antipoverty programs dragged on. Nixon still sought the end of the Office of Equal Opportunity because, Chisholm suspected, he wanted to keep conservative congressional Republicans in his corner. In this case, Chisholm's efforts were less successful. The Committee on Education and Labor, seeing the futility of passing an OEO extension bill, wrote a "compromise bill" (H.R. 14449) that would preserve OEO programs but dismantle the OEO itself. It would create a new Community Action Administration within Health, Education, and Welfare. Chisholm was resigned to the changes. The new bill had taken "a lot of blood sweat and tears . . . and this is not the bill I would like to have written," Chisholm said. But it was, she felt, the only option for preserving the Community Action Programs, given the opposition to an independent antipoverty agency among conservative colleagues.[86]

Chisholm remained committed to welfare reform even as Nixon's administration sought to impose its own changes. She continued to see welfare's shortcomings as a Black women's issue that had wide resonance for all Americans. She argued that women of color were more likely to be heads of household and also more likely to be working poor or poor due to unlivable wages. Therefore, they were more likely to need welfare. However, the welfare system showed a bias against women of color in how it treated its recipients.[87] She had a mixed review of the Nixon administration's new plan, termed "welfare replacement" rather than welfare reform. When she addressed the New York State Welfare Association's conference late in 1974, she praised the part of the plan that would move the responsibility of distributing welfare checks from Health, Education, and Welfare to the Department of the Treasury, arguing that welfare recipients would benefit from a reduction in invasions of privacy. As the Congressional Black Caucus proposal had done, she advocated for a reverse income tax of sorts, with checks issued though the Internal Revenue Service. However, she reminded those present that the underlying motivation of the Nixon administration in proposing such a change was to reduce the funds devoted to antipoverty efforts.[88]

Chisholm made a deeper criticism of the welfare system, however, when she charged that its very existence depended on the perpetuation of racism and sexism. She remained frustrated by the invisibility of women heads of households in debates over welfare. "When people are talking about the skyrocketing welfare rolls," she pointed out, "what they are really talking about are the female heads of household who have had to resort to welfare because they could not make it in the economic market place."[89] Because of discrimination and lack of opportunity, women who wanted to work were unable to find jobs, or worked long hours for tiny wages and no job security. Therefore, she saw welfare itself as a symptom and direct cost of the corrosive effects of racism and sexism: "What has not been accepted and dealt with in any of the welfare reform [and] welfare replacement formulas which have been advanced is the fact that the welfare rolls are a part of and a testimony to the overall pattern of discrimination against women, especially minority women, in this country."[90]

Chisholm went on to conclude that any plan to end welfare would have to tackle not only structural obstacles, like childcare and education, but would also have to eradicate these interlocking concerns. The chronic lack of childcare and the failure of the 1971 Comprehensive Child Development Act were direct results of sexism and "indifference to the poor," she explained. White men lawmakers assumed that women only had to work when they wanted to and not because they needed to in order to support families. The United States lagged far behind peer nations in providing access to childcare, she pointed out, despite large amounts of wealth in the country. Due to a laissez-faire-above-all ideology, somebody was always going to be out of work in the American economy, and it was usually people of color and/or women. This hit poor women of color especially hard. The "entire system of employment and hiring is a stacked deck against women," Chisholm pointed out, and she advanced an argument very much like ones Frances Beal (1970) and Audre Lorde (1984) used when they maintained that oppressed groups were used as "surplus labor" in the United States. The very least the nation could do was ensure a basic standard of living for all.[91]

However, Chisholm explained, most Americans thought receiving welfare and unemployment were personal failings. Absent an understanding of the political economy, welfare could seem undeserved and unnecessary. The Ford administration was indifferent at best, putting enemies to antipoverty programs in charge of the federal agencies that administered them ("we are putting an arsonist in charge of the fire department," she complained). But the basic problem was that antipoverty programs had been built on New Deal programs, which in turn were built on the assumption that "welfare must somehow be correlated with work." And, in a labor market that unemployed or underemployed millions, following that premise would leave unmet need. Chisholm believed that a solution lay in providing fair wages to all and in increasing local power and accountability over programs for the poor.[92] She was to remain frustrated throughout her career by the persistent power maneuverings of her congressional peers that left concerns of everyday people, and especially nonwhite and poor people, out of decision-making processes.[93] Like welfare rights activists, she named the main problem as lack of access to well-paying jobs and competent childcare, not laziness or family dysfunction.[94]

Although she was likely relieved to see Nixon eventually resign and leave office in August, the high point of Chisholm's summer of 1974 was seeing the memorial to her hero Mary McLeod Bethune unveiled in Lincoln Park. Chisholm had introduced the federal bill to get the monument built, and now it had been completed and was standing at the other end of the park from Abraham Lincoln himself, who had been repositioned to turn toward the Bethune statue. It was the first monument to a Black person or woman in the District and was unveiled before 20,000 spectators, all sweating in the 94-degree day for the ninety-minute ceremony. Chisholm introduced Dorothy Height, who officially presented the monument to the secretary of the Interior. The ceremony was followed by a parade to the Capitol and a 2,000-person banquet. Unfortunately, Chisholm was admitted to the hospital July 24 with sunstroke, likely exacerbated by the heat at the statue unveiling ceremony several days before. She was hospitalized at Washington's then Freedmen's Hospital for a week and complained that it took over a month for her to feel like herself again.[95]

When Nixon resigned in August, an event that Chisholm had been predicting since February, Chisholm declared herself open to working with Gerald Ford. "This is a time for conciliation and healing," she announced. "Partisanship has no place in this hour of history." Even though she disagreed with Ford's conservative record on the issues, she was hopeful that, like Lyndon Johnson, Ford would rise to the occasion and be a willing ally.[96] Chisholm enthusiastically supported the nomination of her sometimes ally New York Governor Nelson Rockefeller as Ford's vice president. Likely preferring a more liberal Republican she knew she could work with, and perhaps due to calculated pragmatism, she seemed to think he would be the best GOP option for the job. She released a statement of support, sent letters to the entire House membership, sent memoranda to the House Judiciary and Senate Rules committees, and attempted to convince all of the CBC members to support the nomination as well. She acknowledged what she called a "Black mark and a human tragedy" in his handling of the Attica prison rebellion in 1971. Her argument was a pragmatic one: no nominee would be perfect, and this one had a better record than most.[97] Rockefeller did get appointed, but whether his presence in the White House was helpful to Chisholm remains unclear. Ford himself would prove as much of an obstruction as Nixon; Ford vetoed dozens of bills from Congress that expanded domestic programs, even when there was broad support for them, saying that they cost too much.[98]

Chisholm herself ran for and won a fourth term in a newly redrawn Twelfth District. The NAACP had sued to change the districts after the GOP-led state legislature redrew them, and won its case in January. Chisholm was pleased to see that the result would be a second majority-Black and brown congressional district.[99] "I am not interested in trying to save my current district as it now exists," she told Simon Anekwe of the *New York Amsterdam News*. "I am interested in broader representation for all minority groups— Blacks as well as Puerto Ricans . . . I have no monopoly on any political seat, nor does any other politician." The redrawn lines split Bedford-Stuyvesant in two: one part in Chisholm's Twelfth District would be 72.6 percent Black, and another in the new Fourteenth District would be 64.6 percent Black. But few Black candidates entered the race in the Fourteenth, and far fewer Black residents voted there compared to the Twelfth. Chisholm reportedly turned down the option to run there in favor of the redrawn Twelfth, even though her Crown Heights home was in the Fourteenth. The seat in the Fourteenth District would be won in November by white city council member Fred Richmond.[100] She was endorsed for her own race by the *New York Amsterdam News*, which called her "by far the best candidate" and placed her "in a class by herself."[101] She handily turned away a primary challenge by a former aide of her nemesis Sam Wright in September and won the general election in a landslide, 80 percent to her opponent's 14 percent.[102] Wright did not run himself because he was engaged in a campaign to be reelected to city council.[103] But he was still a thorn in her side, and now he accused her of engineering the Twelfth District lines to create a safe seat for herself. He had developed his own political machine: a Council of Black Elected Officials and a wide patronage network of government jobs and board positions that he ran with "autocratic control." He supported candidates against Chisholm's allies in state races.[104]

BLACK FEMINIST POLITICAL POWER IN CONGRESS, 1975–1976

In the new Ninety-Fourth Congress, Chisholm had more structural power. She was assistant secretary of the House Democratic Caucus, the first member of the now seventeen-strong Congressional Black Caucus to have such a leadership position.[105] Bella Abzug and Patricia Schroeder of Colorado began efforts to convene a caucus of the now eighteen women in Congress, an initiative that Chisholm joined and publicly praised, with caveats. She acknowledged that not all women's concerns would be the same, but that on some issues involving education, families, and health, women could form coalitions.[106] Her caution reflected the limits of her relationship with white feminists. She was willing to collaborate with the women's caucus, such as when she cosponsored Abzug's 1975 bill to fund a National Women's Conference. But she would not extend a helping hand in electoral matters, and in 1976, Chisholm would decline to endorse her one-time collaborator as Abzug's Senate campaign struggled. When a reporter asked whether Chisholm's lack of endorsement was related to Abzug's failure to endorse her in the 1972 presidential race, Chisholm was blunt. "I never expected all of the women or all of the Blacks to support me, but I did expect the support of a militant feminist," she acknowledged. She continued: "People have to remember, in this political business, that one good turn deserves another. . . . And that one bad turn sometimes deserves another."[107] Abzug's bid for the Senate seat was not successful, and she would retire from the House after the end of her term. Meanwhile, Chisholm's alliance with the National Women's Political Caucus continued, but because of her travel schedule and the lukewarm support she had received from the organization, she chose to send her legislative aide to meetings instead of attending herself.[108]

It was becoming clear that feminist politics were losing momentum. The Equal Rights Amendment (ERA) battle was not yet won, and Chisholm was beginning to think it might not ever be. She did not think that the ratification campaign was strong enough and felt that the National Organization for Women's (NOW's) leadership was not taking it seriously enough. This and other issues led to distance between Chisholm and NOW. She was deeply invested in intersectional economic justice, while she felt that NOW's emphasis fell too heavily on issues facing professional women.[109] But she herself did advocate for the ERA. She specifically exhorted Black women to make common cause with white women over it. The amendment would benefit Black women, who worked for wages in great numbers, by providing a strong legal basis to dispute workplace discrimination. And fighting sexism was not working against Black men. "We are smart enough to realize that Black men are not in control of the power structure and are not responsible for setting the parameters for discrimination in this country," she said. "However, that does not mean that we as Black women must step aside for Black men or anyone else. We are talented human beings who have a contribution to make to this society. We can best do that in an environment which tolerates no forms of discrimination."[110]

Instead of hanging her hopes on the ERA alone, Chisholm sought policies that met women at the intersections of race and class. Her concerns were with working-class and poor women, and she took up issues that she thought could make a material difference in their lives. Black women needed support. Proportionally, Black women were overrepresented as female heads of households, a status that correlated with poverty. "If we are going to become an unconquerable race we need the sisters and brothers together holding each other up," she told one 1975 audience. A few specific interventions would mitigate the economic risks of single mothers: comprehensive childcare, equal access to vocational education, and equal pay.[111] She leveraged the good relationship she had developed with Carl Perkins, chair of Education and Labor, to be named chair of a series of hearings on sex discrimination in vocational training. The Vocational Education Act was up for renewal, and Chisholm, Patsy Mink, and Alphonzo Bell were determined to use the opportunity for greater gender equality in vocational programs. The three had requested the hearing from Carl Perkins. Chisholm's priority was to solve real problems for working-class women. She lined up witnesses who would explain the inadequacy of vocational training for well-paid jobs for women. They would show how the increasing numbers of women in the paid labor force were restricted to a limited number of jobs, and how the jobs in which the most women were employed tended to be the lowest paid. The testimony would emphasize that women, especially women of color, were working out of necessity and demonstrate the need for access to quality day care. Her eventual aim was to add a provision to the law that would help women escape traditional women's roles. The hearings, held over three days, had unusually high turnout.[112] Chisholm prevailed: the renewed Vocational Education Act would contain a provision that established offices that would oversee and promote sex equality in state programs.[113] It would also contain a provision for bilingual education, a result of Chisholm's efforts as well. Chisholm's success on this front was in large part due to her willingness to collaborate with colleagues across the ideological spectrum. She made what to some was a surprising alliance with conservative John Tower of Texas, whose state had a large population of Spanish-speaking residents.[114] She would be honored that July by El Congreso, the Latinx lobbying group, for her work.[115]

Chisholm also pushed for better enforcement of Title IX. The Nixon and Ford administrations had yet to issue Title IX anti–sex discrimination regulations for publicly funded programs. Despite the fact that the Higher Education Act had been enacted into law in 1972, it had taken until the spring of 1974 for Health, Education, and Welfare to issue enforcement regulations. Those regulations were seen as incomplete and unclear to many feminists, including Chisholm, and hearings were held in June to determine whether they upheld and conformed to the spirit of the legislation. Chisholm questioned witnesses extensively. She sparred with the football coaches at the University of Texas and the University of Nebraska on whether athletic programs ought to be held to the same standards of nondiscrimination as other educational activities (she thought so; they were unashamed to say they didn't). Much of the football coaches' argument rested on the fact that their programs did not directly receive federal funds, but Chisholm pointed out that the athletic programs were indeed part of the institutions that did receive federal funds. She also cross-examined her colleague William Goodling, a Republican from Pennsylvania. When he said that he feared regulations might force the creation of coeducational teams and cause confusion, Chisholm was skeptical. "The Federal regulations per se do not require coeducational physical classes, would you say that?" she asked Goodling. "Yes," he replied. "Well then, what?" Chisholm shot back. Goodling stammered an inadequate answer. Chisholm rested her case, arguing that such a position rested on nothing more than custom and entitlement. "Those individuals who have been the beneficiaries of the status quo are likely to be the individuals who are opposed to change," she said. She explicitly rejected the reasoning of witnesses who had said that athletics did not receive federal funds, because they were part of institutions that did. And, as for the danger to revenue from sports, she thought the basic right to nondiscrimination was far more of a priority than maintaining sales from basketball and football game ticket receipts. The fact that women were increasingly essential wage earners for their families suggested that they needed equal access to higher education. The Ford administration did produce a set of Title IX rules in July that exempted revenue-producing athletic programs, though Chisholm voted in the minority to reject them on the grounds of the exemption.[116]

Chisholm frequently used her own voice in advocating for Black feminist power, and she was also willing to lend her voice to antirape activism. Twenty-year-old Joan Little was on trial for having killed a white jailer in Beaufort County, North Carolina, the previous August. Little had stabbed the jailer, she explained, in an act of self-defense when he attempted to rape her. In the months before the trial, Little's attorney began a concerted effort to emphasize the racism of Beaufort County's justice system and build the case for Little's innocence into a national campaign. Soon it had captured the attention of Black, feminist, and prison reform activists and tapped into both a decades-long history of antirape activism and newer activist energy. Two weeks before the trial was set to begin, Chisholm urged

Attorney General Edward Levi to intervene. It was clear that the death had occurred in self-defense, she argued, and Little's incarcerated status at the time had no bearing on that fact. Furthermore, the lack of Black people on juries in the county was unfair, she said. It was an unfair disadvantage to Little, because "many, many Caucasian people hold the worst sort of prejudices against Black women." She, like Little's defense attorneys, wanted the charges dismissed or at least a change of venue. Her effort to have the Justice Department intervene and dismiss the charges was unsuccessful, although Little's case eventually was. Little would be unanimously acquitted by a jury in Raleigh that July.[117]

Likewise, she was willing to use her platform to amplify poor women of color's voices. In collaboration with the National Committee on Household Employment, Chisholm chaired hearings on women in low-waged jobs, called the Speakout for Economic Justice: Poor Women in the Economy, in early September. The intent was to show that the most recent recession had not lifted for some women workers, many of whom were women of color. Women from a spectrum of racial and ethnic groups, employed in largely service or agricultural jobs, spoke on what it was like to be poor, female, and unemployed or underemployed. In opening remarks, Chisholm pointed out that two-thirds of welfare recipients were women and children, and that a similar percentage of households receiving food stamps were headed by women. Overall, about 37 percent of Black families were female-headed, and a large percentage of Puerto Rican families were, too. Therefore, she said, it is important to realize that women were often the sole source of income for a family. The assumption that women were working for supplemental wages only was wrong.[118]

While Chisholm's commitments had remained consistent, the broader political context was changing. In the 1976 presidential campaign, Chisholm noticed that previous political consensus about the role of government was beginning to erode. In the speeches of Ronald Reagan and Gerald Ford, federal government spending on domestic social programs came under fire as government overreach. "I find a dangerous trend throughout the country as I travel and meet with people," she noted. "There is a broad shift to the right taking place politically, and the campaign issue which is emerging as the most important has to do with [the] federal government's role in social service and social welfare problems." Candidates, including some Democrats, had begun to argue for reducing the scope of government. Chisholm herself did not think that there was a need for less government, but she did "believe we need better government, more responsible government, and a federal government which takes into account the needs of those among us who have been relegated to second-class citizenship because of their race or ethnic origin."[119] She would continue to advocate for more democratic government for the rest of her time in office.

PERSONAL AND POLITICAL TESTS

Chisholm's personal life was in upheaval in the mid-1970s. At Gerald Ford's 1974 Christmas Ball for members of Congress, Chisholm had caused some surprise by arriving with a man who was not her husband. She was escorted instead by the tall, handsome Arthur Hardwick, the same Arthur Hardwick who had served with her in the New York State Assembly and whose wife had died two years ago. Chisholm's official explanation was that Conrad was not interested in the social swirl of Washington and had elected to stay in Brooklyn for that reason.[120] But now, in July 1975, the *New York Amsterdam News* blared a front-page headline: "Shirley Chisholm to Divorce Hubby." The author was her old nemesis Andy Cooper, assisted by Sara Slack, who had perhaps interviewed a reluctant Chisholm. It was unclear how the paper had discovered the story. Chisholm had told the reporter, "There is a real possibility that I will be entertaining a divorce. Conrad and I are not getting along." Chisholm made the case that such things happened to couples, that she and Conrad were still cordial, and that the news had no bearing on her ability to do her job. "True, all is not well between the congresswoman and her husband," she said, using her characteristic third-person language. "Yet, I don't have to share my private life with everyone. My record is good and speaks for itself. I carry myself as a lady with great dignity."[121] The story flared up again in early 1977. "Whether I'm divorced or re-wed is my personal business," she emphatically stated when asked about her marriage during a speech in January.[122]

The reason for the divorce, it seemed, was the handsome widower Arthur Hardwick. He and Chisholm had been keeping in touch at least since their public appearance at Gerald Ford's Christmas Ball in 1974. In 1975, Chisholm had purchased a building lot near Buffalo, New York, where Hardwick still lived.[123] The local paper picked up the story in 1976, announcing that Chisholm was building a $162,000 house in the town of Amherst and reminding readers that Chisholm was a "personal friend" of Hardwick. It did not, however, seem to be aware of Chisholm's impending divorce. Chisholm had told the Buffalo reporter that she planned to spend some time in the new home, but it was an investment and she was not planning a permanent move. She had "lots of friends up there, both male and female," she said, and she liked the area around the University at Buffalo's Amherst campus. Meanwhile, the house taking shape seemed like a major investment in a dream home: 4,000 square feet, with an elaborately graded and landscaped backyard.[124]

Notwithstanding Chisholm's protestations, she had fallen, or was in the process of falling, "head over heels" for Arthur Hardwick.[125] The two had had a warm relationship since they met in Albany in 1967. They had met at the restaurant where legislators often had breakfast, where it seemed that she had felt an instant attraction. She "saw this tall, good-looking man. . . . And he came over and he was very manly. He was a real gentleman." Hardwick introduced himself as a freshman legislator and Chisholm offered to help him. They bantered a little more; he jokingly offered her money for her help and she shot back that the first thing about politics is to never let anyone see you passing money. The two became friends, and she did mentor him in getting his first bill passed.[126]

Later in life, Chisholm reflected on why she had chosen the men she had. In some ways, Conrad and Arthur were "exact opposites," but they were also both "rather complacent, passive gentlemen." Chisholm acknowledged that she was not a helpmate type of wife. If she had married a "gentleman who had the [same] personality that I had, I wouldn't have stayed married. I just wouldn't. Because of the kind of person I was." She acknowledged that Conrad was "passive, complacent, humorous, he didn't let anything worry him."[127] Conrad "supported me all the way. . . . I cannot say that he did not support me," she admitted. But there were other problems:

He became insanely jealous. Insanely jealous of me. And it got to the point that also, where I really felt that I really felt afraid of him. So I had to get out. . . . You see, as the years went by I became more popular. And it seemed to me, he felt badly and left in the background. Although he went with me to all the functions. But he still, there was something there. And I saw it in his face, in his eyes. I, in turn, began to get a little frightened. Yeah, and we divorced. And my second husband, he was marvelous. He was really marvelous.[128]

"I'm not claiming that politics *caused* the final breakup," she disclosed later. "Our marriage was deteriorating, but politics *did* help to escalate the problem." There was no time to resolve conflicts in her hectic schedule.[129] The impetus for the divorce was from Shirley and not Conrad. The latter, for his part, still seemed to be in love with his wife. Years later, he recalled her "inner strength" and that she was "wonderful, wonderful." He was proud of her and saw himself as "the wonder man behind a good woman."[130] The divorce would be final the following February.[131] He would not remarry.

As if personal life changes were not enough, she faced the toughest primary fight since her first congressional campaign. Sam Wright, her longtime nemesis and now a city council member, finally became a direct political opponent. Now, in July 1976, Wright announced his intention to run for the Twelfth District seat. Chisholm, notwithstanding her earlier predictions that she would retire from Congress in 1976, was ready for the fight. "I can win," Chisholm declared, "but I want to win big. It will be a sign to Sam Wright that he can't be no. 1." Chisholm cast him as a politician in the old boss-structured, Tammany mold. Wright went on the offensive, claiming that Chisholm's national ambitions and pursuit of speaking fees had led her to neglect the district and left a "void in the political and community leadership." The press, for its part, lamented the fragmentation of Black political power in the district that the Chisholm-Wright rivalry represented. Some feared that white candidates could be elected in the absence of Black unity. A third candidate in the primary, Puerto Rican antipoverty worker Luz P. Vega, ran on criticism of Wright and Chisholm, casting them as too distracted by power struggles to support the community effectively. Carlos Russell, activist, Brooklyn College faculty member, and doctoral student (who had been the one to criticize her in 1972 for "vaginal politics"), blamed "deep-rooted enmity and distrust."[132]

The two finally met for a debate days before the primary balloting, in Bedford-Stuyvesant's Varick Memorial AME Zion Church. Chisholm's ten minutes of remarks criticized Wright's reliance on patronage and old-style organization politics to gain power. She herself, alternatively, had focused on bringing national resources to the district rather than keeping "a finger in every pot" and making people beholden to her, as she said Wright did. Wright lashed back, predicting that Chisholm's frequent absences from the district would "destroy" it.[133] Chisholm would prevail, however. Percy Sutton endorsed her, citing her seniority in Congress, which would help her be more influential in committees. Aided by the stalwart Mac Holder, her emotional connection with voters, her easily mobilized women supporters, and a major effort in Wright's former Fifty-Fourth Assembly District won the day. The night of September 14, Chisholm declared victory, admitting that it had been "one of the toughest races of my political career." She went on to an easy win in the general election.[134] Wright would lose his city council seat in 1978 after a criminal conviction in a corruption scandal.[135]

After the 1976 election, despite having won, Chisholm was frustrated with Brooklyn politics. "I never saw Mrs. Chisholm really irate or upset," Carolyn Smith recalled, "except when she used to run . . . every two years—I can't think of that man's name. I think his name was Sam something."[136] The Sam that Smith referred to was, of course, Sam Wright. But it was not just Wright who disappointed Chisholm. The potential for political power that Chisholm saw in Black and brown Brooklyn was untapped, she felt, because candidates and officials had not figured out how to identify and use power. In her opinion, Harlem politicians had a better handle on wielding real political power. In an interview with Carlos Russell, she agreed with his assessment that the conflict between herself and Wright drained resources from the community as a whole. But she would not take blame for the squabbling. The "divisiveness and pettiness" is due to "fantastic, massive insecurity on the part of many elected officials, insecurity pertaining to their own personal egos," she asserted. Still, she conceded that it might soon be time for her to step aside and allow new political leadership.[137]

There would be new national political leadership in 1976, and Chisholm was optimistic. The new president-elect, Jimmy Carter, was publicly committed to universal voter registration, nationwide health care, diversity in government, and the right to full employment. Chisholm publicly supported him.[138] She published an endorsement in her congressional mailer, with a photo of Chisholm shaking hands with a smiling Carter. Her hope was that unified government in 1977 would finally be an opportunity for legislative progress toward her Black feminist goals.

18

FIGHTING THE TIDE, 1977-1982

★

In the spring of 1980, Chisholm sat down in her Rayburn Building office with John Lewis Jr., a reporter for the *New York Amsterdam News*. She was starting her last congressional campaign and willing to speak freely to a journalist from a paper that had both supported and attacked her over the past decade and a half. She was fifty-five years old, divorced and remarried, and sitting on the most powerful committee in the House of Representatives, the Committee on Rules. Her most daunting challenge, she told Lewis, was that she had to "fight on so many fronts at the same time." She considered fighting for the people her highest priority, and her constituents' needs came first. But they were also overwhelming. Her weekends at home were filled with mediating between multiple groups in Brooklyn and trying to pack as many meetings as possible into a few short days. Added to this was the persistent fact that as a Black woman politician she still had to wrangle racist white colleagues and sexist Black colleagues. "Sometimes," she told Lewis, "I don't know how much longer a 105 lb. black woman advancing in years, even though she's still somewhat energetic, can continue this fight on every circle around her."[1]

Indeed, Chisholm was fighting on even more fronts than she named within the interview. The Committee on Rules was powerful but time and energy consuming. She faced detractors and rivals at home in her district. She had moved out of Annie Pharr's house and was now on her own in a D.C. apartment. She had relocated to a new home with a new husband upstate and was now in a commuter marriage between Washington, Brooklyn, and Buffalo. After a disappointing single term of Jimmy Carter and deepening economic recession, she would have to swim hard against Ronald Reagan's conservative tide. She continued to advocate for equity, expanding her concerns to Black people outside the United States. But she was only willing to stay so long. In 1982, after years of hinting at her imminent retirement, she finally made the decision. At the time she was the most senior woman in the Democratic congressional delegation.

Before 1982, Chisholm perpetually searched her soul about whether to continue. As she watched other Black women in the House leave for other endeavors—Jordan for academia and Brathwaite-Burke for California state politics—she considered leaving herself. She was briefly a front-runner for the top position in the New York City school system and interviewed to lead the City University of New York. She came close to not seeking reelection in 1978. This would change, however, after a chance encounter on the plane from Washington to New York. A woman sitting next to Chisholm, as she recounted it, told Chisholm that "I was all that she had—an idol with an unconquerable spirit." The remark jolted Chisholm from her fantasies about quitting Congress. "Then and there, I began to rethink my decision," she told *Ebony* magazine in a rare moment of self-disclosure. In the late 1970s she felt a renewed sense of pride in her accomplishments on behalf of her district, including steering federal dollars to it in the form of grants and passing minimum wage legislation that helped her constituents. And she acknowledged her seniority: she was now the most senior Democratic woman and secretary of the Democratic Caucus; she was on the Rules Committee, and she was vice chair of the Congressional Black Caucus. Not only that, she had learned more about wielding power and had earned trust and respect from her colleagues. "In Washington, above all places, power is what counts," she wrote. "Nothing else matters. Real power is never given; it must be taken." She still saw herself as a militant, but emphasized the need for "effective militancy": the capacity to move beyond rhetoric to get material resources. And at that moment in 1978, she declared her intention to remain a militant on Capitol Hill.[2] She would postpone her decision to retire for two more terms.

It was a good thing that Chisholm felt a renewed sense of energy, because she would need it in her later terms as a legislator. Several persistent problems arose again and again. For one, the United States was in a deep recession, and Chisholm's district was at the epicenter. Simultaneous increases in both inflation and unemployment, as the manufacturing sector contracted, had led to the new crisis called "stagflation" in the mid-1970s. In the late 1970s, the energy crisis and weakening automobile industry further eroded confidence in the economy and stranded Americans in poverty.[3] In Chisholm's congressional district, unemployment was up to 38 percent, a deeply alarming figure.[4] Chisholm's constituents desperately wrote to her seeking help finding work, and her own district exploded into chaos during the summer of 1977 when a blackout spread over the entire city. Looting and arson were citywide, but Crown Heights and Bushwick, inside the Twelfth District, were hardest hit. Chisholm was "deeply troubled" by the violence and lamented that it exacerbated the "general deterioration" of those neighborhoods. "I will not rationalize the violence," she declared, but hastened to add that "I also will not rationalize a system which can allow upwards of 80% of our young people to be unemployed." She would continue to worry that another urban uprising would burst into flames.[5]

In addition to economic depression, Chisholm was running into a wall of conservative resistance. Having entered the federal government on a tide of hope for additional bold programs that would reduce inequality in America, by 1980 Chisholm was admitting that "we should have known that it was too good to last." In hindsight, she saw that the high tide of that antipoverty, antidiscrimination, education, and health legislation was before 1968 and that, by the time she was sworn in, most legislative battles were over preserving funding for such programs and not creating new ones. She had held out hope that the administration following Nixon's and Ford's would return to a bold vision of equality, but she would be "deeply disappointed by the ineffectiveness of the Carter team" and frustrated by the Reagan administration.[6] As historian Duchess Harris has pointed out, the "backlash movement against liberalism that emerged with Nixon was fully consummated with the election and presidency of Ronald Reagan in the 1980s."[7]

Chisholm recognized the tide turning against liberal reforms and further civil rights legislation in real time. "It must be recognized," she said in one speech on racism in 1976, "that many of the gains made by blacks in the 1960s were in securing things that whites already had such as voting rights, access to public accommodations, and educational opportunity and hence did not come at the expense of whites." Now, however, "given the national conservative mood and a sluggish economy," the economic agenda of Black activists was "in direct competition with whites." The continuing economic harms of racism were justified by a "cultural myth of white supremacy" and enabled by lax enforcement of existing civil rights laws.[8] In 1978 she would write that "liberalism is dying," in a backlash against recent social movements, and that any coalition between those movements had fractured.[9] By her last term, she would state simply that past gains were in danger from "a national mood turning mean." Reagan was taking away those gains "one by one."[10] She feared that a civil rights coalition in the House that reauthorized the Voting Rights Act in 1981 might have come together for the last time.[11]

Nonetheless, Chisholm capitalized on her formidable confidence and, quietly, became respected as an analytical mind in the committee rooms of the House. The big problems she wanted to solve—racism, sexism, and economic inequality—she battled in the minutia of writing, evaluating, and debating bills and procedures. While the days of big visions for sweeping change passed with the Nixon and Ford administrations, Carter's incrementalism, and Reagan's New Right assault, Chisholm kept pressure on her colleagues. Chisholm did not give up on winning material change and political power for America's most vulnerable residents. From domestic programs to immigration policy, she pushed back against the rightward turn in national politics. In the mid-1970s, for a short time, she ruled uncontested over Brooklyn politics. Sam Wright was indicted in April 1977 on extortion charges (some, given the bitterness of the 1976 campaign, suspected that Chisholm was behind the investigation), and Tom Fortune fought a fraud indictment for allowing welfare recipients to stay on his payroll. Chisholm donated $1,000 of her and Hardwick's personal funds to Fortune's defense.[12] Notwithstanding her efforts on the Hill and at home, Chisholm's press in New York was becoming more critical. At the *New York Amsterdam News*, editor Fred Weaver teamed up with her old nemesis Andrew Cooper and rising political opponent Al Vann. The three began a campaign to discredit Chisholm's motivations and convict her of political opportunism.

NEW HUSBAND, NEW STAFF, NEW INFLUENCE

Chisholm's personal life was also changing. Chisholm and Hardwick got engaged in the summer of 1977, after her divorce was final. Chisholm was famously private, and at the time she married Hardwick most of her colleagues did not even know that she had divorced Conrad. In July, Speaker Tip O'Neill had a reception at Dumbarton Oaks to celebrate majority whip John Brademas's marriage earlier that month. With Arthur at the party, Chisholm shocked all present by saying that she herself had just gotten engaged.[13] The wedding was held at the Sheraton Inn on the east side of Buffalo on the afternoon of November 26. A host of dignitaries were invited, including local officials and then representative Jack Kemp (R-NY). Chisholm's family was not present; the matron of honor, Mary Jarrett, was the wife of Arthur's best man and longtime friend, Albert Jarrett. Thaddeus Garrett had become an AME minister and officiated, reading from both the Bible and Khalil Gibran's *The Prophet:* "Together you shall be forevermore . . . but let there be spaces in your togetherness. . . . Love one another but make not a bond of love. . . . Sing and dance together and be joyous, but let each of you be along alone." Chisholm wore a light beige dress, and the couple stood with Garrett under an archway of flowers. There was dinner of a carved steamship round of beef, Salmon Bellevue, and a champagne toast for each of the 150 guests, plus an open bar.[14] When Chisholm tossed her garter from the balcony overlooking the hotel's courtyard, it was caught by none other than Annie Pharr, in whose house Chisholm had resided until 1974. Laura Murphy called Hardwick "one of the most handsome men I've ever met. And I was happy for her." Chisholm herself seemed "ecstatic," declaring that she had been waiting for "a long, long time" for that moment.[15] The two had declared their intention to live in Brooklyn, but they settled into their

Shirley Chisholm and Arthur Hardwick on their wedding day, November 1977. Courtesy of the Shirley Chisholm estate.

expansive three-story Buffalo house. They held a reception in Brooklyn for their New York City well-wishers on December 4.[16]

Inside the D.C. office, talented young politicos helped Chisholm keep up the Good Fight. She functioned as an othermother, and they responded by performing filial duties, especially those that helped Chisholm maintain her aesthetics. For the price of shuttling their nondriving boss in their personal cars (Chisholm had exacting standards for the cleanliness of the car and the quality of the driving), dropping off dry cleaning and wigs, and occasionally needing to retype letters that Chisholm had smudged Fashion Fair makeup on, the late 1970s/early 1980s cohort was thrilled to have the opportunity to work in the heart of the action.[17] For her part Chisholm saw the young people who worked for her as her own children. She did not have personal photos of her own family on her desk; she merely had a signed photo of Jimmy Carter and photos of children of staff members.[18] Later she identified mentoring her young staff and seeing their subsequent achievements as one of the great pleasures of her job.[19]

In addition to several long-timers, a few new faces had arrived. Bevin Dufty, a young white man whose parents were involved in Harlem cultural life, had been hired on as an intern in 1976. He joined the permanent staff and was in charge of driving Chisholm to the Democratic Caucus meetings when she was secretary, plus doing her basic shopping. But his favorite parts of the job were driving Chisholm out to shop in the new Bloomingdale's at the brand-new White Flint Mall and the witty (and sometimes bawdy) repartee in the D.C. offices.[20] Dufty in turn hired a young intern, Paul Cunningham, in 1978, who became a legislative assistant the following year. Cunningham was drawn to the inclusive climate of the office and the chance to work on fighting oppression through the legislative process. He would become Chisholm's aide on the Rules Committee in 1981.[21] Laura Murphy, a native of Baltimore, joined the office in 1977 after graduating from Wellesley and working for Parren Mitchell for a short time. The daughter of a "very political family," one branch of which published the *Baltimore Afro-American,* had grown up tagging along on her parents' campaigns and had met Mitchell while working on her father's campaign for a judgeship in 1970. Mitchell promised Murphy a legislative assistantship after her graduation from Wellesley, and when she graduated in 1976 she became one of the youngest legislative assistants on the Hill. She loved the job but was rankled by Mitchell's refusal to pay women staffers as much as men. This was why Bevin Dufty was able to recruit her to Chisholm's office, where Murphy immediately received a raise of several thousand dollars. She worked on tracking noncommittee assignment–related issues, and when Chisholm was assigned to the Rules Committee, Murphy also had the job of briefing her boss on the array of bills that came through. She loved the job and her boss, excited by the opportunities she got from the moment she was hired. For her it was a thrill to be a part of a cadre of women following their boss through the halls of Capitol Hill, watching Chisholm's combination of charm and strength in action.[22]

Press secretary Bob Frishman arrived in Chisholm's office in 1980. He had worked for John Conyers for seven years but had recently quit. He stopped by Chisholm's offices one day to recruit help on the Jerry Brown presidential campaign, and his friend Brenda Pillors asked him, "Oh, Bobby, are you here for the job?" "What job?" Frishman replied. Pillors sent him home to get a coat and tie for the interview, and he finished the day as Chisholm's new press secretary and speechwriter. Despite his official role, however, he also found himself as Chisholm's principal driver in an old Jaguar that he kept parked under the Rayburn Building. Chisholm was particularly delighted when people thought it was her car, as happened when she attended a reception at the vice president's Naval Observatory mansion. Frishman and his wife, Jeanne Schinto, on occasion felt filial responsibility for his boss. The couple took the congresswoman for dinner once, and, in a rare moment of self-disclosure, Chisholm mentioned her difficult relationship with her mother and sisters. Memorably, one day Bob received a letter that requested he give Chisholm a kiss on the writer's behalf. After he briefed her, to Frishman's surprise, Chisholm declared, "You may," and tilted her cheek toward him. He obliged and left the office bearing the inevitable makeup smudges. Years later he, too, recalled the respect and affection he received in the office. In contrast to others on the Hill, Chisholm had no unpleasant private persona that differed from her public one. "I never really felt like she was my boss anyway. . . . I felt pretty much that we were colleagues and she made me feel that way," he remembered.[23]

Carolyn Smith was still the center of the office, keeping things running and her boss on track. Smith worked on Chisholm to decrease the makeup and return to wearing her natural hair. "Mrs. Chisholm, you got to do something about this makeup, you got it from one side of your head to the other," Smith recalled telling her boss. Chisholm did visit Smith's stylist, who shampooed and styled the congresswoman's natural hair. Chisholm seemed pleased with the look, but on the way back to the Capitol she pulled her wig out of her bag and placed it back on her head. Back in the office, Smith was waiting for her boss, having talked with the salon on the phone about how well the styling session had gone. When Chisholm walked in wearing the old wig, Smith was taken aback. Under questioning, Chisholm admitted that she thought people liked her hair when she wore the wigs. Furthermore, she was starting to go grey. Eventually, Smith and Chisholm worked out a compromise. The salon would shampoo Chisholm's hair regularly, and the stylist at the wig shop would begin adding a few grey hairs here and there over time.[24] Chisholm was all too aware that, in an era of rapid-time media, appearance mattered; for Black women, it was especially critical.

Chisholm had accrued hard-won seniority and gravitas on Capitol Hill. Perhaps in consideration of her support for his bid for Speaker, the new Majority Leader Tip O' Neill of Massachusetts named her to the powerful Rules Committee. The fifteen-member committee had never had a woman serve on it since its creation in 1880. It had evolved from a narrowly defined charge of refereeing the Rules of the House to a body that decided the legislative schedule and what legislation would reach the floor of the House for debate and a vote. It also determined whether a bill could or could not be amended on the floor. In other words, it determined the priorities of the House for the session. She was now at the center of power in the House and would remain there for her final three terms. The workload was high enough that members could serve that committee only. However, although she was no longer on Education and Labor, Chisholm still felt pressure to continue to be involved in that committee because of its relevance to Black, brown, young, female, and poor people. Staffer Muriel Morisey volunteered to remain working on education issues, and Chisholm retained influence on that committee.[25]

On Rules, Chisholm had to set ground rules of gender equality during committee proceedings. At the first meeting, Chair James Delaney, a fellow New York Democrat, continually referred to Chisholm as "Shirley" while referring to the other (male) members as "Mr." Delaney dismissed her request to be called by her title and last name. "Why Shirley, you and I have been intimate for years," he cajoled, to the laughter of other members. Chisholm responded with her customary edgy humor. "Jim, we don't have to let the public know it," she retorted. Delaney immediately and permanently began referring to her as "Mrs. Chisholm."[26]

Chisholm's pragmatism suited the Rules Committee. She did not mind wading into the arcane procedural questions that the committee took up, and used the appointment to practice Black feminist power politics. She saw her presence on the committee as ensuring that the needs of women and Black people, along with those of other disempowered groups, would be considered before legislation reached the floor. The rules of the House were no mere abstraction in her mind; she vocally supported a set of procedures that would increase public participation in regulation making.[27] She also seemed to relish the nuts and bolts of the legislative process, such as the ethics of House members' outside income or the processes by which Congress should raise the debt ceiling. On the outside income issue, a 1977 House bill proposed that earned income be limited to $15,000 over the congressional salary, while no limit would be placed on income from investments. If earned income were to be limited, she asked, should not all types of income be limited? She was outvoted on that occasion, but she had indicated her willingness to find the underlying logic and fight for what she saw as the most fair decision.[28] The respect that her colleagues developed was evident by her second term on the committee, when she was delegated to chair hearings on federal program review.[29]

Away from the Hill, Chisholm preached a Black feminist power message of coalition with other movements for political power. When she spoke to the Independent Black Women's Caucus in 1978, she exhorted Black Americans to take advantage of the political power that they had shown in the 1976 elections and to support "candidates—be they Democrat or Republican—*who have something to offer us* in return for our votes" She reminded her audience that power is usually not given but it is assumed by those who hold it: "The only running we are going to do is running toward the power that must be seized and held to control our destinies."[30] Chisholm did her best to bridge feminism and the ongoing Black freedom struggle, urging Black men and Black women to work for common cause. She explained the necessity of Black men and women to work together on an equal footing. "The black woman who is educated and has ability cannot be expected to put said talent on the proverbial shelf when she can utilize these gifts side by side with the black man," she pointed out. Furthermore, the simultaneous struggles against racism and sexism had equipped Black women to participate in the Black freedom struggle. Establishing national day care centers and reforming welfare would directly benefit Black families and thereby all Black people.[31] When she addressed an audience of Black businesswomen, she urged them to work with white women in their communities and benefit from the gains of feminism.[32] She had a similar message for Spelman undergraduates about the ERA. "If we take it upon ourselves to say we want to be removed from any kind of struggle that will help us to move just a half step upward, it means that . . . the white women, who have been pushing the ERA, decide what the final outcome is going to be. And if we have not been inside observing and making our contributions, we can't go around wringing our hands and complaining, 'What they done did to us again.'" She went on to say that she had experienced conflict with white feminists because, as a Black woman, she refused to allow them to define her priorities—but that she stayed connected to white feminists so that she could be on the inside of advocating for change. "Remember, black sisters . . . ," she exhorted them, "God helps those who help themselves."[33]

These later terms started out with a sense of hopefulness. January 1977 brought in a new era of united government, with Carter in the White House and a continued Democratic Congress. Chisholm had reason to expect that a Democratic administration, the first that she had served under, might be far more friendly to progressive policies. Carter's election "makes me feel that perhaps we will see many more things done on behalf of black people," she predicted. Furthermore, she was pleased when Carter remembered the Black support he had received during the campaign and appointed large numbers of Black people, as well as women, to positions in his administration.[34] She saw Carter as "a light at the end of the tunnel."[35]

As she had done since 1968, Chisholm kept working on antipoverty legislation. She continued to work through Education and Labor, though she no longer sat on the committee. Chair Carl Perkins and other colleagues continued to seek her accumulated expertise and counsel, and she actually questioned witnesses during a subcommittee hearing on the extension of desegregation funding and was frequently called to testify on issues ranging from learning disability programs, school safety, IRS regulations and private schools, youth employment, and standardized testing. But in the late 1970s her most significant intervention was to preserve and strengthen Title I of the Elementary and Secondary Education Act of 1965. The legislation funded school districts serving low-income students (according to a formula developed by the Social Security Administration's star statistician Mollie Orshansky), and some in Congress wanted to expand eligibility beyond the poorest districts. She undertook a campaign to preserve the original intent of Title I, publishing an op-ed and advocating for a Title I enforcement bill in front of the Subcommittee on Elementary, Secondary, and Vocational Education. Addressing the committee, she waded deep into the weeds of policy that would expand and improve the funding, toughening supervision of the program's requirements and increasing parental involvement.[36]

Chisholm also allowed the House effort regarding the food stamp program to be run out of her office, with Patsy Fleming working as staff liaison. Dismayed at the myth of food stamp fraud that had taken hold of the national narrative, and in the context of the recession, she told the Domestic Marketing, Consumer Relations, and Nutrition Subcommittee to work on creating local awareness of the necessity and reality of food stamp programs, in alignment with the findings of Mollie Orshansky's poverty calculations. She also advocated eliminating the requirement that recipients purchase food stamps. The policy created hardship for women heads of households, who often could not afford their full allotment, she argued. Furthermore, she made the case that the cost of childcare ought to be deducted from income when determining recipients' allotments. She pledged her own and the Black Caucus's guidance on a food stamp reform bill then in committee, but hastened to point out that most food stamp recipients were white, that fraud was relatively rare, and that, in fact, almost half of the people eligible for food stamps did not obtain them. She was later able to use her appointment to the Committee on Rules to bring a 1979 food stamp appropriations increase bill to the House floor, where it passed. However, she would have to keep fighting cuts to food stamps and child nutrition programs the following year.[37]

The consequences of poverty were becoming ever more dire in Brooklyn in 1977. On July 13, a sweltering summer day, much of the electrical grid in New York City failed. While the lights were off, violence erupted. Chisholm was dismayed, both at the violence and at the 80 percent youth unemployment rate that engulfed the city and was blamed for the chaos. When her ally Fred Richmond led New York's congressional delegation in a tour of the worst-hit areas in Harlem, Bushwick, and Bedford-Stuyvesant, she went along. The members of Congress and the federal Small Business Association promised store owners that they would quickly approve loan applications for rebuilding. But the greater problem was high unemployment, the same problem Chisholm, with Charlie Rangel and Herman Badillo, had identified the year before. Chisholm would attempt to mitigate the staggering unemployment numbers.[38] Absent good jobs, the burden on welfare programs would remain. In November, Chisholm appeared in New York before a joint subcommittee on welfare reform made up of members from Agriculture, Education and Labor, and Ways and Means. With Fred Richmond as chair, the hearings were held in Lower Manhattan, and he again brought in his Brooklyn ally. She emphasized that no one wanted reform of the welfare system more than poor people themselves, who preferred jobs so that they could leave the system altogether. As manufacturing left cities, more good jobs needed to be provided, as well as more funding for those unable to find work, especially single parents with heavy childcare responsibilities. As always, she pointed out that most of those single parents were women, who were far more likely to be in badly paid jobs that did not cover the cost of childcare. She agreed with Richmond that welfare reform would not solve any problems without day care, job training, and jobs themselves. And she expressed frustration that voters and politicians, including Hubert Humphrey and Augustus Hawkins, sponsors of a full employment bill, did not realize the necessity of day care for reducing poverty and getting many more people into the paid workforce.[39] She would continue efforts to expand programs for poor families for the rest of her tenure.[40] In 1978 some of Chisholm's work paid off in major legislative victories: the passage of a watered-down Hawkins-Humphrey full employment bill and an extension of the Elementary and Secondary Education Act with the Title I provisions.[41]

Unfortunately, Chisholm was already disillusioned with President Carter as his attempts to move to the center clashed with her own legislative goals. Ironically, it was not Republicans themselves who dashed Chisholm's hopes for a new era of progressive change. While Chisholm continued to prioritize the same legislative issues, she had become adept at identifying slivers of common ground on which to build. What frustrated Chisholm was the hesitancy of Democrats to pursue bold anti-poverty policy initiatives that served her longtime constituents. Her colleagues seemed to be walking on eggshells to avoid antagonizing those on the right. As staffers would attest, Nixon had been frustrating but represented a concrete obstacle to Chisholm's policy goals. Now it was even more frustrating to have a cordial relationship and a professed alliance but little political will to enact the legislation Carter's Black supporters needed. He also continued to cut funding from welfare and education programs, citing fears of inflation. Ron Dellums put it bluntly: Carter had "totally abdicated the agenda of 1976" and "embraced a right-wing analysis of American economic problems." For example, Chisholm found Carter's welfare reform timid and inadequate. Her 1976 campaign stumping had paid off when she got a private meeting with Carter in the Oval Office to discuss it. Carter had a plan to replace public assistance with both a job program and cash assistance of $4,200 per year. Chisholm informed the president that families needed comprehensive childcare, health care, and job skills training to make his plan work.[42] As the year continued she became frustrated with the president, who did not seem to listen to her. Laura Murphy recalled that whenever she picked Chisholm up from the White House the congresswoman would be livid. She felt treated as "invisible" by the men around the cabinet table and eventually refused to attend.[43] She was mad that Carter refused to fight for increased appropriations for antipoverty programs. She suspected that Carter "has foregone his commitment to the poor and working class on these 'lunch pail' issues." In September, after a meeting in which Carter stated his priorities as reducing inflation and for balancing the budget even at the expense of reducing unemployment, she criticized his politics as mirroring those of conservatives. And after the next January's State of the Union address, she asserted that Carter's insulation from the problem of poverty in America was leading him to make unrealistically optimistic statements about domestic stability.[44]

Carter earned some goodwill when he eventually signed the Hawkins-Humphrey full employment bill in late 1978, although only after much pressure from the Congressional Black Caucus to put his weight behind it in Congress. But throughout the summer and fall of 1979, Chisholm and Black legislators debated whether to continue to support Carter. Chisholm was leaning against. She was appalled that a president she had hoped would be an ally for progressive change was repeating conservative talking points such as balancing the budget through domestic spending cuts. He invited Chisholm in a group of legislators to Camp David for a "relaxed weekend" in the summer of 1979. But then he squandered some of the good feelings when he summarily moved Patricia Roberts Harris from secretary of Housing and Urban Development, where she had become a useful ally to Chisholm and other Black legislators, to Health, Education and Welfare. He began to seem increasingly out of touch with the concerns of Black voters. His speech on energy fell flat in Harlem, where "people either did not listen to the speech, fell asleep during the speech, or could not make heads or tails out of what Carter was trying to get the public to do . . . or how far he wanted them to go."[45] Carter kept taking actions that frustrated Chisholm. He decided to separate a Department of Education from the Department of Health, Education, and Welfare, a move Chisholm strongly condemned, because broad expertise would be lost and an existing labor–civil rights coalition would no longer be able to advocate for the interests of children of color and poor children. She thought the bill was Carter's gift to the National Education Association in return for the organization's endorsement.[46] Chisholm broke for Kennedy that December.[47]

POLITICAL AND PERSONAL CHALLENGES AT HOME

Political alliances at home seemed to be going better. Her support of the new mayor of New York, Ed Koch, was rewarded when he named her as his top choice to take over as chancellor of schools. Chisholm seemed delighted, telling the *New York Amsterdam News* that she was deeply committed to New York's schoolchildren and that she, as a "creative and imaginative person" with wide contacts and deep experience, was ready for the "big, tough job." She thought that a logical next step in her career was to create a legacy through educating the city's children.[48] City officials, the *New York Amsterdam News*, and a broad section of parents seemed to agree. Her status as front-runner would be short lived, however. Albert Shanker, still president of the American Federation of Teachers and the United Federation of Teachers, had not forgotten her support for community schools in the 1969 Ocean Hill-Brownsville crisis. He announced that he opposed her on the grounds that, despite her years as a teacher and administrator, she was not experienced enough in education or administration, and unprepared to manage the $3 billion budget for the school system. A week after Koch's announcement, Herman Badillo, now Koch's vice mayor, called to tell her that Shanker had threatened to obstruct Koch's education legislation in Albany if

Chisholm's nomination went forward. Koch was dropping his support. Chisholm saw that the fix was in. In a move that came as a shock to many, she withdrew. Koch's second choice, Frank Macchiarola, won the position instead. To Chisholm, it was clear that Shanker's long-standing antipathy toward her and Black education activists in New York City motivated him to obstruct her appointment. He feared that he could not control her, she explained to a reporter, and did not "want a Black woman controlling a $3 billion education budget." She was losing patience with Koch, too, and would issue criticism of his treatment of poor, Black, and brown New Yorkers in his early months as mayor, pointing out that his actions did not match his verbal claims of caring about them.[49]

Political rivals still looked for opportunities to dethrone Chisholm as the controlling force in Black Brooklyn politics. Rumors of potential primary opponents proliferated. Critics began to advance the idea that Chisholm was insufficiently responsive to Black constituents, a charge that she vehemently denied. Her attendance (at 80 percent, just under the Congressional Black Caucus average of 81.8 percent) and bill introduction records also came under attack. Chisholm had to go on the defensive. After the Reverend Herbert Daughtry accused Chisholm of lacking accountability to Black New Yorkers, Chisholm retorted, "They're mixing up the fact that I'm not responsive to some of the political and ideological doctrines of some Black groups in the 12th District." She went on: "They confuse my right to dissent with them on my record of accountability to my Black constituency," she said, echoing years of power struggles she had had with other Black leaders. Decisions she had made not to support Percy Sutton or Arthur Eve in the New York and Buffalo mayoral races, respectively, reflected prior political commitments and not a lack of support for Black constituents' needs. Her rivals, however, saw her endorsement positions as political failures and an opportunity to possibly unseat her.[50] Then there were rumors, spread by Andy Cooper, that Chisholm would resign after the 1978 primary and name her protégé Ed Towns as a substitute.[51] Cooper's employer, the *New York Amsterdam News*, did not endorse Chisholm and added a scathing editorial comment, after its list of endorsements for the 1978 primary races. The "troublesome Mrs. Chisholm" had been serving the district well enough, but her nonsupport of several of the *News's* chosen candidates, and of Sutton the year before, was unforgivable. "We must," the anonymous writer said, "make her accountable to a higher standard of political wisdom and loyalty, or . . . mount a serious effort to remove her." He or she hoped that the rebuke in the pages of the *News* would make her rethink her actions.[52]

Chisholm pushed back, writing a letter to the *Amsterdam News* to set the record straight. "As a Black female politician," she wrote, "I have learned over the years that there is one set of rules for me and another set for others." She pointed out the double standard that she was expected to support Vann and Owens while they did not support her, and that other Black politicians had supported white ones with no criticism from the paper. She also asserted that she had been avoiding the "national limelight" while making a deliberate effort to legislate for more resources in her district and other poor communities. Furthermore, she stated that Major Owens had ostensibly gathered petition signatures on her behalf in the most recent primary, but somehow had acquired only 250 valid signatures for her while collecting 4,500 for himself, implying that he had used her name to benefit his own candidacy.[53] Al Vann replied in kind, claiming in the pages of the *News* that Chisholm had lied about Vann's encouragement of a primary challenger. Owens, however, did not deny the allegations about his petitions.[54] Notwithstanding her detractors, she won the 1978 primary and went on to win the general election in a landslide.

Her 1978 victory was in spite of a major attack from an old foe days before the election. Over twenty years after their first run-in, the conflict between Andy Cooper and Chisholm flared up again. Cooper, with a Major Owens staffer named Wayne Barrett and another journalist, Gabrielle Patrick, published an excoriating article about Chisholm's political loyalties on the front page of the *Village Voice*. The article explained that while "blacks in this town are sentimentally attached to her," Chisholm was really not who she appeared to be. Instead of being "unbought and unbossed," Chisholm had practiced a politics of opportunism and cast her lot with the city's party bosses. Cooper and Barrett presented a long list of examples that the authors said were evidence of Chisholm's neglect of people in her district. Excavating the past two decades, the authors cited every instance they could find that might suggest Chisholm's incompetence and opportunism. Their main point of evidence was Chisholm's failure to endorse local and state Black, women, and reform candidates. Instead, they argued, she had become the consummate organization politician that she professed to reject. They also claimed that she had been on the wrong side of, or had ignored, an assortment of issues over the past ten years. The authors advanced three theories about why this was. They argued that Chisholm's own psychological insecurity was the primary driving force behind her political career. Then they posited that she was now under the thumb of Brooklyn party leader Meade Esposito and Buffalo leader Joseph Crangle. Later, they suggested she was trying to pit different Black political circles against each other to gain leverage. Cooper, writing in the first person, revived his grievances from their Unity Democratic Club days and declared that Chisholm had always been an opportunist, while claiming that his own case and not *Wells v. Rockefeller* had been the one to create the Twelfth District. The article ended with a series of quotes from Chisholm's political rivals and the conclusion that Chisholm's pettiness came from paranoia.[55] In addition to the original article, which was quite long, the *New York Amsterdam News* appeared to have received advance copy and did not hesitate to point out and summarize the *Voice* article to its own readers. It "would appear further to weaken [*sic*] her apparently eroding political stance in Brooklyn," Executive Editor Bryant Rollins reported darkly.[56]

Chisholm's private world was shaken the following spring when Arthur Hardwick was in a serious car crash. He was about twenty minutes from their home in Buffalo when a nineteen-year-old tow truck driver swerved into Hardwick's lane. His 1977 Lincoln Continental was pushed off the road and into a tree. The car was nearly demolished and so was Hardwick; he sustained broken bones in his left leg, pelvis, ribs, and arm, and a contusion to his right lung. But he was miraculously alive. Chisholm rushed to his side. "He was bandaged from head to toe," she recalled, and " the only unbandaged part of him was his nose and that had a tube coming out of it." Standing at the doorway to his room she felt herself getting faint. "Come on in here, baby," Arthur called out to her. "I ain't goin' nowhere." Chisholm took some sedatives to calm her nerves and reluctantly decided to return to work in Washington. After two surgeries, Hardwick landed in intensive care in the Millard Fillmore Suburban Hospital. The other driver was uninjured and cited for failing to yield the right of way and driving with inadequate brakes. But Hardwick's recovery would be long. A month after the accident, doctors were still worried about saving the broken leg, even though a steel plate had been installed. Hardwick would eventually accept a settlement payment from the owner of the truck, a local car dealership.[57] Chisholm was back at work, but months later was still summoning the strength to deal with the "almost complete destruction of my husband." She later admitted that she cried "every night for a year." Hardwick was finally out and about, "walking well" on both legs, later in 1980.[58]

THE ELECTION OF 1980

1980, an election year, would be Chisholm's final campaign. It was also a presidential election year, and she started the season by stumping on Kennedy's behalf. Kennedy had "fought the good fight" on behalf of Black Americans, she argued. The primary race was tight and remained contested until the second night of the 1980 Democratic National Convention, which was held in New York City. Kennedy had won New York, and Chisholm was cochair of the New York state delegation, so she was "all fired up and ready to do battle" on behalf of her candidate.[59] But Kennedy conceded. Chisholm fell in line behind Carter. Backing him against Reagan was not simply "the less of two evils," she insisted, but because she did share common goals with the incumbent. She hosted Carter at the Concord Baptist Church in Bedford-Stuyvesant, where Kennedy himself and Muhammad Ali made an all-out effort to reassure and rally Black voters.[60] Despite these heroics, Carter would go on to a major defeat by Ronald Reagan in the general election. To make matters even worse, the Senate would pass into Republican hands for the first time in nearly three decades.

Chisholm was frustrated. She deplored Reagan's politics. Reagan's "utterances and his practices indicate subconsciously or otherwise a proclivity for the business sector as contrasted to the consumer sector," she said, as well as hostility to government's instruments for reducing inequality and "a preoccupation with the symptoms rather than the causes of poverty."[61] He wanted to enact a "dream of the 18th Century," she told the Urban League's Seventieth Anniversary conference, implying that Reagan did not disapprove of slavery.[62] She also, she admitted after her retirement, thought he was charismatic but mentally "limited." "I'm amazed at his limitations," she told a reporter. "Everyone says it in Washington, but they don't say it openly," she added.[63] Reagan's campaign tried unsuccessfully to get an endorsement from Chisholm, and once he won the election rumors flew that she might take a political appointment in his administration. The transition team was eager to dispel fears, generated by Reagan's nods to racism on the campaign trail, that Black repression would return to post-Reconstruction levels. Transition officials were looking for Black faces to fill various posts.[64] Chisholm responded to the rumors with an op-ed in the *Washington Post* a few weeks after the election. "I hope I have been wrong about Ronald Reagan," she began. "I hope I have been totally wrong about his new conservative economic policies." But she went on to point out that she thought his policies were not up to the task of reducing "the plague of structural unemployment." While criticizing the inadequate implementation of liberal policies, she had even less faith in the "pro-business, anti-regulation, and anti-welfare" aims of Reagan's incoming administration. If those policies did turn out to reverse unemployment, she would support the administration, but if they did not, she called for conservatives to be willing to concede that they were wrong.[65] None of the rumors about her place in the new administration came true.

She was also frustrated with her colleagues. Black politicians had sold out their support "for handshakes, vague promises, or a few federal dollars" during the 1980 Democratic National Convention. These same politicians had not earned true leadership, she wrote in a scathing *New York Amsterdam News* editorial. Instead, they were too self-interested to act effectively on behalf of the masses of Black people and had descended to "squabbling, backstabbing, and microphone-grabbing." The challenge now, she asserted, was to overcome the lack of coordinated leadership in the face of a conservative resurgence.[66]

FIGHTING REAGANOMICS

At the same time, she herself had won her seat back by over a 10 to 1 margin. As the Reagan era began, Chisholm spent much of 1981 fighting Reagan's supply-side economics. Reagan was on the vanguard of a new Republican emphasis on tax cuts and government cutbacks, emanating from the libertarian agenda that was beginning to captivate the Right.[67] He and others justified the cuts on the basis of the bruising economic slump of the Carter era. He shifted blame to Carter in particular and liberal policies in general, but with a sleight-of-hand that labeled government itself as the problem. He and his supporters cast themselves as the saviors of the nation from frivolous and misguided policies (read antipoverty, antidiscrimination, and environmental legislation) that stood on the necks of middle-class (read white middle-class) voters. To add insult to injury, the narrative went, those voters were forced to pay for these programs through their hard-earned taxes. This last point was a political winner, as he had learned as governor of California during the Proposition 13 campaign to slash property taxes in 1978. Antitax fervor had spread nationwide and became a New Right coalition bedrock issue. A cadre of supply-side economists had rejected New Deal Keynesian ideas for the orthodoxy that cutting business and wealthy people's taxes would grow the economy, an idea that was eagerly embraced by those constituencies. Reagan had won the presidency by uniting these New Right conservatives with the growing Religious Right. Now in office, he embarked on a crusade to cut taxes, convinced that it was not only a winning political issue but also a winning economic strategy. Cutting taxes was a useful way to justify cutting social services. Reagan, aware that many social programs were popular, was able to cast them as worthless drains on middle-class budgets and the growing economy.[68] He also evoked images of out-of-control, lazy, and sexually promiscuous Blackness, old racist images revised for a new age. In case anyone missed the point, on the campaign trail in 1976 and 1980 he repeatedly exaggerated the story of one Black fraudster, the infamous Linda Taylor of Chicago, whom he said was stealing $150,000 per year in welfare, food stamps, and veterans' benefits. Notwithstanding the fact that prosecutors had only been able to prove a total of $8,000 in fraud, and that Taylor was an isolated case, the message was clear: those on welfare were criminal cheaters.[69] Those who supported public benefits were the ones who enabled such grift. And not only that: the welfare state was actually harming recipients and society at large.[70]

Unsurprisingly, Chisholm and a remarkably unified Congressional Black Caucus (CBC) strongly disagreed with Reagan. They immediately grasped that Reaganomics was less about freeing the people from intrusive government than moving funds from social programs to corporations and the highest earners. Chisholm recognized Reagan's attempts to minimize the role of the federal government as a new permutation of an old states' rights argument.[71] As the budgeting process got underway, the eighteen-strong CBC, now chaired by Walter Fauntroy, met with the new president. Determined to avoid a standoff like the one Nixon created in 1969, Reagan met with the group less than two weeks into his term and promised a regular series of meetings thereafter. Chisholm told the gathered press that administration officials would be consulting with the CBC on proposed legislation. Reagan had not backed away from his campaign promises to reduce federal spending, but he did promise that the cuts would be equally felt by all.[72] Chisholm expressed a wait-and-see attitude. "Where there's life, there's hope," she told the *New York Times*. "You have to give someone an opportunity to see whether or not his word is his bond."[73]

When President Reagan announced his budget proposal to a joint session of Congress on February 18, it was clear that his word was not worth much. CBC input had not been incorporated. The cuts would not be equally felt by all but largely fell on those whom the CBC had sought to protect. Reagan announced blanket cuts of 30 percent on domestic spending. Chisholm's decade-plus advocacy work on behalf of antipoverty programs looked like it might be undone in one federal budget year. The budget became the top legislative priority for 1981.[74] The CBC got to work preparing an alternative budget. Reagan's budget cuts were "radical and severe," Chisholm commented when the budget was introduced in the House, and instead of solving the problems Reagan named, they would create new ones. There was no evidence that they would reduce the size of government, and they would certainly harm those who most needed economic help. She was dubious about supply-side economics, saying that the theory had "praiseworthy goals but shaky foundations."[75] On a practical level, she opposed specific cuts to over $10 billion in programs over the next two years, from solar energy to mass transit.[76]

Chisholm and the CBC would become very busy in House hearings as committees began to deal with Reagan's proposed budget. She testified on cuts to student aid, the National Endowments for the Arts and the Humanities, unemployment insurance and public assistance, and other health and human services budgets.[77] Her arguments all pointed out negative consequences for the poor as a result of the cuts—consequences that seemed to matter little to the current administration. Outside the hearing rooms, the

CBC was in the process of writing an alternative budget that took up a challenge issued by Reagan: if another method for balancing the budget while preserving domestic programs could be devised, Congress should consider it. The budget that the CBC produced would prioritize funding for domestic antipoverty programs and progressive taxation. It restored $27 billion of Reagan's cuts and found $34 billion in savings elsewhere while increasing defense spending.[78] It was at risk of getting no hearing, but Chisholm's place on the Rules Committee proved to be decisive when she negotiated time for the CBC's proposal to be deliberated as an amendment on the House floor. She had threatened House leadership that the CBC would vote en masse against the budget proposal unless the alternative budget could be offered on the floor.[79]

Reagan's all-out attack on domestic spending via the budget withered in the House in 1981, but he had plenty of options remaining. Reagan began targeting individual agencies for defunding, starting with the Legal Services Corporation, the national legal aid nonprofit. Then Republican reconciliation amendments in June overrode months of committee work that had hammered out a budget, to Chisholm's frustration.[80] She watched as the supply-side theory gained traction. Despite low support for Reagan's program early in 1981, an assassination attempt in March had raised his popularity and approval ratings. While the steep cuts had been headed off, middle-class white voters slowly began to adopt his idea that a tax cut that disproportionately benefited the wealthy would help their bottom lines, too, even as Chisholm vehemently argued the opposite. It did not hurt that he was calling for all tax rates to be cut by 25 percent. Democrats compromised and passed Reagan's tax bill that summer. That left a budget shortfall and necessitated the cuts that Reagan wanted. Despite Chisholm's efforts in the Rules Committee to block enactment of Reaganomics, Congress did approve about $25 billion in budget cuts to antipoverty programs.[81]

On another front, Chisholm was as determined as ever to challenge Reagan's belief that racial justice was the responsibility of the states, not the federal government. "Of course," she told an interviewer, "those of us who are minorities in this country—particularly the Black and Hispanic minority—know that if it were not for the federal government intruding, if you will, in our lives, we would not have had the massive compensatory education programs that have helped us move out in terms of catching up." Neither would there have been a Civil Rights Act or a Voting Rights Act, she reasoned, because history suggested local officials could not be trusted to support equity. Reagan's states' rights reasoning erased decades of progress. "In fact," she said in response to these dismantling attempts, "in all my days in the political arena, I have never, never seen such political arrogance." She firmly pushed back on Reagan's assertion that the Voting Rights Act was too strong and disapproved of his instructions to the Senate to weaken it before he would sign a reauthorization.[82] She disputed his criticisms of affirmative action for federal contractors, angry that he had no other suggestions for reducing employment discrimination.[83]

DEFENDING THE DIASPORA

Chisholm's concerns grew increasingly transnational in her last term, and she worked on behalf of the international Black diaspora. In the last years of Carter's term, Chisholm had become especially concerned with the United States' treatment of Haitian asylum seekers. To her, the systematic detention and deportation of these Black refugees was a clear example of racism. The Nixon administration had begun a policy of classifying those who fled from Jean-Claude Duvalier's repressive regime as economically motivated migrants, not refugees, in 1973. Under a clear double standard, in which Cubans were daily admitted as refugees from Castro's regime, Haitian arrivals who arrived by boat were systematically denied the same treatment and often incarcerated. Chisholm almost immediately joined the activist effort to change this policy. She expressed public concern as early as 1974, when she was a headlining speaker at a rally in protest of imprisonment of and denial of work permits to recent Haitian migrants. She began correspondence with New York immigration activist Ira Gollobin, and in 1976 she had been one of eight Democratic members of the House to call for the end of deportations and detentions of Haitian exiles, plus legal worker status while asylum cases were pending.[84] The Carter administration relented for two years, but then reenergized detention and created expedited deportation proceedings, a policy called the Haitian Program. In response, the Congressional Black Caucus created a Haitian Task Force and named Chisholm its chair. In July 1979, she released a scathing statement about the actions of the Immigration and Naturalization Service (INS). Haitians had experienced "deplorable" treatment in INS hearings of 150 asylum seekers at a time. A "voluntary return" policy had already sent 600 Haitians back to Haiti, though returnees were coerced into leaving and they faced harsh reprisals on return. And the denial of work permits had resulted in the social services capacities of Miami-Dade County being strained beyond capacity.[85] Chisholm's task force had notably gained passage of and Carter's signature on the Refugee Act, which expanded the definition of refugee to conform to the United Nations standard.[86] A group of 4,000 asylum seekers also won a class-action suit against the attorney general in July 1980, halting the Haitian Program. But these signs of hope would not end up curbing the large-scale incarceration of Haitian migrants. The act did not help new refugees from

Haiti, the administration soon figured out ways around the court ruling and planned to appeal it, and the Bureau of Prisons and the INS created a new agreement to detain Haitian refugees in federal prison facilities.[87]

In the spring and summer of 1980, Chisholm had watched, dismayed, as the crisis deepened. Beginning that April, about 15,000 Haitian refugees arrived at the same time as the Mariel boatlift from Cuba, which brought 100,000 migrants to southern Florida. Both groups sought political asylum, but in practice Haitians did not receive the same treatment as Cubans, who were automatically considered asylum seekers. Instead, Haitians were by default considered undocumented and directed toward exclusion proceedings, as well as having less access to sponsorship and thus higher rates of incarceration.[88] Chisholm castigated these practices before the Immigration, Refugees, and International Law Subcommittee, detailing the human rights abuses Haitians encountered at home in the Duvalier regime. She also described the lack of due process for Haitian asylum seekers and called for use of the emergency provisions in the Refugee Act on their behalf. The hearings had some effect; the same day, Congress passed an appropriations bill that reimbursed states for the costs incurred providing services to both Haitian and Cuban refugees. Three days after Chisholm's testimony, Carter agreed to offer parole to Haitian arrivals between April and October 10 in the Cuban-Haitian Entrant Program.[89] Ultimately, Carter never treated Haitians as asylum seekers on par with Cubans, and after losing to Reagan in November 1980, he left office without doing so.

Chisholm resumed her advocacy on behalf of Haitian asylum seekers as their situation grew worse. The Reagan administration would reinstitute a policy of immigrant detention as well as initiate a policy of interdiction, the practice of intercepting vessels carrying would-be refugees from Haiti on the water. Still arguing that the refusal of the executive branch to recognize that migrants were fleeing political repression constituted racism, she filed a bill to grant legal refugee status. She denounced Reagan's proposed interdiction policy and labeled immigration proceedings as a "kangaroo court." She also criticized treatment of African refugees and the administration's dishonoring its international commitment to admit more.[90] Then things went from bad to worse. The INS began mass deportation hearings against the 6,000 Haitians who had arrived after October 10, 1980, the cutoff date for special legal status. Immigration attorneys were barred from the courtrooms, where as many as thirty-five defendants were adjudicated at a time. The previous year's class-action legal decision was summarily disregarded by a Miami immigration judge, who claimed that lawyers seeking to represent immigrants were only looking to drum up business and conducted the hearings behind closed doors. Chisholm immediately sent a letter to the attorney general, William French Smith, calling for an immediate halt to the hearings. Her efforts brought some success; Associate Attorney General Rudolph Giuliani announced that hearings would thenceforth be conducted in open court.[91] But the problem continued. The overcrowded Krome detention camp in Miami began sending detainees to federal prisons as far away as New York and Texas, a move Chisholm called "a cruel, unjust, and seemingly racist policy."[92]

Indeed, it seemed that while Carter had been frustratingly indifferent to Haitian asylum seekers, Reagan was actively hostile. Chisholm's CBC task force on refugees had to renew calls for immigrants' human rights, a duty she carried out in Capitol Hill hearings and public statements. In front of the Senate's Judiciary Committee on Immigration in July, she bluntly pointed out the conditional nature of the United States as a refuge for asylum seekers. Despite lofty rhetoric, the United States was far less willing to accept refugees on the basis of humanitarian need and, apparently, when the immigrants in question were Black or brown.[93] She testified on interdiction policy in front of the Subcommittee on Coast Guard and Navigation in September as well. She warned that by carrying out interdiction the Coast Guard would "stain the image of the agency" in the manner that refusing Jewish refugees of the Nazis had in 1939.[94] She did not utter such warnings lightly. "I don't say everything is racism, I do my homework," she explained. "And I know now that this policy is racist."[95]

Despite widespread criticism, including a CBC letter criticizing the policy, Reagan issued an executive proclamation directing the Coast Guard to begin interdiction in late September 1981 and stationed a ship near Haiti to do so. The task force issued a position paper, and Chisholm took the floor of the House to no avail.[96] Reagan also reinstated large-scale immigration detention, putting in place an unprecedented policy of imprisonment for all undocumented Haitians without bond. As of February 1982, over 2,000 Haitian immigrants were incarcerated, some of whom had been detained for almost a year.[97] Chisholm introduced a refugee asylum bill in response. She made a trip to Haiti that summer with Walter Fauntroy and also sent representatives of her office to the new organization National Emergency Coalition for Haitian Refugees (NECHR) meetings.[98] Chisholm would leave office with the crisis unresolved, though she continued to serve on the NECHR's executive committee, and her successor Edolphus Towns would take up the cause.

Meanwhile Chisholm took up the economic rights of international migrant workers in the form of a bill she called the Farmworker Bill of Rights. She introduced H.R. 4453 in September, a bill that would charge a commission to monitor basic safety, health care, housing, and education for migrant workers. This legislation was an effort to harness the free-market turn in politics and create incentives for growers that respected labor rights. The commission would create a "Bill of Rights" for workers and a voluntary label for produce marketed by employers who complied. But there would be no consequences for those who did not. She invited colleagues to join her as cosponsors, explaining that one-half of these workers were Latinx, a third were Black, about 10 percent were Native American, and the rest were white. Notwithstanding the appeal, no cosponsors emerged. Chisholm introduced the bill on the floor of the House, calling migrant workers "the most exploited and impoverished group of workers in America" and listing the human rights that workers lacked.[99] The bill was referred to the Education and Labor's Subcommittee on Labor Standards. In the meantime, Chisholm testified before the Subcommittee on Housing and Community Development about the substandard housing that many migrant workers were forced to inhabit. She discussed her own legislation, but also reminded her colleagues that her bill was not the entire solution to the problem: enforcement of existing laws was weak, and additional laws might be passed. Notwithstanding the modest scope of her legislation, however, the Farmworker Bill of Rights did not make it out of committee.

Chisholm also cultivated international relationships in her later career. She had developed some Chinese contacts after serving as one of the hosts of a delegation of Chinese diplomats to Brooklyn in 1979. She and others had welcomed Wang Bingnan, ambassador plenipotentiary and president of the Chinese People's Association for Friendship with Foreign Countries, and his entourage to the Restoration Corporation building. Echoing earlier calls for Black American–Asian solidarity, both Wang and Chisholm recognized the possibilities for coalition as nonwhite people. Chisholm made a point of noting that "we are not interested in other people interpreting for us what the relationship must be that we want to develop with the Third World."[100] Several months later, she made an official visit, and she traveled again in June 1981, this time with Hardwick.[101]

She took another international trip in the service of Black solidarity in August, this time to six African countries over eighteen days. Her most contentious experience would be in South Africa. Chisholm had called in the past for boycotting the South Africa apartheid government and had strong criticisms for the United States' hypocrisy in seeking business relationships with the apartheid government under the guise of anticommunism. In 1977, she said the South African tennis team, which was all white, should not be allowed to compete in a major international tournament held in the United States.[102] Now she and her colleagues were in the country, and she had been granted "honorary white" status so that she could stay in hotels and eat with the rest of the delegation. This was a small comfort. She could "never forget . . . I shared with my people there a visible badge of inferiority."[103] The delegation tangled with Foreign Minister Roelof Botha about whether they could visit Nelson Mandela at Robben Island's infamous prison. Botha refused, and during a meeting with him things "turned acrimonious." Botha lashed out at Chisholm in particular: "What are you doing over here in South Africa, Ms. Chisholm, when you have got enough problems in your country with your blacks?" He accused her of trying to interfere where she had no business. She pointed out that at least Black people in the United States had freedom of movement, unlike South African people forced to live three hours from their workplaces. By the end, Botha was unwilling to answer any questions from the chair of the House Subcommittee on Africa, Howard Wolpe (D-MI), and afterward he released an angry statement accusing the Americans of "arrogance" and "obvious intolerance." Chisholm felt the same about him, calling him "the most arrogant white political figure I have ever met in my life." When the delegation made plans to visit a Black settlement between Nyanga and Crossroads in Cape Town, Botha had it bulldozed before they could arrive. The delegation was turned back at a police roadblock, but could see the bulldozers flattening the makeshift housing and children fleeing after their mothers beyond the barriers. Chisholm was deeply shaken. In tears at the airport, she expressed her horror at "what had been done to black mothers and children." "I was just not prepared," she said in a press release, "for the first-hand evidence of harsh repression and discrimination" she saw there. And she returned home, she said, "even more committed to ending any semblance of American support for it."[104] Some weeks later she would sign a letter protesting the loosening of human rights requirements in a foreign aid bill and serve on the conference committee for reconciling the House and Senate versions.[105]

"TEDIOUS AND FRUSTRATING": LEAVING CONGRESS

She was still under fire from the press at home. By the fall of 1981 she had forgiven Ed Koch and endorsed him for mayor again. She explained her decision in a press release: it was a pragmatic one, based on the idea that Reagan's New Federalism meant that city officials would have increasing power and alliances with them were strategically necessary. Fred Weaver of the *Amsterdam News* was predictably incensed, as was Andy Cooper. "Every Black and Puerto Rican person knows that Koch is not a supporter," Weaver fumed, and Chisholm was one of them. She had supported Koch nonetheless, however, because she was "playing footsey" with him over political patronage. Weaver and Cooper reprised their previous complaints about Chisholm's support of white candidates over Black ones in the past. In a City Hall march and rally against Reagan and Koch, Chisholm's rival Major Owens called her a "Judas" outright.[106]

Chisholm had had enough. She fired off two letters to the *Amsterdam News*, one addressed to Executive Editor John F. Davis and an enclosed open letter for publication. The *News* published both. In the letter for Davis, Chisholm complained about Weaver, Cooper, and Barrett's "deliberate, concerted, vitriolic, and unwarranted attack" and their multiple distortions of the truth. She suggested that the writers represented one side of a Brooklyn power struggle and thus had not allowed her to present her side. In the open letter, she elaborated: Al Vann and Major Owens sought political power in Brooklyn and operated using patronage tactics. In other words, they were making their own strategic power broker decisions behind closed doors, and happened to disagree with hers. Those writers who supported their stories ignored Chisholm's own press releases that documented her performance and then accused her of doing little in Washington. They also spread the lie that Chisholm was spending all of her time at her new home with Arthur. Chisholm was counting, and in the four years since her marriage, she had spent forty-two days in the Buffalo house. The motive, she was certain, was that she continued "to be an unbought and unbossed Black woman, outside of the 'old-boy' network and beyond their pernicious control." She apparently had plenty of supporters remaining; a group calling itself "Outraged Group of Concerned Citizens" sent a blistering letter to the *Amsterdam News* accusing the newspaper of sexism and bias in its coverage of her. Refusing to allow Chisholm to have the last word, the *News* wrote its own editorials in response. One denied accusations of sexism and called Koch "anti-Black," while Fred Weaver's signed response called Chisholm "the little lady from Brooklyn," called Frishman Chisholm's "white mouthpiece," criticized her decision to hire him in the first place, and accused him of writing the unsigned letter in Chisholm's defense. However, Weaver would not survive to the end of Chisholm's last term; by April, he had passed away at the age of sixty-nine.[107]

But the "nonstop sniping," as one anonymous friend told the *Washington Post,* was draining, and came on top of other problems. In addition to castigation from enemies in the press, commuting was becoming a major burden. She saw very little of Arthur and returned most weekends to an empty apartment in Brooklyn. She was still, over a dozen years into her congressional career, subject to racist harassment. She was accosted by two young white men at Washington National Airport on May 28. They approached her while she was waiting in line for the Eastern Airlines shuttle to New York, "shouted a few racial epithets at me, at close range, and then left the area," she wrote to the airport's manager. She requested that she be allowed to proceed directly to the departure lounge instead of waiting in line, at least for the next few weeks, and recommended a greater security presence in the area.[108] She openly courted a new opportunity to leave Washington, this time interviewing for president of the City College of New York. She did not get the position, however, despite strong support from her old ally Herman Badillo.[109]

Despite not having a new position lined up, Chisholm was done with politics. The fights in Congress had grown "tedious and frustrating": the conservative tide of "individualistic selfishness," the endless commuting, the hostile press and rival politicians in the district, and the time away from Arthur. "Mrs. Chisholm outgrew Brooklyn," Smith recalled. Chisholm grew weary of cynicism she perceived in her constituents, a tit-for-tat bargaining that she needed to do things for them in order to get their vote. The district came to feel like it "owned" her, Smith recalled, "and nobody owns Shirley, you know?" Also, Arthur wasn't well. He also "wanted her to branch out" because he perceived that her constituents were "driving her crazy."[110]

In January 1982 she was feeling "very politically depressed" by watching so many of the policies she had fought for get erased or threatened. She was tired of disappointing her constituents and tired of being disappointed by her liberal House colleagues. By February, she had decided not to run for office again. Bob Frishman called Jane Perlez at the *New York Times* and offered her the exclusive. Perlez visited Chisholm's Washington office, where the congresswoman said bluntly that she was frustrated with the Reagan administration's hostility to pursuing equality: "I find myself in a position where I can't help [my constituency]." The coalitions that she had relied on to get legislation done had evaporated in the aftermath of the Senate's flip to the Republicans. Now former allies were afraid of losing their own seats, and she was unable to be as effective at shifting policy as she once had been. She was also frustrated with the lack of protest by citizens themselves, noting the rise of conservatives' successful uses of the media. Right-wing appeals effectively deployed a trio of concepts that served to stifle dissent: family, morality, and the flag. Chisholm thought that her voice could be used outside of Congress against this movement. "I want people to know that this is not a funeral, politically," she said.[111]

Although Frishman and Perlez had agreed on an embargo of a few days, Perlez went right to press. Suddenly the office was thrown into chaos, without a finalized press release and a deluge of phone calls from report-ers.[112] Frishman hastily put out a press release. Chisholm was proud of what she had accomplished and her "role as a leader and a symbol." She planned to write and teach in order to help change what she called a "national state of mind."[113]

The Perlez interview was the first of a series of candid ones she gave at the end of her career. She was lonely, she told the *Boston Globe*, unable to take a weekend off to relax, living by herself in both Washington and Brooklyn, and only able to see her husband during congressional breaks. The *Globe* reporter had also discovered the rift between Chisholm and her mother. Chisholm had endured the emotional "pain of rejection and intimidation" and felt her belief in herself and in God had kept her going.[114] She told *Essence* magazine the same thing, that she had been "completely misunderstood and maligned by a lot of Black politicians." She also char-acterized some of her constituents as "abusive." But she claimed that her main reason for retiring was personal: it had been difficult to spend the ten months while Arthur had been in the hospital after the accident away from him in Washington. "He's recovered now, so I want to go home," she said. "I owe this to him," she told the reporter. She did mention the political frustra-tion of the Reagan administration, too. "We try not to appear negative when our constituents visit us in the Capitol," she said, "but this president is really out to hurt Black people." And it was difficult to give up working directly on behalf of the people, some of whom felt abandoned. She was haunted by a recent call from a ninety-year-old man who said to her desperately, "You can't do this." Nevertheless, her decision was final.[115]

Chisholm began a farewell tour of sorts, feted by colleagues and friends in the district, in Washington, across the country, and even internationally. She appeared at a fundraiser for the Rosa Parks Cultural Institute in Detroit, held in Manhattan. Along with Parks herself, Lena Horne was present. Horne and Arthur had both been raised on the same street in Chattanooga and had gone to the same school.[116] With Arthur, she took a trip to Barbados with the Brooklyn-based Shirley Chisholm Cultural Institute for Children, which she had founded. Chisholm herself made the rounds of local dignitaries, spoke to the local National Organization for Women chapter, and visited with her sister Muriel, who had moved to the island—the only one of her three sisters with whom she was on speaking terms.[117] There were receptions for her in New York, at the CBC's Third Annual Caribbean Seminar, hosted by her district office manager Arlene Doren, by her protégé Ed Towns at a Brooklyn private home, and by the Shirley Chisholm Cultural Institute for Children.[118] Then-assembly-woman Maxine Waters, chair of the Black Women's Forum in Los Angeles, held a "West Coast Farewell" for her when she visited for a conference keynote. Over thirty-five organizations and companies from across the state participated in putting on the event, which was also a fundraising kickoff.[119]

The CBC's Annual Legislative Weekend included a large farewell reception at the Sheraton cosponsored by the tobacco company Philip Morris. The following evening she was announced as the winner of the CBC's William Dawson Award, named for that iconoclastic representative from Chicago Chisholm encountered in 1969. She delivered an emotional acceptance speech in front of an applauding audience of 1,500, including dignitaries Jesse Jackson, Coretta Scott King, Ruby Dee and Ossie Davis, and Earl Graves.[120] "My friends, my brothers and sisters, my colleagues," she began. "If all of you could have been my delegates at the Democratic Party convention in 1972, we might have eaten some of our black caucus dinners over at the White House." She described the arc of her career as a complete circle: from "that loud and angry Shirley Chisholm" in 1969, to the 1970s institutionalist trying to preserve Great Society programs and make government work for the people, and now "angry and outspoken once again" about the militarism and greed of Reagan's administration. She was leaving Congress, she said, to take her righteous anger "out to the people of this great land."[121]

Chisholm's last term ended with a tribute to her on the House floor, led by her fellow New York representatives Geraldine Ferraro, Charlie Rangel, and Sam Stratton. Over three dozen colleagues, including members of the Congressional Black Caucus, inserted laudatory remarks into the *Congressional Record*. All friction appeared to have vanished; only admiration for Chisholm's dedication, intellect, and skills was in evidence. Colleagues from both parties participated, with multiple contributors saying that they disagreed with Chisholm on the issues but enjoyed working with her nonetheless.[122] Behind the scenes, she sold the contents of her Washington apartment, offering the discounted furnishings to her staff first. Items ranged from a white bedroom set trimmed in gold for $150 down to various dishes for a quarter each.[123]

In January, Chisholm's nemesis Major Owens was sworn in as the new U.S. representative for the Twelfth District. Owens had narrowly beaten Chisholm's endorsee Vander Beatty in the primary and had gone on to win the general election.[124] Ed Towns had initially announced he would seek the Twelfth District seat. When it became clear that Owens had momentum, Towns ran instead next door in the Eleventh District, which was Fred Richmond's old turf, winning the primary over two Latinx men candidates. He went on to win the general election and moved into Chisholm's old Capitol Hill apartment. Chisholm's reign in Brooklyn was over.[125]

Despite her protestations that her career was not yet over, Chisholm was already thinking about her legacy. In June 1982, Chisholm agreed to fill in for popular call-in-show host Barry Gray on WMCA radio. Listeners were able to ask the retiring congresswoman any questions they had, and one asked about how she wanted to be remembered. "I would like to be remembered for the fact that I was a catalyst for change," she told the caller. "Although misunderstood, maligned, and sometimes abused, I had the audacity and the courage and the nerve to stand up for what I believe and to fight very hard for that which I believe."[126]

19
PROFESSOR AND CHAIR

★

Finally freed from the biennial campaigning and local feuds of holding office, Chisholm would embark on two main efforts to build Black feminist power during her postretirement years. One was in the academy, in the form of a named visiting professorship at Mount Holyoke College and teaching courses at Spelman and Buffalo State Colleges. The other was in institution building, as the first chair of the National Political Congress of Black Women. At times she said that she was working on a memoir, "*The Illusion of Inclusion*," though she would never publish it and no manuscript has been found.[1] She continued the rounds of public appearances, accepting awards and making speeches throughout the country, aided at first by Bob Frishman as speechwriter, to whom she provided detailed notes for transformation into spoken prose. She was based with Arthur at their spacious home in Buffalo but was sometimes in Brooklyn, most often at the Shirley Chisholm Cultural Institute for Children, the mentoring organization that she had founded her first year in Congress. And she was a regular at the annual Congressional Black Caucus Weekend each September.[2]

For much of Chisholm's last year, mystery surrounded what would be her next move. When rumors circulated that she was angling for the presidency of CUNY's Medgar Evers College, she was insulted that people said she was "going around knocking on doors looking for a job."[3] In early August, she announced her decision to accept Mount Holyoke College's offer of a distinguished temporary position, the Purington Professorship. The position had been held in the past by the renowned writers W. H. Auden, Arna Bontemps, and Bertrand Russell. She had delivered the 1981 commencement address and been awarded an honorary doctorate. Now the relationship developed into a mutually beneficial arrangement. The college was not too far from her house and husband in Buffalo, nor was it a long distance from Brooklyn. She would be required to teach three courses on politics over the academic year, and eventually stayed on for three years.[4]

After retirement she maintained mentoring relationships and stayed in touch with staffers, some more than others. Bob Frishman was still working for her immediately after her retirement, and the two corresponded about upcoming speeches. She was perhaps closest to Carolyn Smith, attending Smith's daughter's high school graduation and wedding, where she danced with abandon. They talked one to three times per week.[5] Smith recalled that Chisholm finally abandoned her wigs because she no longer had a staff to bring them to the shop for maintenance.[6] She continued mentoring up-and-coming talent, such as James T. Conolly, district leader in Brooklyn's Forty-Second Assembly District, whom she had known since his youth and who had worked on her late 1970s campaigns.[7] Ada Smith, who also worked in the district, won a New York State Senate seat in 1988.[8] Barbara Lee, the enthusiastic Oakland volunteer from 1972 and erstwhile Ron Dellums staffer, won a California State Assembly seat in 1990 with Chisholm's help on the campaign trail. Chisholm was more than a political ally to Lee; the older congresswoman had become a close personal mentor who was there for each of Lee's achievements. When Lee won a state senate seat in 1996, Chisholm announced at the victory ball that Lee was destined to become a member of Congress. She was correct: Dellums announced his retirement and Lee was elected to his seat in 1998. To Chisholm's delight, Lee introduced a resolution in 2001 to formally recognize Chisholm's achievements in the House. It garnered seventy-one cosponsors and passed, 415–0.[9] She also received birthday and Mother's Day cards from her district staffer and mentee Victor Robles. And she helped pay for college for at least four students in the 1980s. "I am a highly paid lecturer," she said in a 1986 speech, "and I use what I earn to leverage black people."[10]

THE NATIONAL POLITICAL CONGRESS OF BLACK WOMEN

In addition to the Purington Professorship, Chisholm served as a political consultant after retirement, most notably to the next Black American to run for president, Jesse Jackson. She liked that Jackson had bypassed the Black political establishment in his 1984 campaign and made an appeal directly to the grassroots. Despite several other candidates' requests for her endorsement—and a few nibbles regarding her as a possible vice presidential running mate—she held out to aid Jackson. When he announced his candidacy in Washington, D.C., Chisholm introduced him to the cheering crowd. She would appear with him on stage at various campaign stops through the primary season. She planned to persuade him to add a white liberal woman to his ticket as the vice presidential nominee if he did gain the nomination, she said.[11] She had hopes for a coalition like one that she imagined in 1972. And, as in 1972, Chisholm watched Jackson struggle to get political establishment figures to fall behind him. She was frustrated by Black leaders' attempts to dissuade Jackson from running on the grounds that he was a long shot.

Shirley Chisholm and Jesse Jackson, 1988.
Courtesy of the Shirley Chisholm estate.

"If you think he shouldn't run because he will not win," she cautioned, "do what you have to do on Election Day, but please keep your mouth shut instead of going public with your feelings about the man."[12] Like Chisholm's campaign, Jackson was not only running for the nomination but hoping to build political infrastructure: more voters involved in politics. Once Jackson's candidacy seemed unlikely to capture the nomination, Chisholm put the word out that grassroots Black voters still had power in the 1984 election. They should continue to vote for Jackson in the remaining primaries so that he had bargaining leverage at the Democratic National Convention. They could then unite behind the eventual nominee in order to defeat Reagan in November.[13]

Although Jackson did not win the nomination, he had amassed enough clout to force the convention's rules committee to institute reforms that would increase Black and Latinx participation. Among these was a concession to add Chisholm as an honorary cochair.[14] Despite this gesture, she and other Black women there were frustrated. Hundreds of Black women were at the convention as Jackson/Rainbow Coalition delegates. Black women, they knew, were the most loyal demographic to the Democratic Party. There was a "sentiment of unity" among them, but no structure or organization.

However, Mondale's actions precipitated a greater unity. He had not interviewed any Black women as potential vice presidential running mates, despite getting half a dozen names, including Chisholm's, from Jackson. (Chisholm herself was "quite annoyed at not being considered.") The result was a firestorm of indignation from Black women at the convention. "By arrogantly excluding us from consideration as his running mate," journalist and activist Jean Wiley explained, "by excluding us even from consultation and advice, Mondale touched a nerve we didn't know was there."[15] Then, as the party platform and nominating procedures were hammered out, it became clear that Black women still did not have real power at the convention. The Rainbow Coalition had negotiated with feminist groups that they all would cooperate to support Jackson's planks on jobs and health care, plus a procedural rule that would have ensured a woman vice presidential nominee. Once Mondale named Geraldine Ferraro as his running mate, feminists stopped supporting the planks. Black women were angry, but also energized and now convinced that they would have to go it alone.[16]

Sensing a tipping point, DNC Black Caucus Chair C. Delores Tucker convened thirty-five of those disaffected Black women two weeks later into a new organization at the National Alliance of Postal and Government Employees building in Washington, D.C. The meeting was emotional. "We don't need brokers anymore," Tucker said. "We will broker for ourselves." Chisholm spoke, too. "We're going to have to realize we can no longer be timid or reluctant," she declared. "We have to form our own organization. I'm 60 years old and I'm at the end of my rope in trying not to upset Black men . . . not to upset white women." The next day, a steering committee met to hammer out a statement of purpose, mission, organizational structure, and temporary budget and proposed Chisholm as chair.[17]

The group, eventually named the National Political Congress of Black Women (NPCBW), was Chisholm's outlet for institution building for the next eight years. She had already been part of several Black women's political groups in the early 1980s. In 1981 she and Mona Bailey, president of Delta Sigma Theta, had convened a Black Women's Summit at Howard University. The over 700 women present participated in a series of workshops and lectures designed to share knowledge and spark political action. The conveners had self-identified the gathering as the first summit of Black women since the 1895 meeting that created the National Association of Colored Women's Clubs and self-consciously echoed that earlier gathering's language of picking up "the fallen torch of national leadership."[18] In 1982 she and Bailey traveled to Bellagio, Italy, for an international conference of Black women convened by the Los Angeles–based Pan-African Women's Secretariat.

California Assemblywoman Maxine Waters and an international list of Black women dignitaries attended.[19]

Now, in the wake of Jackson's campaign and the snub at the 1984 DNC, she and Tucker were cofounding an organization that would foster Black women's political careers and advocate for their interests. The group was explicitly focused on gaining power in the electoral arena, unlike other Black women's groups. It would encourage Black women as voters and as candidates, policy makers, and fundraisers. Initially called the National Black Women's Political Caucus, the group was a virtual who's who of Black women in politics and public life at the time. Tucker had been named secretary of state by Pennsylvania governor Milton J. Shapp in 1971. Eleanor Holmes Norton was a member, as were Mary Frances Berry, Cardiss Collins, Dorothy Height, and Maxine Waters. They hired a twenty-nine-year-old Jackson campaign staffer from New Orleans, Donna Brazile, to be their executive director.[20]

The group followed up at another meeting in a Rayburn House Office Building hearing room one week after the founding meeting, finalizing the statement of purpose. After multiple attendees described how inspirational Chisholm was to them and to all Black women, the group voted by acclamation to designate her as national chair. She "accepted in her usual forthright and gracious manner stating how the [NPCBW] is a long-term dream of hers and how honored she was to serve." The meeting temporarily adjourned for a press conference, where she read the new statement of purpose and took questions from the press. When they reconvened, the founders made pledges to the operating budget, named committees and additional officers, and planned their next meeting the following month.[21]

The organization was immediately a source of excitement to Black women nationally. Letters congratulating the founders began to pour in, asking how to become a member and how to get involved. Some local chapters galloped ahead, forming before the executive committee could form policies. Over 600 individuals had signed up for membership. The national office quickly devised a system to create local chapters and started planning a first convention to elect officers and create bylaws. The group held its first public event, a breakfast, at the Washington Hilton on September 30. Chisholm addressed the gathered women with language that was alternately inspirational and organizational. She quoted Langston Hughes, declaring that the dream he wrote of in his poem *Harlem* "will not be deferred because on August 2nd, 1984, Black women who have long been beacons of progressive political change met . . . to form a national organization committed to achieving political empowerment for black women." Invoking Anna Julia Cooper, she told her audience that "black women should not assume a passive subordinate position. . . . We must take a stand for ourselves." The organization drew from women's leadership across class lines, she explained, having involved the National Council of Negro Women, trade unions, church groups, voter registration groups, children's advocates, educational leaders, and grassroots activists. "There will be no room for elitism of any kind," she decreed, going on to ask all present to struggle past "disillusionment" and "apathy" to create change. She finished with a status report on the formation of the organization itself, explaining that the name might have to be changed, and praising the overwhelming desire of women to become members immediately and their patience while bylaws, charter, and structure were created. The breakfast raised $28,000.[22]

Behind the scenes, the challenges in building the organization from scratch, with the volunteer effort of busy women, and with little funds became evident. Eleanor Holmes Norton had agreed to chair the Bylaws Committee, but the committee took a long time to review a draft. The breakfast had made a significant dent in the projected six-month budget of over $43,000, but did not meet it. And the group had realized that the name had to be changed. A similarly named group, the National Black Women's Political Leadership Caucus, was founded in the early 1970s by Nelis James Saunders, attorney Zenobia Hart, Helena R. Mons of Philadelphia, Lillian Huff of Washington, D.C., and Juanita Dandridge. They had held their first annual conference in the Cannon House Office Building in the spring of 1975. Chisholm, as well as other Congressional Black Caucus members, had been present. After hearing of the new group, Saunders and the current executive secretary dashed off letters to Chisholm. Saunders was supportive of the new group, she explained, but must the name be so similar to the existing group? The executive secretary was more blunt; she was threatening legal action.[23] Chisholm's group eventually would be incorporated as the National Political Congress of Black Women in February 1985. In addition to financial and naming issues, communication and lines of authority were easily muddled, and the measurable goals and strategy for the organization and annual meeting were not yet formed five months after the founding.[24]

Even as the organization was still being assembled, developing political events needed a rapid response. A slew of state and local races over the next two years required decisions about where to target organizing efforts. Conservative chair of the federal Commission on Civil Rights, Clarence Pendleton, had recently criticized Black progressive leaders, which demanded a response. Apartheid in South Africa demanded a response, too, and the group decided to endorse the Free South Africa movement. Tucker told the executive committee that they should all march and go to jail, which

Chisholm had just done for demonstrating in a restricted area outside the South African embassy. There were the problems of nuclear proliferation and Reagan's court appointees. And still the concrete goals of the group needed to be prioritized.[25]

Then there was the ever-present need to plan national meetings. The first major test of the NPCBW's organizing skills was the 1985 National Assembly. Early on, Spelman College in Atlanta was chosen as the location. Chisholm had developed a working relationship with the college; she addressed a Spelman convocation in October 1983 and would teach a course entitled "Congress, Power, Politics" at Spelman in the spring of 1985. The conference was conceived of as a series of workshops on how to run candidates for political office, raise funds, and discuss issues.[26] "History has provided Black women with many role models," the call read,

> who will inspire us on the first weekend in June, 1985 when Black women assemble to set a political agenda that will carry us into the 21st century. We will be guided by the legacy of such Black woman as *Harriet Tubman, Sojourner Truth, Ida B. Wells, Mary McLeod Bethune, Fannie Lou Hamer and Patricia Roberts Harris.* . . . Black women from all walks of life, and of every political persuasion who want to advance their cause and the cause of Black people through the political process are urged to join the National Political Congress of Black Women and to attend the National Assembly.[27]

Four hundred and fifty women attended the three-day conference in June, which featured a statement of support from Jesse Jackson and then-mayor Andrew Young, a tribute to Dorothy Height, and a keynote address by Chisholm herself. Chisholm's speech was both inspiration and exhortation. She had wanted to convene Black women together for at least two decades. "We can't wait any longer," she said now. And the time for mere talk was over: "There is no point in jawboning—regardless of how poetic it might be—about whether the black man wants to integrate with America, because we are involved so inextricably with America that sensible black men and women accept it as a mandate. And we, as sensible black women, accept it as a mandate to work for a change that is written in the way of things."[28]

Height, Mary Frances Berry, and Angela Davis led a three-part workshop on civil rights. The attendees held a hotly contested election for the permanent board, though Chisholm ran unopposed for chair. Other winners showed the spectrum of Black women's political thought—Davis, Eleanor Holmes Norton, and Republican Gloria Toote—and the board held its first official meeting. The organization adopted politics, the preamble read, to "address the aspirations and concerns of the Black community, with special attention to the unique and particular needs of Black women." It would serve as a "voice and instrument for change . . . and as a catalyst for the election of Black women at all levels of government." The meeting seemed to be a great success, though there was some "minor bungling" in organization, such as the long delay in counting votes for the board election.[29]

Once the group was off and running, local chapters were granted charters. Chisholm started traveling to many of them, an activity that would eventually lead to a main source of revenue for the organization. Donna Brazile won a scholarship to attend the United Nations Conference on the Status of Women in Nairobi, Kenya, on behalf of NPCBW. The Political Planning Committee, chaired by Maxine Waters, began to strategize for the 1986 elections. In early 1986 the NPCBW founded a political action committee that supported five Black women congressional candidates.[30] Even as the organization grew, the challenges of institution building loomed. A unified agenda was elusive. Board member attendance at meetings was uneven. Finances would be a constant difficulty, with unpaid dues and high overhead constantly challenging the balance sheet. The board also worried about accepting donations from entities who did business in South Africa, especially as they raised funds to establish a foundation for voter registration and candidate education and for the organization's operating expenses.[31]

The growing problems in the NPCBW came to a head at the same time Chisholm's own world was in turmoil. Arthur, it turned out, was gravely ill with prostate cancer. He was hospitalized at first and then at home in a bedroom that had been converted into a hospice, and Chisholm was not willing to leave his side. She withdrew from the daily administration of the NPCBW. The first annual meeting (as opposed to its biennial national assemblies) was held in Indianapolis in June, but Chisholm could not be there. In her absence, the board of directors meeting grew rancorous. Several of the women present had strong criticism for Donna Brazile, complaining about her approach to organizing the meeting and treatment of the local chapter members. Brazile angrily delivered a farewell speech near midnight during one of the sessions. She resigned within the week. At the same time, seeking to stem the financial bleeding, Chisholm directed the second vice chair Gloria Toote to close the Washington office and move the organization into temporary, borrowed quarters. The result was a firestorm of criticism directed at Toote and the formation of an Ad Hoc Committee of Concerned NPCBW Members.[32]

Chisholm was otherwise occupied with caring for her once-dapper husband as he withered away to eighty-two pounds. In August 1986, Arthur died at age seventy:

I knew that he was going to die because the night before, at twelve o'clock, he was sitting by the window and a bird was up in the tree, flying about and everything, and all of a sudden, the bird dropped dead. Right by the place he was sitting. And they say whenever a bird drops from a tree dead right by a person, the person's going to die. And he passed on. And he said to me, the night before, Shirley, he said, I don't want to leave you here. And I said, I know you don't. But he said, but listen, be careful. Because I'm frantic and I'm going, you know. He thought I couldn't take care of myself. I'm so afraid to leave you. And he died with that, you know, I don't want to leave you. And I said, I'll be all right, I'll make it. And he passed away.[33]

Chisholm was bereft. Arthur had been "too good to be true," and although Chisholm did survive nearly twenty years after his death, she missed him the entire time. The dream house that had been their haven together no longer provided comfort, and she would sell it within a few years. His funeral was held at the St. John Baptist Church in Buffalo, followed by entombment in the Birchwood Mausoleum in the expansive Forest Lawn Cemetery. The tomb held an empty spot reserved for Chisholm's own remains.[34]

The grieving Chisholm was back at work with the NPCBW within two months. She presided over the October board meeting, gratefully acknowledging the sympathy that she had received from the members and explaining that it was she who had closed the national office for financial reasons.[35] She now had the task of reuniting the fractious and demoralized group. As the dust of the summer settled, she was finding an able ally in board member Portia Perry Dempsey. Dempsey, a native of Baltimore and former Department of Defense worker, had convened a chapter of NPCBW in suburban Burlington County, New Jersey, and become a member of the national board of directors as well as state director for New Jersey.[36] After a trip to address Dempsey's chapter's 1985 Champagne Brunch and the state conference in 1986, Chisholm was impressed with the enthusiasm and diligence of the New Jersey Congress and with Dempsey as its leader. She designated Dempsey as the organizer for that year's biennial conference, to be held just across the river from Philadelphia in Cherry Hill, because Dempsey had the "necessary people-power" for pulling it off.[37]

Like the 1985 national assembly, the goals of the 1987 Cherry Hill conference were to recruit more Black women into political participation and leadership and educate them through workshop sessions.[38] The meeting was star studded. After opening remarks by Tucker, Chisholm, and Dempsey, Ruby Dee and Coretta Scott King spoke on the first night. Susan Taylor, editor in chief of *Essence* magazine, Angela Davis, and new Spelman president

Johnetta Cole also gave keynotes. There were workshops on setting up chapters, the electoral and political process, economic empowerment, youth, family, and health. The conference ended with rousing closing remarks by Chisholm. "We must organize in order to empower ourselves," she exhorted the several hundred women present. She had again won the office of chair unopposed.[39]

Chisholm made a round of appearances that fall. She presided over the NPCBW brunch at the Congressional Black Caucus's 1987 Legislative Weekend, and she endorsed Doris Smith's successful campaign for a state court office in Pittsburgh.[40] She delivered one of her rousing speeches on Smith's behalf: "Women must be resilient . . . tough . . . and stop being fluttering butterflies," she told the crowd. She recognized that Smith had not been supported by the local party, just as Chisholm herself had experienced in 1968.[41] Chisholm and Tucker were also on the offensive against harassment of Black leaders nationwide. They appeared together on behalf of Clarence and Michael Mitchell, two brothers and Maryland state senators indicted for obstructing a congressional investigation into a federal defense contract. "All over the nation," Chisholm said at the Baltimore rally, "strong Black officials, like the Mitchell brothers, are under harassing federal investigations and indictments as the Reagan Justice Department plots to drive them out of office and destroy the tremendous gains we've made." The nationwide fight against harassment of Black officials formalized into the National Campaign for Justice, cochaired by Tucker.[42]

The organization was back on firmer administrative footing, particularly because Portia Dempsey had stepped in as acting executive director. While Dempsey was formally tasked with administering the NPCBW, she was becoming Chisholm's right-hand woman. She was unafraid to pursue accounts payable and dues, sometimes to the consternation of chapter leaders. Dempsey moved the NPCBW headquarters near to her home outside of Camden, New Jersey, started a newsletter, and began to administer activities with a firm hand: fundraising, recruiting Black women electoral candidates, and sending Black women delegates to the Democratic National Convention in 1988.[43]

In 1988, Chisholm and Tucker were ready to take advantage of the fact that Jesse Jackson was running for president again, this time with more uniform Black support, and that his coattails would bolster the visibility and viability of down-ballot candidates. Jackson had written to Chisholm directly to ask for her and the NPCBW's support in August 1987, and the organization began to plan a major effort to both support him and promote Black women running for office.[44] Chisholm herself took the stage at Jackson rallies in twenty different states. She led New York Women for Jesse Jackson and hosted a

Left to right: Rosa Parks, Coretta Scott King, Shirley Chisholm, Dorothy Height, and C. Delores Tucker celebrate Parks's seventy-fifth birthday, likely at an NPCBW event, 1988.
Courtesy of the Shirley Chisholm estate.

major fundraiser for him in New York City with Gloria Steinem.[45] Multiple NPCBW members served on the Jackson campaign, as Jackson delegates, and in state Democratic Party leadership positions. Dempsey reserved two Amtrak train cars to transport East Coast NPCBW members to the convention in Atlanta that July. Chisholm combined the 1988 DNC with the founding of an NPCBW chapter in Atlanta, with a membership of over one hundred.[46]

Jackson lost the nomination to Michael Dukakis. However, perhaps because Donna Brazile was on his campaign staff, Dukakis made a deliberate effort to reach out to Black leaders. He invited Chisholm to a Washington meeting that focused on a large-scale voter registration drive.[47] Chisholm was supportive of Dukakis and even recorded a radio ad for him, but she predicted a difficult fight in the general election. While polls showed a majority of women preferring the Massachusetts governor, Chisholm expected that gap to narrow as the election drew near. Furthermore, women who preferred Dukakis might not actually vote.[48] Chisholm would prove correct, as Dukakis lost the general election, narrowly losing among women, too.

Chisholm was still flirting with the idea of holding public office again. In 1988, no fewer than twenty-seven New Yorkers approached Chisholm to run for mayor against a floundering Ed Koch the following year, she said. She was bemused by the resulting curiosity in the press, observing that "my life has been filled with rumors." She warned the NPCBW board that October that she was seriously considering a run. But she was reluctant, hesitant about giving up her "very quiet life" and occupied by her consulting duties to Jesse Jackson's campaign as he prepared for the Democratic National Convention.[49] She did hire a campaign manager, Arthur Nitzburg, and supporters apparently raised enough money to keep Chisholm flirting with campaigning through the end of the year. The New York City and Vicinity chapter of the NPCBW held its inaugural conference in September, and she spoke there.[50] But she had no interest in running against Manhattan Borough President David Dinkins, and when he finally announced his candidacy she stepped back. Dinkins defeated Ed Koch in the primary and went on to win the general election.[51]

Chisholm served as national chair of the NPCBW for five more years, though she was frequently frustrated by members' delinquency in paying dues and with inconsistent volunteer labor that the organization relied on. She reduced her duties to recruiting new chapters to grow the nearly-1,300-strong membership and speaking at fundraisers. Dempsey did her best to make the load light on Chisholm, handling her calendar and paperwork for speaking appearances (Chisholm's fees were paid directly to the NPCBW).[52] Eventually, Chisholm stepped away entirely in 1992, taking the title of chair emeritus and handing over duties to C. Delores Tucker. That year's NPCBW brunch honored Chisholm with an array of luminaries paying tribute. Melba Moore and Dionne Warwick performed the national anthem, Dorothy Height presented Chisholm with an award, and both Rosa Parks and Jesse Jackson gave remarks (the latter was introduced by the newly elected U.S. congresswoman Maxine Waters). Rev. Willie Barrow of Operation Push gave a benediction.[53]

The chair emeritus was still busy for the rest of the year, taking up campaigning for Bill Clinton's presidential run in 1992. Despite neglecting to invite her to the Democratic National Convention, the Clinton campaign asked her to stump for him in front of Black, brown, and women voters. She was happy to support his run against George H. W. Bush, touting the importance of the economy and jobs in the aftermath of the Bush Recession and the need for federal investment in childcare.[54] When Clinton won, the NPCBW submitted a set of Black women's names for his transition team to consider as administration appointees.[55] Her efforts would be rewarded when President Clinton nominated her to be ambassador to Jamaica in July

President Bill Clinton and Shirley Chisholm meet in the
Oval Office regarding the Jamaica ambassadorship, 1993.
William J. Clinton Library, National Archives and Records Administration.

1993. Initially she was ready to take the job. She called Victor Robles, asking
him to come work for her. But Robles, who was then a city council member,
declined. Her sister Muriel Forde counseled against taking the position,
arguing it had large risks and few rewards. Chisholm then learned that she
would be required to learn to shoot a gun and sleep with one by her side.
She withdrew from consideration, citing failing eyesight as the reason she
would not be able to serve.[56]

Chisholm really was in the process of withdrawing from public life. She
moved out of the state of New York entirely in 1992, leaving for Palm Coast,
Florida, and taking up residence next to Portia and Calvin Dempsey's new
home. Her contacts in New York City were disappearing. Mac Holder died
in March 1993 at the age of ninety-six. His funeral was a gathering of who's

who in Black New York politics; Chisholm herself attended, as did her political friends and enemies from the past decades. While Mayor Dinkins and Victor Robles eulogized Holder, Chisholm did not.[57] She also attended the 1993 NPCBW Conference in Washington, D.C. Congresswoman Maxine Waters presided, while Chisholm presented an award to Senator Carol Mosely-Braun, Coretta Scott King presented one to Rosa Parks, and Dorothy Height presented one to Virginia Governor Douglas Wilder. The organization's new committee on gangster rap and misogyny in hip-hop music announced their formation and requested support from those present. But this time Chisholm was neither in charge nor at the center of the events. She would attend few NPCBW functions from then on, skipping the 1994 Founder's Day reception and the 1995 biennial meeting.[58]

NPCBW's erstwhile executive director Portia Dempsey and her husband, Calvin, had deepened their friendship with Chisholm, who had come to trust Portia implicitly. The two had become a team at NPCBW, and Portia only lasted about a year after Chisholm's retirement. When Dempsey did resign in early 1993, Chisholm helped her friend by drafting a resignation letter—which referred both to Calvin's recent illness and the difficulty of running the office with unreliable cash flow and "the daily grind of misplaced accusations."[59] The Dempseys and Chisholm had, by then, moved to Florida together. When the Dempseys bought a house in the upscale Halifax Plantation development in nearby Ormond Beach, Chisholm bought one next door.[60]

By the turn of the twenty-first century, Chisholm was mostly out of the public eye. She still got requests for speeches but turned most of them down, making exceptions for local venues: a Black history class at nearby Bethune-Cookman College in honor of her inspiration, Mary McLeod Bethune; at the Dempseys' church; to the Flagler County NAACP; and to a local Unitarian Universalist congregation. The latter speech would be her last. She was still as blunt as ever, telling the mostly white audience that if they really wanted to fight racism, they ought to have held their event in a Black community (the speech, nevertheless, got a standing ovation). She sat for hours of interviews with filmmaker Shola Lynch and a documentary film crew that came to her home in 2000 and 2003. "I've become something like a couch potato," she told them in 2003. She had turned down a request for a meeting with then Florida Governor Jeb Bush. "I don't want any more politics, no more politics in my life. No more. Had enough," she stated emphatically.[61] Although she had been asked to speak out on various issues in Brooklyn, she had turned down these invitations in favor of staying at home reading political biographies. She had 3,000 books, by her estimation, in her home library. To her dismay she saw the historical moment of the early 2000s as one of "retrogression" in the rights of Black people and women.[62]

Chisholm's health was becoming more challenging due to diabetes-related complications. In 2000, she claimed that she felt like she was thirty years old.[63] But sometime in 2003, Carolyn Smith called her friend and was alarmed at how frail she seemed. Smith began making plans to visit, but Chisholm convinced her that was unnecessary. Portia Dempsey had taken over much of Chisholm's care, and there were also some home health aides visiting the house. While Smith was not quite convinced she did not need to visit, she honored her old boss's wishes. The last time they spoke, Chisholm admitted that she was not feeling well. In 2004, she had several small strokes, necessitating a short stay in a local skilled nursing facility.[64] But she returned to her home for the rest of the year. On New Year's Day, 2005, Chisholm was discovered to have died overnight at home. She was eighty years old.[65]

Five years earlier, filmmaker Shola Lynch had asked her an open-ended question: who is Shirley Chisholm? "Shirley Chisholm is a little black woman who has tremendous confidence in herself," the congresswoman replied in her characteristic third-person style.

A little black woman who relies on her own abilities and talents and versatilities. And pays absolutely no attention to what is said about her. Of course, Shirley Chisholm would like to feel that she's well-loved and she knows that is not true in some instances. Shirley Chisholm would like to know that people can accept her for what she is and she knows that is not so in some instances. But Shirley Chisholm is a down to earth woman who likes people, who enjoys people and who hopes that in her lifetime, she has made some contributions while she was here.[66]

Chisholm had several memorial services. The funeral itself was at Portia and Calvin Dempsey's AME church in Palm Coast, Florida. About 150 mourners packed the small space, including seven members of Congress, multiple Florida state legislators, and other elected officials from around the country. The ninety-two-year-old Rosa Parks, former president Bill Clinton, and former New York mayor David Dinkins sent letters to be read during the two-hour-long service. Muriel Forde was there, too, accepting the flag that had draped her sister's casket after a congressional honor guard had brought it out of the church and a twenty-one-gun salute was given (although there was a moment of hesitation in which Forde thought the flag was about to be handed to Portia Dempsey).[67] After the service, Chisholm's body was sent to Buffalo to be entombed next to Arthur Hardwick at Forest Lawn Cemetery.

The Congressional Black Caucus held its own memorial service February 15 on the Hill, hosted by Barbara Lee and Ed Towns. Nancy Pelosi, then the Democratic leader, and Melvin Watts, CBC chair, welcomed the attendees. Walter Fauntroy, Ron Dellums, Hilda Solis, Charlie Rangel, Eleanor Holmes Norton, Maxine Waters, Hillary Clinton, Chuck Schumer, and Stephanie Tubbs-Jones were all legislators who offered tributes. Carolyn Smith and Chisholm's cousin offered reflections, and an excerpt from the new documentary by Shola Lynch was shown.[68] Memories and accolades poured in: from Carol Moseley Braun, who said that Chisholm inspired her 2004 presidential run, and from Barbara Lee, Maxine Waters, Geraldine Ferraro, Gloria Steinem, Eleanor Smeal, Elijah Cummings, John Lewis, Jesse Jackson, and George H. W. Bush.[69]

On the night of February 7, viewers across the country watched the debut of Lynch's film *Chisholm '72: Unbought and Unbossed* on PBS stations.[70] Chisholm had missed the broadcast by just five weeks.

EPILOGUE
Bring a Folding Chair

Fifty years to the day after Chisholm was sworn in as the first Black congresswoman, a class of fifty-one women of color, including twenty-four Black women, were sworn in for the 116th Congress.[1] Returning to Congress on January 3, 2019, were Chisholm's mentee Barbara Lee; her allies Eleanor Holmes Norton and Maxine Waters; and Yvette Clark, who now occupies the seat representing Crown Heights. Chisholm's old district has been redrawn into two, and House Democratic Caucus Chair Hakeem Jeffries was sworn in for his fourth term representing the part of Brooklyn that includes Bedford-Stuyvesant. And then there were the four first-timers who would become known as The Squad: Ayanna Pressley, a Boston city council member who won a seat out from under the Democratic incumbent; Ilhan Omar from Minneapolis, who immigrated from Somalia as a child; Rashida Tlaib, who won John Conyers's Detroit seat after his retirement in 2017 due to allegations of sexual misconduct; and Alexandria Ocasio-Cortez, a dynamic newcomer who won an upset victory over the incumbent in her Bronx district.

The Squad explicitly embraced Chisholm's Black feminist power legacy and invoked her as they began their terms. Pressley was proud to move into the Longworth office suite that was one of those Chisholm had used during her incumbency and took a photo with Chisholm's official portrait.[2] Ocasio-Cortez decided to wear white during her swearing-in, believing that Chisholm, like suffragists, had worn white, too (Chisholm had in fact worn a red suit trimmed in black velvet). They also embraced Chisholm's focus on redistributing resources and power equitably among the American people. They attracted much media attention with their outspoken progressive rhetoric, which drew a sharp contrast to cautious colleagues who seemed afraid of offending conservatives. And, like Chisholm, they attracted negative attention for refusing to follow existing etiquette within the House that they viewed as interfering with their mission. Future historians will evaluate The Squad and their impact on the political era of their lifetime, but it is without a doubt that they—and so many feminists in and beyond formal politics—were influenced by Shirley Chisholm.

Meanwhile, Chisholm retains enormous symbolic power. Donna Brazile, who presided over the 2016 Democratic National Convention as acting party chair, has often recited a quote that she attributes to Chisholm: "If they don't give you a seat at the table, bring a folding chair."[3] Although Chisholm left no written record of the statement, it has caught on as hers—and it certainly sounds like something she would have said. The *New York Times* declared 2019 the year of Shirley Chisholm, alluding to a new state park in Brooklyn, the planned monument in Prospect Park, as well as available merchandise featuring her name and likeness. When California senator Kamala Harris announced her bid for the Democratic Party presidential nomination—only the third Black woman to do so—she called on Chisholm's legacy. She did so again when she accepted the nomination for vice president of the United States at the 2020 Democratic National Convention.

Chisholm is increasingly invoked as a symbol of universal access to economic and political power. Despite her existence in a body that did not confer birthright power within the United States, Chisholm understood how to wield political power. As she quoted Frederick Douglass more than once, "Power concedes nothing without a demand." She proceeded accordingly, broadcasting her intentions and teaching others to do the same. Her career was a moment of possibility when substantive change seemed like it might happen. Her priorities carried immense resonance in her time as an extension of Black Power and feminism, but they also do in ours. As we confront white supremacist oligarchy and kleptocracy in the twenty-first century, marginalized Americans are looking for ways to deploy our own power on behalf of democracy. Chisholm's life is one road map—or perhaps a North Star—for those who would use politics to recommit the nation to freedom, equality, and justice.

And yet Chisholm's story is a reminder of lost opportunities: the moment of her rise into national politics is now, in hindsight, an apex of political possibility for left, feminist, and antiracist politics. While Black women have more representation within the legislative branch, the policies that they have sought have become more and more elusive. In 1971, Chisholm nearly succeeded in establishing universal childcare in the United States. In 2021, paying for childcare kept working families in poverty. In 1974, she not only helped raise the minimum wage but she also expanded it to more workers. As of this writing, the minimum wage will not have been raised for over a decade and a half. Fiscal policy has realigned priorities away from providing opportunities to all Americans to redistributing wealth upward. Conservative obstruction of legislation that creates more equitable living conditions, coupled with moderates' guardedness, has stifled most bold policy on the left. Chisholm, of course, saw the tide turning and issued warnings, but could only watch with dismay.

With good reason, she had hopes that those she had mentored could carry on the fight, but she was too much of a pragmatist to imagine that power would concede this time. If she had recovered from her strokes enough to watch the young senatorial candidate from Illinois, Barack Obama, keynote the 2004 Democratic National Convention, she might have recognized in his hopeful speech a strain of her own dreams of a coalition made possible because Shirley Chisholm envisioned it. Such is the legacy of Chisholm and her commitment to Black feminist power politics.

ACKNOWLEDGMENTS

I first encountered Shirley Chisholm as a child in my own family's collection of photos. There, in black-and-white with younger versions of my parents, was an elegant, dark-skinned woman with an infectiously broad smile. Mistaking her for my father's sister, he corrected me: "That is Shirley Chisholm. She ran for president, and when you grow up you can, too." My mother had volunteered as the treasurer for Chisholm's presidential bid in Massachusetts, while my father was a young reporter at the time and covered the campaign. But I gave Chisholm little thought, even as I became a historian and wrote my first book, until looking for a biography of her to assign to an undergraduate seminar in 2007. I was perplexed to find that, apart from Chisholm's own two memoirs, *Unbought and Unbossed* and *The Good Fight*, there was no book that I could assign. At least there was a documentary film: Shola Lynch's 2005 *Chisholm '72: Unbought and Unbossed*. But there was no historically grounded biography. Given how well-known she is, and how often she is invoked as a foundational figure, I was intrigued. The result, fifteen years later, is this book.

Carol Skricki has walked beside me at every phase of this undertaking with loving generosity, and it is to her that this book is dedicated. My parents, Steve Curwood and Wendy Zens, first introduced me to Chisholm and the ideas I have come to call Black feminist power politics. They have also been manuscript critics and sources of endless encouragement. Thank you to other family members who have helped sustain me during this process:

From left: Steve Curwood, Wendy Curwood, Jean Rubenstein,
and Shirley Chisholm in Cambridge, Massachusetts, 1972.
Michael Dobo / Dobophoto.com.

Ken Brown, Jennifer Stevens-Curwood, Sarah E. Curwood, Susan Moore, James Curwood, Noah Kabbara, and Amira, Alex, Alya, and Amel Batista. Michael Dobo, a family friend and professional photographer, took photos of both Chisholm and my folks, including the one that started this project and the one that appears on the cover. Thank you also to Taco, Biggie, Glen, Crescent, Hazel, Rufus, Mocha, Clementine, Cowboy, Leo, Zippy, and Zeph. Thank you to my friends and teachers from the equestrian world, Karen Isberg, Megan Edwards, Joan Gariboldi, Heather Gillette, Amy Wise, Lainey Johnson, Linda Strine, and the Strides for Equality Equestrians steering committee and supporters.

Mark Simpson-Vos at the University of North Carolina Press waited for this book's completion with great patience. I am grateful for his wise advice and that of the truly dedicated anonymous reviewers who combed through a very long manuscript with sharp eyes and insightful analysis. The highly skilled and professional UNC Press team has been delightful to work with. Thank you to freelance editor and historian Stephanie Gilmore for stepping in at a crucial revision stage with much-needed perspective that helped me find the core of my argument, and then serving as doula to this very overdue book.

Researching this book was incredibly enjoyable, made even more so by the willingness of so many to help. Thank you to those who have provided information in interviews, archival materials, or both: Muriel Forde, Valarie Bacon, Shirley Downs, Carolyn Jones Smith, Muriel Morisey, Bob Frishman, Jeanne Schinto, Bevan Dufty, Paul Cunningham, Andrea Tracy Holmes, Laura Murphy, Patsy Fleming, Virginia Kerr, Marion Humphrey, and Barbara Lee. I had assistance from many libraries and librarians: Ron Becker at Archibald S. Alexander Library, Special Collections and University Archives, Rutgers, The State University of New Jersey; the Schlesinger Library and Houghton Library at Harvard University; the Department of the Archives of Barbados; and the University of Kentucky Libraries. Thank you to Barbara Winslow for creating and donating to the Shirley Chisholm Collection in the Brooklyn College Special Collections and for being a stalwart supporter of this project for many years. Thank you to Shola Lynch for donating the materials from *Chisholm '72: Unbought and Unbossed* to the collection and, as curator at the Schomburg Center, providing access to the Shirley Chisholm materials in the oral history project tapes.

This book was begun at Vanderbilt University, where I had encouragement from Tracy D. Sharpley-Whiting, Gilman Whiting, Tiffany Patterson, Houston Baker, Hortense Spillers, Trica Keaton, Tara Williams, Dennis Dickerson, and Brooke Ackerly and the Global Feminisms Collaborative. I received fellowships from the Institute for Citizens and Scholars and from the James Weldon Johnson Institute for the Study of Race and Difference at Emory University during work on this project. At Emory, I was grateful for Carol Anderson, Calinda Lee, Mary Frederickson, Leslie Harris, Brett Gadsden, Andra Gillespie, Michan Connor, Sherie Randolph, Scot Brown, Eric Pritchard, Joe Crespino, Pellom McDaniels III, and Randall Burkett. Having moved to the University of Kentucky in 2014, I have been lucky to be a part of the Department of History and the Program in African American and Africana Studies. I thank my friends and colleagues Melynda Price, Amy Taylor, Gerald Smith, Jeremy Popkin, Karen Petrone, DaMaris Hill, Chamara Kwakye, Nazera Wright, Lisa Cliggett, George Wright, David Blackwell, Christian Brady, Anna Bosch, Cristina Alcalde, Mark Kornbluh, Francis Musoni, Steve Davis, Francie Chassen-Lopez, Mel Schroeder-Stein, Vanessa Holden, Kathy Newfont, Nikki Brown, Derrick White, Bert Louis, Eladio Bobadilla, Akiko Takenaka, Pearl James, Crystal Wilkinson, Frank X. Walker, Reinette Jones, Aria Halliday, Regina Hamilton, Kamahra Ewing, JWells, DeBraun Thomas, Michelle Del Toro, Alycia Sullivan, and Tina Hagee. My graduate students have all been sources of inspiration, and Austin Zinkle and Jillean McCommons have assisted with research and provided insights. Bruce Holle did not live to see this book published, but he was a somewhat ruthless cheerleader for it and is a much-missed friend. I also appreciate support and feedback from colleagues at other institutions: Ellen Fitzpatrick, Claude Clegg, LaDale Winling, Will Kuby, Robert Self, and Nan Woodruff. Thank you also to sister-colleagues who have collaborated, read work, and offered affirmation: Erin Chapman, Francoise Hamlin, Nadia Brown, Wendy Smooth, Evelyn Simien, Nikol Alexander-Floyd, Niambi Carter, Zinga Fraser, Kim Warren, the Black Women Biography Genius group (convened by Ashley Farmer and Tanisha Ford), Imaobong Umoren, Amrita Myers, Beverly Guy-Sheftall, Crystal Feimster, Ula Taylor, and my forever teacher Nell Irvin Painter.

Finally, this book was inspired by the ambition and optimism of a young Black girl who thought she could grow up to be president someday. She became a historian instead, but she wrote this story so that Black girls of the present and future would know just how high they can aim.

APPENDIX

Table A.1. Results of the 1972 Democratic primaries

Date	State	Candidate	Number of votes	Percentage of votes
March 7	New Hampshire	Edmund S. Muskie	41,235	46.4
		George S. McGovern	33,007	37.1
		Sam Yorty	5,401	6.1
		Wilbur D. Mills*	3,563	4.0
		Vance Hartke	2,417	2.7
		Edward M. Kennedy*	984	1.1
		Hubert H. Humphrey*	348	.4
		Henry M. Jackson*	197	.2
		George C. Wallace*	175	.2
		Others	1,557	1.8
March 14	Florida	Wallace	526,651	41.6
		Humphrey	234,658	18.6
		Jackson	170,156	13.5
		Muskie	112,523	8.9
		John V. Lindsay	82,386	6.5
		McGovern	78,232	6.2
		Shirley Chisholm	**43,989**	**3.5**
		Eugene J. McCarthy	5,847	.5
		Mills	4,539	.4
		Hartke	3,009	.2
		Yorty	2,564	.2
March 21	Illinois	Muskie	766,914	62.6
		McCarthy	444,260	36.3
		Wallace*	7,017	.6
		McGovern*	3,687	.3
		Humphrey*	1,476	.1
		Chisholm*	**777**	**.1**
		Jackson*	442	–
		Kennedy*	242	–
		Lindsay*	118	–
		Others	211	–
April 4	Wisconsin	McGovern	333,528	29.6
		Wallace	248,676	22.0

Table A.1. *(continued)*

Date	State	Candidate	Number of votes	Percentage of votes
		Humphrey	233,748	20.7
		Muskie	115,811	10.3
		Jackson	88,068	7.8
		Lindsay	75,579	6.7
		McCarthy	15,543	1.4
		Chisholm	**9,198**	**.8**
		Others	2,450	.2
		Yorty	2,349	.2
		Patsy T. Mink	1,213	.1
		Mills	913	.1
		Hartke	766	.1
		Kennedy*	183	–
		Others	559	–
April 25	Massachusetts	McGovern	325,673	52.7
		Muskie	131,709	21.3
		Humphrey	48,929	7.9
		Wallace	45,807	7.4
		Chisholm	**22,398**	**3.6**
		Mills	19,441	3.1
		McCarthy	8,736	1.4
		Jackson	8,499	1.4
		Kennedy*	2,348	.4
		Lindsay	2,107	.3
		Hartke	874	.1
		Yorty	646	.1
		Others	1,349	.2
April 25	Pennsylvania	Humphrey	481,900	35.1
		Wallace	292,437	21.3
		McGovern	280,861	20.4
		Muskie	279,983	20.4
		Jackson	38,767	2.8
		Chisholm*	**306**	–
		Others	585	–
May 2	District of Columbia	Walter E. Fauntroy	21,217	71.8
		Unpledged delegates	8,343	28.2
May 2	Indiana	Humphrey	354,244	47.1
		Wallace	309,495	41.2
		Muskie	87,719	11.7

Table A.1. *(continued)*

Date	State	Candidate	Number of votes	Percentage of votes
May 2	Ohio	Humphrey	499,680	41.2
		McGovern	480,320	39.6
		Muskie	107,806	8.9
		Jackson	98,498	8.1
		McCarthy	26,026	2.1
May 4	Tennessee	Wallace	335,858	68.2
		Humphrey	78,350	15.9
		McGovern	35,551	7.2
		Chisholm	**18,809**	**3.8**
		Muskie	9,634	2.0
		Jackson	5,896	1.2
		Mills	2,543	.5
		McCarthy	2,267	.5
		Hartke	1,621	.3
		Lindsay	1,476	.3
		Yorty	692	.1
		Others	24	–
May 6	North Carolina	Wallace	413,518	50.3
		Terry Sandford	306,014	37.3
		Chisholm	**61,723**	**7.5**
		Muskie	30,739	3.7
		Jackson	9,416	1.1
May 9	Nebraska	McGovern	79,309	41.3
		Humphrey	65,968	34.3
		Wallace	23,912	12.4
		Muskie	6,886	3.6
		Jackson	5,276	2.7
		Yorty	3,459	1.8
		McCarthy	3,194	1.7
		Chisholm	**1,763**	**.9**
		Lindsay	1,244	.6
		Mills	377	.2
		Kennedy*	293	.2
		Hartke	249	.1
		Others	207	.1
May 9	West Virginia	Humphrey	246,596	66.9
		Wallace	121,888	33.1

Table A.1. *(continued)*

Date	State	Candidate	Number of votes	Percentage of votes
May 9	Maryland	Wallace	219,687	38.7
		Humphrey	151,981	26.8
		McGovern	126,978	22.4
		Jackson	17,728	3.1
		Yorty	13,584	2.4
		Muskie	13,363	2.4
		Chisholm	**12,602**	**2.2**
		Mills	4,776	.8
		McCarthy	4,691	.8
		Lindsay	2,168	.4
		Mink	573	.1
May 16	Michigan	Wallace	809,239	51.0
		McGovern	425,694	26.8
		Humphrey	249,798	15.7
		Chisholm	**44,090**	**2.8**
		Muskie	38,701	2.4
		Unpledged delegates	10,700	.7
		Jackson	6,938	.4
		Hartke	2,862	.2
		Others	51	–
May 23	Oregon	McGovern	205,328	50.2
		Wallace	81,868	20.0
		Humphrey	51,163	12.5
		Jackson	22,042	5.4
		Kennedy	12,673	3.1
		Muskie	10,244	2.5
		McCarthy	8,943	2.2
		Mink	6,500	1.6
		Lindsay	5,082	1.2
		Chisholm	**2,975**	**.7**
		Mills	1,208	.3
		Others	618	.2
May 23	Rhode Island	McGovern	15,603	41.2
		Muskie	7,838	20.7
		Humphrey	7,701	20.3
		Wallace	5,802	15.3
		Unpledged delegates	490	1.3
		McCarthy	245	.6
		Jackson	138	.4

Table A.1. *(continued)*

Date	State	Candidate	Number of votes	Percentage of votes
		Mills	41	.1
		Yorty	6	–
June 6	California	McGovern	1,550,652	43.5
		Humphrey	1,375,064	38.6
		Wallace*	268,551	7.5
		Chisholm	**157,435**	**4.4**
		Muskie	72,701	2.0
		Yorty	50,745	1.4
		McCarthy	34,203	1.0
		Jackson	28,901	.8
		Lindsay	26,246	.7
		Others	20	–
June 6	New Jersey	**Chisholm**	**51,433**	**66.9**
		Sanford	25,401	33.1
June 6	New Mexico	McGovern	51,011	33.3
		Wallace	44,843	29.3
		Humphrey	39,768	25.9
		Muskie	6,411	4.2
		Jackson	4,236	2.8
		None of the names shown	3,819	2.5
		Chisholm	**3,205**	**2.1**
June 6	South Dakota	McGovern	28,017	100.0
	Totals	Humphrey	4,121,372	25.8
		McGovern	4,053,451	25.3
		Wallace	3,755,424	23.5
		Muskie	1,840,217	11.5
		McCarthy	553,055	3.5
		Jackson	505,198	3.2
		Chisholm	**430,703**	**2.7**
		Sanford	331,415	2.1
		Lindsay	196,406	1.2
		Yorty	79,446	.5
		Mills	37,401	.2
		Fauntroy	21,217	.1
		Unpledged delegates	19,533	.1
		Kennedy	16,693	.1
		Hartke	11,798	.1
		Mink	8,286	.1

Table A.1. *(continued)*

Date	State	Candidate	Number of votes	Percentage of votes
		None of the names shown	6,269	–
		Others	5,181	–
			15,993,965	

Source: Robert A. Diamond, ed., *Congressional Quarterly's Guide to U.S. Elections* (Washington, D.C.: Congressional Quarterly, Inc., 1975), 346–49.
Note: Alabama and New York had delegate-selection primaries, but delegate preferences were not printed on the ballots. The remaining twenty-eight states held caucuses, not primaries. Percentages do not always add up to 100.00, likely due to rounded figures in the original data.
*Write-in

Table A.2. 1972 Democratic National Convention first ballot results (before shift)

	McGovern	Jackson	Wallace	Chisholm	Sanford
California	271	–	–	–	–
South Carolina	6	10	6	4	6
Ohio	77	39	–	23	3
Canal Zone	3	–	–	–	–
Utah	14	1	–	–	3
Delaware	5.85	6.5	–	0.65	–
Rhode Island	22	–	–	–	–
Texas	54	23	48	4	–
West Virginia	16	14	1	–	4
South Dakota	17	–	–	–	–
Kansas	20	10	–	2	1
New York	263	9	–	6	–
Virginia	33.5	4	1	5.5	9
Wyoming	3.3	6.05	–	1.1	–
Arkansas	1	1	–	–	–
Indiana	26	20	26	1	–
Puerto Rico	7	–	–	–	–
Tennessee	–	–	33	10	–
Pennsylvania	81	86.5	2	9.5	1
Mississippi	10	–	–	12	3
Wisconsin	55	3	–	5	–
Illinois	119	30.5	0.5	4.5	2
Maine	5	–	–	–	–
Florida	2	–	75	2	–
New Hampshire	10.8	5.4	–	–	–
Arizona	21	3	–	–	1
North Carolina	–	–	37	–	27
Massachusetts	102	–	–	–	–
Nebraska	21	3	–	–	–
Georgia	14.5	14.5	11	12	1
North Dakota	8.4	2.8	0.7	0.7	–
Maryland	13	–	38	2	–
New Jersey	89	11.5	–	4	1.5
Vermont	12	–	–	–	–
Nevada	5.75	5.25	–	–	–
Michigan	50.5	7	67.5	3	1
Iowa	35	–	–	3	4
Colorado	27	–	–	7	–
Alabama	9	1	24	–	1
Alaska	6.5	3.25	–	–	–
Hawaii	6.5	8.5	–	1	–
Washington	–	52	–	–	–

Table A.2. *(continued)*

	McGovern	Jackson	Wallace	Chisholm	Sanford
Minnesota	11	–	–	6	–
Louisiana	10.25	10.25	3	18.5	2
Idaho	12.5	2.5	–	2	–
Montana	16	–	–	1	–
Connecticut	30	20	–	–	1
District of Columbia	13.5	1.5	–	0.5	–
Virgin Islands	1	1.5	–	0.5	–
Kentucky	10	35	–	–	2
Missouri	24.5	48.5	–	–	–
New Mexico	10	–	8	–	–
Guam	1.5	1.5	–	–	–
Oregon	34	–	–	–	–
Oklahoma	10.5	23.5	–	1	4
Total	1,728.35	525	381.7	151.95	77.5

Source: Robert A. Diamond, ed., *Congressional Quarterly's Guide to U.S. Elections* (Washington, D.C.: Congressional Quarterly, Inc., 1975).
Note: States are listed in order of balloting.

Table A.3. 1972 Democratic National Convention first ballot results (after shift)

	McGovern	Jackson	Wallace	Chisholm	Sanford
California	271	–	–	–	–
South Carolina	10	9	6	–	6
Ohio	77	39	–	23	3
Canal Zone	3	–	–	–	–
Utah	14	1	–	–	3
Delaware	5.85	5.85	–	0.65	–
Rhode Island	22	–	–	–	–
Texas	54	23	48	4	–
West Virginia	16	14	1	–	4
South Dakota	17	–	–	–	–
Kansas	20	10	–	2	1
New York	278	–	–	–	–
Virginia	37	5	–	2.5	8.5
Wyoming	3.3	6.05	–	1.1	–
Arkansas	1	1	–	–	–
Indiana	28	19	25	–	–
Puerto Rico	7	–	–	–	–
Tennessee	5	–	32	7	–
Pennsylvania	81	86.5	2	9.5	1
Mississippi	23	–	–	2	–
Wisconsin	55	3	–	5	–
Illinois	155	6	–	1	–
Maine	5	–	–	–	–
Florida	4	–	75	1	–
New Hampshire	10.8	5.4	–	–	–
Arizona	22	3	–	–	–
North Carolina	–	–	37	–	27
Massachusetts	102	–	–	–	–
Nebraska	21	3	–	–	–
Georgia	14.5	14.5	11	12	1
North Dakota	10.5	2.1	–	0.7	–
Maryland	13		38	2	–
New Jersey	92.5	11	–	3.5	–
Vermont	12	–	–	–	–
Nevada	5.75	5.25	–	–	–
Michigan	51.5	7	67.5	2	1
Iowa	35	–	–	3	4
Colorado	29	2	–	5	–
Alabama	9	1	24	–	1

Table A.3. *(continued)*

	McGovern	Jackson	Wallace	Chisholm	Sanford
Alaska	6.5	3.25	–	–	–
Hawaii	6.5	8.5	–	1	–
Washington	–	52	–	–	–
Minnesota	43	–	–	4	1
Louisiana	25.75	5.25	3	4	1
Idaho	12.5	2.5	–	2	–
Montana	16	–	–	1	–
Connecticut	30	20	–	–	1
District of Columbia	13.5	1.5	–	–	
Virgin Islands	1	1.5	–	0.5	–
Kentucky	10	35	–	–	2
Missouri	24.5	48.5	–	–	–
New Mexico	10	–	8	–	–
Guam	1.5	1.5	–	–	–
Oregon	34	–	–	–	–
Oklahoma	9.5	23.5	–	2	4
Total	1,864.95	485.65	377.5	101.45	69.5

Source: Robert A. Diamond, ed., *Congressional Quarterly's Guide to U.S. Elections* (Washington, D.C.: Congressional Quarterly, Inc., 1975).
Note: States are listed in order of balloting.

NOTES

ABBREVIATIONS USED IN THE NOTES

BDA   Anglican Church Records, Department of the Archives, Barbados

BG   *Boston Globe*

BOHC   Ralph Bunche Oral History Collection, Moorland-Spingarn Research Center, Howard University, Washington, D.C.

CC   Shirley Chisholm Collection, Brooklyn College, Brooklyn, NY

CD   *Chicago Defender*

CP   Shirley Chisholm Papers, Alexander Library, Rutgers University, New Brunswick, NJ

CPP   Shirley Chisholm Personal Papers, Ormond Beach, FL

CR   *Congressional Record*

CT   *Chicago Tribune*

HMP   Houghton Mifflin Papers, Houghton Library, Harvard University, Cambridge, MA

JP   Thomas Russell Jones Papers, Schomburg Center for Research in Black Culture, New York Public Library, New York, NY

LAS   *Los Angeles Sentinel*

NYAN   *New York Amsterdam News*

NYT   *New York Times*

PC   *Pittsburgh Courier*

PEP   Pam Elam Papers, Special Collections Research Center, University of Kentucky, Lexington

SL   Shola Lynch

SLRI   Schlesinger Library, Radcliffe Institute, Harvard University, Cambridge, MA

SOHP   Schomburg Center for Research in Black Culture, Oral History Project, New York Public Library

WP   *Washington Post*

INTRODUCTION

1. Chisholm told the story of the $42,500 episodes on film in the 1974 documentary *Chisholm: Pursuing the Dream.* "Shirley Chisholm had guts": James Barron, "Shirley Chisholm, 'Unbossed' Pioneer in Congress, Is Dead at 80," *NYT*, January 3, 2005.

2. My framework of considering Chisholm's life in tandem with her status as a symbol was inspired by Nell Irvin Painter's biography *Sojourner Truth*. Another famous Black woman whose humanity is sometimes lost in the mythology of the Strong Black Woman, Truth's biography traces both the lived experience and iconography of its subject.

3. This practice was first theorized by Darlene Clark Hine in 1989 as a form of self-protection from sexual and intimate partner violence. In a recent analysis by Shoniqua Roach, Hine's concept of a culture of dissemblance carries an implicit call for recognizing both Black women's right to privacy and the assaults to which Black women have been vulnerable. See Hine, "Rape and the Inner Lives of Black Women," and Roach, "(Re)turning to 'Rape and the Inner Lives of Black Women.'"

4. Chisholm donated a modest collection to Special Collections and University Archives in the Archibald S. Alexander Library at Rutgers, the State University of New Jersey, in New Brunswick, though it is far smaller than collections of other members of Congress of the same vintage. While she has about four cubic feet of material, her Brooklyn colleague Frank Brasco, for instance, has ten times that amount at the Rutgers repository. The Shirley Chisholm Project on Brooklyn Women's Activism, founded by Barbara Winslow and now run by Zinga Fraser, has collected oral histories and other materials related to Chisholm. Shola Lynch seeded the collection with the papers generated by producing *Chisholm '72*. As a historian of Black women and gender, I am accustomed to cobbling together an archive, and I have been able to do just that: from a series of oral histories I conducted between 2008 and 2012, from published sources such as newspapers and the *Congressional Record*, and from the papers remaining in Chisholm's estate. This latter cache of materials remains privately held by Chisholm's family, who have been generous in allowing me access to the papers that remained in Chisholm's home when she died in 2005.

5. It was not until 2013 that Barbara Winslow published the first scholarly biography of Chisholm, *Shirley Chisholm*. Prior to that point a series of academic articles and chapters appeared. Paula McLain, Niambi Carter, and Michael Brady pioneered contemporary scholarly work on Chisholm with their 2005 article "Gender and Black Presidential Politics." Tammy Brown published "'A New Era in American Politics'" in *Callaloo* in 2008 (and included a chapter about Chisholm in her 2015 *City of Islands*). Joshua Guild wrote "To Make That Someday Come: Shirley Chisholm's Radical Politics of Possibility," in the 2009 edited volume *Want to Start a Revolution?* Julie Gallagher published "Waging '*The Good Fight*': The Political Life of Shirley Chisholm, 1953–1982" in the *Journal of African American History* in 2007, as well as a chapter about Chisholm in her 2012 *Black Women and Politics in New York City* and the useful "How Did Shirley Chisholm, the First African American Woman Elected to the U.S. Congress, Advance an Inclusive Feminist Politics in the 1960s and 1970s?" in *Women and Social Movements in the United States, 1600–2000*. Zinga Fraser, current director of Brooklyn College's Shirley Chisholm Project, completed a 2014 Northwestern University dissertation, "Catalysts for Change: A Comparative Study of Barbara Jordan and Shirley Chisholm." Ellen Fitzpatrick published a chapter, "Shirley Chisholm: 'Shake It Up, Make It Change,'" in *The Highest Glass Ceiling*. Evelyn Simien analyzed Chisholm's decision to run for president in *Historic Firsts* in 2016.

6. Harris, *Black Feminist Politics from Kennedy to Trump*, 9.

7. The first scholarly articulation of the term "intersectionality" was in Kimberlé Crenshaw's 1989 essay "Demarginalizing the Intersection of Race and Sex." Scholars across disciplines have continued to build on the framework. See Collins, *Intersectionality as Critical Social Theory*.

8. Chisholm quoted in Joseph Rosenbloom, "Chisholm Says Voters 'Upset, Disturbed,'" *BG*, April 6, 1972.

9. Author interview with Laura Murphy.

10. Collins, *Black Feminist Thought*, 178–83.

CHAPTER 1

1. SL interview with Shirley Chisholm, April 29, 2003, CC, Box 9, Part 3: 18. The dates and occasions for Chisholm's meetings with Bethune and Roosevelt remain unknown.

2. Like Chisholm, Bethune's symbolic presence has at times eclipsed her actual skills and accomplishments, and there is relatively little scholarly engagement with her work. For an analysis of Bethune's life and ideas in context, see McCluskey and Smith, *Mary McLeod Bethune*, 3–20.

3. For extensive analysis of the planter oligarchy in Barbados and the effects of systemic racism on the lives of Black Barbadians, see Browne, *Race, Class, Politics;* Carter, *Labour Pains; and* James, *Holding Aloft the Banner of Ethiopia*, 15–47, 355.

4. SL interview with Muriel Forde, CC, Box 9, Tape 1; birth certificate of Charles Christopher St. Hill, No. 1684 [Guyana, December 9, 1898], and baptism certificate of Charles Christopher St. Hill, March 14, 1910, Muriel Forde Family Collection, Barbados.

5. For the marriage of Sarah Jane and George, see BDA RL2 v. 23, p. 449 (Mark Crawford, Sarah Jane's father, had a third, somewhat illegible name: Smith or Small); for the birth of Thomas, see BDA RL2 v. 36, p. 420; for the marriage of Thomas and Mary Malvina St. Hill, see BDA RL2 v. 110, p. 354; author interview with Muriel Forde, August 8, 2012.

6. James, *Holding Aloft the Banner of Ethiopia*, 38; Beckles, *A History of Barbados*; see also Beckles and Shepherd, *Caribbean Freedom.*

7. When Mary Malvina died in 1915, she was living on Waverly Road in Christ Church, and she was buried at the same church where she was baptized: Christ Church Parish Church. Burial: BDA RL2 v. 176, p. 377; baptism: BDA RL2 v. 33, p. 225. Charles's brother Thomas Jr. would own a quarter of an acre in Below Rock, too. Thomas Jr. willed his land to Charles, naming Charles's mother-in-law, Emmeline Seale, as the executrix. See last will and testament of Thomas St. Hill, December 27, 1931, Muriel Forde Family Collection, Barbados.

8. Emmeline was not baptized until 1888, and the clerk made an error, writing that she had been born the same year. Her grandmother Angelina Chase (later Hollingsworth) had her baptized at the Christ Church Parish Church. They lived on Lodge Road, near the church atop the hill in Oistins. Angelina was not married at the time, and there is no name of Emmeline's father given. BDA, RL2 v. 97, p. 502.

9. See Burton Lloyd Seale, "Barbados: My Island Home: A Genealogical Survey" (unpublished manuscript, 1992), Shilstone Library, Barbados Museum and Historical Society, Bridgetown, Genealogical Files.

10. The King family on Fitzherbert's paternal side eventually gave their land to the present-day Church of Christ, which stands next to the house Muriel Forde owned and occupied until her death in 2019. David Wiltshire King was baptized in 1858 (author interview with Muriel Forde, August 8, 2012; BDA RL2 v. 27, p. 108). The record of the birth of Ruby Leotta Seale is found in BDA RL2 v. 136, p. 409. She was born on August 31, 1901, and baptized on October 27, 1901. Fitzherbert and Emmeline were married by the rector W. Alleyne Allder. Fitzherbert signed his name as "Fitz Seales." It was witnessed by Edward and William Yard. BDA RL2 v. 137B, p. 342.

11. James, *Holding Aloft the Banner of Ethiopia*, 45.

12. SL interview with Muriel Forde, CC, Box 9, Tape 1: 14–15.

13. Charles St. Hill passport, Muriel Forde Family Collection, Barbados.

14. Marshall, *Triangular Road*, 67; James, *Holding Aloft the Banner of Ethiopia*, 355, 362–63.15. Watkins-Owens, *Blood Relations*, 24–25; Marshall, "Black Immigrant Women in *Brown Girl, Brownstones.*"

16. Marshall, *Triangular Road*, 65–66.

17. Chisholm, *Unbought and Unbossed*, 3. Charles's and Ruby's heights were noted on the passenger manifest of the SS *Munamar* and SS *Pocone*, respectively.

18. Marshall, *Triangular Road*, 65.

19. "List or Manifest of Alien Passengers for the United States Immigration Officer at Port of Arrival," SS *Pocone*, Passengers sailing from Barbados, departed February 28, 1922, arriving at Port of New York March 8, 1922; "Record of Detained Aliens," SS *Pocone*, March 8, 1922, Ellis Island Passenger Database, *www.ellisisland.org* (accessed October 23, 2012); Shirley Chisholm interview, SOHP Tape C-160, Part V.

20. "List or Manifest of Alien Passengers for the United States Immigration Officer at Port of Arrival," *SS Munamar*, Passengers sailing from Antilla, Cuba, departed April 6, 1923, arriving at Port of New York April 10, 1923, Ellis Island Passenger Database, *www.ellisisland.org* (accessed October 23, 2012).

21. Muriel Forde specifically cited Marshall's novel *Brown Girl, Brownstones* and Marshall's essay "From the Poets in the Kitchen," *NYT*, January 9, 1983, as close reflections of her childhood in Brooklyn. Author interview with Muriel Forde, August 8, 2012.

22. Shirley Chisholm interview, SOHP Tape C-160, Part II; Chisholm, *Unbought and Unbossed*, 4.

23. Cohen, "Cultural Diaspora," 23–24.

24. Marshall, *Triangular Road*, 86–87.

25. Watkins-Owens, *Blood Relations*, 66–71; Marshall, *Brown Girl, Brownstones*, 173, 220. Chisholm owned a signed 1959 copy of *Brown Girl, Brownstones* (CPP).

26. "What's in Your Head Can't Take Out": SL interview with Muriel Forde, CC, Box 9, Tape 1: 6–7; author interview with Muriel Forde, August 2, 2012. On the 1:30 Saturday afternoon talks, see Shirley Chisholm interview, SOHP Tape C-160, Part V.

27. Marshall, "From the Poets in the Kitchen."

28. James, *Holding Aloft the Banner of Ethiopia*, 93–119, 258–61; Browne, *Race, Class, Politics*, 90, 96. For more on the transnational world that Caribbean migrants made between the two world wars, see Putnam, *Radical Moves*; Grant, *Negro with a Hat;* and Ewing, *Age of Garvey.*

29. Chisholm, *Unbought and Unbossed*, 76–77.

30. City of New York Office of the City Clerk Certificate of Marriage Registration 10608-1924, "Charles Christopher St. Hill of 1087 Fulton St., Brooklyn, Age 24, married Ruby Leotta Seale of 1800 Dean St., Brooklyn, Age Unknown, on June 29, 1924," Protestant Episcopal Church, N. Peterson Boyd (duplicate certificate of January 3, 1991). Chisholm, *Unbought and Unbossed*, 3.

31. "Muriel St. Hill born Feb 18 1928," certificate no 06885 (birth certificate issued December 20, 1990). Odessa Leotta St. Hill was born in March 1926 (Funeral Order of Service, estate of Muriel S. Forde); Shirley Chisholm interview, SOHP Tape C-160.

32. SL interview with Shirley Chisholm, April 1, 2000, CC, Box 9, Part 1: 33–34.

33. SL interview with Shirley Chisholm, April 29, 2003, CC, Box 9, Part 3: 10.

34. Shirley Chisholm interview, SOHP Tape C-161, Part I; SL interview with Shirley Chisholm, April 1, 2000, CC, Box 9, Part 3: 10, Part 1: 33–34.

35. Marshall, *Brown Girl, Brownstones*, 47.

36. Shirley Chisholm interview, SOHP Tape C-160, Part II; SL interview with Muriel Forde, CC, Box 9, Tape 1: 10.

37. SL interview with Muriel Forde, CC, Box 9, Tape 1: 1–3. Chisholm recalled that this ship was the *Vulcania* in *Unbought and Unbossed*, but she was mistaken; the *Vulcania* was an Italian ship that made transatlantic runs. She also forgot or omitted her four cousins from the trip.

38. "339 Take to Lifeboats as Liner *Vestris* Sinks; Rescuers Find Some Survivors in Darkness; Nine Vessels Scour Sea at Disaster Scene," *NYT*, November 13, 1928, 1; "Survivors on Three Ships: Report All Children and Most of Women Were Swallowed in Sea," *NYT*, November 15, 1928, 1; "Puts *Vestris* Blame on Carey and Crew: Inspector General Hoover's Report on Federal Inquiry Finds Lack of Discipline," *NYT*, December 15, 1928, 4; "*Vestris* Found Unfit; Three Men Accused," *NYT*, August 1, 1929, 1; "Only One of Bodies Still Unidentified: Twelve More, Six Passengers and Six of Crew, Recognized Among 21 and Morgue," *NYT*, November 17, 1928, 3.

39. Mildred Headly's father was James Headly of Harlem, who had arrived in New York two weeks after Charles St. Hill did. See "List or Manifest of Alien Passengers for the United States Immigration Officer at Port of Arrival," SS *Munargo*, Passengers sailing from Antilla, Cuba, departed May 2 [*sic*], 1923, arriving at Port of New York, May 2, 1923, Ellis Island Passenger Database, www.ellisisland.org (accessed October 23, 2012). SL interview with Muriel Forde, CC, Box 9, Tape 1: 3.

40. SL interview with Muriel Forde, CC, Box 9, Tape 1: 1–3.

41. Chisholm, *Unbought and Unbossed*, 5; SL interview with Shirley Chisholm, April 1, 2000, CC, Box 9, Part 1: 32.

42. SL interview with Muriel Forde, CC, Box 9, Tape 1: 18–21.

43. Author interview with Muriel Forde, August 2, 2012; SL interview with Muriel Forde, CC, Box 9, Tape 1: 11–12.

44. SL interview with Shirley Chisholm, April 29, 2003, CC, Box 9, Part 3: 11; Muriel Forde personal communication to author, August 1, 2012.

45. Author interview with Muriel Forde, August 2, 2012; Muriel Forde personal communication to author, August 1, 2012; SL interview with Muriel Forde, CC, Box 9, Tape 1: 17–18.

46. SL interview with Shirley Chisholm, April 29, 2003, CC, Box 9, Part 3: 1–5.

47. Chisholm, *Unbought and Unbossed*, 7–8; Shirley Chisholm interview, SOHP Tape C-160, Part III; SL interview with Muriel Forde, CC, Box 9, Tape 1: 9. Chisholm recalls being just four years old when her grandmother sent her to school, also in *Unbought and Unbossed*, 7.

48. Browne, *Race, Class, Politics*, 4.

49. Chisholm, *Unbought and Unbossed*, 8–9.

50. Gerson, "Building the Brooklyn Machine," 158, 160, 171–72; Lewinson, *Black Politics in New York City*, 81.

51. Chisholm, *Unbought and Unbossed*, 12, 16; Shirley Chisholm interview, SOHP Tape C-160, Part VII.

52. Chisholm, *Unbought and Unbossed*, 13, 20–21; Shirley Chisholm interview, SOHP Tape C-160, Part VI.

53. Lutz, "Legacy of Migration," 100–101; Chamberlain, "Family and Identity," 157.

54. Ol' talk features prominently in the writings of Paule Marshall. See Marshall, *Triangular Road*, 87–89; Marshall, "From the Poets in the Kitchen," *NYT*, January 9, 1983; author interview with Muriel Forde, August 8, 2012.

55. SL interview with Muriel Forde, CC, Box 9, Tape 2: 4–6.

56. The 1940 census listed him as a laborer in the textile industry and said that he made $600 during 1939. Muriel also remembered Charles's deep engagement with politics. "He was very interested in the world outside. Very much so. When a lot of people were not even thinking about what was going on in Europe and so on . . . he was really interested. He used to talk to us a lot around the dinner table. . . . And that all came through his alliance with the Marcus Garvey movement. Marcus Garvey opened the ideas of black people in general." SL interview with Muriel Forde, CC, Box 9, Tape 1: 22–23, 28–29; SL interview with Shirley Chisholm, April 29, 2003, CC, Box 9, Part 3: 16–17; Chisholm, *Unbought and Unbossed*, 14–16, 21.

57. SL interview with Shirley Chisholm, April 29, 2003, CC, Box 9, Part 3: 13; SL interview with Muriel Forde, CC, Box 9, Tape 2: 25–26. In *Unbought and Unbossed*, Chisholm wrote that her school in Brownsville had been PS 84, but in another interview, she gave it as PS 144 (Shirley Chisholm interview, SOHP Tape C-160, Part II). PS 144 was indeed a public school in existence in Brownsville and played an instrumental part in the Ocean Hill–Brownsville strike, so I have concluded this must have been Chisholm's school. See Podair, *Strike that Changed New York*, 74, 81, 88.

58. SL interview with Shirley Chisholm, April 29, 2003, CC, Box 9, Part 3: 9; SL interview with Muriel Forde, CC, Box 9, Tape 1: 27; Chisholm, *Unbought and Unbossed*, 14–15, 18–19.

59. This is the address where the family lived at the time of the 1940 census.

60. Schwartz, *New York Approach*, 51–60; Bloom, *Public Housing that Worked,* 59, 93, 270.

61. SL interview with Shirley Chisholm, April 29, 2003, CC, Box 9, Part 3: 6–7, 15; SL interview with Muriel Forde, CC, Box 9, Tape 2: 7; Shirley Chisholm interview, SOHP Tape C-160, Part IX.

62. Shirley Chisholm interview, SOHP Tape C-161, Parts VII, VIII; Chisholm, *Unbought and Unbossed*, 18.

63. Shirley Chisholm interview, SOHP Tape C-161, Part V.

64. SL interview with Muriel Forde, CC, Box 9, Tape 2: 28–29.

65. SL interview with Muriel Forde, CC, Box 9, Tape 2: 4, Tape 1: 28–31.

66. SL interview with Shirley Chisholm, April 29, 2003, CC, Box 9, Part 3: 6–7, 15; SL interview with Muriel Forde, CC, Box 9, Tape 2: 7; Shirley Chisholm interview, SOHP Tape C-160, Part IX; *Blue and Gold* (Girls' High School yearbook), 1942, CPP.

CHAPTER 2

1. Shirley Chisholm interview, SOHP Tape C-161, Part IX; Chisholm, *Unbought and Unbossed*, 21; Hicks, *Honorable Shirley Chisholm*, 32. Brownmiller's fictionalized account suggests that Shirley willingly chose Brooklyn College. On the college's founding and double admission standard, see Winslow, *Shirley Chisholm*, 21–22.

2. Shirley Chisholm interview, SOHP Tape C-161, Part IX. In this interview, she stated her major as "social work," but the Brooklyn College yearbook (*Broeklundian*, Brooklyn College Library, Archives and Special Collections) of 1947 states her major as sociology. Chisholm, *Unbought and Unbossed,* 23, 26.

3. *Broeklundian*, 1946, 5, Brooklyn College Library, Archives and Special Collections.

4. Leberstein, "Purging the Profs."

5. Chisholm, *Unbought and Unbossed*, 27.

6. Chisholm listed the Harriet Tubman Society, Ipothia, and the Political Science Society in *Unbought and Unbossed* (22–26), but the *Broeklundian* listed Harriet Tubman Society, the Social Science Club, and Ipothia.

7. Chisholm, *Unbought and Unbossed*, 26.

8. Chisholm, *Unbought and Unbossed*, 26.

9. Brownmiller, *Shirley Chisholm*, 49–50.

10. Chisholm, *Unbought and Unbossed*, 24–25.

11. SL interview with Shirley Chisholm, April 1, 2000, CC, Box 9, Part 1: 32; National Visionary Leadership Project interview with Shirley Chisholm, n.d., circa 2000, *www.vision aryproject.com* (accessed December 20, 2021). Chisholm named Stanley Steingut, son of Irwin Steingut and future Speaker of the New York State Assembly, but because the son was deployed in the navy, it was most likely his father. See also Chisholm, *Unbought and Unbossed*, 27.

12. Shirley Chisholm interview, SOHP Tape C-161, Part IX; Chisholm, *Unbought and Unbossed*, 25–26.

13. Chisholm, *Unbought and Unbossed*, 25.

14. Branda Pillors memorandum to Chisholm, May 11, 1981, CP, Box 7, Folder 15. Chisholm handwrote her answer to a question from a journalist writing a story on famous women's worst jobs.

15. This version, titled "Pawn," is undated but was written early in her marriage to Conrad Chisholm. Shirley Chisholm, "Pawn" (unpublished manuscript, n.d.), CPP.

16. Chisholm, *Unbought and Unbossed*, 43–45. Chisholm wrote that this "was the start of a nearly five-year-long romance (44)." However, it only lasted between 1946 and 1948.

17. Chisholm, "Pawn," 2.

18. Chisholm, *Unbought and Unbossed*, 44.

19. Curwood, *Stormy Weather*, 84, 91–107.

20. SL interview with Shirley Chisholm, April 29, 2003, CC, Box 9, Part 3: 19.

21. Shirley Chisholm interview, SOHP Tape C-161, Part X.

22. Shirley Chisholm interview, SOHP Tape C-161, Part X; Chisholm, *Unbought and Unbossed*, 28. Although Chisholm gave the location as 121st Street and Edgecombe, Edgecombe Avenue and 121st Street do not intersect. It seems more likely that the center was where Nancy Hicks recorded its location, 140th Street and Edgecombe, because Mt Calvary Methodist Church is at 116 Edgecombe. See Hicks, *Honorable Shirley Chisholm*, 35–37.

23. Hicks, *Honorable Shirley Chisholm*, 36–37.

24. Brownmiller, *Shirley Chisholm*, 56.

25. Chisholm, *Unbought and Unbossed*, 45; Brownmiller, *Shirley Chisholm*, 57. In contrast to Chisholm, who wrote that she met Conrad while walking to class, Brownmiller reported that she met Conrad, who was a graduate student, at a Saturday night dance.

26. SL interview with Conrad Chisholm, CC, Box 9: 1–6; Chisholm wedding diary, CPP. On Calabar High School, see "About Calabar: History," www.calabaralumni.org/about -calabar/history (accessed October 4, 2013); "Jamaica, Civil Registration 1880–1999," index and images, FamilySearch, https://familysearch.org/pal:MM9.1.1/XN81–59W (accessed October 7, 2013).

27. Chisholm, "Pawn," 2–3.

28. Chisholm, "Pawn," 3–7.

29. Chisholm, "Pawn," 7–8.

30. "Expose BWI Smuggling Plot," *NYAN*, October 16, 1948; "Pleads Guilty to Helping Slip Jamaicans into America," *Baltimore Afro-American*, October 23, 1948.

31. Chisholm, "Pawn," 8–9.

32. Chisholm, *Unbought and Unbossed*, 45.

33. Chisholm, *Unbought and Unbossed*, 45.

34. Chisholm, *Unbought and Unbossed*, 45–46; Chisholm wedding diary; Hicks, *Honorable Shirley Chisholm*, 36–37. SL interview with Conrad Chisholm, CC, Box 9: 24–26. As of September 5, 1950, their address was 974 Park Place according to his naturalization petition in the Index to the Naturalization Petitions for the United States District Court for the Eastern District of New York, 1865–1957. They also lived in a Bedford-Stuyvesant brownstone at 468 Putnam Avenue at one time early in the marriage, according to Chisholm's "Pawn" manuscript.

35. SL interview with Conrad Chisholm, CC, Box 9: 22–23.

36. SL interview with Muriel Forde, CC, Box 9, Tape 1: 33–34.

37. SL interview with Conrad Chisholm, CC, Box 9: 27–30.

38. Author interview with Carolyn Smith, 28.

39. Hicks, *Honorable Shirley Chisholm*, 39–40.

40. Shirley Chisholm interview, SOHP Tape C-160, Part VIII; Hicks, *Honorable Shirley Chisholm*, 41–42. Although Chisholm told this story as something that had happened immediately after her graduation from college in the Schomburg interview, Hicks places the event seven years later, when Chisholm was applying for an administrative position.

41. Hicks, *Honorable Shirley Chisholm*, 44.

42. Shirley Chisholm interview, SOHP Tape C-160, Part XI; Winslow, *Shirley Chisholm*, 28; Brownmiller, *Shirley Chisholm*, 61–62; Hicks, *Honorable Shirley Chisholm*, 43–44.

43. Edward Thompson III interview with Shirley Chisholm, May 2, 1973, BOHC.

CHAPTER 3

1. SL interview with Shirley Chisholm, April 29, 2003, CC, Box 9, Part 3: 20; Hicks, *Honorable Shirley Chisholm*, 47.

2. Woodsworth, *Battle for Bed-Stuy,* 98.

3. Lewinson, *Black Politics in New York City*, 35–45, 58–62; see also Weiss, *Farewell to the Party of Lincoln.*

4. Lewinson, *Black Politics in New York City*, 67–76. For a comprehensive discussion of building Black political power in New York Democratic politics in the 1940s, see Biondi, *To Stand and Fight*, 39–42.

5. Gerson, "Building the Brooklyn Machine," 158, 160, 171–72; Lewinson, *Black Politics in New York City*, 81.

6. Gerson, "Building the Brooklyn Machine," 179–81.

7. Gerson, "Building the Brooklyn Machine," 182–85.

8. Regarding the Scottsboro case, see Goodman, *Stories of Scottsboro*, and Carter, *Scottsboro.*

9. Gerson, "Building the Brooklyn Machine," 186–90.

10. Gerson, "Building the Brooklyn Machine," 216–21.

11. Biondi, *To Stand and Fight*, 51.

12. Lewinson, *Black Politics in New York City*, 84–85; Biondi, *To Stand and Fight*, 54.

13. Biondi, *To Stand and Fight*, 141; *NYAN*, October 29 and September 24, 1949, cited in Biondi, *To Stand and Fight*, 216–17.

14. Winslow, *Shirley Chisholm*, 31; Gerson, "Building the Brooklyn Machine," 229; Vivienne McGuire, "Reminiscences of Wesley McDonald Holder," Oral History Archives, Rare Book & Manuscript Library, Columbia University, 16.

15. Gallagher, *Black Women and Politics*, 93–94, 223n28.

16. Chisholm, *Unbought and Unbossed*, 34; Haskins, *Fighting Shirley Chisholm*, 79–80; Gerson, "Building the Brooklyn Machine," 229, 235, 243; Biondi, *To Stand and Fight*, 216–17; McGuire, "Reminiscences of Wesley McDonald Holder," 17–18.

17. See Gill, *Beauty Shop Politics*; Chisholm, *Unbought and Unbossed*, 31–32. Chisholm implies in *Unbought and Unbossed* that she met Holder during her senior year of college. But in her later Schomburg interview, she recalls meeting him in 1954, and this is also what she told biographer Nancy Hicks. Shirley Chisholm interview, SOHP Tape C-160, Part XIII; Hicks, *Honorable Shirley Chisholm*, 46.

18. Chisholm, *Unbought and Unbossed,* 31.

19. McGuire, "Reminiscences of Wesley McDonald Holder," 1–13; J. Zamgba Browne, "The 'Dean' of Brooklyn Politics Dies at Age 96," *NYAN*, March 27, 1993; "Organizer for Black Politicians Honored," *NYT*, June 27, 1971; Simon Anekwe, "Wesley Holder—The King Maker," *NYAN*, July 10, 1976; Sheila Rule, "Dean of Black Brooklyn Politics a Power at 85," *NYT*, October 10, 1982; Sam Roberts, "Marcus Garvey and Ed Koch in Perspective," *NYT*, May 26, 1988; "Geoghan-Liebowitz Fight Recalls Feud," *Brooklyn Eagle*, September 15, 1935; Gerson, "Building the Brooklyn Machine," 297–300; Gerson, "Bertram L. Baker."

20. Chisholm, *Unbought and Unbossed*, 47.

21. Chisholm, *Unbought and Unbossed*, 34. On page 31 Chisholm says that Skeete first introduced the two in Chisholm's senior year of college.

22. Gerson, "Building the Brooklyn Machine," 225, 236–38, 253.

23. Chisholm, *Unbought and Unbossed*, 29–30.

24. In *Unbought and Unbossed*, she notes the appointment of Magistrate Clarence Wilson, an event that took place in 1953. Chisholm, *Unbought and Unbossed*, 32, 36.

25. Chisholm, *Unbought and Unbossed*, 29–30. Gerson disagrees with Chisholm's analysis, arguing that Chisholm's portrayal of the regulars' hostility to Black political participation is exaggerated. Gerson, "Building the Brooklyn Machine," 245–46.

26. Chisholm, *Unbought and Unbossed*, 29–31.

27. Gerson, "Building the Brooklyn Machine," 256–72.

28. Chisholm, *Unbought and Unbossed*, 35; "Aims and Purposes of the Bedford Stuyvesant Political League," Testimonial Dinner Program, JP, Box 2, Folder 10.

29. Chisholm, *Unbought and Unbossed*, 35.

30. "Election Express" flyer, December 9, 1958, CP, Box 3, Folder 24; Photo, *CD*, August 11, 1956; Jeffrey Gerson interview with Tom Jones, June 10, 1993, JP, Box 1, Folder 6: 12.

31. Daphne Sheppard, "King's Diary," *NYAN*, June 15, 1957.

32. Chisholm, *Unbought and Unbossed*, 39–40; McGuire, "Reminiscences of Wesley McDonald Holder," 21; "Election Express" flyer, December 9, 1958, CP, Box 3, Folder 24. Andrew W. Cooper and Wayne Barrett in "Chisholm's Compromise," *Village Voice*, October 30, 1978, blamed Chisholm's bid for the presidency as the cause of the BSPL's demise.

33. In *Unbought and Unbossed*, she says only that her "interest in politics grew gradually" in the late 1940s and as a result she joined, around the time she enrolled at Columbia, which was 1947, and stayed on "even though I was active in the BSPL." She also asserts that she was already part of the Democratic Club when Mac Holder formed the Bedford-Stuyvesant Political League (BSPL) in 1954. The earlier join date chronology is repeated in Haskins, *Fighting Shirley Chisholm*, 71–73, 76–78, who wrote that Chisholm was already dismissed from the board of directors and her third vice president position before she joined the BSPL. But in a 1968 interview for the SOHP, she said that she did not join the club until 1954 or 1955 (Part XV). This chronology is also echoed by Hicks, *Honorable Shirley Chisholm*, which implies that she did not join the regular club until after her falling-out with Holder in 1958 (48). She was, however, present at a 1956 UADA meeting. See *The Guardian* [UADA newsletter], n.d. [March 1956], JP, "Unsorted Papers" Folder, Box 22.

Chisholm also wrote in *Unbought and Unbossed* (32–34, 36) that she joined the regular club while she was still in her twenties, which would have had to have been by 1954. She told Carlos Russell that she joined when Carney was leader, which would have been from 1953 to 1960 (*Perspectives on Power*, 235). And Holder mentioned Chisholm's election as vice president of the Seventeenth AD Club as occurring in 1956. See Holder, "Election Express" flyer, CP, Box 3, Folder 24. In light of the existing evidence, this author believes that Chisholm was involved in the Seventeenth AD Club from approximately 1954 through 1960.

A critical article about Chisholm written by Andrew Cooper and Wayne Barrett in 1978 suggested that Chisholm's officer status in both clubs was a sign of dishonesty. Cooper and Barrett, "Chisholm's Compromise."

34. Chisholm, *Unbought and Unbossed*, 33; SL interview with Shirley Chisholm, April 29, 2003, CC, Box 9, Part 3: 21, 24–25.

35. Chisholm, *Unbought and Unbossed*, 34; SL interview with Shirley Chisholm, April 29, 2003, CC, Box 9, Part 3: 21.

36. Edward Thompson III interview with Shirley Chisholm, May 2, 1973, BOHC; Chisholm, *Unbought and Unbossed*, 38.

37. Gerson, "Building the Brooklyn Machine," 309.

38. Thomas Jones interview in Russell, *Perspectives on Power*, 46–48, 78; Sewell Chan, "Thomas R. Jones, 93, Judge Who Agitated for Urban Revival," *NYT*, November 1, 2006; Gerson, "Building the Brooklyn Machine," 289–93.

39. Gerson, "Building the Brooklyn Machine," 292–97; Chan, "Thomas R. Jones."

40. Gerson, "Building the Brooklyn Machine," 302–3.

41. Gerson, "Building the Brooklyn Machine," 304–5, 316, 407–8; Russell, *Perspectives on Power*, 46–49.

42. "Minutes of Strategic Committee of Thomas Russell Jones Campaign," April 12, 1960; "Dear Friend," Letter, Thomas R. Jones Committee, March 15, 1960; and Joint Committee for Jones and Rowe press release, May 12, 1960, all in JP, Box 2, Folder 15. Chisholm, *Unbought and Unbossed*, 47; Gerson, "Building the Brooklyn Machine," 318. In her interview with Russell, Chisholm recalled that there were "seven or eight" founding members, and that she "was one of the founders, one of the persons that was involved in pulling together the Unity Democratic Club." Russell, *Perspectives on Power*, 321. Tom Jones, Andrew and Jocelyn Cooper, and Ethelyn Dubin recalled that Chisholm was in the regular Seventeenth AD Club until 1962. Russell, *Perspectives on Power*, 52, 260–61, 350.

43. Thomas R. Jones to Edna Kelly, August 17, 1960, JP, Box 2, Folder 17.

44. Gerson, "Building the Brooklyn Machine," 304–5, 310; Russell, *Perspectives on Power*, 53.

45. Gerson disputes Chisholm's and others' claims that the Seventeenth AD Club was exclusionary to Black participants, and argues that population shifts rather than changing power dynamics caused the eventual succession to Black leadership. He also suggests that personal dislike for Sam Berman pushed many members and voters toward UDC. Gerson, "Building the Brooklyn Machine," 245–46, 261–62, 275, 306, 319.

46. Gerson, "Building the Brooklyn Machine," 309–12; Russell, *Perspectives on Power*, 50; Dawkins, *City Son*, 31.

47. Gerson, "Building the Brooklyn Machine," 313–16.

48. Chisholm, *Unbought and Unbossed*, 47–49; Gerson, "Building the Brooklyn Machine," 316, 320–27; Russell, *Perspectives on Power*, 151.

49. Stokely Carmichael, the future president of the Student Nonviolent Coordinating Committee (SNCC) during its more nationalist years, had visited the UDC at some point. Unity Democrat, April 1961, JP, Box 2, Folder 26; UDC Ledger, JP, Box 2, Folder 31; Thomas R. Jones to Chisholm, December 4, 1962, JP, Box 2, Folder 25; Russell, *Perspectives on Power*, 52.

50. Gerson, "Building the Brooklyn Machine," 333–34, 337, 339, 342–49; Russell, *Perspectives on Power*, 55.

51. Cooper and Barrett, "Chisholm's Compromise."

52. Ruth Goring interview in Russell, *Perspectives on Power*, 162; Gerson, "Building the Brooklyn Machine," 335–36; Mary [Woods] to Thomas R. Jones, September 27, 1962, JP, Box 2, Folder 19.

53. Gerson characterized Chisholm's actions as "nefarious" ("Building the Brooklyn Machine," 352). Still, it is possible that personal dislike for Chisholm, combined with Chisholm's political ambitions, fueled the overwhelmingly negative opinions in Gerson's dissertation. For instance, James Shaw remembered Goring and Chisholm being "at each other's throat [*sic*]" (Gerson, "Building the Brooklyn Machine," 356). See also Gerson, "Building the Brooklyn Machine," 334–36, 340, 352. Cooper strongly disliked her as well (see "Chisholm's Compromise").

54. SL interview with Shirley Chisholm, April 29, 2003, CC, Box 9, Part 3: 9, 25.

CHAPTER 4

1. On Chisholm's grief, see Shirley Chisholm interview, SOHP Tape C-160, Part V. Charles St. Hill passed away in Kings County Hospital of hypertensive cardiovascular disease on June 9, 1960. His occupation was listed as textile worker on the City of New York Certificate of Death no. 156-60-312063. Forde did not see Chisholm as Charles's favorite: "Even though my father was very proud of her . . . he made no distinction between us." He talked to her about politics and "backed her up." They had conversations about events at the political clubhouse. SL interview with Muriel Forde, CC, Box 9, Tape 1.

2. SL interview with Shirley Chisholm, April 1, 2000, CC, Box 9, Part 1: 34–35.

3. SL interview with Conrad Chisholm, CC, Box 9: 9.

4. Chisholm, *Unbought and Unbossed*, 55; SL interview with Shirley Chisholm, April 1, 2000, CC, Box 9, Part 1: 34–35, 15–16. Chisholm told Nancy Hicks that the funds came in the form of a $10,000 life insurance policy. Hicks, *Honorable Shirley Chisholm*, 54.

5. Joshua Guild's dissertation, "You Can't Go Home Again," describes the political landscape in Brooklyn. In the early 1960s conflict over control of the Restoration Corporation pitted older activist women against younger activist men. He uses the periodical *Central Brooklyn Coordinator* and the television show *Inside Bedford-Stuyvesant*, currently housed in New York City's Museum of Television and Radio.

6. See Purnell, *Fighting Jim Crow in the County of Kings*.

7. "Key Women's Banquet of All Nations Sunday," *NYAN*, September 29, 1962; "Key Women Will Salute Jackie Robinson's Mom," *NYAN*, September 8, 1962; "Key Women to Fete Aged Folk," *NYAN*, June 8, 1962; Daphne Sheppard, "Kings Diary," *NYAN*, September 21, 1963, October 19, 1963, and February 29, 1964; Gallagher, *Black Women and Politics*, 165.

8. For comprehensive historical examinations of the CBCC, see Woodsworth, *Battle for Bed-Stuy*, and Guild, "You Can't Go Home Again." "Operation Teens Rapidly Nearing Goals for Summer," *NYAN*, July 26, 1958; Simon Anekwe, "Stuyvesant Leaders Score City Planning Officials," and "Say Commission Moves Is Step in Right Direction," *NYAN*, September 29 and October 6, 1962; "Council Elects Officers," *NYAN*, November 10, 1962.

9. Woodsworth, *Battle for Bed-Stuy*, 100, 119, 126, 140–43; "Leaders Praise Big 3," *NYAN*, October 20, 1962; "Council to Act on Boro Problems," *NYAN*, February 3, 1963; Dave Hepburn, "Say They Were Bypassed in Labor Setup," *NYAN*, June 15, 1963; "Council Wants Slum Housing Clearance," *NYAN*, March 16, 1963; "Council's Youth Services Project Gets in Motion," *NYAN*, August 24, 1963; "B'klyn Council Gets $66,000 Youth Grants: CBCC To Study Youth Problems; Get A Home," *NYAN*, November 9, 1963; "CBCC to Study Youth Problems, Get a Home," *NYAN*, February 1, 1964; Guild, "You Can't Go Home Again," 289–90.

10. Gerson, "Building the Brooklyn Machine," 357; Russell, *Perspectives on Power*, 68, 71–72. Later in her career, Jones was also displeased with Chisholm's performance in Congress, hinting that she was merely paying lip service to solving problems of education, drugs, and youth unemployment. Russell, *Perspectives on Power*, 82. On Jones disappearing, see Russell, *Perspectives on Power*, 204.

11. Russell, *Perspectives on Power*, 196.

12. Shirley Chisholm interview, SOHP Tape C-161.

13. SL interview with Shirley Chisholm, April 29, 2003, CC, Box 9, Part 2: 2–4, .

14. Shirley Chisholm interview, SOHP Tape C-161; *NYAN*, photo, May 16, 1964; "Results of City Primary Contests," *NYT*, June 3, 1964.

15. Orleck, "Introduction," 2, 4.

16. Sundquist, *On Fighting Poverty*, 7–8, 19–29; Patterson, *America's Struggle against Poverty*, 99–111; Mittelstadt, *From Welfare to Workfare*, 148

17. Shirley Chisholm, "Law of the Land," *NYAN*, September 5, 1964.

18. Dittmer, *Local People*, 285–302.

19. Dawkins, *City Son*, 40; Pat Carter interview in Russell, *Perspectives on Power*, 194, 206; Andrew and Jocelyn Cooper interview in Russell, *Perspectives on Power*, 248, 256.

20. Purnell, *Fighting Jim Crow in the County of Kings*, 249–78, 280–82; Abu-Lughod, *Race, Space, and Riots*, 171–81. Abu-Lughod's account relies extensively on Shapiro and Sullivan, *Race Riots*. On activism against police violence prior to the 1964 riots, see Guild, "You Can't Go Home Again," 286.

21. Guild, "You Can't Go Home Again," 289–90, 292–94; Dawkins, *City Son*, 41.

22. "3 Men to Face Jury for Attempted Holdup," *Buffalo Courier-Express*, July 9, 1957, CPP.

23. Advertisement, *NYAN*, October 10, 1964; "Citizens Union Rates Candidates in City for State Senate and Assembly," *NYT*, October 11, 1964; "2nd Masonic District Holds Dinner Dance," *NYAN*, October 31, 1964; "State and City Tally for President, Senator, and Other Offices," *NYT*, November 5, 1964; Rosemarie Tyler Brooks, "Washington Round-Up," *CD*, November 23, 1964; "6 in Assembly, 3 in Senate," *NYAN*, November 7, 1964.

24. Daphne Sheppard, "The Lady Is Also a First," *NYAN*, November 7, 1964; Andrew Cooper, Letter to the Editor, *NYAN*, December 5, 1964.

25. "Bedford-Stuyvesant Moves to Elect Its Congressman: Legislators Pledge Gerrymander Help," *NYAN*, December 26, 1964.

26. Thomas P. Ronan, "Steingut Still Considering Race for Speaker's Post in Assembly," *NYT*, November 18, 1964; Layhmond Johnson, "Democrats Split over Leadership," *NYT*, December 4, 1964; Ronald Sullivan, "Buckley Is Key," *NYT*, December 23, 1964.

27. Ronald Sullivan, "Session Is Opened," *NYT*, January 7, 1965; Chisholm, *Unbought and Unbossed*, 56–57; R. W. Apple Jr., "Travia Elected Speaker; G. O. P. Vote Again Decisive as Steingut Is Defeated," *NYT*, February 5, 1965.

28. "Legislators Are Split over Party Leadership" and "Look Closely!" (editorial), *NYAN*, January 2, 1965; "'I Took No Bribe' Baker!" *NYAN*, January 30, 1965, "Vote for Assembly Chief," *NYT*, February 5, 1965.

29. Chisholm, *Unbought and Unbossed*, 57–60. Barbara Winslow identifies this colleague as Howard Shakin, a former Brooklyn College classmate of hers, in *Shirley Chisholm*, 47.

30. Ruth Goring interview in Russell, *Perspectives on Power*, 162; Allan Fagan interview, SOHP Tape C-165.

31. Shirley Chisholm, "The Albany Impasse of 1965," *NYAN*, April 10, 1965.

CHAPTER 5

1. A large and growing body of work on the so-called second wave exists: Evans, *Personal Politics* and *Tidal Wave*; Echols, *Daring to Be Bad*; Gilmore, *Feminist Coalitions*.

2. "4 Negro Chairmen in Legislature," *NYAN*, February 20, 1965; "Set Talks on Addiction," and "Youths Launch Drive," *NYAN*, February 27, 1965; Photo, *NYAN*, April 3, 1965; "5-Block Cleanup Operation," *NYAN*, June 26, 1965; "Parents and Teachers Discuss Children," *NYAN*, April 10, 1965; "News of Churches," *NYAN*, June 5, 1965; "Community Supports Woman Lawmaker," *NYAN*, April 24, 1965. On doing homework in the DeWitt Clinton Hotel, see Chisholm, *Unbought and Unbossed*, 62; Hicks, *Honorable Shirley Chisholm*, 55; and Winslow, *Shirley Chisholm*, 49, who quotes Brownmiller, *Shirley Chisholm*, 76–77.

3. Dinkins and Knobler, *A Mayor's Life*, 59.

4. On her exclusion from fellow legislators' socializing, see Winslow, *Shirley Chisholm*, 49, and Haskins, *Fighting Shirley Chisholm*, 100–101.

5. Chisholm, *Unbought and Unbossed*, 63; Brownmiller, *Shirley Chisholm*, 80. On the figure of the Jezebel, see *White, Ar'n't I a Woman?*, 29, and Collins, *Black Feminist Thought*, 81–83.

6. *Shirley Chisholm's Report from Albany*, March 1965, CP, Box 3 Folder 23.

7. *Shirley Chisholm's Report from Albany*, April 1965, CP, Box 3, Folder 23; Gallagher, "How Did Shirley Chisholm," Docs. 2A, 2C, and 2D.

8. "Coordinating Council Warring on Poverty," *NYAN*, December 5, 1964; "Events Today," *NYT*, June 3, 1965; Guild, "You Can't Go Home Again," 296–99.

9. See Curwood, *Stormy Weather*, 70, and Lindquist, *Race, Social Science, and the Crisis of Manhood*, 180. Reportedly, after receiving a copy of the report, one "high administration official" said, "Pat, I think you've got it." Rainwater and Yancey, *Moynihan Report and the Politics of Controversy*, 16.

10. Rainwater and Yancey, *Moynihan Report and the Politics of Controversy*, 18–32; Self, *All In the Family*, 4.

11. U.S. Department of Labor, Office of Policy Planning and Research, *Negro Family (the Moynihan Report)*, 3–4; Self, *All in the Family*, 4.

12. U.S. Department of Labor, Office of Policy Planning and Research, *Negro Family (the Moynihan Report)*, 29–42.

13. See, for example, Wallace, *Black Macho and the Myth of the Superwoman*.

14. Edward Thompson III interview with Shirley Chisholm, May 2, 1973, BOHC, 22–24.

15. Letters to the editor, *NYAN*, August 21 and 28, 1965.

16. Haskins, *Fighting Shirley Chisholm*, 107; Thomas P. Ronan, "US Court Voids State's 1961 Law on Redistricting," *NYT*, May 11, 1967.

17. Haskins, *Fighting Shirley Chisholm*, 107–8; "Wright Wins in Brooklyn," *NYAN*, September 18, 1965; "A Salute to Him" (photo), *NYAN*, December 18, 1965.

18. Guild, "You Can't Go Home Again," 274–81; Woodsworth, *Battle for Bed-Stuy*, 200; Steven J. Roberts, "Redevelopment Plan Set for Bedford-Stuyvesant," *NYT*, December 11, 1966; Ralph Blumenthal, "Brooklyn Negroes Harass Kennedy," *NYT*, February 5, 1966; Susan Brownmiller, "This Is Fighting Shirley Chisholm," *NYT*, April 13, 1969.

19. Dinkins and Knobler, *A Mayor's Life*, 61; Daphne Sheppard, "Kings Diary," *NYAN*, March 5 and April 9, 1966; "B-S Again Raps Gypsy Cab Ban," *NYAN*, January 1, 1966; Richard Witkin, "Negro Democrats Seek 2nd Place on State Ticket," *NYT*, September 3, 1966.

20. Peter Kihss, "Farmer Rejects Liberals' 2d Spot," *NYT*, September 5, 1966.

21. Ralph Blumenthal, "Assembly Passes School Book Plan," *NYT*, May 17, 1966.

22. "Flouting the Constitution," *NYT*, May 18, 1966. Chisholm would continue to argue against aid to religious or private K–12 schools in the U.S. Congress, as she explained to Kuriansky and Smith (see *Shirley Chisholm*, 16).

23. "Legislators Will Amend, or Kill Education Bill," *NYAN*, May 28, 1966; Will Lissner, "Travia Drafting Bill to Aid City U.," *NYT*, May 16, 1966.

24. Dinkins and Knobler, *A Mayor's Life*, 60; Ralph Blumenthal, "Sutton Criticizes Bill to Aid City U.," *NYT*, June 7, 1966; "Honoring a Champion of Equality," CUNY Newswire, November 11, 2011, www.cuny.edu/mu/forum/2011/12/02/honoring-a-champion-of -equality/#.VO9TAVdJa1E.gmail (accessed February 27, 2015).

25. Rules Committee Introductory No. 6124, June 8, 1966, Assembly Introductory Record, *New York Legislative Record and Index*, Vol. 189, 1966; Ralph Blumenthal, "Full Aid Specified for City University in New State Bill," *NYT*, June 9, 1966; Nelson Rockefeller, Message of June 22, 1966, *New York State Legislative Annual*, 1966, 332–33; Sidney Schanberg, "Rockefeller Backs Bill to Aid City U.," *NYT*, June 22, 1966; Sidney Schanberg, "Bill Voted to Aid City University," *NYT*, June 23, 1966; Sidney Schanberg, "City U. Expansion Voted in Albany," July 2, 1966; Leonard Buder, "Program for Poor at City U. Expands," *NYT*, August 12, 1966; "YIA Boasts Most College Enrollees," *NYAN*, October 29, 1966; "Low Dropout Rate in SEEK Program," *NYAN*, December 30, 1967.

26. The Assembly Introductory Record in the *New York Legislative Record and Index*, vols. 188–91, documents thirty-eight single-author bills that Chisholm introduced.

27. Chisholm, *Unbought and Unbossed*, 61; Brownmiller, *Shirley Chisholm*, 81–83; "City University Opens Two New Dorms for Disadvantaged," *NYAN*, September 23, 1967. According to Brownmiller, 8,000 students were served by SEEK in its first two years, 1966 and 1967. But the total was about half of that, suggesting that Brownmiller's information was incorrect—or that she exaggerated the total in her eagerness to tell a triumphant story.

28. Hicks, *Honorable Shirley Chisholm*, 55–59; Richard Johnston, "Legislative Panel Will Investigate Sale by L. I. U. and Dismissals at St. John's," *NYT*, October 10, 1967; M. A. Farber,

"L. I. U. Asked to Sell Center to Unions," *NYT*, October 24, 1967; "Legislative Unit Urges L. I. U. Split," *NYT*, December 13, 1967; "City U. Said to Drop L. I. U. Purchase Plan," *NYT*, May 3, 1968.

29. "Boroites Urge Support for Negro Congressman," *NYAN*, April 9, 1966.

30. Lewis, DeVine, Pitcher, and Martis, *Digital Boundary Definitions of United States Congressional Districts, 1789–2012, Districts 89 and 90*; Sokol, *All Eyes Are Upon Us*, 138.

31. Lewis, DeVine, Pitcher, and Martis, *Digital Boundary Definitions of United States Congressional Districts, 1789–2012*.

32. "Bedford-Stuyvesant Is Called a Victim of Gerrymandering," *NYT*, June 24, 1966; "U.S. Panel to Hear Charge of Poll Bias in Brooklyn Line-Up," *NYT*, August 11, 1966.

33. Decision, August 9, 1966, and Docket for *Cooper v. Power*, 66C 594 (EDNY, 1967).

34. Andrew W. Cooper and Wayne Barrett, "Chisholm's Compromise," *Village Voice*, October 30, 1978, 42.

35. *Wells v. Rockefeller*, 273 F. Supp 984 (SDNY 1967); Sidney Zion, "A Suit by Liberals Attacks State Congressional Lines," *NYT*, June 6, 1966.

36. Thomas P. Ronan, "US Court Voids State's 1961 Law on Redistricting" and "Excerpts from the Reapportionment Decision," *NYT*, May 11, 1967; Thomas P. Ronan, "Liberals Ask Special Legislature on Redistricting," *NYT*, May 12, 1967.

37. Decision, March 21, 1968, *Cooper v. Power*, 66C 594 (EDNY, 1967).

38. Cooper and Barrett, "Chisholm's Compromise." Cooper's version of events is also told in Dawkins, *City Son*, 52–55., and Cooper's 2002 obituary also credited his suit with creating the Twelfth District. Thomas J. Lueck, "Andrew W. Cooper, 74, Pioneering Journalist," *NYT*, January 30, 2002.

39. Ethel Payne, "Women Show Their Mettle in Politics," *CD*, June 28, 1967; "Negro Elected Officials to Meet Here," *CD*, September 26, 1967.

40. Purnell, *Fighting Jim Crow in the County of Kings*, 100.

41. Self, *All In the Family*, 107–11.

42. Assembly Introductory Record, *New York Legislative Record and Index*, vols. 188 and 190 (1965, 1967); 1965 Assembly bills 1932, 2558, 2560, 3603; 1967 Assembly bills 1248, 1250. See also Gallagher, "How Did Shirley Chisholm," Documents 2A–3A.

43. Self, *All In the Family*, 112–13.

44. Richard L. Madden, "Governor Accepts June 20 Primary," *NYT*, April 12, 1967; Assembly Introductory Record, *New York Legislative Record and Index*, Assembly Bill 2568, reprinted in Gallagher, "How Did Shirley Chisholm," Document 3A.

45. Rosen, *World Split Open*, 73–75, 78.

46. Shirley Chisholm to Betty Friedan, April 20, 1967, Enclosed: "Meet Your State Assemblywoman," circa 1967, original pub. unknown, Betty Friedan Papers, Box 42, Folder 1476, SLRI.

47. Chisholm to Friedan, April 20, 1967.

48. NOW Press Release, April 4, 1967, Tamiment Library, New York University, reprinted in Gallagher, "How Did Shirley Chisholm?," Document 3B; New York State Temporary State Commission in the Constitution Convention, Report 14: Individual Freedoms, March 31, 1967, in *Proceedings of the Constitutional Convention of the State of New York*, vol. 12 (Index), 63 (1967); "Propose Sex Bias End Here," *NYAN*, June 10, 1967; G. Donald Covington, "Constitutional Convention Briefs," *NYAN*, May 20, 1967; "NY State Constitution Urged to Bar Job Bias," *NYAN*, July 22, 1967; Thomas Ronan, "Charter Report on Schools Filed," *NYT*, April 28, 1967.

49. NOW Press Release, April 4, 1967; Jean Faust, letter to delegates, April 18, 1967; and Jean Faust, letter to Hulan Jack, May 25, 1967, Tamiment Library, New York University,

reprinted in Gallagher, "How Did Shirley Chisholm," Documents 3B–3D. Proposal II was introduced as Proposition 450 by Dollie Robinson. *Proceedings of the Constitutional Convention of the State of New York*, Vol. 7, 302 (May 23, 1967).

50. *Proceedings of the Constitutional Convention of the State of New York*, Vol. 2, 187–88 (June 12, 1967).

51. Photo, *NYAN*, April 15, 1967.

52. Robinson and Jones, on the other hand, were both in favor. Ultimately, the new charter was defeated in a 3–1 margin on Election Day. Viewed as too partisan and slanted toward Democrats, and unwilling to vote for the entire package, most Republicans and many Democrats voted against it. Richard L. Madden, "Committee Votes to Offer Charter in Single Package," *NYT*, September 26, 1967; Editorial, "The Convention Comes Up With an 'All or Nothing' Constitution," *NYT*, October 1, 1967; Thomas P. Ronan, "Negro Delegates Praise Charter," *NYT*, October 20, 1967; Thomas A. Johnson, "State's NAACP Opposes the War and New Charter," *NYT*, October 23, 1967; George Barner, "Now Up to Voters: Controversy, Confusion, Bias, Politics Surround New Charter," *NYAN*, November 4, 1967; "Charter Vote 3–1," *NYT*, November 8, 1967.

53. Payne, "Women Show Their Mettle."

54. It is not clear whether Sutton also convened this conference. "Negro Elected Officials to Meet Here."

CHAPTER 6

1. Podair, *Strike that Changed New York*, 9–12.

2. Podair, *Strike that Changed New York*, 5, 8.

3. "More Black Candidates Eye Congress," *CD*, March 16, 1968.

4. "200 Black Democrats Eyeing Nov. 5 Election," *CD*, October 10, 1968.

5. See Perlstein, *Nixonland*, and Cohen, *American Maelstrom*.

6. Joseph, *Waiting 'til the Midnight Hour*, 205; Marable and Mullings, *Let Nobody Turn Us Around*, xix–xx; Joseph, "Black Power Movement," 753–54, 755; Lee, "Guns, Death, and Better Tomorrows."

7. Edward Thompson III interview with Shirley Chisholm, May 2, 1973, 22–24, BOHC.

8. SL interview with Susan Brownmiller, CC, Box 9: 6.

9. 389 U.S. 421 (1967).

10. 66C 594 (EDNY, 1967).

11. Daphne Sheppard, "Kings Diary," *NYAN*, January 13, 1968; Susan Brownmiller, "This Is Fighting Shirley Chisholm," *NYT*, April 13, 1969; Thomas Fortune interview in Russell, *Perspectives on Power*, 294.

12. Woodsworth, *Battle for Bed Stuy*, 254–55; Simon Anekwe, "Bed-Stuy Launches Afro-Congress Drive," *NYAN*, June 3, 1967; Daphne Sheppard, "Afro-American Congressman Search Brings Many Choices," *NYAN*, December 2, 1967; Daphne Sheppard, "CNC Picks Shirley Chisholm for Congress Race," *NYAN*, December 30, 1967.

13. Shirley Chisholm interview, SOHP Tape C-161; Chisholm, *Unbought and Unbossed*, 66.

14. Sheppard, "CNC Picks Shirley Chisholm for Congress Race."

15. Etheline Dubin interview in Russell, *Perspectives on Power*, 352–54.

16. Chisholm, *Unbought and Unbossed*, 67; Haskins, *Fighting Shirley Chisholm*, 114; Martin Tolchin, "Brooklyn Shifts, So Do Democrats," *NYT*, June 12, 1968. Shirley Chisholm interview, SOHP Tape C-161; White, *Making of the President 1968*, 67; Allan Fagan interview, SOHP Tape C-165. Chisholm would also say later that the slogan came about because she was approached by multiple people who wanted to give her campaign money but "for a price." See SL interview with Shirley Chisholm, April 29, 2003, CC, Box 9, Part 1: 4.

17. Gallagher, *Black Women and Politics*, 126, 127, 130; Ethel Payne, "Jesse Jackson Emerging as Poor Campaign's Hero," *CD*, June 1, 1968; "Bertram Baker Backs Mrs. Robinson in Race," *NYAN*, March 30, 1968; "Robinson Stock Up; Rev. Taylor Falls In," *NYAN*, April 20, 1968; Tolchin, "Brooklyn Shifts, So Do Democrats"; Winslow, *Shirley Chisholm*, 62; Shirley Chisholm interview, SOHP Tape C-161; Daphne Sheppard, "Kings Diary," *NYAN*, April 20, 1968.

18. Farmer, *Lay Bare the Heart*, 311–14.

19. Brownmiller, "This Is Fighting Shirley Chisholm"; Thomas P. Ronan, "Farmer Will Run for a House Seat," *NYT*, March 9, 1968; John Kifner, "G.O.P. Names James Farmer for Brooklyn Race for Congress," *NYT*, May 20, 1968; "Farmer Receives GOP Congressional Nod," *NYAN*, May 25, 1968; Hudson Reed interview, SOHP Tape C-162; "Farmer's Chances are Good," *NYAN*, June 1, 1968.

20. George Barner, "Albany to Consider Powell Seat," *NYAN*, January 6, 1968.

21. Ethel Payne, "So this Is Washington," *CD*, October 19, 1968.

22. Lewis, DeVine, Pitcher, and Martis, *Digital Boundary Definitions of United States Congressional Districts, 1789–2012.*

23. Martin Arnold, "A Brooklyn Negro May Go to Congress," *NYT*, February 23, 1968; "Rush Congressional Districting," *NYT*, February 24, 1968; Sokol, *All Eyes Are Upon Us*, 149–50; "Gerrymander Forever!" *NYT*, February 27, 1968; Sidney Schamberg, "State Reshapes House Districts; Court Fight Due," *NYT*, February 27, 1968; "No Blues in Albany," *NYAN*, March 9, 1968.

24. White, *Making of the President 1968*, 66; Farber, *Chicago '68*, 86, 92–93, 99–100.

25. "Holder Chisholm Coordinator," *NYAN*, March 23, 1968; Chisholm, *Unbought and Unbossed*, 68; Haskins, *Fighting Shirley Chisholm*, 115; Brownmiller, *Shirley Chisholm*, 95; Hicks, *Honorable Shirley Chisholm*, 67; Kuriansky and Smith, *Shirley Chisholm*, 4.

26. SL interview with Victor Robles, CC, Box 10, Part 1: 6–7.

27. Allan Fagan interview, SOHP Tape C-165.

28. Daphne Sheppard, "Who's Who in the Upcoming Primary Elections June 18," *NYAN*, June 8, 1968.

29. SL interview with Conrad Chisholm, CC, Box 9: 9–10.

30. "Fortune Backs Chisholm for Congressional Seat," *NYAN*, January 13, 1968.

31. "Chisholm Endorsed Again," *NYAN*, February 24, 1968; Earl Caldwell, "3 Negroes Weigh House Race in New Brooklyn 12th District," *NYT*, February 26, 1968.

32. Brownmiller, *Shirley Chisholm*, 86–87; Hicks, *Honorable Shirley Chisholm*, 63–64; Shirley Chisholm interview, SOHP Tape C-161.

33. Annie Bowen interview, SOHP Tape C-163.

34. Daphne Sheppard, "Kings Diary," *NYAN*, May 11, 1968.

35. Annie Bowen interview, SOHP Tape C-163.

36. No endorsement by James Brown has been found. "Chisholm Endorsed Again"; Annie Bowen interview, SOHP Tape C-163.

37. Daphne Sheppard, "First Black Woman in Congress Looms: Chisholm Gets Labor Backing for Congress," *NYAN*, November 2, 1968.

38. Marshall Dubin interview, SOHP Tapes C-164 and C-165.

39. Marshall Dubin interview, SOHP Tapes C-164 and C-165.

40. Marshall Dubin interview, SOHP Tapes C-164 and C-165; Judith Berek interview, SOHP Tape C-164.

41. Daphne Sheppard, "Kings Diary," *NYAN*, January 20, 1968; Sady Sullivan interview with Pete Beveridge, Brooklyn Historical Society, http://cb*BG*.brooklynhistory.org/ohms /viewer.php?cachefile=bhs_2011.019.032_Beveridge-Pete_20120523_x_0.xml (accessed August 12, 2015.

42. "CNC Blasts-Off Chisholm Campaign," *NYAN*, January 27, 1968.

43. Photo, *NYAN*, February 3, 1968.

44. Daphne Sheppard, "Kings Diary," *NYAN*, March 2, 1968.

45. Chisholm, *Unbought and Unbossed*, 74; Daphne Sheppard, "Kings Diary," *NYAN*, April 13, April 20, and June 1, 1968.

46. Sokol, *All Eyes Are Upon Us*, 139, 146–50, Celler quoted on 146.

47. Brownmiller, "This Is Fighting Shirley Chisholm"; Haskins, *Fighting Shirley Chisholm*, 127–28.

48. Shirley Chisholm interview, SOHP Tape C-161; Brownmiller, "This Is Fighting Shirley Chisholm"; Hicks, *Honorable Shirley Chisholm*, 66.

49. Sokol, *All Eyes Are Upon Us*, 152; Shirley Chisholm interview, SOHP Tape C-161.

50. "Rocky's Programs Leading to Unrest, 7 Negroes Charge," *WP*, March 15, 1968; "Criticize Middle Class," *NYAN*, June 8, 1968; "Warns on Extremists, Militants Taking Over," *NYAN*, June 8, 1968; "Wrong Group," *NYAN*, June 15, 1968. Chisholm's speech about the Black middle class was at the National Association of College Women, later the National Association of University Women, a Black-led organization parallel to the American Association of University Women. She gave a similar speech at a luncheon honoring a former Panamanian ambassador the next day.

51. Shirley Chisholm interview, SOHP Tape C-161; Dolores Alexander, "Women Seeking to Alter the Power Structure," *Newsday*, January 24, 1968; Brownmiller, "This Is Fighting Shirley Chisholm."

52. John Kifner, "Abortion Reform Dies in Assembly," *NYT*, April 4, 1968; Leroy Aarons, "New Abortion Bill Filed in N.Y. Legislature," *WP*, December 14, 1968.

53. Brownmiller, *Shirley Chisholm*, 103–4; Daphne Sheppard, "Bed-Stuy Primary Round-Up Shows Sweep by New Breed," *NYAN*, June 29, 1968; Daphne Sheppard, "Ex-Teacher Aims at Congress Seat," *NYAN*, June 22, 1968; figures cited are from Hicks, *Honorable Shirley Chisholm*, 67, and "Results of Contests for Senatorial Nominations and Other Primary Contests," *NYT*, June 20, 1968; Chisholm, *Unbought and Unbossed*, 70.

54. Sheppard, "Ex-Teacher Aims at Congress Seat"; Martin Tolchin, "Negro Support of O'Dwyer Weighed," *NYT*, June 22, 1968; Sydney H. Schanberg, "Seymour and Celler Win House Contests," *NYT*, June 19, 1968; Martin Arnold, "Variety of Issues Debated in Primary Races Here," *NYT*, May 26, 1968.

55. Sheppard, "Bed-Stuy Primary Round-Up Shows Sweep by New Breed"; George Barner, "Elected Democrats Issue Warning to Party," *NYAN*, February 3, 1968; Haskins, *Fighting Shirley Chisholm*, 120; Brownmiller, "This Is Fighting Shirley Chisholm."

56. Chisholm, *Unbought and Unbossed*, 71–72; Brownmiller, "This Is Fighting Shirley Chisholm"; Shirley Chisholm interview, SOHP Tape C-162; Hicks, *Honorable Shirley Chisholm*, 68–69; Etta Lynch and DeLinda Harrell, "Only Through Faith" (unpublished manuscript), CPP.

57. "Democrats Will Name Black Woman," *NYAN*, August 3, 1968; Richard Madden, "New York Caucus Puts Off Clash," *NYT*, August 27, 1968; Richard Madden, "English Is Elected as National Committeeman," *NYT*, August 28, 1968; Brownmiller, "This Is Fighting Shirley Chisholm," and *Shirley Chisholm*, 106; "Shirley Chisholm Dem Nat'l Committeewoman," *NYAN*, August 31, 1968; Chisholm interview, SOHP Tape C-162.

58. SL interview with Conrad Chisholm, CC, Box 9: 10–11; Shirley Chisholm interview, SOHP Tape C-162; Chisholm, *Unbought and Unbossed*, 73.

59. Chesly Manly, "Nixon Rejects Hubert Bid," *NYT*, September 3, 1968.

60. Manly, "Nixon Rejects Hubert Bid"; "Humphrey in Talks With Party Chiefs," *NYT*, September 3, 1968.

CHAPTER 7

1. "Governor Endorses James Farmer Race," *NYT*, October 7, 1968.

2. "Campaign Opened by James Farmer," *NYT*, July 26, 1968; "Farmer Kickoff Rally," *NYAN*, July 27, 1968; John Kifner, "Farmer and Woman in Lively Bedford-Stuyvesant Race," *NYT*, October 26, 1968; "Black Poll Shows Rocky Favorite over Nixon, Humphrey," *NYAN*, July 20, 1968; "Farmer Hits Nixon; Will Be Independent," *NYAN*, July 13, 1968; "Urges Elks to Start Own Insurance," *NYAN*, September 7, 1968.

3. Farmer, *Lay Bare the Heart*, 311–14.

4. Sokol, *All Eyes Are Upon Us*, 151–52.

5. Shirley Chisholm interview, SOHP Tape C-162.

6. SL interview with Shirley Chisholm, April 29, 2003, CC, Box 9, Part 1.

7. SL interview with Shirley Chisholm, April 29, 2003, CC, Box 9, Part 1: 1–2.

8. Allan Fagan interview, SOHP Tape C-165.

9. Chisholm, *Unbought and Unbossed*, 76; Hudson Reed interview, SOHP Tape C-163; Allan Fagan interview, SOHP Tape C-165; Marshall Dubin interview, SOHP Tape C-162; Susan Brownmiller, "This Is Fighting Shirley Chisholm," *NYT*, April 13, 1969.

10. Clayton Knowles, "Bonds Proposed to Aid Poor Areas," *NYT*, September 1968; *Shirley Chisholm's Report from Albany*, April 1965, CP, Box 3, Folder 23; "Farmer Wants More Insurance Action," *NYAN*, September 28, 1968.

11. Andrew and Jocelyn Cooper interview in Russell, *Perspectives on Power*, 252; Carmichael and Hamilton, *Black Power*.

12. Guild, "You Can't Go Home Again," 330–31.

13. Podair, *Strike that Changed New York*, 81–89. On the ideology of community control, see 36–47.

14. Podair, *Strike that Changed New York*, 101–45.

15. "Criticize Middle Class," *NYAN*, June 8, 1968; "Warns on Extremists, Militants Taking Over," *NYAN*, June 8, 1968; "Wrong Group," *NYAN*, June 15, 1968.

16. Sara Slack, "Two Congressional Candidates Back Bd.," and "'Children Victims': Farmer," *NYAN*, September 28, 1968; Gene Currivan, "Citizens' Group Formed to Keep Decentralization in Ocean Hill," *NYT*, October 4, 1968.

17. Purnell, *Fighting Jim Crow in the County of Kings*, 236–37; Abubadika, *Education of Sonny Carson*, 182–86.

18. Ollie Leeds, Letter to the Editor, *NYAN*, September 14, 1968; Marshall Dubin interview, SOHP Tape C-164.

19. SL interview with Shirley Chisholm, April 29, 2003, CC, Box 9, Part 1: 2–3; Kifner, "Farmer and Woman in Lively Bedford-Stuyvesant Race." "Of course we have to help black men": quoted in Brownmiller, "This Is Fighting Shirley Chisholm," 107.

20. Chisholm, *Unbought and Unbossed*, 74–75.

21. "Congress: Brooklyn, Queens," *NYT*, October 17, 1968; Kifner, "Farmer and Woman in Lively Bedford-Stuyvesant Race."

22. Kifner, "Farmer and Woman in Lively Bedford-Stuyvesant Race"; Editorial, "For Congress," *NYAN*, October 26, 1968.

23. Pauli Murray to Esther Peterson, October 29, 1968, Esther Peterson Papers, Box 27, Folder 507, SLRI. Murray sent her letter to Irene Barlow, Catherine East, Dr. Gardiner C. Means and Caroline F. Ware, Patricia R. Harris, Mary Gresham, Mildred Fearing (Murray's sister), Maida Springer-Kemp, Aileen Hernandez, Marchette and Joy Chute, Eva Schindler-Rainman, Mary Eastwood, Caroline Bird, Eleanor Rawson, Laura Bornholdt, Phineas Indritz, Dorothy Kenyon, Marritt and Ann Hedgeman, Morag Simshak, B. Ruth Powell, Edna and Gene Rostow, Dorothy Haener, Marie Rodell, and Henry and Ruth Morganthau

("sent Jim Farmer contribution early in his campaign but were shocked at the news story"); Pauli Murray Papers, Box 119, Folder 2130, SLRI.

24. Pauli Murray to Shirley Chisholm, October 30, 1968, Pauli Murray Papers, Box 119, Folder 2130, SLRI. It is unclear whether Murray and Chisholm ever met; a September 15, 1969, letter from Murray to Chisholm suggests that they had not yet met at that point. Pauli Murray Papers, Box 119, Folder 2130, SLRI.

25. On Chisholm's debating skills, see Hicks, *Honorable Shirley Chisholm*. See also Shirley Chisholm interview, SOHP Tape C-162, and "Chisholm, *Unbought and Unbossed*, 77.

Chisholm's words at the Emma Lazarus meeting have been preserved by a remarkable series of audio recordings of the last weeks of the campaign. In October and November of 1968, cognizant of the historic nature of the campaign, the Schomburg Center for Research in Black Culture of the New York Public Library sent an unnamed oral historian into the streets. The result was a set of recordings of rallies and speeches, as well as conversations with Chisholm's campaign team and anonymous interviews with attendees and bystanders. In addition to the Emma Lazarus Federation speech, recordings from a rally against George Wallace, a Democratic rally, and a Chisholm-Farmer debate survive. Chisholm speech to the Emma Lazarus Federation, SOHP Tape C-167; Joyce Antler, "Emma Lazarus Federation of Jewish Women's Clubs," *Jewish Women's Archive Encyclopedia*, http://jwa.org/encyclopedia/article/emma-lazarus-federation-of-jewish-womens-clubs (accessed January 8, 2016).

26. Chisholm speech to the Emma Lazarus Federation, SOHP Tape C-168.

27. Shirley Chisholm interview, SOHP Tape C-162.

28. Hicks, *Honorable Shirley Chisholm*, 72–73.

29. Farmer- Chisholm debate at Community Church, SOHP Tape C-166.

30. Chisholm speech at anti–George Wallace rally, SOHP Tape C-169; "Anti-Wallace Rally at Friendship," *NYAN*, October 19, 1968.

31. Advertisement, *NYT*, October 27, 1968; Edmund Muskie speech at anti–George Wallace rally, SOHP Tape C-167.

32. Chisholm speech at Newman Memorial Church, [October 30, 1968], SOHP Tape C-167.

33. James Farmer street rally, SOHP Tape C-169.

34. Shirley Chisholm street rally, SOHP Tape C-170.

35. Bedford-Stuyvesant voter interviews, SOHP Tape C-170.

36. "Endorses Farmer," *NYAN*, November 2, 1968.

37. Hicks, *Honorable Shirley Chisholm*, 73–74.

38. Guthrie and Jennings, *Statistics for the Presidential and Congressional Election*.

39. Daphne Sheppard, "Chisholm Overwhelms Farmer in House Race," *NYAN*, November 9, 1968; George Todd, "Farmer Graciously Bows to First Lady," *NYAN*, November 9, 1968; "Make Way for Mrs. Chisholm!" *NYAN*, November 7, 1968; Richard L. Madden, "Mrs. Chisholm Defeats Farmer, Is First Negro Woman in House," *NYT*, November 6, 1968; Brownmiller, *Shirley Chisholm*, 109–10.

40. Sheppard, "Chisholm Overwhelms Farmer."

41. SOHP Tape C-165.

42. "To Honor Chisholm at Ninth Annual Tea," *NYAN*, November 23, 1968; "Poor to Honor Shirley," *NYAN*, December 30, 1968; Daphne Sheppard, "1,000 Honor Shirley at Victory Salute Gala," *NYAN*, December 28, 1968; Brownmiller, *Shirley Chisholm*, 114–15; Hicks, *Honorable Shirley Chisholm*, 74.

43. Edith Evans Asbury, "Freshman in Congress Won't Be Quiet," *NYT*, November 6, 1968; regarding the house and the piano, see Brownmiller, *Shirley Chisholm*, 115; SL interview with Muriel Forde, CC, Box 9, Tape 1: 33.

44. Brownmiller, *Shirley Chisholm*, 112, 113; Esther Peterson to Shirley Chisholm, November 12, 1968, Esther Peterson Papers, Box 5, Folder 152, SLRI. Emphasis in original.

45. Asbury, "Freshman in Congress Won't Be Quiet."

46. Beatrice Berg, "Brooklyn Freshman," *WP*, December 8, 1968.

47. Chisholm interview, SOHP Tape C-162.

48. Berg, "Brooklyn Freshman"; David Holmstrom, "Shirley Chisholm Goes to Congress," *Christian Science Monitor*, December 24, 1968.

CHAPTER 8

1. Kuriansky and Smith, *Shirley Chisholm*, 20.

2. Chisholm, *Unbought and Unbossed*, 88–90.

3. Photo, *CD*, January 6, 1969.

4. Chisholm, *Unbought and Unbossed*, 100–101; Elizabeth Shelton, "Shirley's Still Fighting," *WP*, January 4, 1969; "Feminist to Be Honored," *WP*, December 27, 1968; Ethel Payne, "So This Is Washington DC," *CD*, January 11, 1969.

5. SL interview with Shirley Chisholm, April 29, 2003, CC, Box 9, Part 4: 7; Chisholm, *Unbought and Unbossed*, 78–9.

6. Regarding the $42,500 salary, see this book's introduction. SL interview with Shirley Chisholm, April 29, 2003, CC, Box 9, Part 4: 15–18; SL interview with Victor Robles, CC, Box 10, Part 1: 19–20; ABC news interview with Chisholm, aired January 29, 1969, Vanderbilt Television News Archives, Nashville, TN.

7. Shirley Chisholm and Marcia Ann Gillespie, "The Unsinkable Shirley Chisholm," *Essence*, November 1972, 81.

8. The initial staff was in part Carolyn Jones (later Smith), Shirley Downs, Travis Cain, Alice Pannell, Pauline Baker, and Karen McRorey. As of October 1970 she also employed Pat Watkins as Downs's legislative secretary, Pauline Middleton and Joan Middleton as general secretaries, and Sylvia Taylor as a receptionist. Chisholm Constituent Newsletter [October 1970], CP, Box 4, Folder 9; SL interview with Shirley Chisholm, April 29, 2003, CC, Box 9, Part 4: 2–3, 9–10; Chisholm, *Unbought and Unbossed*, 79–80; Pauli Murray to Shirley Chisholm, September 15, 1969, Pauli Murray Papers, Folder 2130, SLRI; Susan Brownmiller, "This Is Fighting Shirley Chisholm," *NYT*, April 13, 1969; SL interview with Carolyn Smith, CC, Box 10, Part 1.

9. Author interview with Carolyn Smith, 2–3, 5, 15; SL interview with Carolyn Smith, CC, Box 10, Part 1.

10. SL interview with Carolyn Smith, CC, Box 10, Part 1.

11. SL interview with Carolyn Smith, CC, Box 10, Part 1.

12. Brown and Lemi, *Sister Style*, 7.

13. Author interview with Carolyn Smith, 11, 26; author interview with Andrea Tracy Holmes, Part 1: 4.

14. Beatrice Berg, "The Brooklyn Freshman," *WP*, December 8, 1968.

15. Author interview with Shirley Downs, July 16, 2012, Part 2: 8.

16. SL interview with Carolyn Smith, CC, Box 10, Part 1; Ben A. Franklin, "City of Fear and Crime: Nixon Faces Capitol Test," *NYT*, January 22, 1969; Diggs Datrooth, "National Hotline," *CD*, February 1, 1969; Brownmiller, "This Is Fighting Shirley Chisholm"; "Chisholm Apartment Ransacked," *WP*, January 15, 1969.

17. SL interview with Carolyn Smith, CC, Box 10, Part 2: 23; author interview with Shirley Downs, July 16, 2012, Part 2: 8; Mary Weigers, "Home from the Hill: Where the New Congressmen Live," *WP*, June 8, 1969; Brownmiller, "This Is Fighting Shirley Chisholm." Pharr was a 1946 graduate of Florida A&M College (now University) and had earned a graduate degree from McGill University in Montreal, Canada. She rose to several administrative

posts at Freedman's Hospital. Her house was on Farragut Street NW, near the intersection with Kansas Avenue in the neighborhood of Petworth. See Kanya Stewart, "FAMU Receives $266,000 from Washington, D.C. Alumni for Scholarships," *FAMU Forward*, July 1, 2016, www.famunews.com/2016/07/famu-receives-266000-from-washington-d-c-alumni-for-scholarships/; Ancestry.com, U.S. Public Records Index, 1950–1993, vol. 1, www.ancestry.com/search/collections/1788 (accessed December 18, 2017).

18. "Brilliant": SL interview with Shirley Chisholm, April 29, 2003, CC, Box 9, Part 3: 11; SL interview with Carolyn Smith, CC, Box 10, Part 1; Brownmiller, "This Is Fighting Shirley Chisholm."

19. SL interview with Shirley Downs, CC, Box 10: 19; author interview with Shirley Downs, July 16, 2012, Part 1: 9–12.

20. SL interview with Shirley Downs, CC, Box 10: 4–5, 12; author interview with Shirley Downs, March 24, 2016.

21. Kuriansky and Smith, *Shirley Chisholm*, 19.

22. SL interview with Shirley Downs, CC, Box 10: 20–22; author interview with Shirley Downs, July 16, 2012, Part 1: 21, and Part 2: 7; author interview with Shirley Downs, March 24, 2016.

23. Author interview with Shirley Downs, July 16, 2012, Part 1: 13, 16–19; author interview with Carolyn Smith, 1.

24. SL interview with Shirley Downs, CC, Box 10: 12–13, 16–17, 33; author interview with Shirley Downs, July 16, 2012, Part 2: 2.

25. Author interview with Laura Murphy; SL interview with Shirley Downs, CC, Box 10: 24; author interview with Shirley Downs, July 16, 2012, Part 1: 7, 28.

26. Author interview with Carolyn Smith, 12.

27. SL interview with Shirley Downs, CC, Box 10: 13–15, 30; author interview with Carolyn Smith, 6, 28.

28. Author interview with Andrea Tracy Holmes, Part 1: 1–2; Chisholm Constituent Newsletter [October 1970], CP, Box 4, Folder 9; Kuriansky and Smith, *Shirley Chisholm*, 21.

29. Author interview with Carolyn Smith, 14–17; SL interview with Carolyn Smith, CC, Box 10, Part 2: 10–11.

30. Author interview with Andrea Tracy Holmes, Part 1: 5.

31. Author interview with Carolyn Smith; Chisholm, *Unbought and Unbossed*, 101.

32. "When I'm disturbed": "Congress' Pepperpot," *BG*, July 31, 1970; SL interview with Carolyn Smith, CC, Box 10, Part 2: 5–6; SL interview with Conrad Chisholm, CC, Box 9: 12–14; Shirley Chisholm Reports to Constituents [October 1970], CP, Box 4, Folder 9.

33. SL interview with Shirley Chisholm, April 29, 2003, CC, Box 9, Part 3; SL interview with Carolyn Smith, CC, Box 10, Part 2: 7; SL interview with Victor Robles, CC, Box 10, Part 1: 8.

34. Author interview with Carolyn Smith, 4; author interview with Shirley Downs, July 16, 2012, Part 1: 5.

35. Elizabeth Shelton, "Shirley Chisholm: Our Fair Share Now," *WP*, April 28, 1969; SL interview with Carolyn Smith, CC, Box 10, Part 1.

36. "Shirley Chisholm's First Chi Visit This Saturday," *CD*, June 11, 1969. Chisholm also inserted the text of her speech into the 115th *CR* (1969), 15972–73.

37. Kuriansky and Smith, *Shirley Chisholm*, 19.

38. "Chisholm Urges Women's Revolt," *CD*, February 18, 1969.

39. "Negro-Student Coalition Seen Saving America," *WP*, April 17, 1969.

40. "Shirley Chisholm Says Blacks Fed Up With Racism," *CD*, June 16 1969.

41. Doris E. Saunders, "Gentlewoman in Congress Packs a Mighty Punch!" *CD*, June 17, 1969.

42. SL interview with Shirley Downs, CC, Box 10: 15–16.

43. Payne, "So This Is Washington."

44. Clay, *Just Permanent Interests*, 112–15.

45. Richard L. Madden, "Powell Seated, Fined $25,000 and Denied Seniority," *NYT*, January 4, 1969; Payne, "So This Is Washington DC"; Daphne Sheppard, "Chisholm Charges Bias against Powell's Power," *NYAN*, July 12, 1969; 115th *CR* (1969), 15–34; Chisholm, *Unbought and Unbossed*, 109.

46. Norman C. Miller, "Negroes in the House Join Forces to Speak for Black Interests," *Wall Street Journal*, March 31, 1970.

47. SL interview with Shirley Downs, CC, Box 10: 23; author interview with Shirley Downs, July 16, 2012, Part 1: 7; Chisholm, *Unbought and Unbossed*, 109–10.

48. Chisholm, *Unbought and Unbossed*, 149–50.

49. Chisholm, *Unbought and Unbossed*, 81; Richard L. Madden, "House Farm Panel to Get Urban View," *NYT*, January 18, 1969; William Greider, "A Tree in Brooklyn; A Gold Pitchfork," *WP*, January 26, 1969.

50. "House Negro Rids Self of Unwanted Job," *CT*, January 30, 1969.

51. Chisholm, *Unbought and Unbossed*, 82–83.

52. Richard Madden, "Mrs. Chisholm Gets Off House Farm Committee," *NYT*, January 30, 1969; Chisholm, *Unbought and Unbossed*, 83–85.

53. Chisholm, *Unbought and Unbossed*, 86, 87–88; ABC, CBS, and NBC evening news broadcasts, January 29, 1969, Vanderbilt Television News Archive.

54. "Shirley Chisholm Bucks Hill System," *WP*, January 30, 1969; Chisholm, *Unbought and Unbossed*, 85.

55. "Rep. Chisholm Defies Rule," *CD*, February 15, 1969.

56. "Mrs. Chisholm Is Elected to a Veterans Committee," *NYT*, February 19, 1969; Chisholm, *Unbought and Unbossed*, 86–87.

57. Payne, "So This Is Washington."

58. SL interview with Carolyn Smith, CC, Box 10, Part 1; "Rep. Shirley Chisholm Makes U.S. History," *Philadelphia Tribune*, February 4, 1969; "Chisholm Dislikes Comm. Post," *Cleveland Call and Post,* February 8, 1969; "Congresswoman Chisholm Rejects Committee Post," *LAS*, February 13, 1969; "Mrs. Chisholm Balks at Seat on Ag. Committee," *PC*, February 8, 1969.

59. SL interview with Susan Brownmiller on Shirley Chisholm, CC, Box 9: 11, 13–15, 18.

60. Brownmiller, "This Is Fighting Shirley Chisholm."

61. "Celebrities Deck Their Trees (With and Without Holly)," *NYT*, November 26, 1969; "Mrs. Chisholm's Tree Enjoys Star Company," *CD*, December 1, 1969.

62. Metcalf, *Up from Within*; George Metcalf to Shirley Chisholm, March 6, 1970, and March 20, 1970, and Chisholm to Metcalf, March 12, 1970, George Metcalf Papers, Box 1, Folder 12, Schomburg Center for Research in Black Culture, New York Public Library; Brownmiller, *Shirley Chisholm*; Hicks, *Honorable Shirley Chisholm*; Haskins, *Fighting Shirley Chisholm*.

CHAPTER 9

1. Rustin, "From Protest to Politics."

2. Author interview with Andrea Tracy Holmes, Part 2: 7.

3. Self, *All in the Family*, 22–23.

4. Self, *All in the Family*, 4, 17.

5. Author interview with Shirley Downs, July 16, 2012, Part 1: 27.

6. Chisholm's essays were "The Speech against the War"; "How I View Congress"; "Facing the Abortion Question"; "The Lindsay Campaign and Coalition Politics"; "Black Politicians

and the Black Minority"; "A Government that Cannot Hear the People"; "Women and Their Liberation"; and "Youth and America's Future."

After its first published articulations in the 1830s, Black feminist thought continued to develop in the United States. In the late 1960s and early 1970s, Black feminism reconceived itself within the context of the civil rights movement and second wave feminism. Several scholars have traced this historical development in addition to Springer (*Living for the Revolution*), Roth (*Separate Roads to Feminism*), and Cooper (*Beyond Respectability*). Joy James and T. Denean Sharpley-Whiting have documented transformations within Black feminism since the 1830s and have noted a "transformative Black feminism" marked by engagement with Black women's sexuality, intersectionality, and political, economic, and social roles in the late 1960s and early 1970s. See their "Editors' Introduction," *The Black Feminist*, 3–4. Deborah Gray White has documented the transformations across and within Black feminism since the turn of the twentieth century and the emergence of the National Black Feminist Organization in *Too Heavy a Load*. Beverly Guy-Sheftall similarly observes "the beginning of a clearly defined Black women's liberation movement" signaled by Toni Cade Bambara's *The Black Woman*—an antisexist, antiracist, and anti-imperialist anthology from 1970. See Guy-Sheftall, *Words of Fire*, 14–15. See also Taylor, "Historical Evolution of Black Feminist Theory and Praxis."

7. For the historical development of Black feminism, see Roth, *Separate Roads to Feminism;* Breines, *Trouble between Us*; and Taylor, "Historical Evolution of Black Feminist Theory and Praxis," 245, 246. For demands and strategies of welfare rights activists, see Nadasen, Mittelstadt, and Chappell, *Welfare in the United States,* and Orleck, *Storming Caesar's Palace*, 108–15.

8. Taylor, "Negro Women Are Great Thinkers," and "Introduction" (to Amy Jacques Garvey section), 89–90; Springer, *Living for the Revolution*, 44.

9. Beal, "Double Jeopardy," in Guy-Sheftall, *Words of Fire*, 146–56 (originally published in Bambara, *Black Woman*, 109–22); Taylor, "Historical Evolution of Black Feminist Theory and Praxis."

10. House Joint Res. 736, 115th *CR* (1969), 13341, and Extensions of Remarks, 115th *CR* (1969), 13380–81. Chisholm revised these remarks into the essay "Women and Their Liberation" in *Unbought and Unbossed*, 178.

11. Chisholm, testimony before the Special Subcommittee on Education, on Section 805 of H.R. 16098, July 1, 1970, U.S. House of Representatives, *Discrimination against Women*, 617–22. She also submitted the text of her speech, "The 51% Minority," presented in January 1970 to NOW's Conference on Women's Employment, as evidence to the subcommittee (907–15). This speech was nearly identical to Chisholm's "Racism and Antifeminism," *Black Scholar*, January–February 1970.

12. Convened by Edith Green (D-OR), the hearings were concerned with a bill that would outlaw discrimination against women in any program receiving federal funds or employed in education; expand the Equal Pay Act; and add sex to the categories covered by the U.S. Commission on Civil Rights. Testimony of Shirley Chisholm and of Frankie Freeman, July 1, 1970, U.S. House of Representatives, *Discrimination against Women*.

13. Shirley Chisholm, "A Visiting Feminine Eye," *McCall's,* August 1970 (reprinted in Gallagher, "How Did Shirley Chisholm," Document 7); "Cong. Shirley Chisholm Says Her Race Much Less a Drawback than Her Sex," *Atlanta Daily World*, July 23, 1970; "Sex Bias Worse than Racial in Politics—Rep. Chisholm," *BG*, July 22, 1970.

14. Randolph, *Florynce "Flo" Kennedy*, 2.

15. Springer, *Living for the Revolution*, 26; Hartmann, *Other Feminists*, 178.

16. Shirley Chisholm, "Women in Elective Office," in Norton, *Women's Role in Contemporary Society*, 63; 116th *CR* (1970), 1717.

17. She addressed Brooklyn chapters of both organizations, and met with their national heads, in 1970. Unity member Etheline Dubin was a chair of the Black Independent Women's Political League chapter in Brooklyn. Untitled photograph of Chisholm with Dorothy Height, *Atlanta Daily World*, April 5, 1970; "Chisholm Keynotes Program," *NYAN*, March 14, 1970.

18. "N.Y. Congresswoman Shirley A. Chisholm Arrives in Los Angeles; Busy Schedule Ahead," *LAS*, January 8, 1970; "Chisholm Speaks; Displays Broad Knowledge of Issues," *LAS*, January 15, 1970.

19. Rudy Johnson, "United Black Women Organize and Consider Racism Issue in Mayoral Race," *NYT*, September 14, 1969; "Black Women in Politics," *NYAN*, August 30, 1969.

20. House Joint Res. 736, 115th *CR* (1969), 13341. The ERA would not be passed by the House until 1971, however, after Martha Griffiths gathered enough signatures on a discharge petition to get it out of the Judiciary Committee. See Hartmann, "Equal Rights Amendment."

21. Shirley Chisholm, "Notes on Minority Women and the Equal Rights Amendment" speech [n.d.; ca. 1970], CP, Box 2, Folder 32.

22. Mac Holder to Nancy Dowling, May 27, 1970, Women's Equity Action League Records, Box 1, Folder 54, SLRI.

23. 115th *CR* (1969), 36765-67, 38592-94.

24. Margaret A. Hagen to Shirley Chisholm, January 22, 1970, and Shirley Chisholm to Delores Alexander, February 25, 1970, Delores Alexander Papers, Box 8, Folder 7, SLRI. On NOW's endorsement of Chisholm for the Judiciary Committee, see *off our backs*, May 30, 1970.

25. "Sponsoring Sisters," *NYT*, August 23, 1970.

CHAPTER 10

1. Perlstein, *Nixonland*, 360, 370-73, 388. Indeed, many legislators, including Chisholm and other Black congresspeople, were on Nixon's first infamous "enemies list." See "The First Enemies List," EnemiesList.info, www.enemieslist.info/list1.php (accessed June 20, 2016).

2. Edward Thompson III interview with Shirley Chisholm, May 2, 1973, 18, BOHC.

3. "Local Women Back Shirley Chisholm on War," *Philadelphia Tribune*, March 25, 1969; David R. Boldt, "Women Protesters March on Capitol," *WP*, March 27, 1969.

4. 115th *CR* (1969), 7765.

5. Chisholm, *Unbought and Unbossed*, 93-97; "Butter, Not Guns: Rep. Chisholm," *CD*, March 27, 1969; Marjorie Hunter, "White House Pickets, House Speakers Score War," *NYT*, March 27, 1969; Boldt, "Women Protestors March on Capitol"; Mary McGrory, "Kennedy Silent in ABM Tiffs," *BG*, March 21, 1969; NBC News, March 26, 1969, Vanderbilt Television News Archive.

6. Chisholm, *Unbought and Unbossed*, 98-99; "Rep. Chisholm Takes Guns, Butter Stand," *CD*, March 27, 1969; Women Strike for Peace Advertisement, *NYT*, April 14, 1969.

7. Hendrick Smith, "Lodge Sees Hope for a New Phase in Vietnam Talks," *NYT*, May 16, 1969; 115th *CR* (1969), 12726.

8. "Remove Band-Aids," *CD*, March 27, 1969.

9. Marjorie Hunter, "Mitchell Opposed to New Laws on Student Unrest," *NYT*, May 21, 1969.

10. John W. Finney, "45 in Congress Seek Rein on Military," *NYT*, June 2, 1969; "Report Warns Congress Must Check Military Colossus," *BG*, June 2, 1969; "Blacks Join Attack on War Units," *CD*, June 2, 1969; Bernard D. Nossiter, "Military Priority Assailed," *WP*, June 2, 1969.

11. Claudia Levy, "20 Seized in Hill War Protest," *WP*, June 12, 1969.

12. "Arrest 15 Viet War Protesters in Washington," *CT*, June 19, 1969; 115th *CR* (1969), 15995–96, 17366, 17369–70.

13. 115th *CR* (1969), 18319.

14. 115th *CR* (1969), 19178–79.

15. "Congress Balks at Draft Reform," *NYT*, August 17, 1969.

16. "Draft Evasion in High Places," *NYT*, October 10, 1969; 115th *CR* (1969), 28566–75.

17. "Muskie Endorses Oct. 15 War Protest," *WP*, October 4, 1969; "War Protest on Wednesday Expected to Be Generally Peaceful," *NYT*, October 12, 1969; Thomas A. Johnson, "Whitney Young, Ending Silence, Condemns War," *NYT*, October 14, 1969; Homer Bigart, "Massive Protest on Vietnam War Expected Today," *NYT*, October 15, 1969; 115th *CR* (1969), 30023–24.

18. 115th *CR* (1969), 32468; "Breakthrough for Draft Reform," *NYT*, October 19, 1969; Richard L. Lyons, "House Passes Draft Lottery Bill," *WP*, October 31, 1969.

19. Ethel Payne, "Black Legislators Side with Draft Reform Opposition," *CD*, November 6, 1969; 115th *CR* (1969), 32464.

20. David E. Rosenbaum, "Thousands Due in Capitol in War Protest This Week," *NYT*, November 8, 1969; William Chapman, "Relatively Few Participate in Protests around Nation," *WP*, November 15, 1969; Richard Harwood, "Largest Rally in Washington History Demands Rapid End to Vietnam War," *WP*, November 16, 1969; Perlstein, *Nixonland*, 429, 440.

21. Perlstein, *Nixonland*, 393.

22. Author interview with Shirley Downs, July 16, 2012, Part 2: 2.

23. "8 House Negroes Write President," *NYT*, April 4, 1969.

24. Glen Elassasser, "Rights Leaders Rap Haynsworth for Court Post," *CT*, September 26, 1969; Fred P. Graham, "Negroes in House Oppose Haynsworth," *NYT*, September 26, 1969; Ethel Payne, "Dawson Tells Why He Nixed 'Black Paper,'" *CD*, September 29, 1969. For general info on the Haynsworth nomination, see Kotlowski, "Trial by Error"; Chisholm's quoted recollections in Chisholm, *Unbought and Unbossed*, 110–11.

25. Perlstein, *Nixonland*, 459.

26. Perlstein, *Nixonland*, 466.

27. "Carswell Critics Add 10th Senator," *NYT*, February 20, 1970.

28. Perlstein, *Nixonland*, 471–72, 474.

29. Walter Unna, "Senators' Whims Delay Appointments," *WP*, June 1, 1969.

30. 115th *CR* (1969), 17457–58.

31. Perlstein, *Nixonland*, 362, 421, 464–65.

32. Perlstein, *Nixonland*, 471; "'Paying Southern Debts' Says Shirley," *NYAN*, April 4, 1970.

33. Display Ad, *NYT*, May 28, 1969; "162 Black Americans Rap S. Africa Flights," *CD*, May 31, 1969.

34. Photo, "Rep. Chisholm Speaks to Group Protesting Poverty Program Cuts," *Norfolk Journal and Guide*, May 3, 1969; "54 in House Urge Tax Reform Drive," *NYT*, May 15, 1969; "Anti-Poverty Conference at Columbia," *NYAN*, January 17, 1970.

35. "Give Money, Not Stamps, Rep. Chisholm Urges," *CD*, February 15, 1969; "Woman Congressman Raps Food Stamps," *Cleveland Call and Post*, March 8, 1969.

36. Eileen Shanahan, "13 in House Back Drive to Put Public Members on G. M. Board," *NYT*, May 1, 1970; 115th *CR* (1969), 19489, 20407.

37. UPI photo, *WP*, September 22, 1969, and *CD*, September 23, 1969.

38. John Kifner, "Inquiry into Slaying of 2 Panthers Urged in Chicago," *NYT*, December 6, 1969; "Panthers Say an Autopsy Shows Party Official Was 'Murdered,'" *NYT*, December 7, 1969; Ethel Payne, "U.S. Moves on Hampton Probe," *CD*, December 9, 1969; Aldo Beckman, "Nixon Urged to Prolong Violence Unit," *CT*, December 10, 1969; "Inquiry Is Urged," *NYT*,

December 10, 1969; "6 in Congress Set Probe," *CD*, December 11, 1969; William Chapman and Joseph D. Whitaker, "Chicago Raid: Versions Clash," *WP*, December 14, 1969; Toni Anthony, "Ready Congress's Panther Hearing," *CD*, December 20, 1969; "Panther Case Probed by Black Congressmen," *WP*, December 21, 1969; Haas, *Assassination of Fred Hampton*, 123–25; Clay, *Just Permanent Interests*, 128–31.

39. Shirley Chisholm Testimony, March 17, 1970, in U.S. House of Representatives, *Hearings Related to Various Bills*, 3028–39.

40. Fisher, *Detention of U.S. Citizens*, 1–3.

41. "Experts Due Here for 'Earth Day,'" *BG*, April 19, 1970; "Rep. Chisholm Talks at Wellesley College," *BG*, April 21, 1970.

42. Bird, along with twenty other Panthers, was arrested in 1969 on charges of conspiracy and had yet to go to trial eighteen months later. Two Panthers, Richard Moore and Afeni Shakur (mother of Tupac), had been released after fundraising efforts, but Bird remained in custody on $100,000 bail. Rudy Johnson, "Mrs. Chisholm Joins Campaign to Collect Bail for Joan Bird," *NYT*, June 9, 1970; "free joan bird! [*sic*]," *off our backs*, June 26, 1970.

43. Self, *All in the Family*, 39.

44. Nadasen, Mittelstadt, and Chappell, *Welfare in the United States*, 47.

45. Advertisement, Taxpayers Committee to Federalize Welfare, *NYT*, March 29, 1969; 115th *CR* (1969), 13803.

46. Wilbur Mills, Democrat of Arkansas and chair of the Ways and Means Committee, introduced the bill on behalf of Nixon. 116th *CR* (1970), 6220; Warren Weaver Jr., "House Unit Backs Nixon Welfare Plan," *NYT*, April 15, 1970.

47. 116th *CR* (1970), 12091–92.

48. Warren Weaver Jr., "President's Welfare Plan Passes House, 243–155," *NYT*, April 17, 1970; Warren Weaver Jr., "Welfare Reform Is Delayed Again," *NYT*, August 5, 1970.

49. Martin Tolchin, "U.S. Moves to Sell Navy Yard to City for $22.5 Million," *NYT*, January 25, 1969; "Congresswoman Chisholm Reports to Constituents," [October 1970], CP, Box 4, Folder 9; "Chisholm Urges Follow-Up Meeting," *NYAN*, January 31, 1970.

50. "Chisholm Wins Bias Hearing," *NYAN*, February 7, 1970.

51. Barnard Collier, "Pupil Expose of City Blight Wins Pledge of Cleanup," *NYT*, April 10, 1969.

52. "Hospital Tinderbox," *NYT*, February 24, 1969; "Strikers in Charleston Are Gaining Wide Support," *CD*, May 10, 1969; Shirley Chisholm and Percy Sutton, Letter to the Editor, *NYT*, April 21, 1969; Daphne Sheppard, "Balky Group Costs Chisholm Refusal," *NYAN*, May 24, 1969.

53. Ethel Payne, "So This Is Washington," *CD*, April 5, 1969; Walter Pincus and Jan Krause, "100 Candidates Haven't Filed on Funds," *WP*, February 27, 1969; Clayton Knowles, "Democrats Here Issue Guidelines on Averting Election Split," *NYT*, March 7, 1969.

54. Susan Brownmiller, "This Is Fighting Shirley Chisholm," *NYT*, April 13, 1969.

55. Roland Black, "Black Candidates 'Doing Their Thing,'" *Cleveland Call and Post*, May 3, 1969; Richard Reeves, "Broderick to Run for Controller on Chisholm-Heuer Slate," *NYT*, April 6, 1969.

56. Brownmiller, "This Is Fighting Shirley Chisholm"; Richard Reeves, "Carey Supported on Mayoral Race," *NYT*, March 21, 1969; Sara Davidson, "N.Y. Mayor Lindsay Faces Stiff Opposition in Reelection Bid," *BG*, April 3, 1969; "Black Mayoral Hopefuls List Grows as Stokes Makes Bid for Re-Election," *CD*, May 3, 1969. Brooklyn's Democratic Party had a changing of the guard in 1969. Steingut's influence had waned to the point that a new county leader, Meade Esposito, was elected. Esposito was, like Chisholm, a Brooklyn native who had gone through the borough schools and became a bail bondsman.

57. "Shirley Blasts Leaders," *NYAN*, May 31, 1969.

58. Hunter-Gault, "Black and White."

59. Lizzi, "'My Heart Is as Black as Yours.'"

60. "Mrs. Chisholm Says She Backs Lindsay," *NYT*, July 21, 1969; Clayton Knowles, "Shirley Chisholm to Announce Endorsement of Lindsay Today," *NYT*, July 22, 1969.

61. "Mrs. Chisholm, as Expected, Backs Lindsay," *CD*, July 23, 1969.

62. "Mrs. Chisholm, as Expected, Backs Lindsay"; Richard Reeves, "Democrats Act over Defections," *NYT*, July 24, 1969; Richard Reeves, "Procaccino Urges Democratic Unity," *NYT*, July 25, 1969; Daphne Sheppard, "Democrats Upset by Shirley's Move," *NYAN*, July 26, 1969; Daphne Sheppard, "Chisholm Defends Backing Lindsay," *NYAN*, August 2, 1969; "New Dems for Shirley," *NYAN*, August 16, 1969.

63. "Will Not Discipline Chisholm," *CD*, July 29, 1969; "New Dems For Shirley," *NYAN*, August 16, 1969; "national liberal symbol" in Reeves, "Democrats Act Over Defections."

64. Martin Tolchin, "Lindsay Presses Navy on Yard Jobs," *NYT*, July 25, 1969; Martin Tolchin, "Mayor Took Company Plane; Impropriety Denied," *NYT*, August 21, 1969; Clayton Knowles, "Mrs. Chisholm Again Proclaims Support for Lindsay Campaign," *NYT*, September 22, 1969.

65. "Rep. Chisholm, Graves Supporting Samuels," *NYAN*, January 31, 1970; Thomas Ronan, "2 in Race Oppose Bid By Goldberg," *NYT*, March 11, 1970.

66. The first version was presented in Dexter D. Eure, "Black Leaders on the State Ticket?" *BG*, April 14, 1970, and corroborated by Homer Bigart, "Ambro Links Shirley Chisholm to 'Sinister Cabal,'" *NYT*, May 29, 1970; Richard Reeves, "Democrats Pick Goldberg But He 'Waives' Selection," *NYT*, April 2, 1970. The second was written by columnists Rowland Evans and Robert Novak in "Shirley's Little Game," *BG*, June 18, 1970; Francis X. Clines, "A Color Line Seen in Dual Posters: Goldberg, Denying Racism, Says He Will 'Look Into' Rep. Chisholm Charge," *NYT*, June 19, 1970. Present at Chisholm's charges of racism against the Goldberg campaign were Charles Rangel, Allan Fagan, Annie Bowen, and Harry Belafonte. On primary results, see "Vote in Samuels Areas Too Light to Win Race," *NYT*, June 25, 1970.

67. "Congressional Vote in the City," *NYT*, November 5, 1970.

68. William E. Farrell, "2 Unknowns Facing Vocal Incumbent in Brooklyn," *NYT*, October 19, 1970; Kuriansky and Smith, *Shirley Chisholm*, 5–6.

69. John Sibley, "Prisoners Seize Hostages, Take Over Jail in Queens," *NYT*, October 2, 1970; Robert McFadden, "Rioting Spreads to a Fourth Jail," *NYT*, October 4, 1970; "The Nation," *NYT*, October 4, 1970. On Attica, see Thompson, *Blood in the Water*, 15–17.

CHAPTER 11

1. For a discussion of this skepticism, see Popkin, "Historians on the Autobiographical Frontier."

2. This analysis owes much to Smith and Watson's *Reading Autobiography*, especially chaps. 1 and 7.

3. Craig Wylie to Joyce Hartman, December 20, 1968; Joyce Hartman to Shirley Chisholm, April 15, 1969; Joyce Hartman to Mac Holder, May 2, 1969; Joyce Hartman to Richard McAdoo, June 17, 1969; Joyce Hartman to Mac Holder, June 25, 1969; Richard McAdoo to Wendy Holdren, November 3, 1969; Richard McAdoo to Mac Holder, November 5, 1969, all in Shirley Chisholm Correspondence, Folder 1, HMP.

4. Joyce Hartman to David Harris, March 23, 1970; Richard McAdoo to Joyce Hartman, March 31, 1970, Shirley Chisholm Correspondence, Folder 1, HMP.

5. Author interview with Shirley Downs, March 24, 2016.

6. Lee Hickling to Joyce Hartman, March 31, 1970; Richard McAdoo to Joyce Hartman, April 7, 1970; Joyce Hartman to Lee Hickling, April 10, 1970; Joyce Hartman to Richard McAdoo, April 23, 1970; Richard McAdoo to Joyce Hartman, April 27, 1970; Joyce Hartman

to Lee Hickling, April 28, 1970; [Unsigned] to [Joyce Hartman], undated memo, all in Shirley Chisholm Correspondence, Folder 1, HMP; Shirley Chisholm to Diane Schluger, July 16, 1970; Joyce Hartman to Shirley Chisholm, September 1, 1970, Shirley Chisholm Correspondence, Folder 3, HMP.

7. SL interview with Muriel Forde, CC, Box 9, Tape 1; birth certificate of Charles Christopher St. Hill, No. 1684 [Guyana, December 9, 1898], and baptism certificate of Charles Christopher St. Hill, March 14, 1910, Muriel Forde Family Collection, Barbados.

8. In the 1968 interview for the SOHP, she said that she did not join the club until 1954 or 1955. Chisholm interview, SOHP Tape C-161, Part XV. This chronology is also echoed by Hicks in *Honorable Shirley Chisholm*, which implies that she did not join the regular club until after her falling out with Holder in 1958 (48). She was, however, present at a 1956 United Action Democratic Association (UADA) meeting. See *The Guardian* [UADA newsletter], n.d. [March 1956], JP, "Unsorted Papers" Folder, Box 22. Chisholm also wrote in *Unbought and Unbossed* (32–34, 36) that she joined the regular club while she was still in her twenties, which would have had to have been by 1954. She told Carlos Russell that she joined when Carney was leader, which would have been from 1953 to 1960 (Russell, *Perspectives on Power*, 235). And Holder mentioned Chisholm's election as vice president of the Seventeenth Assembly District Club as occurring in 1956. See Holder, "Election Express" flyer, CP, Box 3, Folder 24. In light of the existing evidence, this author believes that Chisholm was involved in the Seventeenth Assembly District Club from approximately 1954 through 1960.

A critical article about Chisholm written by Andrew Cooper and Wayne Barrett in 1978 suggested that Chisholm's officer status in both clubs was a sign of dishonesty. Cooper and Barrett, "Chisholm's Compromise," *Village Voice,* October 30, 1978.

9. *Unity Democrat*, April 1961, JP, Box 2, Folder 26; Unity Democratic Club (UDC) Ledger, JP, Box 2, Folder 31; Thomas R. Jones to Shirley Chisholm, December 4, 1962, JP, Box 2, Folder 25; Shirley Chisholm interview in Russell, *Perspectives on Power*, 52.

10. Shirley Chisholm interview, SOHP Tape C-161; Chisholm, *Unbought and Unbossed*, 66.

11. Chisholm, *Unbought and Unbossed*, 100–112.

12. Chisholm, *Unbought and Unbossed*, 113–22.

13. Sara Davidson, "Lindsay Wins Key Democrat," *BG*, July 23, 1969; Chisholm, *Unbought and Unbossed*, 138–40.

14. Chisholm, "The Lindsay Campaign and Coalition Politics," in *Unbought and Unbossed*, 123–32.

15. Chisholm, *Unbought and Unbossed*, 133–34.

16. Chisholm, *Unbought and Unbossed*, 134–46.

17. On radicalism as addressing the root of a problem, see Ella Baker quoted in Ransby, *Ella Baker and the Black Freedom Movement,* 1.

18. Ransby, *Ella Baker and the Black Freedom Movement*, 146–51; Bond, "Black Experiences in Politics," 11–13.

19. Chisholm, *Unbought and Unbossed*, 155–62.

20. Chisholm, *Unbought and Unbossed*, 167; Chisholm, "Racism and Antifeminism," *Black Scholar*, January–February 1970, 45. She also presented a speech with nearly identical text titled "The 51% Minority" to NOW Chicago's Conference on Women's Employment, on January 24, 1970, and submitted it as evidence in House subcommittee hearings on H.R. 16098.

21. Chisholm, *Unbought and Unbossed*, 163–69.

22. Charlayne Hunter, review of *Unbought and Unbossed*, *New York Times Book Review*, November 1, 1970; Glendora Putnam, "Shirley Chisholm: *Unbought and Unbossed,*" *BG*, October 25, 1970; review by Marietta Tree, *WP*, October 10, 1970; Robert K. Walsh, "The

Outspoken Shirley Chisholm," *Washington Evening Star*, October 13, 1970 (Tree and Walsh reviews reprinted in Chisholm constituent newsletter, [October 1970], CP, Box 4, Folder 9); Carolyn Amussen memo, September 10, 1970, Shirley Chisholm Correspondence, Folder 3, HMP; Marcia Janulewicz, "Just Too Much Message," *Boston Herald*, December 27, 1970, found in Shirley Chisholm Correspondence, Folder 5, HMP.

CHAPTER 12

1. Kuriansky and Smith, *Shirley Chisholm*, 6 (for a full list of floor votes by Chisholm in 1971, see 28–30); Ethel Payne, "Woman Power in House," *CD*, January 12, 1970; Joseph Kraft, "Larger Caucus Role," *WP*, January 21, 1971.

2. "Rep. Chisholm Says Negroes Want 'Their Share of America,'" *Atlanta Daily World*, January 6, 1970; "More Blacks Want Piece of American Dream Pie," *CD*, January 6, 1970.

3. See author interview with Shirley Downs, July 16, 2012, Part 2: 1–2 (on voting rights and bilingual education); author interview with Barbara Lee; author interview with Laura Murphy.

4. Members included Chisholm, Bill Clay (MO), Louis Stokes (OH), John Conyers Jr. (MI), Charlie Diggs (MI), Augustus Hawkins (CA), Robert Nix (PA), and George Collins (IL; after being elected to finish the term of the deceased Daniel Ronan). William Dawson (IL) did not always align with the group. Clay wrote that it was his December 31, 1970, memo to the Democratic Select Committee that precipitated the group's formalization. Clay, *Just Permanent Interests*, 117.

5. Clay, *Just Permanent Interests*, 121.

6. CBC Press Release, August 6, 1971, CP, Box 5, Folder 9; Paul Delaney, "Blacks in House Seeking Negro Leadership," *NYT*, March 29, 1971; Thomas Foley, "Black Caucus Flexes Muscle of Leadership," *Los Angeles Times*, March 28, 1971.

7. Singh, *Congressional Black Caucus*, 2, 54–57, 80; Dellums and Halterman, *Lying Down with Lions*, 74; "Origins of the CBC," A Voice: African American Voices in Congress, avoiceonline.org/cbc/history.html (accessed September 25, 2012).

8. SL interview with Ronald Dellums, April 7, 2003, CC, Box 9, Part 1: 11–12.

9. "2000 Honor Powell, Who Says He'll Run," *NYT*, February 1, 1970; Clayton Knowles, "Powell Predicts a 3–1 Victory," *NYT*, June 17, 1970; William Kling, "Internal Rift Hits Black Caucus of House: Diggs Is New Chief," *CT*, January 24, 1971; "H. R. A. Aide Resigns Here," *NYT*, May 1, 1971; "Black Caucus Plans Fund Raising Dinner," *NYT*, May 29, 1971; Paul Delaney, "Dinner Nets Black Caucus $250,000," *NYT*, June 20, 1971; Clay, *Just Permanent Interests*, 169; Mary McGrory, "Black Caucus Takes on the Pentagon," *BG*, November 21, 1971. There was some discord over whom to hire as the staff director, with John Dean named first by Diggs but the other CBC members naming Howard T. Robinson. James Naughton, "McCarthy Said to Lean toward Entering Several Democratic Primaries," *NYT*, July 23, 1971.

10. "Women's lib support": Thomas Johnson, "Mrs. Chisholm Chides Black Caucus," *NYT*, November 20, 1971; SL interview with Shirley Chisholm, April 29, 2003, CC, Box 9, Part 3: 13–16; Clay, *Just Permanent Interests*, 197.

11. Edward Thompson III interview with Shirley Chisholm, May 2, 1973, BOHC: "psychological needs," 11; "isolated enclaves," 17–18; Chisholm, "Coalitions—The Politics of the Future," 85: "ever mindful," 93; "belief that on many issues," 90.

12. John S. Carroll, "Nixon Faces Tough Talk with Blacks," *BG*, February 21, 1971; "12 Came Knocking," *NYT*, February 21, 1971.

13. Clay, *Just Permanent Interests*, 143; Perlstein, *Nixonland*, 388.

14. Ethel Payne, "So This Is Washington: Black Caucus Greeting Inside the White House," *CD*, April 3, 1971.

15. Paul Delaney, "President Agrees to a Meeting with 12 Black House Members," *NYT*, February 19. 1971; Carroll, "Nixon Faces Tough Talk with Blacks"; Clay, *Just Permanent Interests*, 143–44.

16. Clay, *Just Permanent Interests*, 147; Paul Delaney, "Blacks in House Get Nixon Pledge," *NYT*, March 26, 1971; "Blacks Await Nixon Reply," *Austin Statesman* (via AP), March 27, 1971.

17. Paul Delaney, "Nixon Defended on Rights Record," *NYT*, May 20, 1971; Robert B. Semple Jr., "Nixon's Racial Stance," *NYT*, May 21, 1971; "Nixon Answers Caucus," *NYAN*, May 22, 1971; "White House Forms Its Own Black Caucus to Counter 13 Democrats," *NYT*, June 2, 1971.

18. Ethel Payne, "Caucus Denies Report of Split; Nixon's Reply is 'Saddening,'" *CD*, May 25, 1971; "Blacks in House Are Critical of Nixon's Reply to Demands," *CT*, May 25, 1971; Bruce Winters, "House Black Caucus Taking Deeper Plunge into Politics," *Baltimore Sun*, May 25, 1971.

19. Shirley Chisholm Press Release, May 27, 1971, CP, Box 5, Folder 9; Albin Krebs, "Judgeship Opposed," *NYT*, May 26, 1971; "Opposition to Appointment of Watson as Judge Rises," *NYT*, May 27, 1971; Fred P. Graham, "Nixon Reportedly Drops Plans to Nominate Watson as Judge," *NYT*, May 28, 1971.

20. "Nixon Racial Policy Scored," *NYT*, June 28, 1971.

21. Nixon's Family Assistance Plan bill was introduced by Wilbur Mills (D-AR) and John Byrnes (R-WI) as H.R. 1 on January 22, 1971.

22. 117th *CR (1971)*, 20742–44.

23. 117th *CR (1971)*, 20741–42.

24. Warren Weaver Jr., "20 in House Seek Welfare Plan Giving $6500 to a Family of 4," *NYT*, April 7, 1971; 117th *CR* (1971), 7927, 9829, 20741–42.

25. Weaver, "20 in House Seek Welfare Plan"; Ethel Payne, "So This Is Washington," *PC*, May 22, 1971; Warren Weaver Jr., "Welfare Project Backed by Negro," *NYT*, June 6, 1971; "Showdown on Welfare," *NYT*, June 22, 1971; Warren Weaver Jr., "House Approves Welfare Reform by 288–132 Vote," *NYT*, June 23, 1971; Thomas A. Johnson, "McGovern to Seek a Floor on Incomes," *NYT*, July 30, 1971; Self, *All in the Family*, 40.

26. SL interview with Ronald Dellums, n.d., CC, Box 9, Tape 2: 5–8, and SL interview with Ronald Dellums, April 7, 2003, CC, Box 9, Part 1: 15–17; Payne, "So This Is Washington," *PC*, May 22, 1971; Mary McGrory, "Black Caucus Takes on the Pentagon," *BG*, November 21, 1971.

27. Thomas Johnson, "Military Race Relations Held 'Explosive,'" *NYT*, November 18, 1971.

28. "Caucus Plans Bias Inquiry in Europe," *WP*, June 4, 1971; "Shirley Checks into Black GI Treatment Overseas," *NYAN*, June 12, 1971; News Release, June 11, 1971, CP, Box 5, Folder 9; Thomas Johnson, "10 in Black Caucus Visit Bases in Study of Charges of Bias," *NYT*, November 16, 1971; "100 Blacks Arrested at Fort McClellan," *BG*, November 16, 1971 (reprinted from *WP*); McGrory, "Black Caucus Takes on the Pentagon"; Stur, *Beyond Combat*, 208–9; Thomas Johnson, "Organized Servicemen Abroad Intensify Drive against Racism," *NYT*, November 19, 1971; "Defense Aide on Rights Chosen; Goal Is to End Military Racism," *NYT*, November 20, 1971. On Chisholm's House testimony and votes, see Kuriansky and Smith, *Shirley Chisholm*, 7, 27nn17–22.

29. Martin Nolan, "Democrats Have a Showdown Today," *BG*, October 13, 1971.

30. Martin Nolan, "A Tough One to Explain in South," *BG*, October 15, 1971; Robert Healy, "Democratic Party Doesn't Need This Kind of Victory," *BG*, October 17, 1971.

31. Mary McGrory, "A Black for Vice President?," *BG*, November 7, 1971.

32. Grace Lichtenstein, "The Abzug-Farbstein Contest: Plenty of Colors," *NYT*, October 30, 1970; "Bella S. Abzug of Peace Strike to Run against Rep. Farbstein," *NYT*, March 14, 1970. For Abzug's biography, see Zarnow, *Battling Bella*, and Levy, *Political Life of Bella Abzug*.

33. "East Side Democrats Hold Spirited Brunch," *NYT*, January 25, 1971.

34. Judy Flander, "It's a Wild, Wild Life for Bella's Brood," *BG*, August 21, 1971.

35. Author interview with Andrea Tracy Holmes, Part 1: 1; author interview with Carolyn Smith, 30.

36. U.S. House of Representatives, *Hearings before the General Subcommittee on Labor*, 303; Letter from Bella Abzug, Shirley Chisholm, and Patsy Mink to "Friends," n.d. [1971], PEP, Box 6, Folder 2; Hill, "Equal Employment Opportunity Acts of 1964 and 1972," 49–50. For Chisholm's floor debate and vote, see 117th *CR* (1971), 32091–113 (September 16, 1971). She did, however, vote in favor of the bill after the conference report: 118th *CR* (1972), H1870 (March 8, 1972).

37. SL interview with Shirley Downs, CC, Box 10: 27.

38. "Statement of Purpose Adopted by the National Women's Political Caucus," July 11, 1971, PEP, Box 35, Folder 16; NWPC memo: "NWPC Organizing Information," September 1, 1971, PEP, Box 34, Folder 8; Remarks by Sen. Fred Harris [D-OK], 117th *CR* (1971), 24519–26 (July 12, 1971, reprinted in Gallagher, "How Did Shirley Chisholm", Document 11A). Harris submitted the NWPC's press release and twenty-point program to be included in the *CR*, along with the text of Friedan's speech from the meeting, the text of two of Chisholm's speeches ("Do Women Dare?" and "Economic Justice for Women"), and a statement by Abzug. "Women Planning Political Drive in 1972 Election," *Baltimore Sun*, July 11, 1971; Eileen Shanahan, "200 Women Organize for Political Power," *NYT*, July 11, 1971.

39. Carroll, "National Women's Political Caucus," 276–78.

40. Shanahan, "200 Women Organize for Political Power"; "Goals Set By Women's Political Caucus," *NYT*, July 13, 1971.

41. "Woman President? It's No Joke, Bub," *NYAN*, July 17, 1971 (reprinted in Gallagher, "How Did Shirley Chisholm" Document 11B).

42. Aileen Jacobson, "Women's Political Caucuses in D.C., VA, MD," *WP*, October 24, 1971.

43. "Women's Caucus Target of White House Jokes," *NYT*, July 14, 1971; Jack Anderson, "President Nixon and the Women," *Parade* magazine in *BG*, October 31, 1971; "Woman President? It's No Joke, Bub."

44. Jacobson, "Women's Political Caucuses"; author interview with Shirley Downs, July 16, 2012, Part 1: 30.

45. Robert Self has pointed out that for the state, accepting state-sponsored childcare would admit to the necessity of women's work and recast the state's relationship to the market. Some feared that government childcare would be used to force women into work. The bill was "quietly revolutionary" because it accounted for female characteristics and extended full economic citizenship to mothers. It also represented a coalition between "the New Deal, the black freedom and Chicano movements, the Great Society, and the women's movement." As such, it was "a merging of social contract politics with feminist politics," to broaden positive rights. Self, *All in the Family*, 128–29 (quotations on 129). The bill was H.R. 6748, or H.R. 16098, section 805.

46. SL interview with Shirley Downs, CC, Box 10: 27.

47. Eleanor Blau, "Mrs. Abzug Backs Child-Care Plan," *NYT*, February 23, 1971. See also 117th *CR* (1971), 15666–85 (Abzug's Extension of Remarks; includes testimony from New York hearing), 15696–15704 (Chisholm's Extension of Remarks).

48. Testimony of Bella Abzug and Shirley Chisholm, U.S. House of Representatives, *Hearings before the Select Subcommittee on Education*, 62–109; "Mrs. Chisholm, Mrs. Abzug Introduce Child Care Bill," *NYT, M*ay 18, 1971 [their version was H.R. 8402]; 117th *CR* (1979) 15246, 15666–85, 15696; Chisholm Press Release, November 5, 1971, CP, Box 5, Folder 9; author interview with Shirley Downs, July 16, 2012, Part 2: 5.

49. The Senate version was S. 2007. Self, *All in the Family*, 129–30; author interview with Shirley Downs, July 16, 2012, Part 2: 5; Kuriansky and Smith said that Quie was "one of her closest friends in Congress," *Shirley Chisholm*, 23. Staffer Muriel Morisey corroborated this. U.S. House of Representatives interview with Muriel Morisey, Senior Legislative Assistant, Representative Shirley Chisholm of New York, April 19, 2017, Oral Histories of African Americans in Congress, History, Art, and Archives, U.S. House of Representatives, Washington, D.C.

50. Self, *All in the Family*, 119 (quote), 129–30.

51. Roth, *Politics of Daycare*, 27–29; Self, *All in the Family*, 130.

52. "Advocates of Child Care Bill Press Nixon to Sign It, But a Veto Appears Likely," *NYT*, December 9, 1971; "Excerpts from Nixon's Veto Message," *NYT*, December 10, 1971; Roth, *Politics of Daycare*, 30; Self, *All in the Family*, 131, 276–78; "a radical piece of social legislation": MacLean, *Freedom Is Not Enough*, 137.

53. "Household Workers Unite, Form National Association," *Milwaukee Star*, August 28, 1971.

54. Randolph, *Florynce "Flo" Kennedy*, 176; Chisholm, "Foreword," in *Abortion Rap*, vii–xi.

55. Author interview with Shirley Downs, March 24, 2016.

56. Blumenthal, *Let Me Play*, 29–34, 37–40; author interview with Shirley Downs, July 16, 2012, Part 3: 6–10. The House bill was 92 H.R. 1748. For floor debate on Title X, see 117th *CR* (1971), 39248–63. Note that what would become Title IX was, in the November 4 version of the bill, Title X. Chisholm on school busing: "You know, let me bring it right down front to you. The fact of the matter is racism is so inherent in the bloodstream of this country that you cannot see beyond a particular limit. You are only concerned when whites are affected. If you were indeed concerned about the busing of young children for the sake of getting educational equality, your voices would have been raised years ago in terms of the fact that black and Chicano, Spanish-speaking children were getting an inferior education by being bused right past the white schools in their neighborhoods in which they lived to the dilapidated schools in the outlying districts." 117th *CR* (1971), 39310.

57. Blumenthal, *Let Me Play*, 47; Mansbridge, *Why We Lost the ERA*, 10. The 1971 version, introduced by Griffiths, was H.J. Res. 208.

CHAPTER 13

1. Chisholm, *Good Fight*, 140.

2. Chisholm, *Good Fight*, 125–27.

3. SL interview with Shirley Chisholm, April 29, 2003, CC, Box 9, Part 1: 13, 19, 20. The symbolic aspect of her candidacy has been remarked on often, then and in the intervening years, while its hope for building a coalition at the Democratic National Convention is often overlooked. See, for example, the contemporary article by A. S. Doc Young, "Shirley Chisholm: The Case of the Winning Loser," *LAS*, May 25, 1972.

4. SL interview with Shirley Chisholm, April 29, 2003, CC, Box 9, Part 1. Opponents tried to prevent her from getting delegates because they feared her using them as barriers to someone getting the nomination. She was offered bribes, she said (30).

5. SL interview with Robert Gottleib, CC, Box 10, Part 2: 9–11.

6. Chisholm, *Good Fight*, 3.

7. SL interview with Ronald Dellums, 2003, CC, Box 9, Part 2: 9.

8. Author interview with Shirley Downs, July 16, 2012, Part 1: 22–23.

9. SL interview with Shirley Chisholm, April 29, 2003, CC, Box 9, Part 2: 17.

10. SL interview with Shirley Chisholm, April 1, 2000, CC, Box 9, Part 2: 5.

11. SL interview with Shirley Chisholm, April 1, 2000, CC, Box 9, Part 2: 17.

12. SL interview with Barbara Lee, CC, Box 10: 31.

13. SL interview with Shirley Chisholm, April 29, 2003, CC, Box 9, Part 1: 17–18.

14. SL interview with Shirley Chisholm, April 1, 2000, CC, Box 9, Part 1: 8–9.

15. "Extremists Alien to America, Mrs. Chisholm Says at Douglass," *NYT*, June 5, 1969; Vincent Paka, "Howard 'On Trial for Life,' Graduates Told," *WP*, June 7, 1969; Ethel Payne, "Rep. Chisholm Is Cheered by Howard Grads," *CD*, June 9, 1969; Fred M. Hechinger, "Negro Leaders and Opponents of War Play Major Role as Graduation Speakers," *NYT*, June 9, 1969; "Rep. Chisholm Sees Nation's Collegians 'Ripe for Agitators,'" *NYT*, June 12, 1970.

16. Chisholm, *Good Fight*, 3, 10–11, 15 ("When are we going to change things?"), 22–23.

17. Edward Thompson III interview with Shirley Chisholm, May 2, 1973, 4, BOHC.

18. Thomas Johnson, "Black Nationalists Now Focusing on Politics," *NYT*, September 11, 1971.

19. Shirley Chisholm, "Welfare Reform or Enforce Poverty," National Welfare Rights Organization, July 31, 1971, quoted in Kuriansky and Smith, *Shirley Chisholm*, 15.

20. Lucinda Smith, "1200 of Nation's Poor Convene in R.I.," *BG*, July 29, 1971; Lucinda Smith, "Rep. Chisholm Considers Race for Presidency," *BG*, August 1, 1971; Thomas A. Johnson, "Rep. Chisholm Declares that She May Run for President in 1972," *NYT*, August 1, 1971; James Naughton, "McCarthy Said to Lean toward Entering Several Democratic Primaries," *NYT*, July 23, 1971.

21. Merelice K. England, "Black Leader Maps '72 Strategy," *Christian Science Monitor*, April 19, 1971; "Demands, Patterns Plague Network," *LAS*, April 21, 1971; Ethel Payne, "Black Caucus Is Cool to 3rd Party Formation," *CD*, May 8, 1971; "Black Caucus Airs Demands on Network," *PC*, May 22, 1971.

22. Howard Romaine, "Why a Black Man Should Run," *Nation*, September 27, 1971, 264–68.

23. Chisholm, *Good Fight*, 24–25.

24. Romaine, "Why a Black Man Should Run"; "Just permanent interests": James T. Wooten, "New Black Caucus in the South Aloof from Presidential Race," *NYT*, August 16, 1971.

25. Chisholm, *Good Fight*, 28–30.

26. Paul Delaney, "Negroes Eye Presidential Races," *NYT*, September 20, 1971; Robert Maynard, "Black Political Leaders Plan Own Convention," *BG*, September 26, 1971; Joseph Rosenbloom, "Blacks Urged to Form Block of Votes," *BG*, December 12, 1971.

27. SL interview with James Richardson, CC, Box 10, Part 1: 38–39.

28. Karen Peterson, "A Ms. President?" *BG*, November 17, 1971.

29. Chisholm, *Good Fight*, 37–38, 41.

30. In multiple retellings, the number of men in the group ranges between two and four. Shirley Chisholm and Marcia Ann Gillespie, "The Unsinkable Shirley Chisholm," *Essence*, November 1972, 42; Chisholm, *Good Fight*, 30–33.

31. The Associated Press report on Cherry's endorsement ran in the *Orlando Star, Tallahassee Democrat, Daytona Beach News,* and *Winter Haven News-Chief* on September 29 and in the *Gainesville Sun* on September 30, 1971. On the CBC conference, see Thomas Johnson, "Mrs. Chisholm Chides Black Caucus," *NYT*, November 20, 1971; Thomas Johnson, "Black Caucus Calls National Political Convention," *NYT*, November 21, 1971; Paul Hope, "Rep. Shirley Chisholm Outflanks Her Black Political Brothers," *BG*, November 30, 1971; Clay, *Just Permanent Interests*, 195–97.

32. Mary McGrory, "A Black for Vice President?" *BG*, November 7, 1971.

33. "Lindsay Joins in a Tribute to Representative Chisholm," *NYT*, November 12, 1971.

34. "Plans Revealed by Mrs. Chisholm," *NYT*, November 15, 1971.

35. "Shirley Chisholm Says No to Koch," *BG*, November 8, 1971.

36. Martin Nolan, "McGovern Presses Honesty as New Theme for '72 Campaign," *BG*, December 5, 1971.

37. SL interview with Carolyn Smith, CC, Box 10, Part 1: 20; SL interview with Shirley Downs, CC, Box 10: 28; SL interview with Muriel Forde, CC, Box 9, Tape 1: 34-35.

38. SL interview with Shirley Chisholm, April 29, 2003, CC, Box 9, Part 2: 14.

39. SL interview with Shirley Chisholm, April 29, 2003, CC, Box 9, Part 1: 20. Muskie drew early fire for saying in October 1971 that a ticket with a Black vice presidential candidate wouldn't win in 1972. Art Seidenbaum, "Black Man at Capitol," *Los Angeles Times*, October 20, 1971. Patsy Mink, Chisholm's Democratic colleague in the House from Hawaii, also ran a limited primary campaign in one state, Oregon.

40. SL interview with Jules Witcover, CC, Box 10: 22-23.

41. SL interview with Shirley Chisholm, April 29, 2003, CC, Box 9, Part 3: 33-34.

42. SL interview with Shirley Chisholm, April 1, 2000, CC, Box 9, Part 2: 6-7.

43. "Polls Will Determine Candidate Protection," *Los Angeles Times*, January 28, 1972; "A Question of Protection," *Los Angeles Times*, January 30, 1972.

44. "5 Democratic Candidates Get Guards," *BG*, March 21, 1972; SL interview with Carolyn Smith, CC, Box 10, Part 2: 8; SL interview with Conrad Chisholm, CC, Box 9: 12, 17-19; SL interview with Victor Robles, April 2003, CC, Box 10, Part 1: 22.

45. Dorothy Townsend, "Black Support Hard for Her to Win," *Los Angeles Times*, May 20, 1972; SL interview with Conrad Chisholm, CC, Box 9: 17; Haskins, *Fighting Shirley Chisholm*, 175-76; Secret Service Binder, CPP.

46. SL interview with Shirley Chisholm, April 29, 2003, CC, Box 9, Part 2: 9-10, 30; SL interview with Carolyn Smith, CC, Box 10, Part 2: 13; Stephen Curwood, "Mrs. Chisholm Has a Vision," *Boston Phoenix*, February 23, 1972; SL interview with Robert Gottlieb, CC, Box 9, Part 1: 35-36.

47. SL interview with Robert Gottlieb, CC, Box 9, Part 2: 14-15.

48. Henry Bubar, Northampton, Massachusetts, Letter to the Editor, *BG*, February 3, 1972.

49. Wilbur Hicks, Letter to the Editor, *NYT*, June 11, 1972.

50. SL interview with Shirley Chisholm, April 1, 2000, CC, Box 9, Part 1: 19.

51. Geri Joseph, "Shirley Chisholm's Candidacy: A 'Surprise Package' for Miami Beach?" *WP*, May 15, 1972.

52. Haskins, *Fighting Shirley Chisholm*, 160; SL interview with Shirley Chisholm, April 1, 2000, CC, Box 9, Part 1: 14; Winslow, *Shirley Chisholm*, 111; SL interview with Victor Robles, CC, Box 10, Part 1: 4, 10, 30; SL interview with Robert Gottlieb, CC, Box 9, Part 1: 12-13. Chisholm's campaign office and congressional staff in Washington in the spring of 1972 were Helen Butler, Lori Collier, Alberta Hamilton, Andrea (Tracy) Simmons (later Holmes), Deborah Alexander, Shirley Downs, Carolyn Smith, Jean Davis, Barbara Dory, Thad Garrett, Gary Elson, Lizabeth Cohen, Roger Barr, and Daniel Butler, per Secret Service Binder, CPP.

53. SL interview with Robert Gottlieb, CC, Box 9, Part 1: 9-10, 16, 18-19, 28, 47, 50; Part 2: 2.

CHAPTER 14

1. "Shirley Chisholm for President? She Must Be Kidding!," campaign flyer, Betty Friedan Papers, Box 35, Folder 1211, SLRI.

2. SL interview with Shirley Chisholm, April 29, 2003, CC, Box 9, Part 1.

3. SL interview with Ronald Dellums, 2003, CC, Box 9, Part 2: 7. Dellums maintained support for Chisholm throughout the first half of 1972 while coming under tremendous pressure to endorse McGovern, which he eventually did at the convention. Chisholm, *Good Fight*, 109-10.

4. Chisholm, *Good Fight*, 108–9.

5. SL interview with Shirley Chisholm, April 1, 2000, CC, Box 9, Part 1: 10–11; SL interview with Robert Gottleib, CC, Box 9, Part 2: 5–7. On the connections between Black Power critiques and strategies and the women's movement, see Randolph, *Florynce "Flo" Kennedy*.

6. SL interview with Wilson Riles, CC, Box 10, Part 1: 18.

7. SL interview with Shirley Chisholm, April 29, 2003, CC, Box 9, Part 1: 35–36, 37–38; Edward Thompson III interview with Shirley Chisholm, May 2, 1973, 5, BOHC.

8. SL interview with Shirley Chisholm, April 29, 2003, CC, Box 9, Part 2: 7–8.

9. SL interview with Shirley Chisholm, April 1, 2000, CC, Box 9, Part 2; SL interview with Wilson Riles, CC, Box 10, Part 1: 20; Clay, *Just Permanent Interests*, 221.

10. Clay, *Just Permanent Interests*, 219, Bond quote at 221; Shirley Chisholm and Marcia Ann Gillespie, "The Unsinkable Shirley Chisholm," *Essence*, November 1972, 41.

11. A. S. Doc Young, "Shirley Chisholm: The Case of the Winning Loser," *LAS*, May 25, 1972. Russell would go on to write his 1978 doctoral thesis ("Project Demonstrating Excellence") on politics in Brooklyn by conducting a series of oral histories. The result was *Perspectives on Power: A Black Community Looks at Itself*, the source of several oral histories cited in this book.

12. Frank Lynn, "What Makes Shirley Run?" *NYT*, January 30, 1972.

13. SL interview with Shirley Chisholm, April 29, 2003, CC, Box 9, Part 2: 19, 27 ("vicious").

14. "Mrs. Chisholm in Maryland Race," *NYT*, March 17, 1972; "Shirley Gains Support as She Enters Maryland Fight," *New York Recorder*, March 25, 1972.

15. Thomas A. Johnson, "Blacks, in Shift, Forming Unit for Mrs. Chisholm," *NYT*, February 4, 1972.

16. For more on the Gary convention, see chapter 15. This theory was advanced by NAACP's Labor Director Herbert Hill at a May 1972 panel. See Austin Scott, "Analysts Discern Shifts in Black Voting Trends," *WP*, May 13, 1972.

17. Edward Thompson III interview with Shirley Chisholm, May 2, 1973, 25, BOHC; SL interview with Arlie Scott, CC, Box 10, Part 2: 17–18; SL interview with Robert Gottleib, CC, Box 9, Part 2: 15.

18. "The Chisholm Trail," *NYAN*, March 11, 1972; "Mrs. Chisholm Asks Help of Students in Georgia," *NYT*, March 4, 1972; Jon Nordheimer, "16 Georgia Blacks Name Delegates," *NYT*, March 12, 1972. Muskie did not get any, though thirty uncommitted delegates remained. Julian Bond and Governor Jimmy Carter were two of the uncommitted ones who won. "Muskie's Backers Shut Out in GA," *BG*, March 12, 1972; "Wallace Gets No Delegates in Georgia District Elections," *WP*, March 12, 1972; Boyd Lewis, "Machine Politics Crumbles at Convention as Chisholm-Pledged Delegates Take Slate," *Atlanta Voice*, March 18, 1972 (Woodruff Library Biographical File); Chuck Andrews, "Politics in Black," *NYAN*, May 6, 1972.

19. The convention took place March 10–12. Paul Delancy, "Rep. Stokes Heads the Black Caucus," *NYT*, February 9, 1972.

20. "Shirley Will Miss Gary Parley," *CT*, March 8, 1972.

21. Chisholm and Gillespie, "Unsinkable Shirley Chisholm," 42–43.

22. SL interview with Shirley Chisholm, April 1, 2000, CC, Box 9, Part 1; Edward Thompson III interview with Shirley Chisholm, May 2, 1973, BOHC, 13–14.

23. Ethel Payne, "After Gary, What?" *CD*, March 14, 1972; Erwin A. Jaffe, "Coming Together in Gary," *Nation*, April 3, 1972, 422–26.

24. "Nominee Doubted at Black Parley," *NYT*, March 8, 1972; Chuck Andrews, "Politics in Black," *NYAN*, February 26, 1972; Byron Rollins, "Where I'm Comin' From," *NYAN*, March 11, 1972; "The Job at Home," *NYAN*, March 18, 1972. According to Rollins, there was "great concern that Cong. Chisholm has made no effort to relate to the New York delegation [which numbered 339 people and included Sonny Carson]; and that she might take an

endorsement and use it along with other support to ultimately support a white presidential candidate such as John Lindsay or George McGovern."

25. Thomas A. Johnson, "We Met, Therefore We Won," *NYT*, March 12, 1972; "Black Assembly Voted at Parley," *NYT*, March 13, 1972; Arthur Jones, "8000 Blacks Cheer Split of Democrats, Urge Their Own Party," *BG*, March 12, 1972; "Getting It Together in Gary," *BG*, March 15, 1972.

26. Jack White, "Lookout Democrats, Black Power Gon' Get Your Momma . . . Maybe," *Race Relations Reporter*, January 3, 1972, 8–11.

27. Jurate Kazicas, "Women's Rights Appeal Rides Campaign Trail," *Los Angeles Times*, March 31, 1972.

28. Donald Fraser to Lawrence O'Brien, DNC Chair, November 29, 1971; Doris Meissner memo, February 1972; Joann Foley Martin, "Women Stand for Being Seated," *Chicago Today*, January 3, 1972. All in Gloria Steinem Papers, Box 168, Folder 4, Sophia Smith Collection of Women's History, Smith College, Northampton, MA.

29. SL interview with Shirley Chisholm, April 1, 2000, CC, Box 9, Part 1: 13.

30. SL interview with Shirley Chisholm, April 1, 2000, CC, Box 9, Part 1: 17.

31. Laurie Johnston, "Women's Caucus Has New Rallying Cry: 'Make Policy Not Coffee,'" *NYT*, February 6, 1972; "Dream for Women: President Chisholm," *NYT*, February 14, 1972. At the southern NWPC meeting in Nashville in February, Abzug called Chisholm's candidacy "one of the most effective ways to press our demands." Eileen Shanahan, "Democratic Women in South Challenge Rules on Picking Convention Delegates," *NYT*, February 14, 1972.

32. SL interview with Carolyn Smith, CC, Box 10, Part 1: 24; Part 2: 25–26.

33. SL interview with Susan Brownmiller, CC, Box 9: 37, 45.

34. SL interview with Shirley Chisholm, April 1, 2000, CC, Box 9, Part 1: 10–11.

35. Hennessee, *Betty Friedan*, 169–70; Chuck Andrews, "Politics in Black," *NYAN*, July 1, 1972.

36. SL interview with Carolyn Smith, CC, Box 10, Part 1.

37. Albin Krebs, "Notes on People," *NYT*, January 13 and 25, 1972. Steinem's Papers contain a file for McGovern, with personal correspondence. See George McGovern to Gloria Steinem, February 29, 1970, and April 1, 1970. There are detailed documents about his schedule at the 1968 convention, suggesting she was involved with his campaign then. Gloria Steinem Papers, Box 182, Folder 1, Sophia Smith Collection of Women's History, Smith College, Northampton, MA.

38. Bella Stumbo, "Kate Millett Speaks Out," *Los Angeles Times*, May 8, 1972.

39. Randolph, *Florynce "Flo" Kennedy*, 100–101, 114, 150, 171, 179, 187 ("never occurred to her": 101).

40. Randolph, *Florynce "Flo" Kennedy*, 187–89, 198–203.

41. Statement by Boston chapter of the Feminist Party, n.d. [1972], Patricia Gold Papers, Box 3, Folder 51, SLRI.

42. Press release, Boston Feminist Party, Patricia Gold Papers, Box 3, Folder 51, SLRI; "New Boston Feminist Party Chapter Backs Rep. Chisholm for President," *BG*, March 3, 1972; Bill Fripp, "Medley," *BG*, March 11, 1972.

43. Chisholm and Gillespie, "Unsinkable Shirley Chisholm," 78.

44. SL interview with Shirley Chisholm, April 1, 2000, CC, Box 9, Part 1: 4–5. However, the "youth vote scare," which was the fear/hope that 25 million new voters would sway elections, never materialized. See SL interview with Jules Witcover, CC, Box 10: 27.

45. SL interview with Shirley Chisholm, April 29, 2003, CC, Box 9, Part 3: 24, 29, 30–31.

46. SL interview with Shirley Chisholm, April 1, 2000, CC, Box 9, Part 1: 23. Later in her congressional career Chisholm would cosponsor multiple bills that attempted to add sexual

orientation as a protected group to the Civil Rights Act of 1964. See U.S. House of Representatives, *Civil Rights Amendments Act of 1979*, 110–12.

47. SL interview with Ronald Dellums, 2003, CC, Box 9, Part 1: 23, 26–27.

48. Liddy, *Will*, 273, 277.

49. Haskins, *Fighting Shirley Chisholm*, 161; Lucinda Inskeep, "Lori Collier's Off on the Chisholm Trail," *Louisville Times*, March 14, 1972.

50. Shirley Chisholm, Presidential Campaign Position Paper 1, "Foreign Aid," Paper 2, "The Middle East Crisis," and Paper 3, "Equality of Commitment—Africa," CC, Box 5. "Foreign Aid" was released January 13, 1972 (see Eileen Shanahan, "McGovern Calls for Tax Reform," *NYT*, January 14, 1972).

51. Shirley Chisholm, Presidential Campaign Position Paper 4, "The Economy," CC, Box 5.

52. Shirley Chisholm, Presidential Campaign Position Paper 5, "Justice in America," CC, Box 5.

53. Shirley Chisholm, Presidential Campaign Position Paper 6, "The Environment," and Paper 7, "Consumerism," CC, Box 5.

54. SL interview with Shirley Chisholm, April 1, 2000, CC, Box 9, Part 1: 24.

55. McGovern scored 96, Muskie 85, Humphrey 89, and Mink 92. "High Rating Is Given to Kennedy by ADA," *NYT*, January 9, 1972; "ADA Rates Kennedy 100% for Performance in 1971," *BG*, January 7, 1972; "Democrats Rate Poorly as Conservatives," *Los Angeles Times*, February 7, 1972; Kay Mills, "Chisholm Tops, Say Consumers," *BG*, January 9, 1972.

56. Mary McGrory, "A Ball of Fire from Brooklyn," *BG*, January 30, 1972; "Symbolic Candidacy," *NYT*, January 27, 1972.

CHAPTER 15

1. George Gallup, "Muskie Pulls Ahead of Kennedy," *BG*, January 23, 1972; R. W. Apple Jr., "Muskie Is Victor in Iowa Caucuses," *NYT*, January 26, 1972; R. W. Apple Jr., "Heavy Turnout by Iowa Students Said to Have Had Role in Outcome of Democratic Precinct Caucuses," *NYT*, January 27, 1972.

2. Frank Lynn, "New Hat in Ring: Mrs. Chisholm's," *NYT*, January 26, 1972; Martin Nolan, "Rep. Chisholm Enters Race for President," *BG*, January 26, 1972.

3. Statement of Candidacy for the Office of President of the United States by the Honorable Shirley Chisholm, January 25, 1972 (reprinted in Gallagher, "How Did Shirley Chisholm," Document 13).

4. C. Gerald Fraser, "Black Women Form a Group for Political Leverage," *NYT*, January 30, 1972; "Symbolic Candidacy," *NYT*, January 27, 1972.

5. "Symbolic Candidacy," *NYT*, January 27, 1972.

6. "An Editorial: Welcome Mrs. Chisholm, *NYAN*, January 29, 1972.

7. Martin Nolan, "Right on the Chisholm Trail," *BG*, January 28, 1972; Editorial Notes, *BG*, January 29, 1972.

8. Mary McGrory, "A Ball of Fire from Brooklyn," *BG*, January 30, 1972.

9. Edward Thompson III interview with Shirley Chisholm, May 2, 1973, BOHC, 7–8.

10. New York Mayor John Lindsay, Chisholm's ally, was dismayed that Chisholm would campaign there also. His staffers complained that Chisholm's candidacy would take Black votes that the Lindsay campaign was counting on. Lindsay himself tried a more personal dissuasion campaign. He summoned Chisholm to Gracie Mansion and implored Chisholm, "Do you have to go into Florida?" Frank Lynn, "Lindsay Dislikes Mrs. Chisholm's Plan to Enter Florida Primary," *NYT*, January 1, 1972; Chisholm, *Good Fight*, 52–53.

11. Haskins, *Fighting Shirley Chisholm*, 161, 165–66.

12. Chisholm, *Good Fight*, 59–61.

13. Christopher Lydon, "Liberals in Florida and Pennsylvania Favor McGovern," *NYT*, January 23, 1972; Larry Mahoney, "Chisholm: Influence for Change," *Miami Herald*, March 2, 1972.

14. The largest offices were in Tampa, Miami, Jacksonville, and Tallahassee. Gerald Fraser, "Mrs. Chisholm Completes 3-Day Campaign in Florida," *NYT*, February 28, 1972; "Supporters Gain Force over State," *Florida Star*, February 5, 1972; "Shirley Chisholm Office Is Opened on Duval Street," *Florida Star*, February 12, 1972; "Rep. Chisholm Is Unitarian Guest Speaker," *Florida Star*, February 26, 1972.

15. Stephan Lesher, "The Short, Unhappy Life of Black Presidential Politics, 1972," *NYT*, June 25, 1972; "Chisholm Irks Some in Women's Lib," *WP* (AP), February 10, 1972.

16. Chisholm, *Good Fight*, 64–65; "Amateur campaign" in SL interview with Robert Gottlieb, CC, Box 9, Part 1: 48; airport story in SL interview with Shirley Chisholm, April 1, 2000, CC, Box 9, Part 1: 12. In Jim Pitts's telling, the two drivers were women. Pitts quoted in Winslow, *Shirley Chisholm*, 111.

17. SL interview with Shirley Chisholm, April 1, 2000, CC, Box 9, Part 1: 19; Chisholm, *Good Fight*, 58–59.

18. Chisholm, *Good Fight*, 65–66; "Still Another Congressman Stumps for Rep. Mills," *NYT*, February 25, 1972.

19. The decision was *Bradley v. Richmond* [VA] *School Board*. S. Micciche, "Busing—A Shadow over the Florida Primary," *BG*, March 12, 1972; "Poll Reports Wallace Leading 2–1 in Florida," *BG*, March 7, 1972; Kenneth Reich, "Busing Furore [*sic*] Overshadows Florida Vote," *Los Angeles Times*, March 2, 1972; Chisholm, *Good Fight*, 62; "Busing in an Angry Glare," *Life*, March 3, 1972.

20. Jules Witcover, "Politics of a Hot Issue," *Los Angeles Times*, March 5, 1972; Stuart Auerbach, "Wallace Lauds Rep. Chisholm," *WP*, March 11, 1972; Chisholm, *Good Fight*, 62–64.

21. "Shirley Will Miss Gary Parley," *CT*, March 8, 1972.

22. Richard Reeves, "Eleven Alligators in Florida's Political Swamp," *New York Times Magazine*, March 12, 1972; Joan Bingham, "The Chisholm Trail," *NYAN*, March 18, 1972.

23. Lesher, "Short, Unhappy Life of Black Presidential Politics."

24. SL interview with Alcee Hastings, CC, Box 10. In this interview, he said he did not remember whether Chisholm was on the Florida ballot. Given that Hastings himself had planned to run as favorite son, this seems unlikely (6–10). Martin Waldron, "Busing Held Key Issue for Blacks in Florida Primary," *NYT*, March 3, 1972; Paul Delaney, "Chisholm Appeal Divides Blacks," *NYT*, March 14, 1972.

25. Lowell Langford, "Nixon Defeated," UPI (*Ft. Lauderdale News, Jacksonville Journal, Florida Times-Union*), October 20, 1971.

26. Clay, *Just Permanent Interests*, 223; Delaney, "Chisholm Appeal Divides Blacks."

27. Beverly Bruce Havard, Letter to the Editor, *Baltimore Afro-American*, April 1, 1972; SL interview with Alcee Hastings, CC, Box 10: 6.

28. The two Black lawyers were lawyers Remus Allen and Ike Williams. Martin Crutsinger, "Rep. Chisholm Urges Economic Rights Bill," *Jacksonville Journal*, March 9, 1972.

29. Chisholm, *Good Fight*, 67–69; Gary Brown, "Shirley: Making it Count," *CD*, March 14, 1972; Gary Brown, "Shirley Stimulates Black Fla. Voters," *CD*, March 15, 1972; Joan Bingham, "The Chisholm Trail," *NYAN*, March 18, 1972.

30. "Seven Democratic Rivals to Debate in Florida," *NYT*, March 5, 1972; "Black Woman Candidate Scores," *Florida Star*, March 18, 1972.

31. Fraser, "Mrs. Chisholm Completes 3-Day Campaign in Florida"; "Wants to Teach after One More Term," *BG*, February 27, 1972; "I'm Ready to Quit," *Los Angeles Times*, February 27, 1972.

32. Richard Weintraub, "Contest Developing for Mass. Caucus," *BG*, January 9, 1972; Richard Weintraub, "Chisholm May Run in Bay State," *BG*, January 12, 1972; Richard Weintraub, "Mass. Youth Want Grassroots Action," *BG*, January 9, 1972; David Nyhan, "The Week that Was," *BG*, January 23, 1972; William Goldsmith, "The Academic View," *BG*, February 21, 1972.

33. "The Mass Caucus '72," Press Release, Patricia Gold Papers, Box 3, Folder 51, SLRI.

34. Chisholm telegram to James Pitts, CC, Box 12, Folder 25. On the new law, see Richard Weintraub, "Political Points," *BG*, January 30, 1972; Michael Kenney, "Senate Revises Primary," *BG*, February 17, 1972; Michael Kenney, "Mass. Ends Winner-Take-All Policy Used by Delegates: Will Affect April 25 Primary," *BG*, March 10, 1972. On the coalition slates, see "Here Comes Shirley Chisholm!" Flyer, CPP; Richard Weintraub, "Liberal Caucus Picks Sen. McGovern," *BG*, January 16, 1972; Rachelle Patterson, "McGovern-Chisholm Slate Eyed in 8th District," *BG*, January 17, 1972; Richard Weintraub, "McGovern, Muskie Backers Trying to Place Delegates," *BG*, January 17, 1972; Steve Curwood, "McGovern-Chisholm Coalition Foreseen for Primaries," *Bay State Banner*, January 20, 1972. The Second and Third Districts did not form coalition slates, but the Eighth did. McGovern supporters were Alvatore Albano, John Elder, Barbara Ackerman, Katharine Kane, and Andrew Puglia. Shirley Chisholm supporters were: Saundra Graham and Charles N. Pierce of the Cambridge School Committee. Sandra E. Fagot was an alternate. Although she was on the coalition slate for McGovern and Shirley Chisholm, she planned to run uncommitted. Richard Weintraub, "4 McGovern District Delegate Slates Finished," *BG*, January 22, 1972; Editorial, "Will Caucus Win Prove Real Gain for McGovern?," *BG*, January 22, 1972; "Mrs. Ackermann Plans to Run Uncommitted," *BG*, January 23, 1972. McGovern's slates, including the coalition ones, were evenly split between men and women, and contained grassroots politics people who for the most part did not hold elected offices. At the same time, Muskie's slate read like a who's who of Massachusetts politics. Richard Weintraub, "Drinan Will Head McGovern Slate" *BG*, January 26, 1972.

35. Chisholm telegram to James Pitts, CC, Box 12, Folder 25; Richard Weintraub, "Liberal Caucus Picks Sen. McGovern," *BG*, January 16, 1972; Rachelle Patterson, "McGovern-Chisholm Slate Eyed in 8th District," *BG*, January 17, 1972; Richard Weintraub, "McGovern, Muskie Backers Trying to Place Delegates," *BG*, January 17, 1972; Steve Curwood, "McGovern-Chisholm Coalition Foreseen for Primaries," *Bay State Banner*, January 20, 1972.

36. In an interview printed just a few days before her arrival in Boston, she had stated that only North Carolina and Florida were confirmed as states where she would campaign, and perhaps California and New York. See "Shirley Chisholm: A Voice for the Voiceless," *WP*, February 13, 1972.

37. "Shirley Chisholm: A Voice for the Voiceless"; Michael Kenney, "Rep. Chisholm's Presidential Campaign Rolls into Mass.," *BG*, February 16, 1972. Kenney estimated 300 attendees at the Community Center rally while Curwood of the *Boston Phoenix* estimated "over 400." See Stephen Curwood, "Mrs. Chisholm Has a Vision," *Boston Phoenix*, February 23, 1972; meeting notes, Citizens for Shirley Chisholm Committee, February 28, 1972, CC, Box 12, Folder 19.

38. March 25, 1972, Order of Service, Patricia Gold Papers, Box 3, Folder 51, SLRI. On that visit, Chisholm also visited the Cardinal Cushing Spanish Speaking Center, a function at a private home in Newton, Walsh Junior High School in Framingham, and the Merrimac Valley NAACP's twenty-fifth anniversary meeting. See handwritten itinerary, CC, Box 12, Folder 24, and letter from Bennie Armstrong to James Pitts, CC, Box 12, Folder 25.

39. Haskins, *Fighting Shirley Chisholm*, 171.

40. SL interview with Shirley Chisholm, April 1, 2000, CC, Box 9, Part 1: 21.

41. SL interview with Shirley Chisholm, April 1, 2000, CC, Box 9, Part 1: 21–22.

42. SL interview with Shirley Chisholm, April 29, 2003, CC, Box 9, Part 1: 33, 35.

43. SL interview with Shirley Chisholm, April 1, 2000, CC, Box 9, Part 1: 23; SL interview with Shirley Chisholm, April 29, 2003, CC, Box 9, Part 1: 34.

44. Massachusetts Itinerary, April 5–6, CC, Box 12, Folder 19; Broadside, CC, Box 12, Folder 22; Joseph Rosenbloom, "Chisholm Says Voters 'Upset, Disturbed,'" *BG*, April 6, 1972. See also "Mark Solomon on Knowing Shirley Chisholm," Shirley Chisholm Project, February 5, 2015, https://www.youtube.com/watch?v=D3uIzczA_T8 (accessed June 3, 2020).

45. "Democratic Hopefuls Concentrate on Mass., Pa.," *BG*, April 22, 1972; Viola Osgood, "Speaks on Boston TV," *BG*, April 23, 1972; List of scheduled appearances, Patricia Gold Papers, Box 3, Folder 51, SLRI; Jean Dietz, "Pioneer Suffragette Likes Shirley Chisholm," *BG*, April 7, 1972; Richard Weintraub, "McGovern Paces Democrats in Organization for Mass. Primary," *BG*, March 26, 1972. The Fourth Congressional District in Massachusetts included Newton, Brookline, Weston, Wayland, and Sudbury, and traditionally voted liberal. Up to a quarter of the attendees at the Massachusetts liberal caucus in January had been from the Fourth.

Chisholm had delegates throughout the district, where she was campaigning on "who is the 'real' liberal?"—a clear dig at McGovern. Chisholm's pledged delegates were: Barbara R. Cantrill, Leominster; Norman J. Faramelli, Waltham; Jack Hoffman, Framingham; Helen S. Johnson, Brookline; Edna E. Pruce, Newtonville; Mark Solomon, Newton; and Merylees K. Turner, Lincoln. Her alternates were Grainger Browning Jr., Fitchburg; David Ecklein, West Newton; Edward Gonzales, Maynard; and Judith J. Hendricks, Brookline. See Richard Weintraub, "'New' 4th Looks Good for McGovern," *BG*, April 9, 1972.

In the Eighth District, represented by Congressman Tip O'Neill, were several wards in Boston: Back Bay/Beacon Hill, East Boston, Charlestown, Brighton, Allston, Arlington, Belmont, Cambridge, Somerville, and Watertown. O'Neill was a staunch Muskie supporter, but he feared McGovern would win because of the 200,000 students in the district and the voting age had just been lowered to eighteen. A liberal coalition had just come into Cambridge city government, including Henry Owens and Barbara Ackermann.

One possible outcome was going to be that the Chisholm-McGovern combined slate would win but that the delegates themselves would have to vote for "someone else" on the first ballot in Miami. See Richard Weintraub, "How Will They Vote April 25 in Rep. O'Neill Country," *BG*, April 13, 1972.

In the Fifth District, pledged to Chisholm were James D. Pitts III and Jean Rubenstein. Those nineteen delegate candidates said that they felt Shirley Chisholm or McGovern were the best choices for president because they would end the Vietnam War. In the Eleventh District Shirley Chisholm had one pledged delegate, Joel Kugelmas. "Democratic Convention Delegate Hopefuls," *BG*, April 18, 1972; "19 Democrats for Chisholm or McGovern," *BG*, April 20, 1972; "11th District Delegate Candidates," *BG*, April 21, 1972.

The Ninth District was much of Boston, including the Black neighborhoods (North End, South End, South Boston, and parts of Dorchester, Roxbury, Jamaica Plains, and West Roxbury), plus the suburbs of Canton, Dedham, Dover, Needham, Westwood, Norwood, and Walpole. The suburbs were slightly majority Democrat, while the Boston wards were heavily Democrat. Chisholm could possibly affect the results here via the 20,000 Black voters in the district. However, her fate was tied to the more local politics of who would replace school desegregation lightning rod Louise Day Hicks in the House. Chisholm did have a number of prominent Black figures on her slate. Supporters of Massachusetts Advocates for Children founder Hubie Jones would probably vote for her, while supporters of Mel Miller (publisher of the *Bay State Banner*) would probably vote for Muskie. Those pledged to Chisholm were: Patricia Bonner-Lyons, Mel King, Byron Rushing, Warren Moore, Frieda Garcia-Wright, and Anna May Cole, all of Boston, plus Mary Ann Del Grosso of Roslindale. Alternates were Sonia Ingram, Samuel Nelms, and Vincent Perrelli of Boston, and Patricia Harris of Dedham. See Richard Weintraub, "The Ninth," *BG*, April 24, 1972.

46. Shirley Chisholm, "The Congressional Black Caucus Speaks," *BG*, April 25, 1972.

47. Bill Kovach, "Dakotan in Sweep," *NYT*, April 26, 1972; Bill Kovach, "Bay State Delegates All Go to McGovern," *NYT*, April 27, 1972.

48. Kovach, "Bay State Delegates All Go to McGovern"; David Nyhan, "McGovern Leaves Democratic Chaos for Ohio," *BG*, April 27, 1972; Richard Weintraub, "67% of State Delegates to Stand by McGovern," *BG*, April 27, 1972; Richard Weintraub, "McGovern Piles Up Delegates," *BG*, April 29, 1972.

49. Richard Weintraub, "Drinan to Lead Mass. Democrats to Miami," *BG*, May 22, 1972.

50. In the lawsuit brought by the Center for Political Reform, each primary candidate in both parties was represented by a plaintiff who was a California citizen. Thomas J. Foley, "Winner-Take-All Primary to Face Suit," *Los Angeles Times*, April 21, 1972.

51. Ethel Payne, "So This Is Washington: Shirley Chisholm to Shun Calif. Primary," *Tri-State Defender*, January 22, 1972. Chisholm would recall later that when she began her campaign in California, she was not aware that it was a winner-take-all state. By the time she realized, it was too late. She was very upset when she found out, and "oh, that hurt me." Had she known, she would not have run there. Had she gotten proportional delegates, she would have gotten about twenty-eight (SL interview with Shirley Chisholm, April 1, 2000, CC, Box 9, Part 1: 25). One report was that her final decision to enter came from the advice of the first Black California Democratic Coalition president, Nate Holman. See "A Pragmatic View of Emotional Politics," *San Francisco Sun Reporter*, February 19, 1972.

52. Chisholm, *Good Fight*, 100–101. Because she did not have a campaign organization formed yet, her supporters missed an early-January meeting with the state Democratic chair about delegate selection procedures. Richard Bergholz, "Kennedy to Appear at Democratic Rally in L.A. Next Month," *Los Angeles Times*, January 12, 1972.

53. SL interview with Arlie Scott, CC, Box 10, Part 2: 10–11; Howard Seelye, "10 in County Picked for Chisholm Slate," *Los Angeles Times*, March 5, 1972. Chisholm polled in second place (16 percent) behind McGovern (40 percent) in a poll of students at fifteen California universities. "Nixon Trails McGovern in Poll Held at 15 California Campuses," *Los Angeles Times*, March 14, 1972.

54. SL interview with Wilson Riles, CC, Box 10, Part 1: 14, 16.

55. SL interview with Wilson Riles, CC, Box 10, Part 1: 10.

56. Chisholm for President Inner City [Los Angeles] Committee, Letter to the Editor, *LAS*, June 1, 1972.

57. "Register to Vote for Shirley Chisholm," *Black Panther*, May 13, 1972. Chisholm was originally on the roster for the Black Community Survival Conference, but had to cancel her late March California visit. See advertisement, *Black Panther*, March 25, 1972.

58. Mary Ellen Leary, "The Candidates Discover the People," *Nation*, May 29, 1972, 693.

59. SL interview with Wilson Riles, CC, Box 10, Part 1: 17.

60. Lin Hilburn, "Shake Off the Yoke of White Paternalism," *LAS*, June 1, 1972.

61. James Sawyer, "Mervyn Dymally, California State Senator, Scouts Miami for Humphrey," *Miami Times*, December 31, 1971.

62. Mary McGrory, "McGovern Woos Vote of Blacks," *BG*, May 31, 1972.

63. Leary, "Candidates Discover the People," 689–93.

64. Richard Bergholz, "McGovern Wins CDC Support But Falls Short of Endorsement," *Los Angeles Times*, March 20, 1972.

65. SL interview with Arlie Scott, CC, Box 10, Part 1: 25–26; Chisholm, *Good Fight*, 109.

66. The investigation into the fake press releases was requested by Special Prosecutor Archibald Cox. FBI File 56-HQ-4714 Section 1, FBI Reports in Chisholm Press Release File and Discovery-3500 Material-Segretti in US vs. Chapin, Records of the Watergate Special Prosecution Force (RG460) Dirty Tricks Task Force, Federal Bureau of Investigation Records, National Archives and Records Administration, College Park, MD; SL interview with Arlie Scott, CC, Box 10, Part 2: 3–5. For her part, Chisholm "remained focused" (SL interview with Shirley Chisholm, April 29, 2003, CC, Box 9, Part 2: 21).

67. SL interview with Barbara Lee, CC, Box 9: 1–2, 6, 12–13; SL interview with Sandra Gaines, CC, Box 10: 1–3; Willie Monroe, "Shirley Chisholm Talks of Women in Politics," *San Francisco Sun Reporter*, January 15, 1972; "Bargaining Power Is Goal of Shirley Chisholm Campaign," *Oakland Post*, January 20, 1972. She reiterated her goal to bring influence to the DNC in her Whitter College speech ("More Muskie Support," *NYT*, January 15, 1972).

68. SL interview with Shirley Chisholm, April 1, 2000, CC, Box 9, Tape 1: 27.

69. Chisholm, *The Good Fight*, 102, 105; SL interview with Barbara Lee, CC, Box 10: 5–6, 7, 14, 37.

70. SL interview with Barbara Lee, CC, Box 9: 7–8.

71. Chisholm, *Good Fight*, 103; SL interview with Arlie Scott, CC, Box 10, Part 1: 28–29; SL interview with Wilson Riles, CC, Box 10, Part 1: 18.

72. SL interview with Sandra Gaines, CC, Box 9: 5; SL interview with Wilson Riles, CC, Box 10, Part 1: 3–5, 19, 21. Scott was officially appointed California coordinator April 3, according to a UPI report. "Mrs. Chisholm Names Aide," *NYT*, April 4, 1972.

73. SL interview with Bobby Seale, CC, Box 10: 2, 22. Seale recalled later that the political campaign was his idea.

74. SL interview with Bobby Seale, CC, Box 10: 22–26, 32, 41, 48–49 ("I'm just proud" quote, 49); "Huey Newton Backs Race by Mrs. Chisholm," *NYT*, April 28, 1972.

75. "Press Statement Read by Chairman Bobby Seale," *Black Panther*, May 6, 1972, reprinted in Huey Newton FBI File, HQ 105-165429, Federal Bureau of Investigation Records, National Archives and Records Administration, College Park, MD.

76. Leroy Aarons, "Black Panthers Set to Endorse Chisholm," *WP*, April 26, 1972; "Black Panther Party for Shirley Chisholm," *WP*, April 28, 1972.

77. SL interview with Shirley Chisholm, April 1, 2000, CC, Box 9, Part 1: 26.

78. Chisholm, *Good Fight*, 107; SL interview with Shirley Chisholm, April 29, 2003, CC, Box 9, Part 1: 40. She did not remember the fundraiser in this interview, although she did in the above-cited 2000 interview with SL.

79. SL interview with Barbara Lee, CC, Box 10: 24.

80. Guest List for Newton Cocktail Party, Huey P. Newton Foundation, Inc., Collection, Series 2, Box 9, Folder 9, Special Collections and University Archives, Stanford University, Palo Alto, CA; Huey Newton FBI File, HQ 105-165429, Section 19, Federal Bureau of Investigation Records, National Archives and Records Administration, College Park, MD. Oakland supporters (including the owner of Jimmy's Lamp Post, the party's regular hangout) also held a fundraiser on June 2. See Invitation, Huey P. Newton Foundation, Inc., Collection, Series 2, Box 9, Folder 9, Special Collections and University Archives, Stanford University, Palo Alto, CA; SL interview with Arlie Scott, CC, Box 10, Part 2: 13–14; "Democrats Seek to Retain the Young," *WP*, May 20, 1972; "Chisholm Given $1,000 By Panthers," *NYT*, May 20, 1972; "Vote for People's Candidates," [advertisement], *Black Panther*, May 27, 1972.

81. Gwen Fontaine to David Schneiderman, May 24, 1972, and "Why We, the Black Panther Party, Support Sister Shirley Chisholm," Huey P. Newton Foundation, Inc., Collection, Series 2, Box 9, Folder 9, Special Collections and University Archives, Stanford University, Palo Alto, CA.

82. SL interview with Sandra Gaines, CC, Box 9: 6–7; SL interview with Wilson Riles, CC, Box 10, Part 1: 23, Part 2.

83. SL interview with Wilson Riles, CC, Box 10, Part 1: 11.

84. SL interview with Ronald Dellums, 2003, CC, Box 9, Part 1: 30.

85. SL interview with Ronald Dellums, 2003, CC, Box 9, Part 1; SL interview with Barbara Lee, CC, Box 9: 24, 29.

86. Bill Robertson, "Political Roundup," *LAS*, January 13, 1972; Chisholm NOW Fundraising Letter, December 18, 1971, Betty Friedan Papers, Box 35, Folder 1211, SLRI; "Rep. Chisholm Confident on State Primary," *Los Angeles Times*, January 15, 1972; "Women Adopt Resolutions," *Los Angeles Times*, October 4, 1971.

87. "Shirley Chisholm Visits LA; Gets Enthusiastic Support," *LAS*, January 20, 1972; SL interview with Arlie Scott, CC, Box 10, Part 1: 8, 11–12.

88. Jean Murphy, "Driver behind the Chisholm Campaign," *Los Angeles Times*, May 9, 1972.

89. "'It Can Be Done' Says Shirley Chisholm," *Sacramento Observer*, January 20, 1972; "Shirley Chisholm Visits LA; Gets Enthusiastic Support," *LAS*, January 20, 1972; "Rep. Chisholm Confident on State Primary," *Los Angeles Times*, January 15, 1972.

90. Jean Murphy, "'Fighting Shirley' Faces the Big Test," *Los Angeles Times*, January 24, 1972.

91. SL interview with Arlie Scott, CC, Box 10, Part 1: 13.

92. Murphy, "Driver behind the Chisholm Campaign;" SL interview with Arlie Scott, CC, Box 10, Part 1: 21. The transcript reads "fifty thousand," but the actual requirement was 14,694 by March 24. Richard Bergholz, "Democrats Changing State Primary Rules," *Los Angeles Times*, November 8, 1971; Richard Bergholz, "Democratic Hopefuls Scramble to Get into California Primary," *Los Angeles Times*, March 16, 1972. In the San Fernando Valley, a local group led by Perry King opened a headquarters at 7105 Havenhurst, Annex, in Van Nuys: Bill Robertson, "Political Roundup," *LAS*, February 17, 1972. In Compton, Aresta Howard led Chisholm supporters along with "Mrs. Morgan" in the Thirty-Fifth *Congressional District* and "Mrs. Shaefer" in the Twenty-Third Congressional District, and would also be a California delegate to the upcoming Black Political Convention in Gary, Indiana: "L.A. Delegation Chosen for Black Political Convention," *LAS*, March 2, 1972; "Cong. Chisholm to Speak in Compton," *LAS*, May 18, 1972. Lynette Hewett Griffin, wife of Booker, was on the Chisholm campaign steering committee and also a delegate to Gary's Black Political Convention: "Booker Griffin Announces for 53rd Assembly District," *LAS*, March 9, 1972.

93. SL interview with Arlie Scott, CC, Box 10, Part 1: 22–24 and Part 2: 2, 6–7; "dominating the whole scene": Chisholm, *Good Fight*, 104–5; SL interview with Barbara Lee, CC, Box 9: 24.

94. SL interview with Arlie Scott, CC, Box 10, Part 1: 29–30, and Part 2: 14–15, 20; Carroll and Morris, *Legs Are the Last to Go*, 131; SL interview with Barbara Lee, CC, Box 9: 18–19; "Gertrude Gibson's Candid Comments," *LAS*, April 20, 1972; Bill Lane, "People, Places, and Situwayshuns," *LAS*, May 11, 1972.

95. "It's a Two-Man Bout in California Race," *BG*, June 4, 1972; Martin Nolan, "4-Way Calif. Debate Today," *BG*, June 4, 1972; "U.S. Court Rules Mrs. Chisholm Must Receive Equal Time on TV," *NYT*, June 3, 1972; SL interview with Tom Asher, CC, Box 9: 5, 9–10, 11–13. Chisholm recalled that it was Tom Asher who called her, not the other way around, to fight her exclusion from the California debate. SL interview with Shirley Chisholm, April 29, 2003, CC, Box 9, Part 1: 28.

96. Bill Boyarsky, "Mrs. Chisholm Wins Equal Time; Yorty Loses Plea," *Los Angeles Times*, June 3, 1972; Jim Stingley, "Rep. Chisholm, Wallace Aide, Yorty to Join Primary Debate," *Los Angeles Times*, June 4, 1972; Wallace Turner, "Democrats Firm on Prisoner Issue in Coast

Debate," *NYT*, June 5, 1972; William Sumner, "Lady from New York Carried the Day," *St. Paul Dispatch*, June 6, 1972; SL interview with Shirley Chisholm, April 1, 2000, CC, Box 9, Part 2: 4.

97. "S.C.L.C. West Rates Local Candidates," *LAS*, June 1, 1972; Chisholm, *Good Fight*, 110; Diamond, *Congressional Quarterly's Guide to U.S. Elections*, 349.

98. The delegates were chosen in "open community meeting[s]" on March 27, two days before Chisholm opened her campaign. Chuck Andrews, "The Chisholm Trail," *NYAN*, March 25, 1972 and April 1, 1972.

99. Frank Lynn, "New York Filings Led by M'Govern [*sic*]," *NYT*, May 12, 1972.

100. Sadie Feddoes, "Please Be Seated," *NYAN*, January 15, 1972.

101. "Black Women Set Harambee for Shirley," *NYAN*, February 12, 1972.

102. Attendees at the Belafontes' party included Sydney Poitier, Richard Roundtree, Dorothy Height, Ron Dellums, and Bella Abzug. "Brooklyn Women Seeking Money for Chisholm," *NYAN*, February 26, 1972; Sadie Feddoes, "Please Be Seated," *NYAN*, March 4, 1972 and March 11, 1972.

103. "Benefit to Aid Shirley's Run," *NYAN*, April 1, 1972; Sadie Feddoes, "Please Be Seated," *NYAN*, April 29, 1972.

104. "Coalition of 100 Set Sat. Meeting," *NYAN*, January 29, 1972; "Politics in Black," *NYAN*, February 5, 1972; Photo, *NYAN*, May 20, 1972.

105. "AM News Supports Shirley," and "The *Amsterdam* Interviews the Candidates," *NYAN*, March 11, 1972. The editorial board explained that it was fully aware that Chisholm was a long shot. "We believe, however, that a united national campaign by Blacks in support of her candidacy can help unite Black people across the country in ways that will help elect local Black candidates everywhere" and that her candidacy would increase Black political involvement.

106. People for Chisholm campaign brochure, 1972, Betty Friedan Papers, Box 35, Folder 1211, SLRI; "Political Roundup," *NYAN*, May 6, 1972.

107. Chuck Andrews, "Politics in Black," *NYAN*, March 4, 1972.

108. J. Zamgba Browne, "'I May Run vs. Shirley . . . ' Says Breadbasket Leader," *NYAN*, January 29, 1972; Shirley Chisholm, "Shirley Hits Back at Breadbasket Leader," *NYAN*, February 5, 1972; Chuck Andrews, "Politics in Black," *NYAN*, February 12, 1972. For his part, Jones claimed that the *NYAN* had mischaracterized his remarks, but chastised Chisholm for her angry response. "Rev. Jones Re-Blasts Cong. Shirley Chisholm," *NYAN*, February 12, 1972.

109. "Politics in Black," *NYAN*, April 1, 1972 and April 8, 1972; Simon Anekwe, "Shirley Backs Beatty for 53rd State Senator," *NYAN*, April 29, 1972; "7 Primary Delegates Balk at Support for Shirley," *NYAN*, May 6, 1972; Tom Buckley, "Mrs. Chisholm Finds District Leaders in Opposing Camp," *NYT*, May 24, 1972; George Todd, "Foes Invaded My Office!!" *NYAN*, May 27, 1972; Les Ledbetter, "Brooklyn Primary Vote Pitting Two Black Forces," *NYT*, September 15, 1972.

110. Carlos Russell, "A Funny Thing Happened," *NYAN*, May 6, 1972.

111. According to Jacqueline Ceballos, Chisholm was "very angry because we asked for seed money for her campaign party—$300.00—in order earn a few thousand!" Ceballos to Betty Friedan, n.d. [1972], Betty Friedan Papers, Box 35, Folder 1211, SLRI.

112. Gerald Fraser, "Mrs. Chisholm Starts Campaign in State," *NYT*, March 30, 1972; "Names and Faces in the News," *BG*, March 19, 1972; Francis X. Cline, "Black Group Says Democratic Women Ignore Minorities," *NYT*, April 10, 1972; Display Ad, *NYT*, April 30, 1972. "Shirley is the only one": Rosa Guy, "Black Perspective: On Harlem's State of Mind," *NYT*, April 16, 1972.

113. "150 Businessmen Salute Youth Group at Hilton Luncheon," *NYAN*, June 10, 1972. Sharpton had known Chisholm since he was thirteen years old in 1968. See "Reverend Al

Sharpton on Shirley Chisholm's Influence," Shirley Chisholm Project, December 3, 2015, https://www.youtube.com/watch?v=2zlUA-6r8X0 (accessed June 3, 2020).

114. Flyer, Betty Friedan Papers, Box 35, Folder 1211, SLRI; Steven R. Weisman, "5 Gay Candidates Are in State Contests," *NYT*, June 16, 1972; Advertisement, *NYAN*, June 17, 1972.

115. "Election Coverage," *NYAN*, June 10, 1972; Alfonso Narvaez, "Housing Is Scored by Mrs. Chisholm," *NYT*, June 14, 1972; Alfonso Narvaez, "Mrs. Chisholm Presses for Key Convention Role," *NYT*, June 15, 1972; Alfonso Narvaez, "Mrs. Chisholm Envisions Power to All the People," *NYT*, June 16, 1972; Alfonso Narvaez, "Rain Cancels Chisholm Rallies But Her Spirits Are Undampened," *NYT*, June 18, 1972.

116. Her choice for state senator to run against Waldaba Stewart was Vander L. Beatty. She endorsed Anna V. Jefferson to run against Tom Fortune for district leader and Woodrow Lewis to run against Sam Wright for assembly. Gerald Fraser, "Brooklyn Toured by Mrs. Chisholm," *NYT*, June 18, 1972; Michael Knight, "Campaigning Cut by Mrs. Chisholm," *NYT*, June 19, 1972; Advertisements, *NYAN*, June 3, 10, and 17, 1972.

117. Stephen Isaacs, "Wins 240 Convention Delegates: McGovern Sweeps N.Y. Primary," *WP*, June 21, 1972; Frank Lynn, "McGovern Victory a Blow to State's Party Leaders," *NYT*, June 22, 1972.

118. Stephen Isaacs, "McGovern Making Hay in Jersey," *BG*, June 5, 1972; Secret Service Binder, CPP.

119. Jon Nordheimer, "16 Georgia Blacks Names Delegates," *NYT*, March 12, 1972.

120. "Mrs. Chisholm in Tennessee," *NYT*, April 20, 1972; Bill Kovach, "Wallace Is Victor in Tennessee Vote," *NYT*, May 5, 1972; Bill Kovach, "Tennessee Spurs Wallace Backers," *NYT*, May 6, 1972; "Wallace Wins Easily in N.C. Primary Vote," *BG*, May 7, 1972.

121. One group headed by John Wilson, who had run Fauntroy's D.C. delegate campaign, sought John Lindsay to oppose Fauntroy. Chisholm said that if Lindsay ran, she would, too. See David Boldt, "Favorite Son Fauntroy Opposed," *WP*, January 21, 1972; Ethel Payne, "So This Is Washington: Fauntroy Urged to Drop Candidate Bid," *Tri-State Defender*, February 12, 1972.

122. Edward Thompson III interview with Shirley Chisholm, May 2, 1973, 9–10, BOHC; Haskins, *Fighting Shirley Chisholm*, 167–68; Ethel L. Payne, *Tri-State Defender*, January 1, 1972. Fauntroy denied having ever pledged his fifteen D.C. delegates to Chisholm. Bill Clay wrote that Chisholm had agreed, in a deal brokered by Percy Sutton, not to run in any areas where a Black "favorite son" candidate was running for president. Clay, *Just Permanent Interests*, 223. See also Ethel Payne, "So This Is Washington: 3,000 Diners Jammed R. J. Brown Testimonial," *Tri-State Defender*, February 19, 1972.

123. The "reform" slate was led by John Wilson and contained Rev. Channing Phillips, who was the first Black person nominated for president at the 1968 DNC. "Fauntroy Slate Win in D.C. Primary," *BG*, May 3, 1972. His only challenge was an uncommitted slate that favored McGovern and Chisholm.

124. "Mrs. Chisholm Visits Wallace," *NYT*, June 9, 1972.

125. Richard Cohen, "Rep. Chisholm Pays Visit to Wallace in Md. Hospital," *WP*, June 9, 1972; Martin Nolan, "Wallace's Wheelchair Speech," *BG*, June 2, 1972.

126. John Herbers, "President Concerned Over Shooting," *NYT*, May 16, 1972; R. W. Apple Jr., "Wallace Rivals Set to Resume Campaign," *NYT*, May 17, 1972; Ben A. Franklin, "Kennedy Guarded by Secret Service" *NYT*, May 16, 1972; Nolan, "Wallace's Wheelchair Speech"; "Mrs. Chisholm Grateful," *NYT*, May 17, 1972.

127. "U.S. President–D Primaries [1972]," Our Campaigns, https://www.ourcampaigns.com/RaceDetail.html?RaceID=46950 (accessed July 23, 2020); Sally Quinn, "Chisholm Trail," *WP*, June 22, 1972; R. W. Apple Jr., "Triumph in State Brings M'Govern [sic] Widening

Support," *NYT*, June 22, 1972; Haskins, *Fighting Shirley Chisholm*, 176; Secret Service Binder, CCP.

CHAPTER 16

1. There had been two DNC commissions to draft reforms. The Commission on Rules was led by Michigan Representative James G. O'Hara and recommended new allocations of delegates and committee members based on state populations, the equal representation of women as officials and committee members, and new floor procedures. The other, more famous commission was that on Party Structure and Delegate Selection, initially led by George McGovern and later by Minnesota Representative Donald M. Fraser. These were the regulations that dictated greater representation of women, youth, and nonwhite people among delegates. Though there were other regulations on disclosure and access for the delegate selection process, it was the requirement that states field delegations "in reasonable relationships" to their population demographics that led to the most challenges brought to the Credentials Committee. In the two weeks prior to the convention, there were eighty-two challenges from thirty states. Diamond, *Congressional Quarterly's Guide to U.S. Elections*, 113–14.

For detailed accounts of the 1972 DNC, see Thompson, *Fear and Loathing on the Campaign Trail '72*; White, *Making of the President*; Miroff, *Liberals' Moment*.

2. R. W. Apple Jr., "Delegate Reforms Bring New Types to the Convention," *NYT*, July 9, 1972.

3. Chisholm, *Good Fight*, 124–45.

4. SL interview with Shirley Chisholm, April 29, 2003, CC, Box 9, Part 2: 24–27. Evelyn Simien has explained that Chisholm was "intersectionally marginalized"—that is, she experienced lack of support due to sexism among Black leaders and due to racism (and perhaps sexism also) among feminist leaders. Simien, *Historic Firsts*, 29–31.

5. Joe Harris, "Convention," *Black Coalition Weekly*, July 14, 1972.

6. George Frazier, "Chisholm, Go to Your Room," *BG*, May 31, 1972; Jeanne Arrondondo and A. M. Perchard, Letters to the Editor, *BG*, June 5, 1972.

7. George S. McGovern interview, *NYAN*, March 4, 1972.

8. Don Oberdorfer and William Chapman, "McGovern Woos 185 to Win Nomination on First Ballot," *WP*, June 22, 1972.

9. SL interview with Wilson Riles, CC, Box 9, Part 1: 25.

10. For a contemporary analysis of the state of Black political strategy, see Austin Scott, "Black Voter Strategy Is Split Four Ways," *WP*, May 8, 1972.

11. Oberdorfer and Chapman, "McGovern Woos 185 to Win Nomination on First Ballot"; Paul Delaney, "Black Bloc Decides to Back McGovern," *NYT*, June 22, 1972.

12. Austin Scott, "Fauntroy Says He Has Pledges to Assure McGovern Victory," *WP*, June 26, 1972; Clay, *Just Permanent Interests*, 226–27.

13. S. Micciche, "Platform Key to Democratic Unity: Success or Failure of Reforms Rests with McGovern, Wallace Power Blocs," *BG*, June 18, 1972.

14. Philip Warden, "Democrats Start Building Party Platform Planks," *CT*, June 25, 1972; Olga Corey, "Platform Committee Told Americans Have No Faith in Government," *Milwaukee Star*, July 6, 1972; S. J. Micciche, "Humphrey Warns on Platform Elitism," *BG*, June 25, 1972.

15. Transcript, *Meet the Press*, July 9, 1972, CPP, 35.

16. Chisholm, *Good Fight*, 112–13; Secret Service Binder, CPP.

17. SL interview with Shirley Chisholm, April 1, 2000, CC, Box 9, Part 1: 28.

18. Clay, *Just Permanent Interests*, 230.

19. Paul Delaney, "Blacks Are Split at Miami Beach," *NYT*, July 9, 1972.

20. SL interview with Shirley Chisholm, April 1 2000, CC, Box 9, Part 1: 28.

21. SL interview with Carolyn Smith, CC, Box 10, Part 2: 11–12.

22. "Wallace Pulls Out of 'Meet Press,'" *BG*, July 6, 1972; Transcript, *Meet the Press*, July 9, 1972, CPP, 32–34. The panel of interviewers were David S. Broder of the *WP*, James J. Kilpatrick of the *Washington Star*, James B. Reston of the *NYT*, Carl T. Rowan of the *Chicago Daily News*, and Frank McGee of NBC News.

23. Transcript, *Meet the Press*, July 9, 1972, CPP, 36.

24. Transcript, *Meet the Press*, July 9, 1972, CPP, 34, 37–38.

25. SL interview with Wilson Riles, CC, Box 9, Part 1: 26; Chisholm, *Good Fight*, 115; Austin Scott, "In Waning Hours, Mrs. Chisholm Courted 1st-Ballot Support," *WP*, July 13, 1972.

26. Scott, "In Waning Hours." Baraka would later issue a scathing criticism of Chisholm and her supporters: "Black people in Miami acted about Mrs. Chisholm as if she were actually running for President, and not in reality running to line up at the McGovern pay-window!!!" He spared none of the other Congressional Black Caucus (CBC) members either, characterizing them as elites who did not have the real interests of Black people in mind. See Baraka, "Toward the Creation of Political Institutions for All African Peoples," *Black World,* October 1972. A group called "Friends of the Black Congressional Caucus" sent copies of the article to CBC members in early November with a cover letter that cautioned them to be "aware of what Baraka thinks of us." Friends of the Black Congressional Caucus to Brothers and Sisters, November 10, 1972, CPP.

27. Shirley Chisholm to James Pitts, June 13, 1972, CC, Box 12, Folder 25. The first Chisholm strategy meeting at the DNC was planned for Sunday, July 9, at 2 p.m. at the Deauville Hotel (where her campaign was headquartered). "HHH Releases Black Delegates, Stirs Controversy in Black Caucus," *WP*, July 11, 1972.

28. Chisholm, *Good Fight*, 115–16.

29. Vernon Jarrett, "Rep. Chisholm's Plea Rocks Black Caucus," *CT*, July 10, 1972 and "Shirley Chisholm's Convention," *CT*, July 30, 1972. In the later article, Jarrett's tone had shifted, and he argued Chisholm had "practically alienated all of her support among the 13 black congressmen and the leadership of the Black National Convention held in Gary last March" because she "unleashed a vicious blast" at her opponents during the speech. His criticism was gendered. "Few male orators ever used a bludgeon as forcefully as Rep. Chisholm," Jarrett wrote. "At one point she described her toughness by attributing to herself a slang sexual term normally reserved for supervirile men of great nerve and durability." Most quotes are from Jarrett, except "younger and more militant" (Chisholm, *Good Fight*, 117).

30. "HHH Releases Black Delegates, Stirs Controversy in Black Caucus."

31. SL interview with Ronald Dellums, April 7, 2003, CC, Box 9, Part 2: 31; SL interview with Ronald Dellums, n.d., CC, Box 9, Tape 2: 38, 48 ("If there's any kind of way that"); SL interview with Ronald Dellums, April 7, 2003, CC, Box 9, Part 1: 20–25. In his recollection, he endorsed McGovern after the party platform was established and Chisholm's candidacy could no longer sway its contents. But, in fact, Dellums endorsed McGovern on the night before the convention began.

32. "Dellums Shifts From Chisholm to McGovern," *Los Angeles Times* (UPI), July 10, 1972. Wilson Riles recalled hearing privately that Dellums did not approve of Chisholm negotiating with southern senators for delegates. SL interview with Wilson Riles, CC, Box 9, Part 1: 36.

33. Percy Sutton delivered the nomination speech. Hixon and Rose, *Official Proceedings*, 374. Chisholm took pains to state that Dellums had "understood what [she] was doing

from the start and supported [her] almost all the way." His last-minute endorsement of McGovern did not preclude her from making five mentions of him as a stalwart supporter in *Good Fight* (31, 50, 73, 74, 101); SL interview with Wilson Riles, CC, Box 10, Part 1: 29–30, 38.

34. SL interview with Wilson Riles, CC, Box 9, Part 1: 34, 41.

35. Invitation, CC, Box 12, Folder 22.

36. Freidan was reportedly dismayed that she had not been chosen as spokesperson. See Hennessee, *Betty Friedan*, 168. Bella Abzug form letter, n.d. [April 1972], PEP, Box 6, Folder 2.

37. Ephron, *Crazy Salad*, 42.

38. Ellen Goodman, "Women Delegates Caucus, Hopefuls Woo Their Votes," *BG*, July 11, 1972.

39. SL interview with Arlie Scott, CC, Box 10, Part 2: 26–27; SL interview with Susan Brownmiller, CC, Box 9: 23.

40. Vivien Leone, "The Elusive Miami Beach Democratic National Transitory Soap Button Opera," *off our backs*, September 1972, 6–8; Gloria Steinem, Letter to the Editor, *off our backs*, December 1972, 22.

41. SL interview with Susan Brownmiller, CC, Box 9: 29–31.

42. SL interview with James Richardson, CC, Box 10, Part 1: 8.

43. SL interview with Wilson Riles, CC, Box 9, Part 1: 26, 30.

44. SL interview with Arlie Scott, CC, Box 10, Part 2: 22–23; SL interview with Wilson Riles, CC, Box 10, Part 1: 30–31.

45. Hixon and Rose, *Official Proceedings*, 174–77, 195; SL interview with James Richardson, CC, Part 1: 28; SL interview with Wilson Riles, CC, Box 10, Part 1: 31–32.

46. SL interview with Arlie Scott, CC, Box 10, Part 2.

47. SL interview with Barbara Lee, CC, Box 10: 27–29.

48. Diamond, *Congressional Quarterly's Guide to U.S. Elections*, 114.

49. Chisholm, *Good Fight*, 119.

50. Chisholm, *Good Fight*, 119.

51. "Caucus Urges Solid Black Support for Rep. Chisholm," *CT*, July 11, 1972; "HHH Releases Black Delegates, Stirs Controversy in Black Caucus," *WP*, July 11, 1972; Paul H. Wyche Jr., "Baraka Hits Humphrey Chisholm Confab Plan," *Los Angeles Herald-Dispatch*, July 20, 1972 (CPP, Clipping, Album 1); Stephen Green, "D.C. Delegates Uneasy on Backing McGovern," *WP*, July 11, 1972; Paul Delaney, "Humphrey Blacks to Vote for Mrs. Chisholm First," *NYT*, July 11, 1972. Reports varied on whether Humphrey had ninety-three or ninety-seven Black delegates to release.

52. Vernon Jarrett, "Little Black Support for Shirley," *WP*, July 13, 1972.

53. Chisholm Delegates Memorandum, PEP, Box 9, Folder 3; Chisholm, *Good Fight*, 117–18.

54. Hixon and Rose, *Official Proceedings*, 250–85 (Pitts speech 281–22).

55. Hixon and Rose, *Official Proceedings*, 294–307.

56. Hixon and Rose, *Official Proceedings*, 328.

57. Hixon and Rose, *Official Proceedings*, 328–33 (quoted language on 328).

58. Diamond, *Congressional Quarterly's Guide to U.S. Elections*, 115.

59. It had taken a concerted effort to make Chisholm eligible for nomination at the DNC and gather the minimum of fifty delegates who endorsed the nomination. Liz Cohen form letter, June 9, 1972, PEP, Box 6, Folder 2.

60. Scott, "In Waning Hours"; Chisholm, *Good Fight*, 118, 121. Delegates from other states were also pledged by law to other candidates, but their home state law enforcement had no jurisdiction in Florida.

61. Hixon and Rose, *Official Proceedings*, 374–75.

62. Hixon and Rose, *Official Proceedings*, 376.

63. Hixon and Rose, *Official Proceedings*, 377.

64. Minnesotans were especially concerned about showing support for Chisholm after Humphrey delegates were released to vote for her. See Peter Ackerberg, "Vote Switching Had Minnesota Result in Doubt," *Minneapolis Star*, July 13, 1972, CPP.

65. The fourteen states who reduced their votes for Chisholm were South Carolina, New York, Indiana, Mississippi, Florida, New Jersey, Colorado, Minnesota, Virginia, Tennessee, Illinois, Michigan, Louisiana, and Oklahoma. See appendix. Hixon and Rose, *Official Proceedings*, 382–97, On southern support see Chisholm, *Good Fight*, 123–24.

66. For the full first ballot count, see appendix. Diamond, *Congressional Quarterly's Guide to U.S. Elections 1974*, 173.

67. Denby and Warner, *Chisholm: Pursuing the Dream*.

68. SL interview with Victor Robles, CC, Box 10, Part 1: 24–26.

69. Hixon and Rose, *Official Proceedings*, 395.

70. SL interview with Shirley Chisholm, April 1, 2000, CC, Box 9, Part 1: 30.

71. Chisholm, *Good Fight*, 131, 159, 161–62.

72. Shirley Chisholm, "Is It Worth It?" *Glamour*, October 1972 (reprinted in Gallagher, "How Did Shirley Chisholm," Document 15).

73. Chisholm, *Good Fight*, 124–25, 128–30, 157.

74. Gloria Steinem, "The Ticket that Might Have Been: President Chisholm," *Ms.*, January 1973, 73, 120–24.

75. Scott, "In Waning Hours."

76. Billy Rowe, "Billy Rowe's Notebook," *NYAN*, July 15, 1972.

77. SL interview with Ronald Dellums, n.d., CC, Box 9, Tape 2: 28–31, 34–35.

78. SL interview with Barbara Lee, CC, Box 9: 26.

79. SL interview with Barbara Lee, CC, Box 9: 30, 32–33.

80. Clay, *Just Permanent Interests*, 230–31.

81. Vernon Jarrett, "Two Black Leaders Hail V. P. Choice," *CT*, July 14, 1972.

82. Chisholm was present at the Extraordinary Session, which was held August 8 at the Sheraton Park Hotel in Washington, D.C. Hixon and Rose, *Official Proceedings*, 474–501.

83. SL interview with Jules Witcover, CC, Box 10: 55, 65.

84. SL interview with James Richardson, CC, Box 10, Part 1: 29–31.

85. David S. Broder, "Candidate Ponders His Running Mate," *WP*, July 13, 1972.

86. "Clergyman Asserts Dems Not Using Black Youth," *NYAN*, August 19, 1972.

87. "Rep. Chisholm Bars Taking Active Role in McGovern Drive," *NYT*, September 20, 1972; Austin Scott, "Snubbed by McGovern, Mrs. Chisholm Says," *WP*, September 21, 1972; "Chisholm Not to Actively Campaign for McGovern," *Milwaukee Star* (National Black News Service), September 28, 1972.

88. Ronald Smothers, "Effort by Blacks for McGovern Gets a Belated Start," *NYT*, October 18, 1972; Jim Squires, "McGovern Charges Nixon with Sabotage," *CT*, October 20, 1972; Thomas Ronan, "Shirley Chisholm Gives McGovern Drive a Push," *NYT*, October 20, 1972.

89. Chisholm, "Is It Worth It?"

90. *Our Record*, November 7, 1972, CP, Box 4, Folder 9.

91. James F. Clarity, "Comparison of the Former and New Congressional District Lines in City and Suburbs," *NYT*, March 20, 1972.

92. Editorial (" . . . and Brooklyn . . ."), *NYT*, October 30, 1972; Diamond, *Congressional Quarterly's Guide to U.S. Elections*, 873; "Row Heading for Showdown," *NYAN*, October 21, 1972; "Beatty Is Victor in Brooklyn Race," *NYT*, September 20, 1972; Ronald Smothers, "Two 'Winners' Seen in Beatty Victory," *NYT*, September 21, 1972; George Todd, "Beatty Crushes

Stewart," *NYAN*, September 23, 1972; George Todd, "Chisholm, Beatty, Fortune Win Landslide Victories," *NYAN*, November 11, 1972; Ronald Smothers, "Rep. Chisholrn Emerges with Power," *NYT*, November 19, 1972.

93. SL interview with Ronald Dellums, 2003, CC, Box 9, Part 2: 33–34.

CHAPTER 17

1. Edward Thompson III interview with Shirley Chisholm, May 2, 1973, BOHC, 10, 29; Penda Saxby, "I Want to Be Left Alone," *CORE* [Congress of Racial Equality] *Magazine*, Summer 1973. Despite her anger with most of her Congressional Black Caucus colleagues, Chisholm would continue to cooperate with them in the House and behave cordially toward them. This even included Walter Fauntroy, her staffer recalled. Author interview with Carolyn Smith, 12.

2. Chisholm, "The Relationship between Religion and Today's Social Issues," 117.

3. Edward Thompson III interview with Shirley Chisholm, May 2, 1973, BOHC, 26–27.

4. Edward Thompson III interview with Shirley Chisholm, May 2, 1973, BOHC, 14–16. She took an interest in reforming the House of Representatives to become more democratic. Reforms in the House Democratic Caucus occurred in 1973–74 in the aftermath of Watergate. See Peabody, "Committees from the Leadership Perspective," 133–46; Orenstein, "Towards Restructuring the Congressional Committee System," 147–57; Davidson and Oleszek, *Congress Against Itself*. A Select Committee on Committees was formed, with Richard Bolling (D-MO) as chair, and suggested fairly far-reaching reforms. Bolling presented the reforms for a vote on the House floor in October 1973. Chisholm had served on the first House reform committee chaired by Julia Hansen in 1970, but she now wanted reform to go further. When Hansen offered a more moderate proposal, Chisholm and other younger and more liberal members sided with the Bolling Committee. See 119th *CR* (1973), 34406–69.

5. Author interview with Laura Murphy.

6. Simon Anekwe, "Show Me $750,000 and I'll Run for President," *NYAN*, December 4, 1974; "Presidential Race Ruled Out," *NYT* (UPI), June 9, 1975; Odessa McClary, "Shirley Skips '76," *NYAN*, October 22, 1975.

7. Conflict over publicity with Houghton Mifflin, who published *Unbought and Unbossed*, led her to choose a new house, Harper and Row. Houghton was interested in a second book, but Chisholm wrote that she was "less than satisfied" with Houghton's work with the first book. Joyce Hartman to Marcia Legrue, April 6, 1972; Shirley Chisholm to Joyce Hartman, September 21, 1972, Houghton Mifflin Company Correspondence, Box 52, Folder 3, HMP.

8. Chisholm, *Good Fight*, 10.

9. Chisholm, *Good Fight*, 140–48.

10. Chisholm, *Good Fight*, 149–58.

11. Around the same time, she also authorized a biography by James Haskins, an author of dozens of short biographies of famous Black figures. Haskins interviewed Chisholm in February 1973. He also relied on extensive newspaper research and a large packet of speeches and clippings provided by Chisholm's D.C. office. Chisholm provided a few personal photos for the volume. Haskins successfully sold it to Dial Press, which specialized in young adult books. Chisholm seemed happy with the result ("It captures my life beautifully!" she wrote in a note to Haskins). *Fighting Shirley Chisholm* was published in 1975. Wesley Holder to James Haskins, April 5, 1972; Arlene Doring to James Haskins, January 23, 1973; James Haskins to Shirley Chisholm, February 3, 1973, James Haskins Collection, Box 57, Folder 23, Howard Gotlieb Archival Research Center, Boston University. Shirley Chisholm to James Haskins, n.d., James Haskins Collection, Box 27, Folder 4, Howard Gotlieb Archival Research Center, Boston University. Wesley Holder to James Haskins, February 23, 1973;

James Haskins to Shirley Chisholm, April 28, 1973; Shirley Chisholm to James Haskins, n.d. [February 1974], James Haskins Collection, Box 57, Folder 23, Howard Gotlieb Archival Research Center, Boston University.

12. Ronald Smothers, "Brooklyn Parade Attracts 150,000," *NYT*, September 5, 1972.

13. Edward Doucette was discovered by police in the basement with burglary tools after the house's alarm system alerted them. "Metropolitan Briefs," *NYT*, October 15, 1972; "Chisholm Home Hit," *WP*, October 15, 1972; Sadie Feddoes, "Please Be Seated," *NYAN*, November 25, 1972. Title record, 1028 St. Johns Place, Brooklyn, NY, 11213, Property Shark, www.propertyshark.com/mason/Reports/showsection.html?propkey=152832 (accessed May 30, 2013).

14. Bob Gottleib felt that the venom from Black politicians served to take the wind out of Chisholm's sails after the 1972 campaign. He did not feel she was as "active [and] influential" afterward, for that reason. SL interview with Robert Gottleib, CC, Box 9, Part 2: 17–18.

15. Martin Tolchin, "Mrs. Chisholm Plans to Retire from Politics, 'Definitely' by '76," *NYT*, July 6, 1973; "See Shirley Chisholm as Next NYC School Chancellor," *NYAN*, March 10, 1973.

16. "Chisholm Endorses Badillo," *NYAN*, June 16, 1973; Charlayne Hunter, "Mrs. Chisholm and Basil Paterson Support Beame's Candidacy," *NYT*, October 12, 1973.

17. Tom Buckley, "Mrs. Chisholm Finds District Leaders in Opposing Camp," *NYT*, May 24, 1972.

18. Buckley, "Mrs. Chisholm Finds District Leaders in Opposing Camp"; Charlayne Hunter, "Chisholm-Wright Feud in Brooklyn Is Eroding Blacks' Political Power," *NYT*, March 20, 1976; Maurice Carroll, "Challenge by Velez Turned Back Easily," *NYT*, September 15, 1976.

19. Edward Thompson III interview with Shirley Chisholm, May 2, 1973, 18, BOHC. She also expressed hope that the Watergate scandal might lead to "somebody's salvation around the corner" (19).

20. "Chisolm [*sic*] Voices Impeachment Views," *Baltimore Afro-American*, June 30, 1973; "Entire Black Caucus on Nixon's 'Hit List,'" *NYAN*, July 7, 1973.

21. Thomas P. Ronan, "Urban Congressman Takes on Farm Post," *NYT*, May 10, 1975.

22. SL interview with Carolyn Smith, CC, Box 10, Part 1: 23.

23. Chisholm boasted of her major grants for the Bedford-Stuyvesant Restoration Corporation, two neighborhood health centers, and a new community center, as well as smaller grants for other institutions. "Rep. Chisholm Brings Boro $$$ from D.C.," *Chisholm Record* [campaign newsletter], September 1974, CC, Box 4, Folder 10.

24. Lesley Crosson, "Candid Conversations: Shirley Chisholm: Unbought, Unbossed, and Undaunted," *NYAN*, December 8, 1973.

25. "Mess Hall Is Seized by Blacks," *WP* (AP), September 20, 1972; Paul Delaney, "Inmates in Capital Seize 10," *NYT*, October 12, 1972, and "Order to Shift Juveniles Broke Capital Jail Revolt," October 13, 1972; Haynes Johnson, "Jail Rebels Free All Hostages after Airing Grievances to Judge," *WP*, October 12, 1972; William L. Claiborne, "They Led Me into a Hall, Saying 'Don't Hurt Him,'" *WP*, October 12, 1972, and "Tragedy Averted by Talks," *WP*, October 13, 1972.

26. She sought increased Head Start funding in the bill, along with legal services funding. 118th *CR (1972)*, 4105, 4125, 4298.

27. Edward Thompson III interview with Shirley Chisholm, May 2, 1973, 17, BOHC.

28. Nat Sheppard, "The Congressional Black Caucus in Search of a Role," *Race Relations Reporter*, March 1973; Crosson, "Candid Conversations."

29. "Stokes, Chisholm Continuing Feud," *CD*, November 6, 1973; Ethel Payne, "The Potomac Scene," *CD*, November 24, 1973.

30. 119th *CR* (1973), 1622.

31. Crosson, "Candid Conversations."

32. U.S. House of Representatives, *Discrimination in Employment*, 222.

33. [Delegate from U.S. Virgin Islands] Ron de Lugo to Shirley Chisholm, December 3, 1972, CP, Box 3, Folder 26. There was also a campaign to get Chisholm elected caucus chair. "Give your chair to a lady" was her campaign slogan. U.S. House of Representatives interview with Muriel Morisey, Senior Legislative Assistant, Representative Shirley Chisholm of New York, April 19, 2017, 36, Oral Histories of African Americans in Congress, History, Art, and Archives, U.S. House of Representatives, Washington, D.C.

34. Author interview with Shirley Downs, July 16, 2012, Part 3: 3.

35. U.S. Senate, *Nominations—July–September*, 126, 129.

36. Author interview with Patsy Fleming; Philip G. Hilts, "Clinton Picks New Director of AIDS Policy," *NYT*, November 11, 1994; U.S. House of Representatives interview with Muriel Morisey, Senior Legislative Assistant, Representative Shirley Chisholm of New York, April 19, 2017, 24–25, Oral Histories of African Americans in Congress, History, Art, and Archives, U.S. House of Representatives, Washington, D.C.

37. Author interview with Carolyn Smith, 6.

38. Charles E. Price, "Whatever Happened to Shirley Chisholm?" *Atlanta Daily World*, March 7, 1974.

39. Jim Squires, "Barbara's Cold, Calculating, and Very Competent," *CT*, February 6, 1973.

40. "2 Black Women Head for House," *NYT*, October 7, 1972.

41. Author interview with Carolyn Smith, 11–12.

42. Author interview with Andrea Tracy Holmes, Part 2: 7–8. For an extended comparison analysis of Chisholm and Jordan, see Fraser, "Catalysts for Change."

43. Leroy F. Aarons, "Legislator with a Subtle Touch," *WP*, October 22, 1972. Other women who joined Chisholm were Patricia Schroeder (D-CO), fellow Brooklynite Elizabeth Holtzman (D-NY), and Paula Hawkins (R-MD). Southern Christian Leadership Conference leader Andrew Young (D-GA) was added to the number of Black representatives.

44. Louise Hutchinson, "Yvonne Can't Kick the Barrier-Breaking Habit," *CT*, January 30, 1973.

45. Lilliam Wiggins, "Women in Politics and UL Convention," *Baltimore Afro-American*, August 4, 1973.

46. News Release, July 10, 1973, CP, Box 5, Folder 11.

47. House Joint Res. 736, 115th *CR* (1969), 13341. The ERA would not be passed by the House until 1971, however, after Martha Griffiths gathered enough signatures on a discharge petition to get it out of the Judiciary Committee. See Hartman, "Equal Rights Amendment," 155–56.

48. Elizabeth Bennet, "Steinem Wants Out and a New Group In at the National Women's Political Caucus," *Houston Post*, February 9, 1973, PEP, Box 33, Folder 13; "Women: Trouble for ERA," *Time*, February 19, 1972; W. H. Stickney, "Chisholm Claims Nixon Disregards Congress's Will," *Houston Chronicle*, February 9, 1972, PEP, Box 33, Folder 13; Nicholas C. Chriss, "Shirley, Betty, Bella, Gloria: Women's Lib Superstars Ask Rank-and-File to Take Over," *Los Angeles Times*, February 10, 1973; Summary of Opening Remarks at 1973 Houston NWPC Convention, n.d., PEP, Box 35, Folder 1; [Associated Press,] "Chisholm's Challenge to Women," *San Francisco Chronicle*, February 10, 1973 (reprinted in Gallagher, "How Did Shirley Chisholm," Document 17).

49. "Contact Shirley Chisholm: Your Voice in Congress," campaign pamphlet, Muriel Forde Family Collection, Barbados.

50. "Contact Shirley Chisholm: Your Voice in Congress," 107–10, 118–19.

51. U.S. House of Representatives, *Proposed Elimination of OEO*, 305–6, 349–51.

52. 119th *CR* (1973), 8591–92; Ethel Payne, "OEO Head Gets Lumps from Cuts," *CD*, March 3, 1973.

53. U.S. House of Representatives, *Proposed Elimination of OEO*, Part 2: March 26 and 27, 1973 (Chisholm's questioning on 1054–55, 1078–79, 1088, 1111, 1146–47, 1168–70). See also "Congressional Unit Hears How Cutbacks Affect NYC," *Baltimore Afro-American*, March 31, 1973.

54. Crosson, "Candid Conversations."

55. "Statement by the Honorable Shirley Chisholm (D-NY) on the Proposed Flat-Grant System of Welfare Payments Currently under Consideration by the Washington, DC, City Council," News Release, August 21, 1972, CP, Box 5, Folder 9 (see also Gallagher, "How Did Shirley Chisholm," Document 9c); "Shirley Blasts Welfare System," *NYAN*, August 26, 1972.

56. Fisher, "Congress, the Executive, and the Budget," 102–13.

57. 119th *CR* (1973): CBC member remarks, 2830–54; Chisholm's remarks, 2836–37.

58. 119th *CR* (1973), 13363–65. In April, Chisholm also criticized the president for his proposed cuts to Medicare and Social Security and the Department of Health, Education, and Welfare for new social services guidelines, and she placed a forceful argument for the extension of the Emergency Employment Act of 1971 (H.R. 4204) in the *CR* (the House declined to consider it). 119th *CR* (1973), 11492–93, 13095–97, 13374–75, 13363–65; News Release, April 28, 1973, CP, Box 5, Folder 10.

59. "Minimum Wage Bill Sought for All Domestic Workers," *Baltimore Afro-American*, May 27, 1972; "Domestics at Sessions Ask Gains," *NYT*, October 10, 1972.

60. "A Way Out of the Poverty Mess: A Full Days Wage for a Full Day's Labor," 119th *CR* (1973), 13846; 119th *CR* Index (1973), 1985.

61. Martin Tolchin, "Mrs. Chisholm Led Fight for Domestics' Base Pay," *NYT*, June 21, 1973; Marian Christy, "The Fire Inside Rep. Chisholm," *BG*, July 9, 1982, CP, Box 8, Folder 6. Chisholm would look back on the bill as her "greatest legislative achievement." See Shirley Chisholm to Art Garso, December 21, 1981, CP, Box 7, Folder 4.

62. These workers, she explained, were the working poor and were the majority (80 percent) of poor families. Only about 20 percent of poor families were receiving public assistance. 119th *CR* (1973), 13846. She was discussing H.R. 4757 that day, but the bill that would eventually be passed was introduced three weeks later as H.R. 7935. Both bills were introduced by her Education and Labor colleague John Dent (D-PA).

63. 119th *CR* (1973), 13847–58. See also Lawrence Feinberg, "110,000 Here Work below Poverty Level," *WP*, April 9, 1973 (reprinted in 119th *CR* (1973), 13857), and Crosson, "Candid Conversations."

64. 119th *CR* (1973), 18340–41. Also in June, Chisholm argued for continued appropriations to local legal services organizations until a comprehensive legal services bill could be passed. 119th *CR* (1973), 20148–49.

65. Even erstwhile critic Roy Wilkins credited Chisholm with the victory in the domestic worker fight. Wilkins, "How It Can Be Done," *Los Angeles Times*, July 6, 1973. Bill Clay, alternatively, refused to credit her. Ethel Payne, "The Potomac Scene" and "Minimum Wage Fight," *CD*, December 1, 1973.

66. 119th *CR* (1973), 30366–67, 30392.

67. For coinage of the term "intersectional," see Crenshaw, "Mapping the Margins."

68. Shirley Chisholm, "The Politics of Coalition," *Black Scholar*, September 1972, 30–33.

69. Edward Thompson III interview with Shirley Chisholm, May 2, 1973, 23, BOHC.

70. Shirley Chisholm, "Black Women in Politics" [typed statement, July 24, 1973], CP, Box 1, Folder 28. She appears to have given versions of this speech in 1974 and 1978: "The Black Woman in Contemporary America," University of Missouri–Kansas City, June 17, 1974,

http://americanradioworks.publicradio.org/features/sayitplain/schisholm.html (accessed January 13, 2011); and "The Contemporary Black Woman," September 16, 1978 (audience unknown), CP, Box 1, Folder 39.

71. Chisholm, "Black Women in Politics."

72. Chisholm directly quoted Beal on at least two occasions, in "The Contemporary Black Woman" (1978) and "The Black Woman In Contemporary America" (1974). See Beal, "Double Jeopardy," in *The Black Woman*. Chisholm's copy of *The Black Woman* remains in her estate's collection of her books (CPP).

73. Author interview with Andrea Tracy Holmes, April 11, 2010.

74. Chisholm, "Facing the Abortion Question," in *Unbought and Unbossed*, 136.

75. Anne Williams, "unconquerable," and Fran Pollner, "Warmth and Heat," *off our backs,* December–January 1974; Barbara Campbell, "Black Feminists Hold Parley Here," *NYT*, December 2, 1973; Shirley Simpson, "Chisholm Advises Feminists at New York Conference," *Bay State Banner*, December 20, 1973.

76. Rita LaPorte, "Notes Prompted by the National Black Feminist Organization," *off our backs*, February 1974, 2–3.

77. Mae Dell, "Sister Shirley Says," *off our backs*, March 1974, 9, 25.

78. There were only three members at the hearing's first day: Subcommittee Chair Augustus Hawkins (who admitted that, had seniority rules not been in place, Chisholm would be chair), Patsy Mink, and Chisholm. The five other subcommittee members, including Bill Clay, were absent. Mink authored the bill on the premise that civil rights legislation did not provide the means for developing equal opportunities for women and, significantly, eradicating gender stereotypes. Clay would attend the second day of the hearing, September 26. U.S. House of Representatives, *Women's Educational Equity Act*, 4–5.

79. U.S. House of Representatives, *Women's Educational Equity Act*, 6, 36, 161, 235, 281.

80. Martin Tolchin, "Shirley Chisholm Facing U.S. Inquiry into 3 Areas," *NYT*, November 16, 1973, and "Agency Sees 'Apparent Violations' in Funds," *NYT*, November 17, 1973; Les Ledbetter, "Representative Planning to Seek Re-Election," *NYT*, November 17, 1973. Chisholm disputed some of Tolchin's account per William Claiborne, in "GAO Alleges Violations by Chisholm," *WP*, November 17, 1973, and in Crosson, "Candid Conversations." The Office of Federal Elections did share its September 7, 1973 report with Watergate investigators. See cover note from Delores McCarthy, secretary to Philip S. Hughes (director, Office of Federal Elections) to Roger Witten, assistant special prosecutor, Records of the Watergate Special Prosecution Force, RG 460, National Archives and Records Administration, College Park, MD. The *NYAN* stood behind her, saying that it was her very closeness to the grassroots that meant her nonprofessional staff had made some accounting mistakes. "Our Duty to Shirley," *NYAN*, November 24, 1973. In addition, it was not only federal officials who initiated investigations; the Massachusetts attorney general also corresponded with the treasurer of the campaign in that state about an alleged failure to file "proper statements." Paul A. Good to Wendy K. Curwood, July 6, 1973 (collection of author).

81. "Shirley Tells All about Campaign Spendings," *NYAN*, January 26, 1974; "Chisholm Group Defends Itself," *NYT*, January 24, 1974; Martin Tolchin, "Inquiry Clearing Rep. Chisholm of Election Campaign Charges," *NYT*, April 24, 1974; Ethel Payne, "Chisholm Beats Funds Rap," *CD*, April 25, 1974. Some members of the press thought Chisholm had been unfairly targeted, including G. W. Westerman of the *Panama Tribune*, who wrote a letter of support. G. W. Westerman to Shirley Chisholm, May 6, 1974, CP, Box 3, Folder 26.

82. "Minority Youth Day in Brooklyn," *NYAN*, March 2, 1974.

83. Lawrence Van Gelder, "Screen: Ali, Shirley Chisholm Subjects of Studies," *NYT*, May 3, 1974. Werner would go on to be a major television producer as an executive at ABC and

then cofounder of a production company that made popular series such as *The Cosby Show*, *Roseanne*, and *3rd Rock from the Sun*.

84. "Domestic Workers Bill Up to Nixon," *NYAN*, March 30, 1974; David E. Rosenbaum, "Congress Raises Minimum Wages," *NYT*, March 29, 1974; R. W. Apple Jr., "President Signs Rise in Pay Base to $2.30 an Hour," *NYT*, April 9, 1974.

85. John W. Lewis Jr., "Fighter, Chisholm: 'I Get Adrenalin from the People,'" *NYAN*, April 19, 1980.

86. The OEO bill was H.R. 14449. John W. Lewis Jr., "Capital Comment: Impeachment Politics Hit OEO," *Baltimore Afro-American*, May 11, 1974; "OEO's Fate Tied to Impeachment," *NYAN*, May 11, 1974. Other successful cosponsored bills in 1974 included Youth Conservation Corps (H.R. 14897; Lloyd Meeds (D-WA), twenty-four cosponsors); Government employees' workers' compensation (H.R. 13871; Dominick Daniels (D-NJ), twenty-two cosponsors); Older Americans Act amendment to fund nutrition programs (H.R. 11105; John Brademas (D-IN), twenty-five cosponsors); the Menominee Restoration Act (H.R. 10717; Harold Froehlich (R-WI), twenty-three cosponsors); Extension of the Drug Abuse Education Act of 1970 (H.R. 9456; Meeds, nine cosponsors); National Foundation on the Arts and Humanities amendments (H.R. 3926; Brademas, thirteen cosponsors, passed as S. 795); House Committee broadcasting (H.R. 1107; Wayne Owens (D-UT), ten cosponsors); Request for info on bombing Cambodia from Department of Defense (H.R. 379; Robert Leggett (D-CA), fifteen cosponsors).

87. Shirley Chisholm, untitled speech before the New York State Welfare Conference, 1974, CP, Box 3, Folder 10, 8–9; see also Chisholm, "Social Justice and the Politics of Welfare," undated speech, [1974–76], CP, Box 2, Folder 54.

88. Chisholm, untitled speech before the New York State Welfare Conference, 1974, CP, Box 3, Folder 10, 3–4.

89. Chisholm, untitled speech before the New York State Welfare Conference, 1974, CP, Box 3, Folder 10, 6.

90. Chisholm, untitled speech before the New York State Welfare Conference, 1974, CP, Box 3, Folder 10, 9.

91. Chisholm, "Social Justice and the Politics of Welfare," speech [1976], CP, Box 2, Folder 54; Beal, "Double Jeopardy," in Guy-Sheftall, *Words of Fire*, 149; Lorde, "Age, Race, Class, and Sex," 284–91. Chisholm also advocated nonviolent direct action means for bringing about employment justice. She supported a boycott of the cosmetics company Posner Labs after it moved its manufacturing plant to avoid increasing wages to its largely Black and brown female employees. "Shirley Chisholm Joins Boycott of New Jersey Cosmetic Firm," *San Francisco Sun Reporter*, September 23, 1976.

92. Shirley Chisholm, "Social Justice and the Politics of Welfare," speech [ca. 1976], CP, Box 2, Folder 54.

93. Chisholm, "Foreword," in *Child Care*, xii.

94. Nadasen, Mittelstadt, and Chappell, *Welfare in the United States*, 49.

95. Photo caption, *CD*, July 27, 1972; Marie Cooke, "Salute to Black Women," *Baltimore Afro-American*, August 10, 1974; "Chisholm Office Ransacked Again," *CD*, August 10, 1974; Shirley Chisholm to James Haskins, September 9, 1974, James Haskins Collection, Box 57, Folder 23, Howard Gotlieb Archival Research Center, Boston University.

96. Chisholm had been hearing murmurs in the House cloakroom that Republican members had been hearing from angry constituents at home and would not continue to support Nixon should those complaints continue. See "Mrs. Chisholm Predicts Nixon Will Quit in April," *NYT*, February 23, 1974. "Rep. Chisholm Urges Support for Ford," *Atlanta Daily World*, August 16, 1974.

97. Linda Charlton, "Rep. Chisholm Drive for Rockefeller," *NYT*, December 17, 1974; Endorsement of Nelson Rockefeller, CP, Box 3, Folder 25; U.S. House of Representatives, *Nomination of Nelson A. Rockefeller*, 677–79.

98. Richard L. Madden, "Congress Votes to Override Ford on Pupil Lunch Aid," *NYT*, October 8, 1975.

99. "Appease Restless Boro Natives—Mrs. Chisholm," *NYAN*, March 23, 1974.

100. Francis X. Clines, "Albany Meets Wednesday on Brooklyn Redistricting," *NYT*, May 26, 1974; Simon Anekwe, "I Have No Monopoly on Any Political Seat, Nor Does Any Other Politician," *NYAN*, May 18, 1974; Frank Lynn, "Rooney Imperiled by District Plan," *NYT*, May 28, 1974; Barone, Ujifusa, and Matthews, *Almanac of American Politics 1976*, 574–75.

101. Editorial, *NYAN*, August 31, 1974.

102. Grace Lictenstein, "Brooklyn's Congress Delegation Altered," *NYT*, September 12, 1974; Charlayne Hunter, "Blacks Reported Resigned to Giving Vote to Carey," *NYT*, October 16, 1974; George Todd, "Chisholm, Wright, Fortune, Vann, Hamilton, Lewis, and Pinkett Are Winners in Brooklyn," *NYAN*, November 9, 1974; Diamond, *Congressional Quarterly's Guide to U.S. Elections*, 878. The battle between Wright and Chisholm also extended into the down-ballot races for district leader and the New York State Assembly. Chisholm supported Edolphus Towns as district leader, while Sam Wright, in a twist of fate, supported Mac Holder's protégé Lloyd Mapp. A social worker by training, Towns was an administrator at the Beth Israel Medical Center. See Andy Cooper, "One Man's Opinion: The Political Scene," *NYAN*, September 7, 1974, and *Chisholm Record*, September 1974, CC, Box 4, Folder 10.

103. "Map Maker, Sam Likes to Run—Without Risks," *Chisholm Record*, September 1974.

104. Charlayne Hunter, "Chisholm-Wright Feud in Brooklyn Is Eroding Blacks' Political Power," *NYT*, March 20, 1976.

105. Austin Scott, "Black Caucus Alters Tactics," *WP*, February 15, 1975.

106. "Women in Congress May Form a Caucus to Increase Influence," *NYT* (AP), December 26, 1974.

107. Martin Tolchin, "Mrs. Abzug Getting Help of Some of Her Colleagues, But Not Their Endorsements," *NYT*, June 10, 1976.

108. Author interview with Shirley Downs, July 16, 2012.

109. Author interview with Shirley Downs, March 24, 2016.

110. Shirley Chisholm, "Notes on Minority Women and the Equal Rights Amendment," n.d. [ca. 1970], CP, Box 2, Folder 32. The venue for this speech is not known. She visited the University of Missouri in Columbia to deliver remarks on this topic, and it is possible this speech was delivered then, on March 7, 1975. See "Chisholm Boosts Feminists," *LAS*, March 13, 1975.

111. Shirley Chisholm, "Minority Women and Economic Parity," undated speech [1975], CP, Box 2, Folder 33.

112. The hearings were held on March 17, April 21, and April 28. Chisholm was absent on April 28 due to her plane from New York being delayed. Shirley Downs staffed the hearings. News Release, [week of March 10, 1975], CP, Box 5, Folder 10; U.S. House of Representatives, *Sex Discrimination and Sex Stereotyping*, March 17, April 21, 28, 1975; Nancy Hicks, "Women Criticize Sex Bias Efforts," *NYT*, April 22, 1975; author email communication from Shirley Downs, July 22, 2019; Shirley Downs and Carol Burris, "What Congress Can Do for You (Or to You), *Ms.*, February 1975, 97–100; SL interview with Shirley Downs, CC, Box 10: 27. According to Alice Kessler-Harris, these hearings were necessary in the aftermath of the Moynihan Report: a focus on Black men's opportunities to be breadwinners eclipsed women's rights to equity. See Kessler-Harris, *In Pursuit of Equity*, 270.

113. The measures passed as S. 2657 (Ninety-Fourth Congress) in October 1976. See also H.R. 12835.

114. Thomas P. Ronan, "Certain Legislation Gets Backers Left and Right," *NYT*, May 17, 1975.

115. Jeanette Smyth, "El Congreso's Salute," *WP*, July 18, 1975.

116. Nancy Hicks, "House Panel Rejects Some Rules on Sex Discrimination in Schools," *NYT*, July 9, 1975; U.S. House of Representatives, *Sex Discrimination Regulations*, 50–53, 65, 153 (quote).

117. Cathy Steele Roche, "U.S. Action Asked in Joan Little Case," *WP*, April 16, 1975; "Ms. Little's First Lawyer Withdraws from Her Case," *Atlanta Daily World* (UPI), April 18, 1975; "Joanne Little Seemed to Be Winning Points," *Baltimore Afro-American*, April 26, 1975. For a sustained analysis of the Joan Little case, see McGuire, *At the Dark End of the Street*, 246–78. Chisholm also signed on her colleague Herman Badillo's letter on behalf of three Puerto Ricans jailed in the Dominican Republic, allegedly for transporting anti-Dominican Republic guerillas. Diplomatic Cable, Department of State to Santo Domingo, September 21, 1975, Department of State Central Foreign Policy Files, 1973–1979, National Archives and Records Administration, College Park, MD; "3 Jailed for Aiding Dominican Rebels," *NYT*, August 2, 1975.

118. "Congressmen to Hear Testimony of Women," *Atlanta Daily World*, September 4, 1975; "Poor Women Decry Job Conditions," *WP*, September 6, 1975; "Poor Women in the Economy," Feminist Radio Network (WGES), September 5, 1975. Also appearing on the program were Linda Andersen, Gloria Johnson of the Coalition of Working Women, Geraldine Gardner, and Edith Barksdale-Sloane of the National Committee on Household Employment.

119. Shirley Chisholm, "Social Justice and the Politics of Welfare," speech [ca. 1976], CP, Box 2, Folder 54.

120. "Rep. Chisholm Picks Escort for Gala White House Party," *Jet*, January 23, 1975, CPP. Essie Clark Hardwick died in October 1972. U.S., Social Security Death Index, 1935–2014, Ancestry.com, https://www.ancestry.com/search/collections/3693 (accessed March 30, 2022).

121. Andy Cooper and Sarah Slack, "Shirley Chisholm to Divorce Hubby," *NYAN*, July 3, 1976, CPP.

122. Major Robinson, "My Marriage Is My Own Business," *NYAN*, January 15, 1977, CPP.

123. Real Estate Settlement Statement, August 1975, CPP.

124. Dale C. English, "Shirley Chisholm Purchases $162,000 House in Amherst," *Buffalo Courier-Express*, July 23, 1976, CPP; Dick Dawson, "Amherst Has Own Brick-Wall Issue—At New Home of Mrs. Chisholm," *Buffalo Evening News*, September 28, 1976, CPP.

125. Author interview with Andrea Tracy Holmes, Part 2: 8. Holmes, like many of Chisholm's staffers and colleagues, did not know that Chisholm and Conrad were divorcing until she heard about the house in Buffalo.

126. SL interview with Shirley Chisholm, April 1, 2000, CC, Box 9, Part 2: 16–17.

127. SL interview with Shirley Chisholm, April 29, 2003, CC, Box 9, Part 2: 16.

128. SL interview with Shirley Chisholm, April 1, 2000, CC, Box 9, Part 1: 36–37.

129. Alfred Duckett, "Retirement of Shirley Chisholm as Controversial as Her Politics," *National Leader*, August 19, 1982, CP, Box 8, Folder 6.

130. SL interview with Conrad Chisholm, CC, Box 9: 33–36.

131. Lamont Flanagan, "Bells Toll for Chisholm," *NYAN*, December 3, 1977.

132. Hunter, "Chisholm-Wright Feud in Brooklyn Is Eroding Blacks' Political Power"; Thomas P. Ronan, "Wright Enters Seat for Chisholm Race," *NYT*, July 10, 1976; Ronald Smothers, "Rep. Chisholm Battling Wright in Showdown Race in Brooklyn," *NYT*, August 30, 1976; Maurice Carroll, "Challenge by Velez Turned Back Easily," *NYT*, September 15, 1976.

133. Ronald Smothers, "Wright, Mrs. Chisholm Trade Charges in Face-to-Face Debate in Brooklyn," *NYT*, September 3, 1976.

134. Carroll, "Challenge by Velez Turned Back Easily." Chisholm won in a landslide, with 41,297 votes to the Republican candidate's (Horace Morancie) 5,336.

135. "Samuel D. Wright, 73, Former Assemblyman," *NYT*, February 1, 1998.

136. SL interview with Carolyn Smith, CC, Box 10, Part 2: 13.

137. Russell, *Perspectives on Power*, 317–40; *Congresswoman Shirley Chisholm Reports from Washington*, August 1975, CP, Box 5, Folder 5.

138. Jimmy Carter, "Our Nation's Past and Future," Address Accepting the Presidential Nomination at the Democratic National Convention in New York City, in Gerhard Peters and John T. Woolley, The American Presidency Project, https://www.presidency.ucsb.edu /node/244286 (accessed March 27, 2019).

CHAPTER 18

1. John W. Lewis Jr., "Fighter, Chisholm: 'I Get Adrenalin from the People," *NYAN*, April 19, 1980. Chisholm also kept a copy of the article in her personal papers.

2. Shirley Chisholm, "Shirley Speaks Her Mind," *Ebony*, October 1978, 135–40.

3. Kruse and Zelizer, *Fault Lines*, 26, 30, 38–43.

4. Jimmy Hicks, "Was Anyone Listening? Does Anyone Care?," *Baltimore Afro-American*, March 4, 1978.

5. Shirley Chisholm to Leonard Sypher, April 5, 1982, CP, Box 7, Folder 5; Nye, *When the Lights Went Out*, 105–37; Constituent Newsletter, September 1977, CP, Box 5, Folder 5.

6. Chisholm, "The U.S. Constitution and Black Americans," undated speech [1983], CP, Box 3, Folder 9.

7. Harris, *Black Feminist Politics from Kennedy to Trump*, 30.

8. Shirley Chisholm, handwritten draft speech [1977], CP, Box 7, Folder 9. This draft was similar to a speech given at the University of Wisconsin in 1981; CP, Box 5, Folder 21. She also defended affirmative action as reasonable because "we have not been able to rely on the conscience and morality of those in power to eradicate the inherent racism in our country's bloodstream." It was not a good tool, but a necessary one, because most white Americans would not prioritize ameliorating the disadvantages of racism without being compelled to do so.

9. Chisholm, "Shirley Speaks Her Mind," 136. Chisholm also warned a group of scholars at a University of Pennsylvania conference on the Black church that there was a strong rightward turn in American politics, and that clergy and congregants needed to push back. See Bibian Aluke, "Shirley Chisholm on Religious Leaders: Church Challenged to Halt Conservative Wave," *Baltimore Afro-American*, May 13, 1978.

10. "national mood turning mean": Chisholm, "The Budget and the People II," *Christianity and Crisis*, April 13, 1981, 106–9; "one by one": Tom Wicker, "Subsidizing Racism," *NYT*, January 12, 1982.

11. *Independent Action PAC* newsletter [March 1982], CP, Box 8, Folder 11.

12. George Todd, "Wright's Supporters Demonstrate at Courts," *NYAN*, April 8, 1977; Lamont Flanagan, "Politicians Rally around Fortune," *NYAN*, December 10, 1977. When Wright got out of federal prison, Chisholm and Fortune would cochair the welcome back reception in his honor. Sadie Feddoes, "Sam Wright Honored," *NYAN*, July 14, 1979,

13. Author interview with Shirley Downs, July 16, 2012, Part 1: 6. Downs recalled that the engagement occurred around Easter Sunday, and the two were indeed spotted on Easter Sunday at St. John's Baptist Church by a *New York Amsterdam News* photographer (1977). However, *Jet* magazine reported that the couple had gotten engaged July 4 (but also misspelled Hardwick's name and claimed that he was an architect). "Shirley Chisholm Announces Engagement to Architect," *Jet*, September 1, 1977. And the *WP* reported

Brademas's engagement party was July 31, with Chisholm and Hardwick in attendance. Judy Bachrach, "Brademases: Receiving at Dumbarton Oaks," *WP*, August 1, 1977.

14. Lamont Flanagan, "Bells Toll for Chisholm," *NYAN*, December 3, 1977; Marci Rix [Sheraton Inn Buffalo East] to Shirley Chisholm, August 30, 1977, CPP.

15. Author interview with Laura Murphy; Flanagan, "Bells Toll for Chisholm"; Program for wedding and function contract, CPP; Anthony Cardinale, "Chisholm Trail Leads Her to WN as Congresswoman Is Wed to Former Buffalo Assemblyman," *Buffalo News*, n.d. [1977], CPP; "Rep. Chisholm Weds a Buffalo Man," *Buffalo Courier-Express*, November 27, 1977, CPP; "Shirley Chisholm Is Wed to a Buffalo Merchant," *NYT*, November 27, 1977.

16. "It Was a Big, Happy Week for Shirley Chisholm," *Baltimore Afro-American*, December 10, 1977.

17. Fashion Fair cosmetics were launched by Eunice Johnson of the Black-owned Johnson Publishing company (*Ebony, Jet*) in 1973. They were the first to offer a comprehensive set of hues for darker skin. Dennis Hevesi, "Eunice Johnson Dies at 93; Gave *Ebony* Its Name," *NYT*, January 10, 2010.

18. Michelle Bekey, "Distinguished Desk Tops," *WP*, June 12, 1977.

19. SL interview with Shirley Chisholm, April 1, 2000, CC, Box 9, Part 2.

20. Author interview with Bevin Dufty.

21. Author interview with Paul Cunningham.

22. Author interview with Laura Murphy. Murphy remembered several issues in particular: the end of forced, nonconsensual sterilization for women in mental institutions; sanctions against Rhodesia; and domestic worker benefits.

23. Author interview with Robert Frishman and Jeanne Schinto, Part 1: 2–3, 6; Part 2: 1.

24. Author interview with Carolyn Smith, 13. Other staffers later in Chisholm's career were Sue Perry, Deanne Samuels, and Ivy Davis.

25. "Shirley Chisholm Makes History Again; First Woman on Rules Committee," *NYAN*, January 22, 1977; SL interview with Shirley Downs, CC, Box 10: 13–15; Muriel Morisey to Shirley Chisholm, January 14, 1977, private collection of Muriel Morisey; U.S. House of Representatives, *History of the Committee on Rules*, v–vi. Chisholm was replacing Andrew Young, who had been named ambassador to the United Nations. When a special election was held to fill Young's Atlanta seat in Congress, Chisholm enthusiastically campaigned for Student Nonviolent Coordinating Committee activist John Lewis. See "Cong. Chisholm Rouses Group," *Atlanta Daily World*, April 5, 1977.

26. "Notes on People," *NYT*, February 3, 1977.

27. The bill was H.R. 3361, and she testified as one of eighty-seven cosponsors and as vice chair of the Congressional Black Caucus, during U.S. House of Representatives, *Hearings before the Subcommittee on Administrative Law*, 74–81; "Chisholm Backs Bill for Regulatory Agencies," *Baltimore Afro-American*, April 16, 1977.

28. Lewis, "Fighter, Chisholm"; U.S. House of Representatives, *Hearings and Markup*, February 23 and 24, 1977, 59–60, 101, 139–40; Martin Tolchin, "House Code of Ethics Approved with Curb on Members' Income," *NYT*, March 3, 1977; U.S. House of Representatives, "Hearings on Amendments to the Congressional Budget," April 16, 1978, 6, 12–13.

29. U.S. House of Representatives, *Sunset, Sunrise, and Related Measures*, May 23 and June 6, 1979.

30. Shirley Chisholm, speech before the Independent Black Women's Caucus, June 24, 1978, CP, Box 1, Folder 27 (emphasis in original); "Chisholm's Challenge," *Newsday*, June 25, 1978; George Todd, "Chisholm on Blacks: Need to Re-Evaluate," *NYAN*, July 8, 1978.

31. Shirley Chisholm, "The Contemporary Black Woman," September 16, 1978 (audience unknown), CP, Box 1, Folder 39. She gave a similar speech at Women's Day at the Wesley

Center AME Church in Pittsburgh. See Willa Mae Rice, "Chisholm: Women Crushed," *PC*, September 23, 1978.

32. Shirley Chisholm, "Draft Remarks on 'Minority Women in Business . . . Where Do You Fit In?'" speech, [1976–80], CP, Box 2, Folder 35.

33. Shirley Chisholm, "The Political Mind: We Will Rise to the Occasion," *Spelman Messenger*, 1984, 14; Reagon, "Coalition Politics," 356-68. The article was originally a speech given in 1981. Chisholm, "The Contemporary Black Woman," and "Notes on Minority Women and the Equal Rights Amendment," [May 1981], CP, Box 1, Folder 39 and 32; Diane R. Powell, "ERA, Black Struggle Mix Misunderstood," *PC*, May 9, 1981. She was not alone in urging cooperation across gender lines. Toni Cade (Bambara) called for "nonsexist coalitions" among Black men and women in 1970. Bambara cited in Taylor, "Historical Evolution of Black Feminist Theory and Praxis," 250.

34. Simon Anekwe, "Lawmakers Return," *NYAN*, January 8, 1977; Constituent Newsletter, September 1977, CP, Box 5, Folder 5.

35. Beau Cutts, "Rep. Chisholm Sees More Aid to Education," *Atlanta Constitution*, April 4, 1977.

36. U.S. House of Representatives, *Part 4, Emergency School Aid Act* (Chisholm participated on June 15). The bill was H.R. 9968. See U.S. House of Representatives, *Part 19: Title I—Funds Allocation*, 507-13. This testimony took place less than a month after Chisholm found out that a fund for gifted and talented students had been unequally distributed in New York City schools: white-majority schools on Staten Island and in Queens had received nearly $197,000, while majority-nonwhite schools had received only about $16,000. "Rep. Chisholm Charges Bias in School Fund Allegations," *NYAN*, October 22, 1977; Lewis, "Fighter, Chisholm.

37. U.S. House of Representatives, *Food Stamp Program*, March 24, 1977, 567–77; author interview with Shirley Downs, July 16, 2012, Part 2: 15. The 1979 bill was H.R. 4057. 125th *CR* (1979), 18062–82; News Release, May 6, 1980, CP, Box 5, Folder 11.

38. Andrew Cooper, "Officials Tour Ravished Areas," *NYAN*, July 23, 1977; Chisholm, Dear Colleague Letter, March 11, 1980, CP, Box 6, Folder 47.

39. U.S. House of Representatives, *Administration's Welfare Reform Proposal*, November 10, 1977. The bill in question was H.R. 9030.

40. On expanding child welfare programs, see 125th *CR* (1979), 22116; on medical benefits for poor mothers and children, see 125th *CR* (1979), 34111–12.

41. See *Congresswoman Shirley Chisholm Reports to the 12th Congressional District*, June 1978, CP, Box 5, Folder 5. Carter signed the Full Employment and Balanced Growth Act on October 26, 1978, and the amendment to Title I of the Elementary and Secondary Education Act on November 1.

42. However, Chisholm was not on the list of five congressional leaders invited to regular breakfast meetings with Carter, even though the Senate Democratic Caucus secretary was. Vera Glaser, "Rep. Chisholm Excluded from Carter's Meetings," *Detroit Free Press*, January 31, 1977. Chisholm successfully fought to be included in the breakfast meeting but then stopped going.

43. Jacqueline Trescott, "Shirley Chisholm in Her Season of Transition," *WP*, June 6, 1982.

44. "Chisholm Chides Carter for Ignoring Poor People's Concerns," *NYAN*, June 18, 1977; Perry Knight and Evelyn Foster, "Just What Was Achieved at the Carter–Black Caucus Meeting," *NYAN*, September 17, 1977; "Chisholm Attacks Carter," *NYAN*, February 11, 1978. Chisholm also criticized current urban policy at a conference organized by Operation Open City. Judith Cummings, "Harlem Parley Examines Stake in Carter Policies," *NYT*, January 15, 1978.

45. "Minority Groups Feel Unheeded by President Jimmy Carter," *Tri-State Defender*, December 30, 1978; Michael C. Givens II, "City Voices React to Energy Alert," *NYAN*, July 21, 1979; Simon Anekwe, "Applauds Are Light for Carter Changes," *NYAN*, July 28. 1979. Carter did not have a cordial relationship with Congress in general. See Steven V. Roberts, "Carter Discord with Congress," *NYT*, June 5, 1979; Lewis, "Fighter, Chisholm."

46. "Black Group Fights Plan on Education," *NYT* (AP), August 2, 1978; U.S. House of Representatives, *Establishing a Department of Education* [H.R. 13343], August 1, 1978, 378–85. Sherman Briscoe, "Black Caucus Split on New Department," *New Pittsburgh Courier*, July 28, 1979. A bill to establish the Department of Education was introduced in the Senate as S. 210 and was eventually passed in the House in 1979. Chisholm voted against, inserting a letter from Marian Wright Edelman into the *CR* on the shortcomings of a separate department and arguing on the floor that Head Start was one program that did not belong in the new Department of Education because it blended social services, health care, and education (125th *CR* (1979), 6275, 14711). Nevertheless, it was signed into law by Carter in October 1979.

47. "Minority Groups Feel Unheeded By President Jimmy Carter," *Tri-State Defender*, December 30, 1978; Lamont Flanagan, "Chisholm Predicts Kennedy Candidacy," *NYAN*, August 18, 1979; Major Robinson, "Caucus on Verge of Internal Revolt," *NYAN*, September 29, 1979; Irvin Molotsky, "Rangel Expected to Back Carter's Re-Election Bid Today," *NYT*, November 30, 1979; Steven V. Roberts, "Kennedy Shifts Criticisms on Iran, Urging a Public Debate on Asylum," *NYT*, December 6, 1979; Simon Anekwe, "Chisholm in Kennedy Camp," *NYAN*, December 15, 1979.

48. Don Rojas, "Chisholm Says Yes: She's Anxious for Top N.Y. City Education Post," *NYAN*, February 25, 1978.

49. "Confusion over a Chancellor," *NYAN*, March 4, 1978. The *NYT* version of the story blamed GOP legislators and not Shanker for scuttling her nomination. Marcia Chambers, "Rep. Chisholm Out as Schools Nominee," *NYT*, March 2, 1978. Don Rojas, "Was Chisholm Pressured Out?" *NYAN*, March 4, 1978; "Chisholm Hits Shanker Power," *Newsday* (UPI), March 7, 1978; Jose Ananias, "Will Shanker Choose 'Our' Ed Board Head?" *NYAN*, March 4, 1978; Jimmy Hicks, "Our Men Didn't Stand Up for Shirley," *Baltimore Afro-American*, March 18, 1978; "Chisholm Calls Koch Insensitive," *Newsday*, July 15, 1978. Her name was still in circulation as a possible chancellor years later. Angela Jones, "Group Wants a Black School Chancellor," *NYAN*, January 22, 1983.

50. Marguerite Barnett, "Have You Heard from Your Congressman Lately?" *Black Enterprise*, January 1978; "Brooklyn Big Mouth," *NYAN*, January 14, 1978; George Todd, "Dr. Gifford Denied He's Planning to Oust Chisholm," *NYAN*, January 28, 1978; Rob Minor, "Will Simeon Golar Run?" *NYAN*, February 4, 1978; "Rep. Chisholm Blasts Her Critics," *NYAN*, February 4, 1978. Daughtry would identify Mayor Ed Koch as unfriendly to Black New Yorkers and reminded his allies that Chisholm had endorsed Koch for mayor. Anti-Koch sentiment reached a peak when Daughtry made Koch a target of demonstrations in September. See "Koch-Daughtry Clash; 10,000 Expected at Rally," *NYAN*, September 30, 1978.

51. Carolyn Smith had attended North Carolina A&T with him and his wife, Gwendolyn. After Chisholm retired Smith went to work for him, though she still did things "on the side" for her old boss. Author interview with Carolyn Smith, 18–19, 24–25.

52. Andrew Cooper, "Claim Chisholm Will Resign," *NYAN*, July 15, 1978; "*Amsterdam News* Endorsements," *NYAN*, September 9, 1978. Chisholm thought that Editor Fred Weaver was the one who had penned the editorial, though it was likely Bryant Rollins who was then executive editor and had written several previous criticisms of Chisholm. See handwritten draft statement, CP, Box 7, Folder 9.

53. Shirley Chisholm, "A Response from Chisholm," *NYAN*, September 30, 1978.

54. Al Vann, "Vann Says Chisholm 'Lied in Public,'" *NYAN*, October 14, 1978.

55. Andrew Cooper and Wayne Barrett, "Chisholm's Compromise: Politics and the Art of Self-Interest," *Village Voice*, October 30, 1978. Candidates that Chisholm did not support but should have, the authors said, were Robert Abrams for New York attorney general, Bella Abzug for Senate, Carol Bellamy for city council president, Elizabeth Holtzman for Congress, and, of course, Percy Sutton and Arthur Eve for mayors of New York and Buffalo, respectively.

56. Bryant Rollins, "*Voice* Article Attacks Rep. Shirley Chisholm," *NYAN*, October 28, 1978.

57. Alfred Duckett, "Retirement of Shirley Chisholm as Controversial as Her Politics," *National Leader*, August 19, 1982 (CP, Box 8, Folder 6); State of New York Department of Motor Vehicles Report of Motor Vehicle Accident, CPP; "Chisholm Kin Hurt in Crash," *New York Daily News*, April 25, 1979, CPP; J. Zamgba Browne, "Doctors Fight to Save Leg of Shirley Chisolm's Spouse," *NYAN*, May 26, 1979; "Hardwick OKs Settlement of '79 Crash Suit," undated clipping, CPP.

58. Lewis, "Fighter, Chisholm"; Sadie Feddoes, "Congressional Black Caucus Gala Weekend," *NYAN*, October 4, 1980; "every night for a year": Les Payne, "Mrs. Chisholm Calls It Quits," *Essence*, August 1982.

59. Simon Anekwe, "Chisholm Talks about Kennedy," *NYAN*, August 16, 1980.

60. Simon Anekwe, "Carter Coming to Bed-Stuy," *NYAN*, October 18, 1980.

61. Shirley Chisholm, "A Real Challenge for Pres-Elect Reagan: The Galloping Disease of Minority Unemployment," unpublished manuscript, [1980], CP, Box 6, Folder 6.

62. Kevin Thomas, "Ronald Reagan's 'Dream of the 18th Century' Ridiculed by Shirley Chisholm," *Hartford Courant*, August 4, 1980.

63. Rose Ciotta, "Shirley Chisholm: Now, the Buffalo Years," *Magazine of the Buffalo News*, January 30, 1983.

64. Ethel Payne, "Reagan Team Wooing Shirley Chisholm," *Baltimore Afro-American*, December 6, 1980.

65. Shirley Chisholm, "Give Reagan a Chance," *WP*, December 12, 1980.

66. Shirley Chisholm, "Black Leadership Must Be Earned," *NYAN*, December 13, 1980.

67. MacLean, *Democracy in Chains*, 176–77, 186–87.

68. Kruse and Zelizer, *Fault Lines*, 101–4, 106–9. See also MacLean, *Democracy in Chains*.

69. Perlstein, *Invisible Bridge*, 603–4.

70. Schulman, *Seventies*, 235–36.

71. James M. Blount, "Congresswoman Shirley Chisholm: Senior Woman in the U.S. House of Representatives," *About . . . Time*, December 1981, 8–11, 22–24, CP, Box 8, Folder 11.

72. "CBC Meets with the President," *Congressional Black Caucus, Report to the People*, June 1981, CPP; Simon Anekwe, "Reagan Meets Black Caucus," *NYT*, February 7, 1981.

73. Steven R. Weisman, "Reagan Is Reported Ready to Eliminate Urban Aid Program," *NYT*, February 4, 1981.

74. Her list of proposed legislative priorities included budget and the economy, education, civil rights, jobs, economic development, and social services. She attempted to present those priorities at a February 17 CBC meeting, but her agenda item was put off to February 24. Shirley Chisholm to CBC members, February 23, 1981, CPP, Box 7, Folder 4. One proposal floated by the administration and introduced by Jack Kemp and Robert Garcia (D-NY) was to create "Enterprise Zones" of reduced business taxes in poor neighborhoods. Initially, Bob Frishman discouraged Chisholm from considering the bill as a priority, given that it amounted to a tax cut for businesses that would cost much but amount to little benefit in practice. Bob Frishman to Shirley Chisholm, February 17, 1981, CPP, Box 7, Folder 15. When the bill was still under debate later in the year, Chisholm offered revisions that would focus

benefits on small businesses and provide for modification or the end of the program if it was not working as hoped. She published an op-ed, "A Windfall—or Real Hope?," *WP*, December 22, 1981. See also "Chisholm Speaks on Enterprise Zones Bill, Suggests Improvements," News Release, CP, Box 5, Folder 11; George Todd, "Chisholm Urges Tax Break for Small Businesses," *NYAN*, December 19, 1981; Chisholm interview, *Morning Edition*, National Public Radio, January 25, 1982.

75. 127th *CR* (1981), 2932–46 [February 24, 1981] (Chisholm's remarks on 2946).

76. Bob Frishman to Brenda Pillors, February 25, 1981, CP, Box 7, Folder 8.

77. U.S. House of Representatives, *Oversight on Higher Education Budget*, February 24, 1981, 16–31; also quoted in *A Report from Your Congresswoman Shirley Chisholm* [constituent newsletter], Spring 1981.

78. "Blacks in Congress Offer Alternative Budget Plan," *NYT*, March 19, 1981.

79. "House Will Vote on Black Caucus Budget," News Release, April 30, 1981, CP, Box 5, Folder 11; Chisholm, Form Letter, April 15, 1981, CP, Box 5, Folder 11. Fauntroy introduced the alternative budget on May 5. See 127th *CR* (1981), 8508–9, Chisholm's remarks at 8514–16.

80. "Chisholm Statement of Republican Reconciliation Amendments," News Release, June 25, 1981, CP, Box 5, Folder 11.

81. Kruse and Zelizer, *Fault Lines*, 110–12, 113; Schulman, *Seventies*, 231; "Chisholm Tells Education Braintrust to 'Get Active,'" News Release, September 25, 1981, CP, Box 5, Folder 11; *A Report from Your Congresswoman Shirley Chisholm*, Winter 1981–82, CP, Box 7, Folder 11.

82. Blount, "Congresswoman Shirley Chisholm"; 127th *CR* (1981), 22937–38 (October 2, 1981); "Reagan's Voting Rights Stand Irks Lawmakers," *NYAN*, November 14, 1981.

83. "Chisholm Condemns Reagan Attack on Affirmative Action," News Release, August 27, 1981, CP, Box 5, Folder 11; J. Zamgba Browne, "New Job Bias Policy Shocks Black Leaders," *NYAN*, October 3, 1981.

84. "Rally for Haitian Refugees," *NYAN*, June 15, 1974; Ira Gollobin to Shirley Chisholm, October 24, 1975, and December 17, 1975, Ira Gollobin Haitian Refugee Collection, Box 31, Folder 3; and Claude Pepper, Shirley Chisholm, Edward Koch, Frederick Richmond, William Lehmen, Dante Fascell, Charles Rangel, and Charles Diggs to Joshua Eilberg, August 2, 1976, Ira Gollobin Haitian Refugee Collection, Box 22, Folder 14, Schomburg Center for Research in Black Culture, New York Public Library. See also Lindskoog, *Detain and Punish*, 2, 16, 22.

85. News Release, July 19, 1979; "Congressional Black Caucus Statement on United States Relationship with Haiti and Haitian Asylum Claimants for the Honorable Cardiss Collins," News Release, July 19, 1979; and Chisholm, Cardiss Collins, and Walter Fauntroy to [CBC] Network Participants, August 15, 1979, all in Ira Gollobin Haitian Refugee Collection, Box 22, Folder 14, Schomburg Center for Research in Black Culture, New York Public Library.

86. The bill passed the House on the same day Chisholm and the rest of the task force held a colloquium on Haitian refugees on the House floor. 125th *CR* (1979), 35819–20, 37263–67.

87. The decision was *Haitian Refugee Center v. Civiletti*. See Lindskoog, *Detain and Punish*, 29–34. Chisholm also objected to the detours around the *Civiletti* decision. See Shirley Chisholm, "U.S. Policy and Black Refugees," *Issue: A Journal of Opinion*, 1982, 22–24, quoted in Lindskoog, *Detain and Punish*, 164n61.

88. Lindskoog, *Detain and Punish*, 35–36.

89. "Time Is Running Out for Haitians," News Release, March 21, 1980; Cardiss Collins, Shirley Chisholm, Walter Fauntroy, Mickey Leland, John Conyers, and Melvin Evans to Jimmy Carter, April 14, 1980; and Cardiss Collins to Jimmy Carter, May 7, 1980, all in Ira Gollobin Haitian Refugee Collection, Schomburg Center for Research in Black Culture, New York Public Library, Box 22, Folder 14; U.S. House of Representatives, *Caribbean Migration*,

June 17, 1980, 139–81; "Chisholm Disturbed over Refugee Bias," *NYAN*, October 18, 1980; Denise Blackburn, "Cuban/Haitians Entrant Program," *In Defense of the Alien* 6 (1983): 189–99.

90. "Chisholm Calls for Action on Refugees," News Release, May 19, 1981, CP, Box 5, Folder 11; H.R. 3602, 97th Congress.

91. Robert Pear, "Haitian Deportations Start; U.S. Orders Open Hearings," *NYT*, June 6, 1981.

92. "Chisholm Attacks Federal Incarceration of Haitian Refugees," News Release, July 21, 1981, CP, Box 5, Folder 11.

93. "Chisholm Testifies on Refugee Asylum Proceedings" and "Chisholm Criticizes President's Immigration Proposals," News Releases, July 31, 1981, CP, Box 5, Folder 11; U.S. Senate, *United States as a Country of Mass First Asylum*, July 31, 1981, 109–19. For analysis of Reagan's task force, see Maddux, "Ronald Reagan and the Task Force on Immigration, 1981."

94. U.S. House of Representatives, *Coast Guard Oversight—Part 2*, September 17, 1981, 19–33.

95. Blount, "Congresswoman Shirley Chisholm."

96. "Reagan Orders Refugees Halted on the High Seas," *NYT (UPI)*, September 30, 1981; CBC Press Release, August 18, 1981, and Haitian Task Force Position Paper, November 25, 1981, Ira Gollobin Haitian Refugee Collection, Box 22, Folder 14, Schomburg Center for Research in Black Culture, New York Public Library; 127th *CR* (1981), 30733–36.

97. Lindskoog, *Detain and Punish*, 62–63, 71.

98. The bill was H.R. 6071. News Release, April 20, 1982, CP, Box 8, Folder 8; U.S. House of Representatives, *Immigration Reform and Control Act*, April 20, 1982, 348–52, 357–65; NECHR agenda, March 9, 1982, and meeting minutes, June 7, 1982, Ira Gollobin Haitian Refugee Collection, Box 24, Folder 8, Schomburg Center for Research in Black Culture, New York Public Library.

99. Chisholm Dear Colleague Letter, September 9, 1981, CP, Box 6, Folder 48; "Chisholm Introduces the Farmworker Bill of Rights Act," News Release, September 10, 1981, CP, Box 5, Folder 11; 127th *CR* (1981), 20243–45; U.S. House of Representatives, *Migrant and Seasonal Farmworker Housing*, September 17, 1981, 78–80.

100. Sadie Feddoes, "Reception for Chinese," *NYAN*, September 15, 1979; "Chinese Delegation Received Bklyn Welcome," *NYAN*, September 22, 1979. On Black and Asian solidarity, see Wu, *Radicals on the Road*; Frazier, *East Is Black*; Schmidt, *Foreign Intervention in Africa*; Young, *Soul Power*.

101. Photo albums, CPP.

102. "Bar South African Tennis Team: Chisholm," *NYAN*, February 11, 1978.

103. Shirley Chisholm, "South Africa: Land of Fear," December 11, 1982, CPP. This speech was delivered on behalf of Bermuda's South African Fund.

104. The camp had sprung up after a series of raids on *Nyan*ga and Langa townships that had evicted over 1,000 people accused of being illegal migrants. It was set up in protest of those evictions and governed by a committee. Five years later Wolpe would coauthor sanctions against South Africa that were passed over Reagan's veto. Joseph Lelyveld, "South Africa Burns a Black Campsite and Bars U.S. Visitors," *NYT*, August 12, 1981; Chisholm, "South Africa: Land of Fear"; "Chisholm Shocked by View of Apartheid," News Release, August 24, 1981, CP, Box 5, Folder 11; "South African Apartheid Conditions Shock Chisholm," *NYAN*, September 5, 1981; Blount, "Congresswoman Shirley Chisholm."

105. Rangel, "Chisholm Backs Anti-Human Amendments," *NYAN*, December 19, 1981.

106. "Chisholm Explains Endorsement of Koch," News Release, October 20, 1981, CP, Box 5, Folder 11. Chisholm also supported David Dinkins from the start of his campaign for Manhattan Borough president. See Simon Anekwe, "Dinkins Plans Vigorous Campaign to Oust

Stein," *NYAN*, October 10, 1981. Fred Weaver, "The Lash and the Cross," *NYAN*, November 21, 1981; [Andy Cooper], "One Man's Opinion," *NYAN*, October 21, 1981; J. Zamgba Browne, "Solidarity: Hundreds March for Human Dignity," *NYAN*, November 7, 1981.

107. Chisholm, undated handwritten manuscript, CP, Box 7 Folder 9; Chisholm, "Open Letter to the Community," *NYAN*, December 26, 1981; Chisholm, "Open Letter to the Community and the Public-at-Large," December 15, 1981, CP, Box 7, Folder 4; "We Dare You to Print This," Letter to the Editor, December 26, 1981, *NYAN*; Fred Weaver, "The Lash and the Cross," *NYAN*, January 2, 1982; "Editorial in Response to Shirley Chisholm," *NYAN*, January 9, 1982; Wolfgang Saxon, "Frederick S. Weaver; Did Public Relations and Wrote Column," *NYT*, April 5, 1982. Chisholm would also endorse Koch in the following year's gubernatorial race in a detailed news release, September 13, 1982, CP, Box 8, Folder 9.

108. Trescott, "Shirley Chisholm in Her Season of Transition"; Shirley Chisholm to John E. Ogden, June 3, 1981, CP, Box 7, Folder 4.

109. "Shirley Chisholm Interviewed," *NYAN*, February 28, 1981; Samuel Wiess, "Search for New President of City College Is Narrowed to Three Candidates," *NYT*, February 9, 1981.

110. Author interview with Carolyn Smith, 19, 22.

111. "Mrs. Chisholm Weighs Retiring from Congress," *NYT*, January 25, 1982; Jane Perlez, "Mrs. Chisholm Plans to Retire from Congress: Cites Losses by Liberals as Factor in Decision," *NYT*, February 11, 1982; News Release, February 11, 1982, CP, Box 8, Folder 9; Trescott, "Shirley Chisholm in Her Season of Transition."

112. Author interview with Robert Frishman and Jeanne Schinto, 7.

113. News Release, February 11, 1982, CP, Box 8, Folder 9.

114. Marian Christy, "The Fire Inside Rep. Chisholm," *BG*, July 9, 1982.

115. Les Payne, "Mrs. Chisholm Calls It Quits," *Essence*, August 1982. Also see Alfred Duckett, "Retirement of Shirley Chisholm as Controversial as Her Politics," *National Leader*, August 19, 1982, CP, Box 8, Folder 6; James Gilbert, "Roving Camera," *NYAN*, March 20, 1982; SL interview with Shirley Chisholm, April 29, 2003, CC, Box 9, Tape 2: 12. In this interview Chisholm seemed to conflate Nixon's years in office with Reagan's, when she did decide to retire.

116. Anne-Marie Schiro, "Honoring a Modern Civil Rights Leader," *NYT*, June 5, 1982.

117. Sadie Feddoes, "Chisholm Cultural Group Takes a Trip to Barbados," *NYAN*, June 12, 1982; "Chisholm Visits Relatives," *Barbados Advocate News*, June 1, 1982; "It's Tough For Minorities in US," *Barbados Advocate News*, June 2, 1982.

118. Sadie Feddoes, "Towns Friends Fete Chisholm," *NYAN*, September 18, 1982; Sadie Feddoes, "Group Honors Chisholm," *NYAN*, November 27, 1982, and "Elected Dems Fete Cuomo," *NYAN*, November 13, 1982; "U.S. Caribbean Policy Black Caucus Thrust," *PC*, September 11, 1982.

119. The September 3 program was held at the Los Angeles Convention Center and sponsored by Anheuser-Busch. Program, Black Women's Forum, Inc., CPP; "Chisholm Addresses Women's Confab," *NYAN*, August 28, 1982.

120. Sadie Feddoes, "Caucus Was Cookin'," *NYAN*, September 25, 1982; Program, "Shirley Chisholm, A Tribute," September 17, 1982, CP, Box 8, Folder 11, and CPP.

121. Shirley Chisholm, "Speech to C.B.C. Dinner, Washington Hilton, 9/18/82," CPP, and CP, Box 6, Folder 4.

122. 128th *CR* (1982) (December 9, 1982), 29740–48.

123. Chisholm Staff Memo, n.d., CP, Box 7, Folder 9.

124. Beatty was later convicted of election fraud in the primary, though he maintained his innocence. "Beatty Battered By 2 Raps; Denies," *NYAN*, February 19, 1983; Peter Noel, "Beatty Seeks Ouster of Election Fraud Rap," *NYAN*, August 2, 1983; Gerald Bishop, "Beatty Found Guilty of Election Forgery," *NYAN*, December 31, 1983.

125. Richmond's former Fourteenth District had been redrawn into the Latinx-majority Eleventh District. "Owens Joins Race for the House," *NYAN*, May 15, 1982; Ronald Smothers, "2 Ex-State Senators Vie for Rep. Chisholm's Job," *NYT*, September 16, 1982; Angela Jones, "Bklyn Races May Be Bitter and Fierce," *NYAN*, September 18, 1982; Joseph P. Fried, "Reruns Ordered in Brooklyn for Two Disputed Elections," *NYT*, October 22, 1982; Jane Perlez, "Congressional Freshmen Settle In," *NYT*, February 12, 1983.

126. Shirley Chisholm, WMCA, June 18, 1982, recording in author's possession.

CHAPTER 19

1. "Shirley Chisholm Remains a Catalyst for Change," *New Pittsburgh Courier*, March 29, 1986.

2. "Chisholm Set to Speak at Howard Commencement," *NYAN*, May 14, 1983. As late as 2000, she was still sending donations to the Shirley Chisholm Cultural Institute for Children, which struggled to repair its building and cover expenses. Marguerite Johnson Form Letter, June 21, 2000, CPP. Chisholm handwrote on the letter that she had sent a check for $100.

3. Peter Noel, "Job-Hunting Rap Ticks Chisholm Off," *NYAN*, May 8, 1982.

4. Clyde Haberman and Laurie Johnston, "New York Day by Day," *NYT*, August 3, 1982.

5. Author interview with Carolyn Smith, 19–20, 26.

6. Author interview with Carolyn Smith, 20.

7. Simon Anekwe, "Conolly Seeks Seat in the State Assembly," *NYAN*, September 6, 1986; Photo, *NYAN*, September 17, 1988; J. Zamgba Browne, "Chisholm Blesses Political Protégé at Gala," *NYAN*, December 22, 1990.

8. Simon Anekwe, "Ada Smith, Freshman Senator, Is Off and Running in Albany," *NYAN*, February 18, 1989.

9. NPCBW Board Minutes, January 27, 1990, CPP; "Congresswoman Barbara Lee's Reflections on Congresswoman Shirley Chisholm," [2005], personal collection of Laura Murphy; H. Res. 97, 107th Congress.

10. Simon Anekwe, "Chisholm Seeks Niche in Financial World," *NYAN*, January 3, 1987.

11. Ronald Smothers, "Jackson Declares Formal Candidacy," *NYT*, November 4, 1983; Minor Roberts, "Chisholm Backs Jaxon [*sic*] Candidacy," *NYAN*, November 5, 1983; "Miss [*sic*] Chisholm Is Asked about Vice Presidency," *NYT*, March 5, 1984; Ronald Smothers, "Jackson Stumps in Pennsylvania," *NYT*, April 8, 1984.

12. J. Zamgba Browne, "Shirley: It's a Disservice," *NYAN*, November 12, 1983.

13. Joe Spencer, "Chisholm Says Black Votes Can Oust Reagan," *NYAN*, April 9, 1984.

14. Simon Anekwe, "Dems to Meet Monday," *NYAN*, July 14, 1984; Warren Weaver Jr., "Democratic Panel Yields to Jackson Backers," *NYT*, June 27, 1984.

15. Greg Harris, "Black Women Politic for New Power," *National Leader*, November 1984, CPP; Jean Wiley, "Organizing for Power," *Essence*, May 1985.

16. Harris, "Black Women Politic for Power"; Wiley, "Organizing for Power."

17. "Black Women Forming Coalition for Recognition," *NYT*, August 6, 1984; Diane R. Powell, "Call to Arms . . . Women's Caucus Aims to Flex Muscle," *PC*, September 1, 1984; Jo Freeman, "Women at the 1988 Democratic Convention," *off our backs*, October 1988; Harris, "Black Women Politic for New Power"; Wiley, "Organizing for Power"; Dorothy Gilliam, "Political Clout and How to Get It," *Essence*, May 1985, CPP; Dorothy Gilliam, "Womanpower," *WP*, August 6, 1984; Summary of Meeting, National Black Women's Political Caucus, August 9, 1984, CPP.

18. Leslie Bennetts, "Black Women Chart a New Activism," *NYT*, August 2, 1981; Annette Samuels, "Women Confab Issues Challenge," *NYAN*, September 5, 1981, and "Black

Women's Summit," *NYAN*, August 8, 1981; Greg Harris, "Black Women Politic For New Power," *National Leader*, November 1984, CPP.

19. News Release, August 23, 1982, CP, Box 8, Folder 9.

20. Harris, "Black Women Politic for New Power."

21. National Black Women's Political Caucus, Summary of Meeting, August 9, 1984, CPP.

22. Shirley Chisholm and Dolores Tucker form letter, September 20, 1984, CPP; "Message from the National Black Women's Political Caucus National Chair and National Vice Chair," September 30, 1984, CPP; Chisholm speech, "My Sisters," [September 30,1984], CPP; Summary of the Executive Committee Meeting, October 15, 1984, CPP; Donna Brazile to Shirley Chisholm and C. Delores Tucker, November 28, 1984, CPP.

23. "Legislation, Women's Equality Theme of Political Conference," *CD*, April 23, 1975; Eleanor Holmes Norton to Juanita Kennedy Morgan, September 12, 1984, CPP; Summary of the Executive Committee Meeting, October 15, 1984, CPP.

24. For example, Pat Tyson, coordinator of the first national assembly, did not know that Chisholm had asked Tucker to be national chair of the assembly. Barbara Williams-Skinner made strong suggestions to Chisholm that regular meetings between herself, Tucker, Brazile, and Tyson be instituted. Barbara Williams-Skinner to Shirley Chisholm, January 14, 1985, CPP; Donna Brazile to Shirley Chisholm, February 27, 1985, CPP.

25. Summary: Executive Committee Meeting, December 17, 1984, CPP; "Foes of South Africa Arrested," *NYT* (AP), December 18, 1984. Pendelton's fellow commissioner and rival Mary Frances Berry collaborated with program chair Barbara Williams-Skinner to craft a letter demanding Pendelton's resignation. See "Criticism on Black Leaders," *NYT*, November 20, 1984, and Barbara Williams-Skinner to National Black Women's Political Caucus Executive Committee, December 26, 1984, CPP.

26. *Spelman Messenger* 101, no. 1 (1983), and 102, no. 1 (1985); "Conference for Black Women in Politics Is Led by Chisholm," *NYT*, June 9, 1985.

27. NPCBW, "A Call to the National Political Congress of Black Women's National Assembly, June 7–9, 1985, Atlanta, Georgia," CPP; emphasis in the original.

28. Shirley Chisholm, "The Seeds of Freedom," press release reprinted from *Focus* [Joint Center for Political Studies], July 1985, CPP.

29. Bylaws of the National Political Congress of Black Women [1985], CPP; American Arbitration Association, "Election of Officers in the Matter of National Political Congress of Black Women: Certification of Results," July 1, 1985, CPP; Nathan McCall, "Jackson, Chisholm Urge Black Women to Action," *Atlanta Journal-Constitution*, June 9, 1985; Dorothy Gilliam, "Black Women Organize a Political Coalition," *WP*, June 10, 1985; "Organizing For Empowerment: The National Political Congress of Black Women," *Southern Changes*, July–September 1985, CPP.

30. Maxine Waters to Shirley Chisholm, October 18, 1985, CPP; "Black Women's PAC Will Help Candidates," *off our backs*, April 1986.

31. Minutes of the Executive Committee of the National Political Congress of Black Women, July 13, 1985, CPP; NPCBW Quarterly Report, July 1, 1985–September 30, 1985, CPP. Donna Brazile also referred to homophobia and rumors of lesbianism within the organization in private communication with Chisholm. Brazile saw them as an attack on her own personal life ("I doubt that I even have one," she lamented.). See Donna Brazile to Shirley Chisholm, June 20, 1985, CPP.

32. On the closure of the national office and the discord at the 1986 annual meeting, see Minutes of National Board Meeting, June 12–15, 1986; Donna Brazile to Shirley Chisholm, June 19, 1986; Gloria Toote to Shirley Chisholm, June 20, 1986; Constance Street to Shirley

Chisholm, June 26, 1986; Mary Terrell, Jennifer Tucker, and Shirley Wilcher to Shirley Chisholm, July 5, 1986; and Julianne Malveaux to Shirley Chisholm, July 9, 1986, all in CPP.

33. SL interview with Shirley Chisholm, April 1, 2000, CC, Box 9, Part 2: 15–16.

34. Order of Service, August 21, 1986, CPP; SL interview with Shirley Chisholm, April 1, 2000, CC, Box 9, Parts 1 and 2.

35. NPCBW Board Minutes, October 4–5, 1986, CPP.

36. Portia Perry Dempsey obituary, *Daytona Beach News-Journal*, December 29, 2009.

37. Portia Dempsey to Shirley Chisholm, October 31, 1985, and August 28, 1986, CPP; NPCBW Minutes of Board Meeting, May 16, 1987, CPP. After Arthur's death, she joined Hodge Taylor Associates as a political consultant for hire. "Chisholm Joins NYC PR Firm," *NYAN*, December 13, 1986.

38. "2,000 Women to Plan Empowerment Strategy," *NYAN*, August 22, 1987.

39. Draft Schedule, NPCBW Biennial Conference, August 26–30, 1987, CPP; "Chisholm Says Organization Equals Power," *PC*, September 12, 1987.

40. A parade of dignitaries spoke: Rosa Parks, Dorothy Height, Dick Gregory, and Chisholm herself, among others. Cathy Connors, "Caucus Ends in Upbeat Sprit," *NYAN*, October 3, 1987.

41. Robert Moore, "Chisholm Speaks at Smith Fundraiser," *New Pittsburgh Courier*, October 31, 1987.

42. NPCBW Minutes of Board Meeting, January 30, 1988, CPP; "$100,000 Raised for Mitchell Defense Fund," *PC*, January 23, 1988.

43. Minutes of Board Meeting, January 30, 1988, CPP; Shirley Chisholm to Mary Terrell, February 17, 1988, CPP.

44. Jesse Jackson to Shirley Chisholm, August 21, 1987, CPP.

45. Simon Anekwe, "Jesse Kicksoff [*sic*] Campaign Here," *NYAN*, January 24, 1988; "Women, Hispanics Rally Behind Jesse Jackson," *NYAN*, January 30, 1988.

46. Minutes of Board Meeting, June 25, 1988, and "Caravan '88" Itinerary, CPP; Jo Freeman, "Women at the 1988 Democratic Convention," *off our backs*, October 1988.

47. Simon Anekwe, "Duke Plans Massive 42-City Voter Registration Campaign," *NYAN*, September 24, 1988.

48. "Dukakis Signs Jackson to Record Radio Spots," *NYT*, September 24, 1988; "Gender Gap May Fade, N.O.W. Delegates Hear," *NYT*, June 27, 1988; Shirley Chisholm, "Women and the '88 Presidential Elections: Will There Be a Gender Gap?," CP, Box 3, Folder 12.

49. Simon Anekwe, "Chisholm May Run Against Koch," *NYAN*, July 9, 1988; NPCBW, Minutes of Board Meeting, October 9, 1988, CPP.

50. The chapter had been founded in 1986, with Dorothy Height and Gloria Toote elected to the board of directors by seventy attendees. Cathy Connors, "Girl Friend's Benefit Called a 'Good Party,'" *NYAN*, October 4, 1986; "Women's Conference," *NYAN*, August 27, 1988.

51. Simon Anekwe, "Messinger Eyeing Mayoral Seat Takes Shots at Sexism, Racism," *NYAN*, November 19, 1988; J. Zamgba Browne, "Chisholm Vows Better Leadership," *NYAN*, December 10, 1988; "Dinkins Files for Mayor," *NYAN*, January 28, 1989.

52. NPCBW Minutes of the Executive Committee, February 16, 1992, CPP.

53. Program, NPCBW Seventh Annual Awards Brunch, September 27, 1992, CPP. Chisholm had just lost her mother; after decades of not speaking, Ruby St. Hill passed away in St. Mary's Hospital, Brooklyn, on June 19, 1991, at the age of eighty-nine. She still resided at 1094 Prospect Place at the time. City of New York Certificate of Death. No. 156-91-033504.

54. Annette Sanchez, "Chisholm Returns to Campaign for Clinton," *PC*, October 3, 1992; Shirley Chisholm speech, "The Future of Women in the Workplace," September 1992, CP, Box 3, Folder 21.

55. NPCBW Press Release, November 24, 1992, NPCBW Minutes of the Board of Directors, January 16, 1993, CPP; C. Delores Tucker to NPCBW Board, Chapter Chair, and Members, March 16, 1993, CPP.

56. "Post of Jamaica Ambassador to Go to Shirley Chisholm," *NYT*, July 30, 1993; Nadine Brozan, "Chronicles," *NYT*, October 15, 1993; Joe Fodor, "Following the Shirley Chisholm Trail," *Brooklyn Bridge*, March 1999, CPP; author interview with Muriel Forde, August 8, 2012.

57. J. Zamgba Browne, "The 'Dean' of Brooklyn Politics Dies at Age 96," *NYAN*, March 27, 1993; Sadie Feddoes, "People from All Walks of Life Say Final Farewell to Holder," *NYAN*, April 6, 1993.

58. "Reorganized Black Women's Political Congress Takes on Racism, Sexism," *NYAN*, October 9, 1993; "NPCBW Honors Three Living Legends," *New Pittsburgh Courier*, October 23, 1993; C. Delores Tucker to Shirley Chisholm, August 3, 1994, CPP. Chisholm had threatened to withdraw from NPCBW if she was not paid back for funds she had lent to hold the biennial meeting in Detroit, but members lent the organization the funds to repay Chisholm and she remained. See NPCBW Minutes of the Board of Directors, January 16, 1993, CPP.

59. Shirley Chisholm, Manuscript Letter Draft, [1993], CPP.

60. Author interview with Carolyn Smith.

61. SL interview with Shirley Chisholm, April 29, 2003, CC, Box 9, Part 4: 25; Linda Trimble, "Voice from Past Shapes Future: Shirley Chisholm Speaks in B-CC History Class," *Daytona Beach News-Journal*, January 24, 2002; "NAACP Has Annual Holiday Luncheon," *Daytona Beach News-Journal*, December 20, 2003; Order of Service, First AME Church of Palm Coast, February 21, 2004, CPP; John Bozzo, "Chisholm: You Are Fearful of Black People," *Daytona Beach News-Journal*, April 25, 2004. The film, *Chisholm '72: Unbought and Unbossed* (2005), was the first feature-length treatment of her presidential campaign and used interviews with participants, as well as extensive archival footage from the 1974 *Chisholm: Pursuing the Dream* production.

62. Deni Luna, "Shirley Chisholm: Up Close," *Northwest Asian Weekly*, October 18, 1996; Joseph P. Freid, "Following Up: After Politics of Change, Quiet Life for Chisholm," *NYT*, March 24, 2002.

63. SL interview with Shirley Chisholm, April 1, 2000, CC, Box 9, Part 2: 19; author interview with Muriel Forde, August 2, 2012.

64. Author interview with Carolyn Smith; Dorrie Blackmon, "In House List Keeps Visitors Busy," *Daytona Beach News Journal*, July 10, 2004; Statement of Claim, February 7, 2005, Clerk of Circuit Court, Volusia County, Florida, Parcel/Case No. 20005-10310-PRDL; William Murphy and Dan Janison, "Reflecting on Her Legacy, Shirley Chisholm Was a Trailblazer Who Broke Sex and Color Barriers to Become a Political Legend," *Newsday*, January 4, 2005.

65. Randal C. Archibold, "Back Home in Brooklyn, Rivals and Allies Remember Chisholm," *NYT*, January 4, 2005. The *NYT* also published a traditional obituary: James Barron, "Shirley Chisholm, 80, Dies; 'Unbossed' Pioneer in Congress and Presidential Candidate," *NYT*, January 4, 2005.

66. SL interview with Shirley Chisholm, April 1, 2000, CC, Box 9, Part 2: 11–12.

67. Order of Service, "A Celebration of the Life and Legacy of the Honorable Shirley Chisholm-Hardwick," January 8, 2005, CPP; Ludmilla Lelis, "Political Maverick's Life Is Celebrated," *Orlando Sentinel*, January 9, 2005; Eileen Zaffiro, "A Funeral—and a Celebration," *Daytona Beach News-Journal*, January 9, 2005; Eileen Zaffiro, "Many Pay Tribute to Trailblazer," *Daytona Beach News-Journal*, January 12, 2005; author interview with Muriel

Forde, August 2, 2012. Members of Congress present included Barbara Lee, Eleanor Holmes Norton, Annette Rainwater, Julia Carson, and Ed Towns. Obituaries were published nationwide. See Barron, "Shirley Chisholm, 80, Dies."

Forde and the Dempseys would remain in a dispute over Chisholm's estate for the following year. Eventually Forde won the bulk of the estate and began to make arrangements for Chisholm's remaining papers to go to the Shirley Chisholm Cultural Institute for Children, which would create a museum under Bill Howard's leadership. The museum was never formed, however. Instead, a new archive was created: the Shirley Chisholm Collection of Brooklyn Women's Activism at Brooklyn College. Women's studies scholar Barbara Winslow obtained filmmaker Shola Lynch's research materials, plus donations from others who had known and worked with Chisholm and a series of video oral histories. A mediator eventually awarded the Dempseys some liquid assets, but the bulk went to Forde, including the papers and other material related to Chisholm's public life. See Settlement Agreement, May 10, 2006, Clerk of Circuit Court, Volusia County, Florida, Parcel /Case No. 20005-10310-PRDL.

68. Program, Memorial Service Celebrating the Life and Legacy of the Honorable Shirley A. Chisholm, February 15, 2005, personal collection of Laura Murphy.

69. T. Shawn Taylor, "Shirley Chisholm's Admirers Share Fondest Memories," *CT*, January 12, 2005; "Chisholm Hailed as Giant in U.S. History," *Gainesville Sun*, January 4, 2005; Yussuf Simmonds, "Shirley Chisholm Dies," *LAS*, January 6, 2004.

70. "P.O.V.'s 'CHISHOLM '72—Unbought & Unbossed' Makes National Broadcast Premiere, Feb. 7 on PBS," *LAS*, January 6, 2005.

EPILOGUE

1. This number includes House delegates. See "Women of Color in Elective Office," Center for American Women and Politics, https://cawp.rutgers.edu/women-color-elective -office-2020 (accessed April 23, 2020). Since Chisholm was first sworn in, there have been forty-seven Black women who have served in the House or Senate. At this writing there are now fifty-seven Black members of Congress across both chambers, and it was the first Congress that does not include a founding member of the Congressional Black Caucus (the last one to leave Congress was John Conyers, in 2017).

2. Ayanna Pressley, Twitter post, November 16, 2018, https://twitter.com/AyannaPressley /status/1063457917960110080.

3. See "1924–2005: Shirley Chisholm," *People*, January 17, 2005; Brazile et al., *For Colored Girls Who Have Considered Politics*, 49; and Jason Cuomo, "A Seat at the Table: A Discussion with the African American Women Who Shaped the Democratic Party," *Georgetown Voice*, February 1, 2019. References to the quote can also be found on social media. See, for example, NBCBLK, Twitter post, July 28, 2016, 11:55 p.m., https://twitter.com/NBCBLK /status/758873508621406208; TheRoot, Twitter post, January 3, 2018, 9:52 a.m., https:// twitter.com/TheRoot/status/948567858677731329; Kamala Harris, Twitter post, November 30 2017, 11:57 a.m., https://twitter.com/KamalaHarris/status/1068549496664190976; Ayanna Pressley, Twitter post, March 17, 2019, 5:59 p.m., https://twitter.com/AyannaPressley /status/1107401080315498496. There is also a podcast produced by the Arkansas Public Policy Panel titled *The Folding Chair*, dozens of internet memes, as well as T-shirts and mugs for purchase that feature the quote.

BIBLIOGRAPHY

PRIMARY SOURCES

Archival Materials

Barbados
    Department of the Archives, Black Rock, St. James
        Anglican Church Records
    Muriel Forde Family Collection, Silver Sands, Christ Church
    Shilstone Library, Barbados Museum and Historical Society, Bridgetown
        Genealogical Files

Boston, MA
    Howard Gotlieb Archival Research Center, Boston University
        James Haskins Collection

Brooklyn, NY
    Shirley Chisholm Collection, Brooklyn College Archives and Special Collections
        Oral Histories by Shola Lynch, 2000 and 2003
            Tom Asher
            Susan Brownmiller
            Conrad Chisholm
            Shirley Chisholm, April 1, 2000 and April 29, 2003
            Ronald Dellums
            Shirley Downs
            Muriel Forde
            Sandra Gaines
            Robert Gottleib
            Alcee Hastings
            Barbara Lee
            James Richardson
            Wilson Riles
            Victor Robles
            Arlie Scott
            Bobby Seale
            Carolyn Smith
            Jules Witcover

Cambridge, MA
    Houghton Library, Harvard University
        Houghton Mifflin Papers
    Schlesinger Library, Radcliffe Institute, Harvard University
        Delores Alexander Papers
        Betty Friedan Papers
        Patricia Gold Papers
        Pauli Murray Papers
        Esther Peterson Papers
        Women's Equity Action League Records

College Park, MD
   National Archives and Records Administration
      Department of State Central Foreign Policy Files, 1973–1979
      Federal Bureau of Investigation Records
      Watergate Special Prosecution Force Records
Lexington, KY
   Special Collections Research Center, University of Kentucky
      Pam Elam Papers
Nashville, TN
   Vanderbilt Television News Archives
New Brunswick, NJ
   Archibald S. Alexander Library, Special Collections and University Archives, Rutgers,
         The State University of New Jersey
      Shirley Chisholm Papers
New York, NY
   Rare Book & Manuscript Library, Columbia University
      Oral History Archives
         Vivienne McGuire, "Reminiscences of Wesley McDonald Holder," July 21, 1973
   Schomburg Center for Research in Black Culture, New York Public Library
      Ira Gollobin Haitian Refugee Collection
      Thomas Russell Jones Papers
      George Metcalf Papers
      Moving Image and Recorded Sound Division, Oral History Project, 1968
         Judith Berek
         Annie Bowen
         Shirley Chisholm
         Marshall Dubin
         Allan Fagan
         Thomas Fortune
         Hudson Reed
Northampton, MA
   Sophia Smith Collection of Women's History, Smith College
      Gloria Steinem Papers
Ormond Beach, FL
   Shirley Chisholm Personal Papers
Palo Alto, CA
   Special Collections and University Archives, Stanford University
      Huey P. Newton Foundation, Inc., Collection
Washington, D.C.
   History, Art, and Archives, U.S. House of Representatives
      Oral Histories of African Americans in Congress
         Muriel Morisey, April 19, 2017. https://history.house.gov/OralHistory/
            Detail?id=15032449620 (accessed May 24, 2021)
   Moorland-Spingarn Research Center, Howard University
      Ralph Bunche Oral History Collection
         Edward Thompson III interview with Shirley Chisholm, May 2, 1973

Newspapers and Periodicals

About . . . Time
Atlanta Constitution
Atlanta Journal-Constitution
Atlanta Daily World
Atlanta Voice
Austin Statesman
Baltimore Afro-American
Baltimore Sun
Barbados Advocate News
Bay State Banner (Boston)
Black Coalition Weekly
Black Enterprise
Black Panther
Black Scholar
Black World
Boston Globe
Boston Herald
Boston Phoenix
Brooklyn Bridge
Brooklyn Eagle
Buffalo Courier-Express
Buffalo Evening News
Chicago Tribune
Christian Science Monitor
Christianity and Crisis
Cleveland Call and Post
Congressional Record
Congresswoman Shirley Chisholm Reports from Washington
CORE Magazine
Daytona Beach News-Journal
Detroit Free Press
Ebony
Essence
FAMU Forward
Florida Star (Jacksonville)
Florida Times-Union
Ft. Lauderdale News
Glamour
Hartford Courant
Houston Chronicle
Houston Post
In Defense of the Alien
Issue: A Journal of Opinion
Jacksonville Journal

Jet
Los Angeles Herald-Dispatch
Los Angeles Sentinel
Los Angeles Times
Louisville Times
Magazine of the Buffalo News
Miami Herald
Miami Times
Milwaukee Star
Minneapolis Star
Ms.
National Leader
New Pittsburgh Courier
New York Amsterdam News
New York Daily News
New York Legislative Record and Index
New York Recorder
New York State Legislative Annual
New York Times
Newsday
Norfolk Journal and Guide
Northwest Asian Weekly (Seattle)
Oakland Post
off our backs
Orlando Sentinel
Philadelphia Tribune
Pittsburgh Courier
Race Relations Reporter
A Report from Your Congresswoman Shirley Chisholm
Sacramento Observer
San Francisco Chronicle
San Francisco Sun Reporter
Southern Changes: Journal of the Southern Regional Council
Spelman Messenger
St. Paul Dispatch
Georgetown Voice
The Nation
Time
Tri-State Defender (Memphis)
Village Voice

Interviews by the Author

Paul Cunningham, September 20, 2008, Washington, D.C.
Shirley Downs, July 16, 2012, Alexandria, VA, and March 24, 2016, telephone
Bevan Dufty, August 15, 2008, San Francisco, CA
Patsy Fleming, September 6, 2012, telephone
Muriel Forde, August 2 and 8, 2012, Christ Church, Barbados
Robert (Bob) Frishman and Jeanne Schinto, June 29, 2008, Andover, MA
Andrea Tracy Holmes, April 11, 2010, Washington, D.C.
Barbara Lee, August 2, 2012, telephone
Muriel Morisey, May 31, 2021, telephone
Laura Murphy, July 18, 2012, Washington, D.C.
Carolyn Smith, July 19, 2012, Takoma Park, MD

Published Primary Sources

Abubadika, Mwlina Imiri (Sonny Carson). *The Education of Sonny Carson*. New York: Norton, 1972.

Abu-Lughod, Janet L. *Race, Space, and Riots in Chicago, New York, and Los Angeles*. New York: Oxford University Press, 2007.

Bambara, Toni Cade, ed. *The Black Woman: An Anthology*. A Signet Book. New York: New American Library, 1970.

Beal, Frances. "Double Jeopardy: To Be Black and Female." In *The Black Woman: An Anthology*, edited by Toni Cade Bambara, 109–22. A Signet Book. New York: New American Library, 1970.

———. "Double Jeopardy: To Be Black and Female." In *Words of Fire: An Anthology of African-American Feminist Thought*, edited by Beverly Guy-Sheftall, 146–56. New York: New Press, distributed by W. W. Norton, 1995.

Bond, Julian. "Black Experiences in Politics." In *The Black Politician; His Struggle for Power, edited by* Mervyn M. Dymally. Belmont, CA: Duxbury Press, 1971.

Brazile, Donna, Yolanda Caraway, Leah Daughtry, Minyon Moore, and Veronica Chambers. *For Colored Girls Who Have Considered Politics*. New York: St. Martin's Press, 2018.

Brownmiller, Susan. *Shirley Chisholm: A Biography*. Doubleday Signal Books. Garden City, NY: Doubleday, 1970.

Carmichael, Stokely, and Charles V. Hamilton. *Black Power: The Politics of Liberation in America*. London: Cape, 1968.

Carroll, Diahann, and Bob Morris. *The Legs Are the Last to Go: Aging, Acting, Marrying, and Other Things I Learned the Hard Way*. New York: Amistad, 2008.

Chisholm, Shirley. "Coalitions—The Politics of the Future." In *What Black Politicians Are Saying*, edited by Nathan Wright Jr. New York: Hawthorn Books, 1972.

———. "Foreword." In *Abortion Rap, edited by* Diane Schulder and Florynce Kennedy, vii–xi. New York: McGraw-Hill, 1971.

———. "Foreword." In *Child Care: Who Cares? Foreign and Domestic Infant and Early Child Development Policies*, edited by Pamela Roby. New York: Basic Books, 1973.

———. *The Good Fight*. A Cass Canfield Book. New York: Harper & Row, 1973.

———. "The Relationship between Religion and Today's Social Issues." *Religious Education* 69, no. 2 (March–April 1974): 117–23.

———. *Unbought and Unbossed*. Boston: Houghton Mifflin, 1970.

Clay, William L. *Just Permanent Interests: Black Americans in Congress, 1870–1991*. New York: Amistad Press, distributed by Penguin USA, 1992.

Dellums, Ronald V., and H. Lee Halterman. *Lying Down with Lions: A Public Life from the Streets of Oakland to the Halls of Power*. Boston: Beacon Press, 2000.

Denby, Bob, and Tom Werner. *Chisholm: Pursuing the Dream*. New Line Cinema. 1974.

Diamond, Robert A., ed. *Congressional Quarterly's Guide to U.S. Elections*. Washington, D.C.: Congressional Quarterly, Inc., 1975.

Dinkins, David N., and Peter Knobler. *A Mayor's Life: Governing New York's Gorgeous Mosaic*. New York: Public Affairs, 2013.

Dymally, Mervyn M., ed. *The Black Politician: His Struggle for Power*. Belmont, CA: Duxbury Press, 1971.

Ephron, Nora. *Crazy Salad: Some Things about Women*. New York: Knopf, 1975.

Farmer, James. *Lay Bare the Heart: An Autobiography of the Civil Rights Movement*. New York: Arbor House, 1985.

Fisher, Louis. "Congress, the Executive, and the Budget." *Annals of the American Academy of Political and Social Science* 411 (January 1974): 102–13.

———. *Detention of U.S. Citizens, CRS Report for Congress*. Washington, D.C.: Congressional Research Service, 2005.

Guthrie, Benjamin, and Pat Jennings. *Statistics for the Presidential and Congressional Election of November 5, 1968*. Washington, D.C.: U.S. Government Printing Office, 1969.

Haskins, James. *Fighting Shirley Chisholm*. New York: Dial Press, 1975.

Hicks, Nancy. *The Honorable Shirley Chisholm, Congresswoman from Brooklyn*. New York: Lion Books, 1971.

Hixon, Sheila, and Ruth Rose, eds. *The Official Proceedings of the 1972 Democratic National Convention*. Washington, D.C.: Democratic National Committee, 1972.

Kuriansky, Joan, and Catherine Smith. *Shirley Chisholm, Democratic Representative from New York*. Washington, D.C.: Grossman, 1972.

Lewis, Jeffrey B., Brandon DeVine, Lincoln Pitcher, and Kenneth C. Martis. *Digital Boundary Definitions of United States Congressional Districts, 1789-2012*. 2013. Accessed on August 24, 2021. https://cdmaps.polisci.ucla.edu.

Marshall, Paule. *Brown Girl, Brownstones*. New York: Random House, 1959.

———. *Triangular Road: A Memoir*. New York: BasicCivitas Books, 2009.

McCluskey, Audrey T., and Elaine M. Smith. *Mary McLeod Bethune: Building a Better World: Essays and Selected Documents*. Bloomington: Indiana University Press, 1999.

Metcalf, George R. *Up from Within: Today's New Black Leaders*. New York: McGraw-Hill, 1971.

New York (State). Constitutional Convention (1967). *Proceedings of the Constitutional Convention of the State of New York: April Fourth to September Twenty Sixth, 1967*. Albany, NY: The Convention, 1967.

Norton, Eleanor Holmes, ed. *Women's Role in Contemporary Society: The Report of the New York City Commission on Human Rights, Sept. 21-25, 1970*. New York: Avon Books, 1977.

Orenstein, Norman J. "Towards Restructuring the Congressional Committee System." *Annals of the American Academy of Political and Social Science* 411 (January 1974): 147–57.

Peabody, Robert L. "Committees from the Leadership Perspective." *Annals of the American Academy of Political and Social Science* 411 (January 1974): 133–46.

Roby, Pamela, ed. *Child Care: Who Cares? Foreign and Domestic Infant and Early Child Development Policies*. New York: Basic Books, 1973.

Roth, William. *The Politics of Daycare: The Comprehensive Child Development Act of 1971*. Madison, WI: Institute for Research on Poverty, University of Wisconsin, 1976.

Russell, Carlos E. *Perspectives on Power: A Black Community Looks At Itself (Profiles in Political Acumen)*. Project Demonstrating Excellence. Cincinnati, OH: Union Graduate School, Union for Experimental Colleges and Universities, 1978.

Rustin, Bayard. "From Protest to Politics: The Future of the Civil Rights Movement." *Commentary* 39, no. 2 (February 1965).

Schulder, Diane, and Florence Kennedy, eds. *Abortion Rap*. New York: McGraw-Hill, 1971.

Thompson, Hunter S. *Fear and Loathing on the Campaign Trail '72*. San Francisco: Straight Arrow Books, distributed by Quick Fox Inc., 1973.

U.S. Department of Labor, Office of Policy Planning and Research. *The Negro Family: The Case for National Action (the Moynihan Report)*. Washington, D.C.: Office of Policy Planning and Research, 1965.

U.S. House of Representatives. *Administration's Welfare Reform Proposal: Joint Hearings Before the Welfare Reform Subcommittee of the Committee on Agriculture, Committee on Education and Labor, Committee on Ways and Means, U.S. House of Representatives, Ninety-Fifth Congress, First Session, on H.R. 9030*. Washington, D.C.: U.S. Government Printing Office, 1977.

———. *Caribbean Migration: Oversight Hearings Before the Subcommittee on Immigration, Refugees, and International Law of the Committee on the Judiciary, House of Representatives, Ninety-Sixth Congress, Second Session, on Caribbean Migration, May 13, June 4, 17, 1980*. Washington, D.C.: U.S. Government Printing Office, 1980.

———. *Civil Rights Amendments Act of 1979, Hearing Before the Subcommittee on Employment Opportunities, Education and Labor, October 10, 1980*. Washington, D.C.: U.S. Government Printing Office, 1980.

———. *Coast Guard Oversight—Part 2: Hearings Before the Subcommittee on Coast Guard and Navigation of the Committee on Merchant Marine and Fisheries, House of Representatives, Ninety-Seventh Congress, First Session, on Military Readiness and International Programs, September 17, 1981; Management: Problems and Procedures, September 30, 1981; Roles and Missions Study by the Executive Branch, November 10, 1981*. Washington D.C.: U.S. Government Printing Office, 1982.

———. *Discrimination against Women: Hearings Before the Special Subcommittee on Education of the Committee on Education and Labor, House of Representatives, Ninety-First Congress, Second Session, on Section 805 of H.R. 16098 . . . Part 2, Hearings Held in Washington, D.C., July 1 and 31, 1970*. Washington, D.C.: U.S. Government Printing Office, 1971.

———. *Discrimination in Employment (Oversight): Hearings Before the General Subcommittee on Labor of the Committee on Education and Labor, House of Representatives, Ninety-Second Congress, Second Session, on Oversight Hearings on Unemployment and Discrimination in Employment; Hearings Held in Chicago, Ill., October 20, 21; Cleveland, Ohio, October 23, 1972*. Washington, D.C.: U.S. Government Printing Office, 1973.

———. *Establishing a Department of Education: Hearings Before a Subcommittee of the Committee on Government Operations, Ninety-Fifth Congress, Second Session, on H.R. 13343 to Establish a Department of Education and for Other Purposes, July 17, 20, 31; August 1 and 2, 1978*. Washington, D.C.: U.S. Government Printing Office, 1978.

———. *Food Stamp Program: Hearings Before the Subcommittee on Domestic Marketing, Consumer Relations, and Nutrition of the Committee on Agriculture, House of Representatives, Ninety-Sixth Congress, First Session, on H.R. 2412, H.R. 4303, and H.R. 4318*. Washington, D.C.: U.S. Government Printing Office, 1979.

———. *Hearings and Markup Before the Committee on Rules, House of Representatives, Ninety-Fifth Congress, First Session, on H. Res. 287 to Amend the Rules of the House of Representatives and for Other Purposes.* Washington, D.C.: U.S. Government Printing Office, 1977.

———. *Hearings before the General Subcommittee on Labor on H.R. 1746: A Bill to Further Promote Equal Employment Opportunities for American Workers.* Washington, D.C.: U.S. Government Printing Office, March 18, 1971.

———. *Hearings before the Select Subcommittee on Education on H.R. 6748, May 17, 1971. Washington, D.C.: U.S. Government Printing Office, 1971.*

———. *Hearings before the Subcommittee on Administrative Law and Governmental Regulations of the Committee on the Judiciary, House of Representatives, Ninety-Fifth Congress, First Session, on H.R. 3361 and Related Bills.* Washington, D.C.: U.S. Government Printing Office, 1977.

———. "Hearings on Amendments to the Congressional Budget and Impoundment Control Act of 1974." In *Hearings on Congressional Procedures: Hearings Before the Subcommittee on the Rules and Organization of the House of the Committee on Rules, House of Representatives, Ninety-Fifth Congress, Second Session.* Washington, D.C.: U.S. Government Printing Office, 1979.

———. *Hearings Related to Various Bills to Repeal the Emergency Detention Act of 1950: Hearings Before the Committee on Internal Security, House of Representatives, Ninety-First Congress, Second Session, March 16, 17, 19, 23, 24, and 26; April 20, 21, and 22; May 21; and September 10, 1970.* Washington, D.C.: U.S. Government Printing Office, 1970.

———. *A History of the Committee on Rules: First to Ninety-Seventh Congress, 1789–1981.* Washington, D.C.: U.S. Government Printing Office, 1983.

———. *Immigration Reform and Control Act of 1982: Joint Hearings Before the Subcommittee on Immigration, Refugees, and International Law, of the Committee on the Judiciary, House of Representatives, and Subcommittee on Immigration and Refugee Policy of the Committee of the Judiciary, United States Senate, Ninety-Seventh Congress, Second Session, on H.R. 5872, S. 2222, Immigration Reform and Control Act, April 1 and 20, 1982.* Washington, D.C.: U.S. Government Printing Office, 1982.

———. *Migrant and Seasonal Farmworker Housing in the United States: Hearings Before the Subcommittee on Housing and Community Development of the Committee on Banking, Finance, and Urban Affairs, House of Representatives, Ninety-Seventh Congress, First Session, Part 1: September 17; September 19 (Melfa, Va.); and October 9, 1981 (San Antonio, Tex.).* Washington, D.C.: U.S. Government Printing Office, 1981.

———. *Nomination of Nelson A. Rockefeller to Be Vice President of the United States: Hearings Before the Committee on the Judiciary, House of Representatives, Ninety-Third Congress, Second Session, on Nomination of Nelson A. Rockefeller to Be Vice President of the United States.* Washington, D.C.: U.S. Government Printing Office, 1974.

———. *Oversight on Higher Education Budget Fiscal Years 1981 and 1982: Hearings Before the Subcommittee on Postsecondary Education of the Committee on Education and Labor, House of Representatives, Ninety-Seventh Congress, First Session, Hearings Held in Washington, D.C., on February 24, 26; Carbondale, Ill., March 6; and Washington, D.C., March 11, 1981.* Washington, D.C.: U.S. Government Printing Office, 1983.

———. *Part 4, Emergency School Aid Act: Hearings Before the Subcommittee on Elementary, Secondary, and Vocational Education of the Committee on Education and Labor, House of Representatives, Ninety-Fifth Congress, First Session; on H.R. 15, to Extend for Five Years Certain Elementary, Secondary, and Other Education Programs; Hearings Held in Washington, D.C.; June 14, 15, 16, 1977*. Washington, D.C.: U.S. Government Printing Office, 1977.

———. *Part 19: Title I—Funds Allocation; Hearings Before the Subcommittee on Elementary, Secondary, and Vocational Education of the Committee on Education and Labor, House of Representatives, Ninety-Fifth Congress, First Session; on H.R. 15, to Extend for Five Years Certain Elementary, Secondary, and Other Education Programs; Hearings Held in Washington, D.C.; November 1, 2, 3, 8, 9, and 10, 1977*. Washington, D.C.: U.S. Government Printing Office, 1978.

———. *Proposed Elimination of OEO and Related Legislation: Hearings, Ninety-Third Congress, First Session, on H.R. 3641, H.R. 3175, and H.R. 3147*. . . . Washington, D.C.: U.S. Government Printing Office, 1974.

———. *Sex Discrimination and Sex Stereotyping in Vocational Education: Hearings Before the Subcommittee on Elementary, Secondary, and Vocational Education of the Committee on Education and Labor, House of Representatives, Ninety-fourth Congress, First Session, March 17 and April 21, 28, 1975*. Washington, D.C.: U.S. Government Printing Office, 1975.

———. *Sex Discrimination Regulations: Hearings Before the Subcommittee on Postsecondary Education of the Committee on Education and Labor, House of Representatives, Ninety-Fourth Congress, First Session, Review of Regulations to Implement Title IX of Public Law 92-318*. . . . *June 17–26, 1975*. Washington, D.C.: U.S. Government Printing Office, 1975.

———. *Sunset, Sunrise, and Related Measures: Hearings Before the Subcommittee on the Legislative Process of the Committee on Rules, House of Representatives, Ninety-Sixth Congress, First Session, on H.R. 2, H.R. 65*. Washington, D.C.: U.S. Government Printing Office, 1980.

———. *The Women's Educational Equity Act. Hearings Before the Subcommittee on Equal Opportunities of the Committee on Education and Labor, House of Representatives, Ninety-Third Congress, First Session, on H.R. 208, Part 1*. Washington, D.C.: U.S. Government Printing Office, 1973.

U.S. Senate. *Nominations—July–September: Hearings Before the Committee on Commerce, United States Senate, Ninety-Fourth Congress, Second Session*. Washington, D.C.: U.S. Government Printing Office, 1976.

———. *United States as a Country of Mass First Asylum: Hearing Before the Subcommittee on Immigration and Refugee Policy of the Committee on the Judiciary, United States Senate, Ninety-Seventh Congress, First Session, on Oversight on the Legal Status of the Cubans and Haitians who Have Entered the United States and the Policies and Procedures which Should Be Adopted in Order to Handle Mass Asylum Cases and Crises, July 31, 1981*. Washington, D.C.: U.S. Government Printing Office, 1981.

White, Theodore H. *The Making of the President, 1968*. New York: Atheneum Publishers, 1969.

SECONDARY SOURCES

Barone, Michael, Grant Ujifusa, and Douglas Matthews. *The Almanac of American Politics 1976*. New York: E. P. Dutton and Co., 1975.

Beckles, Hilary. *A History of Barbados: From Amerindian Settlement to Nation-State*. 2nd ed. New York: Cambridge University Press, 2007.

Beckles, Hilary, and Verene Shepherd, eds. *Caribbean Freedom: Economy and Society from Emancipation to the Present: A Student Reader*. Kingston, Jamaica: M. Wiener Publishers, 1996 (1st American ed., Princeton University Press).

Biondi, Martha. *To Stand and Fight: The Struggle for Civil Rights in Postwar New York City*. Cambridge, MA: Harvard University Press, 2003.

Bloom, Nicholas Dagen. *Public Housing That Worked: New York in the Twentieth Century*. Philadelphia: University of Pennsylvania Press, 2008.

Blumenthal, Karen. *Let Me Play: The Story of Title IX: The Law that Changed the Future of Girls in America*. New York: Atheneum Books for Young Readers, 2005.

Breines, Wini. *The Trouble between Us: An Uneasy History of White and Black Women in the Feminist Movement*. New York: Oxford University Press, 2006.

Brown, Michael E. *New Studies in the Politics and Culture of U.S. Communism*. New York: Monthly Review Press, 1993.

Brown, Nadia E., and Danielle Casarez Lemi. *Sister Style: The Politics of Appearance for Black Women Political Elites*. New York: Oxford University Press, 2021.

Brown, Tammy. "'A New Era in American Politics': Shirley Chisholm and the Discourse of Identity." *Callaloo* 31, no. 4 (2008): 1013-25.

———. *City of Islands: Caribbean Intellectuals in New York*. Jackson: University Press of Mississippi, 2015.

Browne, David V. C. *Race, Class, Politics and the Struggle for Empowerment in Barbados, 1914-1937*. Forgotten Histories of the Caribbean. Miami, FL: Ian Randle, 2012.

Carroll, Susan. "National Women's Political Caucus." In *Encyclopedia of U. S. Political History*, Vol. 6, edited by Thomas Langston, 276-78. Washington, D.C.: CQ Press, 2010.

Carter, Dan T. *Scottsboro: A Tragedy of the American South*. Rev. ed. Baton Rouge: Louisiana State University Press, 2007.

Carter, Henderson. *Labour Pains: Resistance and Protest in Barbados, 1838-1904*. Forgotten Histories of the Caribbean. Miami, FL: Ian Randle, 2012.

Chamberlain, Mary. "Family and Identity: Barbadian Migrants to Britain." In *Caribbean Migration: Globalised Identities*, edited by Mary Chamberlain, 148-61. New York: Routledge, 1998.

Cohen, Michael A. *American Maelstrom: The 1968 Election and the Politics of Division*. Pivotal Moments in American History. New York: Oxford University Press, 2016.

Cohen, Robin. "Cultural Diaspora: The Caribbean Case." In *Caribbean Migration: Globalised Identities*, edited by Mary Chamberlain, 21-35. New York: Routledge, 1998.

Collins, Patricia Hill. *Black Feminist Thought: Knowledge, Consciousness, and the Politics of Empowerment*. 2nd ed. New York: Routledge, 1999.

———. *Intersectionality as Critical Social Theory*. Durham, NC: Duke University Press, 2019.

Cooper, Brittney. *Beyond Respectability: The Intellectual Thought of Race Women*. Champaign: University of Illinois Press, 2017.

Crenshaw, Kimberlé. "Demarginalizing the Intersection of Race and Sex: A Black Feminist Critique of Antidiscrimination Doctrine, Feminist Theory, and Antiracist Politics." *University of Chicago Legal Forum* 1 (1989): 138-67.

———. "Mapping the Margins: Intersectionality, Identity, and Violence against Women of Color." *Stanford Law Review* 43, no. 6 (1991): 1241-99.

Curwood, Anastasia Carol. *Stormy Weather: Middle-Class African American Marriages between the Two World Wars*. Chapel Hill: University of North Carolina Press, 2010.

Davidson, Roger H., and Walter J. Oleszek, *Congress Against Itself*. Bloomington: Indiana University Press, 1977.

Dawkins, Wayne. *City Son: Andrew W. Cooper's Impact on Modern-Day Brooklyn*. Margaret Walker Alexander Series in African American Studies. Jackson: University Press of Mississippi, 2012.

Dittmer, John. *Local People: The Struggle for Civil Rights in Mississippi.* Champaign-Urbana: University of Illinois Press, 1993.

Echols, Alice. *Daring to Be Bad: Radical Feminism in America, 1967–1975.* American Culture. Minneapolis: University of Minnesota Press, 1989.

Evans, Sara M. *Personal Politics: The Roots of Women's Liberation in the Civil Rights Movement and the New Left.* New York: Knopf, 1979.

———. *Tidal Wave: How Women Changed America at Century's End.* New York: Free Press, 2003.

Ewing, Adam. *The Age of Garvey: How a Jamaican Activist Created a Mass Movement and Changed Global Black Politics.* Princeton, NJ: Princeton University Press, 2014.

Farber, David R. *Chicago '68.* Chicago: University of Chicago Press, 1988.

Fitzpatrick, Ellen, *The Highest Glass Ceiling: Women's Quest for the American Presidency.* Cambridge, MA: Harvard University Press, 2016.

Fraser, Zinga. "Catalysts for Change: A Comparative Study of Barbara Jordan and Shirley Chisholm." PhD diss., Northwestern University, 2014.

Frazier, Robeson Taj. *The East Is Black: Cold War China in the Black Radical Imagination.* Durham, NC: Duke University Press, 2015.

Gallagher, Julie A. *Black Women and Politics in New York City.* Women in American History. Urbana: University of Illinois Press, 2012.

———. "How Did Shirley Chisholm, the First African American Woman Elected to the U.S. Congress, Advance an Inclusive Feminist Politics in the 1960s and 1970s?" *Women and Social Movements in the United States, 1600–2000* 17, no. 1 (March 2013).

———. "Waging '*The Good Fight*': The Political Life of Shirley Chisholm, 1953–1982." *Journal of African American History* 93, no. 3 (2007): 393–416.

Gerson, Jeffrey. "Bertram L. Baker, the United Action Democratic Association, and the First Black Democratic Succession in Brooklyn, 1933–1954." *Afro-Americans in New York Life and History* 16, no. 2 (1992): 17–46.

———. "Building the Brooklyn Machine: Irish, Jewish and Black Political Succession in Central Brooklyn, 1919–1964." PhD diss., City University of New York, 19.

Gill, Tiffany M. *Beauty Shop Politics: African American Women's Activism in the Beauty Industry.* Women in American History. Urbana: University of Illinois Press, 2010.

Gilmore, Stephanie. *Feminist Coalitions: Historical Perspectives on Second-Wave Feminism in the United States.* Women in American History. Urbana: University of Illinois Press, 2008.

Goodman, James. *Stories of Scottsboro.* New York: Pantheon Books, 1994.

Grant, Colin. *Negro with a Hat: The Rise and Fall of Marcus Garvey.* New York: Oxford University Press, 2008.

Guild, Joshua. "To Make That Someday Come: Shirley Chisholm's Radical Politics of Possibility." In *Want to Start a Revolution?: Radical Women in the Black Freedom Struggle*, edited by Dayo F. Gore, Jeanne Theoharis, and Komozi Woodard, 248–70. New York: New York University Press, 2009.

———. "You Can't Go Home Again: Migration, Citizenship, and Black Community in Postwar New York and London." PhD diss., Yale University, 2007.

Guy-Sheftall, Beverly, ed. *Words of Fire: An Anthology of African-American Feminist Thought.* New York: New Press, 1995.

Haas, Jeffrey. *The Assassination of Fred Hampton: How the FBI and the Chicago Police Murdered a Black Panther.* Chicago: Lawrence Hill Books, 2010.

Harris, Duchess. *Black Feminist Politics from Kennedy to Trump.* Cham: Springer International Publishing, Imprint: Palgrave Macmillan, 2019.

Hartmann, Susan M. "Equal Rights Amendment." In *Encyclopedia of U.S. Political History*. Vol. 6, edited by Thomas Langston, 155–56. Washington, D.C.: CQ Press, 2010.

———. *The Other Feminists: Activists in the Liberal Establishment*. New Haven, CT: Yale University Press, 1998.

Hennessee, Judith Adler. *Betty Friedan: Her Life*. New York: Random House, 1999.

Hill, Herbert. "The Equal Employment Opportunity Acts of 1964 and 1972: A Critical Analysis of the Legislative History and Administration of the Law." *Berkeley Journal of Employment and Labor Law* 2, no. 1 (Spring 1977): 49–50.

Hine, Darlene Clark. "Rape and the Inner Lives of Black Women in the Middle West: Preliminary Thoughts on the Culture of Dissemblance." *Signs: Journal of Women in Culture and Society* 14, no. 4 (1989): 912–20.

Hunter-Gault, Charlayne. "Black and White." In *America's Mayor: John V. Lindsay and the Reinvention of New York, New York*, edited by Sam Roberts, 42–52. New York: Columbia University Press, 2010.

James, Joy, and T. Denean Sharpley-Whiting, eds. *The Black Feminist Reader*. Malden, MA: Blackwell, 2000.

James, Winston. *Holding Aloft the Banner of Ethiopia: Caribbean Radicalism in Early Twentieth-Century America*. New York: Verso, 1999.

Joseph, Peniel E. "The Black Power Movement: A State of the Field." *Journal of American History* 96, no. 3 (December 2009): 751–76.

———. *Waiting 'til the Midnight Hour: A Narrative History of Black Power in America*. New York: Henry Holt and Co., 2006.

Kessler-Harris, Alice. *In Pursuit of Equity: Women, Men and the Quest for Economic Citizenship in Twentieth-Century America*. New York: Oxford University Press, 2001.

Kotlowski, Dean J. "Trial by Error: Nixon, the Senate, and the Haynsworth Nomination." *Presidential Studies Quarterly* 1 (1996): 71–91.

Kruse, Kevin Michael, and Julian E. Zelizer. *Fault Lines: A History of the United States since 1974*. New York: W.W. Norton & Company, 2019.

Leberstein, Stephen. "Purging the Profs: The Rapp-Coudert Committee in New York, 1940–1942." In *New Studies in the Politics and Culture of U. S. Communism*, edited by M. E. Brown, R. Martin, F. Rosengarten, and G. Snedeker, 91–122. New York: Monthly Review Press, 1993.

Lee, Chana Kai. "Guns, Death, and Better Tomorrows: New Work on Black Militancy." *American Quarterly* 67, no. 2 (January 2015): 517–28.

Levy, Alan Howard. *The Political Life of Bella Abzug*. Lanham, MD: Lexington Books, 2013.

Lewinson, Edwin R. *Black Politics in New York City*. New York: Twayne Publishers, 1974.

Liddy, G. Gordon. *Will: The Autobiography*. New York: Dell, 1981.

Lindquist, Malinda A. *Race, Social Science and the Crisis of Manhood, 1890–1970: We Are the Supermen*. New York: Routledge, 2012.

Lindskoog, Carl, *Detain and Punish: Haitian Refugees and the Rise of the World's Largest Immigration Detention System*. Gainesville: University of Florida Press, 2019.

Lizzi, Maria. "'My Heart Is as Black as Yours': White Backlash, Racial Identity, and Italian American Stereotypes in New York City's 1969 Mayoral Campaign." *Journal of American Ethnic History* 27, no. 3 (Spring 2008): 43–80.

Lorde, Audre. "Age, Race, Class, and Sex: Women Redefining Difference" (1984). In *Words of Fire: An Anthology of African-American Feminist Thought*, edited by Beverly Guy-Sheftall, 284–91. New York: New Press, 1995.

Lutz, Helma. "The Legacy of Migration: Immigrant Mothers and Daughters and the Process of Intergenerational Transmission." In *Caribbean Migration: Globalised Identities*, edited by Mary Chamberlain, 95–107. New York: Routledge, 1998 .

Lynch, Shola. *Chisholm '72: Unbought & Unbossed*. Beverly Hills, CA: 20th Century Fox Home Entertainment, 2004.

MacLean, Nancy. *Democracy in Chains: The Deep History of the Radical Right's Stealth Plan for America*. New York: Penguin, 2017.

——. *Freedom Is Not Enough: The Opening of the American Work Place*. Cambridge, MA: Harvard University Press, 2006.

Maddux, Thomas R. "Ronald Reagan and the Task Force on Immigration, 1981." *Pacific Historical Review* 74, no. 2 (2005): 195–236.

Mansbridge, Jane J. *Why We Lost the ERA*. Chicago: University of Chicago Press, 1986.

Marable, Manning, and Leith Mullings. *Let Nobody Turn Us Around: Voices of Resistance, Reform, and Renewal: An African American Anthology*. 2nd ed. Lanham, MD: Rowman & Littlefield, 2009.

Marshall, Paule. "Black Immigrant Women in *Brown Girl, Brownstones*." In *Female Immigrants to the United States: Caribbean, Latin American, and African Experiences, edited by Delores M. Mortimer and Roy S. Bryce-Laporte*. RIIES Occasional Papers. Washington, D.C.: Research Institute on Immigration and Ethnic Studies, Smithsonian Institution, 1981.

McGuire, Danielle. *At the Dark End of the Street: Black Women, Rape, and Resistance—A New History of the Civil Rights Movement from Rosa Parks to the Rise of Black Power*. New York: Vintage, 2011.

McLain, Paula, Niambi Carter, and Michael Brady. "Gender and Black Presidential Politics: From Chisholm to Moseley Braun." *Journal of Women, Politics, and Policy* 27, no. 1 (2005): 51–68.

Miroff, Bruce. *The Liberals' Moment: The McGovern Insurgency and the Identity Crisis of the Democratic Party*. Lawrence: University Press of Kansas, 2007.

Mittelstadt, Jennifer. *From Welfare to Workfare: The Unintended Consequences of Liberal Reform*. Chapel Hill: University of North Carolina Press, 2005.

Mortimer, Delores M., and Roy S. Bryce-Laporte. *Female Immigrants to the United States: Caribbean, Latin American, and African Experiences*. RIIES Occasional Papers. Washington, D.C.: Research Institute on Immigration and Ethnic Studies, Smithsonian Institution, 1981.

Nadasen, Premilla, Jennifer Mittelstadt, and Marisa Chappell, eds. *Welfare in the United States: A History with Documents, 1935–1996*. New York: Routledge, 2009.

Nye, David E. *When the Lights Went Out: A History of Blackouts in America*. Cambridge, MA: MIT Press, 2010.

Orleck, Annelise. "Introduction: The War on Poverty from the Grass Roots Up." In *The War on Poverty: A New Grassroots History, 1964–1980, edited by Annelise Orleck and Lisa Gayle Hazirjian*, 1–28. Athens: University of Georgia Press, 2011.

——. *Storming Caesar's Palace: How Black Mothers Fought Their Own War on Poverty*. Boston: Beacon Press, 2005.

Orleck, Annelise, and Lisa Gayle Hazirjian, eds. *The War on Poverty: A New Grassroots History, 1964–1980*. Athens: University of Georgia Press, 2011.

Painter, Nell Irvin. *Sojourner Truth: A Life, a Symbol*. New York: W. W. Norton, 1996.

Patterson, James T. *America's Struggle against Poverty in the Twentieth Century*. Cambridge, MA: Harvard University Press, 2000.

——. *Freedom Is Not Enough: The Moynihan Report and America's Struggle over Black Family Life: From LBJ to Obama*. New York: Basic Books, 2010.

Perlstein, Rick. *The Invisible Bridge: The Fall of Nixon and the Rise of Reagan*. New York: Simon & Schuster, 2014.

———. *Nixonland: The Rise of a President and the Fracturing of America*. New York: Scribner, 2008.

Podair, Jerald E. *The Strike That Changed New York: Blacks, Whites, and the Ocean Hill-Brownsville Crisis*. New Haven, CT: Yale University Press, 2002.

Popkin, Jeremy. "Historians on the Autobiographical Frontier." *American Historical Review* 104, no. 3 (June 1999): 725-30.

Purnell, Brian. *Fighting Jim Crow in the County of Kings: The Congress of Racial Equality in Brooklyn*. Civil Rights and the Struggle for Black Equality in the Twentieth Century. Lexington: University Press of Kentucky, 2013.

Putnam, Lara. *Radical Moves: Caribbean Migrants and the Politics of Race in the Jazz Age*. Chapel Hill: University of North Carolina Press, 2013.

Rainwater, Lee, and William L. Yancey. *The Moynihan Report and the Politics of Controversy: A Trans-Action Social Science and Public Policy Report*. Cambridge, MA: MIT Press, 1967.

Randolph, Sherie M. *Florynce "Flo" Kennedy: The Life of a Black Feminist Radical*. Gender and American Culture. Chapel Hill: University of North Carolina Press, 2015.

Ransby, Barbara. *Ella Baker and the Black Freedom Movement: A Radical Democratic Vision*. Chapel Hill: University of North Carolina Press, 2003.

Reagon, Bernice Johnson. "The Political Mind: We Will Rise to the Occasion." In *Home Girls: A Black Feminist Anthology, edited by Barbara Smith,* 356-68. New York: Kitchen Table: Women of Color Press, 1983.

Roach, Shoniqua. "(Re)turning to 'Rape and the Inner Lives of Black Women': A Black Feminist Forum on the Culture of Dissemblance." *Signs: Journal of Women and Culture in Society* 45, no. 3 (2020): 515-19.

Roberts, Sam. *America's Mayor: John V. Lindsay and the Reinvention of New York*. New York: Museum of the City of New York, Columbia University Press, 2010.

Rosen, Ruth. *The World Split Open: How the Modern Women's Movement Changed America*. New York: Viking, 2000.

Roth, Benita. *Separate Roads to Feminism: Black, Chicana, and White Feminist Movements in America's Second Wave*. New York: Cambridge University Press, 2004.

Schmidt, Elizabeth. *Foreign Intervention in Africa: From the Cold War to the War on Terror*. New Approaches to African History. Cambridge, UK: Cambridge University Press, 2013.

———. *Foreign Intervention in Africa after the Cold War: Sovereignty, Responsibility, and the War on Terror*. Ohio University Research in International Studies Global and Comparative Studies Series. Athens: Ohio University Press, 2018.

Schulman, Bruce J. *The Seventies: The Great Shift in American Culture, Society, and Politics*. New York: Free Press, 2001.

Schwartz, Joel. *The New York Approach: Robert Moses, Urban Liberals, and Redevelopment of the Inner City*. Columbus: Ohio State University Press, 1993.

Self, Robert O. *All in the Family: The Realignment of American Democracy since the 1960s*. New York: Hill and Wang, 2012.

Shapiro, Fred C., and James W. Sullivan. *Race Riots: New York, 1964*. New York: Cromwell, 1964.

Simien, Evelyn M. *Historic Firsts: How Symbolic Empowerment Changes US Politics*. New York: Oxford University Press, 2016.

Singh, Robert. *The Congressional Black Caucus: Racial Politics in the U.S. Congress*. Thousand Oaks, CA: Sage, 1998.

Smith, Barbara. *Home Girls: A Black Feminist Anthology*. New York: Kitchen Table: Women of Color Press, 1983.

———. *Home Girls: A Black Feminist Anthology*. New Brunswick, NJ: Rutgers University Press, 2000.

Smith, Sidonie, and Julia Watson. *Reading Autobiography: A Guide for Interpreting Life Narratives*. 2nd ed. Minneapolis: University of Minnesota Press, 2010.

Sokol, Jason. *All Eyes Are Upon Us: Race and Politics from Boston to Brooklyn*. Amherst: University of Massachusetts Press, 2017.

Springer, Kimberly. *Living for the Revolution: Black Feminist Organizations, 1968-1980*. Durham, NC: Duke University Press, 2005.

Stur, Heather Marie. *Beyond Combat: Women and Gender in the Vietnam War Era*. New York: Cambridge University Press, 2011.

Sundquist, James L. *On Fighting Poverty: Perspectives from Experience*. New York: Basic Books, 1969.

Taylor, Ula Y. "The Historical Evolution of Black Feminist Theory and Praxis." *Journal of Black Studies* 29, no.2 (November, 1998): 234-53.

———. "Introduction" (to Amy Jacques Garvey section). In *Words of Fire: An Anthology of African-American Feminist Thought*, edited by Beverly Guy-Sheftall, 89-90. New York: New Press, distributed by W. W. Norton, 1995.

———. "'Negro Women Are Great Thinkers as well as Doers': Amy Jacques Garvey and Community Feminism in the United States, 1924-1927." *Journal of Women's History* 12, no. 2 (Summer 2000): 104-26.

Thompson, Heather Ann. *Blood in the Water: The Attica Prison Uprising of 1971 and Its Legacy*. New York: Vintage Books, 2017.

Wallace, Michele. *Black Macho and the Myth of the Superwoman*. New York: Dial Press, 1979.

Watkins-Owens, Irma. *Blood Relations: Caribbean Immigrants and the Harlem Community, 1900-1930*. Blacks in the Diaspora. Bloomington: Indiana University Press, 1996.

Weiss, Nancy J. *Farewell to the Party of Lincoln: Black Politics in the Age of FDR*. Princeton, NJ: Princeton University Press, 1983.

White, Deborah Gray. *Ar'n't I a Woman?: Female Slaves in the Plantation South*. Rev. ed. New York: W. W. Norton, 1999.

———. *Too Heavy a Load: Black Women in Defense of Themselves, 1894-1994*. New York: W. W. Norton, 1999.

Winslow, Barbara. *Shirley Chisholm: Catalyst for Change, 1926-2005*. Boulder, CO: Westview Press, 2014.

Woodsworth, Michael. *Battle for Bed-Stuy: The Long War on Poverty in New York City*. Cambridge, MA: Harvard University Press, 2016.

Wu, Judy Tzu-Chun. *Radicals on the Road: Internationalism, Orientalism, and Feminism during the Vietnam Era*. Ithaca, NY: Cornell University Press, 2013.

Young, Cynthia Ann. *Soul Power: Culture, Radicalism, and the Making of a U.S. Third World Left*. Durham, NC: Duke University Press, 2006.

Zarnow, Leandra Ruth. *Battling Bella: The Protest Politics of Bella Abzug*. Cambridge, MA: Harvard University Press, 2019.

INDEX

Vauxhall Primary School, *21*

Vietnam War, 5, 105–10, 119–24, 148, 157, 189, 191–92, 271, 284, 408n45; Chisholm's opposition to, 104–5, 125, 158–61, 172, 215, 258; Vietnam Veterans Against the War, 191–92

Wallace, George, 120–21, 234–37, 265–70, 284–85

War on Poverty, 68–69, 79–80, 181–82, 273. *See also* Great Society; liberalism

Watergate, 275, 278, 292

Wells v. Rockefeller (1968), 88, 95, 98–99, 106, 319–20

Women Strike for Peace, 159

Wright, Samuel, 82, 95, 170, 253, 274, 277–78, 292, 296, 302–4, 413n116, 426n12

Young, Whitney, 160–61

Young voters, 182–83, 206, 225, 232–34, 253–54

Youth in Action (YIA), 71–72, 79–80, 84

Zens, Wendy (Curwood), 238, 355